Windows 7 Made Simple

Kevin Otnes

Apress®

Windows 7 Made Simple

ISBN-13 (pbk): 978-1-4302-3650-4

ISBN-13 (electronic): 978-1-4302-3651-1

President and Publisher: Paul Manning
Lead Editor: Steve Anglin
Development Editor: Matthew Moodie
Technical Reviewer: Peter Membry
Editorial Board: Steve Anglin, Mark Beckner, Ewan Buckingham, Gary Cornell, Morgan
    Engel, Jonathan Gennick, Jonathan Hassell, Robert Hutchinson, Michelle Lowman,
    James Markham, Matthew Moodie, Jeff Olson, Jeffrey Pepper, Douglas Pundick,
    Ben Renow-Clarke, Dominic Shakeshaft, Gwenan Spearing, Matt Wade, Tom Welsh
Coordinating Editor: Kelly Moritz
Copy Editor: Mary Behr, Elizabeth Berry, Seth Kline
Compositor: MacPS, LLC
Indexer: SPI Global
Artist: SPI Global
Cover Designer: Anna Ishchenko

Distributed to the book trade worldwide by Springer Science+Business Media, LLC., 233 Spring Street, 6th Floor, New York, NY 10013. Phone 1-800-SPRINGER, fax (201) 348-4505, e-mail orders-ny@springer-sbm.com, or visit www.springeronline.com.

For information on translations, please e-mail rights@apress.com, or visit www.apress.com.

Apress and friends of ED books may be purchased in bulk for academic, corporate, or promotional use. eBook versions and licenses are also available for most titles. For more information, reference our Special Bulk Sales–eBook Licensing web page at www.apress.com/bulk-sales.

To my wife for believing in and encouraging me, my children for making me proud of them, and my extended family and friends for keeping me in their thoughts and prayers during this epic writing project.

—Kevin Otnes

Contents at a Glance

Contents

Chapter 8: Communicating with E-mail, IM, and Social Networks 297

Chapter 9: Surfing the Web 361

▨ Chapter 16: Protecting Your Computer and Data 649

▨ Chapter 17: Troubleshooting and Maintaining Your Computer 707

About the Author

 **Kevin Otnes,** technical writer and author, was born and raised in the Emerald City. His experience with Windows ranges from assembling and shipping Windows 2.0 retail boxes with 20 floppy disks to a dozen years of writing award-winning online help for Windows, Outlook Express, Internet Explorer, Windows XP Embedded, and Windows Mobile Embedded. During that time, he also contributed to the Windows 95 Help Authoring Kit book, served as a technical reviewer for several Windows and Internet Explorer books, and wrote several technical articles published on Microsoft TechNet. His past and present work includes writing for Laplink, Andrew Corporation, Boeing, and EMC.

He copes with the dietary demands of the tropical Puget Sound climate with salmon, tomatoes, raspberries, krumkake, and rosettes according to season and adapts to the change of seasons with rock salt, bumbershoots, and sunglasses.

About the Technical Reviewer

Peter Membrey is a Chartered IT Professional who holds a masters degree in IT specialising in Information Security. He is the youngest person to have passed the RHCE (which he did when he was 17) and had the honour of working for and with Red Hat for many years. He is currently studying for a PhD in Security Engineering at the Hong Kong Polytechnic University. He lives in Hong Kong with his wife Sarah and son Kaydyn and is still desperately trying (and still failing) to come to grips with Esperanto and the various Chinese languages.

His personal site is at `http://peter.membrey.hk`

Acknowledgments

First and foremost, I must thank the Apress editors for this project. Without them this book would never have been born, nurtured, and completed. I feel really blessed to work with the same folks I worked with previously on the *Getting Started with Windows 7* book. Many thanks to Lead Editor Steve Anglin for this opportunity to write the Windows 7 book for the Made Simple series and for guiding it from a proposal to a real project. Kelly Moritz, our Coordinating Editor, kept the project focused and on track, and she was always available to answer questions or clarify as we went along. Matthew Moodie, our Developmental Editor, was crucial for shaping the outline, structure, format, and content of this book.

I also must thank Peter Membrey, our Technical Reviewer, for his great insight, voice of the user, and occasionally, an extra voice of reason.

Most of all, thanks to Lori for keeping my feet grounded, my heart and soul nourished, and my life balanced.

Part I

Quick Start Guide

On your computer screen is the most exciting new release of Windows in the last 10 years: Windows 7. This Quick Start Guide will get you up and running with Windows in no time. You'll learn what's new in Windows 7, how to find your way around the Windows 7 desktop, where to find your programs and documents, and several ways you can quickly tailor the desktop to suit your needs and tastes. After you get to know your new Windows desktop, you can jump into the top 12 things you'll want to do or set up on your new computer. You'll also learn some basic Windows tasks and skills and where to get more details about them in this book.

Getting Around Quickly

This Quick Start Guide means just what it says. It will help you quickly locate specific information within this book, and it will show you the basics of using Windows 7 and your PC. Very few of us have taken a formal, structured class that taught us everything we need to know about using Windows and computers. Often we learn or are taught on a need-to-know basis by friends or coworkers. It's easy to feel intimidated when we watch others effortless perform tasks like clicking, dragging, copying, pasting, connecting, and printing.

This book is designed so that you can use it *your way*. There's no computer gene that some have and some don't—everybody learns differently and at their own pace. As a result, you will find plenty of written and visual instructions in this book. And, while the chapters are numbered, you don't have to read them in a particular order—or even read all of them. Read this book a la carte; sample a few topics like appetizers when you're hungry for just a little bit of information, or build a seven course meal when you want to consume information until you're stuffed.

What would you like to know? Table QSG–1 describes where to go for more information in this chapter and this book.

Table QSG–1. *Information Location*

To do this...	Go to...
View a short description of each chapter	"How to Use this Book" in the Introduction.
Learn more about the content of a particular chapter	The first page of each chapter describes what you will learn in the chapter. At the end of the chapter, the Summary section describes key skills or features you have learned about, and the Next Steps section suggests related chapters.
Find information in this book	Some people like to search for particular terms or words, and some like to browse things at a heading or outline level. You can do either, whichever suits your preference or current need.
	▪ **Contents at a Glance** at the beginning of the book provides the chapter numbers and names.
	▪ **Contents** at the beginning of the book provides a more comprehensive look at each chapter down to several levels of subheadings.
	▪ The **Index** at the back of the book provides page numbers for key words, concepts, and features in this book.
	▪ If you are reading this book as an eBook, use the *word search*, *text search*, or *full text search* features provided by the eReader. Searching capabilities and features vary by type of eBook.
Twelve things you should do right away	See "A Digital Dozen Things to Do Right Away" in this Quick Start Guide.
Learn about the new Windows 7 features	See "Learning Your Way around the Desktop" and "What Else is New or Improved in Windows 7" in this Quick Start Guide.
Learn about basic Windows, mouse, and keyboard skills through examples of common Windows tasks	See "Learning Basic Windows Skills and Concepts" in this Quick Start Guide.

Learning Your Way Around the Desktop

Your desktop is what fills your screen after you log in to your Windows account: the **Desktop Background, Start button, Taskbar, Notification Area,** and **Desktop Icons**. It is your palette, your gateway, your dashboard, and your organizer. Take a quick look at the new and improved Windows 7 desktop in Figure QSG–1.

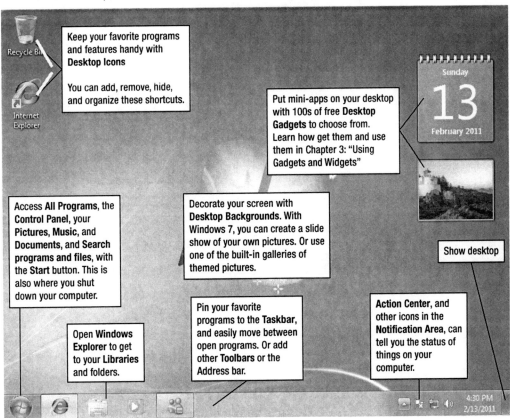

Keep your favorite programs and features handy with Desktop Icons

You can add, remove, hide, and organize these shortcuts.

Put mini-apps on your desktop with 100s of free Desktop Gadgets to choose from. Learn how get them and use them in Chapter 3: "Using Gadgets and Widgets"

Access All Programs, the **Control Panel,** your **Pictures, Music,** and **Documents,** and **Search programs and files,** with the **Start** button. This is also where you shut down your computer.

Decorate your screen with Desktop Backgrounds. With Windows 7, you can create a slide show of your own pictures. Or use one of the built-in galleries of themed pictures.

Show desktop

Open Windows Explorer to get to your **Libraries** and folders.

Pin your favorite programs to the Taskbar, and easily move between open programs. Or add other **Toolbars** or the **Address bar.**

Action Center, and other icons in the **Notification Area,** can tell you the status of things on your computer.

Figure QSG–1. *The desktop is where everything starts (and ends)*

Your desktop is like a first impression—it can set the tone for how you see and view everything about your computer. Use the **Desktop Background** as your palette to display or share with others interesting pictures and colors. It's a gateway to everything you do on your computer; you get to programs, features, settings, files, and libraries through the **Start** button and the **Taskbar**. It's your dashboard: the **Taskbar** tells you what programs are running and which windows are open, and the **Notification Area** gives you the status of important features and settings that are vital to running your computer. It's an organizer: you can bring all of your favorite or most frequently used things up front and center with **Desktop Icons, Desktop Gadgets,** and pinned items on the **Taskbar**.

Desktop Background

This is a picture, design, or color that covers your entire screen area. Everything else on your desktop sits on top of it. Figure QSG–2 shows a desktop background created from one of the built-in themes.

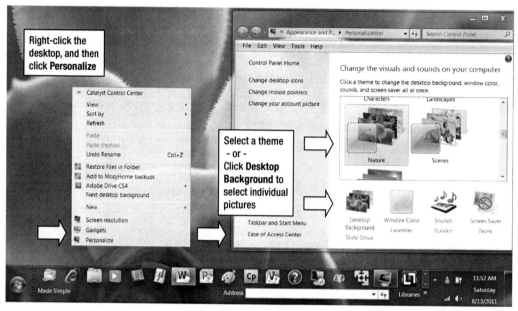

Figure QSG–2. *You can customize your desktop colors, background, and theme in the Personalization window.*

You can change just your background or you can use Themes, which can coordinate a color theme for your program window borders and taskbar with a group of pictures. You can also rotate pictures with a slide show that changes the picture in the background at intervals from every 10 seconds to every day,

To change your background, theme, or colors:

1. Right-click the desktop and then click **Personalize**.

2. In the Personalization window do one of the following:

    Select a theme from the themes list.

    Click **Desktop Background** to select your own pictures or set up a slide show.

To learn more about the desktop, see Chapter 1: "Customizing And Personalizing Windows."

Start Menu

Click the **Start** button to access the **Start menu**. You can get to almost any file, program, feature, or setting on your computer. Figure QSG–3 shows the Start menu, and Figure QSG–4 shows the "other half" when you click **All Programs**.

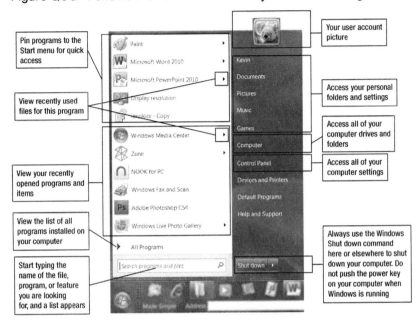

Figure QSG–3. *The Start button provides access to programs, settings, files, folders, and shut down options.*

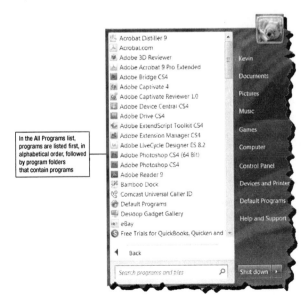

Figure QSG–4. *All Programs on the Start menu*

Taskbar

The **Taskbar** refers to both the entire bar across the bottom (or sides or top if you moved it), and the toolbar area between the Start button on the left and the Notification Area and Show Desktop button on the right, as shown in Figure QSG–5. The Taskbar combines the Quick Launch toolbar and open windows icon buttons that were separate in Windows XP and Windows Vista.

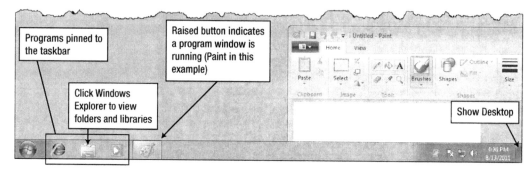

Figure QSG–5. *Program buttons on the Taskbar*

Here are a few things you can do to customize the taskbar:

- To pin a program to the taskbar, click the **Start** menu, locate the program in **All Programs**, right-click the program icon and then click **Pin this program to taskbar**. Or, right-click the program icon of an already open program on the taskbar, and then click **Pin this program to taskbar.**

- To add other toolbars such as the Address bar, Desktop, Links, Libraries, or any other folder, right click the taskbar, click **Toolbars**, and then select a toolbar from the list or select **New Toolbar**.

- To make the taskbar taller, right-click the toolbar, and clear the checkbox for **Lock the toolbar**. Then you can click the top edge of the taskbar and drag it up to the desired height.

- To minimize all windows so that only the desktop background is showing, click the **Show Desktop** button. If you have your desktop set to show desktop icons, or gadgets, or both, these will still show on the desktop.

- To move the taskbar to another side of the desktop, click and drag the taskbar to the desired location. Or right-click the taskbar, click **Properties**, and then select the new location in **Taskbar location on screen**.

Notification Area and Time

The notification area, on the far right side of the taskbar, displays icons that tell you the status and notifications about incoming e-mail, Windows updates, network connection status, and other information about the state of your computer. The Action Center icon notifies you of issues that require your attention.

The time area, to the right of the notification area, displays the clock time, day of the week, and calendar date in a wide variety of formats, as shown in Figure QSG–6. The formats available depend on the language and region your computer is set for.

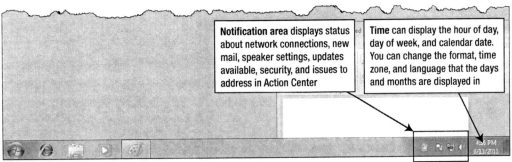

Notification area displays status about network connections, new mail, speaker settings, updates available, security, and issues to address in Action Center

Time can display the hour of day, day of week, and calendar date. You can change the format, time zone, and language that the days and months are displayed in

Figure QSG–6. *Notification and Time areas*

Here are a few ways to customize these areas:

- To change how notifications are displayed, right-click an empty area of the notification area, and then click **Customize notification icons**.

- To change the time settings, right-click the time area on the taskbar, and then click **Adjust date/time**.

- To change the language for the days of week and month names, click the **Start** button, and in **Search programs and files**, type **Region**. In the list that appears, click **Region and Language**.

Desktop Icons and Gadgets

Desktop icons are shortcuts on your desktop to files, folders, programs, and features. Since the desktop itself is a folder, you can also store actual files, folders, and programs there, too.

Desktop gadgets are mini-applications or mini-viewers that you can use directly on your desktop. Desktop gadgets are off when you first install Windows, but it is easy to add them from Windows or get additional gadgets from the Web.

Figure QSG–7 shows some examples of desktop icons and desktop gadgets.

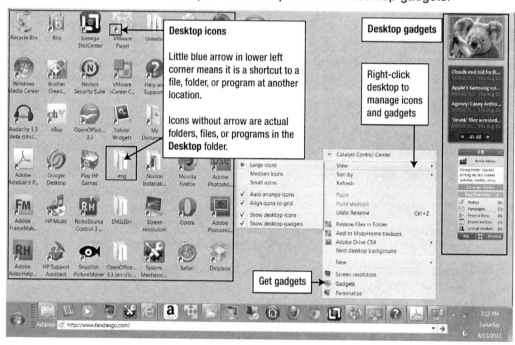

Figure QSG–7. *Desktop icons and desktop gadgets*

- To add icons to the desktop, copy and paste the icons from a folder or hold down the Control key while you click and drag a program icon from the All programs menu.

- To show, hide, or arrange desktop icons or gadgets, right-click the desktop, click **View**, and then select your settings. (Gadgets snap to each other like magnets when you put them close to each other.)

- To get or add gadgets, right-click the desktop and then click **Gadgets**.

To learn more about icons and gadgets, see Chapter 1: "Customizing And Personalizing Windows" and Chapter 3: "Using Gadgets and Widgets."

New or Improved in Windows 7

Windows 7 isn't just a facelift to make Windows look prettier. The changes and improvements make Windows 7 faster, easier, safer, more versatile with new hardware, and better equipped to how we use computers today. See Table QSG–2 for more information.

Table QSG–2. *Changes and Improvements*

Feature	Where to Learn More About It
Backup and recovery	Protect your computer with improved backup and recovery features. See Chapter 16: "Protecting Your Computer and Data."
Finding files and programs	On the Start menu, the **Search Programs and Files** box allows you to find files, folders, or programs by name. You will find examples throughout this book. Many procedures start with using the Search Programs and Files box. It is often much quicker than navigating through a series of menus like "Click the Start button, click Control Panel, and in Control Panel locate the item you want to open."
Homegroup	Share files and printers with other Windows 7 computers on your home network easier with the homegroup feature. See Chapter 15: "Connecting to the Internet and Home Networks."
Libraries	Organize and store your pictures, music, videos, and documents easier, even when they are in multiple folders on your computer or network. See Chapter 2: "Checking Out Libraries."
Make it easier to read what's on your screen	Use **Display** in **Control Panel** to adjust the size of text as it appears on your screen. See Chapter 1: "Customizing And Personalizing Windows."
Multiple monitors	Manage your multiple monitor positions, screen resolution, and screen rotation all in one window. See Chapter 14: "Connecting Monitors and Hardware."
Other network improvements	Manage your home networks and connections through the **Network and Sharing Center**. See Chapter 15: "Connecting to the Internet and Home Networks."

Feature	Where to Learn More About It
Personalizing Windows	Do more with your desktop background, themes, window color, and screen saver. See Chapter 1: "Customizing And Personalizing Windows."
Transferring User Account files and settings from another computer	You can transfer user accounts from your old Windows XP or Windows 7 computer with the Windows Easy Transfer Wizard. See Chapter 12: "Setting Up and Transferring User Accounts."
Windows Live Essentials	Download this free set of programs, if they weren't already installed by your computer manufacturer. They include programs for e-mail, instant messaging, blogging, making movies, and managing your photos. See Chapter 7: "Getting Free Goodies like Windows Live Essentials."
Windows Live Family Safety	Monitor and manage parental controls for all of your computers from a web page. Windows Live Family Safety is free and is part of the Windows Live Essentials pack. See Chapter 7: "Getting Free Goodies like Windows Live Essentials" and Chapter 12: "Setting Up and Transferring User Accounts."
Windows XP Mode and Windows Virtual PC	If you have one of the business editions of Windows 7 (Professional, Ultimate, or Enterprise), you can run most legacy programs in Windows XP Mode or Windows Virtual PC. See Chapter 18: "Using Windows at Work and On the Road."

A Digital Dozen Things to Do Right Away

Windows 7 is a very nice surprise. Many of us toiled away for close to 10 years with the reliable, sturdy, and familiar Windows XP at home and at work. A new and improved Windows was long overdue. While Windows Vista had some shiny new chrome and improvements under the hood, it wasn't enough for most of us or our employers to make the switch from Windows XP.

But Windows 7 came through. We can forget about Vista and pretend it was just a bad dream; we can wave a fond farewell to our faithful companion Windows XP.

So it is understandable if you can't wait to use Windows 7. It really is more fun, more powerful, and in most cases, easier to use. There are no tasks that are harder to do with Windows 7, but even improvements can take some time to get used to. The following sections show why certain tasks are important, how to perform them, and where to find more detailed information on them:

- Set up a backup process and create a system repair disk.
- Create a Password Reset Disk.
- Store your installation disks, product keys, manuals, and warranty information.
- Set up virus protection.
- Make sure Windows Update is set.
- Transfer settings and files from old computer.
- Set up user accounts and parental controls.
- Set up network connections and sharing.
- Set up e-mail and IM.
- Select your web browser.
- Import/export your favorites, passwords, and cookies.
- Install programs.
- Set up your printers.
- Optimize touch screen settings.

Setting Up Backup and Creating a System Repair Disk

From Chapter 16: "Protecting Your Computer and Data"

Backup is like an insurance policy: you hope you never need it, but you should set it up before you do need it. It only takes a few minutes to set up your backup process. Your first backup will take two to three hours; your regular backups after this may take about 30 minutes. In any edition of Windows 7, you can save your backup to an external drive or portable media such as USB flash drives or DVDs. With Windows 7 Professional, Ultimate, and Enterprise, you have the option of storing your backup on a network location.

A **System Repair Disk** is a special boot disk that allows you to start your computer without running Windows on your hard drive. This allows you to restore your entire computer from a disk image.

To set up backup:

1. Click the **Start** button, and in the search box type **Backup and Restore**. In the list that appears, click **Backup and Restore**.

2. Click **Set up backup**. Select a location you want to send the backup to from the list of internal or externally attached local drives, (or network, if you have a business edition of Windows 7), and then click **Next**. In the next page of the wizard you will select what you want to back up.

3. Accept the default, **Let Windows choose**.

4. Click **Next**. The next page in the wizard is where you schedule your backups.

5. Select how often to perform the backup and when. Select a time when you know your computer will be on for several hours. Click **OK** when you are done.

6. Click the **Save settings** button.

   If the button said **Save settings and exit**, when you click the button your settings are saved. In the main Backup and Restore window, click **Back up now**. Backup will begin.

   If the button said **Save settings and run backup**, when you click the button then backup will begin immediately.

To create a System Repair Disk:

1. When backup completes, click **Create a system repair disk**.

   You will need a blank CD or DVD for this.

2. Follow the instructions in the wizard and then click **Create disc**.

   When you finish creating the system repair disk, be sure to label it and store it in safe accessible where you can easily find it if you ever need it.

Creating a Password Reset Disk

From Chapter 12: "Setting Up and Transferring User Accounts"

When you first set up your computer and start adding accounts, create a **Password Reset Disk** in case somebody else who has Administrator-level access accidently or deliberately changes your account, or you forget your password. A password reset disk doesn't have to be a floppy disk (if you can even find one), CD, or DVD. You can also use a USB flash drive or external hard drive.

To create a password reset disk:

1. Click the **Start** button, and in the search box type **password reset**. In the list that appears, click **Create a password reset disk**.

   The Forgotten Password Wizard page appears.

2. Click **Next**.

   The Create a Password Reset Disk page appears.

3. Select which drive to store the password reset disk on, and then click **Next**.

   > **TIP:** If you can't tell what each drive letter is, open **Computer** in another window to find descriptions of each drive.

   The Current User Account Password page appears.

4. Type your current user account password for this account, and then click **Next**.

   A Progress page will appear.

5. When the Progress page reaches 100%, click **Next**.

6. When the wizard completes creating the Password Reset Disk, click **Finish**.

   > **NOTE:** Each user must create their own Password Reset Disk for their account.

7. Be sure to mark or label the disk so that you know that it contains the Password Reset information, and also which computer and which user this reset key is for.

Storing Your Installation Disks, Manuals, and Warranty Information

When you set up a new computer, it's easy to accumulate a big mess of boxes and packing materials, and to misplace or accidently throw out something you will need later. Get organized now to avoid such situations later. If you downloaded installation files, you should select a location on your computer or network to store those too.

What you should save:

- Software installation disks and their product keys

- Hardware and driver installation disks

- System Repair Disk

- Disaster Recovery Disk (from manufacturer or from disk you created when prompted by computer manufacturer to do so)

- Password Reset Disk

- Receipts and warranty information for your computer and any separate hardware you added

- Installation and user manuals

There are lots of different containers you can use to store things:

- **File or folder boxes for your manuals, receipts, and warranties:** If you have a lot of papers, tabbed folders that can be labeled or alphabetized can be helpful, especially for small receipts that otherwise might float around loosely in the box.

- **DVD disk albums with disk sleeves or plastic disk bins:** Be sure to keep your product keys written down with your disks. Index cards are handy for writing down your product keys, and for organizing if you keep them in a bin.

Go digital!

You may be able to store most of your paper things in PDF files.

- If you have a scanner, scan your receipts, product keys, and simple one- or two-page manuals to PDF or graphics files, and then store the files on your computer.

- Look for online PDF versions of your manuals and download them to your computer. You'll often find these available from the hardware or software manufacturer's support site.

NOTE: Even if you can create or download PDF files for your paper items, you will still need to keep your physical installation, repair, and reset disks.

You should also keep installation files for any programs you downloaded from the Internet. There is a handy **Downloads** folder in **My Documents**, or you can create a special folder of your own. If possible, regularly make a backup copy of this folder and store it safely away from your computer.

See Chapter 2: "Checking Out Libraries" to learn how to access the Document library and create your own libraries.

See Chapter 5: "Installing Programs" to learn about storing and protecting installation disks, files, and product keys.

See Chapter 13: "Printing, Faxing, and Scanning" to learn more about using a scanner, optical character recognition programs, and going paperless.

See Chapter 16: "Protecting Your Computer and Data" to learn more about backing up folders and files.

Setting Up Virus Protection

From Chapter 16: "Protecting Your Computer and Data"

Most new computers come with a free 30, 60, or 90 day trial version of a virus protection program or security suite. If you have a trial version, you can usually buy an upgrade to the full version by opening the program and clicking a buy, purchase, or upgrade button or command and providing payment information. If you aren't sure what kind of virus protection you have, and you haven't been bombarded with warning messages from Windows that virus protection is off, you can easily check your security status.

> **TIP:** When you install your antivirus software, or if it is already installed on your computer, make sure you set the software to automatically download and install antivirus software updates.

To check your security status and set up virus protection if needed:

1. Click the **Start** button, and in the search box type **Security status**. In the list that appears, click **Check security status**.

2. In **Action Center**, click the **Security** down arrow to see what virus programs are installed and running.

   If Action Center says your virus protection is on, that's great and you're done here.

   If you don't have a virus protection program installed, you easily find one from the Action Center. Continue to the next step.

3. In the Action Center Security section, click Find a program online.

   Windows will connect to the Internet and access a Microsoft web page listing virus protection and security programs that are compatible with Windows 7.

4. Click the company logos to go to the websites and view the offerings. Most offer a free 30-day trial so you can install the program and try it before you buy it.

5. When you find one that you like, follow the instructions on your screen to purchase, download, and install the software.

> **TIP:** You may be able to get free security software from your employer if you often use your home computers to work from home or connect to the corporate network. Also, many Internet providers offer free or reduced cost security suites for their subscribers.

Setting Windows Update to Automatic

From Chapter 16: "Protecting Your Computer and Data"

Many of the newsworthy mass infections of computers by viruses and Trojan horses could have been prevented if users had kept their computer security up to date with Windows Update and automatic updating of antivirus software. Fortunately, Windows makes it easy for you to "set it and forget it" with Windows Updates.

To set Windows Update to automatically install updates:

1. Click the **Start** button, and in the search box type **Windows Update**. In the list that appears, click **Windows Update**.

2. In the left column of the **Windows Update** window, click **Change settings**.

    The **Change settings** window appears.

3. Click the drop-down list under Important updates, and then select Install updates automatically (recommended).

4. If desired, set how often you want Windows to install updates and at what time.

    If your computer is not on at the scheduled time, Windows will install the updates the next time your computer is on.

Transferring Settings and Files from an Old Computer

From Chapter 12: "Setting Up and Transferring User Accounts"

If your new Windows 7 computer replaces a Windows XP or Vista computer, you can copy all of your personal settings, documents, and preferences to your new one with Windows Easy Transfer.

Windows Easy Transfer is a wizard that will guide you through the process:

1. Run Windows Easy Transfer on your old and new computer. (You may have to download and install Windows Easy Transfer on your old computer if it is running Windows XP. Windows Vista already has Windows Easy Transfer.)

2. Choose a method of transfer—through a network connection, an Easy Transfer cable, or by copying to storage media such as a USB flash drive, external hard drive, or removable discs such as CDs or DVDs.

3. Windows Easy Transfer scans your old computer to determine what can be transferred and the size of the transfer.

4. Choose what to transfer. Windows Easy Transfer suggests what to transfer, but you can customize the list to include or exclude specific files or folders.

5. Transfer the files and settings directly to your new computer (via a Easy Transfer cable or in real time through a network connection) or to a storage location (network share, external hard drive, USB flash drive, or CD/DVD discs) for transfer later to the new computer.

To access the Windows Easy Transfer wizard:

1. On your new computer, click the Start button and in the Search box type Windows Easy Transfer.

2. In the search results list that appears, click Windows Easy Transfer.

3. Follow the instructions in the wizard.

The Windows Easy Transfer wizard works quite well, but there are a lot of things you can do before, during, and after the transfer to make it smooth and successful. Fortunately, we have taken the scariness out of it with extensive instructions and screen shots to walk you all the way through.

> **TIP:** Windows Easy Transfer allows you to transfer one or all user accounts to the new computer. You can save a lot of time for yourself and the rest of your family if you do this right away because you won't have to start all over creating new accounts for them on the new computer— Windows Easy Transfer can do that for you.

Setting Up User Accounts and Parental Controls

From Chapter 7: "Getting Free Goodies like Windows Live Essentials" and Chapter 12: "Setting Up and Transferring User Accounts"

You will want to set these up right away to protect preferences, access, and privacy for each user, and where needed, place controls or restrictions on your children's use.

User Accounts allow you to:

- Assign each user the appropriate permissions level. This will give you control over what programs are installed, and it will prevent the wrong people from accidently doing something that harms the computer or other users.

- Provide each user with their own set of folders in My Documents.

- Let each user have separate desktop backgrounds, color preferences, and other personal customizations.

- Set separate parental control levels for each child.

- Control access to each account by letting users have their own passwords.

To add a user:

1. Click the **Start** button, and in the search box type **User Account**. In the list that appears, click **User Accounts**.

2. In the **User Accounts** window, click **Manage another account**.

> **TIP:** If all you want is a temporary account for a visitor, click **Guest**, and you're done.

3. In the Manage Accounts window, click Create a new account.

    The Create New Account window appears.

4. In the Create New Account window, type the new account name, select Standard user or Administrator, and then click Create Account.

    The new account is displayed.

> **CAUTION:** Neither of the Standard user accounts in this example are password protected, but they should be.

To add a password:

After you add a user account, the user should log in to their account to set the password. Once they are logged in, they can set their own password.

1. Click the **Start** button, and in the search box type **password**. In the list that appears, click **Change your Windows password.**

2. In the **User Accounts** window, click **Create a password for your account.**

3. On the **Create Your Password** page, type the new password in both boxes, and optionally type a password hint that will help you remember but not be obvious for others to guess.

4. Click **Create password.**

5. When you are done, the user account will now display "Password Protected" under the name.

To set up Parental Controls:

1. Log in to Windows with an Administrator account.

2. Click **Start**, and in the **Search programs and folders** box, type **Parental Controls.**

3. In the list that appears, select **Parental Controls.**

4. In the **Parental Controls** window, click the user you want to apply the settings to.

5. In the **User Controls** window, click **On, enforce current settings**.

6. Click **Time Limits**.

7. In the **Time Restrictions** window, select the hours each day that you want to block use of the computer.

8. Click **OK** when you are done with the Time Restrictions.

9. In the **User Controls** window, click **Games.**

10. In the **Games** window, click **Set game ratings.**

11. In the **Game Restrictions** window, set blocking games by rating and content:

    - **Allow or block games with no rating**: Choose one or the other.

    - **Which ratings are ok for user to play**: Choose one level. Your selection includes all of the levels above it.

    - **Block these types of content**: Select none, one, many, or all. By default, none are selected (nothing is blocked). There are about 76 separate checkboxes. Content types are listed alphabetically, not by maturity level.

12. Click **OK**.

13. Click **Block or Allow** specific games.

The Game Overrides window displays what games currently installed on this computer can be played according to the ratings and content descriptions you selected in the Games Control window. If you have several ages of users, such as adults, teens, and younger, you may have games that are not suitable for younger users. You can ensure that those games are blocked if they are not already blocked by the rating level or content blocking.

14. When you are done viewing or making changes, click **OK** twice to exit Game overrides and Games Controls.

15. In the **User Controls** window, click **Allow and block specific programs** if you want to block your child from using specific programs.

16. In the **Applications Restrictions** window, click **<User> can only use the programs I allow**. It takes a few minutes for Windows to complete gathering a list of most of the registered programs on your computer.

CAUTION: This list will appear with no programs selected. If you close this window without selecting programs, when this user logs in, many background programs will not run. Instead, your child will see 20 or 30 message boxes saying that Parental Controls has blocked specific programs.

---

17. A good way to use this list is to click **Check All**, and then clear the check boxes for the specific programs you want to block.

18. Click **OK** when you are done selecting which programs are allowed, and then click **OK** again to close the Parental Controls for this account. Repeat this procedure for each user account you want to set Parental Controls for.

CAUTION: Parental Controls do not include any kind of web or e-mail filtering. Through Parental Controls, you can block specific e-mail programs from running, but you can't block Internet Explorer. However, you can get web filtering and additional parental controls through Windows Live Family Safety, which is part of Windows Live Essentials.

Setting Up Network Connections and Sharing

From Chapter 15: "Connecting to the Internet and Home Networks"

Windows 7 made several improvements that make connecting to a network and sharing with other computers easier. With the Network and Sharing Center, you can quickly see if you are connected to a network and set up a connection if you aren't.

Setting Up Your Network Connections

To check your current connections, go to the Network and Sharing Center:

1. Click the Windows **Start** button, and in the **Start** menu's search box, type **Network**.

2. In the results list, under **Control Panel**, click **Network and Sharing Center**. The Network and Sharing Center appears.

3. At the top of the page, check the diagram under **View your basic network information and set up connections** it should show a computer connected through a network to the Internet. If there is a red X on one of the connections in the diagram or says "You are currently not connected by any networks," you may just need to set up the network connection.

To connect to a home network and then to the Internet, make sure you have the following:

- An Internet Service Provider (ISP)—this is usually your cable or telephone company.

- A cable or DSL broadband modem, usually provided by your ISP for a small monthly rental fee.

- A router to provide wireless or wired access for your computers. Even if you only plan on having one computer, getting a wireless router will give you the freedom to move your computer to almost any room in your house.

> **TIP:** If you are setting up new Internet service, check with your ISP to see if they have combination modem/routers.

To connect to a wired home network:

- Connect an Ethernet cable (also known as Cat5e, Cat6, LAN cable) to your PC and your router. Windows should automatically detect the network and connect to it. If this is your own home network, you shouldn't need a password to connect. If you can't get a network or Internet connection and have everything connected from the computer to the router to the modem to the wall jack where your ISP line comes in, there are several things you can check:
  - Make sure all cable connections are firmly connected.
  - Check your modem and routers to make sure the power is on.
  - Try replacing each cable one by one. Sometimes the cable is defective.

To connect to your wireless home network:

1. Make sure your broadband modem is on.

2. In Windows on your computer, click the **Start** button, and then type **Network** in the **Start** menu's search box.

3. In the list that appears, click **Network and Sharing Center**.

4. Click **Set up a new connection or network**.

5. Click **Connect to the Internet** and then click **Next**.

6. In the Connect to the Internet window, click **Wireless**.

   Windows will detect any nearby wireless networks and list them. If you live in a densely populated area, you may see other wireless networks listed besides your own. The green bars next to each detected network in the list indicate their signal strength. The more green bars, the stronger the signal.

7. Click *your* wireless network.

   The network entry will expand to show a Connect button.

8. Select **Connect automatically** (if this is your own network and you plan to use it all the time when you are at home), and then click **Connect**.

   If you set up security protection when you previously installed your wireless router, you will be prompted for a network security key. Type the network security key and then click **OK**. If you don't remember your network security key, check the documentation that came with your wireless router on how to reset the security key.

Setting Up Network Sharing

If all of your computers are running Windows 7, you can use the new homegroup feature. With homegroup, you can share any, all, or none of your Libraries with other Windows 7 computers or users on your home network. If this is the first Windows 7 computer you have connected to your network, you'll have to create the homegroup. Fortunately, homegroups are easy to create and easy for the other computers to join.

To create a homegroup for the first Windows 7 computer on your home network:

1. Click the **Start** button, and then type **homegroup** in the **Start** menu's search box.

2. Click **Homegroup**. Since this is the first Windows 7 computer on your home network, you will be prompted to create a homegroup.

3. Click **Create a homegroup**. The next screen prompts you to choose what you'd like to share with other computers in your homegroup—music, videos, pictures, and documents. Most items are preselected, except for documents, which tend to be more private or individual. You may want to select documents if you regularly work on many of your documents from more than one computer in your homegroup.

   The settings that you select to share apply only to the current user. Each user must specify their settings by logging on to the computer under his or her own account.

4. Select or clear the check boxes to specify what to share and then click **Next**. In the next screen, Windows displays the password for your homegroup. You will need to type this password on each computer in your home network to join the homegroup. The password is case sensitive.

5. Follow the instructions on your screen and then click **Finish**.

   After you have set up the first computer in a homegroup, when you add other Windows 7 computers to your home network, they will detect the homegroup and offer to join it.

Adding Network Printers

There are many ways to share your printers on your network. With homegroup features, network sharing, network-ready printers, and the growing popularity of network attached storage, you have more choices than ever. See Chapter 13: "Printing, Faxing, and Scanning" for complete steps and diagrams for almost every imaginable way to share printers in your home networks.

Setting Up E-mail and IM

From Chapter 7: "Getting Free Goodies like Windows Live Essentials" and Chapter 8: "Communicating with E-mail, IM, and Social Networks."

Windows 7 doesn't provide any free e-mail or instant messaging programs. However, Microsoft includes them in a group of free programs called **Windows Live Essentials** that you can download and install on Windows 7. Computer manufacturers have the option of pre-installing Windows Live Essentials on their computers, so you may already have it.

You have many choices for free e-mail and instant messaging accounts that you can access from any computer on the Web. If you just want to dive into getting and setting up an e-mail or IM service, the following list provides some of the more popular programs and where to download them from:

- Windows Live Mail and Windows Live Messenger: Download Windows Live Essentials from `http://explore.live.com/windows-live-essentials.` Windows Live Mail can be accessed as a program on your computer or as web-based mail (no installation required) at `http://mail.live.com/`.

- Mozilla Thunderbird: You can download this mail client from `www.mozilla.org/thunderbird`.

- Gmail (Google) is web-based so you can access it by going to their web site in almost any browser: `www.gmail.com`. You can download their instant messaging program, Google Talk, from `www.google.com/talk/`.

- Yahoo! Mail is web-based so you can access it by going to their web site at `www.yahoo.com`. You can also download Yahoo! Messenger from `http://messenger.yahoo.com`.

- AOL Mail is web-based so you can access it by going to their web site at `http://mail.aol.com`. You can download AOL Instant Messenger from `www.aim.com`.

- Meebo is an instant messaging client program that can display all of your IM accounts from Google Talk, AOM. Yahoo!, Windows Live, and many more, all in one window. You can set up Meebo at `www.meebo.com`.

- Trillian is another instant messaging client like Meebo, and it can display most of your IM accounts in one window. You can download it from `www.trillian.im` (Note that is .im at the end, not .com).

Transferring Your Contacts and Address Books

Almost every installation program for e-mail or instant messaging will offer the option to import your contacts and address books from your old e-mail service to your new one (you can also do this yourself later on). Sometimes it's hard to find this feature, but it's usually offered. It would be nice if you could tell your new e-mail program to import contacts or the address book from your old e-mail program.

What you really need to do is the following:

1. In your old e-mail program, find an export contacts or address book command.

2. Export the contacts to a file. There many file formats for contacts, so before you export the contacts, you may need to find out what file formats your new e-mail program can import.

3. Open your new e-mail program and find the import contacts feature.

4. When prompted for the file name and location of the contacts file, browse to the folder where you stored the exported contacts.

The key to success is finding the export command on your old e-mail program and the import command on your new e-mail program.

Selecting and Setting Up Your Web Browser

From Chapter 9: "Surfing the Web"

When you get a new Windows 7 computer, Internet Explorer is usually set up as your default web browser. In some countries and regions, however, the government requires that no browser can be set as the default, so you will be shown a list of alternate browsers you can install instead of Internet Explorer.

Even if Internet Explorer is already set as your default web browser, you still have a choice, and you can install several different web browsers on the same machine. Here are some of the more popular alternatives:

- **Mozilla Firefox,** www.mozilla.com/firefox

- **Google Chrome,** www.google.com/chrome

- **Opera,** www.opera.com

- **Apple Safari,** www.apple.com/safari/download/

NOTE: If you are on a corporate network, check with your IT department before installing a different browser or updating to a newer version of your existing browser. Sometimes internal programs and web sites need to be updated or tested for compatibility with new browsers or versions by your IT department before they will approve and support it.

Import/export your favorites, passwords, and cookies

If you've been using your browser for a long time on your old computer, you probably have a lot of favorite web sites on your Favorites lists. If you are starting with Windows 7 on a new computer, you can export your favorites or bookmarks from your old computer to a file, and then import that file into your browser on your new computer. Many browsers store the favorites in a file named or similar to **bookmarks.htm**.

Some browsers can import all of your browser settings: bookmarks, passwords for web sites, and cookies. You can find import and export options in most browsers. Several browsers also offer syncing of your browser settings (for the same browser) across all of your computers:

- In Internet Explorer, select **File ➤ Import and export**. Sync is available through Windows Live Mesh, a feature available with Windows Live Essentials.

- In Mozilla Firefox, select **Bookmarks ➤ Show All Bookmarks ➤ Import and Backup.** To set up Sync for Firefox, select **Tools ➤ Set Up Sync**

- In Google Chrome, select **Customize** (wrench button in toolbar) **➤ Options ➤ Bookmarks ➤ Bookmark manager**. To sync Chrome settings, select **Customize** (wrench button in toolbar) **➤ Options ➤ Personal Stuff ➤ Sync ➤ Set up sync.**

- In Opera, select **File ➤ Import and Export**. To sync Opera settings, select **Tools ➤ Synchronize Opera ➤ Enable Synchronization.**

- In Apple Safari, select **File ➤ Import Bookmarks** or **File ➤ Export Bookmarks.** To sync Safari settings across all of your Safari installations on other computers as well as your iPad, iPhone, or iTouch, set up MobileMe at www.apple.com/mobileme/setup/pc.html.

TIP: When you use Windows Easy Transfer to move your User Accounts from your old computer to your new Windows 7 computer, you can include your browser settings. This way you don't have to export the settings from your old computer and then import them into your new computer.

Installing Programs 1 – 2 – 3

From Chapter 5: "Installing Programs"

Installing a program may seem as simple as putting a disk in your computer or downloading and file and clicking install. But once in a while something goes wrong during or after installation. Follow these simple steps and you may minimize installation headaches:

1. Prepare for installation:

   a. Check to make sure you have any needed license or activation keys.

   b. Allow time to download and run the installation program.

   c. Check program requirements: memory, disk space, video memory.

   d. Login as an administrator, or have an administrator user nearby who can enter password if required for User Account Control.

   e. Check program compatibility with Windows 7 and other programs on your computer.

   f. Create a System Restore checkpoint if you are installing a large program or several programs in a row.

2. Start the installation:

   a. Locate and run the installation program from the Web, your computer, or a folder on your network.

   b. Review security warnings when they appear. Proceed if you feel safe.

   c. If installation goes okay, you can finish the installation.

      If installation doesn't work, see Chapter 5: "Installing Programs" and Chapter 17: "Troubleshooting and Maintaining Your Computer."

3. Finish the installation:

   a. Even if the installation program doesn't require it, restart your computer when installation is complete.

   b. After restarting your computer, try out the newly installed program.

      If the program doesn't work correctly, uninstall it and then reinstall. Or, run System Restore to restore your computer to a restore point before the install when your computer last worked correctly.

   c. Store your installation programs/disks and product keys in a safe place.

Setting Up Your Printers

From Chapter 13: "Printing, Faxing, and Scanning"

Most printers should just work when you connect them to your computer. Windows detects and identifies the device, and then it installs the right drivers from the set of drivers that are already provided by Windows.

To install a new printer out of the box:

1. Unpack the printer. The box usually contains a power cord, installation instructions, warranty information, a starter ink cartridge set, and an installation disk. Most printers don't come with the USB cord to hook up the printer to your computer.

2. Remove all of the wrapping. Some parts may be taped to keep parts from opening or coming apart during shipping.

3. Follow the installation instructions provided by the manufacturer. There may be important steps to unpack and install the printer cartridges before turning on the printer and connecting it to the computer.

To install an older printer on a Windows 7 computer:

1. Make sure your computer is connected to the Internet.

2. Try installing from the printer's original installation disk, if available, because it may contain print utilities from the manufacturer that are not included in the printer drivers provided by Windows 7.

3. Connect the printer to the computer and turn on the printer. If Windows 7 has the drivers, it will automatically install the printer; you will find it in the Devices and Printers folder.

If Windows 7 can't find the right printer driver, it will attempt to locate a driver from Windows Update. A printer model may be so new that there were no drivers available when Windows 7 was released. Conversely, your printer may be so old or uncommon that drivers weren't included in Windows 7. In either case you can, try installing the driver manually.

To manually install a printer driver:

1. Click the **Start** menu, and in **Search programs and files**, type **Add a printer**.

2. In the list that appears, click **Add a Printer**.

3. In the **Add Printer** wizard, click **Add a local printer**.

4. In the **Choose a printer port** page, make sure **Use an existing port** is selected, and then click **Next**.

5. On the Install the printer driver page, click Windows Update.

6. When Windows finishes updating the list of printers, select the printer manufacturer and printer model, and then click **Next**.

7. Complete the wizard, and then click **Finish**.

Learning Basic Windows Skills and Concepts

Whether you learn better by reading descriptions or seeing illustrations, one of the best ways to learn Windows is with hands on experience. Throughout the book you will find examples and explanations of various skills and techniques integrated with procedures. Chapter 6: "Using WordPad, Paint, and Accessories" provides a wide variety of exercises and explanations to help you learn many basic keyboard and mouse skills.

Table QSG–3 lists skills and tasks that are the basis for a lot of things you do in Windows and on your PC.

Table QSG–3. *Skills and Tasks*

Skills and Tasks	Where to Practice It
Installing programs	In addition to "Installing programs 1-2-3" and Chapter 5: "Installing Programs," there are many other examples throughout the book:
	▓ Chapter 3: "Using Gadgets and Widgets"
	▓ Chapter 7: "Getting Free Goodies like Windows Live Essentials"
	▓ Chapter 9: "Surfing the Web"
	▓ Chapter 16: "Protecting Your Computer and Data"
	▓ Chapter 17: "Troubleshooting and Maintaining Your Computer"
	▓ Chapter 18: "Using Windows at Work and On the Road"
Installing hardware devices and drivers	▓ Chapter 13: "Printing, Faxing, and Scanning"
	▓ Chapter 14: "Connecting Monitors and Hardware"
	▓ Chapter 17: "Troubleshooting and Maintaining Your Computer"
Building keyboard skills	▓ Chapter 6: "Using WordPad, Paint, and Accessories"
Practicing text and paragraph formatting	▓ Chapter 6: "Using WordPad, Paint, and Accessories"

Skills and Tasks	Where to Practice It
Building mouse skills	▨ Chapter 6: "Using WordPad, Paint, and Accessories"
Common Windows hotkeys for file, formatting, and editing commands	▨ Chapter 6: "Using WordPad, Paint, and Accessories"
Using right-click menus	▨ Chapter 6: "Using WordPad, Paint, and Accessories"
Using drag and drop	▨ Chapter 6: "Using WordPad, Paint, and Accessories"
Using CTRL keys	▨ Chapter 6: "Using WordPad, Paint, and Accessories"
Using cut and paste	▨ Chapter 6: "Using WordPad, Paint, and Accessories"
Copying text or pictures between programs	▨ Chapter 6: "Using WordPad, Paint, and Accessories"
Formatting text, characters, and paragraphs	▨ Chapter 6: "Using WordPad, Paint, and Accessories"
Inserting pictures or objects into a document	▨ Chapter 6: "Using WordPad, Paint, and Accessories"
Using the new Office-style ribbon	▨ Chapter 6: "Using WordPad, Paint, and Accessories"
Working with folders and libraries	▨ Chapter 2: "Checking Out Libraries"
Save vs. Save as	▨ Chapter 17: "Troubleshooting and Maintaining Your Computer"

Making Your PC More Touch Friendly

Windows has provided various touch interface features in Windows since 2001 when Microsoft introduced the Windows-based Tablet PC. Originally, touch in Windows meant you could use a stylus to tap the screen in place of using a mouse. Along with handwriting recognition, you could eliminate the need for a mouse and keyboard. But Windows has never been re-designed from the ground up as a touch interface. Windows 7 does provide many features for touch, but they don't yet match the experience of using an iPad or Android-based tablet. Reports in computer publications and information from Microsoft indicate that the next version of Windows will be very touch-friendly.

In the meantime, there are several types of devices you can use for touch input in Windows 7. Understanding what they are designed for and their limitations will help you understand how to get the most out of a touch screen; see Table QSG–4.

Table QSG–4. *Touch Input Devices*

Device	Description
Windows tablets	Many computer manufacturers offer devices that only function as tablets. Some offer docks with keyboards or USB ports so that you can add a keyboard, mouse, etc. These devices often have limited memory and slower hardware, so they're not very suitable for intensive multi-application work or as an overall replacement for your desktop PC or laptop.
Convertible tablet/laptop or netbook	There are several convertible tablets designed (and priced) more for business users. Convertible means the screen flips or rotates so that you can use it in either laptop mode with the built-in keyboard and touchpad, or as a touch screen tablet folded flat. Because these are designed for business users, their performance is similar to that of a regular laptop.
All-in-one touch screen desktops	These tend to be designed as media centers, so they have the memory to do all of your intensive office and graphics-type programs as well.
Touch tablet input devices	You can add graphic tablets like those produced by **Wacom** that provide a small tablet area that sits on your desk. They usually offer finger touch as well as stylus touch support.
Touch-screen monitors	These can be purchased for home use but are probably more often used for things like public kiosks with the keyboard, mouse, and PC itself hidden from view.

Within the limitations of Windows 7, there are several features you can use to make your touch screen friendlier to your touch:

- Simplify your expectations for what you can do with a touch user interface. Use the touch features for uses they do best. While you can type documents, create spreadsheets, and create presentations just using the touch user interface and soft keyboards, those are nont suitable for performing these tasks for hours on end. Choose the programs in each category that work best on touchscreens for viewing pictures, watching videos, listening to music, reading eBooks, browsing, and e-mail

- Set up **Tablet PC** in **Control Panel**. If your computer is sold as a Windows 7 touch device, this should already be in Control Panel. If not, install it through **Control Panel ➤ Programs and Features ➤ Turn Windows features on or off**.

- Download and install Microsoft Touch Pack for Windows 7 from www.microsoft.com/download/en/details.aspx?id=17368. While not essential to using multi-touch, it includes several games and applications that can be helpful in getting proficient with touch.

- Teach your computer to read your handwriting. To open Handwriting Personalization, click **Start ➤ All Programs ➤ Accessories ➤ Tablet PC ➤ Personalize Handwriting Recognition**.

- Pin a shortcut to the taskbar, Start menu, or desktop to the Tablet PC Input Panel. The Tablet Input Panel provides a small input area for handwriting recognition or touch keyboard. You'll find it at **Start ➤ All Programs ➤ Accessories ➤Tablet PC ➤ Tablet PC Input Panel.**

- Pin a shortcut to the taskbar, Start menu, or desktop to the On-Screen Keyboard. This is different from the keyboard in the Tablet Input Panel. You'll find it at **Start ➤ All Programs ➤ Accessories ➤ Ease of Access ➤ On-Screen Keyboard.**

- Learn more about touch gestures and practice them. Click Start ➤ Help and Support and then search for "using touch gestures."

- Build proficiency by practicing. Solitaire and other card games are a great way to practice the actions you would normally do with a mouse. For an even greater challenge, try the editing and formatting exercises with WordPad in Chapter 6: "Using WordPad, Paint, and Accessories."

- Try any touch software provided by your computer manufacturer. These provide quick access to media programs, games, and features designed for touch. For example, Dell provides the Duo Stage software for its Inspiron Duo Tablet PC, as shown in Figure QSG–8.

Figure QSG–8. *Dell Stage touch UI provided by Dell for its Inspiron Duo Tablet PC*

■ Use desktop icons as your main access to programs and files. Use large icons, and thin them out to only a dozen or less. You can add a folder to the desktop and put less frequently used icons there, as shown in Figure QSG–9. To further clean up the desktop, auto-hide the task bar. Right-click **Start** button ➤ **Properties** ➤ **Taskbar** tab ➤ **Auto-hide the taskbar**.

Figure QSG–9. *A few large icons on the desktop provide easy access*

■ Try out different media players, browsers, and mail programs to see which is easiest to use on a touch screen. For example, Windows Media Center with its "10-foot interface" is really good for touch because of its large UI and easy navigation. It was designed for easy use with a remote control, so it's not as dependent on mouse or keyboard input. Figure QSG–10 shows the main page of Windows Media Center.

Figure QSG–10. *Windows Media Center is well suited for touch screens*

- Give your fingers bigger targets on windows and menus. Create a custom theme in Personalization. Customize your windows colors and sizes through the Windows 7 Basic (non-Aero) theme. You can make scroll bars, menus, text, and buttons larger. Right-click the **desktop ➤ Personalize ➤ Windows Color ➤ Advanced appearance settings ➤ Windows Color and Appearance**. When you find the right settings, save them as a custom theme. This way, if there are times you want your desktop to look normal, you can switch back and forth between a standard Aero theme and your enlarged touch UI screen. Figure QSG–11 shows an example of the settings at a larger size.

Figure QSG–11. *Using a Basic (non-Aero) Windows colors setting you can make menus, scroll bars, buttons, and labels extra-large for easier targets*

Summary

With this Quick Start Guide you now have a pretty good orientation to the new and improved desktop and Windows 7 features. Now you know a few quick procedures to get your computer up and running. But we've only scratched the surface of what you can do with Windows 7 and your PC. *Windows 7 Made Simple* is more than a book using Windows 7. It's about how to do much more on your computer, starting with Windows 7.

Next Steps

As mentioned at the beginning of the Quick Start Guide, even though the chapters are numbered, you don't have to use them in order. The closest thing to a list of specific things to do is "A Digital Dozen Things to Do Right Away." Before you dive into the fun things, it really is important that you set up protection for your computer with scheduled backups, a Password Reset Disk, activated virus protection, and security programs and Windows Update set to automatic.

New Users

If you are a new PC or Windows 7 user, after reading this Quick Start Guide, I suggest starting with Chapter 6: "Using WordPad, Paint, and Accessories" to learn and improve your mouse and keyboard skills with the section on WordPad. Then move on to these chapters in whatever order interests you most:

- Chapters 1-11
- Chapters 16-17

Experienced or Advanced Users

Many common computer tasks don't change much between versions of Windows. But several features and functions have improved or change quite a bit. The following chapters will help you with those changes, as well as the more technical or advanced features:

- Chapter 1: "Customizing And Personalizing Windows"
- Chapter 2: "Checking Out Libraries"
- Chapter 12: "Setting Up and Transferring User Accounts"
- Chapter 13: "Printing, Faxing, and Scanning"
- Chapter 14: "Connecting Monitors and Hardware"
- Chapter 15: "Connecting to the Internet and Home Networks"
- Chapter 16: "Protecting Your Computer and Data"
- Chapter 17: "Troubleshooting and Maintaining Your Computer"
- Chapter 18: "Using Windows at Work and On the Road"

Part II

Chapter 1

Customizing and Personalizing Windows

Don't let the word *customizing* scare you. It doesn't mean a lot of tinkering or risks. It's making Windows work for you—and still look pleasing. Customizing can be fun, and you can do as much or as little as you want. When you customize Windows, you're also *personalizing* it—because each person using the computer can personalize it with their own user account, preferences, and documents.

You like soft jazz, soothing landscapes, and you work on a lot of spreadsheets and reports. Your daughter likes pink. And purple. And some other colors the names of which you don't even know. Your son is into video games, and what he likes is dark and scary. If you three share the same computer, good news! You can each have your own background pictures, windows colors, and sounds, thanks to personalization.

> **TIP:** Have you had a chance to browse through the Quick Start Guide? It's a great way to get acquainted with Windows 7 and the desktop. It's also a roadmap to find your way around this book. We'll also share some tips and tricks to get you up and running in no time.

This chapter covers the following tasks to customize Windows for fun and ease-of-use:

- Changing your Welcome screen
- Changing your desktop background
- Setting up your screen saver
- Making the screen easier to read
- Managing Windows sounds
- Making your computer more accessible
- Adjusting your mouse

Changing Your Welcome Screen Picture

The first place you see any kind of personalization in Windows 7 is your Welcome screen. The Welcome screen displays all the user accounts on your computer, as shown in Figure 1–1.

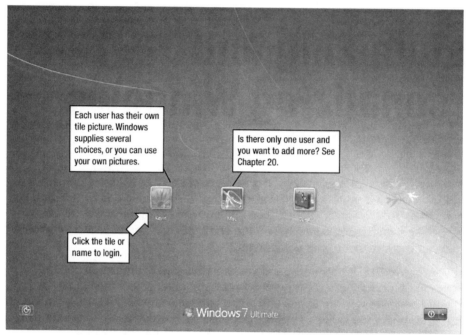

Figure 1–1. *The Welcome screen displays the user accounts on your computer.*

When you click a username or tile, Windows asks you for your password, as shown in Figure 1–2.

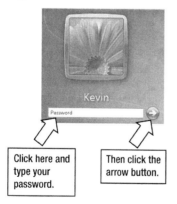

Figure 1–2. *Each user sets their login password and picture. The username and tile also appear at the top of the Start menu.*

> **CAUTION:** Even if you are the only person using your computer, you should always set up your user account to require a password. See Chapter 20 for more information.

Using a Picture Provided by Windows

After you log in, you can change your user tile if you like.

1. Click the **Start** button, and in the **Start** menu's search box, type account picture. In the list that appears, click **Change your account picture**.

    The Change Your Picture window appears, as shown in Figure 1–3.

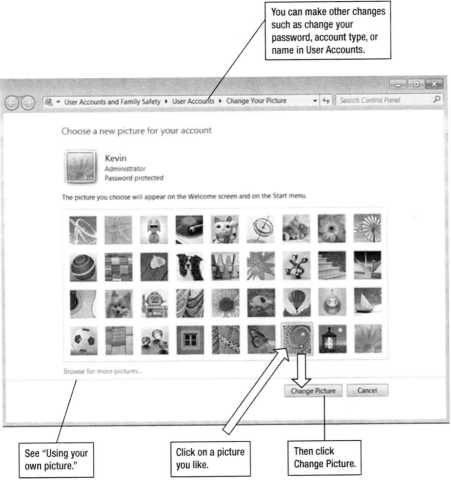

Figure 1–3. *You can choose from a variety of pictures provided by Windows, or you can browse for other pictures on your computer.*

2. Click a picture you like, and then click **Change Picture**. The Change your picture window closes and returns you to the User Account page.

> Your new picture is displayed on your User Accounts page, as shown in Figure 1–4.

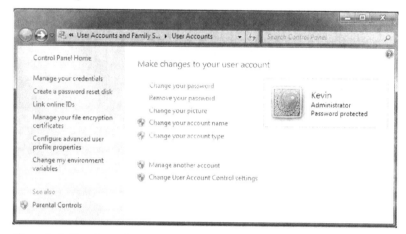

Figure 1–4. *User Accounts page*

It also will appear on your Start menu and login screen, as shown in Figure 1–5.

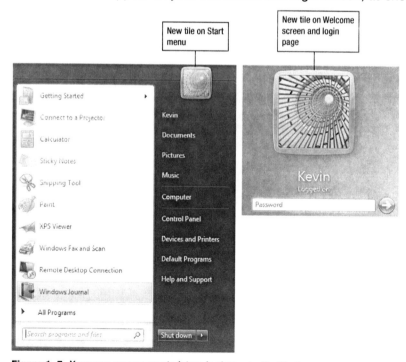

Figure 1–5. *Your new user account picture is shown on the Start menu.*

Using Your Own Picture

But what if you want to use another picture from your computer, not one from the Change Your Picture window? You can select other pictures on your computer, such as pictures in your Picture library. If you haven't had a chance to add your own personal pictures to your computer, try this out with a picture from the Sample Pictures folder in the Pictures Library.

1. Click the **Start** button, and in the **Start** menu's search box, type **account picture**. In the list that appears, click **Change your account picture**.

   The Change Your Picture window appears.

2. Click **Browse** for more pictures.

   An **Open** window appears, allowing you to navigate to the libraries or folders that contain other pictures on your computer.

   For example, the Documents library might not have any pictures, but you will find a Sample Pictures folder in the Pictures library, as shown in Figure 1–6.

Figure 1–6. *Even if your computer is new and you haven't added any personal photos or pictures yet, Windows 7 provides pictures in the Sample Pictures folder.*

3. Locate the picture you want. For example, find the Koala picture shown in Figure 1–7.

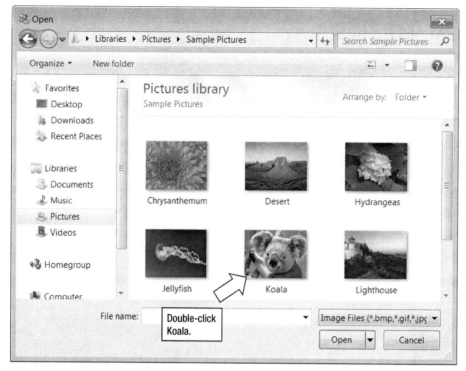

Figure 1–7. *When you locate the picture you want, double-click it.*

4. Double-click the picture you want to use.

In a few moments, Windows displays your User Accounts window where you can see the new picture in place, as shown in Figure 1–8. Windows crops the sides or top and bottom of rectangular pictures to make them fit into the square tile without stretching or distorting the picture. Windows does not crop or alter the original picture file.

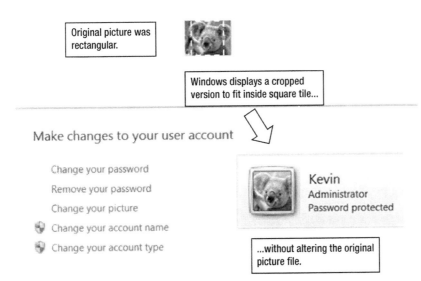

Figure 1–8. *The user account picture was successfully changed.*

Customizing the Start Menu

The Start menu isn't just for getting to your programs. It also provides quick access to your documents, folders, settings, preferences, hardware, and Help. By default, Windows keeps the Start menu short and simple by listing just the most common links, and listing them only as links to open a folder or window, not a menu. You can add to or remove items from the right side of the window, and you can change how the links work. For example, by default the Documents, Pictures, and Music libraries are listed on the Start menu, but a fourth library, Videos, is not. You can add the Videos library to this list.

To customize the Start menu:

1. Right-click the **Start** button, and then click **Properties**, as shown in Figure 1–9.

Figure 1–9. *Opening Start Menu Properties*

2. Click the **Start Menu** tab, and then click **Customize**.

3. In the **Customize Start Menu** window, scroll down the list of settings, as shown in Figure 1–10.

    You will notice there are a number of links listed that do not currently appear on your Start menu because they are set as Don't display this item. For the links that do appear on your Start menu, you will notice that most, if not all, are set to Display as a link. When Set the item to Display as a menu is selected, a small dropdown arrow appears next to the item on the Start menu. With that setting, you can see what is in that folder without opening it, and select an item.

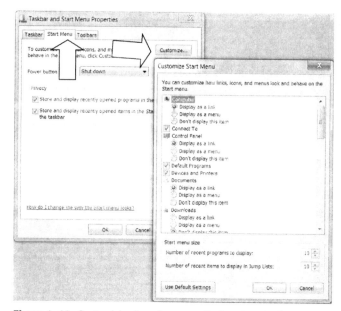

Figure 1–10. *Customizing how items are displayed on the Start menu*

4. Locate the **Control Panel** setting, and select **Display as a menu**, as shown in Figure 1–11.

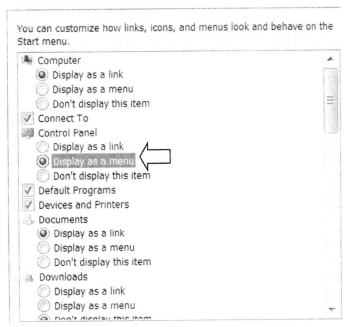

Figure 1–11. *Change the Control Panel setting so it will open as a menu from the Start menu.*

5. Scroll down to the bottom of the list and in **Videos** and select **Display as a link**, as shown in Figure 1–12.

6. Click **OK** twice to close the **Customize Start Menu** window, and then the **Taskbar and Start Menu Properties** window.

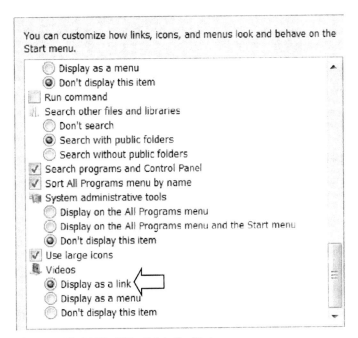

Figure 1–12. *Add the Video link to the Start menu.*

What items to add, and which to make links or menus, is a matter of personal preference.

Adding **Recent Items** makes it easy to get to the files you used last.

Turning **Control Panel** into a menu makes for a very long menu, as shown in Figure 1–13.

Other items such as Pictures, Music, and Videos, are probably not good candidates for displaying as menus because you could have hundreds or thousands of items in those libraries and folders.

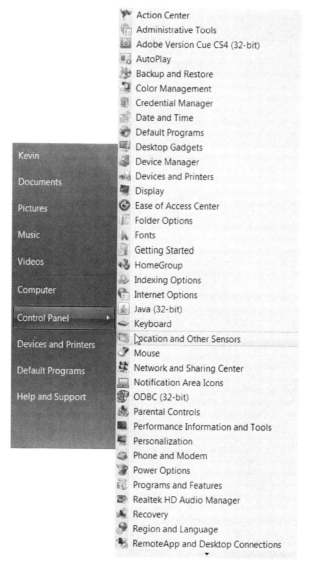

Figure 1–13. *The Videos link has been added, and Control Panel is now a menu.*

TIP: Whether to display items as links or menus is a personal preference. If you know exactly what you are looking for, or the list of items in the folder is very short, displaying an item as a menu can be much more convenient than opening a window. It is also convenient if you have a hierarchy of folders and subfolders.

RECOMMENDATIONS: Add Recent Items. Turn Documents and Computer into menu. Turn Control Panel into menu only if you are very familiar with the items and just want to go to one as quickly as possible. Don't make photos a menu, because you'll probably want to browse them by previewing them in a regular window, not by file name. Remove Music; if you have many songs, you're better off accessing songs through your music player, such as WMP, iTunes, Zune, Rhapsody, etc.

Personalizing Your Desktop

The first things you probably want to change or customize when you have a new computer are the colors and the desktop background. Or you may want to get right down to business and arrange the shortcuts to your favorite programs and features for easy access. There is no right or wrong order in which to customize your computer (other than you need to have your user account already set up).

We'll start with the big picture—the one that covers your screen before you open any programs—your **desktop background**. Windows offers many choices for customization. You can use **themes**, which coordinate a desktop background with a matching window color, sounds, and screen saver. You can also change each of these separately, or even create your own theme.

You can change any of these settings on the **Personalization** window. The easiest way to get to the **Personalization** window is to right-click any place on the desktop, and then on the small menu that pops up, click **Personalize**, as shown in Figure 1–14.

TIP: Can't find an open spot on the desktop to click because open program windows cover everything? Hold down the Windows key and then press D or click the blank button to the right of the notification area in the taskbar.

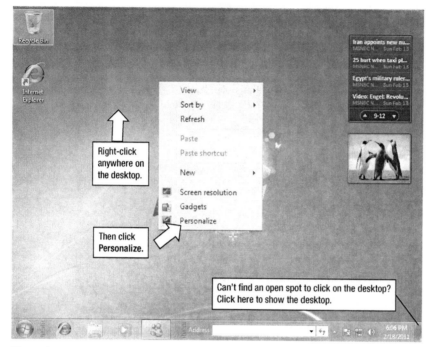

Figure 1–14. *Access the Personalization window by right-clicking the desktop and then clicking Personalize.*

Navigating the Personalization Window

This window allows you to change almost all your visual preferences and many of your sound preferences. The currently selected theme will be highlighted, as the **Unsaved Theme** is in **My Themes** in Figure 1–15. Themes are listed in three groups.

- **My Themes** are any themes you create by specifying your own combination of desktop background pictures, window color, sounds, and screen saver. You can also click **Get more themes online** to download additional themes and desktop backgrounds.

- **Aero Themes** take advantage of Aero effects such as transparency.

- **Installed Themes** are any themes your computer manufacturer designed and installed on your computer or those you have downloaded and installed.

- **Basic and High Contrast Themes** provide simpler desktop backgrounds and Windows colors or high-contrast themes to make the screen, windows, and text easier to view. This group includes the Windows Classic theme (the desktop style from Windows 95 to Windows 2000).

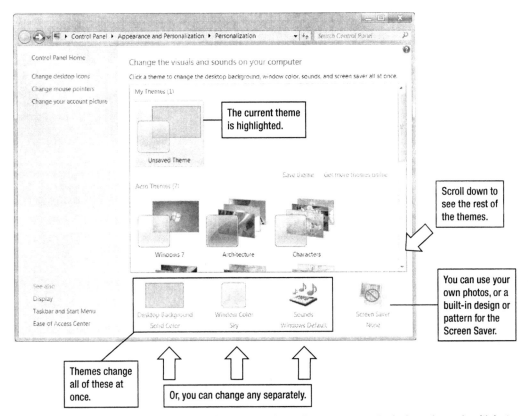

Figure 1–15. *The Personalization window allows you to change how your computer looks and sounds with just a few clicks.*

Choosing a Theme

The themes listed in the **Personalization** window display a preview of the desktop background pictures and the window color for each theme. Each Aero theme contains multiple pictures except the **Windows 7** theme. When you select an Aero theme, the default is to show all the pictures in the theme as a slide show so that the picture changes to another picture within the theme every 30 minutes. This means you'll have a new desktop background every 30 minutes.

To choose a theme:

    ▓   Scroll the themes list as needed, and then click a theme.

Windows will automatically apply the theme you selected. The **Personalization** window stays open, so if you don't like the theme you just selected or you want to check out the other themes, you can easily change it again.

> **TIP:** High-contrast themes are one of many Windows features that can make it easier to view content on your computer. See the "Making Your Screen Easier to View and Read" and "Customizing Windows for Visual, Audio, Mobility, or Cognitive Needs" sections later in this chapter for tips on using these Windows features and the Ease of Access Center.

Fixing Aero

There are several reasons why Aero themes might not be working or might not be available on your computer.

- The entry level **Windows 7 Home Basic** and **Windows 7 Starter** editions do not include Aero. Aero is included in the **Windows 7 Enterprise**, **Home Premium**, **Professional**, and **Ultimate** editions.

- Even if you have an edition that includes Aero, your computer hardware or your current configuration may not support it.

- Some programs may not run at the higher level of resolution required for Aero. If you have an Aero theme and then you start a program that doesn't work with Aero, Windows will automatically revert to a non-Aero theme.

If Aero does not work or has stopped working, try the Aero troubleshooter in **Help and Support**.

1. Click the **Start** button, and in the **Start** menu, click **Help and Support**.

2. In the search box, type **Aero troubleshooter** and then click the **Search** button.

3. In the list that appears, click **Open the Aero troubleshooter**.

4. Review the information and then click the link to start the troubleshooter.

The troubleshooter will examine your edition of Windows 7, your computer's hardware, any programs that may not support Windows 7, and suggest ways to fix the problem.

Viewing or Changing Your Desktop Background

Themes provide a convenient way to set your desktop background, window color, and sounds all at once. But what if you don't want a slide show or want to change which pictures are in a Theme slide show? Or, what if you want to use your own pictures? You can easily change this in the Desktop Background window, as shown in Figure 1–16.

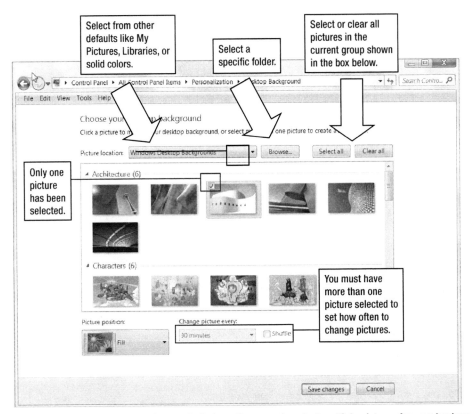

Figure 1-16. *The Desktop Background window allows you to select multiple pictures for your background.*

To change your desktop background:

> **TIP** If you have personal, private, or confidential pictures on your computer that you would not want others to see, be careful about selecting large photo collection folders like My Photos or Photos Library. You may want to create a separate folder just for pictures that are safe for public viewing.

1. In the **Personalization** window, click **Desktop Background**.

2. Select the picture or pictures you want to use in your background. Place the mouse pointer over a picture and a check box will appear momentarily.

   - If the pictures you want to use are not displayed, select a different group from the **Picture location** drop-down list, or click **Browse** to navigate to a different folder on your computer or a shared folder on your network.

▓ If you use **Browse** to select pictures from a location that is not on your computer, such as a shared folder on a homegroup or home network location, the pictures can be displayed only when the location is online and available. If the location requires a username and password, the pictures may not be available the next time you use your computer.

▓ To ensure that your selected pictures are always available, make sure the network location is always online and available and in a public folder that does not require a username and password. Or, copy the picture files from the network location to a local folder on your computer.

When a picture is selected, a check mark appears in the checkbox, as shown in Figure 1–17.

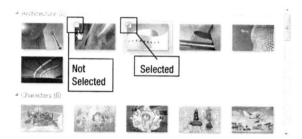

Figure 1–17. *The check mark indicates the picture has been selected.*

3. In the **Picture position** drop-down list, choose how you want the pictures positioned in the background.

▓ **Fill** is the default and works best for most pictures because it doesn't distort the picture to make it fit on the desktop and doesn't leave any blank areas at the top or the bottom. If you have pictures with proportions or shapes that don't match your screen dimensions, experiment with what looks best to you.

▓ If you choose **Fit** or **Center**, the **Change background color** link appears below it so that you can select the color of the background that fills in the sides or top and bottom of the desktop when the proportions of the picture don't match the desktop.

4. If you have selected more than one picture, you can also adjust the following slide show settings:

▓ In the **Change picture every** drop-down list, choose how often you want the pictures to change in the slide show.

- If you want the pictures to change randomly from among the pictures you selected for this desktop background, select **Shuffle**.

- If you want the selected pictures to change in the order they are displayed on the desktop background, deselect **Shuffle**.

- If you are using a laptop and frequently run just on battery power, select **When using battery power, pause the slide show to save power**.

> **TIP:** Your display may drain more power than your hard disk or the CPU. Even the slide show can increase the drain on your battery. Chapter 28 covers how to use the Power Options in Control Panel to provide even more power saving options to reduce battery drain.

5. When you are done setting your desktop background, click **Save changes**.

Viewing or Changing Your Window Colors

Window Color changes the color of the window borders, Start menu, and taskbar. It also allows you to turn off, enable, or adjust the transparency. *Transparency*, sometimes called *glass*, is part of the Aero effects. It allows the background to show through the window borders, Start menu, and taskbar. This cool look has a practical use because it can help you see what is behind the windows without having to move them all over.

When you select **Enable transparency**, you can adjust how much of the background shows through with the **Color intensity** slider. Compare the background window in Figure 1–18 with Figure 1–19. When the slider is all the way to the left, the color of the foreground window border is most transparent, as shown in Figure 1–18. When the slider is all the way to the right, the foreground window border is least transparent, as shown in Figure 1–19.

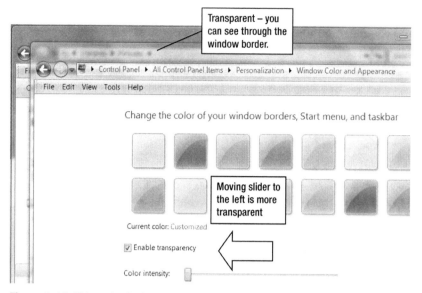

Figure 1–18. *This setting is the most transparent.*

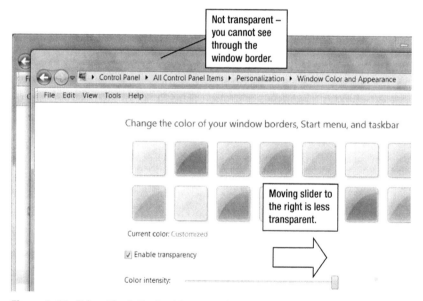

Figure 1–19. *This setting is the least transparent.*

The color combinations provided by Windows themes work well for most people. If you are using a Windows 7 theme with Windows Aero, some of the colors, fonts, and sizes settings can't be changed unless you are using the Windows 7 basic theme or a high-contrast theme. Changing the window color is not difficult or risky, but you'll find that the Windows 7 themes are easier and more satisfying.

If you or the people you are setting up the computer for have special visual, audio, mobility, or cognitive needs, the **Windows Ease of Access Center** is a great resource for customizing the Windows experience. These features are for everybody, not just for those with what people traditionally label as disabilities. With age, hearing and vision decline; young or old, repetitive work or poor ergonomic conditions can affect mobility. Sometimes it's just easier if the computer provides feedback through one type of sensory input and tunes out others. For example, a student may find it distracting to herself or others to hear Windows system sounds or see notifications popping up on the screen. For more information, see "How to Customize Windows for Visual, Audio, Mobility, or Cognitive Needs" section later in this chapter.

Setting Up Your Screen Saver

A *screen saver* animates your screen with pictures or graphics moving across your screen when your computer is on but idle. A Screen saver serves several purposes.

- It helps safeguard your privacy by hiding what is on your screen when you are away from your desk.

- It can work with your power management settings to reduce power use when your computer is on but inactive.

- It can display a custom message.

- It can display a slide show of your favorite pictures.

Originally one of the main purposes of a screen saver was to prevent what is called *burn-in* or *image persistence*. When the image on the screen doesn't change for a long time, the image can get imprinted so that a ghost of that image remains on the screen forever. Older cathode ray tube (CRT) monitors are more susceptible to burn-in. It happens less frequently with today's LCD desktop monitors, televisions, and laptop displays. A screen saver prevents burn-in or image persistence by keeping images moving on the screen so that nothing stays in one place too long. The following steps describe how to use photos for your screen saver, but most of the steps apply to using one of the built-in animation screen savers as well:

1. Open the **Personalization** window if it is not already open from your previous personalization tasks. To open this page, right-click your desktop, and then click **Personalize**.

2. At the bottom of the page, click **Screen Saver**.

    The **Screen Saver Settings** dialog box appears, as shown in Figure 1–20.

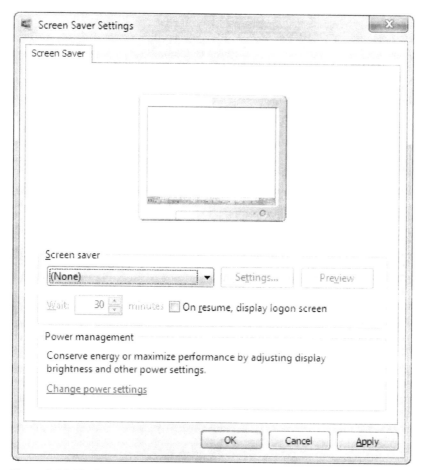

Figure 1–20. *The Screen Saver Settings dialog box specifies which screen saver to use, how long to wait before it comes on, and whether to protect it with your password.*

3. Click the drop-down list under Screen saver, like the one that displays **None** in Figure 1–20.

   Windows includes several built-in screen savers, including a photo screen saver.

4. Click **Photos**, as shown in Figure 1–21.

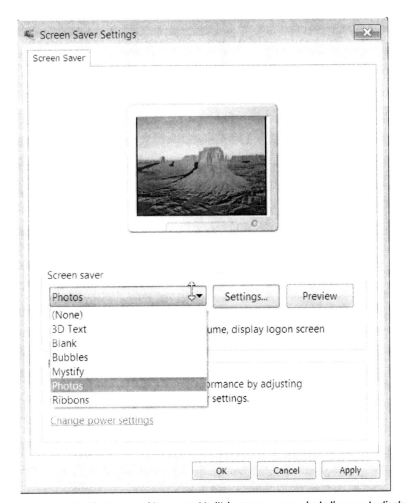

Figure 1–21. *Windows provides several built-in screen savers, including one to display your photos.*

When you select Photos, Windows defaults to the Photos folder in your library. If you do not have any photos there or you want to use other photos, you can specify another folder to use.

TIP: If you have personal, private, or confidential pictures on your computer that you would not want others to see, be careful about selecting large photo collection folders like My Photos or Photos Library. You may want to create a separate folder just for pictures that are safe for public viewing.

5.   Click **Settings**.

The **Photo Screen Saver Settings** dialog box appears, as shown in Figure 1–22.

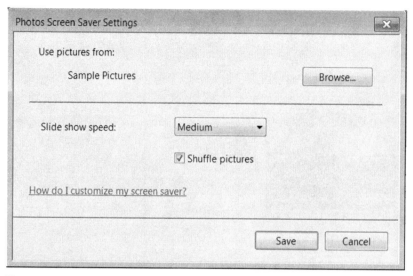

Figure 1–22. *Photos Screen Saver Settings allows you to specify which folder to use pictures from and how you want them shown.*

6. Click **Browse** to specify a different folder to get the pictures from.

7. Click **Slide show speed** to specify how fast to change the pictures: **Slow**, **Medium**, or **Fast**.

8. Select the **Shuffle pictures** check box if you want them displayed in a random order, or deselect this check box if you want them displayed in the order they are listed in the source folder. When you are done with these settings, click **Save**.

9. If you want to see what the screen saver will look like and how fast it changes, click **Preview**. The slide show will run for a bit and stop either when you move your mouse or, if you wait a few moments, by itself.

10. Select how long you want Windows to wait before it starts the screen saver and whether to require you to log on again when you stop the screen saver to resume using the computer.

11. When you are done, click **OK**.

> **NOTE:** As mentioned previously, if you use photos for your screen saver from a folder on another homegroup or home network computer, make sure the folder will be accessible all the time.

Making Your Screen Easier to View and Read

Changing the theme, desktop background, and colors that you see on the desktop makes Windows more enjoyable to look at, but sometimes the details on the screen or the text size may be difficult to view.

The high-contrast themes are often a good solution for those who have difficulty seeing things on the computer screen. But some people may find they can make a few adjustments to their settings and still use one of the standard Aero themes.

Changing the Size of Text and Items in Windows

You can change the size of text and objects on-screen without changing your screen resolution. You can set the size from small (100 percent or normal size) to medium (125 percent) or large (150 percent). This setting is easy to change, but each time you change it, you will need to restart your computer afterward to see the changes in effect.

To change the size of text and items on your screen, follow these steps:

1. Click the Windows **Start** button, and in the **Start** menu's search box, type **Display**.

2. In the results list, click **Display**.

   The **Display** window appears, as shown in Figure 1–23.

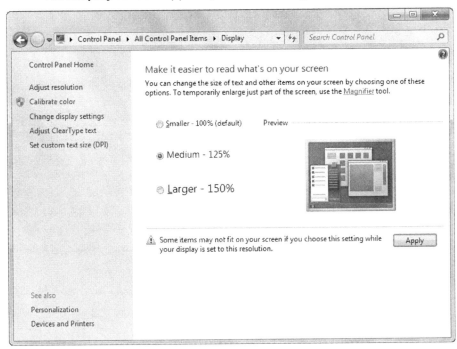

Figure 1–23. *The Display window provides three preset sizes for the size of text and items on your screen.*

3. Click a size to see an example in the **Preview** area.

4. Click **Apply** if you want Windows to make that change. You will need to restart your computer to see the new sizes put into effect.

Changing the Size Of Text in Other Programs

Many programs provide a way to change the size of how things are displayed within the program window, separate from Windows size settings. Sometimes the feature is called *text size*, *magnification*, or *zoom*. The most common places to check are the **View** menu or a slider in toolbar or status bar. Figures 1–24 through 1–27 show examples from several common programs.

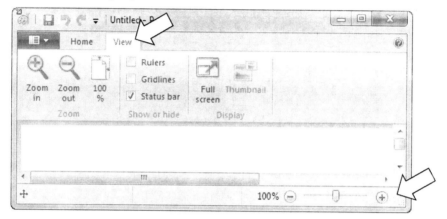

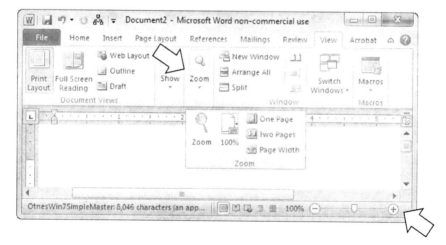

Figure 1–24. *Microsoft Paint (top) and Microsoft Office programs like Word (bottom) provide access to the zoom feature on both the View menu and a slider on the status bar.*

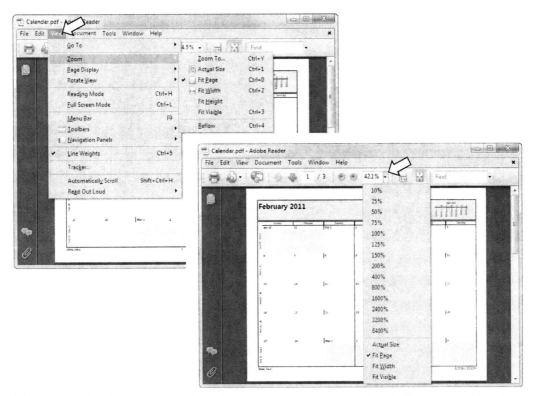

Figure 1–25. *Adobe Reader, used for viewing PDF files, offers a zoom feature from the View menu and from a dropdown on the toolbar.*

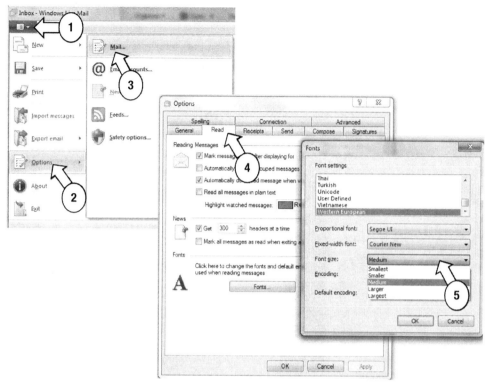

Figure 1–26. *The Windows Live Mail program does not offer a zoom slider or dropdown; you can change the type and size of fonts that are displayed when you read mail messages in about five steps.*

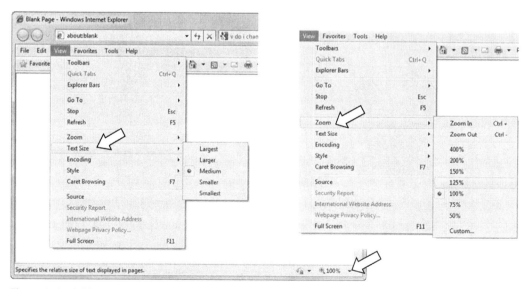

Figure 1–27. *With Internet Explorer and other browsers, you can change the text size, zoom the entire web page, and set other Internet Options to make web pages more accessible. These options are described in detail in Chapter 11.*

TIP: Your computer mouse may also provide a zoom feature. In Office programs or Internet Explorer, hold down the Ctrl key while moving the middle mouse wheel. Learn more about using your mouse in the Quick Start Guide.

Changing Your Screen Resolution

Screen resolution is the level of detail on your display. It is a measurement of how many pixels can fit across the width and height on your screen. *Pixels* are the smallest unit of measurement of the dots of color that make up the images on your screen. The higher the resolution, the finer the detail that can be shown on your display. With high resolutions like 1600×1200 pixels, the details are sharper, objects are smaller, and you can view more objects on your screen. At lower resolutions, such as 800×600, Windows displays fewer objects on your screen but they are larger. Compare Figures 1–28 and 1–29. For some people, high resolution may be too hard to see. At a lower resolution, objects are larger and easier to see, but you can't fit as much on your screen.

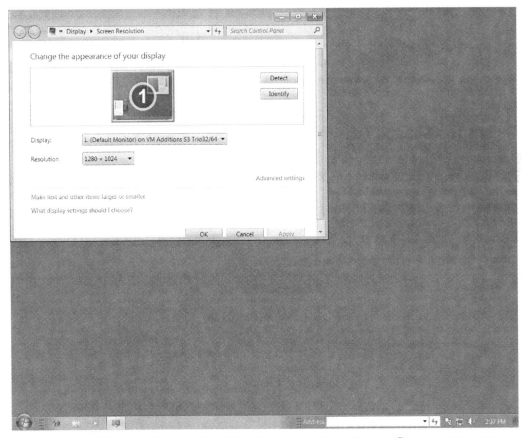

Figure 1–28. *At a higher resolution like 1280×1024, objects are smaller, and you can fit more on your screen.*

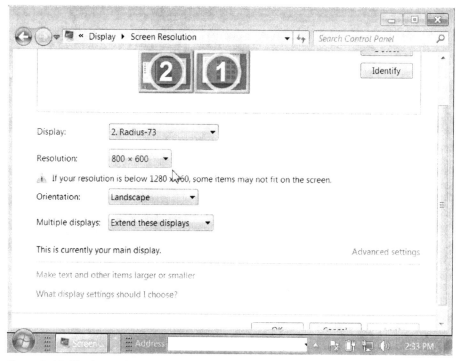

Figure 1–29. *The Screen Resolution window, which took up only part of the screen at 1280×1024, is now too big to fit completely on the screen at 800×600.*

Before You Change Your Resolution...

Sometimes changing your resolution is not the best solution because it may make your monitor look worse or doesn't fix the problem you are trying to solve. Every monitor or laptop screen is designed to look best at a specific resolution, usually called the *native*, *optimum*, or *recommended* resolution. When you connect a monitor, Windows detects the type of monitor and automatically adjusts the screen to the recommended resolution. Table 1–1 lists some alternatives to changing the resolution.

Table 1–1. *Alternatives to Changing Screen Resolution*

Screen/display Problem	Recommendations
I want to pack more things onto my screen. I need to be able to see several program windows at once.	Try a larger monitor, or multiple monitors.
	Studies have shown that using multiple monitors greatly improves your efficiency and productivity when using your computer.
	Chapter 14, Connecting Monitors and Hardware, provides many useful tips for using single and multiple monitors

Screen/display Problem	Recommendations
Everything is too small for me at the "recommended" resolution. If I can make things bigger, it will be easier for me to see and read.	These previous sections will probably give you more satisfying results: "Changing the Size Of Text and Items in Windows" "Changing the Size Of Text in Other Programs" Later in this chapter, read about using the Ease of Access Center in the "Customizing Windows For Visual, Audio, Mobility, or Cognitive Needs" section.
My eyes and neck hurt because I am having to sit so close to the screen	The problems may be ergonomic—related to the position of your chair, your desk, and your monitor. The Web is full of good information on setting up your work area for good ergonomics. Search for "computer ergonomics" and you will find checklists, diagrams, and articles from government occupational safety agencies, medical organizations, colleges, and other groups. If you use a computer all day at work or for hours at a time at home, be sure to give your eyes a break. Some experts recommend getting up and walking away from your computer for 5-10 minutes every hour. If you wear glasses, contacts, or have less than perfect vision, check with an optometrist to see if "computer glasses" might help. Try a larger monitor or multiple monitors.

To change your resolution, follow these steps:

1. Right-click your desktop background (in a blank spot where there are no program windows open), and then click **Screen resolution**.

2. In the **Screen Resolution** window, click the **Resolution** drop-down list. Figure 1–30 displays the resolutions available for this monitor.

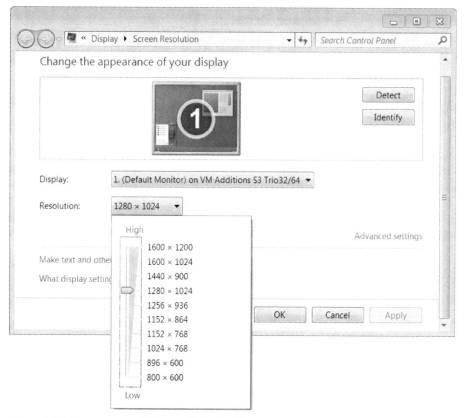

Figure 1–30. *The screen resolutions available for this monitor*

3. Drag the slider up or down. The preview will change in size and shape as you move the slider.

4. Click **Apply** to reset the resolution without closing the **Screen Resolution** window.

A dialog box may appear asking whether you want to keep these changes, as shown in Figure 1–31. This gives you a chance to try it without committing the changes.

Figure 1–31. *When you change your resolution, you have a chance to see what it will look like before committing to the new settings.*

5. Click **Keep changes** if you like the new setting. Otherwise, let it revert.

In some instances, if you select a resolution that is completely incompatible with your monitor or video card, Windows will display a warning message and doesn't even attempt to apply the new resolution.

Wide Screen vs. Normal Aspect

Wide-screen monitors are becoming the norm for desktop PCs and are gaining popularity in laptop computers. The screen resolution list for your computer may include both wide-screen and regular width (sometimes called *normal aspect*) resolutions. As you move the slider up or down, compare the shape in the preview of your monitor. If you use a resolution that doesn't match the height and width ratio of your screen, it may not look right. You may end up with black bars on the top and bottom, part of the desktop off-screen, or all of it on-screen but squished together so everything seems unnaturally tall and skinny.

Additional Features for Multiple Monitors

If you connect your laptop computer to an external monitor or projector or if you have a desktop PC that has a video card that supports multiple monitors, the **Screen Resolution** window provides additional settings and features. Each monitor has its own resolution settings, and you can drag the monitors around in the preview window to match the actual physical position of your monitors. This allows you to move your windows and mouse pointer smoothly between monitors. If your monitors are different sizes and you want to use them side-by-side, you may need to adjust the resolutions on one or both of them so that program windows appear about the same size on both screens.

Multiple monitors are so exciting and fun we've devoted an entire chapter to the topic. In Chapter 25, we'll show you all the tricks for making them work for you.

Cleaning Up and Organizing Your Desktop

You have this nice desktop background and a cool color scheme. But the desktop looks cluttered. There's a grid of little icons like tombstones in a cemetery. And they seem to be multiplying, even though you don't remember putting them there. Those are your *desktop icons*. Figure 1–32 shows a desktop that has become overgrown with desktop icons.

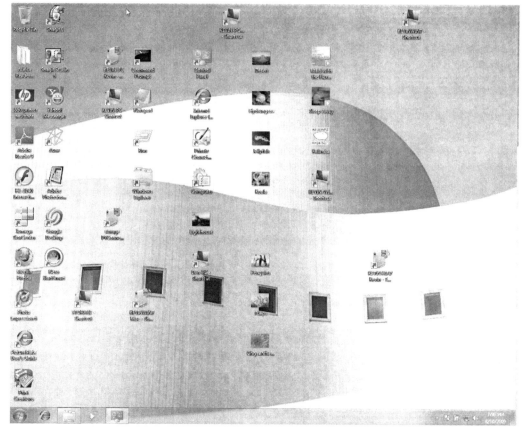

Figure 1-32. *A desktop overrun with too many icons*

Where did they come from, and why are they there? When you buy a new computer, the manufacturer often adds shortcuts to software that you can try or buy. Also, when you add new software or devices, the installation program asks whether you want to place a shortcut on the desktop. Fortunately, you can manage the icons in several ways.

- Organize the icons into tidy rows and columns.

- Hide all desktop icons.

- Delete individual icons you don't need.

- Add a desktop toolbar.

Another View: Desktop Icons Can Be Very Useful

One thing that makes the Apple iPod Touch, the iPhone, and the iPad so popular is their ease of use. You can tap and swipe to access programs and features without going through layers of menus or commands. When you turn on one of these devices, your programs are right on the surface on the *Home* screen. The Apple device's Home screen is the equivalent of the Windows desktop.

> **TIP:** We can't turn your Windows PC, laptop, or netbook into and iPad. But using desktop icons can bring your favorite programs, links, and features to the surface so that you don't have to click menus or the Start menu as often. "Making Your PC More Touch Friendly" in the Quick Start Guide provides many more ways to customize the desktop and Windows features to get the most out of Touch features.

Tidying Up Your Desktop Icons

If you simply need to organize your icons into tidy rows and columns, follow these steps:

1. Right-click an empty area of your desktop.

2. On the menu that pops up, hover over **View**.

   Figure 1–33 shows the submenu that appears, with several commands for organizing and displaying your desktop icons.

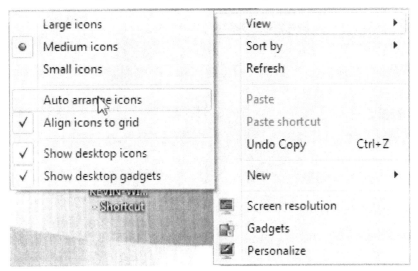

Figure 1–33. *When you right-click the desktop and click View, you can arrange, hide, or resize desktop icons.*

3. Organize the icons as desired.

- To tidy up the icons, select **Auto arrange icons** or **Align icons to grid**, or both.

- **Auto arrange icons** is useful when you've dragged shortcuts to the desktop and they are scattered all over. **Align icons to grid** organizes the icons into uniform rows and columns.

- If you don't want to see any icons on your desktop, clear the **Show desktop icons** check box.

> **NOTE:** Clearing **Show desktop icons** is useful when you have so many icons that they litter the nice desktop background you've chosen or it now takes you a long time to find the icons you want to click. If you like using the desktop as a container to hold all your favorite links and program icons, the "Accessing Your Desktop with a Toolbar" section shows how to get to those links without showing them on the desktop.

Hiding or Showing Common Windows Desktop Icons

Windows includes some common desktop icons for Computer, User's Files, Recycle Bin, Control Panel, and Network that you can select to hide or display through the **Desktop Icon Settings** dialog box. By default, only the Recycle Bin is displayed.

1. Click the **Start** button, and in the **Start** menu's search box, type **desktop icons**.

2. In the list that appears, click **Show or hide common icons on the desktop**.

3. In the **Desktop Icon Settings** dialog box, shown in Figure 1–34, clear or select check boxes as needed.

Figure 1–34. *You can hide or show Windows common desktop icons.*

TIP: You can also add a desktop toolbar to access desktop icons, even if you have hidden the icons on the desktop itself. This is covered in the "Accessing Your Desktop with a Toolbar" section.

Deleting or Moving Desktop Icons

If you like using the desktop to access programs, files, or folders but there are extra icons that you don't want or need, you can delete or move individual icons. As you've seen, you can also hide or show common desktop icons for things such as the Recycle Bin, Computer, Control Panel, User's Files, and Network.

Consider the following before deleting or moving desktop icons:

- Desktop icons can be **shortcuts** to open programs or files located elsewhere on your computer, or they can be actual files or folders located in the desktop folder.

- Deleting a shortcut icon does not delete a program or file or uninstall a program; it just removes the icon from the desktop.

- Deleting a folder or file icon actually deletes the folder or file. If you don't want the folder or file icon on your desktop, move it to one of your libraries, such as Documents.

- If you accidentally delete a file or folder, you may be able to retrieve it by pressing the key combination Ctrl+Z (Undo) or opening the Recycle Bin.

Figure 1–35 shows several types of desktop icons: a common desktop icon (Recycle Bin), a folder icon (New folder), a shortcut icon (Adobe Photoshop), and a picture file icon (Lighthouse). You can identify a shortcut icon by the arrow in the lower-left corner, like the Adobe Photoshop icon.

Figure 1–35. *Several different examples of desktop icons*

To delete or move a desktop icon, follow these steps:

1. Right-click a desktop icon. A context menu appears, as shown in Figure 1–36.

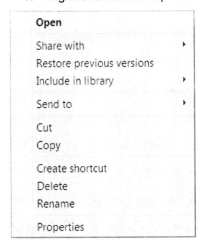

Open

Share with   ▸
Restore previous versions
Include in library   ▸

Send to   ▸

Cut
Copy

Create shortcut
Delete
Rename

Properties

Figure 1–36. *Desktop icon context menu allows you to delete an icon if you don't want it to appear on your desktop.*

2. Complete one of the following:

   a. To delete a shortcut (an icon with an arrow in the lower-left corner), on the right-click menu, click **Delete**. A message similar to Figure 1–37 appears, clarifying that this only deletes the shortcut and does not uninstall the program.

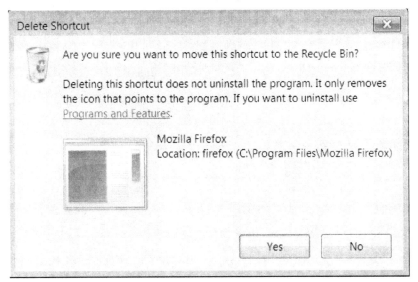

Delete Shortcut

Are you sure you want to move this shortcut to the Recycle Bin?

Deleting this shortcut does not uninstall the program. It only removes the icon that points to the program. If you want to uninstall use Programs and Features.

Mozilla Firefox
Location: firefox (C:\Program Files\Mozilla Firefox)

Yes   No

Figure 1–37. *When you delete a program shortcut, Windows reminds you that this does not uninstall the program. This message is not displayed when you are deleting a browser shortcut to a web site, because web sites are not programs.*

b. To permanently delete a folder or file, on the right-click menu, click **Delete**. A message similar to Figure 1–38 is displayed to confirm that you want to send the folder or file to the Recycle Bin.

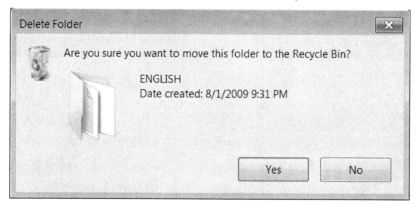

Figure 1–38. *When you delete a file or folder, Windows reminds you that this will place the item in the Recycle Bin.*

c. To move a file or folder, on the right-click menu, click **Cut**, navigate to the folder you want to move it to (destination), and then click **Paste** in the destination folder.

Accessing Your Desktop with a Toolbar

You can hide your desktop icons and still keep them handy for quick access.

1. Right-click the taskbar, click **Toolbars**, and then click **Desktop**, as shown in Figure 1–39.

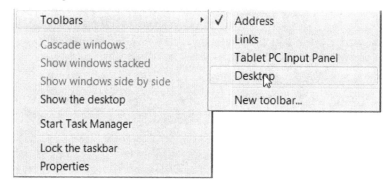

Figure 1–39. *You can access the desktop icons from the taskbar by adding the desktop toolbar.*

2. To access a desktop item from the taskbar, click the double angle brackets, as shown in Figure 1–40.

Figure 1–40. *The desktop icons are now available from the desktop toolbar in the taskbar.*

Customizing Your Computer Sounds

Just as there are visual themes, Windows also provides *sound themes* for events that occur in Windows and other programs. These events include the sounds you hear when starting or exiting windows and when receiving new mail, warnings, and errors, to name a few. There quite a few things you can do with Windows sounds to suit your needs, including the following:

- Turn on or off the sound played at Windows startup.
- Turn off Windows events sounds completely.
- Change the sound scheme.
- Change or turn off the sound assigned to a specific event.
- Mute sounds.

In the next section, you'll learn how to use and change the Control Panel's sound and volume settings.

Changing System Sounds

To change your system sounds, follow these steps:

1. Click the Windows **Start** button. In the **Start** menu's search box, type **Sound**.

2. In the results list, click **Change system sounds**.

    The Control Panel's **Sound** dialog box appears, displaying the **Sounds** tab, as shown in Figure 1–41.

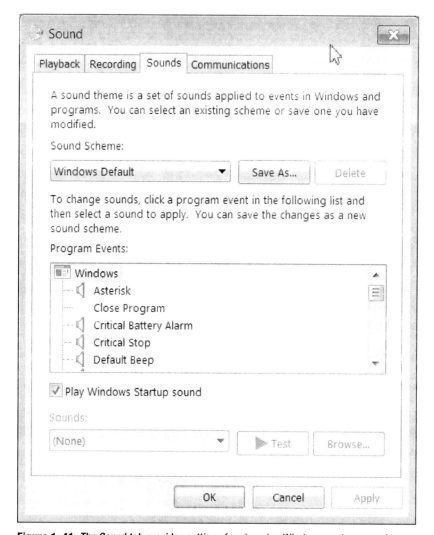

Figure 1–41. *The Sound tab provides settings for changing Windows system sounds.*

3. Change the settings if desired.

   ▪ To turn off the sound that is played when Windows starts, clear the **Play Windows Startup sound** check box.

   ▪ To turn off all Windows sounds for program events, click the **Sound Scheme** drop-down list, and then click **No Sounds**.

   ▪ To change the sound scheme, click the **Sound Scheme** drop-down list, and then click a different sound scheme.

   ▪ To listen to the sound for a specific program event, in the **Program Events** list, click the event, and then click **Test**.

- To change the sound for a specific event, in the **Program Events** list, click the event, click the **Sounds** drop-down list, and then select the sound or select (**None**) at the top of the list if you don't want any sound for that event.

- To save all your changes without overriding the existing sound scheme your changes are based on, click **Save As** to create a new sound scheme.

Using Text or Visual Alternatives for Windows Sounds

The Windows 7 Ease of Access Center provides a feature to use text or visual alternatives for sounds.

To access settings for this feature:

- In the **Start** menu's search box, type **Sounds**. In the list that appears, click **Replace sounds with visual cues**.

For more information about the Ease of Access Center, see "Customizing Windows for Visual, Audio, Mobility, or Cognitive Needs" section later in this chapter.

Adjusting the Volume or Muting Your Computer

You can adjust the volume or mute all sounds from your computer, not just Windows system sounds. For example, you can adjust the speakers, headphones, music, videos, or any other application or device that is currently providing sound on your computer.

To adjust or mute the volume of devices and programs:

1. In the notification area at the bottom right of your screen, right-click the speaker icon, and then click **Open Volume Mixer**, as shown in Figure 1–42.

Figure 1–42. *The Volume Mixer provides controls for the volume and muting of the audio devices and programs currently in use.*

If the icon is not displayed in your taskbar, you can also click the **Start** menu and enter **Adjust Volume** in the **Start** menu's search box.

When the Volume Mixer opens, it displays at least one audio device that produces actual sounds such as speakers or headphones, as well as currently running programs that provide sounds such as System Sounds, Windows Media Player, or Windows Media Center.

2. You can adjust or mute the volume of any or all items. Each item can be changed individually, except **Device**. If you move the slider for the **Device** volume, all other sliders move with it. If you mute **Device**, all other items are muted:

   ▪ To adjust the volume of an item, move its slider up or down.

   ▪ To mute an item, click the speaker icon at the bottom.

   ▪ To adjust the volume of all items at once, move the **Device** slider up or down.

   ▪ To mute everything, click the speaker icon under the device. In Figure 1–43, all items are muted because the **Device** slider for **Speakers** is muted.

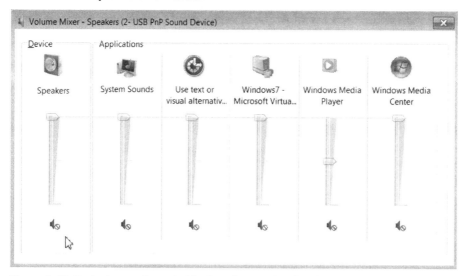

Figure 1–43. *Device is a master control for the volume and muting of all the other mixer controls.*

MUTING A LAPTOP BEFORE YOU TURN IT ON

If you have a laptop computer, this has probably happened to you. You start up your laptop, and before you know it, Windows has announced itself to the world with the "Ta-da!" sound. Here's an easy, low-tech, cheap trick you can use without even turning on your laptop. Plug the sound leak with a dead headphone plug. The next time you throw away a pair of headphones, cut the plug off the end of the cord. Or, get a headphone Y-splitter jack that allows two sets of headphones to share one jack. Insert the plug into your laptop's headphone jack before you start your computer. Your computer thinks you are using headphones or external speakers, and it won't use your laptop's built-in speakers. Ta-da!

Customizing Windows for Visual, Audio, Mobility, or Cognitive Needs

Windows 7's Ease of Access Center provides many features, settings, and programs to fit a wide variety of needs. These capabilities are designed to help you get the most out of your computer through whatever means of input and interaction works best for you. There is no one-size-fits-all technique for visual, audio, mobility, or cognitive needs. The average age of the world's population is increasing, and with age comes a decrease in hearing, vision, mobility, and other abilities. So, many of the traditional definitions of disabilities are blurring.

The Ease of Access Center lists all the features that can make your computer easier to use. If you are not sure what you need, the Ease of Access Center also provides a great assessment tool to survey your needs and, based on your answers, recommends features and settings that will benefit you specifically. Any information gathered by Windows in this process is private and will not be shared or accessible to anybody else outside of your computer.

To open the Ease of Access Center, follow these steps:

1. Click the **Start** button, and in the **Start** menu's search box, type **Ease of Access**.

2. On the list that appears, click **Ease of Access**.

   The **Ease of Access Center** window appears, as shown in Figure 1–44. In this window, you can directly apply many specific settings to make your computer easier to use, explore other settings, or answer a series of questions to help recommend features for you.

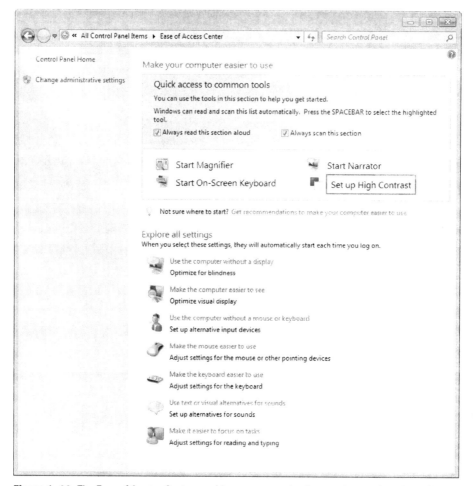

Figure 1–44. *The Ease of Access Center provides many ways to view, explore, and apply a wide variety of tools and features to make your computer easier to use.*

3. If you want some recommendations because you don't know what features Windows offers for your needs, click **Get recommendations to make your computer easier to use**. Again, the questions, answers, and recommendations are private. The results of the answers do not label, name, or group the user into a category, but rather, suggest the specific features and settings that may be of most benefit.

Customizing Program Preferences and Personal Information

Windows 7 provides many ways for you to customize which programs to use and how much personal preference information is saved on your computer and made available to programs and web sites. PC stands for *personal computer*, right? So, almost every chapter in *Windows 7 Made Simple* contains additional information about making your computer personal.

- Chapter 2: "Checking Out Libraries" provides information about sharing and keeping private your libraries and documents across your home network.

- Chapter 4: "Exploring Programs and Features" provides information about choosing which programs to use for your favorite tasks such as browsing the Internet, reading e-mail, listening to music, viewing pictures and video, and writing and viewing documents.

- Chapter 8: "Communication with Email, IM, and Social Networks" provides information about saving and storing personal contact information in e-mail address books.

- Chapter 9: "Surfing the Web" includes information about bookmarking your favorite websites.

- Chapter 12: "Setting Up and Transferring User Accounts" explains how to personalize your user accounts. It also provides information about how to move personal settings including browser cookies and your personal files to your new computer.

- Chapter 16: "Protecting Your Computer and Data" includes information about personalizing your security settings, passwords, and identity information.

Summary

Here's a review of what you've learned in this chapter:

- How to change the picture on your logon screen and the Start menu with user accounts.

- How to select a theme, desktop background, colors, and screen saver with personalization.

- How to change the size of text displayed on screen and the level of detail on the screen with screen resolution.

- How to tidy up your desktop by arranging, removing, or hiding desktop icons.

- How to adjust your Windows system sounds and volume with the Sound dialog box in the Control Panel and the Volume Mixer.

- How to customize for visual, audio, mobility, and cognitive needs with the Ease of Access Center in the Control Panel.

Chapter 2

Checking Out Libraries

Sometimes it seems like the amount of information we put onto our computers is growing faster than we can keep up with. Wouldn't it be nice if every time you add or create information, you could organize it into to tidy containers that are easy to navigate and search? That's what Windows 7 does. It stores files, runs programs, and connects you to other computers and people with the following tools:

- The **Start Menu** and **Taskbar**, which help you find and access the programs that are available or in use on your computer. Chapter 1 shows you many ways to tailor these and other features to make it easy to find and use your programs and Windows features. Chapter 4 shows you how to manage, add, and delete programs and features on your computer.

- **Libraries**, which provide containers for several of the most common types of information you store and use on your computer: documents, pictures, videos, and music. Libraries make it easy for you to decide where to put things on your computer and where to find them later. You can also create your own libraries for additional information and file types that you use frequently and would like to group together.

- **Folders and the file system**—the traditional storage structure for Windows and computers. Folders are still very important for organizing and storing your files, but you no longer need to try to remember a long path name to find your documents. Though this chapter does not depend on a substantial knowledge about folders, drives, and paths, if you need a refresher, take a look at the Computer window section in the Quick Start Guide.

- **Favorites**, which provide links to web sites, network locations, and local folders that you visit and use frequently. Chapter 9 shows you how to add these nifty shortcuts to your repertoire of.

Introduction to Libraries

Libraries are special folders designed to hold your documents, pictures, music, and videos. If you have used previous versions of Windows, you are familiar with special folders such as My Documents, My Music, and My Pictures, which were introduced in Windows 95. Figure 2–1 displays the Library folder with the folders typical to Windows.

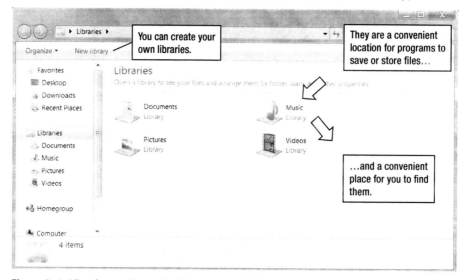

Figure 2–1. *Libraries provide a default location to which programs can automatically save files. This makes it easy for you to find or open the files later.*

When you or a program saves a file to a library, you might not be using the same program to view or edit it. Typical scenarios include the following:

- You download pictures from your *digital camera* to the **Pictures library** and then open the **Pictures library** to view or touch up with your *photo editor or viewer*.

- You download music from a *music service* or *rip a CD* to your computer. The songs or albums are saved to the **Music library**. When you open your *media player*, it looks for songs in the **Music library**.

- You receive a *Microsoft Word document* attached to an e-mail. You save the attachment in the **Documents library**. The next day, you *read and edit the document*. You locate the Word document in the **Documents library** and double-click the document to open it in *Microsoft Word*.

Backing Up Libraries

If something is worth saving and organizing in libraries, it must be worth protecting with a backup. Chapter 18 will show you how to backup to protect your computer and its contents.

Backups Are Important for Libraries

Imagine your computer gets fried from an electrical surge, the hard drive crashes, or your laptop is stolen. You can replace the computer and software. What about the things you typically save in libraries?

- 3000 digital photos from 10 years of family parties, vacations, and special events.

- Hundreds of CDs and thousands of songs that you've accumulated over your lifetime.

- The home videos that you immediately downloaded from your camcorder and then erased from the tape or digital card so that you could reuse it.

- Important work and personal records, documents, and spreadsheets.

You may be able to replace your music from the original CDs if you still have them and just re-purchase the rest. Your photos, home videos, and documents, however, are probably gone. *Forever*. Save yourself the cost, time, and anguish of trying to replace what can be replaced and letting go of what cannot by performing simple backups.

Libraries Are Important for Backups

Libraries are important for backups because they provide an easy way to locate and select which files to back up. Ideally, you should back up your entire computer. Backup programs vary in how they let you select what to back up.

- **Windows Backup and Restore** allows you to select libraries. You don't have to go through a file directory to select things like C:\users\Kevin\My Documents.

- **Backups by type:** Some backup programs allow you to select what to back up via checkboxes for office documents, music files, video files, music files, and all other files. The backup program determines what files fit into these categories either by scanning your computer and selecting these files by file extension or by relying on what you have placed in the My Documents, My Pictures, My Videos, and My Music folders.

■ **Backups by folder location:** Some backup programs provide a standard directory tree where you can select the entire hard drive (like `C:\`) or individual folders on the hard drive (such as `C:\users\Kevin\My Documents`). This isn't the friendliest method, but libraries are still helpful. Use libraries for all of your content. You can find the actual folder path for all of the locations through the **locations** link in a Library window.

One Library: Multiple Folders and Locations

Where libraries differ and improve upon My Documents, My Music, My Pictures, etc. is that each library can include physical folders from multiple locations. Libraries are not single locations; they are a grouping of shortcuts to one or multiple physical locations of the same content type. This gives you a single "bucket" for a content type, like the Pictures library, but you can include other locations besides the default storage location on your computer for pictures; this is typically a username folder, like C:\Users\Kevin\Pictures, and Public Pictures, like C:\Users\Public\Pictures. You can also include picture locations on other computers and network locations, like \\Other_computer\kevin\pictures or \\Storage_device\kevin\pictures.

> **NOTE:** If you include folders on other computers or network locations, those locations must be online in order for you to access content on them. Also, you may need a local user name and password for that location.

Some programs automatically create a folder in the appropriate library. For example, your digital camera or your scanner may create a folder within the Pictures library, as shown in Figure 2–2.

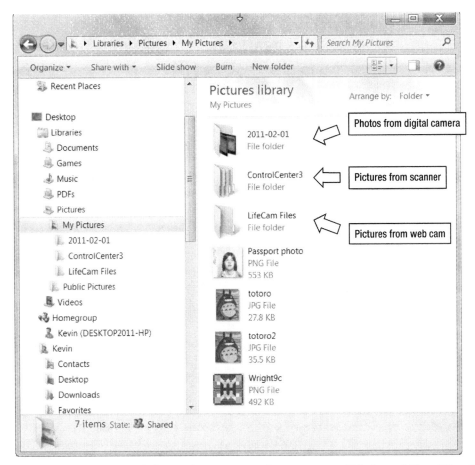

Figure 2–2. *Programs and devices such as cameras and scanners may add their own folder within a library.*

Sometimes a program wants to save its type of documents or files to its own folder outside of a library. You can customize any library to include multiple locations.

By default, each library has two locations, your *personal folder* and a *public folder*. Figure 2–3 shows the Video folder on a new computer; it already includes these two locations.

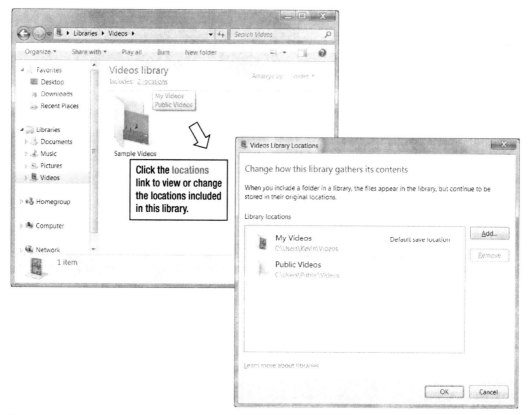

Figure 2–3. *Each of the default libraries includes two locations, the personal folder location and the public folder.*

You can add or remove which folders are included in a library. The folders do not have to be on your computer; you can include folders on your home network or on another computer in your Homegroup.

Later in the chapter, we'll show you how to add other locations to a library and how to create your own libraries. But before we do that, let's take a look at the different ways you can get to your libraries.

Accessing Your Libraries

If you do not already have a folder window open, the easiest way to get to your libraries is from the **Taskbar**, as shown in Figure 2–4.Click the **Windows Explorer** button, and your libraries are displayed.

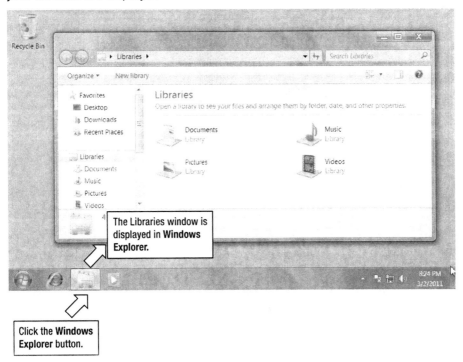

Figure 2–4. *The Libraries window, displaying the default Documents, Music, Pictures, and Videos Libraries.*

You can double-click any of these to open a specific library. In just a bit, we'll show you the difference between each of these libraries and how to create your own libraries.

If you already have a Windows Explorer folder window open, your libraries are also visible in the navigation pane on the left side. So, whether you are looking at the Computer, Favorites, Homegroup, or Network window, you will see it listed. For example, in Figure 2–5, the Computer window shows the libraries in the navigation pane.

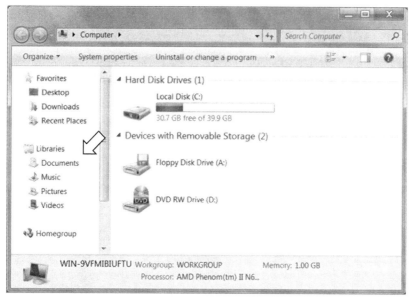

Figure 2–5. *Standard Windows Explorer folder windows, like the Computer window, show Libraries options in the left navigation pane.*

You can also open each of these libraries from the Start Menu, as shown in Figure 2–6.

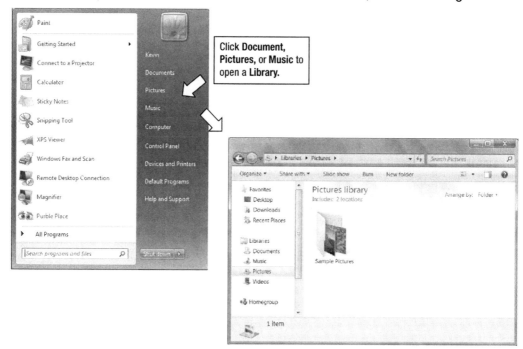

Figure 2–6. *Libraries are displayed on the Start menu as Documents, Pictures, and Music.*

NOTE: You may have noticed a fourth library, Videos, in the Libraries folder but it's not listed on the Start menu. You can add that and other libraries to the Start menu. Chapter 1 explains how you can customize the Start menu, including adding or removing what libraries are listed there.

Adding Shortcuts to Libraries in Other Places

It is pretty easy to get to your libraries through the Start menu or through the navigation pane in Windows Explorer. But maybe those aren't your favorite ways to get to your libraries. When you click the **Windows Explorer** button on the Taskbar, you get the Library window that displays all of your libraries.

When you first start Windows, before you open any programs, there are two places immediately accessible: the **Taskbar** and the **Desktop.** Though you already know how to use the Windows Explorer button on the Taskbar to get to libraries, there are ways to make the Taskbar and the Desktop do more for you, as shown in Figure 2–7.

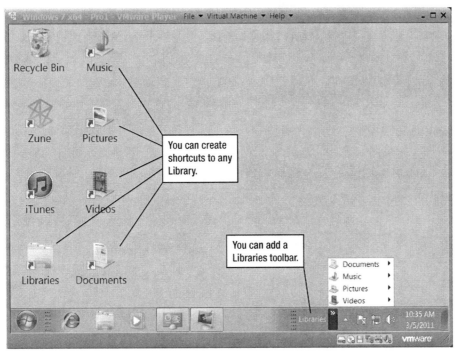

Figure 2–7. *If you like to work as much as possible from the Desktop and Taskbar, you can add shortcuts and toolbars.*

Adding a Library Toolbar to the Taskbar

If you've already poked around with adding toolbars to the Taskbar, you're probably thinking my computer doesn't have a Libraries toolbar. That's because you haven't created it yet. Do you really need one if you already have a button on the Taskbar? Check this out. A Libraries toolbar makes it super easy to go right to any file in your libraries without opening a series of windows.

To add the Libraries toolbar, follow the steps shown in Figures 2–8 and 2–9.

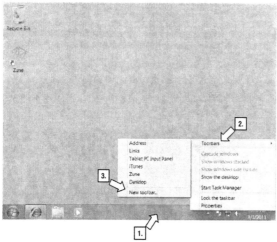

1. Right-click an empty area of the Taskbar.

2. Click **Toolbars**.

3. Click **New** toolbar.

   The **New Toolbar – Choose a folder** window appears, as shown in Figure 2–9.

Figure 2–8. *Adding a new toolbar*

4. Click **Libraries**.

5. Click **Select Folder**.

Figure 2–9. *Click Libraries to select it as the folder you want to create a toolbar for, and then click Select Folder*

The Libraries toolbar appears on the Taskbar, as shown in Figure 2–10. Your Taskbar may look different depending on how many other toolbars you have, your icon sizes, and whether you have the Taskbar locked.

Figure 2–10. *The Libraries toolbar appears on the Taskbar.*

You can click the **double right angle brackets** to the right of Libraries to drill down into the individual libraries, folders, and ultimately, files. In Figure 2–11, you can see how the menus and submenus cascade to the files.

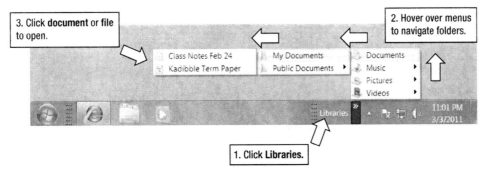

Figure 2–11. *Navigating to files through the Libraries toolbar*

Perhaps you prefer doing all of this navigating through windows not menus, but still like the idea of having more direct access to the specific libraries (Documents, Music, Pictures, or Video) without having to start at the Libraries folder level in Windows Explorer. With just a few more clicks and drags, you can get all of the libraries to show as separate icons in the toolbar. Figure 2–12 shows what this looks like. All you have to do is resize the Taskbar so that there's more room for the Libraries toolbar.

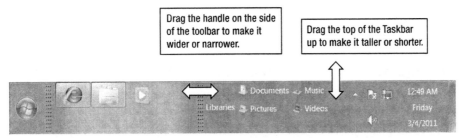

Figure 2–12. *Expanding the Taskbar allows you to enlarge the Libraries toolbar and show them as icons that open up separate windows.*

Adding Shortcuts to the Desktop

You will be amazed how easy this is to do. Drag and drop an icon from the Library folder onto the desktop, as shown in Figure 2–13.

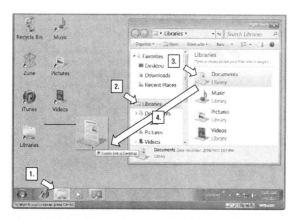

Figure 2–13. *Adding a Library shortcut to the desktop*

1. Open Windows Explorer.

2. Click **Libraries** in the left navigation pane.

3. Click and hold the library icon you want to add to the desktop.

4. Drag the icon to the desktop, and then release the mouse button.

5. Optional: right click the new icon on the desktop and rename it so that it does not say "- Shortcut" at the end of the name.

TIP: You can use this technique to create a shortcut on the desktop for just about anything that appears in a Windows Explorer window.

Using a Library

A library is more than just a name or a convenient place to store similar files or folders. Each library is designed for specific file types and presentation. As mentioned earlier, each library has two default folders, *My* — which is where your personal files go by default, and *Public* —, where you can place items that you want to share with users on your computer or network.

Document Library

The Document library is the default destination for almost every content file that isn't a picture, video, or music file. Many programs create their own folders inside the Document library for storing documents and data files. The following list is a sampling of programs that typically save files to the Documents library:

- **Microsoft Word**: .doc, .docx, .rtf

- **Microsoft Excel**: .xls, .xlsx, .csv

- **Microsoft PowerPoint**: .ppt, .pptx

- **Microsoft Visio**: .vsd, .vsdx

- **Adobe Acrobat/Reader**: .pdf

- **Many other programs that don't fit into the Music, Video, or Picture categories**

Each type of library has a different set of columns available for listing the files and folders. Figure 2–14 describes the parts and features of a Document library.

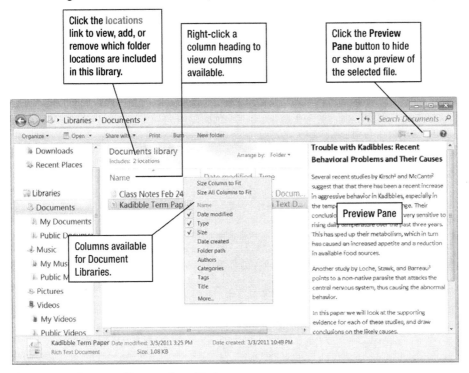

Figure 2–14. *Document library parts and features*

Music Library

When you first open the Music library, the default view is by Folder with small icons, as shown in Figure 2–15. This is not a friendly or useful view.

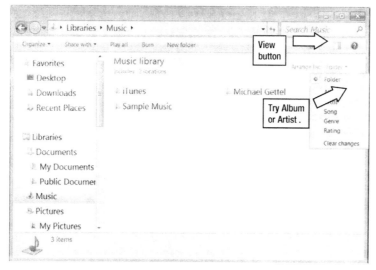

Figure 2–15. *Music library default Folder view*

For a more useful look, click the folder **View** button and choose **Medium Icons**, and then click **Arrange by** and select **Album** or **Artist,** like Figure 2–16.

Figure 2–16. *The Arrange by Artist view uses the album cover art.*

> **TIP:** Learn more about the different music file formats and media players in Chapter 11.

Pictures Library

The Pictures library is the default folder for more than just photos from your digital camera. It's also the place to look for pictures scanned in from your scanner or all-in-one, pictures you've created with drawing or graphic programs, and more. This library is really great for sorting and locating pictures without opening a photo viewer or editing program. Figure 2–17 shows pictures sorted by **Day** with the **View** slider set between **Large Icons** and **Extra Large Icons**.

Figure 2–17. *Sorting by Month, Day, or Tag makes browsing or finding photos in your collection quite easy.*

The Preview Pane is really useful here because you can quickly scroll through smaller icons and then select a file to look at it in more detail, as shown in Figure 2–18.

Figure 2–18. *The Preview Pane also allows you to add tags, a title, or change the date on the picture.*

MORE ABOUT USING PICTURES

There's a lot you can do to organize your pictures with the Pictures library. When you select a picture in the Pictures library, you can view and edit information about the picture (by adding tags or a title, or changing the date). If you want to do more with your pictures, such as crop or make color corrections, Chapter 7 describes how to install and use Windows Live Photo Gallery. Chapter 10 describes more programs for organizing and editing pictures, share them on the web; ordering pictures; or viewing them with programs like Windows Media Player and Windows Media Center.

Videos Library

The Videos library is where programs like Windows Media Player, Windows Media Center, and Windows Live Movie Maker store video files. The standard video file format for Windows is .wmv, or Windows Media files. Other common file formats include .mov, .avi, .mp4, and .mpeg. This library is also a place to save and organize video clips from your digital camera, camcorder, web cam, and downloads from the Internet. Some types of video clips and video formats only work with specific media players. There are several options for arranging the files in the Videos library. Figure 2–19 shows videos arranged by year.

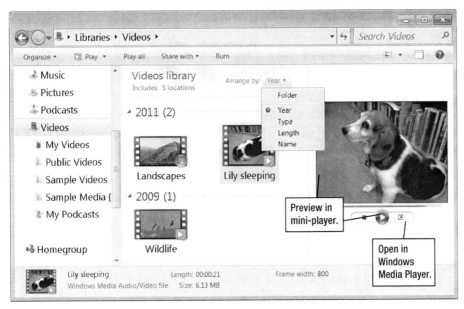

Figure 2–19. *The Arrange by Year option provides a good thumbnail of each video file.*

Experiment with the different ways to arrange and view the items in this window to find the one that works best for you. The Preview Pane offers the option of viewing the video in a mini-viewer or in a separate window such as Windows Media Player.

MORE ABOUT USING VIDEOS

The Video library is a great way to sort, organize, and locate many types of videos. Media players, such as Windows Media Center, Windows Media Player, iTunes, QuickTime, RealPlayer, and others, provide a more complete experience for enjoying your videos and music.

There's so much more to explore with enjoying your music and videos. Section 3 of this book contains several chapters about watching, sharing, and streaming videos and music.

Adding, Changing, and Removing Locations in Libraries

The standard libraries (Documents, Music, Pictures, and Videos) all have two default locations: the public folder and your user folder. Each of these has a real folder path as well as the friendly name you see. For example, Table 2–1 shows the names and paths in my Music Library.

Table 2–1. *Friendly Names and Folder Paths in the Music Library*

Friendly name seen in the window	Actual folder path
My Music	C:\Users\Kevin\Music
Public Music	C:\Users\Public\Music

Both of these locations are local on your computer. You can easily add more locations to any library in order to provide access to the following:

- Folders on a network hard drive, file server, media server, or Xbox.

- Public folders on another computer on your network.

- Content from programs that don't use the standard libraries for the default save location.

ADDITIONAL NOTES ABOUT ADDING LOCATIONS

The files and folders from the added location are not moved. No matter where you add locations from, the files and folders themselves do not move from the physical location. Even if the folders are on another computer or on your network, you can work with the files just like you would any files that are physically on your machine (local).

Accessing files on another computer may slow down the other computer. The other computer may be serving two masters—you and the person using the other computer. Accessing videos may be very demanding both on the computers and the network. Chapter 18 describes better ways to share across a network.

Accessing files across the network requires that the other computer be turned on. To access files on another computer, the other computer must be on and connected to the network.

Adding a folder location to a library doesn't limit what the library will display from that folder. For example, if you take still pictures and videos with a digital camera or camcorder, when you download those files to your computer, they usually go to the same folder. When you add a folder that contains picture and video files to the Pictures library, the video files will also be visible in the library.

To add a location to a library, follow the steps shown in Figure 2–20.

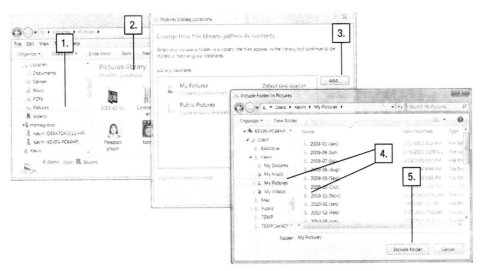

Figure 2–20. *Adding a folder location to a library*

1. Open a library.

2. Under the library name, for example, **Pictures library**, click the **locations** link. The **Picture Library Locations** window appears.

3. In **Picture Library Locations**, click **Add**. The **Include Folder in Pictures** dialog box appears.

4. Select a folder in the navigation pane or the folder list.

5. Click **Include Folder**. The Picture library lists the folders from the new location, as shown in Figure 2–21.

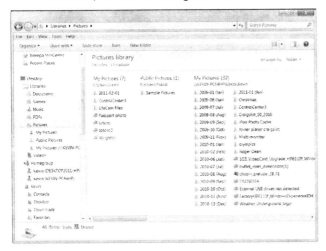

Figure 2–21. *The Pictures library, shown here in Folder view, displays all of the folders added from the new location.*

Adding Locations for Programs That Don't Use the Default Libraries

Photo editing, video editing, camera downloads, music downloads, and other types of programs may create their own structure of subfolders that are not in the Documents, Pictures, Music, or Videos libraries. To get the program's default save location and the libraries to agree with each other, there are several options.

1. Open up the source program, and look in its Properties, Tools, or Configuration to find the default save location.

2. Record the default save folder location the program uses, and add that location to the library. This option does not change or affect the program in any way.

   -or-

   Change the default save location in the program to point to the library you want it to use in the future. Then, move any existing files into an existing folder location in the library such as one of the default library folder locations, the My folder or Public folder. If your program has a most recently used (MRU) list, you may get an error if you try to open a file from that list. If that happens, just use the File ➤ Open command to find it in the new location. Eventually all of the entries in the most recently used list get pushed out by the files you have opened in the new location.

Creating a New Library

You can create your own libraries to make it easier to organize and locate types of information separate from the standard libraries already provided. When you create your own library, you must base it one of *five* library types; Documents, Music, Pictures, Video, and General Items. General does not appear to be much different than Documents and is probably most useful for content that does not fit in any of the other categories. Earlier in this chapter, you learned how each library is optimized for a particular type of content. In the following example, you are creating a new library called Spreadsheets to organize all of your Excel spreadsheet documents. Currently Excel saves these to a folder in the Documents library.

To create a new library, follow the steps shown in Figures 2–22 and 2–23.

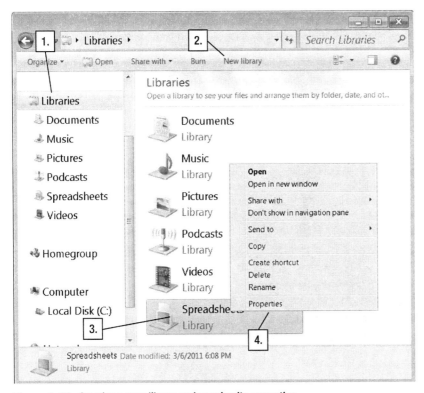

Figure 2–22. *Creating a new library and opening its properties*

1. Open the **Libraries** window.

2. In the title bar, click **New Library**.

    A **New Library** icon appears in the Library window, with the name highlighted so that you can type your own name for the library.

3. Type the name for the library. For example, "Spreadsheets."

4. Right-click **Library** under the **Library** name, and then click **Properties**.

    The Library (Spreadsheets) Properties appears.

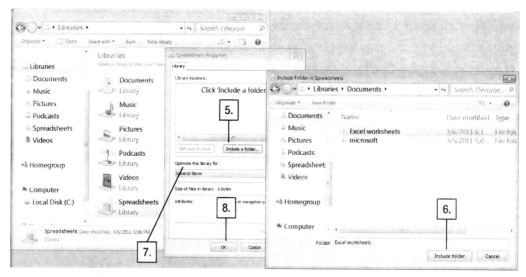

Figure 2–23. *Including a folder and optimizing the library*

5.   Click the **Include a folder** button.

The **Include Folder in (Spreadsheets) dialog box** appears.

> **NOTE:** Adding a location to a library does not automatically create a new folder. If you have not created a folder, you can create one now with the **New folder** link.

6.   Navigate to the folder you want to use, select it, and then click **Include folder**.

The folder location you selected now appears in the Library locations list.

7.   In **Optimize this library for**, select the library type. You can change this later if you want to use a different type.

8.   Click **OK**.

Creating a Separate PDF Library

The Document library can get quite crowded with all sorts of document types such as Word documents, Excel spreadsheets, PowerPoint presentations, and Adobe PDF files. There are two great advantages to creating a separate folder for PDFs, and then creating a library for that folder.

 Adobe Advanced Search—Search all PDF documents in a folder at once.

This Adobe feature, available in both the free Adobe Reader and in Adobe Acrobat, allows you to search all PDF documents in a specific folder. This very powerful full-text search provides a search results list of all matches (see Figure 2–24).

PDF documents are very commonly used to provide documents, user guides, brochures, and books over the web. Many scanning programs provide the option to save to a PDF file. You may have accumulated quite a few PDF documents, even if you don't create them yourself.

Storing all of your PDF documents in their own folder (or folders) and adding their location to their own PDF library makes it much easier to find them later.

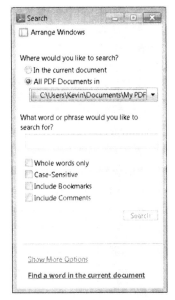

Figure 2–24. *Adobe Advanced Search can search all PDF documents in a folder.*

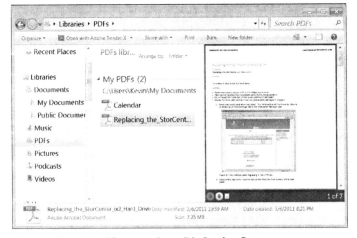

Figure 2–25. *Adobe Viewer works well in Preview Pane.*

Browse PDFs with the Preview Pane

Not all document and media content files have a viewer to preview the file in the Preview Pane (see Figure 2–25). The PDF viewer works quite well. Keeping all PDFs in their own folders, a powerful search tool, and a useful preview pane make it easy to find information in your PDF library.

Summary

In this chapter, you've learned a lot about using libraries. After reading this chapter you should be able to

- Get to the Libraries folder from the Taskbar, Start button, or any Windows Explorer window.

- Understand how important libraries and backups are to each other.

- Know how to create shortcuts to libraries in other places that might be useful to you, such as a Toolbar or the desktop.

- Know the difference between your personal user folders and public folders.

- Know how to use each type of library and understand how each type is optimized for their specific content.

- Understand the difference between libraries and actual folder locations.

- Add locations to a library, including programs that do not normally save to a library

- Create a new library.

Next Steps

Libraries are an integral part of many programs. They not only provide a preview of most of the common types of files and content you use on your computer, they also provide an insight into how useful this content is and what kinds of programs you can use to work with that content. The following chapters will help you explore these programs a little more:

- Chapter 1 for more information about adding libraries to the Start menu.

- Chapter 6 for examples of programs that save files to libraries, like WordPad, which edits documents and stores them in the Documents library, and Paint, which creates and edits bitmap images and pictures and stores them in the Pictures library.

- Chapter 5 for more examples of programs that save or manage files in libraries.

- Chapter 7 for more programs that use libraries to store files, like Windows Live Photo Gallery, which uses the Photo library; Windows Movie Maker, which uses the Video library; and Adobe Reader, which stores PDFs in the Documents library.

■ Chapter 10 to see examples of using the Pictures library to find, preview, and select pictures.

■ Chapter 10 and Chapter 11 to learn more about organizing and previewing content in the Music, Pictures, and Video libraries.

■ Chapter 16 for how to organize your content so that it gets backed up and how to schedule backups of libraries. Libraries probably contain your most valuable and irreplaceable content. Keep them protected with backups.

Chapter 3

Using Gadgets and Widgets

This chapter will show you how to use gadgets and widgets. *Gadgets* and *widgets* are miniature programs that provide information or access to tools directly from the desktop. They are designed to allow you to do or view something quickly without having to open a full-blown program. Gadgets are convenient because they are easy to access, take up very little space on your computer, and they don't use very much of your computer memory. Does this sound like something else you may use in your everyday life, possibly more than your computer, like an iPod Touch, iPhone, iPad, Android Smartphone, or tablet? In some ways, gadgets and widgets are the predecessors to apps for Apple and Android mobile devices. Since the apps you download to touch mobile devices are the heart of what you can do with those devices, out of necessity some of them can be quite powerful. Conventional Windows programs have the luxury of more desktop space to work with and easier multi-tasking. But if you like the idea of small windows and applications that provide quick snippets of information or perform small tasks from a small area of your computer, you've found it: gadgets.

Windows 7 includes several gadgets, such as Calendar, Clock, Weather, Feed Headlines, Slide Show, and Picture Puzzle. You can also get more gadgets from the Web, created by Microsoft or other third parties.

Microsoft Windows Gadgets are not the only game in town. There are also **Google Desktop Gadgets**, and **Yahoo! Widgets**. Both use separate applications to run; they don't use the same application used by Windows 7's built-in gadgets. We will show you how to use all three of these offerings from Microsoft, Google, and Yahoo*!*

> **NOTE:** Gadgets or widgets? Though they use different names and require different programs, gadgets and widgets are the same thing. So unless we are talking specifically about Yahoo! Widgets, whenever we mention gadgets we mean both gadgets and widgets.

Quick Comparison of Gadgets

Table 3–1 summarizes the gadget features offered by Microsoft, Google, and Yahoo! The pictures of the clock gadgets show the relative size as they appear on the desktop. The icons for Microsoft gadgets are larger than those for Google desktop gadgets or Yahoo! widgets.

Table 3–1. *Gadget Features*

Feature	Microsoft Gadgets	Google Desktop Gadgets	Yahoo! Widgets
Installation	Built in to Windows 7 and Windows Vista	Download Google Desktop `http://desktop.google.com`	Download Yahoo! Widgets application `http://widgets.yahoo.com/download/`
Available from Web	About 6,000 listed on gadget downloads page	Not listed on download page	Over 6,000 listed on widgets download page
Operating system requirements	Windows 7 Windows Vista	Windows 7 Windows Vista Windows XP SP2	Windows 7 Windows Vista Windows XP SP2 Windows 2000 SP4 Mac OSX 10.3.9 and up
Sizing and hiding options	Always on top Some gadgets resizable Close gadget	Always on top Font size resizable	Always on top Auto hide Some widgets resizable Close dock
Docking options	Snap to sides, top, or bottom	Sidebar with Gadgets	Widget Dock
Launch at Startup option	✔	✔	✔

Choosing the Best Gadget Program

Though they are similar, there are some differences. Which one is best? Since they are all easy to download and set up, try all three to see which you like best. You can use all three at once; they play together nicely. But you will probably settle on one because then you only have one set of features to learn and manage. All offer many of the same type of gadgets. Which photo viewer do you like best? Which news viewer is most relevant? Which clock is coolest? You may find more gadgets for Microsoft Outlook, Hotmail, or Windows Media Player in the Microsoft gadgets; more gadgets for Google search, Gmail, and Google Docs in the Google gadgets, etc.

Exploring Windows and Gadgets

The rest of this chapter covers how install, download, and use each of these gadget programs:

- Windows 7 Desktop Gadgets
- Google Desktop Gadgets
- Yahoo! Widgets

Using Windows 7 Desktop Gadgets

Of the gadgets and widgets described in this chapter, Windows 7 Desktop Gadgets have the largest icons. If you don't see any on your desktop, don't worry. They are already installed on your computer but are usually hidden by default when you use Windows for the first time.

Windows gadgets were introduced in Windows Vista. Many of the gadgets created for Vista will work on Windows 7, too. All of the Desktop Gadgets provided by Windows 7 will work. Most gadgets download from Microsoft's Desktop and SideShow gadgets page or Windows Live Gallery will work on Windows 7. Microsoft notes some exceptions in Windows Help and Support, and on their Desktop Gadgets download pages.

- Some gadgets created for Windows Vista might not work as well on Windows 7.

- Some gadgets only work on computers running Windows 7.

- Gadgets designed for a 32-bit version of Windows will not work on a 64-bit version of Windows.

In Figure 3–1, you can see four examples of common Windows Desktop Gadgets that are already installed and available on your computer. Most gadgets have controls that appear when you hover over the gadget, like those shown for the news headline gadget. The controls available vary with each gadget.

Figure 3–1. *These four Windows Desktop Gadgets are already installed by Windows 7. When you hover over a gadget, you can view a toolbar with controls and options for that gadget.*

When Microsoft introduced gadgets in Vista, it also included a container to dock them together, called *Windows Sidebar*. This feature was dropped in Windows 7, but Sidebar Gadgets are really still just gadgets. So, don't go looking for a Windows Sidebar in Windows 7, but feel free to try any gadgets that are labeled "Sidebar gadgets" or "designed for Windows Sidebar."

> **TIP:** In Windows 7, gadgets stick to each other and the side of the screen like magnets. Without a sidebar or dock feature such as the ones for Google gadgets or Yahoo! widgets, you can't drag all of your gadgets across the screen together; you have to move them individually. Google Desktop Gadgets offers a sidebar and Yahoo! Widgets offers a dock, both of which allow you to attach your gadgets to each other and move them as a group.

Another Windows Vista feature related to gadgets that might be confusing when you are looking for gadgets on Microsoft's web sites is *SideShow Gadgets*. You can ignore *SideShow Gadgets*; they are specifically designed for *SideShow devices* and were introduced in Windows Vista. They do not work as desktop gadgets. This technology was not widely adopted; in fact, I've never seen a SideShow device.

Adding Gadgets to Your Desktop

Windows 7 provides a few gadgets that you can immediately add to your desktop, but there are many more available on the web. Figure 3–2 displays the Desktop Gadgets window where you can select from gadgets already on your computer. When you download new gadgets from the web, they are added here.

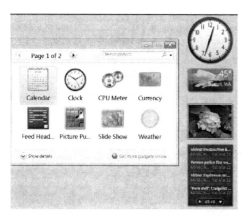

Figure 3–2. *Double-click a gadget in the Desktop Gadgets window or drag it onto your desktop*

To add a gadget to the desktop from the gadgets already on your computer, follow these steps:

1. Click the Start button, and in the **Start** menu's search box, type Gadgets.

2. In the list that appears, click **Desktop Gadgets**. The Desktop Gadgets window displays the gadgets currently installed on your computer.

3. In the Desktop Gadgets window, select a gadget and double-click it to add it to the desktop.

4. Repeat as needed for each installed gadget you want to add to the desktop.

To find more desktop gadgets on the web, use any of the following methods to get to Microsoft web sites that provide additional gadgets:

Figure 3–3. *The Desktop and SideShow gadgets web site*

Go to the **Desktop and SideShow gadgets** web site. In the Desktop Gadgets window, click the Get more gadgets online link.

-or-

Go to `http://windows.microsoft.com/en-US/windows/downloads/personalize/gadgets`

A web page similar to Figure 3–3 will display gadgets you can download.

Figure 3–4. *The Windows Live Gallery web site*

You can also go to the **Windows Live Gallery** web site at `http://gallery.live.com/results.aspx?c=0&bt=1&pl=1&st=5`

A web page similar to Figure 3–4 displays gadgets you can download.

Both of these web pages let you click the gadget image to view more information about it, including reviews by other users. You can also click Get Now or Download to immediately download it, as shown in Figures 3–3 and 3–4.

NOTE: When you select to download a gadget, you will have to click through a series of messages warning about the download. Even though it is on a Microsoft web site, Microsoft can't guarantee the safety of the gadgets. Almost all gadgets are created by third parties (often individual users) and you are more likely to encounter a gadget that is buggy than one that is malicious or dangerous. User reviews can help you sort out gadgets that don't work well.

Showing or Hiding All Gadgets

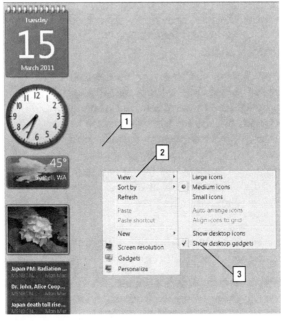

You can hide or show all gadgets on your desktop just like you do your desktop icons.

To show desktop gadgets, follow these steps:

1. Right-click an empty area of the desktop, as shown in Figure 3–5.

2. Click **View**.

3. Select **Show** desktop gadgets.

This toggles all of your Microsoft Windows desktop gadgets on or off. When you select Show desktop icons, they will be displayed whenever you start Windows.

Figure 3–5. *Right-click the desktop to show or hide the desktop gadgets.*

> **NOTE:** The Show desktop gadgets command only controls Microsoft Windows desktop gadgets. This command has no effect on Google Desktop Gadgets or Yahoo! Widgets.

Managing Gadgets

There are several things you can do selectively on a per-gadget basis. These features are available when you right-click a gadget or from the gadget controls toolbar that appears on the right side when you hover over the gadget. Figure 3–6 displays the right-click menu and previously Figure 3–5 displayed the mini-toolbar on the side of the gadget.

Most of the commands on the right-click menu are the same for all gadgets.

- **Add gadgets**: Opens the Desktop Gadgets window, previously described in the "Adding Gadgets to Your Desktop" section.

- **Move**: Allows you to move the gadget across the desktop without clicking and dragging. Use the arrow keys on the keyboard or move it with the mouse pointer. When the gadget is positioned where you want it, click or press the Enter key. Gadgets are "magnetic" and will stick to each other or the side of the window when you bring them close together.

- **Size ➤ Larger size/Smaller size:** Not all gadgets offer size options.

- **Always on top**: When selected, this prevents other windows from covering the gadget. If not selected, then the gadget can be covered by other windows or dragged on top of a window.

- **Opacity ➤ 20% to 100%**: Sets whether you can see through it or not. The lower the percentage, the more transparent. 100% is solid. Regardless of the opacity, when you hover over the gadget, it becomes solid until you move away from it again.

- **Options**: Changes settings for this specific gadget. For example, the options for the clock are to change the clock face style and set the time zone. Not all gadgets have individual options.

- **Close gadget**: Removes the gadget from the desktop. If you want to see it again, then you must add it from the Desktop Gadgets window.

| Add gadgets... |
| Move |
| Size ▸ |
| Always on top |
| Opacity ▸ |
| Options |
| Close gadget |

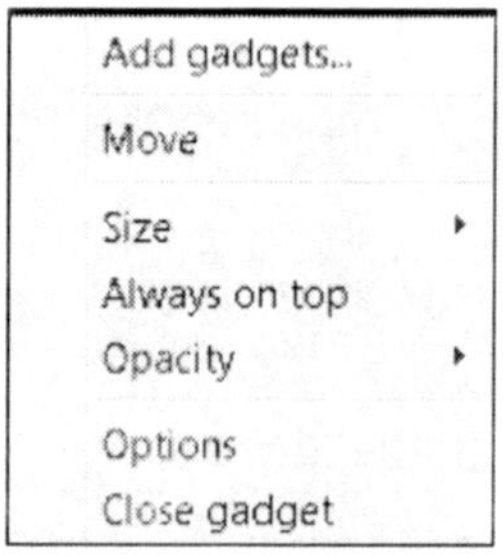

Figure 3–6. *Gadget right-click menu*

Keep it Simple: Making Microsoft Gadgets less Obtrusive

To keep gadgets out of the way when you are not using or viewing them, select the following settings from the right-click menu:

- Click **Size** (if available) and then select **Smaller size**.

- Make sure **Always on top** is cleared (no checkbox).

- Click **Opacity** and set it to **20%**.

In addition:

- Move the gadgets to the side of the screen you use least for your main programs.

Using these settings is a lot less work than closing and re-adding gadgets or toggling Show Desktop Gadgets off and on.

CONGRATULATIONS! Your Windows Desktop Gadgets are now easy to use when you need them and out of the way when you don't.

Using Google Desktop Gadgets

Google includes *Google Gadgets* and the *Sidebar*, shown in Figure 3–7, as part of *Google Desktop*. There are a number of other cool things in Google Desktop besides the Gadgets and Sidebar. For now we'll focus on Google Gadgets—how to download and use them.

Google gadgets work similarly to Windows Desktop Gadgets. There are differences, however.

- The Google sidebar, which helps you organize, move, and manage your gadgets as a group, is like a floating toolbar or menu that contains all of your gadgets (see Figure 3–7).

- Google Gadgets aren't just for Windows 7 and Windows Vista; you can also install gadgets on Windows XP. So if you have computers with different versions of Windows at work, school, and home, you can use most of your favorite Google Gadgets on any of them.

Figure 3–7. *Google Gadgets on the Sidebar*

Downloading and Installing Google Desktop Gadgets

Google Desktop Gadgets is not built into Windows. Before you can use the Google Gadgets, you must install Google Desktop. Google Desktop includes more than gadgets, but you do not have to install every feature that is offered.

To install Google Desktop, follow these steps:

1. In your web browser, go to `http://desktop.google.com`.

2. Click Install **Google Desktop**.

3. Your browser may display a message that the download is being blocked, similar to Figure 3–8.

Figure 3–8. *Internet Explorer warning in toolbar, and dropdown menu that appears when you click it.*

4. Click the message and then click **Download File**.

5. Select **Run**.

   -Or-

   Select **Save**, and when the download completes, select Open.

6. When the Welcome to Google Desktop page appears, you'll see a description of the features and the Google Terms of Service (also called the licensing agreement).

7. Click **I agree**. The Google Desktop Features page appears.

8. Make sure the checkbox for Sidebar with Gadgets is selected, as shown in Figure 3–9. All other features are optional; they are not required for using gadgets.

Figure 3–9. *Google Desktop Features installation options*

9. Click **Done**. Installation is very quick. At the end of installation a Thank you screen appears along with your Google Sidebar, as shown in Figure 3–10.

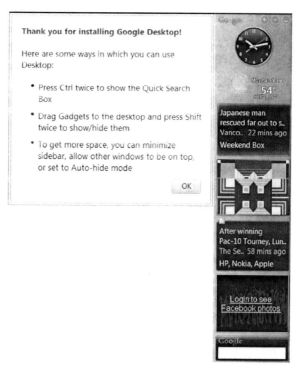

Thank you for installing Google Desktop!

Here are some ways in which you can use Desktop:

* Press Ctrl twice to show the Quick Search Box

* Drag Gadgets to the desktop and press Shift twice to show/hide them

* To get more space, you can minimize sidebar, allow other windows to be on top, or set to Auto-hide mode

OK

Figure 3–10. *The Thank you screen provides some useful tips.*

10. A new Google Desktop icon is added to the Notification area of the toolbar, as shown in Figure 3–11, though it will probably be hidden.

Google Desktop

Customize...

Figure 3–11. *Google Desktop icon in Notifications*

Adding Gadgets to Your Desktop

Once Google Desktop Gadgets is installed, Google provides additional gadgets that you can install from your computer; there are thousands more you can download from the Web.

To add a gadget from those listed on your computer, follow these steps:

1. Click the **Add gadgets** button in the toolbar at the top of the Google sidebar, as shown in Figure 3–12.

Figure 3–12. *On the toolbar at the top of the Google Sidebar, the Plus button is the Add Gadgets button.*

The Add gadgets window appears, as shown in Figure 3–13.

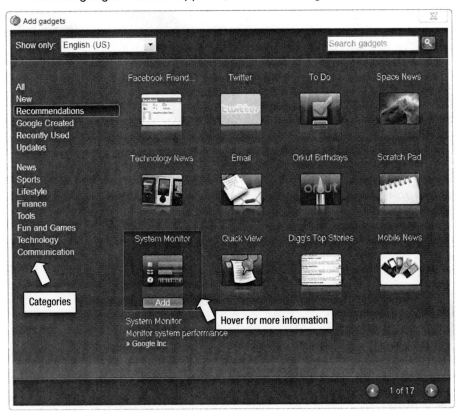

Figure 3–13. *Google Add gadgets window*

2. Browse, select, and add gadgets.

   a. Select gadget categories from the list on the left.

    b.   Hover over a gadget to learn more about it.

    c.   To add a gadget, hover over the gadget and then click Add or double-click the gadget.

    d.   Repeat as needed for each installed gadget you want to add to the desktop.

To add a gadget to the sidebar,

■   Right-click the gadget and then click Dock to Sidebar, as shown in Figure 3–14.

Figure 3–14. *Adding a gadget on your desktop to the sidebar*

To add Google Gadgets from the web, follow these steps:

1.   Go to the Google Desktop Gadgets web site at `http://desktop.google.com/plugins`.

2.   Select gadget categories from the list on the left, as shown in Figure 3–15.

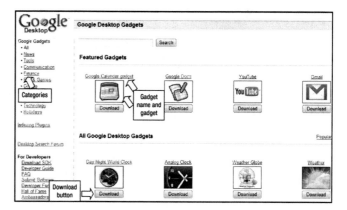

Figure 3–15. *Google Desktop Gadgets web site*

3.   If you see a gadget you want to add, click the Download button under the gadget.

4.   If you are searching for a particular gadget by name, like Facebook, use the Search box.

5.   If you want to know more about a gadget or read user reviews before downloading it, click the gadget or gadget name.

Figure 3–16 shows a gadget description page for a Facebook gadget. On the description page, you can read other user's comments and ratings, find out when it was published, and download it.

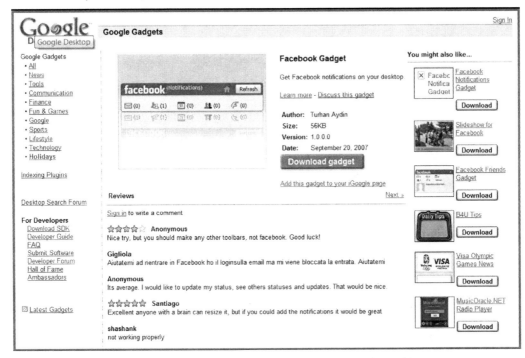

Figure 3–16. *The description page allows you to learn more about a gadget before downloading it.*

NOTE: When you select to download a gadget from the web, you will have to click through a series of messages warning about the download. Even though it is on a Google web site, Google can't guarantee the safety of the gadgets. Almost all gadgets are created by third parties (often individual users), and you are more likely to encounter a gadget that is buggy than one that is malicious or dangerous. User reviews can help you sort out gadgets that don't work well.

Managing Gadgets

Google Desktop is always running when you start Windows. If you close the sidebar, the next time you start Windows you won't see the sidebar but Google Desktop is still running in the background.

To move, hide, or close the Sidebar, follow these steps:

The Sidebar must be docked to the left or right side of your desktop. It can't be docked to the top or bottom of the desktop or float undocked.

You can minimize the Sidebar to the Floating Deskbar. You can also undock and float individual gadgets any place on your desktop.

Table 3–2 describes where and how to select these options.

Table 3–2. *Google Features and How to Use Them*

Perform these tasks	Using these Google features
▨ To dock the Sidebar to the other side of the desktop, click the Sidebar title bar and drag the Sidebar to the other side of your desktop. Or, click the Menu button at the top of the sidebar shown in Figure 3–17; in the menu that appears, click Dock Sidebar ➤ Left or Right.	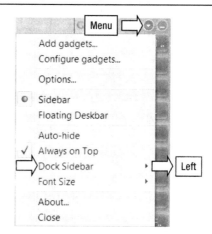 **Figure 3–17.** Click the Menu button on the Sidebar title bar, click Dock Sidebar menu, and then click Left or Right.
▨ To minimize the Sidebar, click the **Minimize** button in the Sidebar shown in Figure 3–18. This minimizes to the Floating Deskbar, shown in Figure 3–19, which can be dragged to any place on the desktop.	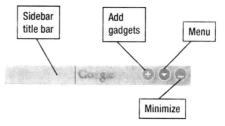 **Figure 3–18.** *Click the Minimize button in the Sidebar title bar to reduce the Sidebar to a Floating Deskbar.*

Figure 3–19. *Gadgets reduced to Floating Sidebar*

- To restore the Sidebar, click the Floating Deskbar menu button shown in Figure 3–20; in the menu that appears, click Sidebar.

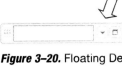

Figure 3–20. Floating Deskbar menu button

- To close the Sidebar, click the **Menu** button at the top of the Sidebar, and then click **Close**, as shown in Figure 3–21.

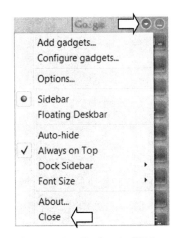

Figure 3–21. *Closing the Sidebar*

- To auto-hide the Sidebar, click the **Menu** button and then click **Auto-hide**, as shown in Figure 3–22.The Sidebar will only appear when you hover at the edge of the screen where the Sidebar was docked.

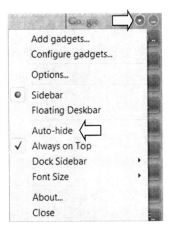

Figure 3–22. Sidebar menu and Floating Deskbar

To collapse or expand, follow these steps:

You can expand or collapse within the sidebar or to the side of the sidebar. You can only collapse or expand gadgets individually; there is no Expand All or Collapse All command for the sidebar.

- To collapse a gadget within the Sidebar, hover over the gadget, click the **Menu** button on the gadget, and then click **Collapse**.

- To expand a gadget to the side of the Sidebar, click the gadget. Some gadgets may offer a further level of detail when you click an item, as shown in Figures 3–23 and 3–24.

- To collapse a gadget back into the Sidebar, click again, almost any place outside of the gadget.

- To remove a gadget from the Sidebar, hover over the gadget, click the **Menu** button on the gadget, and then click **Remove**.

Figure 3–23. *Stock gadget expanded (top) and collapsed (bottom) within the sidebar*

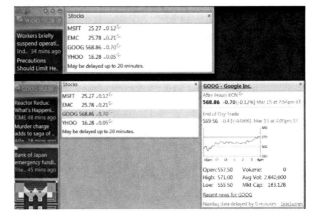

Figure 3–24. *Stock gadget expanded to the side of the sidebar (top) and further expanded (bottom).*

To move, hide, or close gadgets, follow these steps:

- To undock a gadget from the Sidebar, click the gadget and drag it to the desktop.

- To dock a floating gadget, drag it to the Sidebar until it clicks in place.

- To close a gadget, hover over the gadget, and then click the **Close** button on the gadget.

To configure or set additional options, follow these steps:

- To set options for a gadget, click the **Menu** button on the gadget, and then click **Options**.

- To change the default size of text in all gadgets, click the **Menu** button on the Sidebar, and then click **Font Size**.

> **TIP:** You can take it with you. If you like the way you have set up desktop gadgets on one computer, you can save those settings to your Google account. Then those same settings can be applied whenever you log in to your Google account on another computer. Click the **Menu** button on the Sidebar, and then click **Configure gadgets**.

Keep it Simple: Make Google Gadgets less Obtrusive

Using what you just learned about moving, hiding, and closing gadgets and sidebars, you can use the following techniques to keep gadgets handy without taking over your desktop:

- Collapse gadgets you don't use very much.

- Remove gadgets from the sidebar that you have not used for a long time.

- On the Sidebar menu, clear **Always on top**.

- On the Sidebar menu, select **Auto-hide**.

CONGRATULATIONS! Your Google Desktop Gadgets are now easy to use when you need them and out of the way when you don't.

Using Yahoo! Widgets

For the most part Yahoo! Widgets look and work a lot like Microsoft and Google gadgets. But widgets also have several differences in how they are organized and displayed. They are not necessarily harder or easier to use than Microsoft or Google gadgets, but you will need to learn a different way to do some things.

Heads Up Display

Heads Up Display is unique to Yahoo! Widgets and is similar to the Windows Show/Hide Desktop command. When you select Heads Up Display, all other windows are minimized, and all widgets in the Dock are opened on top of a special background on top of the desktop. You can also toggle the Heads Up Display by pressing the F8 key.

Figure 3–25 shows the desktop with Heads Up Display, the Yahoo! Widgets dock, and "shown" widgets.

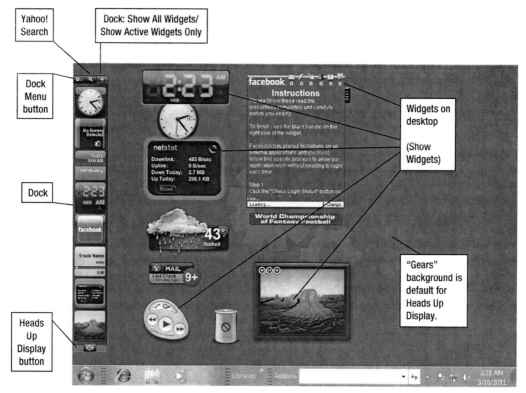

Figure 3–25. *Widget dock and widgets on Heads Up Display*

Overall, Yahoo! Widgets look and work a lot like Microsoft and Google gadgets. But widgets have several differences in how they are organized and displayed. Widgets are not necessarily harder or easier to use than Microsoft or Google gadgets, but you will need to learn a different way to do some things.

Downloading and Installing the Yahoo! Widgets Program

Like Google Desktop Gadgets, Yahoo! Widgets are not built in to Windows. Before you can use the Yahoo! Widgets, you must install the Yahoo! Widgets program.

To install the Yahoo! Widgets Program, follow these steps:

1. In your web browser, go to http://widgets.yahoo.com/ download/.

2. Under **Manual Download**, click **Windows**, as shown in Figure 3–26.

   Your browser may display a File Download Security Warning dialog box, as shown in Figure 3–27, asking if you want to run or save the file.

Figure 3–26. *Widgets program download page*

3. Select **Run**.

   –or–

   Select **Save**, and when the download completes, select **Open**.

4. If Windows displays a User Account Control dialog box, click **Yes** to allow the installation program to run.

Figure 3–27. *Choose Run or Save*

The Yahoo! Widgets Setup page appears.

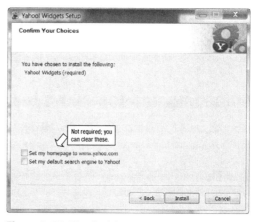

NOTE The wizard will try to hijack your home page and search by automatically selecting Yahoo, as shown in Figure 3–28. If you like your current homepage and search engine, clear these checkboxes.

5. After installation is finished, the first time you use Yahoo! Widgets, you will be asked to accept the license agreement.

Figure 3–28. *You don't have to use Yahoo! for your home page or start page.*

6. Click **I Accept**.

When Yahoo! Widgets opens, the Yahoo! Widgets Dock appears on the right side of your desktop and several widgets open, as shown in Figure 3–29.

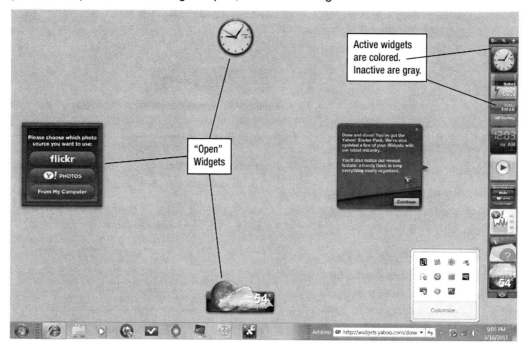

Figure 3–29. *Widgets dock and widgets on desktop*

A Widgets two-gear icon is added to the notification area, as shown in Figure 3–30. Depending on your notification settings, this icon may be hidden.

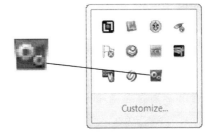

Figure 3–30. *Widget icon in notifications*

To add Yahoo! Widgets from the web:

1. Go to the Yahoo! Widgets Gallery web site at http://widgets.yahoo.com/

2. Find widgets. Figure 3–31 displays several different ways you can browse or find widgets.

   ▪ You can browse the Top Rated or New Widgets lists.

   ▪ You can browse one of the category lists.

   ▪ You can type a key word in the Search box, such as "Facebook." Figure 3–32 shows part of the search results for Facebook.

Figure 3–31. *Yahoo! Widgets Gallery*

Figure 3–32. *Search results for Facebook widgets*

3. If you want to know more about a widget or read user reviews before downloading it, click the widget or widget name. Figure 3–33 shows a description page for a particular Facebook gadget.

4. If you like a gadget, click the Get it! button.

Once widgets have been downloaded to your computer, they are stored by default in My Widgets.

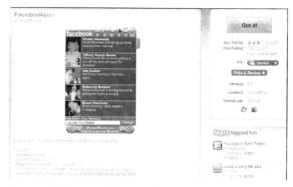

Figure 3–33. *Description page for a Facebook Widget*

Adding Widgets to Your Desktop

The Yahoo! Widgets does not provide a widgets window for picking out gadgets to add to your computer like the Microsoft Desktop Gadgets window or Google Desktop Gadgets Add Gadgets window. If you want to find widgets already on your computer, you can find them in the `My Widgets` folder created by the Yahoo! Widgets installation program. Once the Yahoo! Widgets program is installed, Yahoo! provides thousands more that you can download from the web.

My Widgets

When the Yahoo! Widgets program is installed on your computer, it creates a My Widgets folder in My Documents, as shown in Figure 3–34. Though it uses generic icons instead of thumbnails that actually look like the widgets, it is actually a pretty convenient way to find your widgets if you do not have any open on your desktop at the moment.

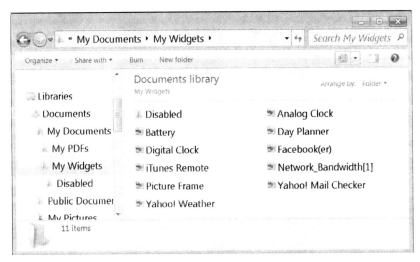

Figure 3–34. *My Widgets folder in My Documents*

Since My Widgets is a folder, it also means you can create a Widgets Library that will show up in your Libraries folder, as shown in Figure 3–35. Chapter 2 tells all you need to know about creating your own libraries.

Figure 3–35. *You can create a Widgets Library for easy access through conventional Libraries folders.*

Or you can add a My Widgets toolbar to your taskbar, as shown in Figure 3–36. The "Customizing and Personalizing Windows" section describes how to do this.

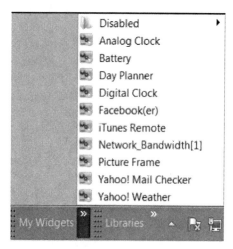

Figure 3–36. *My Widgets toolbar added to the taskbar*

Managing Widgets

Yahoo! offers may options for managing the dock or individual widgets. Table 3–3 describes where and how to select these options.

Table 3–3. *Widget Options*

Perform these tasks	Using these Yahoo! features
To move, resize, or close the dock: The dock can be attached to the top, bottom, left, or right side of the desktop. In addition, you can position the dock within each side of desktop. For example, if you dock to the right side, you can specify the top of the right side, middle of the right side, or bottom of the right side. You can't float the dock in the desktop area away from a side, but you can float individual widgets any place on the desktop.	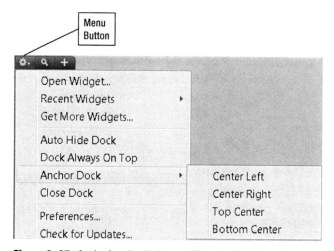 **Figure 3–37.** *Anchoring the dock to a different side of the desktop.*

- To move the dock to a different side of the desktop, click the **Menu** button, and then click **Anchor Dock ➤ Center Left**, **Center Right**, **Top Center**, or **Bottom Center**, as shown in Figure 3–37.

- To specify a docking position other than center of any side, click the **Menu** button, and then click **Preferences**. In Yahoo! Widgets Preferences, shown in Figure 3–38, click the **Dock** tab. Select the **Side** and the **Position**.

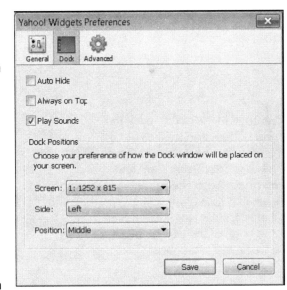

Figure 3–38. *Yahoo! Widgets Preferences*

- To move the dock to a different monitor in a multiple-monitor system, click the **Menu** button, click **Preferences**, and then click the **Dock** tab. In **Screen**, your active monitors are listed by resolution. Select a monitor.

- To close the dock, click the **Menu** button, and then click **Close Dock**.

■ To auto hide the dock, click the **Menu** button, and then click **Preferences**, as shown in Figure 3–39. Click the **Dock** tab, and then select **Auto Hide**, as shown in Figure 3–40. The Dock will only appear when you hover at the edge of the screen where the Dock was attached.

■ To keep the dock always on top, so that no other windows can cover it, click the **Menu** button and then click **Preferences**, as shown in Figure 3–39. Click the **Dock** tab, and then select **Always on Top**, as shown in Figure 3–40.

Figure 3–39. *Accessing Widgets Preferences*

Figure 3–40. *Yahoo! Widgets Preferences*

Heads Up Display:

You can customize some of the Heads Up Display settings in Preferences. Click the **Menu** button at the top of the **Dock**, click **Preferences**, and then click the **General** tab, as shown in Figure 3–41.

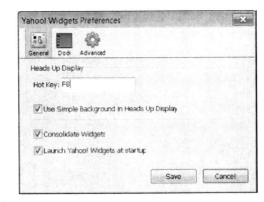

Figure 3–41. *Heads Up Display settings*

To move, close, or hide widgets:

- To add a widget from the dock to the desktop, right-click the widget on the dock, and then click **Show Widget**, as shown in Figure 3–42.

- To remove a widget from the desktop, right-click the widget and then click **Hide Widget**, as shown in Figure 3–42.

- To remove a widget from the dock and your computer, right-click the widget and then click **Delete Widget**.

Figure 3–42. *Showing and hiding widgets on the desktop*

- To move a widget on the desktop, click and drag the widget.

■ To show only open widgets on the dock, click the + button.

■

■ Figure 3–43 shows the dock with only open widgets on the left and shows the dock with all widgets (open and closed) on the right.

■

■ To show all widgets on the dock (open or closed), click the + button again. When closed widgets are displayed on the dock, they are grayed out, as shown on the right side. Open widgets are in color.

Figure 3–43. *Only open widgets (left); all widgets (right)*

To configure or set individual widget options:

- To set options for a widget, right-click the widget on the desktop or click the **Menu** button on the widget on the dock, as shown in Figure 3–44 (the widget must be in the open state on the dock).

- The options and number of tabs may vary in the Widget preferences, but the Window tab shown in Figure 3–45 provides several options to control how the mouse interacts with widgets and to specify the opacity of the widget.

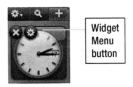

Figure 3–44. *Widget menu button*

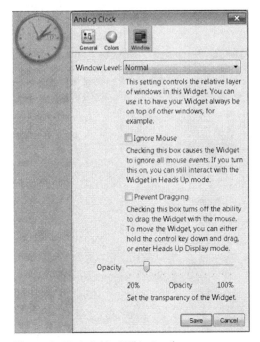

Figure 3–45. *Individual Widget options*

Keep It Simple: Make Yahoo! Widgets Less Obtrusive

Using what you just learned, you can use the following techniques to keep widgets out of the way when you are not using or viewing them:

- Collapse widgets you don't use very much.

- Remove widgets that you have not used for a long time from the dock.

- On the Preferences menu, clear Always on top.

- On the Preferences menu, select Auto-hide.

CONGRATULATIONS! Your Yahoo! Widgets are now easy to use when you need them and out of the way when you don't.

Weather Gadget Challenge

The Weather gadgets provided by Microsoft, Google, and Yahoo! are an easy way to compare and explore features. Try this multiple-choice quiz to test what you have learned. Each question lists the gadgets suites on the left and all the possible answers on the right. Sometimes each suite has more than one answer associated with it, and sometimes they share answers.

1. Add the Weather gadget to your desktop if you haven't already. Where could you look to find weather gadgets?

Gadget Program	How to find a gadget
	a. Right-click the desktop, and then click **Gadgets**.
	b. Right-click any gadget on the desktop, and then click **Add gadgets**.
	c. Click the **+** button at the top of the sidebar.
1. Microsoft	**d.** Click the **Menu** button at the top of the sidebar, and then click **Add gadgets**.
2. Google	
3. Yahoo!	**e.** Click the **Options** menu button at the top of the dock, and then click **Get More Widgets**.
	f. Click the **Search** button at the top of the dock, and then search for **Weather**.
	g. In the taskbar notification area, right-click the program's icon and then select the **Get <?>** or **Add <?>** command.

Answers:

1. Microsoft: you can find a gadget with either a. or b.
2. Google: you can find a gadget with either c. or g.
3. Yahoo!: you can find a gadget with either e. or g.

If you try f. on the Yahoo! Widgets Dock, it is a web search, not a search of the widget library.

2. Match the program with the Weather gadget or widget by city.

Gadget Program	Weather Gadget

1. Microsoft

2. Google

3. Yahoo!

Answers:

1. Microsoft: bottom, New York.

2. Google: top, San Francisco.

3. Yahoo!: middle, Sunnyvale.

3. You probably don't live in at least one of these cities. Change each one to your city. Match the program with the steps.

Gadget Program	Change City

a. Right-click, and then click **Options**.

1. Microsoft

2. Google

3. Yahoo!

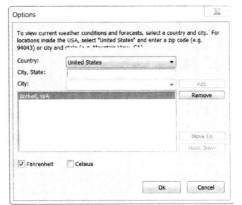

b. Right-click, and then click **Options**.

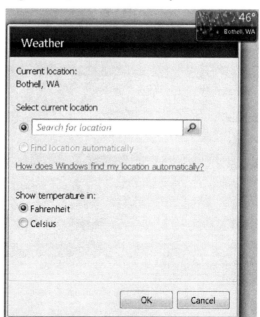

c. Click the city name, and then click **Change Location**.

Answers:

1. Microsoft: b.

2. Google: a.

3. Yahoo!: c.

When you're done, all of your weather gadgets should show the same city, though because they each use different weather services, they might not agree on the temperature.

Keep It Simple: Choose the Gadget Program that is Right for You

1. Set up all three gadget programs.

2. Download the gadgets you like. In some cases, a gadget creator has made the same gadget available on all three services. Or, you may find several gadget offerings for the same thing within a brand of gadgets. For example, if you want a Facebook gadget, Microsoft, Google, and Yahoo! each have many to choose from.

3. Compare how the gadgets work in each version.

4. Play with moving, hiding, docking, and resizing the gadgets.

5. Try the steps provided in each section for changing the location for your weather gadget or widget.

6. When you find the gadget program you like, close the other ones.

CONGRATULATIONS! You've found the gadget program that works best for you and the gadgets you like.

> **TIP:** The gadget programs and individual programs don't take up much space, so don't worry about uninstalling the ones you don't use right away. If you change your mind, it's easy to switch to or show the other gadget programs.

Summary

In this chapter, you have learned about the following three types of gadgets and widgets available for Windows 7:

- Windows Desktop Gadgets
- Google Desktop Gadgets
- Yahoo! Widgets

Though they look similar, each has their own way of doing some things. For each type, you looked at the following:

- Installation of the gadget program, if needed.
- Adding gadgets from your computer or the Web.
- Moving, hiding, docking, and customizing.

Finally, you took a short quiz so that you could test what you've learned and compare how each program presents a Weather gadget.

Chapter 4

Exploring Programs and Features

Programs and Features helps you manage programs already installed; programs and features provided by Windows; and updates installed after you got your computer. Programs and Features replaces **Add/Remove Programs** found in Windows XP and other previous versions of Windows.

> **TIP:** Though this Control Panel has been renamed **Programs and Features**, you can still type **Add/Remove Programs** in the **Start** menu **Search** box and it will get you there.

While you will not be going into Programs and Features every day, there are several great reasons why you should get familiar with how this Control Panel item works.

- **To uninstall or change a program**:
    - Remove programs you don't use.
    - Repair or remove programs that are not working properly.
    - Add optional components such as Office tools that you didn't install when you installed Microsoft Office.
- **To view installed updates**:
    - Check what updates have been installed on your computer to see if you are missing crucial updates.
    - Remove or reinstall updates that might be causing problems.
- **To turn Windows features on or off**:
    - Remove built-in Windows programs like Internet Explorer because you prefer to use other third-party programs instead.

■ Add Windows programs and features that seem to be missing, like Games.

■ Enable specialized services such as networking, remote features, Internet Information Services, or Telnet.

OTHER INSTALLATION-RELATED SECTIONS IN THIS BOOK

If you are looking for information about installing programs on your computer, check out Chapter 5.

Almost all hardware devices attached to your computer require *device drivers* (sometimes just called *drivers*) so that Windows and your device can communicate and work with each other. Device drivers are often installed the same way you install programs from a disk or the Web, but they don't appear as items in your list of installed programs in Programs and Features. You will find out how to install, update, and remove drivers in Chapter 14.

This chapter, Chapter 5, and Chapter 13 provide several options for troubleshooting. When you are having problems with your computer, it's often hard to tell if it's because of Windows, a program, or a device hooked up to your computer. For more comprehensive help with fixing problems, see Chapter 17.

Getting to Programs and Features

You will find **Programs and Features** in the **Control Panel**. There are several ways to get to Programs and Features.

To access Programs and Features through the Start Menu Search:

1. Click the **Start** button, and in the Start menu's search box, type **Programs**.

2. In the list that appears, click **Programs and Features**.

3. To access Programs and Features through the Control Panel, click the `Start` button, and then click **Control Panel**. There are several different views for Control Panel, so choose the step that matches your view.

    ■ If your window displays **View by: Category,** click **Programs**, and then click **Programs and Features.**

    ■ If your window displays **View by: Large icons** or **View by: Small icons,** click **Programs and Features.**

Figure 4–1 displays the Programs and Features window.

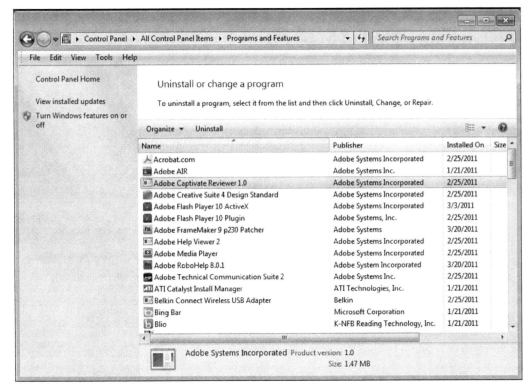

Figure 4–1. *Programs and Features window opens to the "Uninstall or change a program" window.*

Uninstalling or Changing a Program

`Programs and Features` in the Control Panel enables you to uninstall, change, or repair programs or updates already installed on your computer. If, after installing a program or programs, your computer doesn't work right, you can systematically remove your most recently installed programs until you have figured out which program is causing the problem and remove or repair it.

Programs and Features isn't just for fixing problems. Sometimes you may want to remove a program because you don't use it or have never used it. For example, new computers often come with free "lite" or "trial" versions of software that you don't want or need. While each program may not take up much space, they can really clutter up your desktop and Programs menu on the Start menu.

> **NOTE:** Some programs only offer uninstall, while others may offer options to add or remove components and features or repair the program by reinstalling it.

Uninstalling from the Start Menu ➤ All Programs Menu

A few programs also provide an Uninstall option on the All Programs menu. Figure 4–2 displays an uninstall option for Norton Internet Security. This is not very common, so it is better to rely on the Uninstall or change a program page listings.

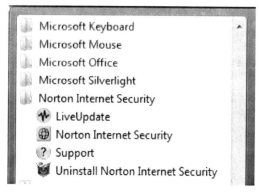

Figure 4–2. *Uninstall option in a program's folder on the Program menu*

Uninstalling from Programs and Features

To remove or repair a program, follow these steps:

1. Select the program you want to remove or repair, then click **Uninstall** or **Change** in the toolbar above the list, as shown in Figure 4–3.

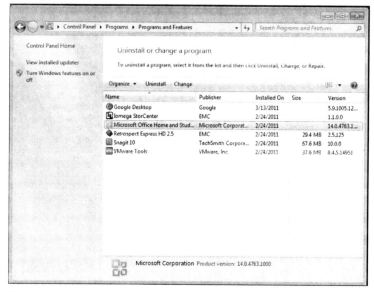

Figure 4–3. *When you select a program in the list, the Uninstall button appears above the list. Some programs offer only Uninstall, and some may also offer Change or Repair.*

When you click Uninstall or Change, the program's *installation* program may start up even though you are *uninstalling, changing, repairing, or modifying*. The installation options for the programs displayed in Figure 4–4 and 4–5 include Add or Remove Features, Modify, and Repair, in addition to Remove (uninstall). Sometimes you don't need to completely uninstall the program to fix a problem. You may want to try reinstalling the program if that option is available. In these two examples, you can reinstall with the Repair option.

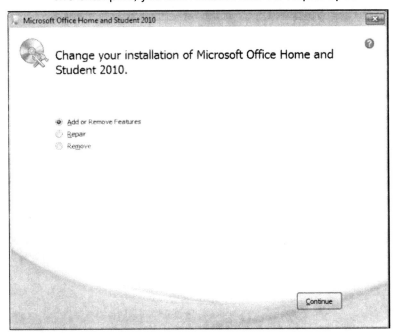

Figure 4–4. *Microsoft Office contains several programs and tools that you can individually add or remove without completely uninstalling the program.*

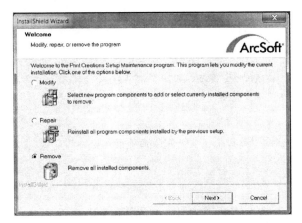

Figure 4–5. *Some programs offer a repair or reinstallation option.*

2. If you are having problems with a program that worked before on another computer or that you think should run on your computer, try the repair or reinstallation option, if available. Not all programs offer a repair option. Other programs may offer only an Uninstall option, as shown in Figure 4–6.

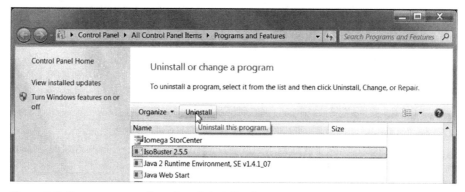

Figure 4–6. *Some programs offer only an Uninstall option.*

3. If the program offers only Uninstall, click the **Uninstall** button. Windows or the installation program may immediately start uninstalling the program, as shown in Figure 4–7, or may ask you to confirm that you really want to uninstall the program. The message and option displayed varies depending on how the software manufacturer designed the program.

Figure 4–7. *The uninstall process may take several minutes, depending on the size and complexity of the program being removed.*

4. When the repair or removal is complete, you may be prompted to restart the computer.

TIP: Even if you aren't asked to, it is a good idea to restart your computer after any installation, repair, or uninstall. If you are changing several programs at once, it may be tempting to wait to restart until you have finished removing or repairing all of them. If you install multiple programs and then have problems after restarting your computer, you may not be able to tell which program change is causing the problem. To be safe, restart your computer whenever you install, remove, or repair a major program, even if it is not required or suggested by the installation program.

Trying Additional Repair Options

If you tried the repair option, used the uninstall/remove option, or reinstalled the program and the program still does not run properly, there are several other things to try.

- **Run the program in compatibility mode**. If a program ran in a previous version of Windows, such as Windows XP or earlier, you may be able to run it in *compatibility mode*. See Chapter 17 for more information.

- **Run the program in XP Mode or in a virtual machine**. These advanced features and products may not be available on your version of Windows 7. **Windows Virtual PC** and **Windows XP Mode** are available for download in the Windows 7 Ultimate, Windows 7 Professional, and Windows 7 Enterprise editions. You can also download VMWare Player for free from www.vmware.com. VMWare Player runs on all versions of Windows 7, Windows Vista, Windows XP, and Windows Server. See Chapter 18 for more information about virtual machines and advanced Windows features for the business environment.

- **Run System Restore**. If you suspect that your issue concerns more than one particular program, or you installed several programs back-to-back, try running System Restore. You can choose a System Restore checkpoint on a day before you started having problems. System Restore does not remove documents or data files, but it will remove any programs and reset any major Windows system changes that occurred after the restore checkpoint date. Then you can reinstall the new programs and updates one at a time. See Chapter 17 for more information.

■ **Run troubleshooters**. Sometimes the program doesn't need to be removed or repaired, but some related settings need to be fixed. For example, a program that connects to the web, such as a chat program, may be blocked by your firewall or other network settings. Running a network or Internet troubleshooter might fix those settings. You can access troubleshooters by clicking the Start button, and in the Start menu's search box, type Troubleshoot. In the list that appears, click Troubleshooting. Also, see Chapter 17.

Viewing Installed Updates

Hopefully when you first set up your Windows 7 computer, you selected the default to automatically download and install Microsoft updates.

> **CAUTION:** If you didn't turn on Microsoft updates, don't wait too long. Microsoft updates are described in Chapter 16.

Typically, Microsoft sends out security updates on the second Tuesday each month, often referred to as Patch Tuesday. Occasionally Microsoft sends out updates in between if there is a serious security issue that needs to be fixed as soon as possible.

If your computer starts acting funny on a Wednesday after Patch Tuesday, it is possible that something did not work right with an update that was just installed on your computer.

While Microsoft makes a good effort to test these patches on as wide a variety Windows configurations as possible, sometimes updates cause problems for a small number of users. In some cases, removing the update, and then going back to the Microsoft Update site and reinstalling the update may fix the problem.

Sometimes an update gets corrupted as it is being installed because the computer was shut down unexpectedly before the installation was complete. This could happen by accident if you had a power outage in the middle of the update, or if you got tired of waiting for installation to complete and went ahead with the shutdown process.

Microsoft Windows Updates are not the only services listed in the updates page. Microsoft Office also lists updates there, as do many Adobe programs. These updates are not tied to Patch Tuesday, so you could still experience problems caused by updates at other times of the month.

Many other third-party programs provide regular product updates but don't show up on the updates list, such as Internet security programs, non-Microsoft browsers, Windows utilities, and Yahoo! Widgets, to name a few. If it is a fairly substantial update, it may show up in the **Uninstall or change a program** list in **Programs and Features**.

Five reasons you might want to uninstall an update:

- You notice problems with your computer immediately after installing an update.

- Your computer was shut down during an update.

- Technical support recommends removing or reinstalling an update.

- You see or hear news reports that a new update is causing problems for many users.

- You just performed a large update, such as a Service Pack or a new version of Internet Explorer.

In an ideal world, you shouldn't have to uninstall updates. But in case you do, it's good to know what is on the **View installed updates** page and how to uninstall an update.

To access the View installed updates page, on the Programs and Features page, click View installed updates. Figure 4–8 displays a list of updates currently installed on my computer. The list contains several pieces of information that can be quite useful in deciding whether to uninstall an update or take other actions.

- **Program**: Is this the program you are having problems with? If several Windows and Office updates were installed on the same date, look first at ones for the program you are having problems with.

- **Help link**: Can link to a web page that explains more about this update (some updates might not have this information).

- **Support link**: Can link to the publisher's support web site (some updates might not have this information).

- **Installed On**: This is when the update was installed on your computer. Is this date prior to when you started having problems?

CAUTION: If you are not sure if an update is causing your problems, it may be safer to perform a System Restore to a date prior to the date when the update was installed or the date when you first started having problems.

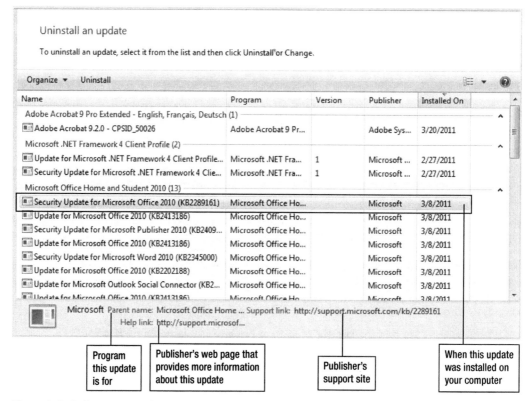

Figure 4–8. *Updates currently installed on this computer, showing additional information about the highlighted update*

Uninstalling an Update

To uninstall an update:

1. Select the update, and then click **Uninstall**.

2. Restart your computer.

> **CAUTION:** While uninstalling an update shouldn't make your computer worse or make it unable to boot, if the update you are removing is quite substantial, you should at least create a System Restore point (described in Chapter 17) and back up your files (described in Chapter 16) before you start the uninstall.

Reinstalling an Update

While you don't want to have the same problems again, in most cases you should try to reinstall the update. Though some updates are optional, many are recommended to keep your computer safe and secure.

To reinstall the update:

1. Restart your computer after uninstalling the update, if you have not done so already.

2. Check your computer to make sure things are operating correctly now. Try to perform the action that was causing problem before and see if the problem has gone away.

3. If the problem is still there, the problem may not have been the update you uninstalled. If you are fairly certain of the date when the problem started happening, perform a System Restore to a date prior to when the problem started.

4. When the problem appears to be gone, create a System Restore checkpoint.

5. In **Control Panel**, open **Windows Update**.

6. Check for updates.

7. Install the critical and recommended updates.

8. When the problem is gone and you have reinstalled updates, create another System Restore checkpoint.

> **NOTE:** Performing a System Restore is not the same as creating a System Restore checkpoint. See Chapter 17 for comprehensive help on using System Restore.

Turning Windows Features On or Off

Windows Features are a little bit different than **Uninstall or change a program** and **Uninstall an update** because it appears in a separate dialog box on top of the **Programs and Features** window. Also, you don't uninstall **Windows Features**; you turn them on or off with checkboxes. Depending on how Windows 7 was installed on your computer, in most cases the features are always installed on your computer and you are just turning their use and visibility on or off. The most common reasons for turning features on or off are the following:

- **Turning off Windows features to use third-party products instead.**
  For example, several Windows programs are on and set as defaults for
  their content types (*Internet Explorer* for web browsing, *Windows
  Media Center* for displaying Music, Videos, and Pictures on large
  screen like a TV, *Windows Media Player* as a music and video player
  and organizer on your computer screen, and *Windows DVD Maker* for
  burning CDs and DVDs). You can turn any of these off to use similar
  third-party products, such as *Mozilla Firefox, Opera, Apple Safari,* or
  Google Chrome as your browser, instead of Internet Explorer. Or you
  could use *Apple iTunes* or *Real Networks RealPlayer* instead of
  Windows Media Player. You do not have to turn the Window feature
  off to use a comparable third-party program; it just hides the Windows
  feature from the Start menu and any place you might normally access
  the program. A related item in the **Control Panel** is **Default
  Programs**. Default Programs specifies the default file types and
  protocols a program can open. For example, you can specify which
  program to use to open music files, picture files, web pages, and
  videos. To learn more about setting the defaults for programs, see
  Chapter 5.

- **Adding Windows programs and features that seem to be missing
  like Games.** Windows has several free built-in games and computer
  manufacturers often add more of their own. It would be very unusual
  for you buy a home computer and not find any games on it. But every
  once in a while, people are assigned a new computer at work and *the
  Games are missing!* Fear not, they are probably there; they've just
  been turned off by the IT department for obvious reasons. In really
  extreme cases, your company might create computer policies that
  completely remove any trace of games from Windows. In that
  environment, the inability to play games on your computer is probably
  the least of your worries.

- **Enabling specialized services such as networking, remote
  features, Internet Information Services, Telnet, etc.** There are a
  number of services that exist for really advanced users. In daily use, if
  the feature was not on when Windows was first installed, you probably
  don't need it. But in case you install a program that requires one of
  these features, and the installation program can't turn the feature on
  by itself, it's handy to know where these are and how to turn them on.

To access Windows Features:

1. In **Programs and Features**, click **Turn Windows** features on or off. Figure 4–9 shows the Windows Features dialog box.

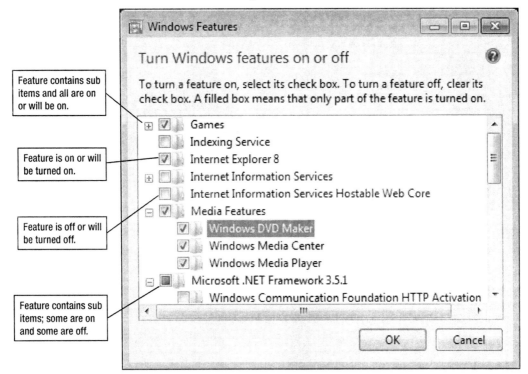

Figure 4–9. *Windows Features dialog box*

2. Turn features on or off as needed.

    ▦ If a plus or minus sign appears next to the feature, that means the feature can be expanded and that there are sub items within that feature that can be selected or cleared. In Figure 4–9, Games, Internet Information Services, Media Features, and Microsoft .NET Framework 3.5.1 all contains sub items.

    ▦ If the checkbox has a checkmark, like Games, Internet Explorer 8, and Media Features, that means that feature and any sub items in it have been selected and will be on when you close this dialog box.

    ▦ If the checkbox is clear, like Indexing Service, Internet Information Services, Internet Information Services Hostable Web Core, and Windows Communication Foundation HTTP Activation, that means that feature and any sub items within it have not been selected and will be off when you close this dialog box.

■ If the checkbox is filled, like Microsoft .NET Framework 3.5.1, then some sub items like Windows Communication Foundation HTTP Activation have not been selected but others have. Only the selected sub items will be on when you close this dialog box.

> **TIP:** If you want to know more about a particular feature, search for the feature in **Help and Support**.

3. When you have completed your changes, click **OK**.

Some changes may require restarting your computer before the changes can take effect. Also, the way that Windows 7 was installed on your computer may require that you insert the original installation disk. If you do not have an installation disk, contact your computer manufacturer, or if this is a work computer, your company's IT department.

Summary

In this chapter you learned how to use Programs and Features to do the following:

■ Uninstall or change a program.

■ View installed updates.

■ Turn Windows features on or off.

With these features you may be able to do the following:

■ Fix programs or updates that are not working properly by uninstalling or repairing them.

■ Check to see what updates have been installed on your computer.

■ Turn features on or off.

Next Steps

You may find the following related chapters useful:

■ Chapter 5 for help with installing programs from disks or the web, and selecting the default programs to use for specific file types and protocols.

■ Chapter 13 for installing and updating device drivers.

■ Chapter 16 for more troubleshooting methods besides those provided in this chapter, including running Program Compatibility to make older programs run in Windows 7.

■ Chapter 18 for ways to use virtual machines such as Windows Virtual PC, Windows XP Mode, or VMWare Player to run programs that are not compatible with Windows 7.

Installing Programs

In Chapter 4, you learned how to manage and remove programs already installed or provided by Windows. Here you'll tackle the age-old questions of

■ Where do programs come from?

■ How do I take care of them?

■ What should I do if they misbehave?

Fortunately, these babies usually *do* come with a manual, or something like it. If not, that's what we're here for. But like children, programs sometimes misbehave or don't get along with their siblings, and it's up to you to bring them under control. This chapter will cover the following topics:

How to install programs from:

■ The Web, a disk, another computer on your network, or a program already on your computer

■ An "Anytime Upgrade"

How to install safely

■ Understanding licensing

■ Moving programs from one PC to another

■ Protecting your computer before, during, and after installation

■ Keeping track of installation programs after installation

Fixing problem programs that:

■ Do not install

■ Do not run

■ Cause problems with other programs

Installation Examples

Most programs use fairly similar installation wizards that walk you through screens where you accept license terms, select installation options, and specify the folder where the program should be installed. This chapter will include examples of installing a game from a disk, and installing Openoffice.org (an office suite of programs) from a web download.

There are many other examples of installation throughout the book.

- See Chapter 3 to learn how to download and install **Google Gadgets** and **Yahoo! Widgets**.

- See Chapter 7 to learn how to download and install **Windows Live Essentials**.

- See Chapter 10 to learn how to download and install other browser programs such as **Firefox**, **Google Chrome**, and **Opera**.

- See Chapter 14 to learn how to download and install **Kindle** and **Nook** programs for reading eBooks on your PC.

- See Chapter 16 to learn how to download and install **iTunes** and **Zune**.

- See Chapter 23 to learn how to download and install antivirus and antispyware programs.

- See Chapter 28 to learn how to download and install virtual machine players from **Microsoft** and **VMWare**.

> **TIP:** Some of what you learn in this chapter can also be applied to installing *device drivers*, the files that help your computer know how to work with hardware and devices. However, finding and installing drivers can be trickier than installing programs, so we have provided additional information about drivers in Chapter 28.

Installing Programs as Easy as 1-2-3

You have probably installed a few programs already. Or you have used Windows for years and have installed many programs. Windows 7 should not be that much different than previous versions of Windows, right? Computers today are more powerful, programs are more sophisticated, and users more experienced. Installation programs seem to work better and smoother. Unfortunately, the more programs we use, the more problems arise from programs not working together well.

Installing programs doesn't need to be scary or dangerous. With a few precautions before, during, and after installation, you can enjoy your new programs without putting your computer in danger.

Think of installation as three tasks, as shown in Figure 5–1.

1. Preparing for Installation.

2. Installing the program.

3. Completing installation with restarts and testing.

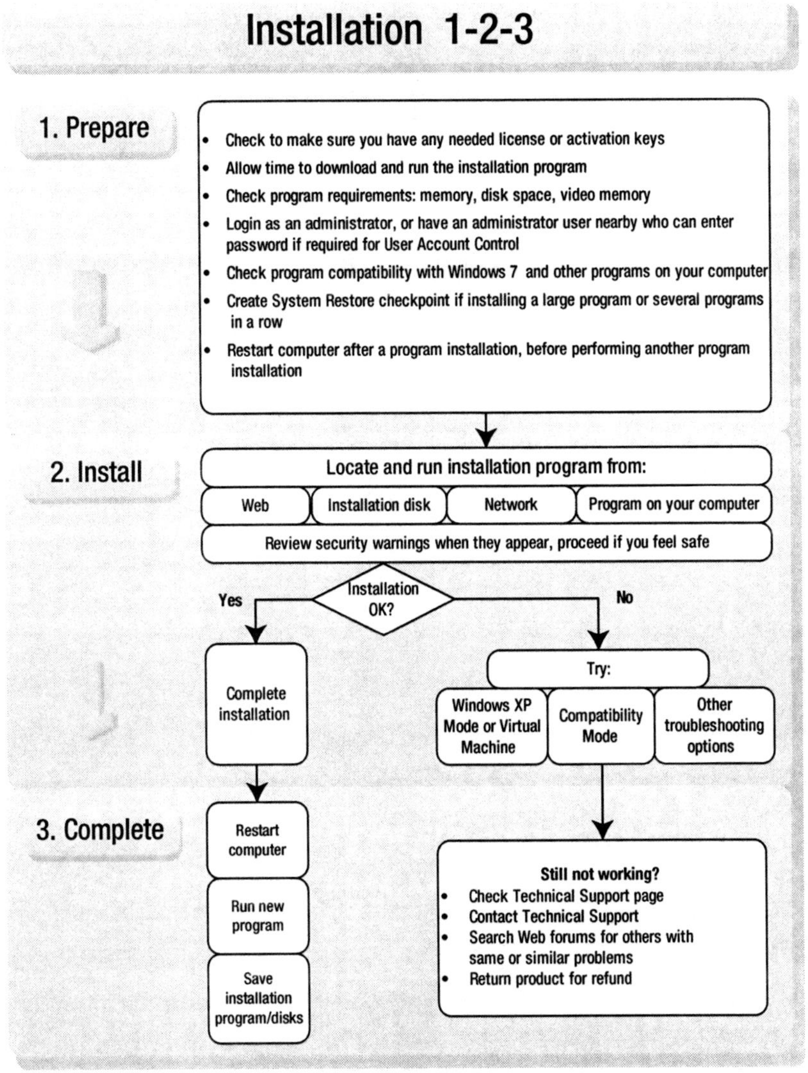

Installation 1-2-3

1. Prepare

- Check to make sure you have any needed license or activation keys
- Allow time to download and run the installation program
- Check program requirements: memory, disk space, video memory
- Login as an administrator, or have an administrator user nearby who can enter password if required for User Account Control
- Check program compatibility with Windows 7 and other programs on your computer
- Create System Restore checkpoint if installing a large program or several programs in a row
- Restart computer after a program installation, before performing another program installation

2. Install

Locate and run installation program from:

| Web | Installation disk | Network | Program on your computer |

Review security warnings when they appear, proceed if you feel safe

Installation OK?

Yes → Complete installation

No → Try:

| Windows XP Mode or Virtual Machine | Compatibility Mode | Other troubleshooting options |

3. Complete

Restart computer

Run new program

Save installation program/disks

Still not working?
- Check Technical Support page
- Contact Technical Support
- Search Web forums for others with same or similar problems
- Return product for refund

Figure 5–1. *Installation is as simple as 1-2-3*

Preparing for Installation

As the cliché goes, this is not rocket science. But planning ahead before you install can save you time, pain, and money later. With so many programs available and large hard drives so common, it is easy to lose control and install everything you can get your hands on. Some people seem to collect programs as a hobby. But why buy more than you want or need?

Keeping it simple is good for you as well as your computer. Installing too many programs that do the same thing can make it harder for you to focus on one program and learn it well. It also can lead to conflicts on your computer as similar programs compete to be your favorite. Windows includes settings to designate what program you want to use as the *default program* for a particular file type or function. Sometimes a newly installed program takes over as the default program. In the "Selecting Your Default Programs" section at the end of this chapter we will show you how to fix it when a rogue program takes over.

Free Screensavers, Desktop Backgrounds, Smileys, and Emoticons

Another cliché applies: there's no such thing as a free lunch. There are many free programs from reputable companies and organizations that are safe to use and download, and several examples are provided in this book. But "free" programs are often a hiding place for viruses, spyware, Trojan horses, and other malicious code. Sometimes free downloads contain *tracking cookies* that record your web activity (which web sites you have visited) or a *keylogger* (a program that records your keystrokes and can use that information to steal your passwords as you log on to web sites or accounts).

Before you download or install that free program, do the following:

- Research the product on the web and see if anybody has reported any issues with it.

- Pay attention to security warnings that open up during download or installation warning that the publisher of the program can't be identified, the certificate is invalid or out of date, or recommending that you don't install it.

- Read the license terms or user agreement very carefully. Most of us don't read these because we usually trust the software publisher. But by accepting that agreement, you may be approving the installation of tracking software that can monitor you web usage.

- Make sure you Internet protection software is enabled to scan downloaded installation files to verify that they are safe.

CAUTION: Make sure that each user on your computer has the right level of user privileges. If you are worried that another family member might install harmful programs, set their login account to Standard, and only assign Administrator accounts to those users you trust to make careful decisions about downloading programs. See Chapter 20, 23, and 28 for more information.

Program Compatibility

It helps to understand how a program you are installing fits in with existing programs so that you don't get surprised with messages during installation. During installation, the new program may request that you uninstall an existing program before installing the new one or make the new program the default program for specific file type or category.

If you have any concerns about whether a program works on Windows 7, a great place to start is to search for the **Windows 7 Compatibility** web site, currently located at www.microsoft.com/windows/compatibility. You can search for the product by product name or category to see if your program is compatible with Windows 7, as shown in Figure 5–2. This web site is also handy for checking to see if your hardware or devices are compatible.

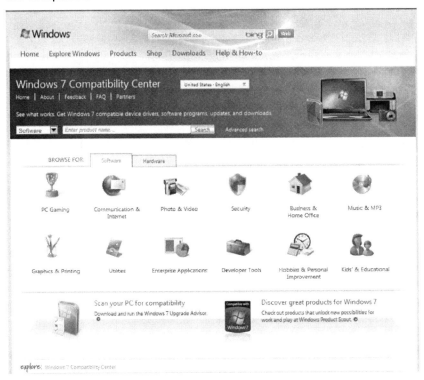

Figure 5–2. *The Compatibility Center is a great place to check whether a program will work with Windows 7.*

NOTE: If your program is not listed on the Windows 7 Compatibility web site, check the software publisher's support site to see if there is an updated version or patch to make it run in Windows 7. You might also be able to run the program in Compatibility Mode.

There are some cases where you should only use only one program because similar programs may conflict if several are installed on your computer. A really common example of conflicting programs is anti-virus software. You only need one. You should only use one at a time. If you want to use a different anti-virus program, uninstall your current anti-virus program before installing the new one. Since your computer is vulnerable to attack when there is no anti-virus program running, be sure to install the new program immediately after installing the old one, or disconnect from the Internet until you have installed the new program. You may need to restart your computer in between uninstalling the old program and installing the new program. Similarly, you only need one firewall program. Windows 7 has a built-in firewall, but most Internet protection suites install their own firewall alongside of their anti-virus program.

Some programs can coexist on the same computer but want to be your default program. For example, Windows Media Player, Windows Media Center, iTunes, and Zune can all play audio files. When you install or use one of these programs for the first time, you are usually prompted to let that player be the default player for a list of audio file types. If you install iTunes, you can make it your default player for .mp3 files. That means when you open an .mp3 file, Windows will use iTunes to play it. You can still use Windows Media Player to play it if you open the file from within Windows Media Player. At the end of this chapter, we will show you how to change or set your preferences in the "Selecting Your Default Programs" section. Figure 5–3 shows a typical dialog box where a program asks if you want to make it the default program for a particular type of file. In this case, Windows Live Photo Gallery is requesting to be the default program to open several picture file types.

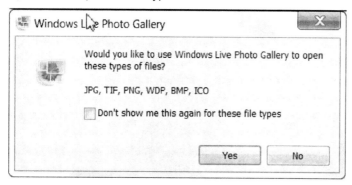

Figure 5–3. You may have several programs on your computer that can open the same file types.

This type of request often pops up when you install a program or use it for the first time. Sometimes two programs are designed to work with the same file types but with different purposes. For example, most digital pictures use the .jpg file format. You may want to use one program to touch up and edit your pictures, such as Windows Live Photo Gallery or Adobe Photoshop Elements, and another to browse your pictures, such as Windows Media Center, Windows Photo Viewer, or the photo viewer built into Microsoft Office 2010. At other times you may want to edit a .jpg file with Paint. Fortunately, you have another option for choosing another program to view or open a file. If for example, you are viewing a picture in the Pictures Library, and you don't want to open it with the default program (for example, Windows Live Photo Gallery), you can right-click the file and select another program to open it with, as shown in Figure 5–4.

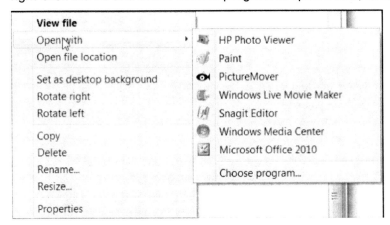

Figure 5–4. *Some types of files can be opened, edited, or viewed by more than one program.*

Licensing

Almost any program you install, even if it's free, will have a license agreement that you must accept before you can install it. Usually software is licensed for use on one computer. Many companies enforce the license with product activation keys and require that you log on to the software provider's web site and activate the copy after installation. Some software programs offer multi-pack licenses so that the software can be installed on multiple computers. The following list describes some common types of licensing for consumer and small business software:

- Single license, which allows installation and use on one computer.

- Single use license, for use on one desktop computer and on one portable (laptop) used by the same person.

- Multiple license packs, suitable for homes that have several members using separate computers on a home network. These multi-packs are cheaper than buying the same number of licenses individually. For example, some Internet protection suites offer three-packs that allow you to install the software on three different computers using the same product key. Microsoft offers Microsoft Office Home and Student 2010 for use on up to three computers for one low price compared to buying separate licenses for each computer when you install the Standard or Professional editions of Microsoft Office 2010. Some products offer a multi-pack that covers all computers in the household for one price, whether it is two or ten.

Large corporations may have additional types of licensing options including:

- Site licensing, where the company pays a flat fee that allows the software to be installed on as many computers in the company as they want.

- Volume licensing, where the company gets a considerable discount for buying large quantities of licenses. They still have to pay a license fee for each installed copy, but the cost per license is much lower.

- Home use license, where software providers have arrangements with large corporations to allow employees to buy a copy of their work software for installation on their home computer. The cost of the home use software disk is usually very small compared to if the employee purchased the software on their own.

> **CAUTION:** Hackers can often find ways to get around the licensing and product activation keys and may offer pirated versions for free or very cheap compared to the legal product. Do not buy, copy, or install pirated software, not only because it is illegal but because the software may carry viruses or other destructive code. Another reason: if you have problems with the software, the real software provider will not help you with it.

Providing Product or Activation Keys

Product or activation keys are essential to many software publishers so that they can enforce their licensing agreements. Typically the product keys are used in this way:

1. When you purchase software, the publisher provides a product key that is good for one or more computers, depending on the license agreement.

2. When you start installation, the installation program will ask for the product key. It will validate that the product key matches an algorithm set for that product version. If it doesn't match, you will be asked to reenter a valid product key. You won't be able to proceed with installation until you have entered a valid key.

3. At the end of installation or the first time you use the program, you will be asked to activate your product. Usually you do this over your Internet connection. Your computer will send the product key you entered during installation to the publisher's servers, where your product key is checked against product keys that are already activated and assigned.

4. In a few moments, you will get a confirmation message that your
    product has been successfully activated.

    If another computer has already been activated with that product key, you will get
    an error message that the product can't be activated. You might also get an
    activation error if you had to reinstall all of you programs on your computer after
    replacing or upgrading your hard drive. After a set number of days, the product
    will stop working. If you feel that the activation failure was in error, usually there is
    a support number you can call to activate over the phone.

Though you should only need to install the software once, make sure to keep your
original installation disks and product keys together and stored safely in case of disaster
recovery of your computer.

> **TIP:** Write the product key on your installation disk (on the label side) with a permanent felt
> marker and also write it on an index card. Sometimes the product key is on a sticker on a retail
> box that could get accidently thrown away.

Moving Programs from One PC to Another

Even if your license is valid for only one computer, you can change the computer on
which it is valid. Say your old computer dies, and you can no longer use it. Or you
bought a new computer and want to use the programs you previously installed on your
old computer. Some software licenses permit you to move your licensed copy to a new
computer, as long as you uninstall or deactivate it on your old computer. If the software
uses product activation over the Web, you will quite likely get an error that the product
can't be activated because the license has already been used. Contact the software
publisher's product support and ask them to help you activate the product. You will
probably have the most success if you can talk to somebody by phone, but many
companies offer live chat sessions. Usually when you explain that you are removing it
from an old computer and want to use it on a new computer, they can give you a new
activation code by phone, in chat, or by e-mail.

> **TIP:** Windows Easy Transfer, a feature of Windows 7, helps you move files and settings from
> your old computer to your new computer. It doesn't move your programs, however. You can
> purchase a third-party program called **PCmover,** available from **Laplink.com**, to move your files,
> settings, and programs to your new computer. See Chapter 12 to learn how to make your
> migration to a new computer easy and painless.

Program Requirements

Before purchasing or installing a program, review the software and hardware requirements and recommendations. You can usually find this on the side of the retail box if you are buying it in a store. If you are buying or downloading from the web, check the product description or go to the manufacturer's web site. Typically the product requirements list includes:

- **Compatibility with Windows versions**: Make sure the product says it works on Windows 7!

- **Memory required**: Though the program runs on Windows 7, it may require more memory than Windows. With a desktop computer, you can usually install or upgrade memory yourself; some laptops can be upgraded without too much technical knowledge. Most netbooks are hard to upgrade yourself, if at all, and to be safe would require a skilled technician.

- **Video memory required**: Some games and video programs require a lot of video memory. On a desktop computer, you can upgrade your computer with a new video card. On a laptop or netbook, the video memory comes from the main computer board and you can't upgrade it.

- **Hard disk space required**: Some programs may temporarily require additional hard drive space to perform the installation on top of the hard disk space that will be used by the program after it is installed. With the large hard drives that are standard on most new computers today, this shouldn't be an issue. Nevertheless, at some point down the road your hard disk space may get filled up and you could run out of room to install more programs.

- **Processor required**: If your computer can run Windows 7, usually the processor should be sufficient for any program running on Windows 7. Netbooks use a less powerful processor that may not be up to the demands of some programs.

> **TIP:** Read user reviews. Another way to evaluate what the program needs or how it runs is to read user reviews on sites like Amazon.com. While user reviews often emphasize the negatives more than the positive, sometimes they give you a better picture of how well the software works in the real world.

Administrator Privileges (UAC)

Make sure you are logged in as an Administrator when you install a program. If you are not, during installation you will be prompted to enter the user name and account of a user with Administrator privileges. While this may seem like a nuisance, it also protects you from unauthorized people or programs trying to install programs that you may not want.

> **NOTE:** Many experts suggest that for regular daily use, log in with a Standard user account and only use an Administrator account when you need to perform more serious tasks like program installation or change Windows system settings.

Set Aside Time for Installation and Restarts

Allow time for installation. Some program installations can take quite some time, especially if you need to download the installation files, uninstall an old version, or download updates from the Web. You don't always need to be at your computer watching the installation all the way through.

Before you start installation, do the following:

- Make sure you can leave your computer on for as long as the installation program needs to complete the installation.

- If you are using a laptop, make sure you have plenty of time left on your battery or that you are plugged into AC power.

- Check your Power Options in Control Panel to make sure that your computer is not going to go into a sleep mode or shutdown in the middle of installation.

System Restore Points

Some installation programs automatically create a System Restore point before starting an install. A System Restore point is a snapshot of the state of your system; this will allow you to turn back your computer's system to the state it was in before the installation. If you are installing several programs or installing a large program, you may want to manually create a System Restore point to be on the safe side. If you have problems with the program after installing, sometimes uninstall does not fix everything. If you have a good System Restore point prior to the installation, you may be more successful fixing your computer with System Restore than with uninstall.

You can learn more about creating and using System Restore points in Chapter 28.

Performing Installation

There are several ways to install programs on your computer. This section will look at installing from

- Web downloads
- Installation disks
- A network
- A program pre-installed on your computer

Installing from Web Downloads

Whether you are buying software or it's free from the software provider, you can download and install just about any software from the Web. For some programs, the Web is the only way to get the software if it is not already pre-installed on your computer.

You can download free office suites, e-mail, browsing, instant messaging, virtual machine, and other programs from well-known and recognizable companies. Many offer free trial versions that work for 30 days so that you can try before you buy, or you can just go ahead and buy the software for download. Most software installation programs are quite similar to each other, so to show you some of the steps you might typically encounter, we will walk you through installing a free program called **OpenOffice.org**.

> **NOTE:** This is not an endorsement of OpenOffice.org. It just provides a good example of a large program installation with several installation options. If you want to practice by installing this program, it is easily uninstalled.

OpenOffice.org is a free productivity suite program, similar to Microsoft Office. It includes **Writer**, a word processing program similar to Microsoft Word; **Calc**, a spreadsheet program similar to Microsoft Excel; **Impress**, a presentation program similar to Microsoft PowerPoint; **Draw**, a drawing program; and **Base**, a database program similar to Microsoft Access. OpenOffice.org can work with files created by Microsoft Office, so many companies and organizations are using it as an inexpensive alternative to Microsoft Office.

INSTALL JUST THE PROGRAMS YOU THINK YOU WILL NEED

OpenOffice.org, like many suites and programs with many components, gives you the option to install everything (Typical Installation) or to select which features or components to install (Custom Installation). It may seem easier to just accept the default Typical Installation and install everything. But why install programs you will never use? Unneeded programs take up *some* disk space, clutter up your All Programs menu with extra entries, and compete for being the default program for their respective file types. For example, though I have been using and installing the complete Microsoft Office suites for years, I have never used or needed one of the included programs, Microsoft Access. So if I am installing OpenOffice.org, I really wouldn't need to install their equivalent program, Base.

If you elect not to install something in a custom installation, you can usually add the feature later in **Control Panel ➤ Uninstall or change a program.** OpenOffice.org provides a **Change** option in **Uninstall or change a program**; Microsoft Office provides an **Add or Remove Features** option. See Chapter 4 to learn how to delete, change, or delete the programs and features that are already installed on your computer.

To install the Openoffice.org productivity suite:

1. Go to the download page. In Internet Explorer or your preferred web browser, go to www.openoffice.org. The OpenOffice.org home page appears as shown in Figure 5–5.

Figure 5–5. *The OpenOffice.org web site*

2. Click the download links or buttons. Sometimes you have to click several times before the download actually starts. In this example, you must click three times.

   ▓ Click the **Download** tab.

   ▓ Click **Download OpenOffice.org**.

   ▓ Click **Download now!**

3. Security settings may block the download, as shown in Figure 5–6. It's easy to miss this notification and then you wonder why your download doesn't start. Check to see if it is there.

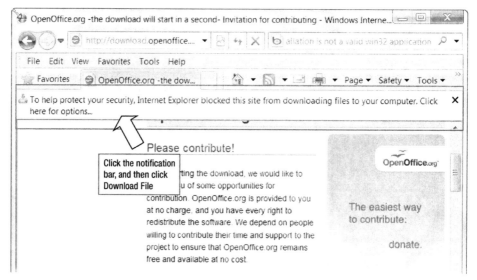

Figure 5–6. *Sometimes the download won't start until you click this little notification, and then click Download File.*

4. Click the notification bar. In the little menu that pops up, click **Download File**. Expect a File Download – Security Warning dialog box to appear, similar to Figure 5–7; that's normal.

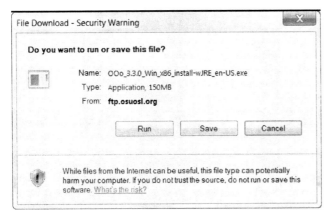

Figure 5–7. *The File Download – Security Warning dialog box is standard.*

5.   Choose whether to Run or Save the file.

    ■   Choose **Run** if you don't need to keep a copy of the installation files and want to complete the installation in this session. It will require a longer download time from the Web because all of the files are downloaded uncompressed. Figure 5–8 is an example of selecting **Run**. It may take a few minutes to download to a temporary folder on your computer.

    ■   Choose **Save** if you want to download the installation files to a local folder on your computer. This enables you to run the installation files now or later from the local file. It will take less download time from the Web because the files are downloaded as a compressed (zipped) file. Once the compressed file is downloaded to your computer, you can open it; Windows should automatically unpack the compressed file and then start the actual installation program. If you save the file, you can also reuse the installation files to install it on another computer on your network without having to download all of the installation files again.

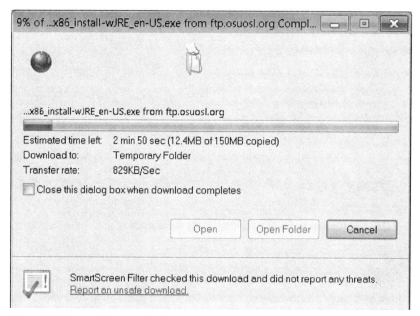

Figure 5–8. *It may take several minutes to download the files to a temporary installation folder on your computer.*

6. When the download completes, a User Account Control dialog box appears, asking for permission to run this program, as shown in Figure 5–9. Click **Yes**.

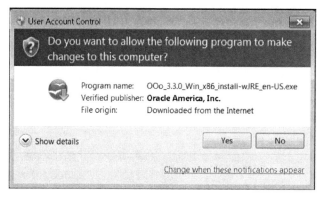

Figure 5–9. *Accessories folder on the Start menu*

7. The Installation wizard begins, as shown in Figure 5–10. Often installation files are in a compressed or "packed" state so that they can download quicker. Once they are on your computer they must be unpacked before installation can begin. Click **Next** to continue.

Figure 5–10. *The download is complete, but the installation files need to be unpacked*

TIP: Sometimes the installation windows disappear behind other windows, especially if you are doing work in other programs while you are waiting. If your installation window "disappears," minimize your other program windows one at a time, or press ALT+TAB to cycle through all of your open programs and windows.

8. When you install a program, it usually asks you where you want to install the program, as shown in Figure 5–11. Note that this installation page also lets you know how much space it will need to install the program. Unless you have a special folder or drive where you prefer to install programs, just accept the default location it suggests. Click **Unpack**.

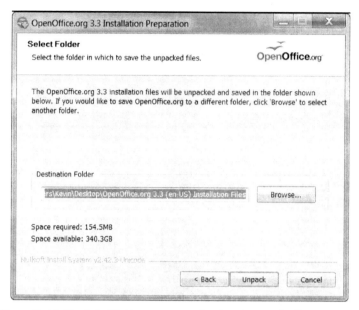

Figure 5–11. *The Select Folder page suggests where to save the files to*

9. Several small windows will pop up and disappear as components required for installation are installed. The actual Installation Wizard page will appear, as shown in Figure 5–12. Click **Next.**

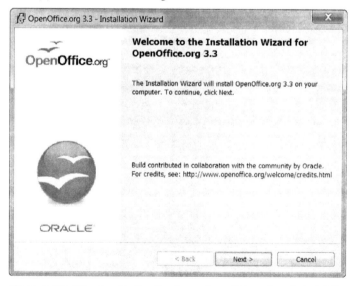

Figure 5–12. *After downloading the files and specifying where to install the program, the actual installation begins.*

10. The Customer Information page is displayed, as shown in Figure 5–13. The program is not looking for personal or private information; the User Name and Organization are used in the file properties for documents you create with OpenOffice.org. Fill in your details here.

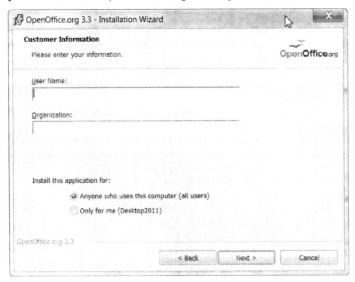

Figure 5–13. *Customer Information is just there to fill in some of the document properties when you create an OpenOffice.org file.*

11. Click **Next**. The next installation wizard page, as shown in Figure 5–14, allows you to choose whether you want **Typical** or **Custom**.

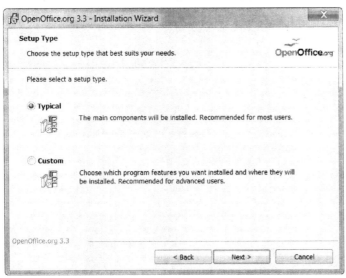

Figure 5–14. *Typical is the default selection.*

12. To install everything, leave **Typical** selected, and then go to step 14. To install some features but not others, select **Custom**. Whichever you choose, click Next.

13. If you selected **Custom**, the Custom Setup page is displayed, as shown in Figure 5–15. In this example, we will install **Writer**, **Calc**, **Draw**, and **Impress**, and will not install **Base** or **Math**.

   a. All six features are still selected and will be installed. On the disk icon next to OpenOffice.org Base, click the down arrow.

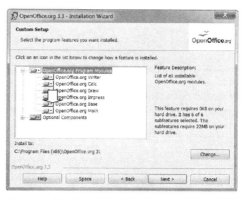

Figure 5–15. *If you select Custom, you can specify which programs and features to install.*

   b. On the submenu that appears, select **This feature will not be available**, as shown in Figure 5–16.

   c. On the disk icon next to **OpenOffice.org Math**, click the down arrow.

   d. Select **This feature will not be available**.

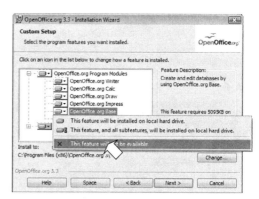

Figure 5–16. *"This feature will not be available" means that Base will not be installed.*

e. Click the words (but not the icon) **OpenOffice.org Program Modules** at the top of the icon list.

In Figure 5–17, note that a red X appears next to Base and Math, meaning they will not be installed. The Feature Description also indicates only four of six features will be installed.

f. Click **Next**. Go to step 14.

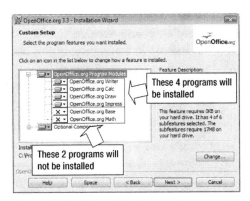

Figure 5–17. *Writer, Calc, Draw, and Impress will be installed; Base and Math will not.*

14. After you have specified the Typical or Custom Setup, you may be prompted to make OpenOffice.org the default program for several types of documents, as shown in Figure 5–18. This wizard page will appear if another program for these types of documents is already installed on your computer, such as Microsoft Office programs. OpenOffice.org installation "plays nicely" because it does not automatically select itself as the default. Make your choices here.

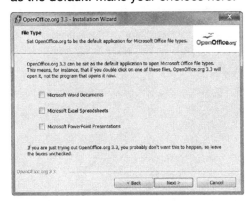

Figure 5–18. *If OpenOffice.org detects another program that handles the same file types, the installation program will prompt you to make OpenOffice.org the default program.*

15. There is one more option to set: whether you want a start link/icon on the desktop, as shown in Figure 5–19. This option to install an icon on the desktop is a common one; some programs may also offer an option to install an icon on the taskbar or pin to the Start menu. If you never use the desktop icons, clear this option. You can easily add an icon to the Start menu or taskbar later by yourself.

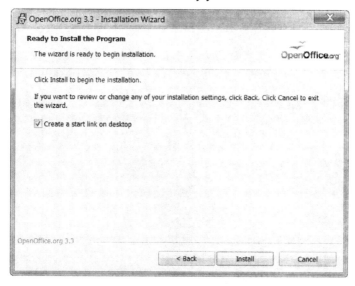

Figure 5–19. *Installation offers the option to add a link to your desktop.*

16. Click **Install**. Installation takes a few minutes. When installation is complete, a final wizard page is displayed, as shown in Figure 5–20.

Figure 5–20. *Click* **Finish***.*

Some installation programs automatically start the new program but in this example, OpenOffice.org does not. When you check your Start menu, the new program should be listed, similar to the example shown in Figure 5–21. A shortcut should also appear on your desktop if you selected that option during installation.

Figure 5–21. *OpenOffice.org on the Start menu*

After installation, the first time you start any OpenOffice.org program you will be prompted to register and sign up for automatic updates. Registration is optional, but you still must click through the pages as shown in Figure 5–22 before you can get to your programs. After you complete registration, you will either see a page asking which program you want to run, or the program you previously selected will be opened, as shown in Figure 5–23.

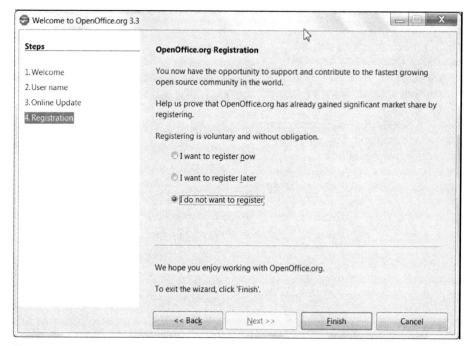

Figure 5–22. *Registration and update options displayed the first time you start an OpenOffice.org program*

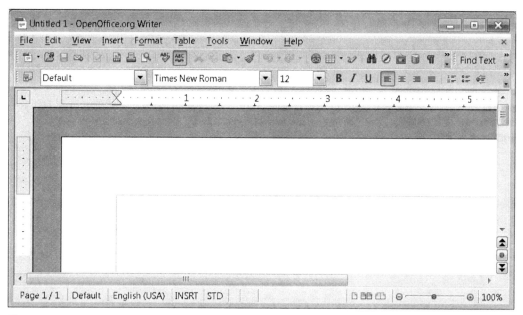

Figure 5–23. *A new OpenOffice.org Writer document*

See the "Complete Installation" section later in this chapter for additional tasks that you should perform after almost any installation.

Installing from Disks

When you install from a disk, you don't have so many warnings and prompts, because you don't need to specify a location for installation files (they're already on the installation disk) and it is assumed that if you inserted the installation disk into the computer it must be safer than files downloaded from the Internet.

To install from a disk:

1. Insert the CD or DVD into the drive on your computer.

2. An installation wizard page should appear. Sometimes the installation program does not automatically start. If after several moments nothing happens, you can start the setup program manually.

   a. Sometimes when you insert an installation disk, your computer may not automatically recognize the setup or installation files on the disk. If so, open **Computer**.

   b. Open the drive that contains the installation disk. Usually, the CD/DVD drive is drive D: or E:.

   c. Double-click **Setup** or **Setup.exe**.

3. Follow the instructions in the installation wizard. Installation options will vary with each program, but you may be prompted to perform, enter, or specify the following:

   - Shutdown all other or specific programs.

   - Product activation key.

   - Program installation folder (the folder where the program will be permanently installed).

   - Automatic update options.

   - Make the program the default program for certain file types.

   - Restart the computer if required.

See the "Complete Installation" section later in this chapter for additional tasks that you should perform after almost any installation.

Installing from a Network

If you have several computers at home, you may want to install a program on all of your computers. For example, you want to install Firefox because you prefer it to Internet Explorer for browsing the web. If your computers are on a home network or in a homegroup, it may be easier to download the installation file to a single location that is shared or available to all of your computers.

> **NOTE:** If you don't have any kind of home network or network attached hard drives, see Chapter 15 to learn the basics of network attached storage (NAS), hard drives attached to a network, and sharing files over the network.

To install from a network:

1. Download the installation file from the Web.

2. When prompted to Run or Save, click **Save**.

3. In the destination dialog box, select a location on your home network.

   ▦ **A network attached storage (NAS) device**: These are becoming more popular in homes and small office networks because they are simpler to use and set up than a home server, but can provide lots of storage space for backups, media files, and any other files you want to always be accessible to computers on your network. With a NAS device, the storage drive is always running on your network because it is not attached to a particular computer.

   ▦ **An external hard drive attached to your router**: Many newer routers allow you to connect a USB printer or hard drive directly to your router so that it is available to all computers on your network.

   ▦ **A shared folder on one of your computers on your network**: You will only have access to that shared folder when that computer is turned on. This may not be an issue if you frequently have that computer on most of the time you are using any computer in your house. Figure 5–24 shows a shared folder on another computer in my home network.

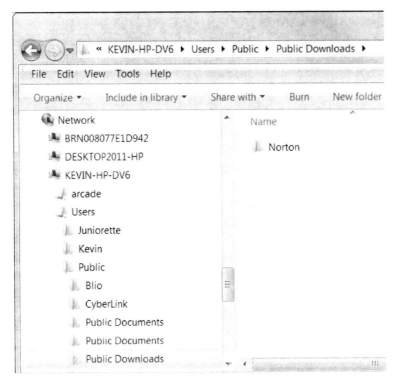

Figure 5–24. *Programs can be installed from a shared folder on another computer on your network.*

> **NOTE:** My Internet provider offers the Norton Security Suite free to its customers. I wanted to install this on all of my computers, so I downloaded the installation files to a shared folder on one of the computers on my network. Since I frequently have several of my computers on at the same time, the shared folders are easy for me to get to whenever I need them.

4. When the download is complete, you can run the installation program on any computer that has access to that network location.

Installing from a Program or Shortcut on Your Computer

Don't be surprised if some of the programs listed on your Start ➤ All Programs menu are not really installed programs. When you click the program, you may be taken to a web page where you can download the program or subscribe to a service. Or, when you click the program, it may display an installation program, not the program itself.

Computer manufacturers are paid to put these links on your desktop or All Programs menu; these links are a form of advertising. Some links, like the Skype shortcut that was on my desktop when I bought a new computer, launch an installation program shown in Figure 5–25.

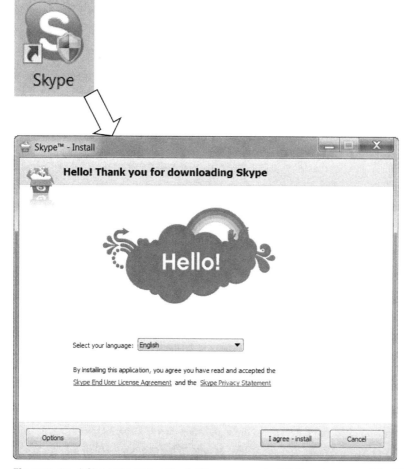

Figure 5–25. *A Skype shortcut on the desktop opens an installation program, not the Skype program itself.*

Performing an Anytime Upgrade or Converting from Trial to Full Version

Microsoft and other software providers have several ways to allow you to use their products for a limited time or with limited features in the hopes that you will convert to a full or better version. In most cases, the installation of the full version is extremely easy because it is already there on your computer. You just need to turn it on by purchasing an activation key or product key.

For example, the Windows 7 computer you are using has the Windows Anytime Upgrade feature. If you are using Windows 7 Home Premium, you can buy a Windows Anytime Upgrade to upgrade to Windows 7 Professional or Windows 7 Ultimate. It is quick and convenient because you don't have to reinstall Windows or go through a long upgrade process.

Microsoft also offers several ways you can buy and activate full versions of Microsoft Office without going through a lengthy installation process. Your computer may come pre-loaded with a version of Office that can be upgraded to full version by purchasing and entering a product activation key.

- Some computers are pre-loaded by the manufacturer with a limited version of Office 2010, called Office Starter 2010. This version contains Microsoft Word Starter 2010 and Microsoft Excel Starter 2010 only, which are stripped down versions of Microsoft Word and Excel that contain some advertising.

- Microsoft also offers trial versions of Microsoft Office 2010 that may be pre-installed on your computer by the manufacturer or can be downloaded from Microsoft. Usually the trial period is 60 days from the date you install it.

Other software providers offer similar programs, such as the following:

- A free "lite" version of the software that you can use indefinitely. The program manufacturer's hope is that you will purchase an upgrade to their full featured version.

- A trial version that will work for 30 to 90 days. Most new computers come with a brand of anti-virus software pre-installed that is good for 90 days. To keep your anti-virus software up to date after the 90 days, you have to purchase a subscription for one year or more.

Most of the time, when you purchase an upgrade to the full version, all you have to do is enter the activation key and possibly restart the program or your computer. In some cases, the trial or lite version is so different from the full version that you must uninstall the old version before installing the new version.

Troubleshooting Programs that Won't Install

Sometimes Windows 7 stops program installation before it even starts. If this happens, there are several things you can try:

- If the program you are trying to install is a fairly recent release, check the software publisher's support web site to see if there are some known issues and suggested solutions. If not, try contacting technical support by phone, e-mail, or online chat.

- Sometimes programs will not install from an installation file you saved to your computer. Downloaded installation files are usually compressed or "zipped" files that need to be uncompressed before they can run. In some cases, Windows or your zip program can't read the zipped file and can't decompress them. Try downloading again, and when prompted to Run or Save, choose **Run**.

- If Windows displays the Program Compatibility wizard, try that first. This often works for programs that were designed for Windows XP and some earlier versions, but it may not work for really old programs that were designed for Windows 95 or Windows 98.

- If the program is not compatible with Windows 7, sometimes you can get a new version from the software publisher.

- If there is no update available, you may want to try running it in Windows XP Mode or Microsoft Virtual PC, which are available as a free download if you have Windows 7 Professional or Windows 7 Ultimate.

- If you do not have Windows 7 Professional or Ultimate, you can download the free VMware Player from www.vmware.com and install an older version of Windows to run in a virtual machine.

- If you are installing a program from your job, check with your IT/help desk to see if the program has been tested to work with Windows 7. Many corporations have programs custom-designed to run on Windows XP that were never updated for Windows Vista or Windows 7.

See Chapter 28 to learn how to use and install Windows XP Mode, Virtual PC, and VMware Player. You will also find more information on installation troubleshooting.

Completing Installation

This is the moment you have been waiting for. You installed the program. Does it work? Before you install any more programs, test the new program to make sure it works.

Sometimes at the end of installation, the new program automatically starts. Many programs, if they don't make major changes to Windows itself, don't require a restart. It is a good idea to restart anyways.

To test the new program:

1. At the end of installation, restart your computer.

2. Find the new program. Is it where you expected it to be on the Start menu, task bar, or desktop? If your Start Menu customization settings specify to highlight newly installed programs, then you should see the new program highlighted when you click All Programs, as shown in Figure 5–26.

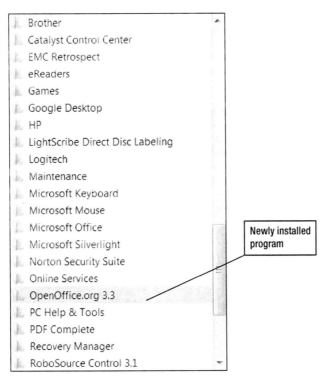

Figure 5–26. *OpenOffice.org 3.3 was recently installed.*

3. Start the program. You may be prompted to:

    ▪ Activate the program.

    ▪ Register the program.

    ▪ Check the Web for program updates, and if any are found, download and install them.

    ▪ Configure settings and preferences.

4. Try out the features of the program to make sure it works.

NOTE: Another good reason to test out the program is to make sure that it is ready when you need it. All too often people install programs to use for a special presentation or occasion and don't check to make sure everything is ready before they actually need it.

Updating and Upgrading

If you want to keep your computer and programs running smoothly and safely, it's a good idea to accept automatic updates when offered by software publishers. Though it may be annoying how often some programs require a new update to be installed, usually they are being pushed because they fix a known security issue or serious program flaw. Though Windows 7 has been available for nearly two years, there are still many new fixes for programs and device drivers to improve compatibility with Windows 7. Most updates don't require uninstalling or reinstalling; you may only have to close the program during the update and sometimes restart your computer afterwards.

Upgrades are usually more substantial because they can be significant improvements in features and functionality. The software publisher may require that the old version be uninstalled, your computer restarted, and then the new version installed. The installation program for the new version may take care of all of this at once; other programs may require that you uninstall the old version, and then come back to the new installation program and run it.

Follow the software publisher's instructions for performing upgrades. If they don't tell you to uninstall first, then don't. If you run into problems afterwards, you may have to manually uninstall and reinstall yourself.

Selecting Your Default Programs

Occasionally a new program takes over as being the main program for a particular type of file when you didn't want it to. Perhaps you installed a new photo editing program to try out but still want your old photo editor to be the default. But the new program took over as the default photo editor, and photos now automatically open with the new program.

You have several options.

- Specify your default programs.

- Associate a file type or protocol with a program.

- Open the file from within the program you want to use.

- Open or edit a file from file context menu in a folder.

To specify a default program:

1. Click the **Start** button, and then click **Default Programs**.

2. Click **Set your default programs**. The Set Default Programs window is displayed.

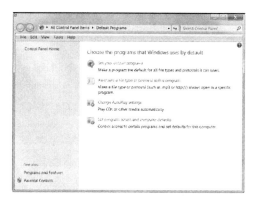

3. Select a program in the list to view information about the current settings.

4. Click **Choose defaults for this program**. The Set Program Associations window is displayed.

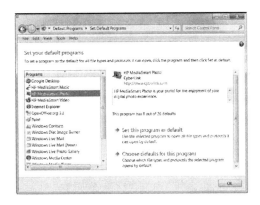

5. If you want to change settings:

   ▪ Clear the checkbox for any file extension you don't want this program to open by default.

   ▪ Select the checkbox for any file extension you want this program to open by default.

6. Click **Save** when you are done.

7. Click **OK** again to close the Set Default Programs window.

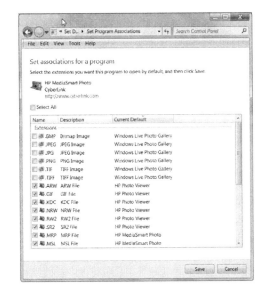

To associate a file type or protocol with a program:

1. Click the **Start** button, and then click **Default Programs**.

2. Click **Associate a file type or protocol with a program**. It will take a few minutes for Windows to create the list of file types and associations. The Set Associations window appears.

3. Select a file name and then click **Change program** to associate the file type with a different program. The Open with window is displayed.

4. Click a different program. Alternatively, if the program you want is not listed, click **Browse** to locate the program on your computer. The **Open with** dialog box opens to C:\Program Files. If you don't see the program's folder, open Program Files (x86). Browse down until you find the folder with the program icon, select it, and then click **Open**.

5. Click **OK** again to close the **Open with** window.

You may want to use several different programs for the same file type, depending on the purpose. For example, you may want to view .jpg photos in one program for photo viewing and browsing, and another program for editing and touching up.

To open the file from within the program you want to use:

1. Open the program. For example, open Windows Live Photo Gallery to touch up a photo.

2. Navigate to the file through the **File open** dialog box or through other file navigation built in to the program.

3. Edit or touch up the file as needed, save changes, and close the program.

4. Open a different program for just browsing, such as the photo viewer program provided by the computer manufacturer.

5. Navigate to the file through the **File open** dialog box or through other file navigation built in to the program.

Open or edit a file from file context menu in a folder:

1. In a Windows Explorer or Libraries folder window, navigate to the file you want to open or edit.

2. Right-click the file. In this example, for the picture file type .jpg, there are three choices for opening or editing this file.

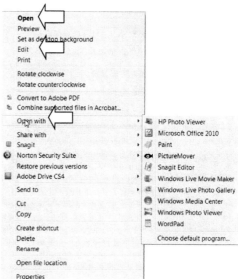

- **Open** on my computer will open it in **Windows Live Photo Gallery**. On your computer, a .jpg may open with a different program.

- **Edit** on my computer will open it in **Paint**. On your computer, a .jpg may open with a different program.

- **Open with** displays a list of programs installed on your computer that are capable of opening the file type.

Protecting and Storing Installation Programs and Information

I have multiple computers at home plus several at work, so I do a lot of program installations and upgrades. I also am called upon to provide technical support to friends and relatives when their computers crash or don't work properly. Over the years I have learned a few tricks and practices to make installing and reinstalling programs easier.

You never know when you might need to reinstall programs because of hardware or software problems. Quite often people end up buying new copies of software they previously bought because they can't find the installation disks or product keys. Table 5–1 lists tips for storing and organizing your installation program disks and files. Some of these tips are really low tech, but simple and effective.

Table 5–1. *Tips for Storing and Organizing Installation Information*

Item	Protection or Storage
Product Keys	Write down product keys on index cards, including the computer(s) on which you installed the program.
	If the installation program came on a disk, you may be able to write the product key on the printed side of the disk with a Sharpie® or similar permanent felt tip pen.
	When you write down a product key any place, recheck the numbers and letters against the original label. Sometimes a "6" can look like "G," an "8" can look like "B," an "O" look like a zero "0," a "1" can look like an "I."
	If the product key was sent to you in e-mail, print a copy of the e-mail to put in with your index cards, and store the e-mail message in an e-mail account that you can access from anywhere (web-based e-mail like Windows Live Mail, Yahoo! Mail, G-mail, etc.)
	TIP: You can buy a handy inexpensive utility that scans your computer and creates a list of the product keys for many programs installed on your computer. Check out **Recover Keys** at http://recover-keys.com.
Installation disks	Buy a simple disk storage box or a DVD/CD notebook to store your disks. As long as the box or notebook is kept in a safe protected place, you don't need to keep the discs in their original boxes or cases. I have used both storage boxes and notebooks; I like the storage box better because it is easier to move them around as you get more disks, and you can use tabbed dividers to alphabetize or organize them.
Downloaded installation programs	Create an Installation Files folder in your Documents library, and back up that folder on another computer or a network location. Installation downloads often have cryptic names. When you download the files, or afterwards, rename the file to something friendly and understandable. So rename that **OC246.32.7.v6.1.exe** file to something like **Program X installation.exe**.

Item	Protection or Storage
	By default, when you download files they go to your Downloads folder. The Downloads folder can get crowded with downloads that you only needed once or twice, and it is easy to either lose track of the installation files or accidentally delete them.
Disk image backups	A disk image backup is a snapshot of your entire hard disk, and can be used to restore the entire hard disk at once. It takes a long time for a backup program to create a disk image, and you will need a backup storage location that has at least as much space available as the size of the disk you are backing up.
	See Chapter 16 to learn how to set up and run backups.
File backups	File backups don't back up programs, but they can back up files created by programs. If you have to reinstall a program, you may also need to restore the files (documents, pictures, spreadsheets, email messages) that were created by the program.
	See Chapter 16 to learn how to set up and run backups.
Create and Safely Store Your Disaster Recovery Disk	Your computer manufacturer should provide you with either a Disaster Recovery Disk or provide a wizard so that you can create your own soon after you start using your new computer. The Disaster Recovery Disk is like a disk image backup, but it only restores your computer to the condition it was in when you bought it. The Disaster Recovery Disk will delete all existing files from your computer. After you perform the disaster recovery you will need to reinstall any programs that you installed after you bought the computer plus recover documents and files from backups that you performed before the disaster.
	See Chapter 16 to learn how to perform disaster recoveries.

Summary

In this chapter you learned about installing programs. Program installation can be easy and painless if you follow a few simple steps before, during, and after installation. You may find it handy to refer to the flow chart at the beginning of this chapter as a reminder of the installation process.

In preparing for installation, you should

- Get license or activation keys if needed.
- Allow plenty of time for download and installation.
- Check program requirements.
- Login as an administrator.
- Check program compatibility with Windows 7.

Create a System Restore point before installation During installation, you should

- Locate and install the program from the Web, installation disk, your network, or a program on your computer.

- If you have problems with installation, you have many options, such as compatibility mode, running in virtual machine, or other troubleshooting options.

After installation, you should

- Restart the computer even if the installation program didn't require it.

- Run the newly installed program to check that it works correctly, register the product, and configure or personalize it as needed.

- If you are installing multiple programs, restart your computer before beginning a new installation. This ensures that the program you just installed is working before you install another one. Otherwise, if you install several programs at once and have problems, you may have to uninstall and reinstall each program to track down which is causing the problem.

- After you are done installing a program, store your installation disks, installation files, and product keys safely in case you need to reinstall them again later.

Next Steps

You may find the following related information helpful for further understanding installation:

- See the "Installation Examples" section at the beginning of this chapter for more examples elsewhere of program installations.

- See Chapter 4 to learn how to remove programs and how to add or change features for a program already installed on your computer.

- See Chapter 18 to learn how to use virtual machines such as Windows Virtual PC, Windows XP Mode, and VMWare Player to run programs that are not compatible with Windows 7.

See Chapter 17 for more troubleshooting methods besides those provided in this chapter, including running Program Compatibility to make older programs run in Windows 7. Also, this chapter provides information about locating, updating, and installing device drivers.

Chapter 6

Using WordPad, Paint, and Accessories

Windows 7 includes many built-in programs and accessories. These programs can be useful tools and aids in helping you become more proficient at using your computer. All of these programs include built-in help systems that explain the features and common tasks. We will show you some tricks and introduce a few small projects that will allow you to explore the features while building important computer skills. While some of these programs may at first appear to be basic "starter" programs, they can be quite useful.

This chapter will cover the following Accessories programs. Table 6–1 explains the different programs.

- WordPad
- Paint
- Calculator
- Games
- System Tools
- Optional Tablet PC Components

Table 6–1. *Highlights of Accessories Programs*

Program	Description
Accessories	The **Accessories** folder on the Programs menu contains many individual programs such as **Calculator**, **Paint**, and **WordPad**. It also contains folders for **Ease of Access** and **System Tools**.
WordPad	**WordPad** is a lightweight word processing program that provides rich text formatting options similar to those offered in e-mail programs. It's a great program for practicing editing and formatting skills to use in e-mail programs, Microsoft Word, and most other programs where you write or edit text.
Paint	**Paint** is a simple bitmap paint program that allows you to create, crop, and edit graphics in a wide variety of formats, including .bmp, .png, .jpg, .gif, and .tif. It's a great program to practice basic graphic editing, including selecting, cropping, combining, and rotating.
Calculator	**Calculator** is more than just a replacement for your scratch pad or a simple handheld calculator. It provides several views that can be useful at all levels of education and work, including general, scientific, programmer, and statistic. The number keys use the same layout as you find on your keyboard, a typical adding machine, or handheld calculator, so it's a great way to build numeric keyboarding skills.
Ease of Access Center	The **Ease of Access Center**, also available through Control Panel, provides a single location for tools and settings to make your computer easier to use. For more information, see Chapter 1.
System Tools	**System Tools** contains programs that help you manage and monitor your computer, as well as several specialized tools and services.
Games	The **Games** folder contains several built-in Windows 7 games plus additional games included by the computer manufacturer. Games are a great way to reduce stress and a fun way to practice mouse skills such as click, double-click, and drag and drop. Even if you long ago mastered those moves with your mouse, try them again with an alternative input device such as a touch pad, touch screen, trackball mouse, or keyboard only!

Using Accessories

The Accessories folder on the All Programs menu lists individual programs as well as subfolders with more programs.

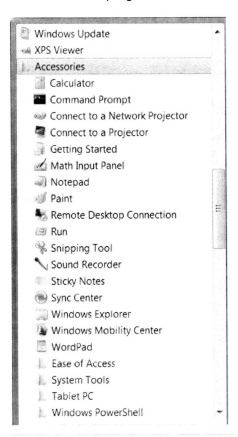

To view the Accessories folder:

1. Click the **Start** button, click **All Programs**, and scroll as needed to the Accessories folder.

2. Click the **Accessories** folder to expand it and view the programs and subfolders.

TIP: The programs shown in your Accessories folder may differ from those shown in the example above. Some programs and folders are only displayed when they are added through **Windows Features**. For example, the Tablet PC folder and Math Input program are added when **Tablet PC Components** is selected in Windows Features. Chapter 4 describes how to add Windows Features.

Using WordPad

WordPad is a lightweight word processing program that provides rich text formatting options similar to those offered in e-mail programs, without the depth of features available in a full-featured program like Microsoft Word. If the last time you looked at WordPad was in Windows Vista or earlier, take a look again. As shown in Figure 6–1, Windows 7 WordPad does away with the old-style menu and toolbars and sports the new "Ribbon"-style of tabbed menus/toolbars introduced in Office 2007.

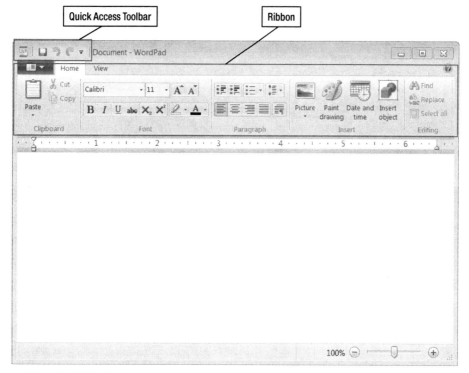

Figure 6–1. *WordPad*

> **TIP:** You can add the commands you use most frequently to the Quick Access Toolbar above the Ribbon. Right-click a command or button, and then click **Add to Quick Access Toolbar**. The Quick Access Toolbar is also available in Paint.

While WordPad will not replace your full-featured word processing program, it's quite useful for small simple documents that don't require fancy layouts.

WordPad is a great for learning how to do the following:

- Use an Office Ribbon-style interface, without the complexity of using a full-featured Office program.

- Build keyboard skills and proficiency.

- Practice text and paragraph formatting.

- Create documents that combine text with pictures, spreadsheets, and content from other programs.

While there is no limit on the length of a document you can create, WordPad does lack some of the features that you may commonly use in Microsoft Word for multi-page documents such as reports, term papers, manuals, or memos.

- **Styles**: You can't save or specify styles, such as Heading 1, 2, 3, Normal, or Body Text, but you can apply formatting to a character, word, line, paragraph, or the entire document to create the look of a style.

- **Manual page breaks**: You can't see or create page breaks on screen, but you can see where the pages will break in Print Preview.

- **Tables**: You can't create tables, but you can use tab stops to line up items in columns. You can also use the Insert object feature to paste or create tables from another program such as Word or Excel.

- **Headers and footers**: You can't create headers or footers, but you can show page numbers.

- **Table of Contents and Index**: You can't tag and generate these.

- **Footnotes**: You can't insert footnotes; however, you can manually add a footnote number to a word by formatting a number as superscript (footnote[1]) and then manually create a footnote list at the end of the document.

- **Spelling checker**: WordPad doesn't have a built-in spelling checker, but you could copy the text from your document to an e-mail message, and then check the spelling using the e-mail program's spelling checker.

> **Tip:** If you need the power of a full featured word processor but don't want to buy the full Microsoft Office suite, **OpenOffice.org** is a free productivity suite that you can download from www.openoffice.org. Chapter 5 uses the installation of OpenOffice.org as an example of downloading and installing a program from the Web.

Thirteen WordPad Keyboard Shortcuts That Can Change Your Life

The keyboard shortcuts in Table 6–2 are almost universal for Windows programs. Once you learn these, you will probably use keyboard shortcut instinctively without looking for a toolbar button or menu command. Formatting and Editing command shortcuts are especially handy because you can type those keys with your left hand while you click and select with your right hand on the mouse.

Table 6–2. *Thirteen Keyboard Shortcuts*

File Commands		Description
Ctrl+N	New	Open a new document.
Ctrl+O	Open	Open an existing document.
Ctrl+S	Save	Save the current file.
Ctrl+P	Print	Print the current document.
Formatting Commands		**Description**
Ctrl+B	Bold	Format the selected text in **bold**.
Ctrl+I	Italic	Format the selected text in *italics*.
Ctrl+U	Underline	Format the selected text with underlining.
Editing Commands		**Description**
Ctrl+Z	Undo	Reverse your last action.
Ctrl+X	Cut	Remove the selected text or content and place it in the clipboard.
Ctrl+C	Copy	Place a copy of the selected text or content in the clipboard and leave the original in place.
Ctrl+V	Paste	Paste the contents of the clipboard into the current location.
Ctrl+A	Select All	Select all content in the document in order to apply formatting or perform an action on all of it at once.
Ctrl+F	Find	Open the Find dialog box to search for text.

NOTE: Many Windows programs list keyboard shortcuts alongside commands on menus, or display them in tooltips when you hover over a toolbar button. Most programs also provide lists of their keyboard shortcuts in their online help system. You don't need to learn them all, but it's handy to memorize shortcuts for commands or features you use frequently.

Editing Text in WordPad

One of the basic skills you can learn from WordPad is how to use the Edit commands: **Cut**, **Copy**, **Paste**, **Select All**, and **Undo**. You might call these universal commands– they are available in almost every level and program in Windows.

NOTE: It might be confusing to see **Cut**, **Copy**, and **Paste** referred to as **Edit** commands, yet in WordPad and in the Office Ribbon menu/toolbar system, those commands are listed in the **Clipboard** group and **Find**, **Replace**, and **Select all** are listed in the **Editing** group. In most Windows programs outside of Microsoft Office, and in older Microsoft programs, the **Edit** menu contains the **Cut**, **Copy** and **Paste** commands.

Select, Cut or Copy, and Paste

Sometimes people just call it "cut and paste." These commands work with the clipboard, which stores your changes in memory and contains the last item you cut or copied.

NOTE: The clipboard only stores the last thing you cut or copied. Each time you cut or copy something, it replaces the contents in the clipboard. However, many programs provide multiple Undo. So if you accidently cut or deleted something a few clicks back, you may be able to click **CTRL+Z** until you get back to where you accidently cut or deleted something.

Understanding how these commands work, and mastering their use, will make Windows programs easier to use. Cut, copy, and paste are not limited to programs that display these commands on a menu or on a toolbar. You can use these commands on almost any object in Windows including files, folders, text, pictures, web pages, and address bars.

WordPad is a great place to practice several ways of doing cut and paste. Table 6–3 compares the different methods.

Table 6–3. *Different Methods of Cut and Paste*

Method	Advantage and Disadvantages	
Command buttons on a toolbar	Pros	▦ Easy to find the commands when toolbar buttons are available.
		▦ Memorizing key combinations not required.
		▦ Easy to do even if original location and destination are on different pages.
	Cons	▦ Many programs don't display toolbar buttons for cut, copy, and paste.
Control key combinations	Pros	▦ Almost universal across all Windows programs.
		▦ May be available even when command buttons and right-click are not available.
		▦ Easy to do even if original location and destination are on different pages.
	Cons	▦ Can be an uncomfortable stretch of fingers if repeated frequently and repetitiously.
Right-click menu	Pros	▦ Entire select–cut/copy–paste can be performed with just the mouse.
		▦ Easy to do even if original location and destination are on different pages.
	Cons	▦ Right-click menu commands may not be available in some programs.
		▦ May be harder to do with notebook touchpad or alternate input device if you are used to using a mouse.
Drag and drop	Pros	▦ Easy to do within same page on screen.
		▦ Works well for dragging and dropping picture files from a folder to the WordPad document window.
	Cons	▦ Can be difficult to drag if you need to scroll the screen up or down from the original location to the destination. Sometimes document scrolls too fast or jumps past where you want to insert.

> **TIP:** Try to learn all of these methods. When you do a lot of cutting, copying, pasting, and selecting with the mouse, these repetitive actions can cause nasty chronic injuries such as Carpal Tunnel Syndrome and RSI (repetitive stress injury). It is good to learn multiple methods so that you can vary your routine, especially if one method starts to hurt.

Using Toolbar Buttons

To cut or copy text and paste it using toolbar buttons:

1. In a WordPad document, select text by double-clicking it or by clicking and dragging the cursor over the text.

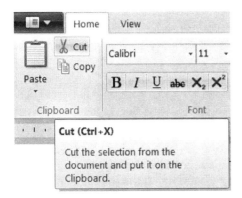

2. Click the **Cut** button.

   The text you selected is now in the clipboard.

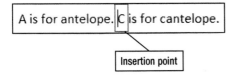

3. Place the cursor where you want to paste the text.

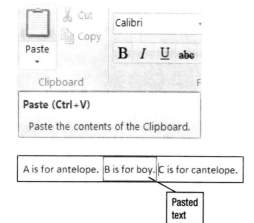

4. Click the **Paste** button.

The text you cut to the clipboard is pasted into the new location.

The text is still in the clipboard, so that you can paste it again someplace else if you want.

NOTE: *Cut* and *delete* are not the same thing. When you *cut* something, it's placed in the clipboard, ready for you to paste it elsewhere. When you *delete* something, it's not placed in the clipboard for pasting. If you accidently delete something you meant to cut, you can usually retrieve it if you immediately use the Undo command, **CTRL+Z**.

Right Hand Select, Left Hand Apply

Look at the location of the editing command keyboard shortcuts on your keyboard. They are all on the left side of the keyboard, in the first and second row up from the spacebar. This allows you to select text or objects with your right hand using the mouse (as shown in Figure 6–2), and then perform an action on the selection with your left hand on these Control key shortcuts (as shown in Figure 6–3). Though most programs, including WordPad, may have toolbar buttons that perform these actions, it can slow you down doing both the selecting and the editing command action with the mouse. It can also lead to more stress on your mouse hand through repetitive motions.

Apply a command with left hand	Select text or insert cursor with mouse

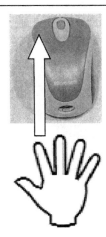

Figure 6–2. *Using left hand, press and hold the CTRL key with little finger, and then press Z, X, C, or V.*

Figure 6–3. *Using right hand, click the mouse and drag the cursor to select text to cut or copy, or click where you want to insert (paste) text that was cut or copied.*

Using the CTRL Keys

To cut or copy text and paste it using CTRL keys:

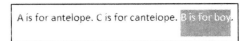

1. Select the text.

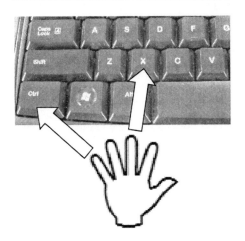

2. Using left hand, press and hold the **CTRL** key with little finger, and then press **X** to cut the text.

    The text you selected is now in the clipboard.

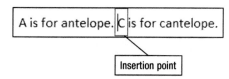

Insertion point

3. Place the cursor where you want to paste the text.

4. Press and hold the **CTRL** key with little finger, and then press **v**.

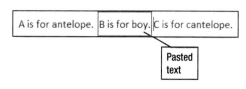

Pasted text

The text you cut to the clipboard is pasted into the new location.

The text is also still in the clipboard so that you can paste it again someplace else if you want.

Using the Mouse and Right-Click

To cut or copy text and paste it using only the mouse:

1. Select the text.

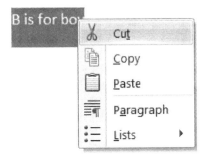

2. Right-click the selection.

   A context menu is displayed.

3. Click **Cut**.

A is for antelope.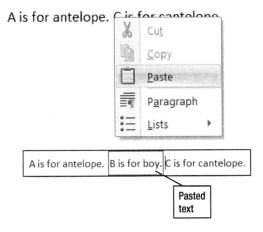

4. Position the cursor where you want to paste the text, and then right-click.

5. In the context menu, click **Paste**. The text you cut or copied to the clipboard is pasted into the new location.

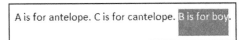

Pasted text

The text you cut to the clipboard is pasted into the new location.

The text is also still in the clipboard so that you can paste it again someplace else if you want.

Using Drag and Drop

Drag and drop can be used for both cutting and copying. The only difference between cutting and copying with drag and drop is that in order to copy, you press the **CTRL** key while you drag the selection to the new location.

> **NOTE:** Drag and drop does not use the clipboard. Whatever was in the clipboard before the drag and drop will still be there afterwards.

To cut and paste text with drag and drop:

A is for antelope. C is for cantelope. B is for boy.

1. Select the text you want to cut, hold down the mouse key, and then drag the selection to the new area.

As you drag the selection, a small rectangle appears at the bottom of the pointer, and the insertion bar moves along to indicate where text will be inserted.

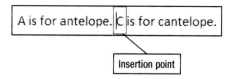

2. Drag until the cursor is where you want to paste the text.

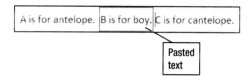

3. When the insertion bar is in the place where you want to paste the text, release the mouse button.

    The text you cut to the clipboard is pasted into the new location.

    The text is also still in the clipboard so that you can paste it again someplace else if you want.

TIP: Using drag and drop to copy text can be really handy if you want to paste the same text repeatedly in several locations.

To copy and paste text with drag and drop:

> **TIP:** Sometimes we accidently drag and drop something without realizing it, and then notice something is wrong. You can use **CTRL+Z** to undo your last drag and drop, whether it is text or pictures within a document. You can also use it to undo drag and drop of files and folders in folder windows.

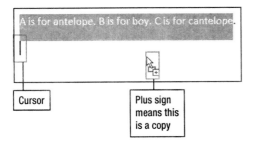

1. Select the text you want to copy, press and hold down the **CTRL** key, hold down the mouse key, and then drag the selection to the new area.

   As you drag the selection, a small rectangle with a plus sign inside appears at the bottom of the pointer, and the insertion bar moves along to indicate where text will be inserted.

2. Drag until the cursor is where you want to place the copy.

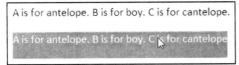

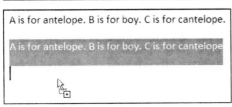

3. When the insertion bar is in the place where you want to paste the text, release the mouse button, but don't release the **CTRL** key yet.

4. If you only want to paste this copy once, release the **CTRL** key.

   If you want to keep pasting a copy of this selection, continue to hold the **CTRL** key and drag the selection to the next location, release the mouse key but don't release the **CTRL** key. Repeat as needed.

Drag and Drop In Other Programs

Drag and drop can be used in many other programs and in Windows folders. It works much like the preceding examples of WordPad. It's as easy as 1-2-3.

1. Click or select what you want to cut or copy.

2. Drag the selection to the new location.

3. Release the mouse button.

Here are some everyday uses of drag and drop:

- Drag and drop a file into an e-mail message, so that you can send it as an attachment.

- Drag and drop an e-mail message attachment to copy a file attachment to a folder on your computer.

- Drag and drop a file from one folder to another.

- Drag and drop a picture file into Word, Excel, PowerPoint, and many other programs to paste the picture directly into the document.

Copying Text or Pictures Between WordPad and Other Programs

All of the copy and paste examples described used text within the current WordPad document. But you can cut and paste between WordPad and other programs. For example, you are researching something on the Web, and you want to copy some information from the web page to your WordPad document. Or, you used WordPad to compose a document, and you want to copy all or part of that document to the body of an e-mail message without attaching a separate document file.

Here are a couple of exercises you can use to sample copying and pasting between programs.

To copy and paste between a web page and WordPad:

1. Open a web page, and select some text or pictures.

2. Copy the selection.

3. In a WordPad document, click where you want to add the content you just copied, and then select the **Paste** command.

> **NOTE:** In some programs, like a web browser, you can only copy from the page and paste it into another document or program. You can't cut content from or paste content into a web page in a web browser.

Chapter 9 describes many different ways to save and copy information from web pages.

To copy WordPad content into an e-mail message:

1. In the WordPad document, select the content you want to copy. If you want to copy the WordPad document contents into the e-mail message, press **CTRL+A** (Select All).

2. Select **Copy** using the toolbar button, **CTRL+C**, or right-click ➤ **Copy**.

3. Click the body of the e-mail message at the location in the message where you want to paste the text.

4. Paste the content from the WordPad document. Which method you use to paste the content depends on your preferences and what methods are available in your e-mail program.

Chapter 8 describes additional ways to send information in e-mail messages, including file attachments.

Formatting Text in WordPad

The Ribbon in WordPad brings almost all features out front so you don't have to dive deeper into layers of menus or dialog boxes. The most frequently used features are in the **Font** and **Paragraph** sections of the Ribbon shown in Figure 6–4.

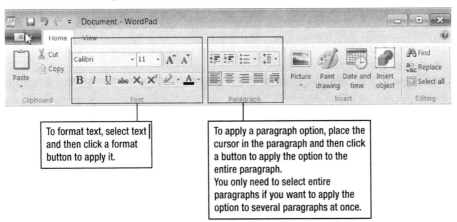

Figure 6–4. *The Home tab on the Ribbon contains most of the features you will need in everyday use.*

Select and Apply

When you want to format text, you can either:

- Insert the cursor where you want the formatting to begin, and select your formatting options. The formatting will be applied to the text as you type, from the insertion point on.

▪ Select existing characters, words, or paragraphs to highlight what will be formatted, and then apply the font characteristics.

When you want to apply a paragraph option to a single paragraph, place the cursor in the paragraph, and then click a button to apply the option.

When you want to apply a paragraph option to multiple paragraphs, select entire paragraphs, and then click a button to apply the option.

> **TIP:** If you don't recognize what a button does, hover over it with your mouse until a tooltip appears.

In the following exercise, practice applying formatting to text. This will introduce you to common formatting options, and at the same time give you practice with several basic mouse skills:

1.   Type the following text: The quick brown fox jumps over the lazy dog.

2.   Select (click and drag your   The *quick* brown fox jumps over the *lazy* dog.
     mouse cursor over) "quick,"
     and then click the **Italic** button
     in the Ribbon. Do the same for
     "lazy." You can also apply italic
     by pressing **Ctrl+I.**

3.   Double-click "fox," and then   The *quick* brown **fox** jumps over the *lazy* **dog**.
     click the **Bold** button in the
     Ribbon. Do the same for "dog."
     You can also apply bold by
     pressing **Ctrl+B.**

4.   Underline "The" and "the." By   <u>The</u> *quick* brown **fox** jumps over <u>the</u> *lazy* **dog**.
     selecting each word separately,
     and then clicking the **U** button.
     You can also apply underline
     by pressing **Ctrl+U.**

5.   Select the word "brown" and then   <u>The</u> *quick* <mark>brown</mark> **fox** jumps over <u>the</u> *lazy* **dog**.
     click the **Text Highlight Color**
     button. Choose a dark color from
     the palette, such as "Dark red."
     Note that black text is hard to
     read on a dark highlight color.

6. Select "brown" if it is not still selected, and then click the **Font Color** button. Pick a contrasting light color from the palette, such as yellow.

The *quick* brown **fox** jumps over the *lazy* **dog**.

7. Select the entire sentence with one click:

The *quick* **brown** fox jumps over the *lazy* **dog.**

Move the mouse cursor to the left of the sentence, in the empty margin area so that the cursor changes to the arrow pointer cursor, and then click once. The entire sentence should be highlighted

8. With the sentence still selected, press **Ctrl+B** once, and the entire sentence is bold.

The *quick* brown fox jumps over the *lazy* dog.

The *quick* brown fox jumps over the *lazy* dog.

Press **Ctrl+B** again, and nothing is bold.

Congratulations! You've used several common formatting options and practiced selecting characters, words, and entire lines with mouse clicks. Explore the other Font buttons such as the font family and size.

> **TIP:** Avoid THE raNsom note look   (Avoid the ransom note look.) New users are often excited by all of the different combinations of formatting, fonts, sizes, colors available. Resist the temptation! It's hard to read and will label you as a "newbie." You can usually create an attractive document with just two different groups of font settings: one font bold and larger for headings, and another font with normal formatting and size for the body.

Paragraph Formatting

Paragraph formatting is a little simpler in that you do not have to select an entire paragraph to format it: place your cursor anyplace in a paragraph or line, and then click a paragraph formatting button. If you want to apply formatting to multiple paragraphs at once, such as a bulleted list or numbered list, you do need to select part of the first paragraph down to part of the last paragraph. When you apply a paragraph option, each time you press the **enter** key the next paragraph continues with the same paragraph options.

Explore the paragraph format buttons:

1. Type several lines.

2. Insert the cursor in the middle of any line.

3. Try the different paragraph buttons to see what each one does.

   When you try the **List** button, you will find it has a dropdown arrow that lists several bullet and number list formats, as shown in Figure 6–5.

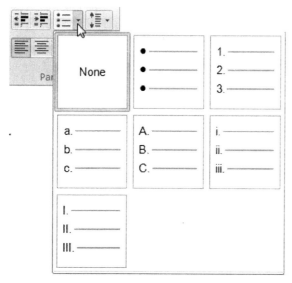

Figure 6–5. *The List button provides bullet, number, and outline lists.*

You can turn list formatting off on a paragraph by clicking the **List** button again.

Inserting Pictures and Objects

The Insert group, shown in Figure 6–6, provides several options for inserting content created by another program, and inserting **Date and time**. Table 6–4 describes the Insert options.

Figure 6–6. *The Insert buttons allow you to insert content from another program or the date and time.*

Table 6–4. *Insert Options*

Insert	Description
Picture	Inserts pictures and provides options to format a picture after it has been inserted. A typical use would be to insert a photo from a folder on your computer.
Paint Drawing	Opens the Paint program so that you can create a bitmap image. When you are done creating a picture, you can save the picture to a file before inserting it into the document.
Date and time	Provides a list of date and time formats, based on the locale (language) your computer is set to.
Insert object	Allows you to create and insert content by using another program as the editor. It is similar to Insert ➤ Paint Drawing. Also allows you to embed a file as an object that you can open and view in another program.
	For example, you can create a Microsoft Excel spreadsheet, a PowerPoint presentation, or a Word document, and then insert it into the WordPad document. When you insert an object, the program used to create and edit that content opens in a separate window. In technical terms, an object is an OLE (Object Linking and Embedding) object. It sounds more techie than it really is. The object types available depend on what programs installed on your computer support OLE objects.

> **TIP:** The **Insert Object** feature in WordPad works well, but if you are going to insert spreadsheets or presentations created by more powerful programs like Excel or PowerPoint, you might as well start with an equally powerful program to create your document—Microsoft Word—instead of WordPad.

The Insert buttons are easy to use. In the following procedures, you will try each one.

To insert the date:

1. Open a new WordPad document.

2. In the **Insert** group, click **Date and time**.

    The Date and Time dialog box appears. Date and time provides many formats for minutes, hours, days, months and years

3. Select a format, and then click **OK**. The available formats listed on your computer may differ depending on your locale and language.

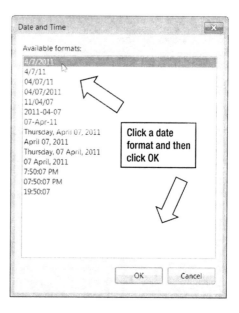

The date is inserted into the WordPad document.

To insert a picture from a folder on your computer:

1. Click the **Picture** button, and then click **Picture**.

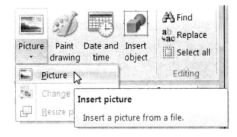

2. In the **Select Picture** dialog box, navigate to **Libraries ➤ Pictures ➤ Sample Pictures**.

3. Select a picture, and then click **Open**.

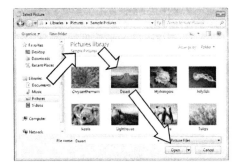

If the actual size of the picture is larger than the page, WordPad will reduce the size so that it fits. This doesn't affect the original picture file.

You can further resize this manually by dragging the handles on the sides or corners. Sometimes it's hard to keep the height or the width from being stretched out of proportion. Fortunately, you can also resize the picture with a dialog box.

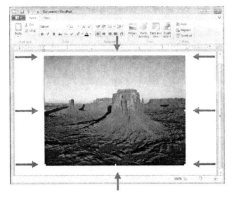

4. Select the picture if it is not already selected, click the **Picture** button, and then click **Resize picture**. the Resize picture command ensures that picture stays in proportion when you resize it.

The Lock aspect ratio check box, which is automatically selected, ensures that whatever change you make to one dimension (height or width) is applied equally to the other dimension (width or height).

5. Set a smaller percentage, and then click **OK**.

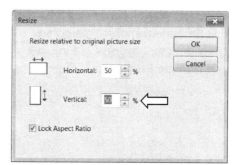

The picture is displayed in WordPad at the new size. You can resize the picture as many times as you want.

To insert a Paint drawing:

1. Click the **Paint drawing** button.

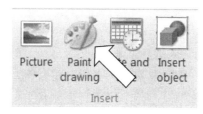

A separate Bitmap Image in Document – Paint window appears outside of the WordPad document.

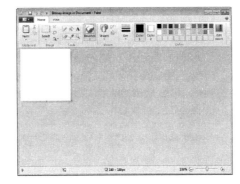

2. Create a drawing. When you are done, click the **Paint** menu, and then click **Exit and return to document**.

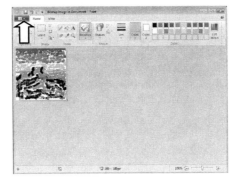

The new Paint drawing is displayed in the WordPad document.

To insert an object:

1. Click the **Insert object** button. The object types listed depend on what programs are installed on your computer. At the very least, you will see **Package**, **Paintbrush Picture**, and **WordPad Document** listed. If you have Microsoft Office installed, you will see more choices available.

2. There are two ways to select an object, **Create New** or **Create from File**.

   ▦ **Create New** opens a new file or document in the program you select in **Object Type**. Create New is selected by default. For this next step, don't change that setting. Figure 6–7 displays four examples of types of programs that might provide objects.

Figure 6–7. *Depending on how many programs you have installed on your computer that provide objects, you may have the three that are available with default Windows 7 (Package, Paintbrush Picture, and WordPad Document) or many more including Microsoft Office, OpenOffice.org, and Adobe programs.*

   ▦ **Create from File** allows you to locate a specific file and insert it as an object.

3. Even if you have other choices available, for this example locate and select **Paintbrush Picture**. The Bitmap Image in Document – Paint window appears, as shown in Figure 6–8.

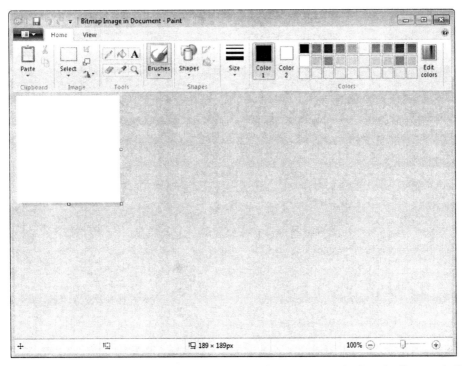

Figure 6–8. *Create your drawing in this separate Paint window; when you're done, it will appear in the WordPad document*

4. Create a drawing. When you are done, click the **Paint** menu, and then click **Exit and return to document**.

> **NOTE:** This example does the same as clicking the Paint drawing button. Paint has its own button because for many Windows users that is the most commonly inserted object.

The **Insert Object ▶ Create New** process is the same for any type of object. The following example illustrates inserting an Adobe Acrobat (PDF file) object:

1. Click the **Insert Object** button.

2. Select the **Object Type**, and then click **OK**.

   In this example, an **Open** file

dialog box will appear.

3. Navigate to a document created or viewed by the Object Type, select the file, and then click **Open**.

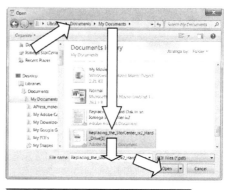

4. The object, a PDF file, appears in a separate window, Adobe Document in Document. In this example, you probably would not be editing the document, so viewing it in this separate window serves to allow you to view and confirm that this is the file you want to embed into the document.

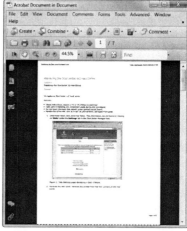

5. When you are done reviewing or changing the document, close the document window to return to the WordPad window.

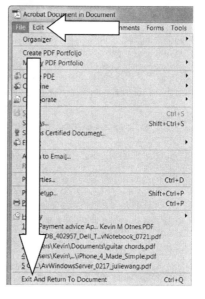

6. When you return to the
WordPad document, the object
is displayed as an image, the
first page of the document, or
an icon.

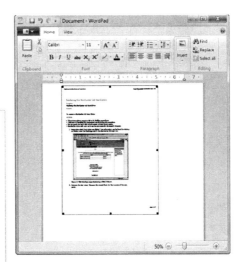

> **NOTE:** If you inserted a multi-page
> document, you may be wondering
> what happened to the rest of the
> pages because you only see the first
> page. They are there in the object.
> When you insert an object, you are
> not just pasting the contents of the
> object. To view all of the pages,
> double-click the object.

You are not limited to inserting object types that are listed. Object types are listed
because they are registered in Windows as objects. For example, there is no object type
listed for Windows movie video files (.wmv). But you can still embed a .wmv file as an
object. The following example inserts a .wmv file into the WordPad document.

To insert a file as an object:

1. Click the **Insert Object** button.

2. Select the **Create from File**,
and then click **Browse**.

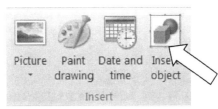

3. Navigate to the file. Click
    **Libraries ➤ Videos ➤ Sample
    Videos**.

    In this example, you are using a
    sample video included with
    Windows.

4. Select the file, and then click
    Open. The Browse window
    closes, and the Insert Object
    dialog box shows the file you
    selected in the **File** box.

5. Click **OK** to close the **Insert
    Object** dialog box.

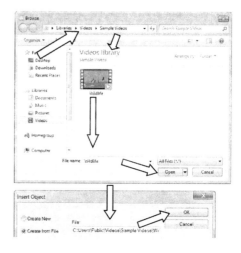

6. Because you are inserting the
    object as a file, it appears as an
    icon in the document. Double-
    click the object to view it. In this
    example, this object type is a
    video so it opens in the default
    video player, which on my
    computer was a mini-Windows
    Media Player window.

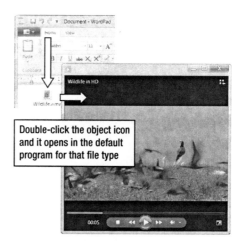

Double-click the object icon
and it opens in the default
program for that file type

Applying What You Have Learned in WordPad to Other Programs

While WordPad is not intended for complex or sophisticated documents, by walking
through some its features you have learned skills and knowledge you can apply to other
Windows programs. These include:

- Using the new Office-style Ribbon.

- Adding frequently used commands to the Quick Access Toolbar.

- Cut, copy, and paste.

- Common text formatting.

- Inserting files and objects.

Using Paint

Paint is a bitmap graphics program that opens most popular picture and image formats. Some common uses for it are creating pictures to add to documents or for light duty touch up or cropping of photos. While it doesn't have the power of a professional graphics program like Adobe Illustrator, Paint also doesn't have the complexity.

Paint uses the Office-type Ribbon, similar to WordPad, but with some different tools. Almost all of the tools and features you need are on the Home tab. The View tab provides controls for zooming in and out, showing rulers, and gridlines, and displaying the picture full screen. Like WordPad, you can also add your most frequently used tools to the **Quick Access Toolbar** above the Ribbon. Just right-click the button or command you want to add, and then click **Add to Quick Access Toolbar**.

Paint vs. "Drawing" Programs

Paint is a bitmap program, which means the picture is made up of tiny bits, mapped across the screen to form the shapes, lines, and patterns you see. You may see different shapes and lines in the picture, but they are all part of one layer, like painting on a canvas. True *drawing* programs use shapes and objects that can be moved or manipulated independently from the background of the drawing. For example, when you use PowerPoint or Visio to create drawings, each object can be moved around without taking the background with it. In Paint, once you draw a shape, it becomes part of the picture. You cannot select a shape as an object; you can select the area of the picture that contains the shape.

To use Paint:

1. Click the **Start** button, and in **Search programs and files**, type **Paint**.

2. In the list that appears, select **Paint**. A new Paint window is displayed.

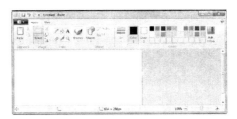

3. Select a tool, such as the **Pencil** or **Brushes**.

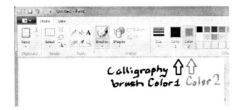

4. Select a color from the **Colors** palette, or use the default colors black and white.

5. Click in the drawing and hold down the mouse key to draw or paint. If you click with your left mouse button as you draw, it will use Color 1. If you click with your right mouse button as you draw, it will use Color 2.

6. Click a shape. When a shape is selected, you can select the type of **Outline**, **Fill**, and line **Size**. The Outline and Fill buttons offer the same choices; Size button offers three thicknesses of lines.

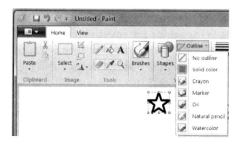

7. If you want to fill the shape with a different color:

   a. Click the **Fill** (paint bucket) button.

   b. Click **Color 1** or **Color 2.**

   c. Click the color in the Color palette.

   d. Click inside the shape.

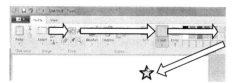

8. If you want to move or change a part of the drawing, click **Select**, drag the mouse over the area,

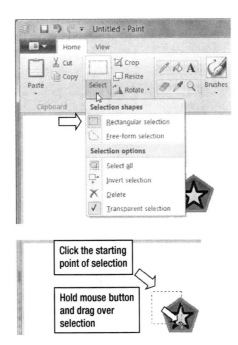

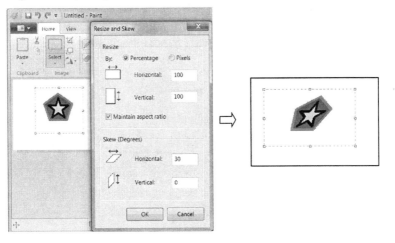

9. Once you have selected the area or object, you can perform any of the following actions:

■ Click **Cut** or **Copy**.

■ Drag the selection to another location.

■ Click **Resize** to resize or skew the selection. Skewing tilts the selection to one side, up, or down. Use positive or negative degrees to specify which direction to skew.

▓ Click **Rotate** to rotate the selection, or flip the selection vertically or horizontally. The selected cylinder shape was rotated right 90 degree. You can rotate in set increments of 90, 180, or 270 degrees.

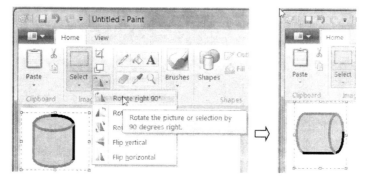

▓ Or you can crop the image. The entire picture on the left was cropped down to the selected area shown on the right.

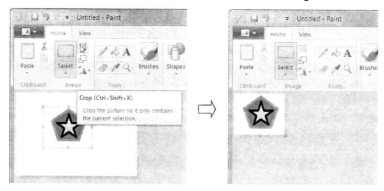

10. You can fix mistakes with the following tools. You can perform multiple undos with the Undo button or command. The eraser is handy when you have drawn a line or shape too far, or you just want to remove an area.

▓ The eraser.

▓ **Undo** (on the Quick Access Toolbar, or **CTRL + Z**).

▓ Selecting and cutting.

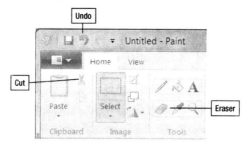

Using the Calculator

When you first open the Calculator it may not seem that impressive. It seems to have the same features as the inexpensive hand calculators often given away as promotional gifts. But the Calculator is actually four calculators, a unit converter, date calculator, and four worksheets for calculating mortgage payments, vehicle lease payments, and fuel economy. The Basic calculator is shown in Figure 6–9.

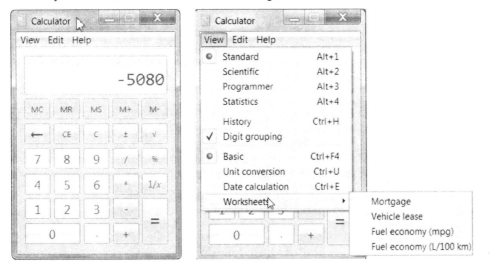

Figure 6–9. *The standard calculator looks like… a standard calculator, until you check the View menu which lists several different types of calculators, conversions, and worksheets available*

To use the Calculator:

1. Click the **Start** button, and in **Search programs and files**, type **Calculator**.

2. In the list that appears, click **Calculator**.

3. Use the keyboard or your numeric keypad to enter numbers. Or click the Calculator keys on screen with your mouse.

4. Click the **View** menu. Figures 6–10 through 6–13 display the many different modes and tools available.

5. You can quickly switch between the different calculator modes with the **ALT + 1** through **ALT + 4** keyboard shortcuts.

Figure 6–10. *ALT+1 displays the standard calculator.*

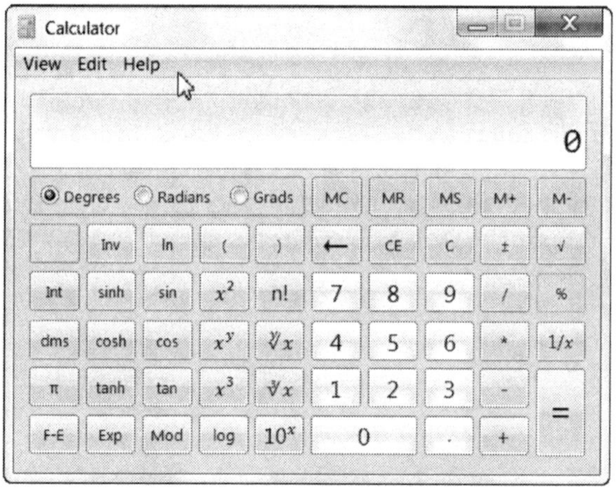

Figure 6–11. *ALT+2 displays the scientific calculator.*

Figure 6–12. *ALT+4 displays the statistics calculator.*

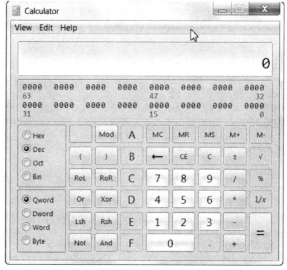

Figure 6–13. *ALT+3 displays the programmer calculator.*

TIP: There are about 90 keyboard shortcuts that you can use in Calculator. To view the list of shortcuts, click the **Start** menu, click **Help and Support**, and search for "Keyboard Shortcuts."

Using Games

Windows 7 provides the **Games Explorer** folder to organize the games installed on your computer, sort of like a Library for games. Microsoft includes several free Windows 7 games. Which games are available and visible on your computer depends on several things.

- **Your version of Windows 7**: Windows Basic/Starter edition, the version installed on many netbooks, does not include several multi-player Internet games, Mahjong Titans, or Chess Titans.

- **Work policy**: Games are not always installed in some business-oriented versions, or because of an employer's policy for work computers.

- **Trial versions**: Additional games may be installed by the computer manufacturer. These programs may be free, trial versions, or require paying a subscription fee to an online game service.

Figure 6–14 shows the free games that Microsoft provides with the premium versions of Windows 7.

Figure 6–14. *Windows 7 games available in Home Premium, Professional, and Ultimate editions*

Installing the Microsoft Games if None Are Showing

Some versions of Windows include games but don't show them by default, so you have to install them through Windows Programs and Features.

To view which games are currently available on your computer:

1.   Click the **Start** button, click **All Programs**, and then click **Games**.

2.   In the list that appears, click **Games**.

If no games are listed, they may be available and they just need to be turned on. See Chapter 4 to learn how to turn Windows features on or off, including Games.

Using Solitaire for Skill Building

There really is a practical use for Solitaire and other games: building computer skills. Games can make learning fun without risking damaging documents or data. Games are also less intimidating than trying to learn an e-mail program or word processing program. With Solitaire, you can build and practice the following computer skills:

- Using program menus to change settings and close programs.

- Using the mouse to click and double-click.

- Using the mouse to click and drag things across the screen.

- Resizing, moving, or snapping a program window.

- Using Help.

- Using alternative inputs, such as trackballs, keyboard input, voice recognition, mouse keys, or touch screens.

To play Solitaire:

1. Click the **Start** button, and in **Search programs and files**, type **Solitaire**.

2. In the list that appears, click **Solitaire**. The Solitaire game appears, as shown in Figure 6–15.

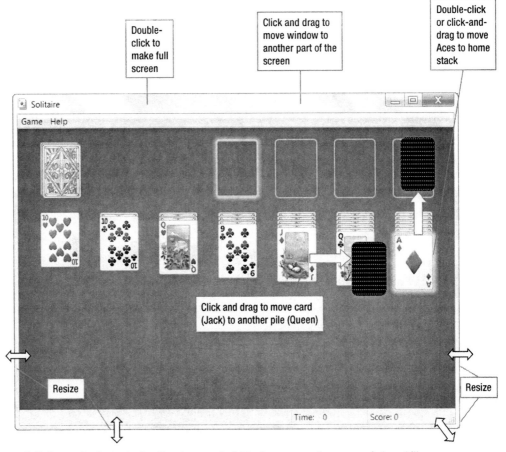

Figure 6–15. *Solitaire can be fun and educational, as you build basic mouse and program window skills*

Here are some suggestions for how to practice Windows skills as you play:

- **Resize or position the window to suit your preferences**:
  - Resize the window by grabbing a corner or side and dragging it in or out.
  - Move the window by clicking the title bar and dragging it to the new location.

- Snap the window to full screen by dragging it to an edge of the screen or by double-clicking the title bar.

- Minimize the Solitaire window to the task bar by clicking the minimize button.

- **Use menus**:

  - Click the Game menu to set options such as how many cards to turn over in the stack, the background pattern, card pattern, and scoring.

  - Click the Help menu for rules and how to play this game.

- **Move cards around**:

  - Double-click an Ace to move it from a column to the home stack.

  - Click and drag a card to move it to another column or to a home stack.

All of these skills will seem very basic when you have been using Windows, computers, and a mouse for a while. Are you really skilled and experienced with a conventional mouse?

Here is a challenge to build your skills with using non-mouse alternative input:

1. Using your mouse, play several games of Solitaire, with the **Game ➤ Options ➤ Standard scoring** and **Timed game** selected.

2. Check your statistics and note your average time and score.

3. Play several more games of Solitaire using another input method that you do not normally use.

   - Use keyboard input only. In Ease of Access Center, turn on MouseKeys.

   - Use your touchpad on your laptop.

   - Use a trackball mouse, where you move a rollerball instead of moving the mouse, to move the cursor across the screen.

   - Use a larger touch pad device such as a Wacom Pen and Touch pad, or a touch screen PC or tablet.

4. After you have played several games, compare your average score and time now with the average you noted when you used your mouse.

Clicking and dragging, and moving the cursor across the screen, can be quite challenging if you have not used one of these other methods before. Solitaire can be a great test and skill builder for improving your proficiency with other input devices besides the mouse.

Getting Additional Games from Microsoft

Microsoft offers many additional free games that you can play online or download from the web. Your computer manufacturer may have installed their own games in addition to the Microsoft games, so depending on where you look you may find links to more Microsoft games, to games offered by the computer manufacturer, or both.

> **NOTE:** The pages and the games offered may change, but in general expect to find links to games you can play online, and to other games you can download.

To get more games from Microsoft:

1. In any Microsoft game already installed on your computer, such as Solitaire, click the **Help** menu, and then click **Get More Games Online.** A web page similar to Figure 6–16 appears.

Figure 6–16. *Microsoft offers many games that you can play online or download.*

2. Click **More FREE Games** for more choices. A web page similar to Figure 6–17 appears.

Figure 6–17. *Lots and lots more free games*

Installing New Games

There are several ways to get and install a new game.

- Install it from a program CD/DVD.
- Download the game program from the Web.
- Log on to an online game service.

Usually when you install a game, the game installation program or Windows will detect if there are incompatibilities with Windows 7. Before installing, check the game program requirements to make sure it will run on Windows 7. Sometimes, with an older games installation disk, you may have to download some additional updates after installation before you can run the game.

With many online multi-player games, you must pay a membership or subscription fee to use their premium services.

Installing Old Games

What's the difference between installing an old game or new game, if it's new to your computer? Game programs have always pushed the limits of what computers and Windows can do, and older programs that were fine-tuned to work in Windows XP or even earlier versions of Windows may not run well—or at all—in Windows 7. Or, they were designed for 32-bit computers, and most new Windows 7 computers today except for netbooks are 64-bit.

Here are some mini-troubleshooting steps to try if you can't get your older game to run in Windows 7:

- **Try running the program with the Program Compatibility Assistant.** When a program doesn't run or install correctly, Windows often detects that there is a problem and offers to try again using the Program Compatibility Assistant. If not, you can run the Program Compatibility troubleshooter: click **Start**, in **Search programs and files** type **compatibility**, and in the list that appears, select **Run programs made for previous versions of Windows**.

- **Try running the program in a virtual machine.** If you have Windows 7 Professional or Ultimate, you can download Virtual PC and Windows XP Mode from Microsoft. If the program ran well on your old computer in Windows XP, you may be able to run the program in Windows XP Mode on your new computer. Virtual PC and Windows XP Mode are not available for Windows 7 Home Premium. However, another virtual machine option is to download the free VMWare Player, which can be installed on any edition of Windows 7, as well as previous versions of Windows.

For more in-depth help on troubleshooting older programs, see Chapter 17. For help with using Windows XP Mode and Virtual Machines, see Chapter 18.

Controlling Access to Games with Parental Controls

Parental Controls can be applied to games. Most games carry ratings to help you determine if the content is acceptable and age-appropriate. Parental Control settings that can be applied to games include:

- **Time limits**: Set what hours of the day and the week when your child can use the computer.

- **Games**: You can specify whether your child can play games, block or allow games by rating and content types, and block or allow specific games.

- **Allow and block specific programs**: This is not just for games; you can apply these settings to your web browser, e-mail programs, instant messaging, or almost any other program on your computer.

To set up Parental Controls for games:

1. Log in to Windows with a Computer administrator account.

2. Click **Start**, and in the Search programs and folders box, type **Parental Controls**.

3. In the list that appears, select **Parental Controls**. The Parental Controls window lists the user accounts on this computer, as shown in Figure 6–18.

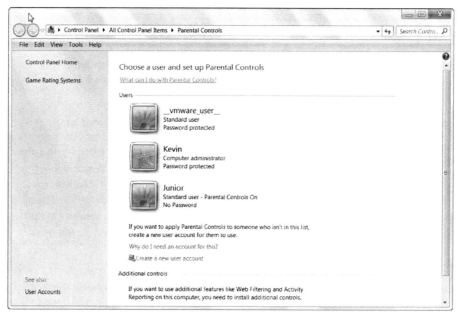

Figure 6–18. *An administrator can apply parental controls to a standard user account. You can't apply parental controls to an administrator account.*

4. In the Parental Controls window, click the user to which you want to apply the settings. The User Controls window displays the current settings and allows you to change the settings, as shown in Figure 6–19.

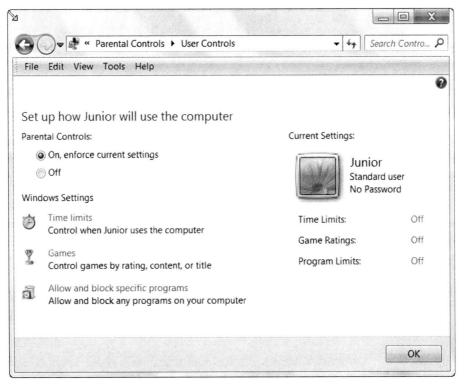

Figure 6–19. *The User Controls window lists the current settings for this user and provides links to change the settings.*

5. Click **On, enforce current settings**, and then click the links under **Windows Settings** as needed.

6. Click **OK** when you are done with the settings for this user.

7. Repeat as needed for each user.

Assigning the right type of account to each user on your computer is very important—not only for controlling your children's access to games, the Internet, and other programs, but also for protecting your computer against dangerous downloads and program installations. See Chapter 12 for more detailed information about setting up user accounts, assigning the appropriate account types, and applying parental controls to accounts.

Controlling Game Fees and Charges

Parental Controls can control access to programs but can't control charges that can be racked up when your kids are playing games. Whenever you sign up for an online service using your credit card, make sure you understand the terms, and monitor your credit card charges after you subscribe. When you sign up for a service, you may also be authorizing automatic payment from your credit card for additional goodies that the game user can purchase to enhance their games. Some services, like Xbox Live, allow you to specify automatic notices be sent to your e-mail account whenever additional services are purchased.

System Tools

You can get to System Tools through the Programs menu. Click **Start ➤ All Programs ➤ Accessories ➤ System Tools**. Most System Tools are programs you don't need or use every day but are handy when you do need them. Table 6–5 tells you a little about each one; in some cases, there is in-depth coverage elsewhere in the book.

Table 6–5. *System Tools*

Program	Description
Character Map	**Character Map** is quite handy when you need to find special characters that don't appear on your keyboard. Select characters from Latin, Cyrillic, Hebrew, and Arabic character sets, as well as symbols, like Registered ®, Copyright ©, fractions ¼, mathematical symbols ±, and degree°.
Computer	**Computer** is the same Computer you see on the desktop, on the Start menu, and in the navigation pane of any folder window. Computer displays the drives located on your computer and network.
Control Panel	**Control Panel** is the same Control Panel you can access from the Start menu. It provides settings and customizations for your computer.
Disk Cleanup	**Disk Cleanup** is a maintenance program that analyzes the files and folders on your computer, and suggests folders, files, and storage that can be cleared to free up disk space and improve performance. You should run this program regularly as part of good computer maintenance. See Chapter 17 to learn how to use this program as part of a good maintenance plan.
Disk Defragmenter	**Disk Defragmenter** is another maintenance program. It analyzes how files are physically stored on your computer's hard drive. Over time, as files are added, deleted, or changed, they become scattered all over your hard drive. This can lead to many small chunks of unused disk space and poorly organized file storage. Eventually your hard disk runs slower and less efficiently. Disk Defragmenter moves the files around on your hard drive to create larger chunks of usable free disk space and better organization of the used disk space. Depending on the size of your hard drive and how much defragmenting is required, it may take several hours for defragmenting to run. While it is

Program	Description
	running, your computer may run considerably slower, so often people run this program overnight when they are not using their computer. See Chapter 17 to learn how to use this program as part of a good maintenance plan.
Internet Explorer (No Add-ons)	**Internet Explorer (No Add-ons)** allows you to open Internet Explorer without add-ons. Add-ons are Active X controls, browser extensions, browser helper objects, or toolbars that provide additional functionality to your browsing. Sometimes one or more add-ons causes problems. Running Internet Explorer (No Add-ons) may help you isolate problems caused by add-ons. See Chapter 9 to learn how to use, add, and disable add-ons.
Private Character Editor	**Private Character Editor** allows you to create or modify your own special characters, which you can then insert into your documents with Character Map. It has a very specialized use for some people; most of us will never need to use it.
Resource Monitor	**Resource Monitor** displays the current status of CPU, disk, memory, and network usage. This information may be more relevant to technical support people than the everyday user as it can be useful for technical and advanced troubleshooting.
System Information	**System Information** lists the specifications and versions of the operating system, hardware, processor, memory, and other information about your computer. This information may be more relevant to technical support people than the everyday user, and can be useful for technical and advanced troubleshooting.
System Restore	**System Restore** is very valuable for fixing and troubleshooting problems with your computer, especially if you recently started having problems after a program installation or update. See Chapter 17 to learn how to use this program to fix a computer that recently started having problems.
Task Scheduler	**Task Scheduler** allows you to set your computer to run a task or program on a recurring basis (daily, weekly, etc.). Some programs, such as backup programs, calendars, etc., may already have some kind of scheduling options built in. For example, you could schedule Disk Defragmenter to run once a month.

Program	Description

> **NOTE:** Your computer must be on and logged on at the time the task is scheduled to run. Task scheduler will not start the computer in order to run the task.

Windows Easy Transfer Reports	**Windows Easy Transfer Reports** provides reports about what was transferred in Windows Easy Transfer, as well as reports on programs you will need to reinstall on your new computer. See Chapter 12 to learn how to access and understand how to use these reports.
Windows Easy Transfer	**Windows Easy Transfer** is a nifty tool that allows you to transfer files, user accounts, and other personal settings from another computer—usually your old computer running Windows XP, Windows Vista, or Windows 7—to your new Windows 7 computer. It doesn't transfer Windows itself or your programs, but it makes it a lot easier to move to a new computer. See Chapter 12 to learn how to use this tool and to learn many helpful tips for making this move as smooth as possible.

Optional Tablet PC Components

Your **Accessories** folder may include a **Tablet PC** folder with several programs and components, including handwriting recognition, that are useful for computers and devices that use touch input.

Summary

In this chapter you learned how to find and use Accessories such as:

- WordPad
- Paint
- Games Explorer
- Parental Controls
- Ease of Access
- Other accessories
- System Tools

You built computer skills using common Windows user interface elements such as:

- The new Office-style Ribbon in WordPad and Paint

- Standard menus in Solitaire

- Moving and resizing windows in Solitaire

- Where to find help

You also learned techniques that can be used in most Windows programs and folders, such as:

- Editing techniques with several methods for cut, copy, and paste.

- Text formatting techniques.

- Thirteen universal Windows keyboard shortcuts.

Next Steps

The following chapters provide additional information about many of the features discussed in this chapter:

- See Chapter 1 to learn how to use the Ease of Access Center.

- See Chapter 4 to learn how to add Windows Features such as Games and Tablet PC components.

- See Chapter 12 to learn how to use the Windows Easy Transfer wizard.

- See Chapter 18 to learn how to use virtual machines such as Windows Virtual PC, Windows XP Mode, and VMWare Player to run games and other programs that are not compatible with Windows 7.

- See Chapter 17 to learn how to use Program Compatibility to make older games run in Windows 7 and how to use Disk Cleanup and Disk Defragmenter to keep your computer running smoothly.

Getting Free Goodies like Windows Live Essentials

Everybody likes free, especially if you get something worthwhile and useful. Windows Live Essentials is all that. It's a free group of programs and features for e-mail, instant messaging, photo organizing and editing, and video editing. Even though Windows Live Essentials may already be installed on your computer, it is not actually part of the Windows 7 installation. If Windows Live Essentials is already installed, great! If not, it is easy to download and install, and we will show you how.

This chapter will introduce you to Windows Live Essentials and get you started with

- Windows Live Mail
- Windows Live Messenger
- Windows Live Movie Maker
- Windows Live Photo Gallery
- Windows Live Writer (for blogging)
- Windows Live Mesh

Windows Live Essentials also includes Windows Live Family Safety which is discussed in more detail in Chapter 12.

Windows Live Essentials Programs

Windows Live Essentials packs quite a few programs into the installation. Some of these features may appear directly on your Programs menu while others may not be available unless you have an associated program already installed. Figure 7–1 displays the feature descriptions provided by Microsoft on their download page.

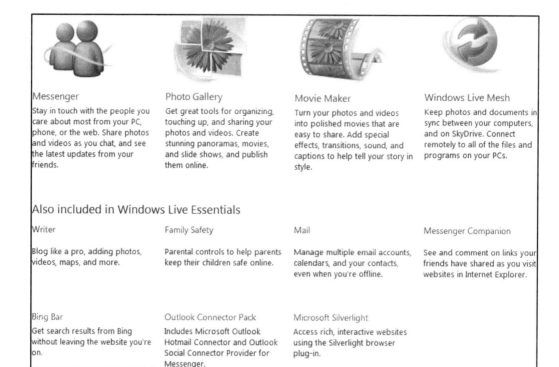

Messenger

Stay in touch with the people you care about most from your PC, phone, or the web. Share photos and videos as you chat, and see the latest updates from your friends.

Photo Gallery

Get great tools for organizing, touching up, and sharing your photos and videos. Create stunning panoramas, movies, and slide shows, and publish them online.

Movie Maker

Turn your photos and videos into polished movies that are easy to share. Add special effects, transitions, sound, and captions to help tell your story in style.

Windows Live Mesh

Keep photos and documents in sync between your computers, and on SkyDrive. Connect remotely to all of the files and programs on your PCs.

Also included in Windows Live Essentials

Writer

Blog like a pro, adding photos, videos, maps, and more.

Family Safety

Parental controls to help parents keep their children safe online.

Mail

Manage multiple email accounts, calendars, and your contacts, even when you're offline.

Messenger Companion

See and comment on links your friends have shared as you visit websites in Internet Explorer.

Bing Bar

Get search results from Bing without leaving the website you're on.

Outlook Connector Pack

Includes Microsoft Outlook Hotmail Connector and Outlook Social Connector Provider for Messenger.

Microsoft Silverlight

Access rich, interactive websites using the Silverlight browser plug-in.

Figure 7–1. *Microsoft's descriptions of the Windows Live Essentials programs, from their download page*

Use Table 7–1 to better understand what each of these programs does and to evaluate if you need or want them.

Table 7–1. *Descriptions of the Windows Live Essential Programs*

Program	Description
Windows Live Mail	This e-mail program is the successor to Windows XP's Outlook Express. Windows Vista included Windows Mail as the successor to Outlook Express, but it didn't support web-based e-mail accounts like Hotmail. You can also access a Windows Live Mail account through the Windows Live Hotmail web site in just about any browser on any computer. Windows Live Hotmail replaces MSN Hotmail.
	This chapter describes how to set up Windows Live Mail with various types of e-mail accounts. There many other free e-mail program options besides Windows Live Mail, such as Yahoo!, Gmail, and AOL. For end-to-end help with using Windows Live Mail and these other e-mail services, see Chapter 8.

Program	Description
Windows Live Messenger	This instant messaging program replaces MSN Messenger. It allows you to chat with other people in your contacts list who are also currently online. It also allows you connect to social network sites like Facebook, LinkedIn, and MySpace and chat with your friends on those sites. This chapter will show you how to get connected to your social networks and friends.
	There many other free instant message program options besides Windows Live Messenger, such as Yahoo! Messenger, Google Talk, and AOL Instant Messenger. There are also several other programs that allow you to chat from multiple message services at once in one web page, such as Meebo and Trillian. For end-to-end help with using Windows Live Messenger and these other instant messengers, see Chapter 8.
Windows Live Movie Maker	This simple video editing program allows you to combine picture, video, and music files to create your own movies. This chapter will introduce you to Windows Live Movie Maker with a quick exercise of creating your own movie using pictures, video, and music files already on your computer.
Windows Live Photo Gallery	This photo viewer and editor helps you organize, tag, publish, edit, and touch up your photos. This chapter will introduce you to the features. See Chapter 10 for everything you need to know to get started with digital pictures and video.
Windows Live Family Safety	These features enhance the standard Parental Controls already available with Windows 7. These additional features include the ability to monitor and manage your child's permissions online from any computer, without logging onto your kid's PC. It also allows you to apply the same settings to all of the computers in your household at once, as long as Family Safety is installed on each one. Windows Live Family Safety and Parental Controls depends heavily on setting up the appropriate level of user account for each member of the family. See Chapter 12 to learn how set up user accounts with parental controls.
Windows Live Mesh	These features are a new way to think of accessing the files and settings on your computers from anywhere. You can sync the files and settings between your computers, or even with storage in "the cloud" on SkyDrive. You can also connect remotely to your PC from another location
Windows Live Writer	This program allows you to write stuff for your blog and then publish it to your blog on WordPress, Blogger, TypePad, and others.
Bing Bar	This toolbar is a browser add-on that provides a search box plus links to sites and features like news, maps, weather, mail, Facebook, and more. See Chapter 9 to learn more about web searches and browser add-ons.

Program	Description
Outlook Connector Pack	This pack includes Microsoft Outlook Hotmail Connector and Microsoft Outlook Social Connector Provider for Messenger. These two features allow you to manage your Windows Live Mail accounts or access your social networks such as Facebook, LinkedIn, and Windows Live Messenger from within Outlook 2003, 2007, or 2010. See Chapter 8 for information about these features.

Getting Windows Live Essentials

Do you already have Windows Live Essentials? It is easy to find out by checking your Start menu.

To locate Windows Live Essentials programs:

1. Click the **Start** button, click **All Programs**, and then scroll as needed to locate the Windows Live programs and folder.

2. If Windows Live programs are installed, you will find them in two locations; the more popular programs are listed individually, and the other less-frequently used programs are located within the Windows Live folder farther down, as shown in Figure 7–2.

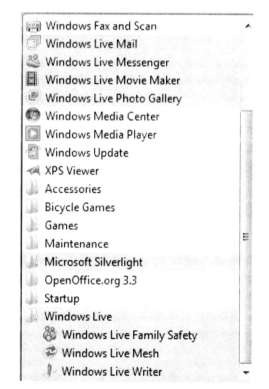

Figure 7–2. *Windows Live programs appear individually and within folders on the Start ➤ All Programs list.*

If you don't see any Windows Live Essentials programs on the Start menu, there are several possible explanations.

- You upgraded or installed Windows using a retail installation disk. Microsoft doesn't include Windows Live Essentials in disks you buy off the shelf or directly from Microsoft.

- Your computer manufacturer chose not to include it.

- You purchased your computer in a country with anti-trust or fair trade commission agreements with Microsoft that restrict the inclusion of Microsoft-branded components like media players, browsers, and instant messaging.

In any case, none of these prohibit you from downloading and installing Windows Live Essentials yourself.

NOTE: Windows Live Essentials will require a computer restart at the end of installation.

To install Windows Live Essentials:

1. Go to the Windows Live Essentials 2011 download site:

   `http://explore.live.com/windows-live-essentials`

   A web page similar to Figure 7–3 is displayed. Scroll through this web page if you want to learn a little more about each feature.

2. Click **Download now**.

Figure 7–3. *Windows Live Essentials download page*

3. When the File Download – Security Warning dialog box appears, as shown in Figure 7–4, click **Run** or **Save**.

   - **Run** downloads the installation files to your computer and starts the installation program as soon as the download completes.

   - **Save** downloads the installation file, usually a compressed folder or cab file, to the location you specify. After downloading

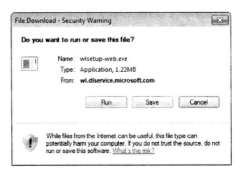

Figure 7–4. *Windows Live Essentials download warning*

the file, go ahead and open the installation file.

4. The User Account Control, shown in Figure 7–5, asks permission to run the Windows Live Essentials installation program. Click **Yes**.

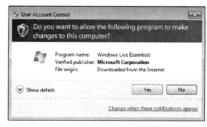

Figure 7–5. *User Account Controls prompt to run the Windows Live Essentials installation*

It will take a few minutes for the installation program to load. The first page, shown in Figure 7–6, lets you install all programs or select which ones to install.

5. Click **Install all of Windows Live Essentials** or **Choose the programs you want to install**.

If you select **Choose the programs you want to install**, the selection options, shown in Figure 7–7, are fairly simple.

Figure 7–6 *Installation options*

> **TIP:** Keep clutter down on your Start menu by only installing programs you think you will need or use. At the very least, install **Messenger**, **Mail**, and **Photo Gallery and Movie Maker**. If no kids can access your computer, you don't need Family Safety. You can run the installation program at a later date if you skip something this time. You can also remove any of these through Programs and Features.

Figure 7–7. *Custom installation options for Windows Live Essentials*

Even with a fast broadband connection, download and installation can take much longer than most other program downloads, so be patient. At the end of installation, you will be prompted to restart your computer.

Windows Live ID

Windows Live ID allows you to sign in once with one ID to access multiple services, including Windows Live Essentials, Hotmail, MSN, Xbox Live, Zune, and more. You may already have an account that you can use for your Windows Live ID. If you have one of the following accounts, you can use the e-mail address and password from that account:

- MSN

- Hotmail

- Messenger

- Xbox Live

- Zune

Typically these accounts are also e-mail accounts, such as yourname@live.com; yourname@msn.com, yourname@hotmail.com, etc. If you don't have any of those accounts, it's easy to get one.

> **NOTE:** Microsoft has renamed Windows Live ID several times over the years. Originally it was named Microsoft Passport, and you may occasionally come across web sites that refer to the Microsoft Passport Network. If you see Microsoft Passport some place, think Microsoft Live ID.

Getting a Windows Live ID

You can get a Windows Live ID by creating a new free live.com or hotmail.com e-mail account. Or, you can also use any e-mail account for your Windows Live ID. For example, yourname@gmail.com, yourname@yahoo.com, yourname@aol.com, etc.

If you want to get a Windows Live ID, the easiest way to get there is when you run Live Essentials Mail or Live Essentials Messenger for the first time. When you are setting up these programs, you will have the option of getting a new Windows Live ID. We will show you how to do this in the next section.

Windows Live Mail

Windows Live Mail is a convenient way to monitor multiple e-mail accounts from many of the popular e-mail services. If you have used Outlook or Outlook Express, you can find your way around Windows Live Mail quite easily because it uses the same *tri-pane window* layout. In the tri-pane view, there are three main areas: the navigation pane on the left, which lists your e-mail accounts and folders; the message list pane on the top right; and the reading pane on the bottom right, which displays the contents of the selected message. Figure 7–8 highlights some of the features of the Windows Live Mail program window.

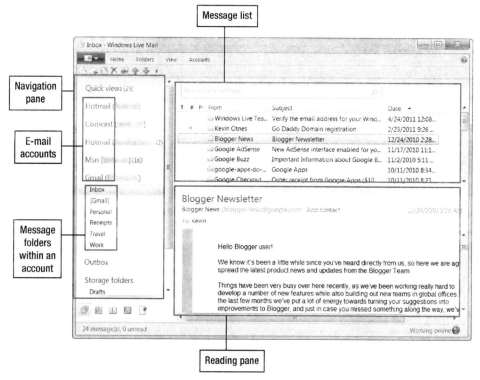

Figure 7–8. *Windows Live Mail window*

TIP: Does your Windows Live Mail window look different than this? See Chapter 8 to learn how to customize the appearance of Windows Live Mail, such as larger toolbar buttons, no message preview, and more. You can also compare other e-mail programs such as Gmail, Yahoo! mail, and Mozilla Thunderbird.

GETTING THE MOST OUT OF E-MAIL

This chapter focuses on getting and setting up Windows Live Essentials programs, like Windows Live Mail. After you have set up Windows Live Mail, see Chapter 9 to get the most out of using e-mail. We will help you avoid common errors that plague new users, and we offer tips and tricks for the experienced user.

Setting Up Windows Live Mail

If you want to get up and running quickly with Windows Live Mail, the easiest way is to use a new or existing Hotmail, Windows Live, or MSN e-mail account. Windows Live Mail can also be used to access many other types of e-mail accounts, including Gmail, AIM, and Yahoo! Plus Mail.

When you add accounts to Windows Live Mail, those settings are for the current user account on the computer. If you want to use Windows Live Mail on your work and home computers, you will need to set up the e-mail accounts on each computer.

> **NOTE:** Typically actual work e-mail accounts use Microsoft Outlook to access mail on company Exchange e-mail servers. Windows Live Mail is not designed to work with Exchange servers.

In the next few pages, we will show several ways to add an e-mail account to Windows Live Mail.

- The "Adding the First E-Mail Account to Windows Live Mail" section describes how to add an existing or newly created Hotmail/Windows Live e-mail account.

- The "Adding an E-Mail Account that Requires Special Server Settings or Configuration" section describes how to add e-mail accounts like Gmail or AIM e-mail.

- The "Adding More E-Mail Accounts to Windows Live Mail" section describes how to add more e-mail accounts or delete accounts.

Adding the First E-Mail Account to Windows Live Mail

In this example, we will show you how to add a Hotmail-type account using either an existing account or by creating a new Windows Live e-mail address.

To add the first e-mail account to Windows Live Mail:

1. Click the **Start** button, click **All Programs**, and then click **Windows Live Mail,** as shown in Figure 7–9.

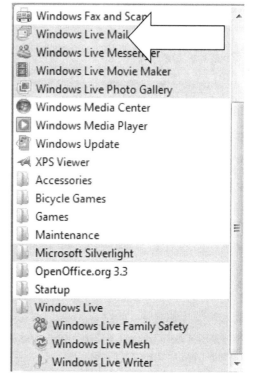

Figure 7–9. *The Windows Live Mail appears individually on the Start ➤ All Programs list*

The first time you open Windows Live Mail after installation, you will be prompted to add your e-mail accounts, as shown in Figure 7–10.

2. To use an existing Windows Live ID account, type the **E-mail address** and **Password** used to access the account, and the **Display name** others will see in the "From" section of the message heading when they receive your e-mail. Then click **Next**, and go to step 6.

To create a new Windows Live ID account, click **Get a Windows Live e-mail address**, and then go to step 3.

3. On the Create your Windows Live ID web page, complete the required information and then click **I accept**.

> **TIP:** See Chapter 9 for tips on creating strong passwords and how to reset and retrieve lost passwords.

Figure 7–10. *You can add an existing e-mail address or create a new Windows Live e-mail address*

Figure 7–11. *Complete the required information to set up the new e-mail address.*

After Windows Live finishes creating your e-mail account, a web page displays information about your account and activities, as shown in Figure 7–12.

4. Close the Hotmail web page, and go back to the **Add your e-mail accounts** window shown previously in Figure 7–10.

Figure 7–12. *When Windows Live is done creating your new account, it takes you to a Hotmail home page listing your activities and e-mail messages status.*

5. Complete the **E-mail address**, **Password**, and **Display name** entries, and then click **Next**.

Windows Live Mail will prompt you whether you want to sign in with this account to Windows Live services, as shown in Figure 7–13. This just makes it easier for you to access other Windows Live services without logging in to each one as you access it.

Figure 7–13. *You can sign in to all Windows Live services with your new e-mail address.*

6. Click **Yes**.

Windows Live Mail starts up, as shown in Figure 7–14.

Windows Live Mail confirms that the new account was added, as shown in Figure 7–15.

If you have more than one e-mail account, Windows Live Mail makes it easy to add more accounts.

Figure 7–14. *Windows Live Mail startup screen*

7. Click **Finish** if you are done adding accounts, or click **Add another e-mail account**.

Figure 7–15. *The confirmation page shows that the e-mail account was added. You can click Finish or add another account.*

TIP Got a bewildering Windows 7 question? Has your computer got you confounded? E-mail me at YourMotherDoesWindows@live.com or visit my blog for tips and articles at www.YourMotherDoesWindows.com. As time allows, I will post questions and answers because others may have the same problems.

Adding E-Mail Accounts that Require Special Server Settings or Configuration

Adding e-mail accounts from Microsoft e-mail services like Hotmail, MSN, or Live.com is relatively easy because Windows Live Mail knows the server settings and configuration to use. After all, they are all Microsoft programs and services. You can also add e-mail accounts from other services; you'll just need to get their server settings.

Mail Protocol Alphabet Soup

There are several different *protocols* that e-mail clients and servers use to send and receive e-mail across the Internet. They use these acronyms like IMAP, POP3, and SMTP. Most of the time, you don't need to care or mess with what these protocols are or do. But sometimes, in order to set up Windows Live Mail (or other e-mail clients) you need to know the e-mail server names and ports used by a particular e-mail server. Fortunately most e-mail services provide that information so that you can set up e-mail client programs like Windows Live Mail. For example, Google's Gmail accounts use IMAP. AOL's AIM mail uses POP3. We will take a look at adding both of these accounts because they are representative of the kinds of server settings you may have to do for non-Microsoft e-mail services.

Adding a Gmail Account

To add a Gmail (IMAP) account to Windows Live Mail:

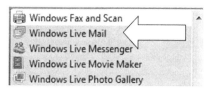

Figure 7–16. *The Windows Live Mail appears individually on the Start ➤ All Programs list.*

1. Click the **Start** button, click **All Programs**, and then click **Windows Live Mail**, as shown in Figure 7–16.

2. If you already have at least one account in Windows Live Mail, click **Accounts** in the toolbar and then click **E-mail** as shown in Figure 7–17. The Add your e-mail account page, shown in Figure 7–18, appears.

Figure 7–17. *Add e-mail accounts through the Accounts tab.*

If this is the first time you have used Windows Live Mail after installation, it automatically starts in the Add your e-mail account page shown in Figure 7–18.

3. Type your Gmail address in the **E-mail address** box.

As soon as you complete typing "…@gmail.com" Windows Live Mail displays a message that you must enable IMAP for this account, as shown in Figure 7–19.

4. Click **Gmail Help** for instructions on how to enable IMAP. Don't close the Windows Live Mail window; you will come back to it later.

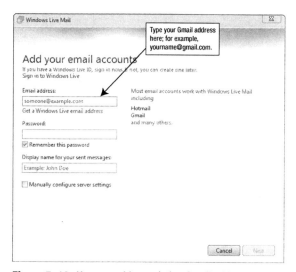

Figure 7–18. *You can add an existing Gmail address.*

If you previously set up
Windows Live Mail on another
computer to access this
particular Gmail account, then
IMAP should already be
enabled for this account and
you can skip ahead to step 6.

Figure 7–19. *Even though adding a Gmail account is not as automatic as adding a Hotmail account, the Gmail Help is… helpful!*

5. Complete the instructions in
   the Gmail Help and Gmail
   Settings pages shown in
   Figure 7–20 to enable IMAP.

6. Click **Save Changes**
   and return to the
   Windows Live Mail
   Add e-mail accounts
   page.

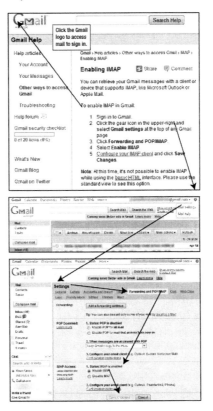

Figure 7–20. *Google's Gmail Help page explains how to enable IMAP through your Gmail account settings so that you can use it in Windows Live Mail.*

7. Type your **Password** and **Display name**, and then click **Next** to finish adding the account, as shown in Figure 7–21.

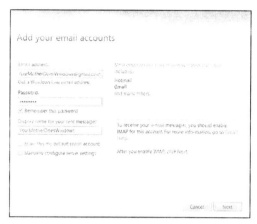

Figure 7–21. *You can complete adding the account when you have enabled IMAP.*

After Windows Live Mail completes the account, a confirmation page shows that the e-mail account was added.

8. Click **Finish** if you are done adding accounts or click **Add another e-mail account**.

Adding an AOL/AIM (POP3) Account

Adding POP3 e-mail accounts like AOL is a little different from Gmail, but it's probably more typical of adding non-Microsoft e-mail accounts. With POP3 accounts, you must find out the e-mail incoming and outgoing server names so that Windows Live Mail knows which servers to contact. You can usually find these settings on the e-mail service provider's web site or in your e-mail account settings.

To add an AOL Mail (POP3) account to Windows Live Mail:

1. Click the **Start** button, click **All Programs**, and then click **Windows Live Mail**, as shown in Figure 7–22.

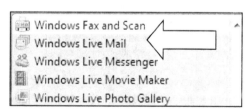

Figure 7–22. *The Windows Live Mail appears individually on the Start ➤ All Programs list.*

2. If you already have at least one account in Windows Live Mail, click **Accounts** in the toolbar and then click **E-mail**, as shown in Figure 7–23. The Add your e-mail accounts page shown in Figure 7–24 appears.

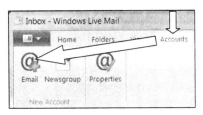

Figure 7–23. Add e-mail accounts through the Accounts tab.

If this is the first time you have used Windows Live Mail after installation, it automatically starts in the Add your e-mail account page shown in Figure 7–24.

3. Type your AOL/AIM **E-mail address**, **Password**, and **Display name**, and then click **Next**. The Configure server settings page is displayed, as shown in Figure 7–25.

Figure 7–24. Enter the e-mail address, password, and display name, and then click Next

Unlike Gmail, when you enter an AOL/AIM e-mail address Windows Live Mail doesn't display a special message. Instead, you must locate and enter AOL's server settings.

Homework time!

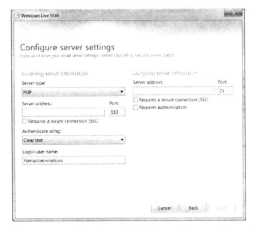

Figure 7–25. Windows Live Mail needs some information about the servers at AOL.

4. Log in to your AOL mail account. In Internet Explorer or your preferred web browser, go to www.aolmail.com and enter your **username** and **password**.

    The AIM Mail window is displayed, as shown in Figure 7–26.

5. Click **Settings**.

    The Settings window is displayed, as shown in Figure 7–27.

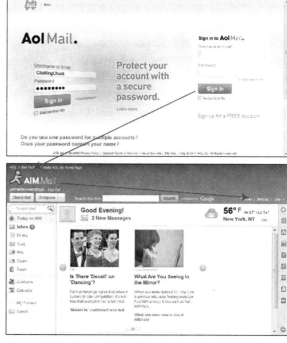

Figure 7–26. *Access AIM Mail*

6. In the left navigation pane, click **IMAP and POP**, and then scroll the page to the **POP Setup Information** section.

7. Arrange the AIM settings and Windows Live Mail Configure server settings windows and copy the settings, as shown in Figure 7–28.

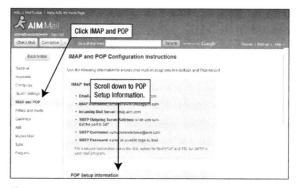

Figure 7–27. *Use the POP Setup Information settings at the bottom of the page.*

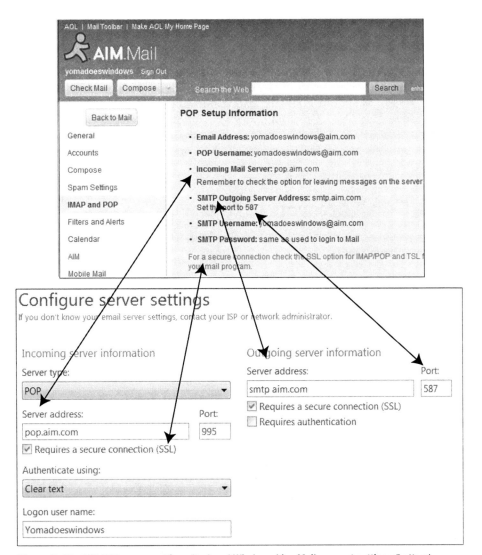

Figure 7–28. *AIM POP server settings (top) and Windows Live Mail account settings (bottom)*

8. Click **Next** to finish adding the account, and then click **Finish** if you are done adding accounts or click **Add another e-mail account**.

Adding a Yahoo! E-mail Account

Yahoo! offers a free, standard web-based e-mail service that, like Hotmail, Gmail, AOL, and other services, can be accessed from just about any e-mail browser. Unfortunately, the free version of Yahoo! Mail does not work with Windows Live Mail. If you want to use Yahoo! Mail in Windows Live Mail, you must upgrade to (in other words pay for) their Yahoo! Plus Mail service, which just enables it to work with POP server accounts. Once you upgrade to Yahoo! Plus Mail, it will work just like AIM Mail and Gmail do within the Windows Live Mail window.

Adding More E-Mail Accounts to Windows Live Mail

You can add more e-mail accounts any time; you don't have to add them all the first time you run Windows Live Mail.

To add another account to Windows Live Mail:

1. Click the **Start** button, click **All Programs**, and then click **Windows Live Mail** as shown in Figure 7–29.

Figure 7–29. *The Windows Live Mail appears individually on the Start ➤ All Programs list.*

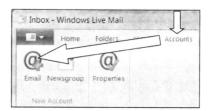

2. Click **Accounts** in the toolbar and then click **E-mail**, as shown in Figure 7–30. The Add your e-mail accounts page appears.

Figure 7–30. *Add e-mail accounts through the Accounts tab*

3. Add the **E-mail address**, **Password**, and **Display name**, and then click **Next**.

4. Enter any other requested information as needed to finish adding the account.

Using Windows Live Mail

Windows Live Mail is great for accessing, organizing, and formatting e-mail. It is really great because the program itself is free, and it works with most popular web-based e-mail services. For personal use, you can't beat free e-mail accounts and a free e-mail program to access them.

Installing Windows Live Mail and adding e-mail accounts is just the start. For some, that is all you needed to know. You are ready to take off and run with your e-mail accounts. But there is much more to using e-mail, regardless of whether you are using MSN Hotmail, Windows Live Mail, Thunderbird, Gmail, AOL, Yahoo!, or e-mail from your cable or high-speed Internet access provider.

To get the most out of using e-mail, see Chapter 8 where you will learn how to do the following:

- Compose and format e-mail messages.

- Use many different types of popular e-mail programs.

- Add, save, and edit e-mail attachments.

- Avoid viruses and deal with junk mail and spam.

- Use good e-mail etiquette.

- Use address books, contacts, and distribution lists.

- Save, import, and export e-mail messages and contacts from one e-mail program to another.

- Use e-mail with mobile devices.

- Miscellaneous tips and tricks that just didn't seem to make it into the documentation that accompanies most e-mail programs.

Windows Live Messenger

Windows Live Messenger is one of many free instant messaging services available. Instant messaging (IM) is a little different from e-mail in that you can communicate in real time with somebody else who is currently online using the same instant messaging network or service. There is no lag time between sending and receiving instant messages as long as you both are online and choose to respond.

To instant message with a friend you both need to:

- **Be online**. You must both be online at the same time. One of the features of any instant messaging program is the ability to see whether somebody is online and available. This is called *status* or *presence*.

- **Be buddies**. You must both have agreed to include each other on your contacts lists or buddy lists. This list can also include contacts from social networks like **Facebook**, **LinkedIn**, and **MySpace**. There are many options for displaying and organizing your contacts list.

- **Belong to a common instant messaging or chat network**. You and the recipient must share a common instant messaging network like Windows Live, AOL Instant Messaging (AIM), or Yahoo! Instant Messaging, or common social network like **Facebook**, **LinkedIn**, and **MySpace**.

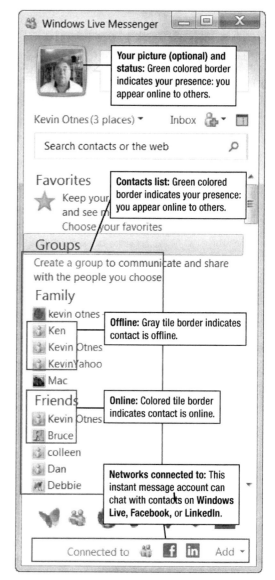

Figure 7–31. *Windows Live Messenger in compact view*

Figure 7–31 shows the compact view of Windows Live Messenger. You might call this the "classic" instant message view. As you set up Windows Live Messenger, you will start off seeing it in the "new" messenger full view shown in Figure 7–32. You can easily switch back and forth between the compact view and full view via a little icon above the search box at the top of the window.

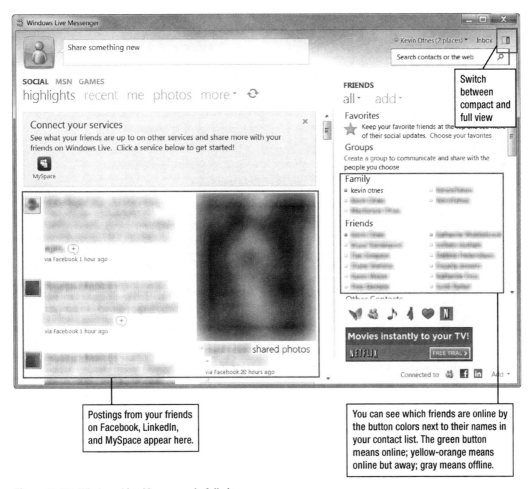

Postings from your friends on Facebook, LinkedIn, and MySpace appear here.

You can see which friends are online by the button colors next to their names in your contact list. The green button means online; yellow-orange means online but away; gray means offline.

Figure 7–32. *Windows Live Messenger in full view*

This web page-like view is similar to social networking sites like Facebook. If you connect your Facebook page to your Windows Live Messenger account, you can see and do almost as much with your Facebook page from within Windows Live Messenger as you can from the Facebook page itself.

Setup

The basic process to set up Windows Live Messenger is:

1. **Select which Windows Live ID to use to log in to Windows Live Messenger on this computer.** The first time you use Windows Live Messenger on a given computer, you may have to complete several one-time steps. You won't need to do these every time you want to use Windows Live Messenger. These are the default settings Windows will use when you open Windows Live Messenger.

2. **Select which social networks you want Windows Live Messenger to connect to with this Windows Live ID.** These preferences stay with this Windows Live ID no matter which Windows 7 computer you use. So if you set up a Windows Live ID for someone@example.com on your computer, and you want to log in to Windows Live Messenger at your workplace computer, your contacts and social network connections through that account will be there. You don't need to specify those every time you use that same account on another computer.

3. **Look for friends to add to your instant messaging contacts list.** These settings also stay with this Windows Live ID whenever you access this account on any computer.

Safety Tips about Installation, Automatic Logins, and Trustworthy Computers

It's fairly easy to install and access your Windows Live Messenger or Mail on somebody else's computer. They may already have the program installed, and all you need to do is log on to your own Windows Live ID or mail account. But be very careful about logging on to personal accounts such as e-mail, instant messaging, bank accounts, or shopping sites as a guest on somebody else's computer or on a public computer.

▪   If you don't trust the computer or the public network you are on, don't use it to access any personal accounts that require a password. Sometimes hackers and criminals install key logger programs that record keystrokes. These can record your username and password.

▪   When you install or log on to a program, make sure you do not select any settings like "Remember me on this computer." Otherwise, the next person who opens that program on that computer may be automatically signed in through your account.

▨   Make sure you log off any e-mail, IM, social network site, or any other accounts you logged onto. Otherwise, if you leave the computer while still logged on, somebody else may be able to access the site or service as you.

Selecting Which Windows Live ID to Use with Windows Live Messenger

To select which Windows Live ID to use with Windows Live Messenger on this computer:

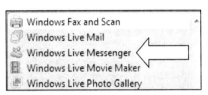

Figure 7–33. *The Windows Live Messenger link appears individually on the Start ➤ All Programs list.*

1. Click the **Start** button, click **All Programs**, and then click **Windows Live Messenger**, as shown in Figure 7–33.

    The first time you open Windows Live Messenger after installation, you will be prompted to sign in with your Windows Live ID, as shown in Figure 7–34.

    -or-

    If the Welcome back login screen appears, as shown in Figure 7–36, skip ahead to step 4.

2. Use an existing Windows Live ID or create a new one:

    To use an existing Windows Live ID account, type the **e-mail address** and **password** used to access the account. Then click **Next**, and go to step 6.

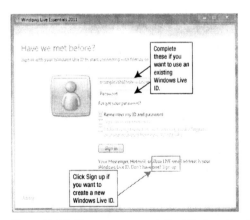

Figure 7–34. *You can use an existing Windows Live ID or create a new one*

NOTE: You can only log into one Windows Live ID account at a time on a given computer in Windows Live Messenger. However, you can log into the Windows Live Messenger with the same Windows Live ID account on different computers or devices at the same time.

To create a new Windows Live ID account, click **Sign up**. When the Create your Windows Live ID page appears, as shown in Figure 7–35, go to step 3.

3. Complete the boxes on this page, and then click **Next**. Note:

   • When you create a Windows Live ID, you are associating an e-mail account with that ID. Your e-mail address is like a user name.

   • You don't have to use a Windows Live e-mail address. You can use any e-mail account e-mail address.

   • When you create a password for your Windows Live ID, you are not being asked for the password you use to access that e-mail address. You can assign any password you want when you create your Windows Live ID.

   • If you select **Or get a Windows Live e-mail address**, see the "Adding the

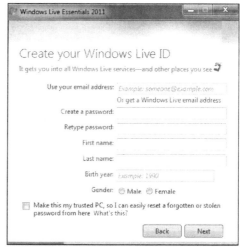

Figure 7–35. *You can associate any e-mail account with a Windows Live ID.*

First E-Mail Account to Windows Live Mail" section earlier in this chapter for help on creating a new Windows Live e-mail account.

4. When the Welcome back page appears (see Figure 7–36), select any options you want, and then sign in.

If you just created this Windows Live ID, you may be prompted to verify the account through the e-mail account you specified, as shown in Figure 7–37. Click OK and complete any additional steps if prompted.

Figure 7–36. *This Windows Messenger sign in page appears when you have a default Windows Live ID set up with your current local user account on this computer.*

Figure 7–37. *If you see this message, open your e-mail.*

5. When your login to Windows Live Messenger is complete the Welcome page is displayed, similar to Figure 7–38.

Figure 7–38. *The Windows Live Messenger Welcome page*

Connecting to Social Networks

To connect to social networks:

1. If you are still on the Welcome page shown in Figure 7–38, click **Social Highlights**.

   If you just opened Windows Live Messenger (but already have the Windows Live ID for this account set up), click **Social highlights**, as shown in Figure 7–39.

Figure 7–39. *Windows Live Messenger default window*

2. If you want to connect to your LinkedIn account, click the **LinkedIn** icon. You can select what you want to share between Windows Live Messenger and LinkedIn, as shown in Figure 7–40.

3. Adjust the settings as needed, and then click **Connect with LinkedIn**.

Figure 7–40. *Sharing options for Linked in and Windows Live Messenger connections*

   You need to give Windows Live Messenger permission to access your LinkedIn account, as shown in Figure 7–41.

4. Enter the **E-mail** and **Password** you use to access LinkedIn.

Figure 7–41. *LinkedIn login information is required in order to allow Windows Live Messenger to access your LinkedIn account.*

Once the login and password are accepted by LinkedIn, you will get the confirmation message shown in Figure 7–42.

Figure 7–42 *Successful LinkedIn connection*

5. If you want to connect to your Facebook account, click the **Facebook** icon. You can select what you want to share between Windows Live Messenger and Facebook, as shown in Figure 7–43.

6. Adjust the settings as needed, and then click **Connect with Facebook**.

Figure 7–43. *Sharing options for Facebook and Windows Live Messenger connections*

You need to give Windows Live Messenger permission to access your Facebook account as shown in Figure 7–44.

7. Enter the **E-mail** and **Password** you use to access Facebook.

8. Once the login and password are accepted by Facebook, you will get the confirmation message shown in Figure 7–45.

Figure 7–44. *Facebook login information is required in order to allow Windows Live Messenger to access your Facebook account.*

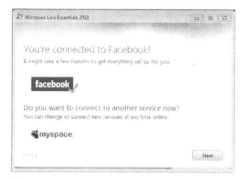

Figure 7–45. *Successful Facebook connection*

9. If you want to connect to your MySpace account, click the **MySpace** icon. You can select what you want to share between Windows Live Messenger and MySpace, as shown in Figure 7–46.

10. Adjust the settings as needed, and then click **Connect with MySpace**.

Figure 7–46. *Sharing options for MySpace and Windows Live Messenger connections*

You need to give Windows Live Messenger permission to access your MySpace account, as shown in Figure 7–47.

11. Enter the **E-mail** and **Password** you use to access MySpace.

12. Once the login and password are accepted by MySpace, you will get the confirmation message shown in Figure 7–48.

Figure 7–47. *MySpace login information is required in order to allow Windows Live Messenger to access your MySpace account*

Figure 7–48. *Successful MySpace connection*

Adding People by Name, E-Mail Address, or from Other Services

You can also add people who are not on your social network friends list by sending them an invitation. They can accept the invitation, and their name will appear on your instant messaging contacts list. Or they can turn down your invitation. If they turn down your invitation, you will not receive any message back from the instant messaging service. You just won't see their name ever appearing in your contacts list.

> **CAUTION:** Instant Messaging has its own variation of spamming. If you receive an invitation or request from somebody you don't know, these are often solicitations for adult web sites. If you don't recognize the e-mail address or name of the person requesting to add you to their buddy list, it's safer to turn down the request. See Chapter 8 for more information about using instant messaging safely.

To add people by name, e-mail address, or from other services:

1. Click the **add** link or icon at the top of the Windows Live Messenger window, and then click **Add people from other services**. Figures 7–49 and 7–50 show where to find this in the compact and full views.

    A Window Live web page is displayed, as shown in Figure 7–51.

Figure 7–49. *Click the messenger icon with the plus symbol at the top of the contacts list when in compact view.*

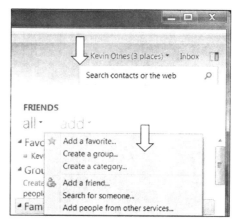

Figure 7–50. *Click the add link at the top of the contacts list in full view.*

2. Locate the person you want to add.

    Depending on which method you use on this page, one or more pages may guide you through entering or selecting an e-mail address for the invitation. To access names from any of the services, you will need to provide a user name and password to log in to that account.

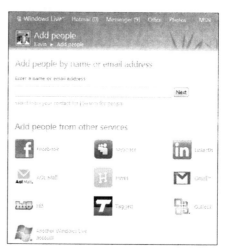

Figure 7–51. *Windows Live Add people page*

3. The **Search for people** link is the least direct method of finding an e-mail address. It uses Windows Live Search to search the info or profile of anybody on Windows Live; search files and documents on your computer; or perform a Web search. Once you have selected a specific name or e-mail address, Windows Live will confirm that you want to send this invitation, as shown in Figure 7–52. Click **Invite**.

Figure 7–52. *Windows Live Messenger prompts you to confirm that you want to send this invitation.*

The person you send the invitation to may receive a notification from within Windows Live Messenger or an e-mail message (as shown in Figure 7–53) asking them to accept your invitation.

If they decline, you will not receive any notification that they declined.

Figure 7–53. *Windows Live Messenger notification and e-mail invite that invitee receives.*

Using Other Instant Messaging Programs

Windows Live Messenger is not the only instant messaging program in town. Yahoo!, Google, and AOL all offer their own instant messaging services and programs. Each one has their advantages and disadvantages. This introduction to Windows Live Messenger will get you started. But there is much more you can do with all of these instant messaging programs. Chapter 8 gets down to the basics of all of them, from emoticons to ROTFL and simple chat windows to voice and video.

Windows Live Movie Maker

With Windows Live Movie Maker you can create your own movies—from simple to sophisticated. Even though this program is free, it's rich with features that can make your home movies really snappy; see Figure 7–54. It's beyond the scope of this book to make you an expert movie maker, but we can take you on a quick tour of some of the features using sample videos, photos, and music already on your computer.

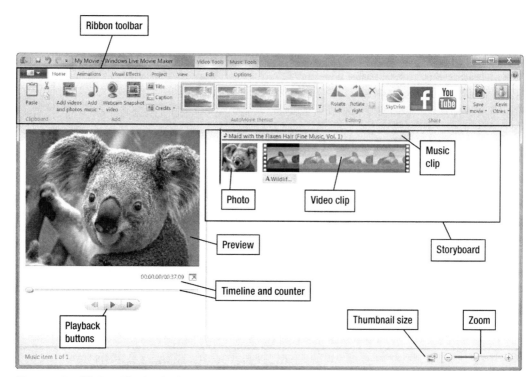

Figure 7–54. *Windows Live Movie Maker sample project with a photo, video, and music soundtrack*

To make a simple movie:

1. Click the **Start** button, click **All Programs**, and then click **Windows Live Movie Maker**, as shown in Figure 7–55.

The Windows Live Movie Maker window appears, similar to Figure 7–54, except it has no content yet.

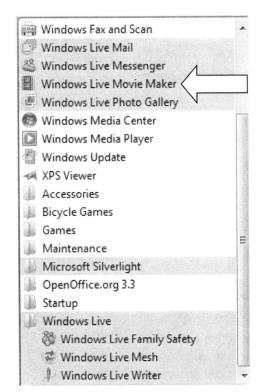

Figure 7–55. *The Windows Live Movie Maker program appears individually on the Start ➤ All Programs list.*

2. Click **Add videos and photos** in the ribbon, as shown in Figure 7–56.

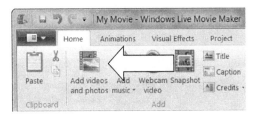

Figure 7–56. *Click the Add videos and photos button on the ribbon.*

3. Navigate to the **Libraries
    ➤ Videos ➤ Sample
    Videos** folder as shown
    in Figure 7–57, and select
    Wildlife.wmv.

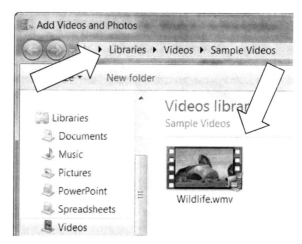

Figure 7–57. *Sample video*

4. Click **Add videos and
    photos** in the ribbon.

5. Navigate to the **Libraries
    ➤ Pictures ➤ Sample
    Pictures** folder as shown
    in Figure 7–58, and select
    Koala.jpg.

Figure 7–58. *Sample photo*

6. Click the **Add music** button in the ribbon, and then click **Add music** in the submenu, as shown in Figure 7–59.

Figure 7–59. *The Add music button on the ribbon*

7. Navigate to the **Libraries > Music > Sample Music** folder as shown in Figure 7–60, and select **Maid with the Flaxen Hair.mp3**.

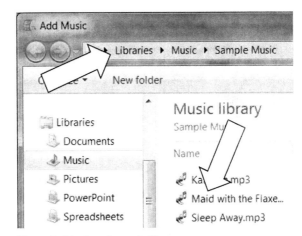

Figure 7–60. *Sample music file*

8. Save the file. Your movie project should look similar to Figure 7–61. You can use this practice file for experimenting with text, editing, and effects features.

9. Hover over the different **AutoMovie themes** buttons in the ribbon. These are quick way to add some pizzazz to your videos.

Figure 7–61. *Windows Live Movie Maker sample project with a photo, video, and music soundtrack*

10. Click the **Play** button to see and hear the movie you've just created.

With this quick tour you used sample files already on your computer to:

- Add videos

- Add pictures

- Add music

- Create a movie quickly with AutoMovie themes

With just those simple steps, you can easily do the same with your own videos, pictures, and music. You can also add your videos and photos through Windows Live Photo Gallery.

For more fun experimenting with your sample project, check out some of these other features. Most of these features offer a preview, like you did with AutoMovie themes, by hovering over each effect.

- On the Animations tab, check out the Transitions and Pan and zoom.

- On the Visual Effects tab, check out 25 different effects.

- On the Format tab, check out the different text effects.

If there are parts of your home videos that you would like to trim down, the **Video Tools** tab allows you to cut, split, and trim segments of your video.

When you are ready to share your video, you can publish directly to your favorite sites like Facebook, YouTube, Flickr, and more. To learn more about publishing and sharing your videos, see Chapter 10.

TIP: Before you go crazy with special effects, check YouTube and similar websites to get a sense of what is too much. Viewer comments on videos similar to yours may tell you what viewers like or tolerate.

Windows Live Photo Gallery

At first glance, Windows Live Photo Gallery resembles the Pictures Library: a folder navigation tree on the left and pictures grouped by date in main window. But it's much more. Windows Live Photo Gallery is a full-fledged photo organizing and editing program. Even if you don't think you take very many pictures, it only takes a few years of digital pictures from holidays, birthdays, and vacations to add up to thousands of pictures. There are quite a few tools here to help you organize and find your pictures. Have you ever gone through a box of old photos and turned over a picture to see the date it was taken and who was in the picture? How do you do that with a picture on your computer? With Windows Live Photo Gallery, you can add visible captions and digital tags to help you identify and sort pictures, as shown in Figure 7–62.

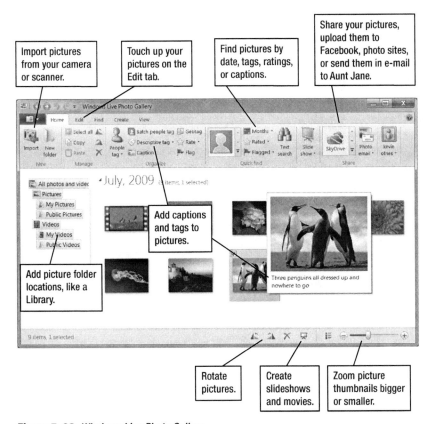

Figure 7–62. *Windows Live Photo Gallery*

This is just a brief introduction to the Windows Live Photo Gallery. See Chapter 10 for more about how to manage your pictures and videos from the time you snap the picture to when it finally ends up on your computer screen, on your favorite picture sharing site, or in e-mail to a friend.

Windows Live Writer

Ideally, when you are writing a blog, you don't want to spend a lot of time formatting, editing, and laying out your articles. So anything that helps you focus on the content is a real help. Windows Live Writer provides a small editing program that makes writing your blog entry as easy as writing an e-mail message. It works with most major blog services, such as WordPress, SharePoint, Windows Live Spaces, Blogger, TypePad, and more. It allows you to draft, preview, and publish your blog article.

Setting up Windows Live Writer

To set up Windows Live Writer for authoring your blog:

1. Click the **Start** button, click **All Programs**, click the Windows Live folder, and then click **Windows Live Writer,** as shown in Figure 7–63.

   Unlike most other Windows Live programs, Windows Live Writer doesn't have its program icon at the top level on the All Programs list. You must scroll down further to the folders and open the Windows Live folder.

Figure 7–63. *Accessing Windows Live Writer for writing your blog*

A series of wizard pages guide you through connecting up to your blog, as shown in Figure 7–64.

2. Follow the instructions in the wizard.

Figure 7–64. *Windows Live Writer setup*

When you have completed the wizard, Windows Live Writer opens, displaying the blank page shown in Figure 7–65.

Write your blog article. When you are done, click the **Preview** tab at the bottom to see how it will look.

Figure 7–65. *Windows Live Writer new post*

3. When you are satisfied with your article, click the Publish button shown in Figure 7–66.

4. Go to your blog and check that the article is there and displays correctly, as shown in Figure 7–67.

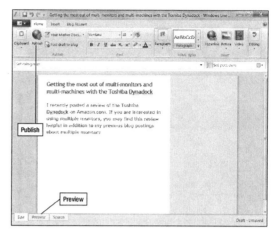

Figure 7–66. *Blog article ready to be previewed and published*

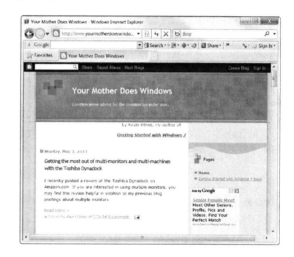

Figure 7–67. *Article successfully published to blog*

You can manage multiple blogs from Windows Live Writer. If you don't have a blog, you can get one for free with some of the major blogging services.

5. To add or create a new blog, click the blog name next to the Publish button shown in Figure 7–68.

Figure 7–68. *Adding a blog to Windows Live Writer*

Summary

In this chapter you learned how to do the following:

- Download and install Windows Live Essentials.

- Get a Windows Live ID.

- Add e-mail accounts to Windows Live Mail, including special configuration for IMAP and POP3 accounts.

- Set up Windows Live Messenger.

- Add social networks like Facebook, LinkedIn, and MySpace to your Windows Live Messenger connections.

- Add people to your contacts in Windows Live Messenger.

- Use Windows Movie Maker to create a simple movie with pictures, video, and music already on your computer.

- Access Windows Live Photo Gallery and explore features.

- Author blog content with Windows Live Writer.

Next Steps

Since some of the sections in this chapter were introductions to Windows Live Essentials features, you will find the following chapters useful:

- Chapter 8 to learn more about e-mail and instant messaging, including other programs from Yahoo!, AOL, and Google.

- Chapter 10 to learn more about importing, editing, organizing, and sharing your pictures and videos with Windows Live Photo Gallery, Windows Movie Maker, and other programs.

- Chapter 12 to learn more about setting up parental controls and using Windows Live Family Safety.

Communicating with E-mail, IM, and Social Networks

This chapter is about keeping in touch and connecting with friends, family, colleagues, and services. It is about using programs and the Internet to share your thoughts, interests, and other things about your life. It is about using your computer to do things you used to do, or never could do, with the telephone and postal (snail) mail. It really is amazing how far we've come from smoke signals, messengers running on foot or on horseback in relays to cover vast distances, or even messages in bottle tossed in the sea. Now we can talk to and see each other instantly, across the world. The world is the same size, yet with these richer, more direct, and quicker forms of communication it seems smaller and more accessible. E-mail has been around much longer than instant messaging and is still the backbone of one-to-one electronic communication in business, large organizations, government, and educational institutions. Social networks are relatively new and build upon a foundation of web sites and both e-mail and instant messaging. This chapter will build upon these communication methods in the same order, telling you about using:

- **E-mail** programs to send and receive messages on your own schedule. You don't have to be on the Internet with somebody at the same time as they are in order to communicate with them.

- **Instant Messaging (IM)** or **Chat** programs to instantly send and receive messages, with one or many friends when both of you are online at the same time.

- **Social Networks** to share your thoughts, pictures, or whatever you want with a few or many friends, or the world.

Using E-mail

E-mail has been around longer than Windows, the Mac, or any other graphical personal computer system. At one time, using e-mail meant you had to learn how to type in a bunch of archaic commands and was limited to composing, sending, and viewing just text, one message at a time.

Today, with most any e-mail provider, you can connect to your e-mail account without installing and using a separate e-mail program. You can access your e-mail account from popular e-mail providers like Windows Live Mail, Gmail, Yahoo! Mail, and AOL using a web browser any place you can access the Internet. You don't even need a computer to use your e-mail—most e-mail providers work with other devices: cellphones like iPhones, Blackberries, and smartphones; and tablets like iPads and Android devices.

E-mail Features

There are many e-mail programs and services available, with a wide variety of features, appearances, and services. Table 8–1 describes common features and how they are used. After that, we will also show you what some of these look like in examples of several popular e-mail programs.

Table 8–1. *E-Mail Program Features*

Feature	What It Does
Address book, contacts, buddy list	This is a list of names, e-mail addresses, phone numbers, mailing addresses, personal web pages or any other type of information about people or organizations you are in contact with. While the main purpose of an address book is to store e-mail addresses of people you exchange e-mail with, you can also store names of people without e-mail addresses. So, you can also use it for storing phone numbers (though you probably store those on your cellphone), or holiday card lists.
	Many e-mail accounts are also used as instant messaging accounts, so your address book may also include your instant message contacts.
	Your e-mail account address book should be available wherever you have access to your e-mail account. So whether you log in to your e-mail account at the library, at work, or at home, you can access your address book.

Feature	What It Does
Advertising	In order to provide free e-mail, popular e-mail services like Gmail, Windows Live Mail, Yahoo! Mail, AOL Mail, display small ads when you access their mail services through a web browser. If you don't like these ads, most e-mail accounts can be added to an e-mail client program like Windows Live Mail or Mozilla Thunderbird. We'll show you some examples in the next section.
Calendar	Most e-mail accounts include an online calendar. Because it is your personal calendar connected to your e-mail account, you can use it to store your appointments, birthdays, holidays, and any other special events. When you enter information on your calendar, you can set reminders, so that you get an e-mail message ahead of time. Your calendar, like your e-mail address book, follows your e-mail account wherever you log in to your account.
E-mail account, address, and password	Your e-mail account is the home for your e-mail address. Your e-mail address is made up of two parts—your e-mail name and your e-mail provider's Internet domain. For example, in the e-mail address Yourname@example.com, *"Yourname"* is your e-mail name at the Internet domain *"example.com."* Your e-mail address is a unique identifier –nobody else can have the same e-mail address with the same provider. When you sign up for an e-mail account, you are asked to provide an e-mail name that becomes part of your e-mail address. Before you are assigned that e-mail name, your e-mail provider will make sure nobody else has already used it. If the name is already taken, the sign up program will prompt you to choose another name and may suggest similar e-mail names that are still available.
	When you create an e-mail account, you will also have to create a password. Don't share your e-mail password with anybody. Since there are so many free e-mail providers, there is no reason for anybody to have to share an e-mail address.

> **CAUTION:** Many web sites require that you create an account using your e-mail address as your user name. When the web site asks you to create a password **it is not asking you for the password you use to access your e-mail**. It uses your e-mail address for your user name because it will be easy for you to remember, and provides them with a way to contact you (if that is okay with you).

Feature	What It Does
E-mail client	Your e-mail client is the program you use to view and use your e-mail. Some e-mail clients are standalone installed programs, like Windows Live Mail or Mozilla Thunderbird, that allow you to view and manager multiple e-mail accounts from different providers. Some e-mail accounts can also be viewed through a web browser. To access your e-mail, you log on to your e-mail provider's web site through your favorite web browser (Internet Explorer, Mozilla Firefox, Google Chrome, Opera, etc.). We'll show you examples of standalone clients and web browser clients in just a bit.
Import/export mail and contacts	Most e-mail account address books can be imported from or exported to other e-mail accounts. So if you have a Windows Live e-mail account, you can export it to another e-mail account, like Yahoo! Mail, Gmail, etc.
	You can also share most mail address books with your social network account. For example, when you create a Facebook account, one of the quickest ways to start your friends list is to let Facebook access your e-mail address book to see if any your stored e-mail addresses match e-mail addresses of people already on Facebook. Then Facebook can suggest them as people you can invite to be friends. Or, Facebook can create invitations to anybody with an e-mail address even though they aren't currently on Facebook. Allowing a social network to access your e-mail address book is completely optional—you have full control and can decline.
Junk mail or spam blocking	This may be one of the most important factors in deciding which e-mail provider to get your e-mail account from. Some providers do a better job than others in detecting and screening out potential junk mail. Junk mail filters examine mail sent to your account for clues that it might be junk mail. Most mild junk mail is automatically directed to a special e-mail folder, usually called your **Junk** or **Spam** folder.

> **TIP:** It is a good idea to check your Junk folder regularly to make sure legitimate e-mail didn't accidently get labeled and sorted to junk mail. Most e-mail providers automatically delete messages from your junk folder after a few days.

You can usually adjust how strongly your incoming e-mail is sorted to the Junk folder. If you are getting too much junk e-mail in your Inbox, you should user stronger settings. If you are having to pull a lot of legitimate mail out of your Junk folder, you may want to use

Feature	What It Does
	weaker settings. Or, you can add a particular e-mail address to your safe senders/do not block list. When you sign up for a mailing list, the sender may suggest that you add their e-mail address to your safe senders list so that you receive their mail.
Mail folders	Most e-mail accounts start with a fairly common list of folders:

Inbox is where your incoming mail goes to, unless you have a filtering rule that sends some e-mail to a different folder in your account.

Drafts is where unfinished messages are stored. If you start composing an e-mail message and then quit your e-mail program before sending it, it may be saved in the Drafts folder.

> **NOTE**: With some web-based e-mail, if you navigate away from or close the page where you were composing the message, you may lose the message. Some e-mail services may warn you that you will lose your message if you navigate away.

Sent is where you can automatically save copies of the e-mail messages you have sent. You can usually turn this off in your e-mail program's settings. If you send a lot of e-mail messages, or frequently send large file attachments, this folder can get quite large quite quickly. If you want to save copies of some sent messages but not all of them all of the time, you could make it a habit of regularly cleaning out your Sent folder and moving the messages you still want to keep to another folder you create for saving or archiving messages. Or, you can turn off the setting to save copies of sent mail, and just add your own e-mail address to the To, CC, or BCC lines of messages that you want to save.

Deleted items/Trash is where your e-mail messages go when you delete them from your message list. Check your e-mail program's settings for this folder. You can usually specify to either leave items in there until you select a command to empty it, or else set your e-mail to automatically empty it when you exit the program or after a set number of days.

Creating Your Own Folders is not a folder name, but the capability to add and name new folders. You can create additional folders to help you sort and store your e-mail so that you don't have everything in one humongous Inbox folder.

Feature	What It Does

> **NOTE:** For those who use mobile devices, smartphones and tablets to access e-mail accounts, these devices may not be able to display custom folders you have created, just your Inbox. If you do regularly sync your mobile device to your e-mail, check to see how extra folders are handled so that you are not unpleasantly surprised later when you can't access an important message from your smartphone because it is not in your Inbox.

Feature	What It Does
Message list	The message list allows you to find out a little bit about the message without opening it up. Each row will display information like the sender, the subject, and date sent, and you can use those headings to sort the list. By default, they are sorted by date, with the most recent messages listed at the top. But in most e-mail programs you can also sort the list alphabetically by sender, subject, or other headings. The message row may also display a paperclip icon to indicate that there is a file attached. The message list also tells you what messages are new and unread. If the row is bold, the message is new and unread. Some programs also display an envelope icon that indicates read (open envelope) or unread (closed envelope). The e-mail program may also include check boxes next to each message so that you can select multiple messages to move, delete, or forward. Depending on what e-mail program you are using, you open a message by clicking or double-clicking it in the message list.
Message viewing pane	The message viewing pane displays the content of the selected message. Some e-mail programs provide the option to display the message list and message body in separate panes, and some programs only display either the list or the body but not both at the same time.
Mobile access	Many e-mail accounts can be set up so that you can access your mail from other devices such as an iTouch, iPhone, Smartphone, iPad or tablet. It is beyond the scope of this book to explain how to set these up because each device, e-mail program, and cellular carrier varies. But if you do want to access your e-mail account from other devices, it may make a difference which e-mail account you use and how you manage your e-mail messages.

Feature	What It Does
Navigation pane	In most e-mail programs, the navigation pane along the left side of the window serves as folder tree for your e-mail account, but may also provide links to other services and features such as: ■ Multiple e-mail account folders ■ Calendar ■ Contacts ■ Instant Messaging
New mail	Most e-mail programs, when you are online, are constantly checking for new mail. When new mail arrives, your e-mail program many notify you in any of these ways: ■ A ding sound (there is a default Windows sound assigned to new mail notifications). ■ A mail envelope appears in the notification area of your taskbar. ■ In your e-mail mailbox folder list, your Inbox folder is bold with the number of new messages in parentheses.
Rules and filtering	In addition to junk mail and spam filtering of messages by your e-mail provider, you can create your own filtering and rules. These features vary with each e-mail program—some programs may offer all or none of these: ■ Rules to copy, move, or delete an e-mail if it contains a specific word in the body or heading or is from a particular person. ■ Safe lists to always allow messages from a specific sender or domain. ■ Block lists to always block and delete messages from a specific sender or domain.
Signature	Many e-mail programs allow you to save a small block of text and/or a graphic that is automatically inserted at the bottom of your message whenever you compose, forward, or reply to an e-mail message. This is completely optional, but an auto signature can serve many uses: ■ List additional contact information such as phone number, web site, job title, certifications, etc.

Feature	What It Does
	▪ Legal disclaimers about the confidentiality of the message.
	▪ Creativity – just expressing yourself.
	Be considerate of your recipients when using graphics in your auto signature. If they get a lot of e-mail from you, the auto signature may become annoying, make your messages harder to send and receive because of the increased message size, and may not even be visible if they have chosen to receive e-mail messages in plain text.
Stationery	Some e-mail programs allow you to select a stationery background or create your own for your messages. Some of the same caveats about using auto signatures apply to stationery. In addition, the some text colors may not display against some colors of stationery.
Themes	Sometimes called *skins*, themes are a way to customize the color and appearance of your e-mail program window. These options vary with each program, but may include selecting a color or background picture for the program window or top banner.

Windows Live Mail

Windows Live Mail provides an e-mail client and e-mail accounts. You don't need a Windows Live, Hotmail, or MSN mail account to view e-mail within the Windows Live Mail client. You can also set up Windows Live Mail to view e-mail from Gmail, AOL, and many other accounts, as well as multiple accounts from the same provider.

Chapter 7: "Getting Free Goodies like Windows Live Essentials" describes how to get a Windows Live ID account and how to add e-mail accounts to the Windows Live Mail client.

Windows Live Mail uses a *tri-pane window* layout. In the tri-pane view shown in Figure 8–1, there are three main areas: the navigation pane on the left, which lists your e-mail accounts and folders; the message list pane on the top right; the reading pane on the bottom right, which displays the contents of the selected message.

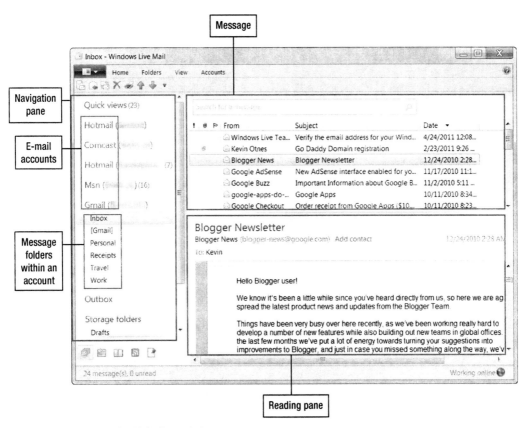

Figure 8–1. *Windows Live Mail client window*

You can also view your Windows Live Mail account in a similar layout within a browser window. With web-based e-mail, you don't need to download and install an e-mail client, you can just go the provider's mail web site. In this browser window version, you can only view one account at a time.

Whether you are using the Windows Live Mail client or browsing your e-mail within a web browser, you have the option of displaying the reading pane on the right, as shown in Figure 8–2, or not at all, as shown in Figure 8–3.

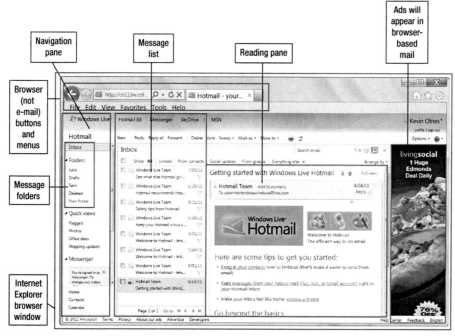

Figure 8–2 *Windows Live Mail in an Internet Explorer 9 browser window, with reading pane on the right*

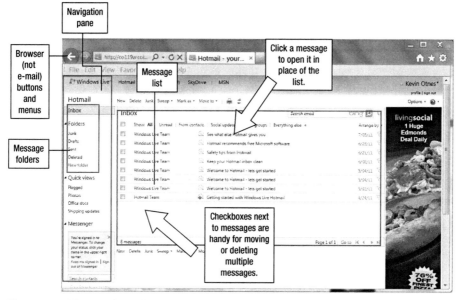

Figure 8–3. *Windows Live Mail in an Internet Explorer 9 browser window, with no reading pane*

Viewing, Sending, and Organizing E-mail

While not everybody will use Windows Live Mail, it is fairly typical of what most e-mail programs provide and how they work. Since it is free, and many computers may already have it installed, it provides a great learning tool. If you do not have Windows Live Essentials, visit the previous chapter, Chapter 7: "Getting Free Goodies like Windows Live Essentials" to set it up.

Checking Your E-mail

One of the first things most of us want to do after we start our computer is check our e-mail. Most e-mail programs highlight unread mail with bold.

> **TIP:** Though sometimes people call unread mail "new" mail, it is not always new. If you have not checked your e-mail for a week, messages that are seven days old are obviously not new, but they are unread. But if you are checking your mail hourly or many times a day, your incoming unread messages will indeed be new to you.

To view your messages

1. Open Windows Live Mail.

2. The Windows Live Mail window is displayed, as shown in Figure 8–4.

   Unread messages are highlighted in bold. In this example, messages are sorted by Date (Conversation), so the Conversation as well as the message are highlighted in bold.

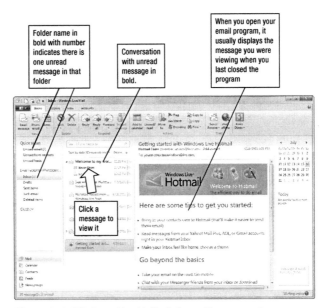

Folder name in bold with number indicates there is one unread message in that folder

Conversation with unread message in bold.

When you open your email program, it usually displays the message you were viewing when you last closed the program

Click a message to view it

Figure 8–4. Windows Live Mail window with an unread message

3. In the message list, click an **unread e-mail message**.

The body of the unread message is displayed in the reading pane, as shown in Figure 8–5. After you open or view the unread message, it is considered read and the bold disappears.

When all unread messages in the folder have been read or deleted, the bold disappears from the folder name too.

After you open or view an unread message, the bold disappears in the message list.

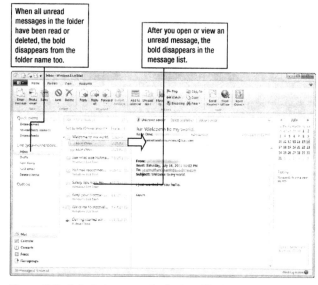

Figure 8–5. *Selected message is displayed in the reading pane*

To view a message in its own window:

In the message list, double-click the message.

A new message window is displayed, as shown in Figure 8–6.

This is a great way to review messages one at a time. With the Previous and Next buttons you can go through your list of messages without returning to the main mail window. This can be especially handy if you have an extremely small screen such as netbook or small laptop.

You can also delete messages as you review them—the message window will stay open and move to the next message in the list.

Delete or respond to messages as you review them.

You can review your messages one at a time and move through your list without having to go back to the mail window.

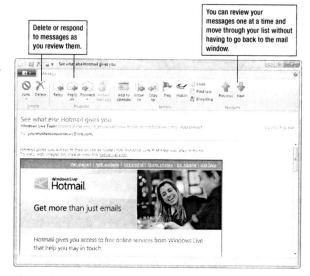

Figure 8–6. *You can review your messages one at a time in a separate window.*

TIP: A *conversation*, also called an *e-mail thread*, is just a group of messages that include an e-mail message and all replies to that message. It is handy for sorting and grouping your messages

You can set Windows Live Mail to automatically check for unread mail whenever you log in to Windows, and at regular intervals after you are logged on, without having to open Windows Live Mail.

CAUTION: If you automatically log in with your Windows Live ID when you start your computer, anybody who has access to your user account on your computer will have access your Windows Live Mail and Windows Live Messenger account. To protect your account and identity, do not share your Windows login or your Windows Live ID login information, and do not allow others to use the PC while you are logged in. See Chapter 12: "Setting Up and Transferring User Accounts" to learn how to set up separate user accounts for each person you want to allow regular access to your computer.

To set Windows Live Mail to automatically check for e-mail:

NOTE: If you are on a dialup phone modem or are charged by minute for Internet connection time, you may not want Windows Live Mail to automatically check for new e-mail.

If you have not set Windows Live Mail to log in when you start Windows, you can set these options in the Windows Live ID login page, as shown in Figure 8–7.

Figure 8–7. *Windows Live ID sign in page*

If you have already signed in and Windows Live Mail is open, or you also want notifications to appear when you have new messages, you can select these settings in the Windows Live Mail options.

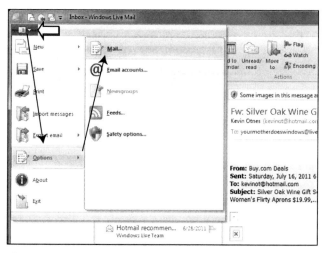

1. In Windows Live Mail, click the **Windows Live Mail** menu, click **Options**, and then click **Mail**, as shown in Figure 8–8.

   The Options window is displayed, as shown in Figure 8–9.

Figure 8–8. *Accessing Windows Live Mail settings*

2. On the **General** tab, make sure the following check boxes are selected:

   ▤ Automatically log on to Windows Live Messenger

   ▤ Play sound when new messages arrive (not required, so turn on or off according to your preferences)

   ▤ Send and receive messages at startup

   ▤ Check for new messages every

3. Click **OK** when you are done.

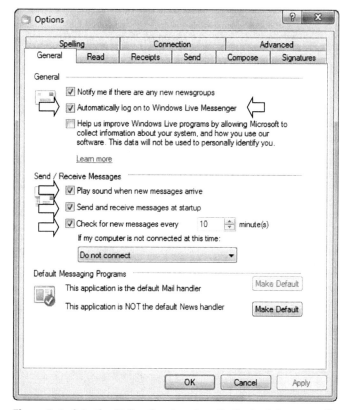

Figure 8–9. *Selecting Mail options to automatically check for new mail*

Once you have selected these settings, any time you log on to your computer and there is new mail, or you are already logged on and new mail arrives, you will see a notification similar to Figure 8–10.

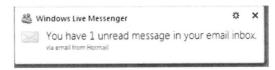

Figure 8–10. *Unread message notification*

You can also turn on Windows Live Mail notifications in the taskbar:

1. Click the **Show hidden icons** button in the notification area, and then click **Customize**, as shown in Figure 8–11.

Figure 8–11. *Customize the notifications*

2. In the Notification Area Icons window, locate Windows Live Mail, and then select **Show icon and notifications**, as shown in Figure 8–12.

3. Click **OK**.

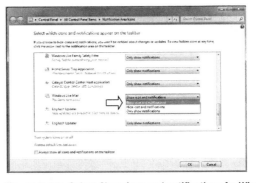

Figure 8–12. *Select Show icon and notifications for Windows Live Mail*

The icon will only be displayed when Windows Live Mail is running. This is handy when you are working in other program windows while

Figure 8–13. *New mail state shows unopened envelope on mail icon*

Windows Live Mail is running but minimized to your taskbar. Figures 8–13 and 8–14 show the icon states when you have new (unread) and read mail.

Figure 8–14. *No unread mail*

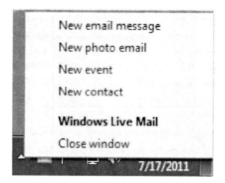

4. You can right-click the notification icon for quick access to several mail features and to open Windows Live Mail, as shown in Figure 8–15.

Figure 8–15. *Right-click the icon for Mail menu*

Sending Messages

There are several ways to create a message within your mail program:

- Compose a new message
- Reply to or forward a message you have received

You may also find commands outside of your mail program to e-mail a file:

- Right-click a file in a Windows explorer or Library window, click **Send to > Mail recipient**, and it will open a new message using your default mail program, and the file you selected will be attached to the message.
- Many programs offer a Send command on the File menu.

To create and send a new e-mail message:

1. Open your mail program, Windows Live Mail.

2. Click **E-mail message**, as shown in Figure 8–16.

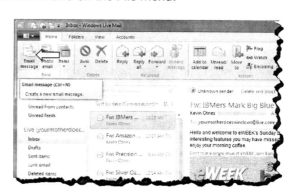

Figure 8–16. *Click E-mail message to create a new message*

A New Message window appears, as shown in Figure 8–17.

3. Type or add the e-mail address for each person to whom you are sending the e-mail. If you want to use a name from your address book, click **To**.

4. Type a short descriptive subject.

5. In the body, write your message. You do all sorts of fun stuff with font formatting, emoticons, and other features in the ribbon.

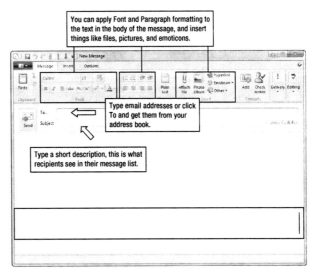

Figure 8–17. New Message window

6. (Optional) Add pictures:

    You can use **Attach file** or insert them in the body of the message with **Photo album** (including captions), as shown in Figure 8–18.

7. When you are done composing the message, click **Send**.

Figure 8–18. E-mail message with picture

USE REPLY ALL SPARINGLY

Unless you are in an e-mail conversation where everybody needs to see everybody else's response, be courteous to others and use **Reply All** sparingly. Many times using **Reply to** with the sender is sufficient, or reply to just of a few of the people who originally received the mail message. Especially in the workplace, it can be annoying to have your Inbox quickly fill up with messages that don't directly involve you or require your input. In some cases, selecting Reply All to a message sent to large distribution list can actually crash the entire e-mail system. An infamous example of this occurred at Microsoft years ago when an employee noticed he was on an e-mail alias (distribution list), and sent an e-mail to the alias asking to be taken off that list. Unfortunately there were 13,000 other people on that list; all of those people received his request to be removed from the list. So a few more people selected Reply All and said "Me too!" It took Microsoft two days to get their internal e-mail back on its feet. Google "Bedlam DL3" to read the full story.

Unfortunately, years after this well-known event, I have seen the same thing happen at other companies. Usually large mailing lists within a company are locked down so that only a few people have privileges to send mail out to the alias. But occasionally somebody forgets to lock down an alias, and a Reply All message gets through to everybody on the list. Then other people start sending Reply All messages to get off of that alias. In a short period of time, several hundred "Me too!" Replies go out to several thousand people and it overloads the e-mail system (and annoys all the people who are getting these replies).

To reply to or forward a message:

1. In Windows Live Mail, select the message you want to respond to, as shown in Figure 8–19.

2. Select one of the following:

   Reply to send a reply to the person who sent you the message. You can add others to the To line or add a CC or BCC line.

   Reply all to send a reply to everybody else who received the same mail. Use this sparingly.

   Forward to send a copy of the message you received, including all attachments to somebody who did not receive the original mail. You can remove attachments before

Figure 8–19. *Select the message in the message list, and then click one of the Respond buttons*

sending.

> **NOTE: Reply** and **Reply all** do not include file attachments from previous message.

A new message window appears, as shown in Figure 8–20.

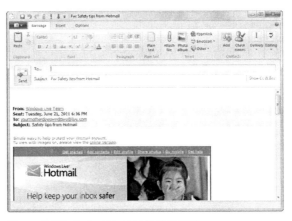

Figure 8–20. *A new message is displayed*

3. Add your comments or reply in the new space that appears at the top of the message, as shown in Figure 8–21.

4. Attach any files you want to send.

5. Click **Send**.

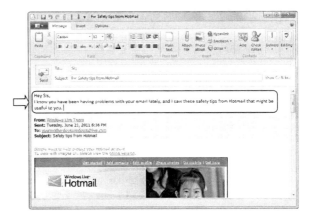

Figure 8–21. *Add your comments*

Saving Mail Attachments

It is not difficult to save mail attachments, but time and time again I hear from friends and family that they were working on a document they had received in e-mail, saved it, and the next time they started the computer they couldn't find it. "But I did save it first. I clicked Save Attachments and it put it in a folder. I saw it."

To save a file attachment:

1. Click the **Windows Live Mail** menu > **Save** > **Save attachments**, as shown in Figure 8–22.

   When you save an attachment using the default folder in the Save dialog box, it usually goes into a Temporary Internet Files Folder.

   For example: "C:\Users\Junior\AppData\Local\Microsoft\Windows\Temporary Internet Files\Content.IE5\L46060AE" as shown in Figure 8–23.

   Do not save to the default location! The folder name Temporary Internet Files is just that—temporary. The contents of that folder are often automatically emptied either because of your Internet Options settings, or by utility programs that regularly empty Temporary Internet Files folders. It also is not an obvious place for you to look for files when you want to open them.

2. Click **Browse**.

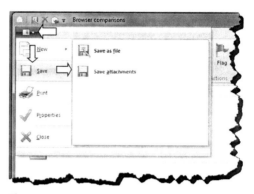

Figure 8–22. *Saving a file attachment*

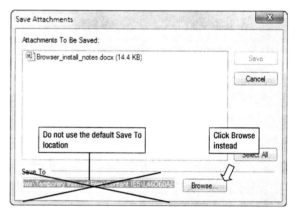

Figure 8–23. *The default save location for file attachments may be a Temporary Internet Files folder*

3. In the **Browse for Folder** dialog box, select a familiar folder like **My Documents** or **Downloads**, as shown in Figure 8–24.

4. Click **OK** to close the Browse for Folder dialog box.

    In the Save Attachments dialog box, the Save To location should look a little friendlier, as shown in Figure 8–25.

5. If everything looks correct, click **Save** to close the Save Attachments dialog box.

    Congratulations! You've saved the attachment to a more permanent location that should be easy to find. If you want to work on the file, open it from the location you saved it to, not from the e-mail message.

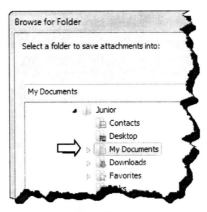

Figure 8–24. *Save attachments to locations that will be easy to find the next time you use your computer.*

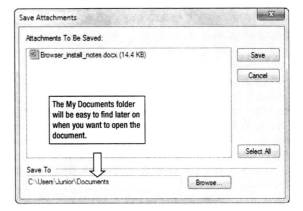

Figure 8–25. *Accessories folder on the Start menu*

Sorting, Organizing, and Customizing

There are many ways to customize and organize your folders, messages, and accounts. In Windows Live Mail, you will find most of the reading, replying, and composing features available on the Home tab. But there are four other tabs that you can explore to change settings, manage folders, change the view of the messages, and manage your e-mail accounts. Table 8–2 highlights those other tabs and points you to some important or interesting things you can do with each. Windows Live Mail uses the Office style ribbon, so the familiar menu names have been replaced with tabs.

Table 8–2. *Extra Tabs in Windows Live Mail*

Tab	Settings and Features
Windows Live Mail	This is the equivalent of the File menu commonly used by most other programs that run on Windows.
	It is quite common for people to have more than one e-mail account or switch from one program to another. **Import messages** and **Export e-mail** help you to share settings, contacts, and messages between them.
	The **Options** command provides access to settings for **Mail**, **E-mail accounts**, **Safety options**, and more.
	In Safety options, you can: adjust the **level of junk mail protection;** manage **Safe Senders** and **Blocked Senders** lists; set **Phishing**, **Security**, and **Virus Protection** levels, and more.
Folders	Create new folders, copy and move messages between folders, and navigate between folders. You can also create message rules to automatically move, copy, or delete incoming messages based on the sender or key words in the subject or message body.
View	Contains many arrangement and layout settings, including how messages are sorted, how the messages lists and reading pane are arranged, and color coding each account.
Accounts	Add e-mail and newsgroup accounts; edit the properties for each account; delete accounts.

Managing Contacts

Your contacts, or address book, are where you store the e-mail addresses and other contact information. As you type a name in the To: line of an e-mail message, Windows Live Mail starts searching for a match and suggests names from your contacts list. You can assign nicknames to any contact, so that instead of typing out a full name, you can create a name like Mom, Sis, Babe, Dude, Jimmy, etc. Figure 8–26 shows the main Contact page.

> **TIP:** When you open a new contact window, the default is the Quick add page. Use the Contact page to add a nickname that is easy to type or remember.

Figure 8–26. *The **Contact** page allows you to add a little more information than the default **Quick add** page.*

There are several ways to add contacts:

- Add contacts when you receive mail.

- Add contacts when you compose e-mail.

- Import contacts from other e-mail programs or accounts.

- Reply to or copy name from previous messages from person you want to send a new message to (not recommended, it doesn't actually save a contact to the Contacts list).

Adding contacts when you receive mail

There are several reasons to save contacts from incoming mail messages:

- To make it easier to find and select names when addressing messages.

- To keep mail from new contacts from going to your Junk/Spam folder.

- To keep mail from services and mailing lists from going to your Junk/Spam folder.

To add a contact from a message you received, right-click or select the name:

1. Right-click the name in the e-mail message header, as shown in Figure 8–27.

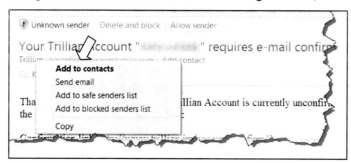

Figure 8–27. *The right-click menu for a contact*

2. Click one of the following:

- **Add to contacts** to add this person's name and e-mail address. You can add other types of information like phone, postal address, company, alternate e-mail addresses, web sites, etc.

- **Add to safe senders list** if you just want to keep e-mails from this sender out of your junk mail, but don't need to send mail back to them. This is useful for mail from companies and mailing lists that you want to keep.

- **Add to blocked senders list** to make sure that any future e-mail from this sender is blocked from your inbox and is treated as junk mail.

   –or–

3. Select the name in the header.

4. Use the links in the header for **Delete and block**, **Allow sender**, or **Add contact**.

Adding Contacts When you Compose E-mail

Somebody tells you, "e-mail me at someone@example.com," or you are given a business card with an e-mail address on it. When you enter their names on the To, CC, or BCC lines as you compose a message, you can add their names to your contacts.

To add a name from a new message you are composing:

1. In the To, CC, or BCC line, type the e-mail address and end it with a semi-colon, like **someone@example.com;** as shown in Figure 8–28.

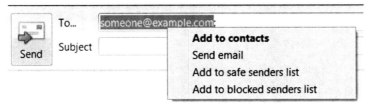

Figure 8–28. *You can add an e-mail address to your contacts as you enter it in your message*

2. Click **Add to** contacts.

3. When the contact page appears, enter any additional information, which can include a nickname that the Contacts list will easily recognize and auto-fill so that you may not even have to type the entire name.

Importing Contacts from Other E-mail Programs or Accounts

Windows Live Mail can import contacts from other e-mail programs if they are exported from the other e-mail program as a contact file compatible with Microsoft Outlook Express 6, Windows Live Mail, and Windows Mail. You will need to open both your old and your new e-mail programs (and accounts) to import your contacts.

> **TIP:** Though you use your contacts with your e-mail and instant message programs, contacts are usually managed by a Contacts program with its own menus. So look for contact import or export features in your Contacts program and menus, not Mail.

Since each mail/contact program has their own user interface and menus, the exact names for these commands will vary depending on which program you are importing from. This is a three step process:

1. Export your contacts from your old e-mail program and account.

2. Import your contacts into Windows Live Mail.

3. Clean up duplicates, if needed.

To export your contacts from your old e-mail program and account:

1. Open the old account, and open the Contacts or Address Book. The contact export and import features may not be available in the Mail/Inbox program or window.

2. Select the **Export** (export contacts, export address book) command.

3. Select one of the following for the contact file format type:

   ▪ Microsoft Outlook or Outlook Express

   ▪ Windows Mail

   ▪ Windows Live Mail

   ▪ Comma Separated Values (.csv)

4. Save the file to a location that you can access from your new account. If the old account and new account are on different computers, you can save the file to a shared home network location or to a portable USB flash drive.

To Import your contacts into your new Windows Live Mail account:

1. In **Windows Live Mail**, click **Contacts** in the navigation pane, as shown in Figure 8–29.

2. Click the **Home** tab.

3. Click the **Import** button, and then click **Comma separated values** (.CSV).

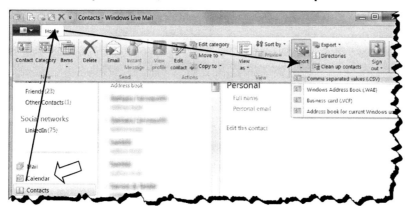

Figure 8–29. *Import the contacts file you exported from your old e-mail program into Windows Live Mail Contacts*

4. In the CSV Import dialog box, click **Browse** and navigate to the folder where you saved the contacts you exported from the other program, as shown in Figure 8–30.

5. Select the file, and then click **Open**. This will return you to the CSV Import dialog box.

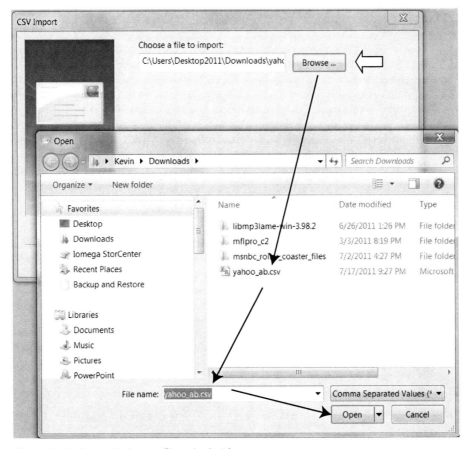

Figure 8–30. *Browse to the .csv file and select it*

6. Click **Next**.

The next screen lists how the fields from your old e-mail program's contacts list will be mapped to the fields in your Windows Live Mail contacts list, as shown in Figure 8–31. If you had some custom fields in your old contacts list, you may want to scroll through the list to see how they will be listed in the new contacts list.

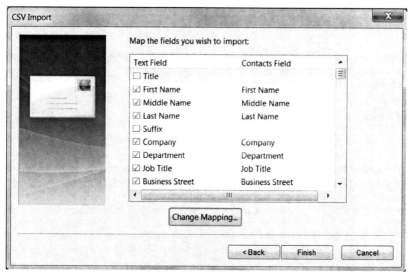

Figure 8–31. *The mappings lists shows how the fields in the old contact list will appear in the new contact list.*

7. When you are satisfied with the mappings, click **Finish**.

8. Review your Windows Live Mail Contacts list to make sure the contacts are correct. If it appears that you have multiple entries for the same person, you can have Windows Live Mail check for duplicates and suggest entries that can be combined.

To clean up duplicates:

1. Click **Contacts**, click the **Home** tab, and then click **Clean up contacts**, as shown in Figure 8–32.

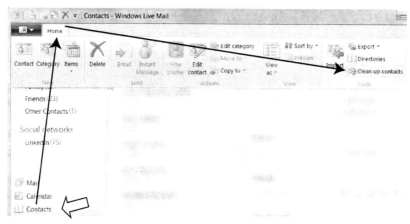

Figure 8–32. *You can clean up duplicate entries in your Windows Live Mail Contacts list.*

Windows Live Mail will retrieve your contacts and show duplicates three sets at a time.

2. Follow the instructions on your screen.

Replying to a Previous Message from Somebody to Send a New Message to Them

Don't do this! Adding names to an address book is really easy, but sometimes people just look for an old e-mail message from the person they want to send the message to, click Reply, and then replace the subject and body, or just the body. This alone doesn't add the e-mail address to your contacts list. And when your friends get a string of e-mail messages that are completely new topics and the subject is listed as "RE: Old topic that I forgot to replace in the subject line," it may make you look silly. Adding their names to your address book will make it easier to create new messages and conversations, and you and your friends will find it easier to manage messages by subject/conversation.

Creating Mailing Lists

You can create your own mailing lists, also known as distributions lists, so that instead of typing a bunch of names, you can create a group and just type the group name. For example, you coach a soccer team with sixteen players and assistant coaches. You regularly send out mail about practice times, game times, etc. It gets tiresome typing each name; sometimes you type one name twice and leave out others. So, you create an alias for your team, **Georgetown Geoducks.**

To create a mailing list:

1. In **Windows Live Mail**, click **Contacts** in the navigation pane.

2. Click the **Home** tab, and then click **Category**, as shown in Figure 8–33.

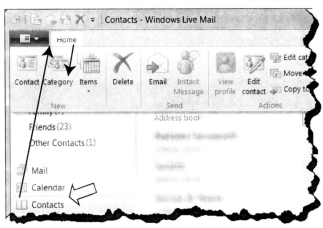

Figure 8–33. *You can create a category for a group of names.*

The Create a new category window appears.

3. Type a name for the category (Geoducks, in this example), and then click names in the list to add them to the group, as shown in Figure 8–34.

TIP: The more unique the name for your category, the quicker Windows Live Mail can autofill it as you enter it in an e-mail message.

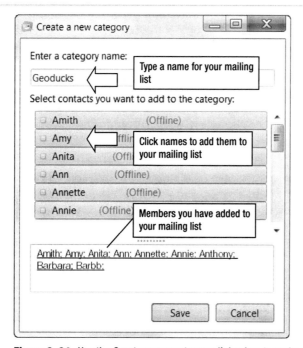

Figure 8–34. *Use the Create a new category dialog box to make your own mailing lists*

4. If your list approaches 50, break the list up and create two or more categories of up to 25 e-mail addresses each.

NOTE: Windows Live Mail/Hotmail limits the number of outgoing messages to 100 a day and limits the number of e-mail addresses a message can have to possibly 50. A category (mailing list) is not considered one e-mail address; each e-mail address in the list is counted separately. When you open a new account, your daily message limit may be much smaller until your e-mail pattern use shows that you are not using the account for spamming.

5. When you are done, click **Save**.

    Your Contacts categories will display your new mailing list, as shown in Figure 8–35.

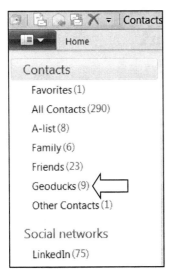

Figure 8–35. *New category is listed under Contacts*

Using a Category As A Mailing List

When you create a new e-mail message, all you have to do is type the name of the category, as shown in Figure 8–36.

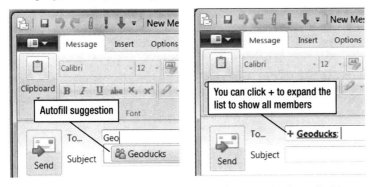

Figure 8–36. *Typing a category name saves typing a bunch of e-mail address every time you send mail to the same people in a group*

If you want to expand the category to display all of the e-mail addresses of the members, click the plus + sign next to the name.

Choosing and Setting Up E-mail Accounts

You have other choices for *e-mail clients* and *accounts* besides Windows Live Mail.

E-mail clients are the programs or windows that display your e-mail accounts and messages. A client can be a standalone program that you install on your computer or web-based (a web page hosted in your browser). **Windows Live Mail** and **Mozilla Thunderbird** are free e-mail client applications that you can download and install. They are opened as separate programs, and you add your e-mail accounts to the program. **Microsoft Outlook** is another e-mail client; it is most commonly used in the workplace. It is designed to work with Exchange servers within a company's internal network but can also be set up to display e-mail accounts from web-based clients like a **Windows Live Mail**, **Gmail**, **AOL Mail**, and **Yahoo! Mail Plus**. Outlook is not free; it is usually purchased and installed as part of a Microsoft Office suite. For web-based e-mail, your browser is the e-mail client, so to access your e-mail account you navigate to a specific web site, such as www.mail.live.com, www.hotmail.com, www.gmail.com, www.mail.yahoo.com, and www.mail.aol.com.

E-mail accounts are what give you an e-mail address through an e-mail provider. Some of the more familiar e-mail providers are **Windows Live Mail**, **Gmail**, **Yahoo! Mail**, and **AOL Mail**. You may also be able to get e-mail accounts from your Internet Service Provider (ISP) or through a web site host if you set up your own—even under your own web domain. Over the next few pages, we'll take a look at some of these e-mail clients and account providers.

> **NOTE:** One of the reasons most web-based e-mail accounts are free is because they are supported by the advertising that appears within the browser window.

Outlook

You can also use Outlook mail, the industrial strength e-mail program that is part of the Microsoft Office family, to host multiple e-mail accounts. This can be convenient if you already use Outlook at work for corporate e-mail and want to access both your work and personal accounts all in one program. Outlook is not a free downloadable e-mail program. You can buy it by itself or as part of a Microsoft Office Professional or Enterprise suite. Outlook is not included in the Microsoft Office Home and Student edition. Figure 8–37 displays Outlook 2003 with a personal Gmail account. Outlook lists e-mail accounts in the left folder pane like Windows Live Mail.

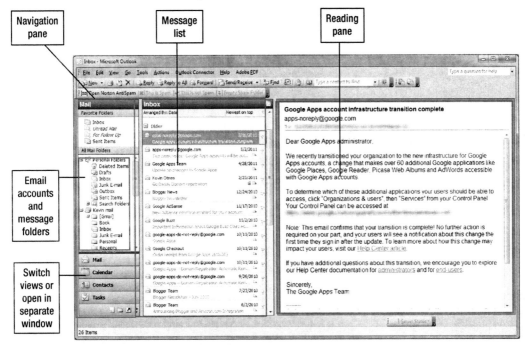

Figure 8–37. *Microsoft Outlook can display multiple e-mail accounts from work accounts and personal accounts such as Gmail, AOL/AIM Mail, Hotmail/Windows Live Mail, and Yahoo! Mail.*

TIP: You do not have to have a corporate (work) e-mail account to use Outlook. You can use it just for personal e-mail accounts at home if you like it better than other e-mail clients.

You can add almost any type of e-mail account to Outlook 2003, 2007, and 2010.

The steps in Table 8–3 vary depending on which version of Outlook you are using, and which type of e-mail account you are adding.

Table 8–3. *Steps to Add Accounts*

To add these accounts	Follow These Steps
Gmail, **AOL/AIM Mail** and many other IMAP and POP3 accounts	1. Search the web for help on adding the e-mail program to Outlook. For example, search for "adding Gmail to Outlook." These instructions should provide you with information you will need when you actually add the account in Outlook such as incoming and outgoing server names, port numbers, and other settings. Some web sites will also include the steps to follow within Outlook. Some e-mail programs have different steps for Outlook 2003, 2007 and 2010. 2. In Outlook, click the **Tools** menu, click **E-mail Accounts**, and then click **Add** (or similar commands depending on which version of Outlook you are using). Follow the instructions in the wizard, using the settings you got from the web for adding this e-mail program to Outlook.
Yahoo! Mail	You have two options: 1. Pay for an upgrade to Yahoo! Mail Plus. Go to `http://overview.mail.yahoo.com/enhancements/mailpl us` for more information and to sign up. 2. After upgrading, search the Yahoo! Mail web site for "Accessing Yahoo! Mail via POP." –or – 1. Download YPOPS! for free from `http://ypopsemail.com/`. This open source program allows you to access your standard free Yahoo! Mail through Outlook, Thunderbird, Windows Live, and many other e-mail clients. 2. After downloading and installing YPOPS! go to their Configuring E-mail Clients page `http://ypopsemail.com/documentation/37-email-configuration` for specific instructions for your version of Outlook. Though Outlook 2010 is not listed, the instructions for Outlook 2007 may work.

To add these accounts	Follow These Steps
Windows Live Mail and Hotmail	1. Install Outlook Hotmail Connector. This is available for download in the Windows Live Essentials 2011 pack. If you have not already installed Windows Live Essentials, you can download the entire pack from `http://explore.live.com/windows-live-essentials`. You can also download just the Outlook Connector Pack from `http://explore.live.com/outlook-hotmail-connector-pack`. For more information about Windows Live Essentials, see Chapter 7: "Getting Free Goodies like Windows Live Essentials." 2. Open Outlook. In the new **Outlook Connector** menu, click **Add a New Account** and follow the instructions in the wizard.

Mozilla Thunderbird

Mozilla Thunderbird, like the Windows Live Mail client, allows you to view and manage multiple e-mail accounts. It also provides a tri-pane layout with similar reading pane options: you can read your messages below (classic view) or to the right (vertical view) of your message list, or with just a message list and no reading pane at all (wide view). Figure 8–38 shows Mozilla Thunderbird in the classic view.

The Thunderbird client offers several folder view options besides the expanding and collapsing list of folders within each account, the All Folders view shown in Figure 8–38. Other folder view options are Unified Folders where the messages from all of your Inbox folders are listed in one message list; Unread folders, which displays only folders that contain unread messages; Favorite Folders; and Recent Folders.

> **NOTE:** Though Figure 8–38 displays the folder, messages lists, and message in the preview pane of a Gmail account, the actual browser view through the Gmail web site will be different—as will the browser views of AOL and Hotmail/Windows Live Mail through their respective mail access web sites.

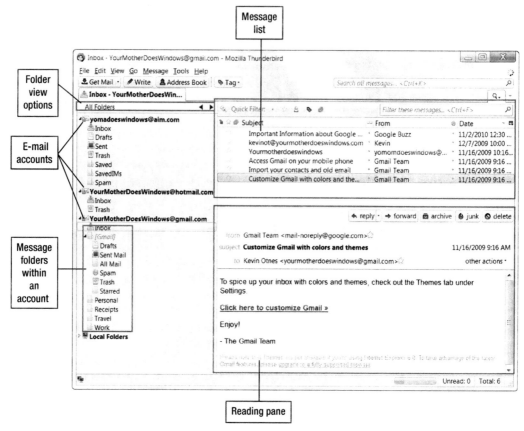

Figure 8–38. *Mozilla Thunderbird client window, with AOL, Hotmail, and Gmail accounts listed*

Gmail

Google's e-mail account service is Gmail. It is browser-based you can access by going to their web site at www.gmail.com. If you forget that web address, you can also access your mail from the regular www.google.com web page; there's a small link at the top for Gmail. If you prefer a regular program window to view your mail, you can add Gmail to your accounts in Windows Live Mail or Mozilla Thunderbird. Figure 8–39 shows a Gmail account accessed through the Gmail web site in Internet Explorer.

Gmail, as of this writing, does not offer a tri-pane view of a folder list, message list, and message body. One alternative is shown in Figure 8–39, where a Gmail theme called Preview (Dense) was applied. This theme displays the subject in the message list, followed by a preview of the first few words of the message body itself. How much of the body is shown depends on how much room is left on the line after the subject.

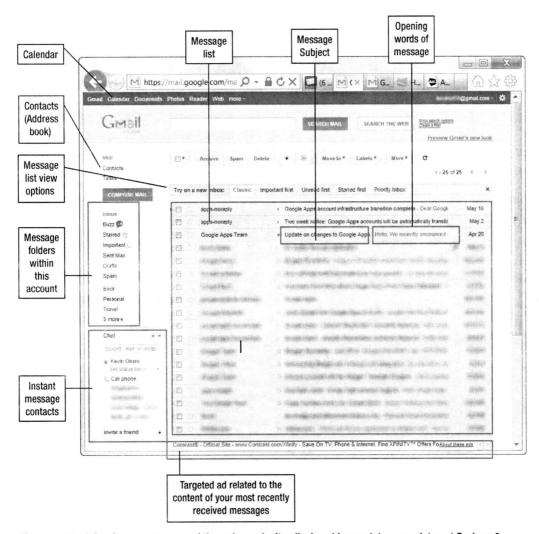

Figure 8–39. *A Gmail account accessed through a web site, displayed in a web browser, Internet Explorer 9*

Yahoo! Mail

Yahoo! Mail is available at two levels of service: Basic, which is free, and Yahoo! Mail Plus, which adds POP access and other services and features, and does away with graphical ads. Free Windows Live Mail, Gmail, and AOL mail accounts can be added to Windows Live Mail and Mozilla Thunderbird e-mail clients. But to access your Yahoo! E-mail account through Windows Live Mail, Thunderbird, or Microsoft Outlook, you must upgrade to Yahoo! Mail Plus. Or you can try a free open source program called **YPOPs!** which emulates a POP3 and SMTP so that you can access your free Yahoo! mail account through your favorite e-mail client such as Windows Live Mail, Mozilla Thunderbird, or Microsoft Outlook. You can download YPOPS! through http://ypopsemail.com/ and other download sites.

The free version of Yahoo! Mail is still a fine e-mail account service. Like Gmail and AOL Mail, it is browser-based so you don't need to install an extra program. In your web browser, go to their mail web site and log in. Yahoo! Mail offers the tri-pane view, just like AOL Mail, Windows Live Mail and Mozilla Thunderbird. By now, the tri-pane view shown in Figure 8–40 should look pretty familiar.

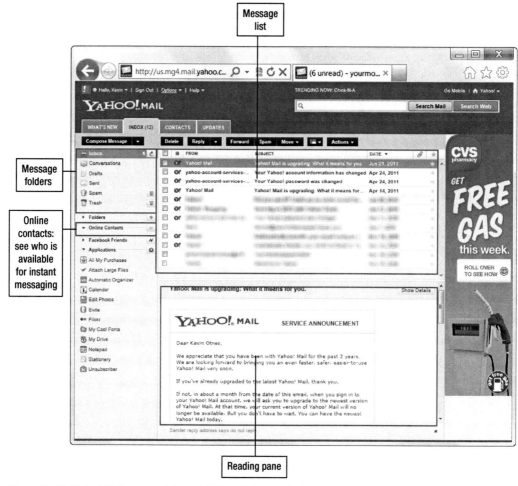

Figure 8–40. *Yahoo! Mail accessed through Yahoo! Mail web site in a regular Internet Explorer 9 browser window*

AOL Mail

AOL Mail is another free web-based e-mail account service. You can access your mail through a web browser, or add your account to Windows Live Mail or Mozilla Thunderbird clients.

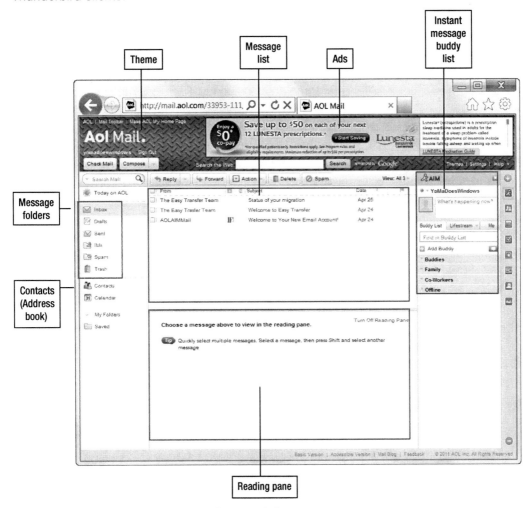

Figure 8–41. *AOL Mail in Internet Explorer 9 browser window*

AOL Instant Messenger, or AIM, is popular so AOL Mail ties into AIM by displaying your AIM buddy list prominently on the right side of the mail window. You can quickly see if your AIM buddies are online by looking at their presence in your buddy list, as you can see in Figure 8–41. If the button next to their name is green, they're online. If it is gray, they are offline. In between other colors may mean they are busy, in a meeting, etc.

Using E-mail Courteously and Safely

None of us like to be made fun of or embarrassed, so we may be hesitant about using e-mail. Everybody has their own pet peeves about how people use or misuse e-mail. My list is subjective, but it is based on my experiences of using e-mail at home and at work for over twenty years, and comments from friends about what they wish they could teach their friends or parents.

- **Check your Junk folder when you log on to your e-mail account.** Most e-mail programs and providers automatically delete a message from your Junk folder after three days. Junk mail filters are not perfect; sometimes when you get mail from a new sender not in your address book, it gets marked as spam.

- **Don't SHOUT.** SHOUTING is typing in all capital letters. It is really hard on the eyes, and there are many other ways to emphasize text with conventional formatting.

- **Don't believe everything you get in e-mail, even if it is from a friend.** There are a lot of myths and hoaxes that spread like wildfire in e-mail because they sound real. Before you forward that story on to all of your friends, check to see if it is true. There are several great web sites for debunking hoaxes and urban legends:

    - Urban Legends Reference Pages, www.snopes.com

    - Urban Legends, www.urbanlegends.about.com

    - TruthOrFiction.com, www.truthorfiction.com

    - Internet Hoaxes, www.internethoaxes.info

    - Hoax Busters, www.hoaxbusters.org

- **Avoid opening e-mail messages that purport to have links to pictures or video about a recent (and often tragic) news event.** Many times these are links to viruses or other harmful downloads. Delete these without opening. If you really want to know about some event, go to a reputable news site like www.msnbc.com, www.cnn.com, or your local newspaper, radio, or television station news site.

- **Beware of e-mail messages from strangers with strange names or subject lines.** These are usually spam, and most of the time your e-mail provider or e-mail program automatically sends these to your Junk folder.

- **Beware of phishing, what it does, and how to spot it.** Phishing uses fake web sites and e-mail messages to fool you into thinking it is from a legitimate organization (bank, shopping web site, etc.) so that you will provide them with your user account and password.

- Do not log onto banking or shopping sites from a link in an e-mail message. If you click a link in an e-mail message and the first thing that you see is a login window, get out of there.

- Visit Wikipedia and review their article on phishing at http://en.wikipedia.org/wiki/Phishing.

- Call your bank if you get an e-mail that sounds suspicious. If an e-mail message says you need to take some specific action immediately, you should be able to do it over the phone.

- Most online banking sites offer a message notification area within your personal banking pages. They avoid sending e-mail messages directly to your account specifically because of the prevalence of phishing and scamming themes.

- **When creating an e-mail name on a new e-mail account, think about who will see it**. Sometimes an e-mail name that is funny to friends may look unprofessional or offensive to prospective employers.

- **Set up separate e-mail accounts for different purposes**. This is really helpful if you send a lot of personal e-mail, receive a lot of e-mail newsletters, visit a lot of special interest forums or web sites, and do a lot of banking or shopping. When you create these accounts, there is no setup box that asks if this is a business, personal, newsletter, or financial/banking account. Those are just labels that you decide upon for yourself as you decide how you will use each account.

  - Create a **business/professional** e-mail account if you need to provide contact information outside of your work e-mail address. Be sure to use a professional-sounding name.

  - Create a **personal** e-mail account for all of your social contacts, friends, and relatives.

  - Create a **newsletter/forum** e-mail account so that any site or e-mail list you subscribe to does not clutter up your personal Inbox.

  - Create a **banking and shopping** e-mail account so that you can set the strongest possible password, and isolate this account from your personal e-mail account. A lot of viruses and nasty stuff is sent to personal e-mail accounts, and sometimes they hack into your address book to snag all of your contacts for spamming.

  - Create a **backup** e-mail account in case one of your other accounts gets compromised. Since most e-mail programs allow you to import and export contacts, you should be able to import all of your contacts from other accounts into this backup account.

- **Don't overreact to e-mail messages**. Since e-mail is not a direct immediate back and forth conversation, it is easy to misread the tone and meaning in an e-mail message. If you get a message that inflames you, cool down before you reply. Even when you compose the reply, let it sit for a while before you send it. Sometimes just the act of writing a reply without sending it helps you vent your feelings without harming anybody. If possible, call the sender on the telephone because you may find that the other person meant something quite different than your interpretation.

- **Spelling and writing do matter**. Even when you are using e-mail just for personal exchanges, people still notice misspellings and errors in your writing. Though they may not say anything, they may be distracted enough that they do not read or actual message or meaning. Also, anything you send to one or more people in e-mail has the potential to be forwarded to hundreds or thousands of people that you never intended it for. So be just as careful how you say it (spelling and grammar) as what you say (the actual content). Once you send a message to somebody, you have no control over where or who they forward it to.

Using Instant Messaging (IM)

In this section, we'll introduce you to IM basics, some of the more popular IM programs, and tips for using them with each other.

Instant messaging is great for short quick messages between people when they are both online at the same time. It can also be used for real-time communication with audio and video. With the surge in use of existing social networks like Facebook and LinkedIn plus upcoming ones from Google and possibly Microsoft, instant messaging can tie into those, too.

In e-mail, you can send and receive messages with anybody else who has an e-mail address. It doesn't matter whether you are using Gmail, Yahoo! Mail, AOL Mail, or Windows Live Mail. You and the other people with whom you exchange e-mail can all use different programs, as long as all of you have access to the Internet and genuine e-mail addresses.

With instant messaging it's more challenging to build and understand your own network of friends and buddies. Though all of the IM programs connect to the Internet, they can't connect or talk to each other as directly because they each use their own protocols for instant messaging. *Protocols* are the formats and methods the instant messaging programs used to talk to each other. In most cases, if you want to instant message with somebody, the two of you not only need to be online at the same time, you may also need to use the same instant messaging program. There are some instant messaging programs that allow you to view most of your IM accounts in one window, though you may still need separate IM programs for each IM network.

There are several methods for getting on the same IM network with your friends:

- If your friend is not using the same IM program and network as you are, you can invite them.

- You can let your IM program search the contacts in your Contacts list of other IM or e-mail programs for people who may already have an IM account compatible with your IM network. Or, you can let your IM program suggest inviting people from your other contacts list who don't currently have an IM account with your current IM network.

- You can use an IM network that works with your IM network, even though they are different companies. For example, Yahoo Instant Messaging accounts and Windows Live (Hotmail) accounts can IM directly with each other, without installing the other's program.

- You can use a program that hosts multiple instant message accounts from different networks at the same time, such as **Meebo** or **Trillian**. This will allow you to see all of your contacts in one list and who is currently online.

Instant Messaging Features

Instant Messaging windows and programs can be an assault on your eyes and senses with all of the information that is thrown at you in one window. Understanding how to use every feature in every instant messaging program could easily require a book all by itself.

As we explore the different IM features and programs, do not feel overwhelmed. Table 8–4 compares several popular IM programs, but most people usually settle on one program—whichever most of their friends are using. Also, social networking sites like Facebook and LinkedIn are integrating with instant messaging programs like Windows Live Mail, Yahoo!, and AIM. You may find yourself using your instant messaging accounts directly from your social network web page more often than from the IM programs themselves.

Table 8–4. *IM Programs*

Feature	What It Does
IM Program Windows and Web Pages	Most instant messaging programs offer similar windows and features. But IM programs also want to be your social network. When you first start your IM program, you may get a web page view that can be a collection of information from several different social network sites, as well as status of your contacts. The following figures show a web page view, Figure 8–42, and a more compact view, Figure 8–43.

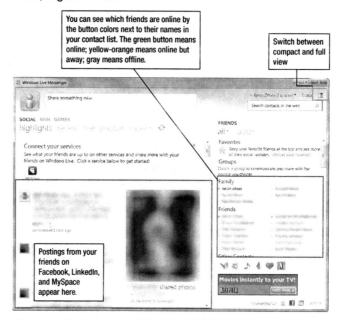

Figure 8–42. *Windows Live Messenger in full view*

Feature	What It Does

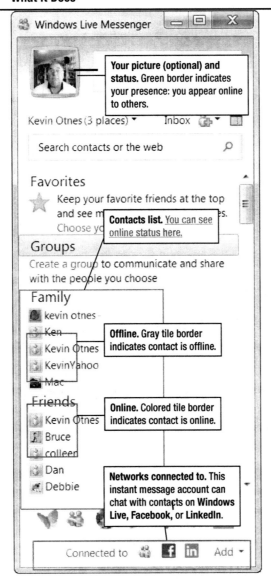

Figure 8–43. *Windows Live Messenger in compact view*

Contact or Buddy List	This is your list of contacts who have instant messaging accounts with the service you are currently using and have agreed to allow you to IM with them. With this list, you can see who is online and available for chatting. If they are not online, most programs let you can double-click their name to send them a regular e-mail message.

Feature	What It Does
Adding individuals to your contact list	To add somebody to your contact list, you must invite them, and they must accept your invitation. Figure 8–44 is a Yahoo! Messenger wizard for adding contacts. Windows Live Mail, Google Talk, and AOL Instant Messenger have similar invitation wizards.

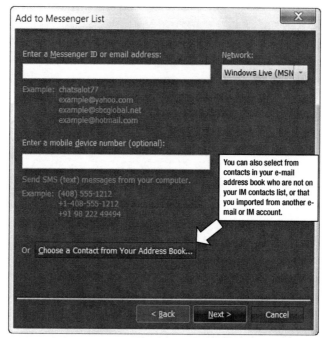

Figure 8–44. *Creating an invite to add a Yahoo! Messenger contact*

The IM service will check the e-mail address you entered to see if they already have an account with your IM service. If the person receiving the invitation already has an account with your IM service, they will receive a message similar to Figure 8–45. Depending on the IM program, the recipient will have options to approve/accept, deny/decline, ignore, or decide later.

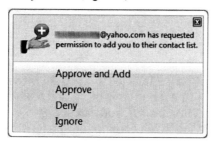

Figure 8–45. *A request from somebody asking permission to add you to their contact list*

Feature	What It Does
	If they don't have an account with your IM service, the invitation wizard will prompt you for more information such as a personal message to include in the invitation, as shown in Figure 8–46.

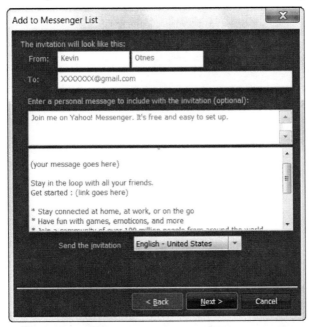

Figure 8–46. *Inviting somebody to install the IM program and add you to their contacts*

When you send the invitation, they will receive an e-mail message similar to the example in Figure 8–47.

Figure 8–47. *The invitation will link to a download page where the recipient can download and install the IM program.*

Feature	What It Does
	Occasionally you may get IM invite requests from people you don't know to join their group or to allow them to be on your contacts list. Figure 8–48 is an example of a pop-up that might appear when you start your IM program or while you are online. These are the IM equivalent of unsolicited junk mail.

Figure 8–48. *Just say No thanks to invitations from people you don't know.*

Feature	What It Does
Blocking or removing contacts	If you change your mind and no longer want somebody on your IM list, you can block or remove them from your contacts list. Usually the IM program doesn't notify them that you have removed them. To the person you dropped, you may appear to always be offline or you may disappear from their contact list. Check the help or search the Web for instructions for your specific IM program because each one is a little different. You can search for "How do I permanently remove instant messaging contacts from <insert name of your IM program>?" If you only want to temporarily keep somebody from seeing you online or sending IMs to you, you can sign in as invisible, a feature available in most programs. We'll explain more about this feature in just a bit.
Presence and Status	**Presence** indicates whether you are online. **Status** indicates whether you are available or busy. The contact's tile color or a small bullet next to their name generally use these colors to indicate presence and status: Green or yellow means online and available for instant messaging Red means online but busy or in a meeting Gray, or no color, means offline and unavailable

Feature	What It Does
	The examples in Figure 8–49 show how different IM programs display your current online status and what others will see.

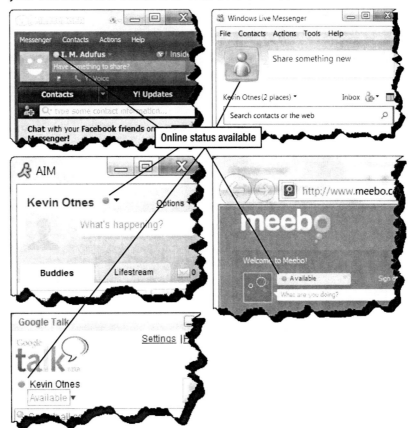

Figure 8–49. *Your own online status is displayed at the top of your IM window; each program is a little different.*

Sign in as invisible **Invisible to everyone**	You control your online status that others see. Sometimes you may not want others to see when you are online. There may be times you want to see who is online but don't want others to see you are online.
	Almost all IM programs offer options to sign in as invisible, as well as change your status to invisible once you are online. You can still IM with your contacts who are online, but you will remain invisible to the rest of your contacts.

Feature	What It Does
Message logs, conversation logs, conversation history	This feature allows you to save a transcript of your instant message conversations. Some programs allow you to save the conversations to a file in a folder on your computer, and some save the conversations as individual messages in a mail folder.

Many people assume that once you close an instant message window and conversation, there is no record of the conversation. So they may be a little more casual (and sometimes careless) in what they say.

NOTE If you are concerned about keeping your IM conversations private from anybody outside of the conversation, some IM programs and IM plug-ins offer OTR (Off The Record). OTR encrypts your conversations in progress. Search the web for OTR or Off The Record for more information.

In some industries and professions, like banking, finance, and stock brokerage, companies and government regulatory agency require that records be kept of all conversations. This includes phone conversations, e-mail messages, and instant message conversations.

Keeping a history of a conversation can be really handy when you need a record of technical information or details. But as a courtesy, if you do turn conversation history logging on, let the people you are IMing with that you are doing so.

> **CAUTION:** In some countries, regions, or cities, there may be legal requirements that both parties be in agreement to allow the recording of any conversation. You may be legally required to disclose to the other party that you are recording (logging) your IM conversation.

Feature	What It Does
Chat Windows	Chat windows are where you enter and view your current conversation. Most chat programs include emoticons that you can insert into your message, as you can see in Figure 8–50.

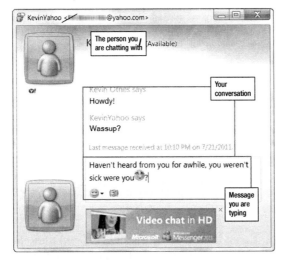

Figure 8–50. *Windows Live Chat window*

You can have multiple chat windows open, one for each person or group with whom you are chatting. You can also invite others to join a chat so that all of you are in the same chat window.

Sharing: **Audio and Video** **Music** **Files** **Desktop**	Instant messaging isn't just for exchanging quick bursts of text and smiley faces. Most IM programs allow you to add audio or video so you can see and hear each other live through a web cam built into your computer or attached to it. The quality of the video depends on the quality of the camera and the Internet connection speeds of the people on both sides of the conversation. With a slow Internet speed, the video may appear choppy instead of a continuous flow like you see when watching TV.
	You may also be able to share the music you are listening to on your computer and send files, such as pictures or documents, back and forth.
	Some instant messaging programs allow you to show people what you have on your computer desktop, or even allow them to control your desktop from their computer. This is sometimes called *desktop sharing*. This is a method that some companies use as a tool to provide technical support. It allows them to directly check settings and log files to troubleshoot what is going wrong. You can also use this with a friend to have them help you with your computer. If the idea of handing over control of your computer is scary to you, it is completely up to you whether to allow them control of your desktop.

GOING BEYOND INSTANT MESSAGING: SERVICES FOR ONLINE CONFERENCING

If you want to do more robust sharing of your desktop, or conduct online conferencing with many people at once, there are commercial grade products for this. They are not free, but they offer more features and capabilities than a personal instant messaging program. Microsoft Office Live Meeting (http://office.microsoft.com/en-us/live-meeting-help/), Webex (www.webex.com), and GoToMeeting (www.gotomeeting.com) are three popular services for online conferencing.

Choosing and Installing Instant Messaging Clients

There are many instant messaging clients to choose from. With e-mail clients and programs that can host multiple accounts, you can keep it simple by handling all of your e-mail with only a couple accounts and programs. With IM, because the different services don't always interoperate with each other, you may end up needing many more accounts with different services if all of your friends don't use the same service.

If you want to keep your IM accounts simple, try one of these tactics:

- Get all of your friends on the same IM service. Or, get them to use either **Yahoo** or **Windows Live** because both of those services can talk directly with each other. Or get them to use either **Google Talk** or **AIM** because both of those offer interoperability.

- Use **Trillian** or **Meebo** to view and manage all of your IM accounts in one program window. For most IM accounts you will still need an account on that service to talk to others on that service, but you can view the online status of your entire account contacts lists in one place.

> **NOTE:** When you access your IM accounts through Trillian or Meebo, you may not have access to unique features only available in the original IM program window. For example, you can't send a Windows Live Messenger or Yahoo! Messenger buzz when you use those accounts from within Meebo.

Most people choose which IM service to use based on what their friends use. But if you and your friends are just starting out with IM, you may want to look around at the different services to see which one works best for you or is easiest to use.

Installation Tips

Installation is fairly easy for any of these IM programs. During installation there are several settings and preferences that you should pay attention to; otherwise you may find your default browser home page, search, and toolbar settings taken over by the IM program. You may also see other settings for preferences on how you want the IM program started. Some of these changes are pre-selected, so you have to be diligent and deselect them as they come up in the installation pages:

- Make (MSN, Yahoo!, Google, AOL) my home page.

- Add (Xxxx) toolbar to my browser.

- Make (Xxxx) my default search provider.

- Start the IM program when I start Windows.

- Import contacts from another address book.

After you install an IM program, most programs offer appearance customizations through themes or skins.

The next few pages offer a quick look at some of the different instant messaging options.

Windows Live Messenger

Windows Live Messenger replaced MSN Messenger a few years ago. Chapter 7: "Getting Free Goodies like Windows Live Essentials" describes how to download and install Windows Live Messenger as part of Windows Live Essentials. Your computer may already have Windows Live Essentials installed. If not, you can download Windows Live Essentials from http://explore.live.com/windows-live-essentials.

Windows Live Messenger can be displayed in a wide web page-like view or in a compact view. These two views are described earlier in this chapter in the "IM Program Windows and Web Pages" section and Figures 8–42 and 8–43.

The networks used by Windows Live Messenger and Yahoo! Messenger can talk with each other. So if you have a Windows Live Messenger account, you can IM directly with other people who have Yahoo! Messenger accounts as well as Windows Live Messenger accounts.

For video and voice calls, you don't need to install a separate program or plug-in.

Yahoo! Messenger

You can download Yahoo! Messenger from http://messenger.yahoo.com.

Yahoo! Messenger and Windows Live Messenger accounts can connect directly with each other. You can use voice and video calling without any add-ins. Like most IM programs, you can play games online with your contacts. Figure 8–51 shows the parts of the Yahoo! Messenger program window.

Figure 8–51. *Yahoo! Messenger program window*

AIM

You can download AOL Instant Messenger from:

`www.aim.com.`

AIM and Google Talk have been building interoperability so that AIM and Google Talk users can talk to each other without logging into both services. The features and capabilities are in transition, so this integration is not seamless yet. See Figure 8–52 for other features.

It appears that the best way for now is to add your Google Friends to your AIM Buddies, and access both from AIM.

You can use audio and video without installing extra plug-ins.

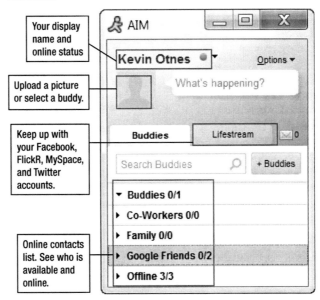

Figure 8–52. *AIM program window*

Google Talk

You can download Google Talk from www.google.com/talk/.

Google Talk and AIM have some interoperability. It appears to be easier to access your Google Talk contacts from within AIM than access your AIM contacts from within Google Talk. You can also initiate IM conversations with your Google Talk contacts through the contact list in your Google Mail window.

Google does not currently integrate voice and video within Google Talk. You can download a separate **Gmail voice and video chat** plug-in, which you can access through your Gmail or iGoogle account. See Figure 8–53 for other features.

You can also add a Google Talk gadget to your Google Gadgets on your desktop. See Chapter 3: "Using Gadgets and Widgets" to learn how to set up and use Google Gadgets.

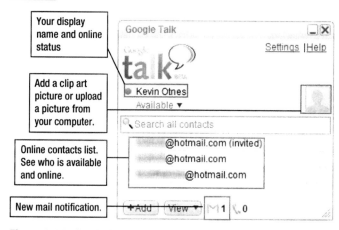

Figure 8–53. *Google Talk program window*

Meebo

You can download Meebo from www.meebo.com. Meebo is free, versatile, and is a great way to tidy up multiple IM accounts (see Figure 8–54). You can add IM accounts from Google Talk, AIM, Yahoo!, Windows Live, and close to 100 other networks. When you add an IM account to Meebo, it stores the user name and password for each account. That way, when you login to Meebo, you are logged into all of your accounts at once. Meebo is browser based, so once you set up your Meebo account, you can log into it (and all of the IM accounts in it) from any PC with web access. You and the other party still need to have accounts with the same IM service or compatible service (Yahoo!/Windows Live, Google Talk/AIM). But you won't need to open each IM program separately or try to remember which network a contact is on. Find the contact in the Buddy List, and then start your conversation.

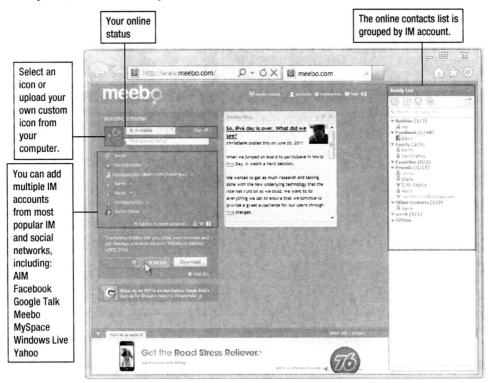

Figure 8–54. *Meebo IM client combines multiple accounts and contact lists into one web browser window.*

Trillian

You can download Trillian from `www.trillian.im/`.

> **NOTE:** The web site is not *.com* — that will take you to an unrelated site.

Like Meebo, Trillian provides the convenience of a single login that logs you into all of your accounts at once. Trillian is a standalone program that runs in its own window; it does not require a web page in a browser (see Figure 8–55). All of your accounts and contacts are provided in a single list, which makes for a very compact view. Trillian can also monitor e-mail accounts to notify you of new mail. The size and views in the Trillian window can be customized, like showing larger or smaller icons, and how much text is shown for each contact or account. You also have many options for how notifications are displayed and how you can respond to them. This versatility in sizing, compact design, the ability to reduce multiple IM accounts and e-mail notifications to a single program window makes Trillian especially appealing for devices like tablets, netbooks, and small laptops that have very little screen size to work with.

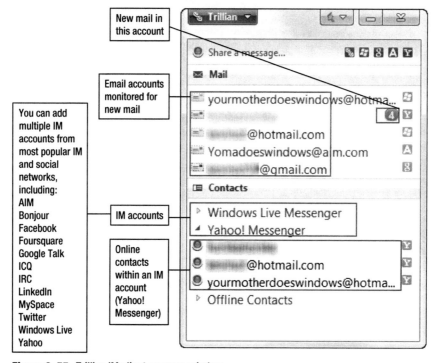

Figure 8–55. *Trillian IM client program window*

Accessing Your IM Accounts from Multiple Locations and Devices

Most IM programs can be set up to work with mobile devices. These features and capabilities may include:

- Sending SMS messages (phone texting) to a cell phone number from your PC. For example, instead of adding and sending to a contact address like example@hotmail.com, you can send to their cell phone number, like (206) 555-1212.

- Sending and receiving instant messages on your IM account through your cell phone using your phone's browser. Some IM services offer apps designed for specific smartphones, such as Windows Phone, iPhone, BlackBerry, Android, and Nokia.

Depending on the IM program, you may be able to sign on to your IM account from multiple locations. For example, you could be logged on to your Windows Live Messenger account on several machines through Meebo or Trillian and through Facebook when you log on to your Facebook page.

IM Fun Stuff: Emoticons and BRB

Texting and instant messaging have developed a new language—a mixture of symbols, numbers, and abbreviations. There is a practical use for this because when you are texting or instant messaging you want to communicate quickly and briefly. If you are pushing tiny buttons on a cellphone, anything that shortens how much you have to type is great. If you think you are missing something in the translation, want to expand your textspeak knowledge, wonder what your kids are really saying when they text PAW or 9, or just want a few good laughs to leave you ROTFL, there are many web sites that can help you. One site to start with is Webopedia, which has lengthy list in an article called "Text Messaging and Online Chat Abbreviations" at
`www.webopedia.com/quick_ref/textmessageabbreviations.asp`.

Communicating with Social Networks

If you already use social networks, you can skip this section. There is only so much that can be written. Trends change very quickly and the best way to learn is to immerse yourself in the actual social network, not read a book about it.

For those who have had little or no experience with social networking, we can provide some background to get you started in the right direction.

Social networks allow people to use the Web to share interests, beliefs, and expressions, with friends, relatives, industry peers, or customers. In the United States, some of the more well know social networks are Facebook, LinkedIn, MySpace, Friendster, and Twitter. Worldwide, many regions and countries have their own social networks.

If you have a Smartphone, iPad, or Android tablet, you've probably seen apps and little icons for Facebook and LinkedIn. But when you started Windows 7, you couldn't find a Facebook program. That's because there isn't one. To regular PCs, Facebook is a web site, not a program.

No worries! You already have at least one, possibly two or more, programs to access social networks on your Windows 7 computer:

- Internet Explorer or your default web browser.
- Windows Live Messenger or other instant messaging programs like Yahoo! Messenger, Google Talk, or AOL Instant Messenger.

The "Using Instant Messaging" section includes information about linking your IM program with social networking sites like Facebook or LinkedIn.

Though we can't explain exactly how to use any specific social network, we can outline the steps to getting there. In the next few pages we'll describe:

1. Choosing a social network
2. Joining a social network
3. Creating your circle of friends and groups
4. Using Your social network

Choosing a Social Network

Before you join a social network, you should decide why you want to join. Are your friends on the network and you feel left out? Do you want to keep in touch and share with far flung friends and relatives that you can't visit or call very often? Are you looking for peers, mentors, potential employers or employees, or colleagues in your profession? Are you trying to reach people (customers) through social marketing?

Are you looking for personal or professional social network sites? Your current and near future choices for personal social networks are the established Facebook and the recently released Google+. Before the rise of Facebook, the leaders had been MySpace and Friendster, but those sites have repositioned themselves so that they are no longer general social networking sites. For professional social networks, LinkedIn and BranchOut are the main choices in the United States.

Though **Facebook** has the largest number of members worldwide, it may not be your best choice for all of your social networking needs. Since people often put very personal information and content on their Facebook page, it may not be the best place for your manager or potential employers to learn more about you. Also, people tend to be much more selective about who they invite or accept as Facebook friends, so using it to sell to friends may not be very popular. On the other hand, many businesses create their own Facebook pages to market and communicate to their customers; celebrities, entertainers, and politicians create Facebook pages to communicate with their fans, followers, or constituents.

Google + is brand new; it just launched on June 28, 2011 to a limited group of users by invitation only. It is too soon to tell how it compares with Facebook and whether people will leave Facebook for it.

MySpace was formerly the top social networking site until Facebook surpassed it. MySpace is no longer a general social networking site; it is now focused on music, movies, entertainment celebrities, and TV.

Friendster was the first social networking site before MySpace and Facebook; it now positions itself as a social gaming site.

LinkedIn is better suited for presenting your professional profile and information. If you are more interested in discussions and topics centered around your career or profession, or you want to network with people in your field, LinkedIn is the place to do so. Many employers and recruiters use LinkedIn as part of their candidate search, and many job seekers look for opportunities there. Most of the activity in LinkedIn is through belonging to groups and participating in discussions there.

BranchOut is a fairly recent offshoot of Facebook aimed at professional networking, like LinkedIn. Because BranchOut is so new, it will take time to build its audience and groups.

Joining a Social Network

There are really two parts to joining a social network: creating an account and making connections to other people as friends or in groups.

To join a social network, go to the appropriate web site:

- Facebook, www.facebook.com
- LinkedIn, www.linkedin.com
- BranchOut, www.branchout.com

When you register with a social network, you need to create a profile. A *profile* is your name, location, birthday, interests, picture, and depending on the site, may also include education, career, and employment information.

> **CAUTION:** Don't rush through completing your profile. Review the site's privacy policies and privacy settings so that you don't expose personal or private information to the wrong people. Also, many employers look at profiles on professional social networking sites, so you want to make sure you project a positive and constructive image.

Creating Your Circle of Friends and Groups

Once you have created an account you need to make connections. There are many ways the social networking sites can assist you in making "friends."

Facebook, for example, may request access to your contact lists from your mail or IM programs; it will look for names and e-mail addresses of people who are already in Facebook and then suggest inviting them. Then Facebook can look at the people already on your friends list and suggest other people connected to your friends that you might know. In some cases, you and the person suggested by Facebook will have one or more mutual friends.

LinkedIn will look at your past or current employers and schools attended to find people from those groups who already belong to LinkedIn; then it will suggest you invite them. Like Facebook, LinkedIn will start looking for friends of your LinkedIn friends.

BranchOut will start out looking in your Facebook friends list, and then look for friends of friends, and other people who work at companies of your friends or their friends. The search is not much different than LinkedIn, but BranchOut highlights more company and employer information. This can be helpful if you are trying to network with somebody at a specific company.

With almost any social networking site, you can also send a simple invitation to somebody via e-mail if they don't currently belong to your social network or if their name didn't come up in previous searches because you have no mutual connections.

Declining an Invitation or Unfriending

You will occasionally receive requests you don't wish to accept—either you don't know the person, or you know them but don't like them. When you decline an invitation, the sender will not receive any notification that you declined. They may notice that they never received a response that you had accepted the invitation. You are not required to explain why you turned down an invitation. Some people may never notice you declined because they send out invitations to anybody and everybody.

Sometimes after we have accepted somebody as a friend, or they accept us, we find that we are tired of seeing their comments, or lack of comments. Or they are making critical, mean, or offensive remarks, and you are tired of reading them on your wall or postings page. You can "unfriend" them—silently delete them from your friends list. Just as when you decline an invitation, there's no notification sent to the person that you removed them from your friends list. They may notice an absence in postings from you, and then notice that you no longer appear on their Friends list. This may be a little bit ruder than the invitation decline, but sometimes you have to do it.

Joining a Group

Most social networks have open and closed groups. Anybody can join an open group. With a closed group, you need to send a request to the group owner for permission to join. Sometimes there are requirements for joining, such as you must be a current or past employee of Company X or an alumnus of XYZ University. The group owner may have access to records to verify that you meet their requirements or may request that you provide some verification.

Once you have joined a group, you can select to be notified by e-mail when there are new postings to the group or you can receive daily or weekly reports of group activity.

Using Your Social Network

That's it! Now you can social network to your heart's content. Well, not quite. You need to jump right in and start using your social network. It's okay if you are quiet for a while and just watch what others are saying and doing. There are general rules of conduct provided by the social network site. But within each group, and each circle of friends, there will be specific rules for courtesy, respect, and decency. Slowly ease yourself in. Most of all, have fun. Even in a professional group, the experience should be positive and enjoyable. One of the things that makes social networks valuable is that you can ask your friends for help using it.

Social Networking on the Go

Years ago, people referred to Blackberry devices as Crackberries because users became addicted to constantly checking their e-mail everywhere they went. Well, Facebook and other social networks can be just as addicting. With the apps built in to Smartphones and high speed wireless access, it's easy to keep up with viewing and posting to your Facebook page anywhere, any time. Whether that is a good thing or a bad thing is completely up to you.

Summary

In this chapter you learned the following about e-mail, instant messaging, and social networks:

- Using e-mail features, including managing your messages and contacts.

- Choosing an e-mail client and the features of some of the more popular e-mail programs.

- Using instant messaging features, including several popular IM programs.

- Making IM programs from different services work together.

- Choosing, joining, and using social networks.

Next Steps

You may find the following related chapters useful:

- Chapter 3: "Using Gadgets and Widgets" for gadgets and widgets for viewing e-mail, instant messaging, and social networks without opening a large program

- Chapter 7: "Getting Free Goodies like Windows Live Essentials" to learn how to install and set up Windows Live Mail and Windows Live Messenger.

- Chapter 10: "Organizing And Sharing Pictures and Videos" to learn other ways to share photos and videos on the Web without using social networks.

- Chapter 18: "Using Windows at Work and On the Road" to learn how to use e-mail, instant messaging, and social networking appropriately in a work environment.

Chapter 9

Surfing the Web

The Web is both a network that connects computers and people across the world and a massive body of information, data, and services. The Web is where you want to go, and your web browser is what will take you there. This chapter is about two things: how to use your web browser to go places, and what you can do when you get there. You have several choices for web browsers: Internet Explorer (often just called IE), which comes with the initial release of Windows 7; and great alternatives such as Mozilla Firefox, Apple Safari, Opera, and Google Chrome.

Microsoft released a new version of IE called IE9 in March 2011. Many Windows 7 users have already upgraded to IE9, and most, if not, all new computers after March 2011 should have it preinstalled by the computer manufacturer. To keep it simple, we will highlight browser features and concepts using IE9 features. But along the way we'll also tell you a little bit about the other browsers. Learn the basics of using IE and you will have no problem using any other browser.

In this chapter, we will show you how to make browsing the Web easy, fun, and safe.

- **Getting started with the Web**: Learn about getting connected to the Internet, and all the cool things you can do on the Web.

- **Getting started with Internet Explorer**: Learn about upgrading to IE 9, the new features, and how to navigate and search the Web.

- **Sharing, saving, and printing web stuff:** Learn how to save or print articles, web pages, and links.

- **Protecting yourself on the Web:** Learn about security, safety, parental controls, privacy, pop-ups, warnings, cookies, and more.

- **Choosing a browser:** Learn about other popular browsers; installation; changing your default browser; and exporting, importing, and syncing settings and preferences.

Getting Started with the Web

The Web changes quickly. In 1994, a hot little program called Netscape Navigator made waves with a graphical, visual way to connect to the Internet. A year later Microsoft launched a revolutionary new version of Windows, Windows 95, and included its own web browser, Internet Explorer (IE). Thus began what is commonly called the browser wars. Initially, Netscape Navigator was the dominant browser, but within a couple years Internet Explorer overtook Netscape. Netscape faded, but out of its ashes, a new challenger emerged: Mozilla Firefox. In some regions of the world, Firefox is more popular than IE, and other browsers like Google Chrome, Opera, and Apple Safari are chipping away for a share of browser usage, mostly at the expense of IE.

While the browser wars raged, a small company in Seattle calling itself Amazon started selling books online. Today, Amazon.com is the largest online reseller (of just about anything imaginable) in the United States. Moving beyond selling and shipping books, they have led the stampede to eBooks with their digital book reader, Kindle. Many of you reading this book are probably doing so on a Kindle, Nook, Sony eReader, or an application on your PC, tablet, or mobile device.

In New York State in the mid-1990s a boy named Mark was learning Atari Basic Programming. Today Mark Zuckerberg is the creator, chief executive, and president of the most popular social networking site, Facebook.

Amazon and Facebook are examples of how quickly our use of the Internet changes from simply a way to access information online to a dominating force in retailing and a new way to communicate and share with friends and family. The next big thing may be on a college student's computer today and spreading like wildfire tomorrow.

According to Wikipedia, about 30 percent of the world (a little over 2 billion people) use the Internet. Browsers have evolved considerably since the IE/Netscape Navigator browser wars. So have the things you can do on the Web. This chapter will take a look at IE and other browsers plus some of the things you can do or visit on the Web.

Connecting to the Internet

We're assuming you have an Internet connection, something like the typical home network shown in Figure 9–1.

> **TIP** Need help setting up a home network or Internet connection? See Chapter 15.

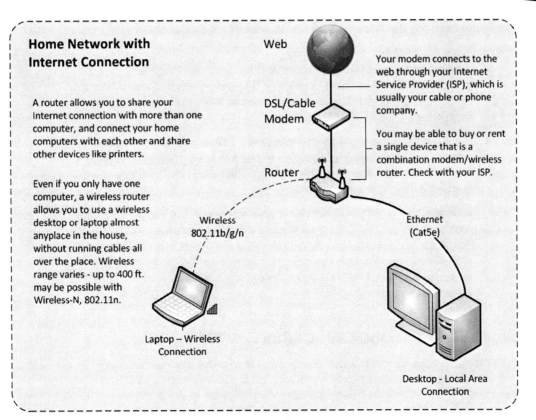

Figure 9–1. *A typical home network with an Internet connection*

Maybe you're not at home. Are you connecting to the Internet through a corporate network at work or at your favorite coffee shop using a Wi-Fi connection? If so, you'll want to read Chapter 18 for more information about using work and public networks.

Where are the Apps?

If you are one of those people who live on their Smartphone, you may be wondering, "Where are all those apps like Facebook, Twitter, and YouTube?" On your computer, they're not apps; they're web sites that you can access through your browser. The convenience of apps on Smartphone has influenced the most recent browser releases, however, so you will find many built-in browser features that make it easier to access your favorite web sites. Also, many of these sites can be accessed on your PC through gadgets and widgets on your desktop, which are a closer to the apps you use on your Smartphone than a full blown program on your PC.

How can you bring the apps experience to your PC and browser?

- **Add gadgets and widgets to your desktop.** See Chapter 3 to learn how to use the **Microsoft Windows Gadgets** included with Windows 7, **Google Desktop Gadgets**, and **Yahoo! Widgets**. All of these are free, easy to install, and fun to use.

- **Pin your favorite sites to the Windows 7 taskbar**. This cool new feature in IE 9 lets you add a site so that it is always one click away. See the "Pinning Your Favorite Sites to the Windows 7 Taskbar" section later in this chapter.

- **Manage the sites you visit most with the New Tab page**. With this new IE 9 feature, your favorite sites are just a click away on the New Tab page. This tab displays the sites you visit most and your favorite web sites. You can also pin sites from the New Tab page directly to your taskbar. See the "Managing Your Favorite Sites with the New Tab Page" section later in this chapter.

What Can I Use Internet Explorer For?

We find more uses for the Internet every day—and more devices and ways to connect to it. If you are just starting out on the Internet, or are a very casual user and have not ventured very far, Table 9–1 shows a sampling of some popular sites and activities on the Internet. This list is not an endorsement of any specific web site nor is it based on any ratings or comparisons.

Table 9–1. *Useful Web Sites*

What You Can Do	Where To Go
Social networking: Connect with friends, colleagues, relatives, professional groups, and social causes.	▓ Facebook, `www.facebook.com` ▓ LinkedIn, `www.linkedin.com` ▓ MySpace, `www.myspace.com` ▓ Friendster, `www.friendster.com` ▓ Twitter, `www.twitter.com`
E-mail: All of the major e-mail services provide web-page based access so that you don't need to install an e-mail program. You just log in to your account from a web page.	▓ Hotmail (Windows Live Mail), `www.hotmail.com` ▓ Gmail (Google), `www.gmail.com` ▓ Yahoo!, `www.mail.yahoo.com`

What You Can Do	Where To Go
Blogging: Share your life, interests, opinions, and expertise. Write it as a diary or as your own personal platform.	▩ WordPress, www.wordpress.org ▩ Typepad, www.typepad.com ▩ Squarespace, www.squarespace.com ▩ Blogger, www.blogger.com

TIP: We talk more about these sites in Chapter 8.

What You Can Do	Where To Go
News: You can get all of your news online any time of day. Local, national, international—you can find news in your language and interests.	▩ MSNBC, www.msnbc.com ▩ CNN, www.cnn.com ▩ New York Times, www.nytimes.com ▩ Wall Street Journal, www.online.wsj.com

NOTE: Some news sites require a paid subscription to access all of their content or for premium content.

What You Can Do	Where To Go
Search and reference: You can search for text, pictures, videos, maps, and more. Most search providers are available directly from your browser search bar. You can also find reference sites from encyclopedias to dictionaries.	▩ Bing, www.bing.com ▩ Google, www.google.com ▩ Ask, www.ask.com ▩ Wikipedia, www.wikipedia.org ▩ MSN Encarta, www.encarta.msn.com ▩ Dictionary, www.dictionary.com ▩ MapQuest, www.mapquest.com ▩ Google Maps, maps.google.com

What You Can Do	Where To Go
Movie tickets and theater times: Find out what's playing, view movie ratings, and purchase tickets.	▨ Fandango, www.fandango.com ▨ Many other movie sites are available for different countries and languages. ▨ Movie theater chains and individual theaters often have their own web sites.
Shopping: You can go directly to shopping sites or you can search price comparison sites for the best prices on a particular item or model.	▨ Amazon.com, www.amazon.com ▨ Staples, www.staples.com ▨ Pricegrabber, www.pricegrabber.com ▨ Yahoo! Shopping, shopping.yahoo.com
Dating: Not to be confused with adult web sites, these sites match people up by interests, profiles, etc.	▨ eHarmony, www.eharmony.com ▨ Match.com, www.match.com ▨ Chemistry.com, www.chemistry.com
Entertaining and services deal of the day: These types of sites are popping up all over; they are usually localized to your area. Some are limited time offers, like daily deals for 50 percent off at a restaurant, spa, dance lessons, etc.	▨ Groupon, www.groupon.com ▨ Living Social, www.livingsocial.com
Selling and buying: Besides the regular online retailers, there are other ways to find and buy stuff or sell your own stuff, such as online classifieds and auctions.	▨ Craigslist, www.craigslist.org ▨ Ebay, www.ebay.com
Employment: You can post your resume and search for jobs in a specific field or category.	▨ Monster.com, www.monster.com ▨ Dice.com, www.dice.com ▨ Local and state government job listing sites

What You Can Do	Where To Go
Travel: You can shop rates and book hotels, rental cars, airlines, tours, and more. Also check hotel chain and airline web sites.	▦ Orbitz, www.orbitz.com ▦ Hotels.com, www.hotels.com ▦ Expedia, www.expedia.com ▦ Priceline, www.priceline.com ▦ Travelocity, www.travelocity.com ▦ Kayak, www.kayak.com
Video posting: Upload your own videos and view others.	▦ YouTube, www.youtube.com

> **TIP:** We'll talk a little bit more about YouTube and other video sharing sites in Chapter 10.

Video streaming: Rent movies, catch up on TV series, stream movies on demand.	▦ Hulu, www.hulu.com ▦ Netflix, www.netflix.com ▦ Blockbuster, www.blockbuster.com
eBooks: You can download eBooks to your PC as well as to your reading device	▦ Amazon Kindle, www.amazon.com ▦ Nook, www.barnesandnoble.com/nook ▦ Kobo eReader, www.kobobooks.com ▦ Sony eReader, ebookstore.sony.com

> **TIP:** If a title is not available in your reader's native format, check with the publisher for PDF versions. Also there are hundreds of free classics available through Project Gutenberg and other sites. See Chapter 11 for additional eBook options and resources.

What You Can Do	Where To Go
Music stores: There are two basic types of services. You can buy music, download it to your PC or device, and you own it. Or you can subscribe to a music service for a monthly fee to download as much music as you want, but you can't keep the music when you quit the service.	▓ Amazon MP3, `www.amazon.com` ▓ iTunes, `www.apple.com/itunes` ▓ Zune marketplace, `social.zune.net/music/` ▓ Rhapsody, `www.rhapsody.com`

> **TIP:** We'll talk a little bit more about media you can download and share on your computer and media center in Chapter 11.

School and online learning: Most colleges and universities use course management software for communicating, turning in papers, group discussions, tests, and grades.	▓ Moodle, `www.moodle.org` ▓ Blackboard, `www.blackboard.com`

Getting Started with Internet Explorer

All browsers are not the same, but if you learn the basics of one, you can easily pick up any of the others. Internet Explorer was for a long time the most-used browser worldwide, but other browsers are eating away at IE's market share with new features and improvements. There are still some technical differences between browsers, so programs and web sites can be designed to work best with a particular browser. This is why you will sometimes see banners on web sites that say "Best viewed with Internet Explorer." Fortunately, this occurs less frequently than it used to because the competing browsers are keeping up with each other's technologies—and the public doesn't like being forced to use a particular browser.

> **NOTE:** If you are using a computer at work or in a large company, before upgrading to the latest version of your browser or switching to a new one, check with your IT department to make sure that the new version is approved, tested, and supported. Depending on how much control your company exerts on your installation rights, you might not even be allowed to perform an upgrade yourself. If you upgrade to an unapproved version, your help desk may not be able to help you if you have problems using company programs or web sites. See Chapter 18 to learn more about using computers in a corporate environment.

Deciding Whether to Upgrade to Internet Explorer 9

When software programs are upgraded, the new versions are supposed to be easier to use. In some cases, they are easier for new computer users to learn, but require experienced users to learn a new way that is different from what they are used to. I have not found anything in IE 9 more difficult to use than the previous version, IE 8. However, IE 9 has several cool new features that make browsing easier. IE 9 is easier to use, so about the only reason not to upgrade is if your company has not approved it yet.

To Install Internet Explorer 9

If you have Windows Updates on, Microsoft will push IE 9 out to you as an Important Update. Install it from Windows Updates: **Control Panel ➤ Windows Update ➤ Install Updates**. If you have updates turned off, you'll have to click **Check for updates** to download the update. You can also go to Microsoft's web site and download it yourself.

To Uninstall Internet Explorer 9

If your new computer came with IE 9, you can't uninstall it and revert to IE 8. But if you installed IE 9 yourself, you can uninstall it if you don't like it. The IE 9 installation is considered an update, not a program installation. So to uninstall IE 9, you must go to **Control Panel ➤ Programs ➤ Programs and Features ➤ View installed updates** or just search for **View installed updates** from the **Start** menu. Scroll down to the **Microsoft Windows** section, and then select **Windows Internet Explorer 9**.

Internet Explorer 9 Highlights

Internet Explorer 9 in its initial default view is very clean and streamlined. If you miss menus, your Favorites bar, and other toolbars, you can add them back. They're not gone; they're just hidden unless you want them to show. Figure 9–2 shows the cleaner, leaner look of IE 9.

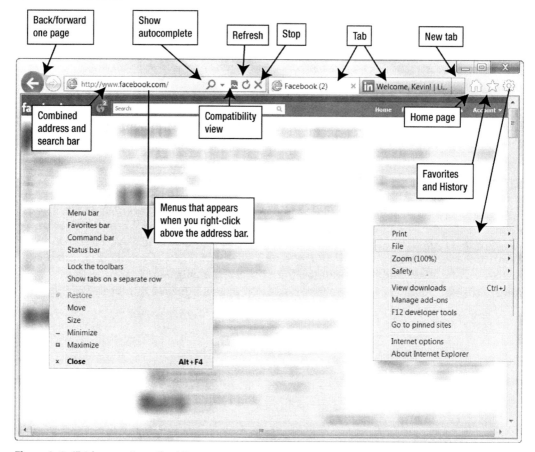

Figure 9–2. *IE 9 is more streamlined than ever.*

Most browsers contain most or all of these features. In a few instances, Microsoft uses a different term in IE than the terms used by other browsers; Table 9–2 highlights common terms.

Table 9–2. *Common Browser Terms*

Back and **Forward**	Go to the last page you visited or move forward one page.
New tab	View another web page in another tab without opening a separate window.
Address bar	Displays the web address of the current page or where you enter a new address to go to another web page. In some browsers, the address bar and search box are combined into one. All of the browsers described in this chapter except Safari allow you to type search words directly in the address bar, regardless of whether the browser had a separate search box.
Autocomplete	Suggests web pages that match what you are typing as you enter a web address.
Compatibility view	Fixes web pages so they display better in the browser when a web site was designed for older browsers.
Refresh(Reload)	Make the browser go back to the web server to get an updated version of the current web page.
Stop	Stop loading or reloading the current web page.
Add to Favorites(Bookmark this page)	Add the current web page to a list of web sites you visit regularly.
Search	Search for web sites related to the search term.
Home page	The default web page when you first open the browser.
Menu bar and toolbars	Almost all of the browsers have a menu bar and additional toolbars for favorites or bookmarks.

Cool IE 9 features

Besides the cleaner browser frame, IE 9 adds other visual improvements such as several enhancements to tabs.

Pin Your Favorite Sites Directly to the Taskbar

Instead of starting IE and then going to the site, you can go directly to a site pinned to the taskbar, as shown in Figure 9–3.

1. Click the tab.

2. Drag the tab (not the title bar) to the taskbar.

3. Release the tab.

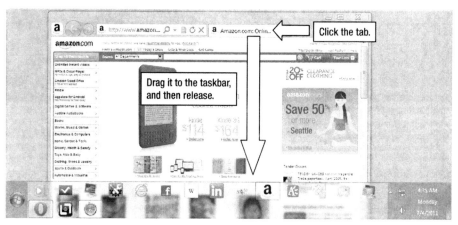

Figure 9–3. *Drag and drop a tab to pin the site to the taskbar.*

The button shows an icon for the site (see Figure 9–4).

Figure 9–4. *Favorite sites pinned to the taskbar*

You can also drag a tab and pin it to the Start menu or to the Favorites bar.

Your pinned site doesn't have to be a single web page. You can add multiple pages to a pinned site. Navigate to the web page you want to add, right-click the icon for the pinned site to the left of the Back button, and then click **Add as a home page.**

Organize Tabs in Windows

There are several ways you can manage tabs.

- Break up multiple tabs into separate windows. Drag the tabs off the window to display them in their own windows.

- Rearrange the order of tabs within a window.

- Give your tabs more space. If you need a little more space for tabs, you can show them in a different row below the address bar. Right-click the toolbar area and then click **Show tabs on a separate row**.

- Use the color coding of similar tabs to further help you view and group them.

The New Tab Page

Click the **New tab** button or press Ctrl+T. The New Tab page displays your most popular sites (the ones you visit the most), as shown in Figure 9–5.

Figure 9–5. *The New Tab page displays your most popular sites.*

Improved Messages and Notifications

Those Information Bar messages in the yellow box under the toolbar above the web page have been moved to the Notification Bar at the bottom of the screen, as shown in Figure 9–6.

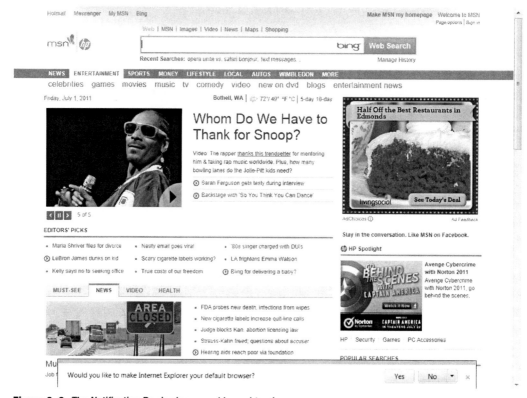

Figure 9–6. The Notification Bar is clearer and less obtrusive.

The messages are clearer, easier to understand, and less obtrusive.

Navigating and Searching the Web

There are several ways to get to web sites through your browser.

■ **Type a web address in the address/search bar**. We see and hear web site addresses in many places, such as newspapers, magazines, television, and radio.

TIP: When using the address bar, if you just type the name of a web site, you can press Ctrl+Enter and IE will add "www" in front of it and ".com" after it.

- **Search the Web**. In the address bar/search bar, type what you are looking for.

> **TIP:** You can add the Address toolbar to the Windows 7 Taskbar so that you can search for a web site or go to a web site without opening your web browser first.

- **Click links in e-mail or documents** (like Word documents or PDF files).

> **CAUTION:** Be careful about links you receive in e-mail. Only click links if you know the sender is trustworthy. Sometimes what appears to be a message from a friend at an e-mail address you recognize may actually be spam sent out fraudulently without your friend's knowledge and approval.

- **Add to and use your Favorites list**. Every browser offers some way to import/export favorites/bookmarks, and you can sync your favorites across all the computers you use. Over time, you can build up quite a large Favorites or bookmarks list.

- **Check your History**. If you visited a web site a few days ago or a few weeks ago and forgot to add it to your Favorites, you may remember enough about the site name that you can find it again. History is accessible through the Favorites (star) button. Or you can start typing what you remember and IE will check the words from the URL or the site's title against those in your History and suggest matches as you match.

- **Read the "What Can I Use Internet Explorer For?" section earlier in this chapter.** Though some of the sites are regional or specific to the U.S., the list gives an idea of the wide variety of web sites out there.

Sharing, Saving, and Printing Web Stuff

It's nice to save a few trees by not printing any more than necessary. But sometimes you want to keep a copy of a web page for a long time, or you want to share it with others.

Even if you only print a few things, the regular settings and steps for printing may leave you with a lot of extra pages and information you don't need. If you want to save the web page as a web file, sometimes that's not much better than printing. And we've all had the experience of clicking a web link we saved or somebody sent us long ago and getting a "Web page could not be found" message.

Fortunately there are several ways you can use printing more efficiently, save web pages to usable files, and share content from web pages with others. We'll show you how to

- Print only the pages you want.

- Print web articles with little or no ads or extra clutter.

- Save web pages to a file that you can save and share today and still be able to view years from now even when you don't have access to the Web or the web site is gone.

Printing Web Pages

As part of the slimming down and tidying up of the toolbars, menus, and buttons, IE doesn't display the print button in the default view. It's not gone; it's just a few clicks deeper.

To access the IE print command:

1. Click the **Settings** button in the toolbar area. In the drop-down menu, click **Print**. In the second menu, click **Print**, as shown in Figure 9–7.

   –or–

   Press Ctrl+P. The Print dialog box appears, as shown in Figure 9–7.

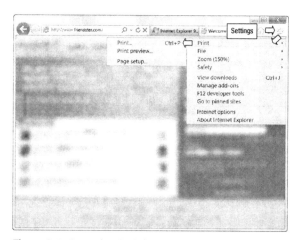

Figure 9–7._Accessing the Print command in IE_

2. Select a printer, as shown in Figure 9–8. Adjust the page range, number of copies, preferences, and any other settings as needed, and then click **Print**.

   Check your printer for the printed pages.

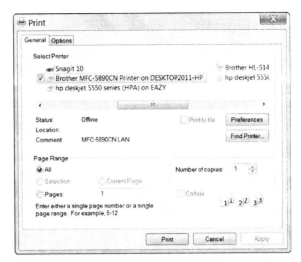

Figure 9–8. *Internet Explorer print dialog box*

If this is a typical web page, you may have 1-2 pages of articles and content, a page of the extra stuff like the links for related information, and maybe even a page with just the web site title in the header and the web site and address in the footer and nothing of value or interest.

Fortunately, you can use the Print preview option to see what is going to be printed before you print it. Then you can specify only those pages when you actually print.

To print only the pages you want:

1. Click the **Settings** button in the toolbar area. In the drop-down menu, click **Print**. In the second menu, click **Print preview**, as shown in Figure 9–9.

   The Print Preview window appears, as shown in Figure 9–10.

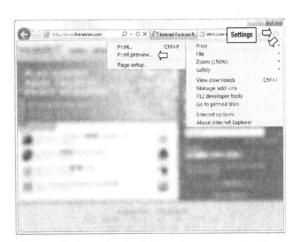

Figure 9–9. *Accessing the Print preview command in IE*

Note that only the first page appears to have useful information.

Review the pages displayed and note which pages you really want or need.

2. Click the **Print** button.

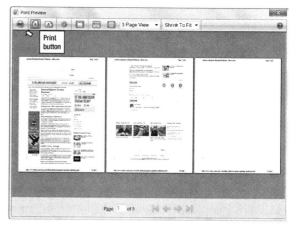

Figure 9–10. *Internet Explorer Print Preview window*

The Print dialog box appears, as shown in Figure 09–11.

3. Select a printer, specify a page or page range, change any other settings as needed, and then click **Print**.

Check your printer for the printed pages.

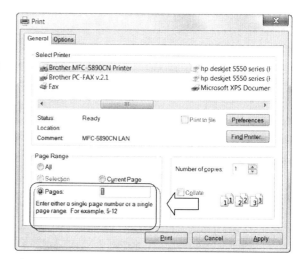

Figure 9–11. *Select a page or page range so that you don't print unneeded pages.*

Printing Printer-Friendly Versions of Web Pages

Another way to reduce or eliminate unnecessary pages when printing is to use a printer-friendly version of a web page. Web pages that are articles or news story content often provide extra links for sharing or saving the web pages. Many web pages have a Print button or link within the web page (as shown in Figure 9–12) that reformats the page to a printer-friendly version (as shown in Figure 9–13).

To print a printer-friendly version of a web page (if available):

1. Look for a **Print** link on the web page, similar to the example in Figure 9–12.

2. Click the **Print** link, and a simple view of the page is displayed, similar to Figure 9–13. There are many different programs that web sites can use to display this in the printer friendly view, so the commands and design of the window will vary.

Figure 9–12. *Some web pages offer a Print link or button within the web page to provide a more readable version when printed.*

Figure 9–13. *Printer-friendly versions of a web page, when available, are created by the web site, not by IE.*

3. On the printer-friendly page, click the **Print** button/link or right-click the page and click **Print Preview** to see what it will look like when printed. Most of the time you won't need to select or specify a page range because the printer-friendly version doesn't usually contain the extra web pages you get when you just print the regular web page.

4. Change other settings as needed in the Print dialog box, and then click **Print**.

Other Handy Links for Sharing Web Pages with Friends

Many web pages also provide links to share a web page. As you can see in the previous example, the web page also provided a **Share** link, which allows you to send a link to the article and the opening paragraphs to a friend through your default e-mail account. Web pages may also include links so that you can share the article on your favorite social network like **Facebook**, **Twitter**, and **LinkedIn**.

Print to Adobe PDF or Microsoft XPS Document Writer

Web browsers also include the capability to save a web page to a file, and we'll show you how to do this in the "Saving a web page to a file" section in this chapter. While this method works, it's not the most convenient way to share or save web pages for future use. Fortunately, there are better ways to save web pages that only require one file, look identical to the original, and don't require a browser to open or view.

- Print to Adobe PDF
- Print to Microsoft XPS Document Writer

Both of these document formats can convert a web page to a portable document that can be viewed on almost any computer.

Adobe PDF

Adobe PDF files can be viewed with the free Adobe Reader program, which is available for almost any computer operating system. To print to PDF, you need a PDF editor program like Adobe Acrobat, which is not free, or another program, some of which are less expensive or even free.

TIP: You can learn more about printing to PDF and how to buy or get free PDF editors in Chapter 13.

Microsoft XPS Document Writer

XPS is short for XML Paper Specification. It is a document format similar to Adobe PDF that allows you to view, save, share, digitally sign, and protect document content. You can create XPS documents by selecting the Microsoft XPS Document Writer when printing a document. Any document or file type that you can send to a physical printer or Adobe PDF, you can print to Microsoft XPS Document Writer. A viewer is included in Windows 7, Office 2007, and Office 2010. The viewer can be downloaded for free for Windows Vista or Windows XP. It is platform independent and available royalty-free, so other companies have created programs for Mac and Linux that you can buy or download for free.

To print to Microsoft XPS:

1. Start one of the following printing procedures:

   ▧ To access the Internet Explorer print command.

   ▧ To print only the pages you want.

   ▧ To print a printer-friendly version of a web page (if available).

2. When the Print dialog box appears, as shown in Figure 9–14, select the printer **Microsoft XPS Document Writer**.

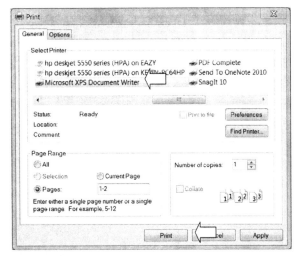

Figure 9–14. *Selecting the Microsoft XPS Document Writer as your printer*

3. Change any other settings as needed, and then click **Print**.

   The Save As dialog box appears. Since you are not actually printing but saving to a file, you must specify a file name and location, as shown in Figure 9–15.

4. Click **Save**.

   Check to see that it "printed" okay by opening the newly created XPS file.

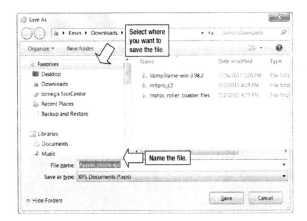

Figure 9–15. *When printing with the Microsoft XPS Document Writer, the Save As dialog box specifies where to save the .XPS file to, and the file name*

5. In a folder window or Libraries window, navigate to the location where you saved the file, as shown in Figure 9–16.

6. Double-click the XPS file.

Figure 9–16. *Find the XPS file and double-click it.*

The XPS Viewer window appears, as shown in Figure 9–17.

The .XPS copy of the web page is searchable, and you can select text to copy and paste into other documents.

Figure 9–17. *A document in the XPS Viewer*

Saving a Web Page to a File

Although web pages can be saved to files, the results are not always convenient or as good as the original. There are several file formats to save a web page, but they either don't save all of it to a single file or the file format isn't readable by other browsers.

To save a web page to the browser file format of "Webpage, complete (.htm, .html)":

1. Click the **Settings** button in the toolbar area. In the drop-down menu, click **File**. In the second menu, click **Save as**, as shown in Figure 9–18.

   The Save Webpage dialog box appears, as shown in Figure 9–19.

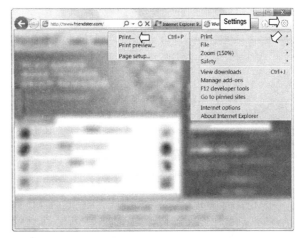

Figure 9–18. *Saving a file in IE*

2. Navigate to the folder where you want to save it.

3. Type an easy-to-remember file name.

4. In **Save as type**, select **Webpage, complete (*.htm; *.html)**, and then click **Save**.

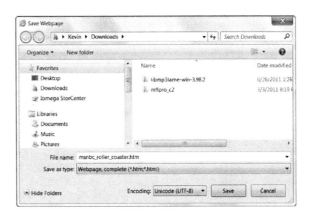

Figure 9–19. *Specify a location, name, and file type*

To open a saved web page:

1. Press Ctrl+O.

    –or–

    If you have Menus on in the
    toolbar, click **File ➤ Open**.

    The Open dialog box appears,
    as shown in Figure 9–20.

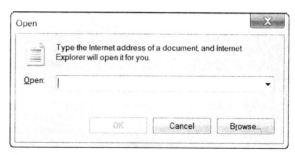

Figure 9–20. *The Open dialog box in IE*

When you save a web page as
Webpage, complete, IE saves
it in several parts using the
name you provided, as shown
in Figure 9–21:

- A folder, which contains
  all of the image files,
  script files, and .htm files
  that make up the page.
  In this example, the
  folder
  msnbc_roller_coaster_file
  s contains 27 files.

Figure 9–21. *The Webpage, complete option saves a web
page in several parts.*

- An .htm file named
  msnbc_roller_coaster.ht
  m brings all those parts
  together into the page
  that you can view.

2. Select the .htm file, click
Open, and then click **Open**
again.

The web page is displayed, as
shown in Figure 9–22. It may
not look exactly like it did
when you previously visited
the page. Notice in the banner
that some of the text overlaps
over "Seasonal Travel" and the
"bing Search" box.

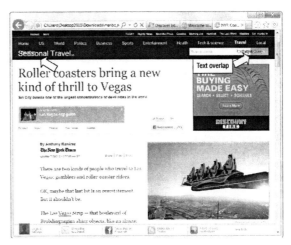

Figure 9–22. *A web page opened from stored web page files may not display exactly like the original.*

> **NOTE:** This is not an ideal way to send web pages to somebody. If you want to send or save the
> entire article, use the Print to Adobe PDF or Print to Microsoft XPS Document option or just send
> them a link to the web page.

Saving and Copying Text and Pictures from Web Pages

It is fairly easy to copy text or pictures from a web page. However, just because it is
easy doesn't mean it's right or legal to copy. I'm not a lawyer and can't give legal
advice, but there are some general rules to follow whenever you copy information from
somebody else's web site.

Be fair and careful about how you copy and save anything from a web page.

- Whether you see a copyright sign © or not on a web page, it is
  copyright protected. Even if you get it from Wikipedia, you need to
  provide the proper citations when quoting works or content.

- Plagiarism is easy to detect. There are numerous web sites and
  programs available for teachers, authors, and students to check
  content for plagiarism.

- A good place to start for making sure you are citing works properly is
  MLA style, www.mla.org. Most college texts for writing research papers
  should also provide guidance on acceptable usage of other's work.

Within Internet Explorer there are several ways to copy or save text or pictures from a web page:

To copy text from a web page into another document

Select the text on the page as you would select text in any other type of document, right-click the selection, and then click **Copy**. Then go to the other document and paste it.

To copy a picture into another document

Select the picture on the page, right-click the selection, and then click **Copy**. Then go to the other document and paste it.

To save a picture

Right-click the picture on the page, and then click **Save picture as** or **Set as background**.

Accessing Internet Options

Internet Options provide access to many important settings for things like temporary files, accessibility, cookies, security, AutoComplete, privacy, pop-ups, Internet connections, preferred programs, search preferences, and other advanced settings.

To access Internet Options: In IE 9, click the **Settings** button and then click **Internet options**, as shown in Figure 9–23.

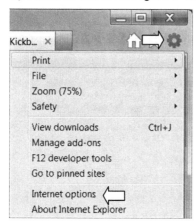

Figure 9–23. *Access Internet Options through the Settings button*

Protecting Yourself on the Web

The Web provides a direct route into your computer, so in addition to the security features in Windows 7, IE provides a number of features to protect your data, identity, and privacy on the Web. In an ideal world we could visit any web site we want, download anything we want, and not be bothered or endangered. Unfortunately, all sorts of dangers lurk on the Web: phishing web sites that try to trick you into revealing your user name and password for your online banking, viruses and spyware that hitchhike on free web downloads, and sites that gather information about your web viewing patterns.

> **NOTE:** IE security settings are not enough by themselves to protect your computer. See Chapter 16 to learn how to set up antivirus, Internet security suites, antispyware, and data protection for your computer.

If you had to figure out how to set every security setting, you would never have any time to actually surf the Web. IE9 makes safety easier by setting many features by default to a high enough safety level for most people without being too restrictive. IE has many security options and privacy settings that can be changed or customized in Internet Options through the General, Security, Privacy, and Content tabs.

Browsing History and InPrivate Browsing

If you need to keep what sites you visit private from others who have access to your computer, there are several IE ways you can protect the privacy of your browsing:

- **Turn on InPrivate Browsing**: Click the **Settings** button, click **Safety**, and then click **InPrivate Browsing**. When you are in InPrivate Browsing, IE doesn't save your browsing history and doesn't save any words in Autocomplete that you used in searches.

- **Delete your browsing history**: Click the **Settings** button, click **Safety**, and then click **Delete browsing history**. In the Delete Browsing History window, you can select whether to keep or delete Favorites, temporary internet files, cookies, history, passwords, and more.

- **Change how IE keeps track of your browser history**: Click the **Settings** button and then click **Internet options.** In the Internet Options dialog box, select the **General** tab. In the Browsing history area, use the settings button to change how IE checks for new versions of files, where those history files are changed, and view what files and objects are stored in the Temporary Internet Files folder.

History can be useful if you want to find a web site you visited yesterday, last week, or last month. It also stores copies of the web pages and content so that the next time you visit the site it loads faster. The history also contains cookies from web sites you visit. The browsing history is stored in the Temporary Internet Files folder and could pose a privacy risk because somebody else with access to your computer could check that folder and see what sites you have visited.

Adjusting Your Overall Internet Security Settings

Although the default security settings in IE work for most people, those settings may be too restrictive or not restrictive enough for others. Maybe you are getting a lot of messages asking if you want to allow this Active X control or that add-in. Maybe you get too many pop-up windows. With Internet Options, you can adjust the overall security level and customize individual security settings.

To change or view security settings:

1. In Internet Explorer, click the **Settings** button and then click **Internet options**.

2. In the Internet Options dialog box, select the **Security** tab shown in Figure 9–24.

The default setting is **Medium-high**.

3. To block more controls, downloads, and content, drag the slider up to **High**, and then click **OK**.

To allow more controls, downloads, and content without prompting for permissions, drag the slider down to **Medium**, and then click **OK**.

As you drag the slider up or down, you will see a description of what that setting allows.

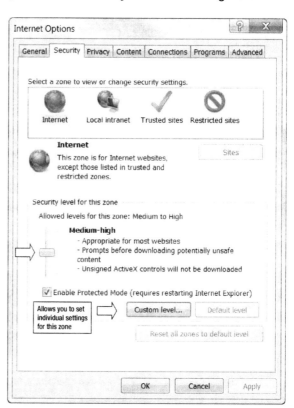

Figure 9–24. *Internet Options dialog box, Security tab*

To adjust individual settings, click **Custom level**.

In the Security Settings list shown in Figure 9–25, locate the setting you want to change, and then select:

- **Disable** if you don't want to ever allow this control or action. You will not be notified when a web site or program requests to use this control or action; IE will just automatically block it.

- **Enable** if you want to allow this control or action. You will not be notified when a web site or program wants to use this control or action; IE will just automatically allow it.

- **Prompt** if you want IE to display a message when a site requests to use this control or action, so that you can decide whether or not to allow it.

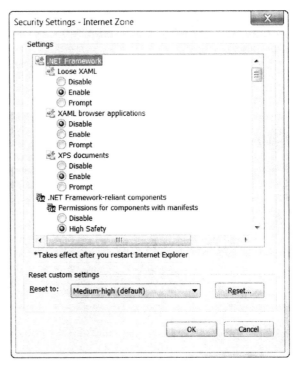

Figure 9–25. *Internet Options security settings*

Managing Your Cookies

Cookies sometimes get a bad reputation because they can be used to store private information and share that data with external web sites. The web sites can then use that information to target specific information based on your browsing habits or history. It can be annoying if not disturbing when the web sites you visit seem to know a little bit too much about you without you explicitly giving anybody information about what city you are in or your interests.

Cookies can also be beneficial. When you log in to a web site that you visit frequently, you may see a checkbox that says something like "Remember my password." If you select that option, your username and password may be stored in a cookie so that the next time you visit the web site, it will find the cookie and won't request that you enter your name and password. If you don't allow any cookies, you will be annoyed at how many sites you regularly visit require that you log in every time.

If you install another browser, you may have the option to import favorites, cookies, and other settings. Otherwise, browsers don't share cookies, so if you switch to another browser, it may seem like you have to start all over again with Windows or your browser remembering your login, password, or preferences for web sites that you regularly visit.

Changing Your Privacy Settings

The privacy settings in Internet Options allow you to change the settings for how cookies, pop-ups, and InPrivate Browsing settings are handled. The default settings work well for most people, but sometimes people want to block cookies or pop-ups from specific sites.

To change your privacy settings:

1. In IE, click the **Settings** button and then click **Internet options.**

2. In the Internet Options dialog box, select the **Privacy** tab shown in Figure 9–26.

3. In the **Settings** area you can:

   ▪ Adjust how IE automatically handles cookies with the slider control.

   ▪ Block or allow cookies from specific sites with the **Sites** button.

   ▪ Import your cookies settings from a file with the **Import** button.

   ▪ Override the automatic cookie handling with the **Advanced** button.

   ▪ In the **Location** settings, you can control whether web sites can request your physical location.

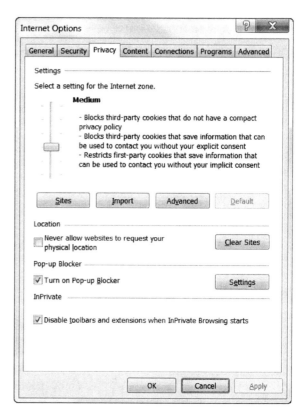

Figure 9–26. *Internet Options dialog box, Privacy tab*

Allowing web site cookies can be beneficial to you for web pages that you visit frequently, so that the web site can remember your preferences. For example, a news site like MSNBC can display things like news, sports, the weather for your city, and stock quotes for specific companies.

In the **Pop-up Blocker** settings, you can turn the blocker on or off and specify sites that you want to allow pop-ups from.

The **InPrivate** settings are useful because toolbars and extensions often send and receive tracking information about your web site activity and provide a backdoor for harmful or malicious software to sneak its way onto your computer. People often use InPrivate browsing when visiting adult web sites, which as a category presents a higher risk to your computer. InPrivate doesn't prevent viruses but it can contain those activities in a sandbox to reduce the chances of cookies associated with those sites popping up ads or windows when you are no longer in an adult viewing domain.

Or maybe you are just gift shopping or planning a surprise for your family and you don't want them to discover the sites you've been visiting!

Parental Controls

Internet Explorer provides several parental controls settings in Internet Options. While these settings can help control and protect your children's computer usage, the Parental Controls features provided with Windows Live Family Safety are even better. See Chapter 7 to learn how to download the free Windows Live Family Safety, and Chapter 12 to learn how to set up full protection not only for web browsing, but for the entire computer.

Choosing a Browser

All of the popular web browsers are free, and in the last couple of years the competition has heated up. This competition is good news for computer users, as each browser works hard to come out with better features, performance, and usability.

In addition to this market competition, it's mandatory in some countries that users be offered a choice of which browser to use as the default browser. For example, since March 2010, as part of a settlement between the European Commission and Microsoft, European users of IE and new computer buyers have been presented a Web Browser Choice screen to make it easier to download and install browsers other than IE.

Which browser should you use? IE, which is included in Windows 7? Mozilla Firefox, which is neck-and-neck with IE in downloads? Or another browser? Each has its fans and detractors. Some are more popular in some areas of the world than others. How well does each browser handle your native language? Fortunately, you can install several or all of these on your computer without too much competition *within* Windows.

> **NOTE:** Every browser wants to be your best friend. So when you install a new browser, it will ask you if you want to make it your default browser. We'll show you how to control which browser is your main browser in a few pages.

Computer manufacturers can add other browsers to your Windows 7 computer. So you may already have another browser besides IE. Figure 9–27 shows the taskbar tiles for Internet Explorer, Firefox, Google Chrome, Apple Safari, and Opera.

Figure 9–27. *Internet Explorer, Firefox, Chrome, Safari, and Opera*

Installing Another Browser

You can't install multiple versions of the same browser (IE 8 and IE9, or Firefox 4 and Firefox 5) on the same computer, but you can install multiple browsers (IE, Firefox, Chrome, Opera, and Safari). Every browser prompts you to make it your default browser during installation or the first time you open it; see Table 9–3. Sometimes it's easy to miss this option and it will become your default browser. If that happens, go to the "Changing Your Default Browser" section to learn how to fix it.

Table 9–3. *Browser Download and Installation Notes*

Browser	Download and Installation Notes
Firefox	▪ Download from www.mozilla.com/firefox.
	▪ "Use Firefox as my default web browser" appears in second page of installation wizard, after choosing Typical Installation.
	▪ After setup is complete, another message appears asking if you want to make Firefox your default browser.
Chrome	▪ Download from www.google.com/chrome.
	▪ "Set Google Chrome as my default browser" is displayed on the Google Chrome Terms of Service page at the beginning of installation.
	▪ The first time you run the browser, a notification banner under the address bar asks if you want set it as the default browser.

Browser	Download and Installation Notes
Opera	▦ Download from www.opera.com.
	▦ Default browser checkbox is pre-selected but doesn't appear on the main wizard page. On the initial **Terms of Service** page, you must click **Options**, and then clear the checkbox.
	▦ The first time you open Opera, it will ask you again if you want to make it your default browser (unless you already allowed it during installation).
Safari	▦ Download from www.apple.com/safari/download/.
	▦ Will require a restart of your computer at the end of installation (none of the other browsers required a restart).
	▦ The first time you open Safari after installation, it will ask you if you want to make it your default browser.

Firefox

Figure 9–28 shows the top of the Firefox browser window, with a minimal amount of toolbars and buttons.

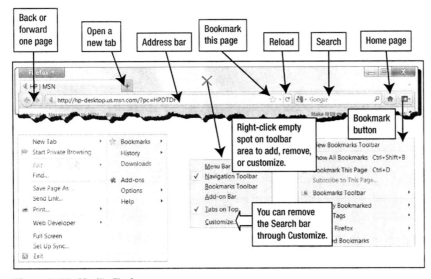

Figure 9–28. *Mozilla Firefox*

Though all of the labels make this look really busy, most of the features you need are out on top, not hidden in menus.

Chrome

Google Chrome simplifies the top of the browser window even more by combining the search with the address bar, as shown in Figure 9–29.

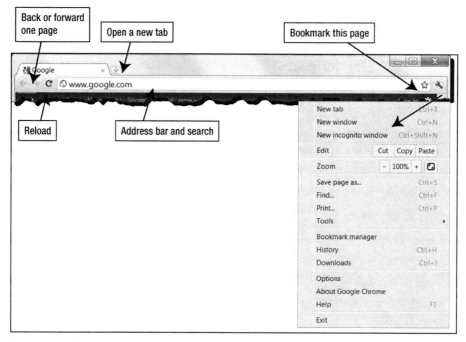

Figure 9–29. *Google Chrome*

NOTE: Many menu commands are also available through keyboard shortcuts.

Opera

The Opera browser has many of the same controls and features as other browsers, but it also offers some interesting unique features. In Figure 9–30, the browser is shown with Panels on the left side. Panels are like a navigation pane providing access to bookmarks, history, widgets, notes, downloads, and Opera Unite. You can customize which panels are available.

Opera provides several free and unique features.

- **Opera Link** allows you to sync Opera browser settings and components between any of your computers and devices that are running the Opera browser.

- **Opera Unite** makes your browser like a personal web server so you can share things like your files, photos, and web pages plus stream music with others on the Web that you grant access to your computer.

- **Opera Turbo** can speed up browsing on slow connections such as dial-up to make it seem more like a broadband connection.

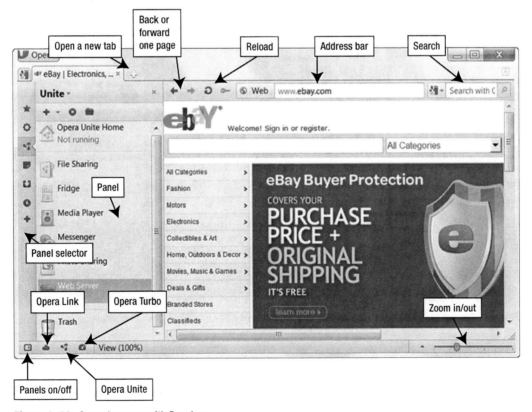

Figure 9–30. *Opera browser with Panels on*

Safari

Apple created its own browser, Safari, for use on its own products as well as on Windows. So if you have a Mac, iPhone, or iPad, Safari should look familiar. Even on Windows, Safari looks very Apple-like. Besides looking distinctively different from other Windows browsers, Safari has some interesting features of its own. One such feature is Top Sites, shown in Figure 9–31. Safari keeps track of the sites you visit most and then adds them to the Top Sites page. It is kind of like a visual Favorites or Bookmarks list. The Bookmarks bar contains web sites as well as Bookmark folders, like the Popular folder in Figure 9–31.

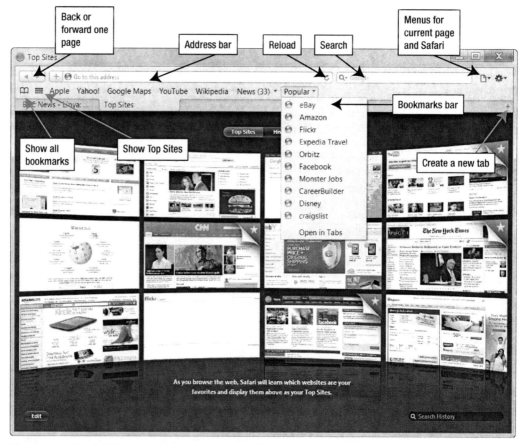

Figure 9–31. *The Safari browser showing the Top Sites list, which is made up of the sites you visit most.*

Changing Your Default Browser

The default browser is the one that Windows uses if you click a link in some other program, like a document, e-mail message, instant message, or an entry in the address bar in the Taskbar. Setting your default browser is a way of telling Windows, "If you need to open a browser, use this one."

Everybody wants to be your browser. And they'll keep asking you to be your default browser, unless you tell all of them no and to go away. Whenever you see a message like the one in Figure 9–32, just say no. Clear the **Always perform this check** checkbox or select **Don't ask again**.

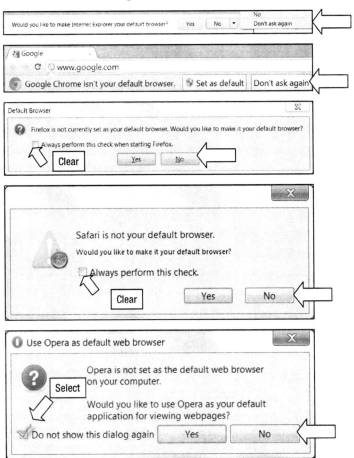

Figure 9–32. *Browser messages requesting to be set as the default*

To set your default browser:

1. Click the **Start** button, and then click **Default Programs**.

2. Click **Set your default programs**.

    The Set Default Programs window is displayed, as shown in Figure 9–33.

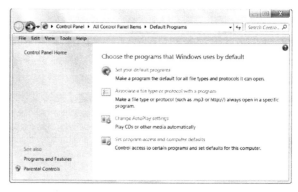

Figure 9–33. *The Default Programs window*

3. Select a browser in the list to view a description.

4. Click the browser you want to use as your default browser, and then click **Set this program as default** , as shown in Figure 9–34.

5. Click **OK** to close the Set Default Programs window.

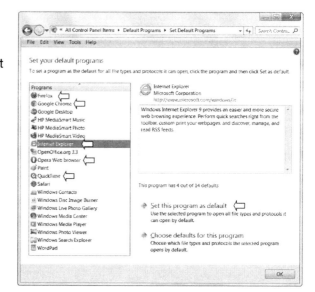

Figure 9–34. *The Set Default Programs window*

Exporting, Importing, and Syncing Settings and Preferences

When you install a new browser, it often asks if you want to import favorites/bookmarks and other settings from another browser on your computer. Some browsers can import cookies from another browser. There is no uniform method that all browsers use for importing and exporting favorites/bookmarks, feeds, and cookies.

Exporting usually means saving these as files. For favorites/bookmarks, it is usually something like bookmark.htm (you can usually name the file whatever you want, like IE_bookmarks.htm, firefox_bookmarks.htm, etc.)

Importing can mean importing a file like a bookmark file. In some cases, the importing browser may read the favorites/bookmarks directly from the other browser.

Several browsers also offer syncing of your browser settings across all of your computers. See Table 9–4 for more information.

Table 9–4. *Browser Export, Import, and Sync Options*

Browser	Export, Import, and Sync
Internet Explorer	Select **File ➤ Import and export** to: ▪ Import from another browser (note that on test computers with IE, Firefox, Chrome, Opera, and Safari installed, IE only listed Safari). ▪ Import from a file: Favorites, Feeds, Cookies. ▪ Export to a file: Favorites, Feeds, Cookies. To sync IE Favorites across all of your computers where IE is installed, use **Windows Live Mesh.** See Chapter 7 to learn how to download and install Windows Live Mesh.
Firefox	Select **File ➤ Import** to: ▪ Import options, bookmarks, history, passwords, and other data. When you install Firefox, you have the option of importing Internet Options, Favorites, cookies, and other settings from IE. To sync your Firefox bookmarks, passwords, preferences, history, and tabs across all of your computers where Firefox is installed, select **Tools ➤ Set Up Sync.**

Browser	Export, Import, and Sync
Chrome	Select **Options ➤ Personal Stuff ➤ Browsing data ➤ Import data from another browser** to:
	▪ Import browsing history, Favorites/bookmarks, saved passwords, search engines
	To sync Chrome settings (Apps, autofill, bookmarks, extensions, passwords, preferences, and themes) across all of your computers where Chrome is installed, select **Customize** (wrench button in toolbar) **➤ Options ➤ Personal Stuff ➤ Sync ➤ Set up sync.**
Opera	Select **File ➤ Import and Export** to:
	▪ Import feed list, Opera bookmarks, Firefox bookmarks, Internet Explorer Favorites, Konqueror bookmarks.
	▪ Export Opera bookmark as an .html file.
	To sync Opera bookmarks and other browser data across all of your computers where Opera is installed, select **Tools ➤ Synchronize Opera ➤ Enable Synchronization.**
Safari	Select **File ➤ Import Bookmarks** or **File ➤ Export Bookmarks**

Summary

In this chapter you have learned about:

▪ Connecting to the Internet.

▪ What you can do on the Internet.

▪ Upgrading to IE 9 and highlights of the new features.

▪ Navigating and searching the Web.

▪ Saving, printing, and sharing web pages.

▪ Protecting your privacy and Internet security settings.

▪ Choosing and installing another browser.

▪ Changing your default browser.

▪ Exporting, importing, and syncing your browser settings and preferences.

Next Steps

You may find the following related chapters useful:

- Chapter 7 to learn how to install Windows Live Family Safety to provide parental controls and Windows Live Mesh for syncing your Internet Explorer favorites, cookies, and settings on all of your computers

- Chapter 12 to learn how to apply parental control settings to your children's accounts.

- Chapter 15 to learn how to set up a home network and share your Internet connection with all of your computers.

- Chapter 16 to learn how to set up Internet security programs.

- Chapter 18 to learn additional conditions you may encounter using Internet Explorer and other browsers in the workplace.

Chapter 10

Organizing and Sharing Pictures and Videos

Digital photography and video has made picture taking and video production easier and more accessible than ever. No more shoeboxes of negatives, yellowed and curled photo albums, and carousels of slides. No more waiting several days for your pictures to come back from the drug store, only to find that some rolls of film never exposed and the pictures that did turn out were not very good. No more guessing how many reprints to get for mom, dad, grandma, and your friends.

Today, you can view your pictures immediately on your camera; take hundreds of pictures without worrying about wasting film; organize, crop, and touch them up on-screen; e-mail or share your pictures on the Web; send them to the drug store; or just print what you like at home. You can do all of this without leaving your desk...well, except to walk across the room to your printer.

This chapter will look at

- Organizing and editing your pictures with

    - Features like the **Pictures Library**.

    - Programs like **Windows Live Photo Gallery, Windows Media Player,** and **Windows Media Center**.

    - Other programs you can purchase and install like **Adobe Photoshop**.

- Web sites for storing, sharing, and printing your pictures, like **Adobe Photoshop Express, Dropbox, Flickr** from Yahoo!, **Picasa** from Google, **Shutterbug, Kodak Gallery,** and **Snapfish** from HP.

- Finding photos to use for your desktop or screen saver.

- Editing your videos with **Windows Live Movie Maker** and sharing them on **YouTube**.

Organizing and Editing Your Pictures

It's a buyer's market for photo viewing and editing options. There are so many choices available for free that printing photos may not cost you anything more than the cost of photo paper and ink for your photo printer. You won't have any problem finding a program; the challenge is to find the one that best meets your needs. Do you just need a place to store, organize, and view your collection? Do you want to be able to crop, touch up, or correct the colors of your pictures? Do you want to share them with friends? There are some programs that allow you to do all of this, and some that are just aimed at displaying and viewing your picture without a lot of other distractions on your screen. But don't be intimidated by the idea of editing your pictures; you don't have to be a digital photography pro to make good pictures look great or to make poorer pictures look good.

If you just want to organize and view your pictures on your computer, **Windows Explorer** and **Windows 7 Libraries** are great solutions. There's nothing to download or install. With libraries, you just point to the folders where you have stored your pictures. From the **Windows Explorer** window or **Pictures** library, you can perform simple tasks such as viewing a slide show of pictures in the folder and previewing a picture. If you right-click a picture, you can perform additional tasks such as rotating, printing, or selecting to open it with an editing program. See Chapter 2: "Checking Out Libraries" to learn how to use the default libraries in Windows 7 and how to add to them or create new ones.

To perform a little touch up and editing, you can download **Windows Live Photo Gallery** for free as part of **Windows Live Essentials** if it isn't already installed on your computer. See Chapter 7: "Getting Free Goodies like Windows Live Essentials" to learn how to download and set up Windows Live Essentials, plus an introduction to Window Live Photo Gallery. In the "Web Sites for Sharing Photos" section later in this chapter, you'll take a look at some web sites that offer sharing and editing tools.

If you want to view a group of pictures as a self-playing slide show, **Windows Media Player** and **Windows Media Center** allow you to select a group or folder of pictures and view them full screen. You can also create a customized picture show with titles, captions, labels, and accompanying music or sound, and save it as a video in **Windows Live Movie Maker**. See Chapter 7: "Getting Free Goodies like Windows Live Essentials" to learn how to download and set up Windows Live Movie Maker plus a sample exercise to create your own video.

For serious photo editing, Adobe Photoshop is a powerful program enjoyed by professionals and home users alike. It's not cheap, nor is it easy to learn. But it offers many more editing options than the free tools available with Windows Live Photo Gallery and other photo sharing sites. In between free and Photoshop there are many other less expensive photo editing programs that offer advanced features. For example, GIMP (GNU Image Manipulation Program) is a free but powerful alternative program available from www.gimp.org. It is available for other operating systems including Mac, Mac OS X, Sun OpenSolaris, and FreeBSD.

Programs for Organizing and Editing Pictures Locally

You can organize and edit your photos locally on your computer without connecting to the web. Several of these programs overlap in their features, so which one you use may depend on whether you just want to view them, or if you want to be able to sort, tag, and edit them in large numbers.

Tagging refers to adding keywords or phrases to the description in the picture file. These tags are not shown when you view just the picture, but they enable you to add a label that can help locate or sort them. For example, you might add tags for the occasion (holiday, vacation, graduation, birthday), a location (Disneyland, Paris, Oregon Coast, Grand Canyon, mountains, beach), or name (Lucy, Delilah, Fido, Dad, Grandma, Mom, John, Jane). Tags can be especially handy if you are putting together a slide show, scrapbook, or picture book with a theme or particular person.

Windows Libraries

Windows Libraries are the new Windows 7 folder organization that replaces the My Documents, My Music, My Pictures, and My Videos buckets in previous versions of Windows. There are now libraries for each of these, as well as fifth library for general items. Libraries have several advantages over the My Documents-type folders.

- **A Library folder is not limited to one path or folder location on your computer or network.** You can include local folders on your computer, network shared locations, or folders on other computers. This way you can bring together all files of a document type and view them in one window, no matter what folder they are in. For example, if you have pictures on your local hard drive under your user account, a public folder, a network location on a server, and a pictures folder on another network computer, you can include all of them in one library.

- **Each Library type (Documents, Music, Pictures, and Videos) provides commands, menus, and sorting options for the specific document type.** For example, in the Pictures library you can view and sort files by month, day, rating, and tag. In the Music library, you can sort files by contributing artists, album, title, song, genre, and rating.

In a Picture Library window, like the one shown in Figure 10–1, there are a number ways you can view and sort pictures, and several ways to change properties for a picture, such as:

- Add other folder location to the Pictures library.

- Adjust the size of the thumbnails in the middle pane picture list.

- Arrange how pictures are listed by Folder, Month, Day, Rating, and Tag.

- Select a picture in the middle pane list to see a larger view of it in the Preview Pane on the right.

- View details about the selected picture in the Details Pane along the bottom. In the Details Pane, you can add or edit tags, change the date, and assign a rating.

- Perform several actions by right-clicking the picture: open, preview, rotate, print, or edit with a specific program.

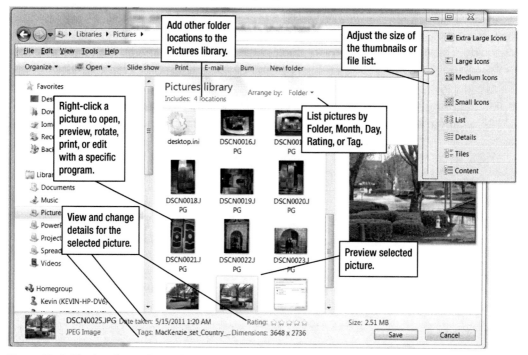

Figure 10–1. *Viewing pictures in the Pictures Library*

See Chapter 2: "Checking Out Libraries" to learn more about customizing and creating libraries.

Windows Live Photo Gallery

Windows Live Photo Gallery is really four tools in one: a central location to view and organize your photos; a photo editor; an online storefront for ordering prints from several vendors; and an easy-to-use portal for sharing your pictures on popular sites and services such as SkyDrive, Facebook, YouTube, Flickr, and Window Live Groups.

Windows Live Photo Gallery has five tabs to group features by use and purpose. The **Home** tab is the place to start for organizing and tagging your pictures, as shown in Figure 10–2. The Home tab brings together some of the most frequently used features. You will find many of these features shown individually on the other tabs.

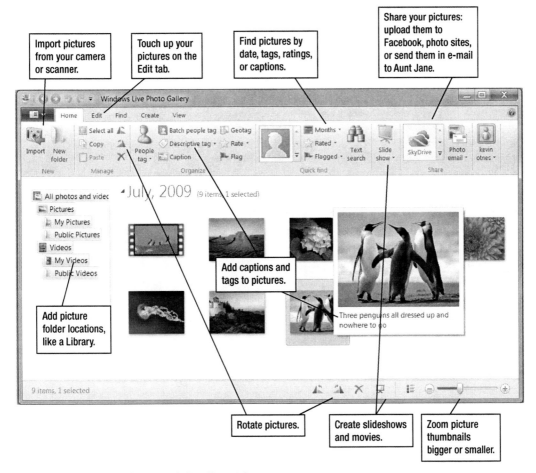

Figure 10–2. *Windows Live Photo Gallery Home tab*

As your picture collection grows, sorting just by folders or date alone will take longer. With the tagging tools, you can add information to each picture or a group of pictures to make it easier to find and sort them.

The **Edit** tab, shown in Figure 10–3, is where you can do color and exposure adjustments, retouching, and straightening to make your pictures brighter and sharper. You can also use special effects to change the overall color and tone of the picture.

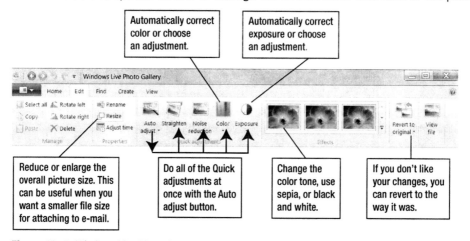

Automatically correct color or choose an adjustment.

Automatically correct exposure or choose an adjustment.

Reduce or enlarge the overall picture size. This can be useful when you want a smaller file size for attaching to e-mail.

Do all of the Quick adjustments at once with the Auto adjust button.

Change the color tone, use sepia, or black and white.

If you don't like your changes, you can revert to the way it was.

Figure 10–3. *Windows Live Photo Gallery Edit tab*

On the Find tab shown in Figure 10–4, you can search for pictures by date, people tagged in it, other tags, rating, text in the file name, etc.

Figure 10–4. *Windows Live Photo Gallery Find tab*

On the Create tab shown in Figure 10–5, you can select ways to use or publish your photos.

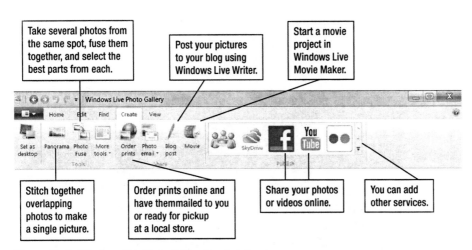

Figure 10–5. *Windows Live Photo Gallery Create tab*

On the View tab shown in Figure 10–6, you can select how you want to browse, arrange, or sort your photos as they are displayed in this window. You can also instantly launch a full screen slide show of the photos currently shown in this window.

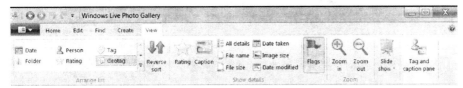

Figure 10–6. *Windows Live Photo Gallery View tab*

Adobe Photoshop Elements

Adobe Photoshop Elements bills itself as the top-selling photo-editing program for consumers. It does more than touch ups and color adjustments. With Adobe Photoshop Elements, you can

- Use People Recognition to organize and find pictures of specific friends and family members.

- Repair pictures by removing clutter from scenes or extending the background.

- Create and print calendars, cards, and photo books.

- Share your pictures and videos on your own web site, Facebook, or online photo albums.

- Store and back up your photo collection online.

Adobe Photoshop Elements has an Organize view (shown in Figure10–7 and Figure 10–8). The Organize view is useful for sorting, organizing, and fixing pictures. It also allows you to create albums to group pictures.

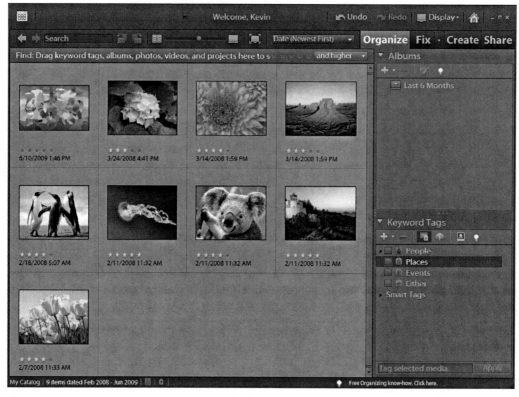

Figure 10–7. *Adobe Photoshop Elements Organize view, the Organize tab*

Each tab provides a different set of options grouped by types of tasks, as shown in Figure 10–8.

Figure 10–8. *Fix, Create, and Share tabs in Photoshop Elements*

In the Edit mode, the Organize and Fix tabs are replaced with the Edit tab, which provides a full set of picture editing and effects tools plus menus, as shown in Figure 10–9.

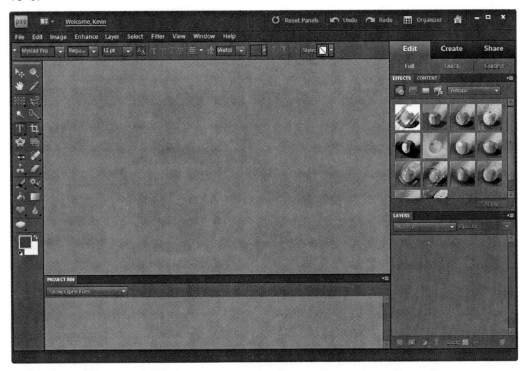

Figure 10–9. *Photoshop Elements Edit mode provides a rich set of editing tools and picture effects.*

Photoshop Elements is not free, but it often comes bundled with other products like printers, touch and pen input tablets, and cameras. You can download a trial version to use for free for 30 days from Adobe at www.adobe.com/go/tryphotoshop_elements.

Adobe offers many free online tutorials, videos, and user community forums to help you get the most out of Photoshop Elements.

Though Photoshop Elements is not free, and requires some dedicated learning, it's well worth the time and money if you want to do much more than just organize or touch up your photos.

Adobe Photoshop

Adobe Photoshop is designed for and used by professionals. It is a standard tool for photographers, graphic design artists, and those with publishing needs. Figure 10–10 shows more controls, tools, and features than Photoshop Elements.

Figure 10–10. *Adobe Photoshop is what the professionals use.*

Home users and consumers can purchase Photoshop, but it costs ten times as much as Photoshop Elements. It also requires much more training than Photoshop Elements or other consumer-level programs. Adobe does have Student and Teacher editions of this and many of their other programs available at a considerable discount through colleges and universities. Adobe provides a lot of good online help and support for Photoshop. Official training books like *Adobe Photoshop Classroom in a Box* are a great way to learn all of the major features.

Programs for Playing and Viewing Your Photos

Windows Libraries are great for organizing and finding your photos on your computer. Windows Live Photo Gallery provides more features, like touch ups and integration with programs to print, share, or create something with your photos. Both of these can be used to just view your pictures, but they're not the showiest way to share these in person, at your desk, or on your TV. Fortunately, Windows 7 also provides two great programs that are designed to do just that: Windows Media Player and Windows Media Center. Windows Media Player allows you easily find your pictures through your Pictures library, and you can show them in a nice window without a bunch of buttons, controls, or menus. If you want to show your pictures in a big way, Windows Media Center is even better. You can see how they'll look on your computer in the next few pages. Chapter 11: "Enjoying Music, Video, and eBooks" goes into more detail about installing and using both of these programs.

Windows Media Player

Windows Media Player isn't just for playing songs or videos. You can also use it to view your photos. Windows Media Player automatically uses the regular Windows 7 Pictures library to locate what pictures are available for display. The Pictures library is displayed in the left navigation column and the content is displayed in the main window, as shown in Figure 10–11. You can sort pictures by title, date, size, tags, and rating; you can also customize the navigation pane to provide a folder view.

Figure 10–11. *Windows Media Player in default Library view*

You can double-click a picture to start a slide show, as shown in Figure 10–12.

Figure 10–12. *Windows Media Player in Now Playing mode.*

Windows Media Center

Windows Media Center can also display your pictures. Windows Media Center is designed to look best when it is a full screen window on a large screen. If you want to share your pictures with friends and family on your big screen TV, Windows Media Center is one of the best ways to view them with Windows 7. But it also looks great on your regular computer monitor. If you've never opened Windows Media Center, it's on the Start menu. The first time you run it, you will be prompted to set it up. It's easy to set up; just select the Express setup option and it will be ready to go in minutes. If you want a little more guidance in setting up Windows Media Center, see Chapter 11: "Enjoying Music, Video, and eBooks."

Figure 10–13 shows the Pictures library selected in Windows Media Center. When you first open Windows Media Center, you won't see the Pictures + Videos listing until you scroll down the list.

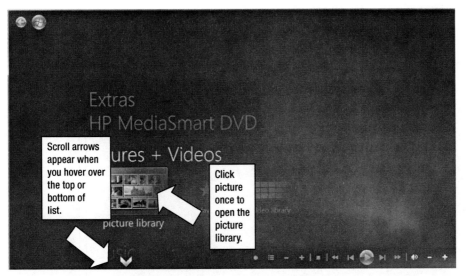

Figure 10–13. *When you open the Windows Media Center main page, scroll down to Pictures + Videos.*

The Windows Media Center page buttons and links work like web pages; you only have to single click an item to open or jump to the next page.

> **TIP:** With its simple menu selection system, single click selection, large icons, and large text, Windows Media Center is a great choice for a Windows 7 touch screen PC or tablet.

When you open the picture library, the default view is to display the pictures in your Pictures folder and all folders listed in your Windows Picture Library, as shown in Figure 10–14.

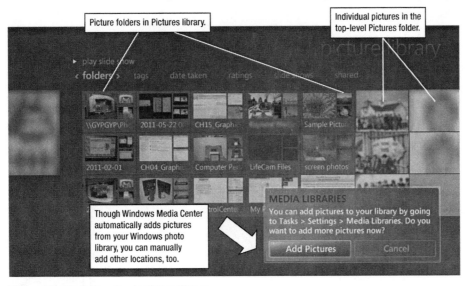

Figure 10–14. *Folder view in Picture library*

It's easy to play a slide show from all of the pictures in your library, or you can open a specific folder. You can even select some music, and then resume the slide show or go back to the pictures library. Figure 10–15 shows a slide show in progress and the current song playing.

Figure 10–15. *You can select music to play in the background during your slide show.*

With the slide show and music shuffle or your favorite music list, you can turn your TV or monitor into a giant photo frame. Moving images and relaxing sounds to fill your room or just provide a background to whatever else you are doing.

Web Sites for Sharing Photos

There are many great benefits to sharing or storing your photos on the Web. There's also a wide variety of services provided by photo web sites. With photo web sites you can

- Save or back up your photo collection.
- Post photos for friends and family to view.
- Edit your photos.
- Send pictures or links by e-mail.
- Print pictures.
- Create scrapbooks.
- Assemble and order picture books.
- Order pictures for pickup at a local store such as Walgreens and Target or have them printed and sent to you by postal mail.

While you can access online sites from any place in the world where you have internet service, if you want pictures and picture projects in a physical form, you should look for services that can deliver them locally to your country or region.

> **TIP:** If you are posting your own photos to the Web for public viewing, be sure to tag them with useful key words so that others can find them in web searches.

Table 10–1 describes some of the more popular services available in the United States.

Table 10–1. *Popular Photo Services*

Photo Service	Features and Services
Adobe Photoshop Express	Available at www.photoshop.com/tools. Sign up with a free Adobe ID, and you can - Store up to 2GB of photos and videos online. - Organize your photos in the gallery and store them online. - Sync your online albums with local folders on your computer. You can sync multiple computers with your online albums. - Access your online storage and gallery directly from Photoshop Elements.

Photo Service	Features and Services
	▓ Share albums with family and friends.
	▓ Edit your photos online. Fix and touch up photos or apply your creativity with effects and enhancements using tools similar to those in Photoshop Elements.
	▓ Access your photos from any web browser.
	▓ Upload pictures from your iPhone or Android phone.
	▓ Download your photos or albums directly to Facebook, Photobucket, Picasa, and Flickr.
Dropbox	Available at xwww.dropbox.com.
	Provides an easily accessible online folder—storage in the cloud—where you can
	▓ Store up to 2GB for free; purchase larger storage of 50 or 100GB
	▓ Open the Dropbox folder as if it were just another folder on your computer.
	▓ Automatically sync the Dropbox folder with all of your computers.
	▓ Share a folder within the Dropbox folder with your friends, family, or coworkers.
	▓ Provide a public link to any file in your Public Folder.
	Dropbox does not provide photo editing, viewing, or organizing tools.
EZ Prints	Available at http://ezprints.com.
	EZ Prints offers photo products such as prints, apparel, skins, stationery, cards, photo books, ornaments, mouse pads, mugs, and more.
	EZPrints does not provide photo editing, viewing, sharing, or organizing tools.
Flickr (Yahoo!)	Available at www.flickr.com.
	Flickr offers
	▓ A web site where you can post and share your pictures with the public. It is not intended to be a photo storage or editing site. With a free basic account you can upload up to 300MB of pictures per month, but you can only view the most recent 200 photos. Also, the photos may be reduced in resolution from the original to keep file size down.

Photo Service	Features and Services
	<ul><li>Paid accounts without storage or resolution limits and storage of the photo in the original resolution.</li><li>Partnership with Snapfish to provide prints and other photo products.</li><li>Settings that allow you limit access to any of your pictures to contacts you have marked as friends or family.</li><li>A "find your friends" feature that checks your Facebook, Gmail, Hotmail, or Yahoo! Mail address books for people who are already Flickr members or sends them an invitation for them to join.</li><li>Several ways to search for pictures among all of the public photos that have been uploaded to the site, as well as links to other photo repositories such as The Commons, where you can access public photo collections worldwide.</li></ul>
Kodak Gallery (formerly Ofoto)	Available at www.kodakgallery.com. Kodak Gallery offers<ul><li>Photo prints, cards, photo books, and photo gifts.</li><li>Sharing with friends and family.</li><li>Unlimited uploads to photo storage, but to continue keeping your photos on their site you must make a minimum purchase at least once every 12 months.</li></ul>
Picasa (Google)	Available at http://picasa.google.com/features.html. Picasa offers<ul><li>A locally installed editing, viewing, and organizing program.</li><li>Online web albums where you can share your pictures and view public pictures shared by others.</li><li>A free basic account that provides 1GB of storage.</li><li>Optional storage upgrade plans that offer 20GB to 1TB.</li></ul>The Picasa program and the Web Albums site don't offer any photo products or services.

Photo Service	Features and Services
Shutterfly	Available at `www.shutterfly.com`. Shutterfly offers ▪ Unlimited picture storage. ▪ Local printing at Walgreens, CVS, and Target stores. ▪ Share sites where you can create special sites for groups like family, sports teams, classroom, events, celebrations, or another type of group of your choosing. ▪ Other photo products such as photo books, cards, stationery, prints, and photo gifts.
Snapfish	Available at `www.snapfish.com`. Snapfish offers ▪ Unlimited photo sharing and storage. ▪ Photo printing, delivered by postal mail, or pickup at local retailers. ▪ Photo books, cards, and gifts.
Windows Live SkyDrive	Available at `https://skydrive.live.com`. This cloud service offers ▪ Storage and sharing of photos. ▪ Storage and collaboration of Office documents. You can open documents from the SkyDrive, work with them locally, and then save and sync with the SkyDrive location. ▪ Public and private sharing. ▪ Partnership with Snapfish for printing, photo gifts, and in-store pickup. ▪ 5GB of free storage.

Finding Photos

With all of the photos posted publically on photo sharing sites like Flickr, social networks like Facebook, and personal blogs and web sites, there's a huge library of pictures waiting to be discovered.

READ THE FINE PRINT ABOUT COPYRIGHTS BEFORE SHARING YOUR OWN CONTENT OR USING OTHER'S CONTENT

Copyright and control (licensing) of content varies internationally and by web site. Read the fine print about who owns the copyright of any material you post to a social networking site, photo sharing site, blog, etc. Assume that anything you see on the web is copyrighted and that you will need permission to reuse any content. However, do not assume that you own the copyright to anything you share through another web site. The terms of service for some sites may require that you agree to a more open license or copyright agreement. With some sites, anything you share may become the property of the web site. For example, in Facebook's Terms of Service (April 26, 2011) it says

"Sharing Your Content and Information

You own all of the content and information you post on Facebook, and you can control how it is shared through your privacy and application settings. In addition:

1.For content that is covered by intellectual property rights, like photos and videos (IP content), you specifically give us the following permission, subject to your privacy and application settings: you grant us a non-exclusive, transferable, sub-licensable, royalty-free, worldwide license to use any IP content that you post on or in connection with Facebook (IP License). This IP License ends when you delete your IP content or your account unless your content has been shared with others, and they have not deleted it."

Some of the more common uses for pictures found on the web are to save the pictures as desktop backgrounds or as themed photo slide shows to run on your computer as your screen saver.

For general image and photo searches, Bing (www.bing.com/image), Google (www.google.com/images), and Yahoo! Image Search (http://images.search.yahoo.com) all work well. Flickr, with its large base of users posting pictures publically, is another good place to check.

If you are looking for sites that specifically provide good quality high resolution photos for public use, check these public agencies, government organizations, and public use collections:

NASA Featured Images and Galleries www.nasa.gov/multimedia/imagegallery/index.html provides a wide variety of space flight, astronomy, and planetary images that are available for public use. There are a few restrictions on their use, so see Image Usage Guidelines at www.nasa.gov/audience/formedia/features/MP_Photo_Guidelines.html. These include images from NASA's Jet Propulsion Laboratory, the Hubble Telescope, Kennedy Space Center, and various missions to Mars, Venus, Saturn, and beyond.

National Park Service: Digital Image Archive www.nps.gov/ pub_aff/imagebase.html provides a wide variety of scenic pictures from national parks.

The Commons on Flickr
www.flickr.com/commons provides access to publicly held photography collections from museums, national archives, national libraries, and cultural heritage institutions from around the world.

Wikimedia Commons
http://commons.wikimedia.org/wiki/Main_Page contains over ten million "freely usable" media files of just about anything imaginable.

> **NOTE:** Even when sites state that they contain public images or those that are freely reusable, be sure to review the specific usage policies at each site.

Sharing Videos on YouTube

You can upload videos to www.youtube.com in just about any common video format. You can upload video files directly from your computer, from mobile devices, live from video or web cam, or from a video editing program. For example, you can create a movie with Windows Live Movie Maker, and when you are done, you can click the YouTube button in the toolbar to upload it. YouTube also offers a free quick-and-dirty online editor, the YouTube Video Editor. It is really bare bones, but it is free, browser-based, and doesn't require as fast and robust a PC as a locally installed video editor.

Before you upload to YouTube for the first time, read and understand the Copyright Tips page and the Community Guidelines. Also, familiarize yourself with how similar videos to yours are handled on YouTube. Doing this homework ahead of time can minimize or eliminate the possibility of posting something that violates copyrights, is not in good taste, or is not up to par in terms of video quality.

YouTube supports

- High Definition and regular video.

- Videos up to 2GB in size.

- Videos up to 15 minutes in length.

- A wide variety of video formats.

Uploading a large video can take a long time, so if your videos fail to complete the upload, YouTube offers an advanced uploader that can handle larger file sizes and resumable uploads; if your server connection times out, when you reconnect the uploader it can resume from where it left off.

YouTube is supported by the ads that run on its web page and as commercials before playing your selection. You can also use YouTube as part of your own advertising strategies and campaigns. Check the Advertising links on YouTube for more information.

Summary

In this chapter you learned about

- Organizing and editing your pictures with free features and programs that you can run locally on your computer: Windows Libraries and Windows Live Photo Gallery.

- Two powerful editing programs you can buy for home use (Adobe Photoshop Elements) and professional use (Adobe Photoshop).

- Built-in Windows 7 programs that are great for viewing or displaying your photos: Windows Media Player and Windows Media Center.

- Web sites for sharing photos.

- How to search for pictures using search engines and several public collections of freely reusable content.

- An overview of sharing your videos on YouTube.

Next Steps

You may find the following related chapters useful:

- Chapter 2: "Checking Out Libraries" to learn how to use Photo Libraries to collect and browse your photos.

- Chapter 7: "Getting Free Goodies like Windows Live Essentials" to learn how to download and set up Windows Live Photo Gallery.

- Chapter 11: "Enjoying Music, Video, and eBooks" to learn more about using Window Media Player and Windows Media Center for music and video; media devices and stores; and eBook reading devices.

- Chapter 21: "Connecting Printers and Other Devices" for installing and updating device drivers.

- Chapter 28: "Troubleshooting Windows, Programs, and Devices" for more troubleshooting methods besides those provided in this chapter, including running Program Compatibility to make older programs run in Windows 7.

Chapter 11

Enjoying Music, Video, and eBooks

Almost everything you want to listen to, watch, or read is available or can be converted to digital formats that you can view with your computer. Your Windows 7 computer can offer a lot of entertainment. Or it can be the hub for other devices dedicated to specific uses. Here are just a few of the ways you can use your Windows 7 computer for your entertainment needs:

- Download, organize, and play music, video, and eBooks.
- Sync your collections between PCs and portable devices.
- Stream audio and video between your PC and other PCs or media devices on your home network.
- View your videos by connecting your PC to your big screen TV.
- Connect your PC to your home stereo system.

Creating a full blown PC-based entertainment center is beyond the scope of this book. But you don't need to be a computer techie, hardcore audiophile, or serious video enthusiast to enjoy audio and video on your PC. You can do some pretty cool stuff with the audio and video players and services available on or for your PC. This chapter will look at:

- Media players that come with Windows 7 or can be downloaded and used for free.
- Music and video stores where you can buy, download, or subscribe to music and video services.
- Popular eBook stores.

Built-in and Free Media Players

Windows 7 provides several basic programs you can use for viewing and organizing your audio and video collections. You can also buy or download for free many other programs with additional features that often are linked to online stores. You have many choices, so which one works best is partly a matter of taste and partly how well it works with your personal devices like your iPhone, Smartphone, MP3 player, or home entertainment system. For example, Windows Media Center provides a nice interface for navigating or playing music, pictures, or video on a large monitor, as the control panel for your home entertainment center. But it is not designed to sync or manage content between your Windows 7 computer and mobile devices like a Smartphone, tablet, or MP3 player.

> **NOTE:** Part of the standard setup for any media player is to add music, videos, and pictures from your Windows 7 libraries to your media player libraries. Adding content to the media player doesn't create duplicate copies of the content, it just tells the media player where to look for it. However, if you run a conversion program, it may create a duplicate copy in the new file format while retaining the original copy in the old format.

Music and Video Formats

The default locations for your music and video files are your Music and Video libraries. When you run or install a media player for the first time, it will search in those locations for content to add to the media player's library. There are several standard music and video file formats, but most PC media players do not view or play all formats. The music and video file formats affect how your computer handles these types of content.

- When you point your media player to look in a Music library for music files, it will ignore file types that your media player does not support.

- When you rip music files from a CD, your media player has a default format to use to save the files. By default, Windows Media Player saves to .wma format, and iTunes saves to .aac. But either one of these programs can save to .mp3, which can play on Windows Media Player, iTunes, and almost all other media players.

- When you buy or download from online music stores, the default file format affects which mobile or personal devices you can play them back on. If you are downloading from iTunes or the Zune store, you may want to set your preferences so that the files are saved or downloaded as .mp3 files so that you can listen to them on almost any device.

For example:

- The **Windows Media Player** default music file format is **.wma**, but it will also play **.mp3** files and many other popular audio formats. However, Windows Media Player *will not* play Apple's default music file format, **.aac**.

- The **iTunes** player default music file format is **.aac,** but it will also play **.mp3** files and many other popular audio formats. However, the iTunes player *will not* play Windows Media Player's default music file format, **.wma**. If you have .wma music files in your music library and you want to import them into iTunes, iTunes can convert your DRM-free .wma files to **.mp3** files.

Similarly, Windows Media Player and iTunes use different default video formats, **.wmv** and **.mpeg-4** respectively.

If you download songs directly to your iPhone but also want to listen to them on your computer, you can't listen to the songs in the default iTunes format of .mp4a in Windows Media Player. Or, if you've been ripping your music collection from CDs to your hard drive in Windows Media Player and now you want all of this music on your iPod, these files need to be converted from .wma files. If you want to find some common ground, you have several choices:

- Use a media player that plays all file formats, like RealPlayer (www.real.com). This does not require duplicating a song in two different formats for playback on your PC but will not fix the problem of being able to play the music on both an .mp3/Zune player and an iPhone/iPod/iPad device.

- Use a music file format conversion program to convert .wma files to .mp4a, or .mp4a to .wma files. If you want to be able to listen to the songs in either player/type of device, you will need to keep two copies of every song: one .wma and one .mp4a. This doubles the amount of storage space you will need for your music collection

- Set .mp3 as the default file format for all players. Your iPhone can play the same .mp3 file as your Windows Media Player, mp3 device, or Zune. On your PC, set your media players to use .mp3 as the default file format when you rip songs from a CD. For all of your existing songs in your library, you can use the free RealPlayer Converter feature in RealPlayer (www.real.com).

```
DIGITAL RIGHTS MANAGEMENT (DRM)
```

Digital Rights Management, or DRM, refers to a wide variety of technologies and standards designed to protect against unauthorized reproduction or copying of digital content. Technically, where this affects you is when you use or try to use content that has DRM protection. Sometimes content that has DRM is only playable on certain devices, which can make it hard for you to move the content from one device to another. When you purchase or subscribe content, be sure to review their DRM policies and implementation. Some online stores will only sell DRM-free content; others may implement DRM for specific uses, such as subscriptions where you lose the use of subscribed content when you quit the subscription services. Many music labels have dropped or reduced the use of DRM protection for content they publish because they often cause technical problems for customers when they are trying to access the content legally.

Windows Media Center

Windows Media Center came into this world as Windows XP Media Center Edition in 2002. Because it had special hardware requirements, it was sold as a separate version of Windows through OEMs. In Window Vista, Windows Media Center was no longer a separate version of Windows but a feature included in Windows Visa Home Premium and Ultimate editions. In Windows 7, it is included in all editions except Starter.

Windows Media Center is designed to be a "10-foot user interface" meaning the words, buttons, and menus should be easy to see and use 10 feet away from a large TV. There are remote control kits, sometimes included with TV tuners, which allow you to control the screen much like you would a TV. That doesn't mean it can't be used on a regular monitor. If you want to use your PC or laptop as an entertainment device, it provides a simpler, cleaner way to access your pictures, videos, music, movies, and television without the extra clutter of the desktop, taskbar, or Start button. This 10-foot user interface is also great if you are looking at a 10-inch netbook or tablet screen from 2 feet away.

With the addition of TV tuner card or USB stick, you can connect your PC to your cable TV, and use it as a Digital Video Recorder. You can learn more about watching your TV on your PC at www.windows.com/pctv.

You can access the Windows Media Center from the Start menu, and you can pin it to your Start menu, Taskbar, or Desktop. The first time you open it, you may be prompted to set it up. Choose the Express settings and you are ready to go. Figure 11–1 shows the Windows Media Center home page.

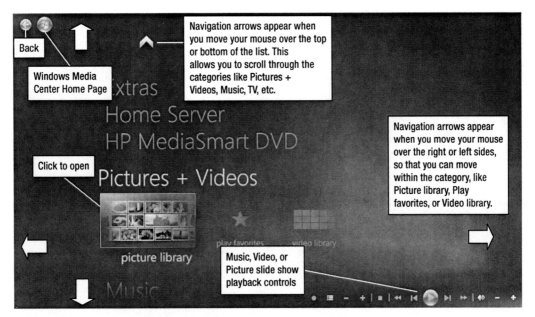

Figure 11–1. *Windows Media Center Home Page*

Within a category, you can navigate to the contents of the library and select an item to play or view it. The Music Library is shown in Figure 11–2.

Figure 11–2. *Inside the Music Library, you can browse by albums, artists, genres, etc.*

Windows Media Center content is available from:

- Files stored in your Windows 7 Music, Pictures, and Video libraries. You can also specify other locations to include in the Windows Media Center libraries.

- Internet TV—live video streaming of some of your favorite television shows.

- Subscriptions to services like Netflix.

- Videos you have downloaded to your PC.

In addition, if you are connected to a Windows Home Server, you can access content stored there and open a console to view information about the server.

Windows Media Player

Windows Media Player is installed and available by default in most countries; a few countries may require that Windows Media Player be off by default so that other players can be offered as alternatives. You can access Windows Media Player from the Start menu ➤ Programs, but if you use it frequently you'll want to pin it to your desktop, taskbar, or Start menu. Figure 11–3 displays a typical Windows Media Player window in Library view.

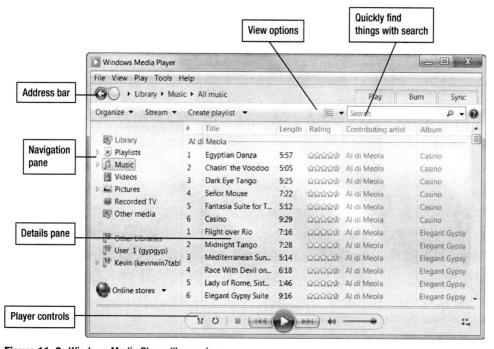

Figure 11–3. *Windows Media Player library view*

There are many ways you can change or customize your view:

- Show or hide the menu bar.

- Switch between Library view, Now Playing, full screen, or minimized to the taskbar with mini-player controls visible when you hover over the program icon.

- In Now Playing, view Visualizations—an assortment of moving shapes and geometric designs that change with the beat of the music.

- Display content list by icons, tiles, or details.

You can shop for music using the **Online stores** link at the bottom of the **Navigation pane**, but you will probably have a better experience shopping or subscribing to Zune Marketplace, iTunes, Amazon Music, Rhapsody, or Napster.

iTunes +QuickTime

Though iTunes is not part of Windows 7, for many people it is a must-have because they also have an iPod, iPhone, or iPad. iTunes is Apple's media player and online store for audio, movies, TV shows, audiobooks, and podcasts, and it syncs your Apple device with your music and video collection. **QuickTime** is a multimedia player that is often required to view high quality video like Internet video and HD movie trailers. You can download iTunes from `www.apple.co/itunes/download/`. When you install iTunes, it also installs QuickTime.

The iTunes player works similar to Windows Media Player and RealPlayer with library navigation on the left side and the contents of albums and song lists in the main pane on the right, as shown in Figure 11–4.

Figure 11–4. *iTunes Library view*

There are many ways you can change or customize your view.

- Switch between Library view, mini player window floating on the desktop, mini player displayed when hovering over the program icon in the Taskbar, or full screen.
- Show the Visualizer—moving shapes and geometric designs that change with the beat of the music.
- Display content as a list, album list, grid, or cover flow.
- Show or hide the Sidebar.

Some players, like iTunes and Zune, have a handy feature that can put together playlists and mixes of related songs and make suggestions of other songs to buy that are similar. In iTunes, this feature is called Genius. To access or turn on Genius, click **Genius** in the **Navigation pane**.

QuickTime, shown in Figure 11–5, complements iTunes. Though QuickTime and iTunes can play most of the same audio and video formats, some formats play on one but not the other. QuickTime is not as noticeable as iTunes. With iTunes, generally you open the program and then locate the music or videos you want to play. With QuickTime, you don't usually see it unless a link on a web page or document requires it to view the content. For example, you see an ad on a web page for a new movie coming out soon. You click a link on the page for the trailer; it opens QuickTime, and then plays the trailer in the QuickTime window.

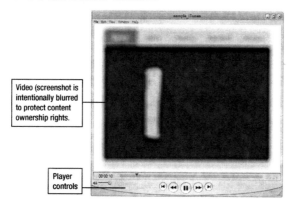

Video (screenshot is intentionally blurred to protect content ownership rights.)

Player controls

Figure 11–5. *QuickTime Player window*

QuickTime is also available in a premium version, QuickTime Pro. QuickTime Pro can convert your home movies and videos to a format that can be used on devices like iPhone, iPod, Apple TV, and more. It also provides advanced recording, editing, and trimming features.

> **TIP:** To get the most out of using iTunes with your Apple devices, check these other great Made Simple books: *iPhone Made Simple*, *iPod Made Simple*, and *iPad Made Simple*.

Zune

Zune is a media player program, a marketplace for buying music and video, and a recently discontinued line of media playing devices from Microsoft. Zune is by no means dead—the software and marketplace integrates with Windows Phone 7, Xbox360, and your Windows PC. The Zune software is free and you can use it as your media player in Windows. In the Zune Marketplace you can purchase songs or albums, or, with a Zune Pass subscription you can download unlimited songs, and keep (to own) ten new songs a month. Go to www.zune.net to download the Zune software, access the Zune Marketplace, or set up a Zune Pass subscription.

The Zune player, shown in Figure 11–6, is a little different from the user interface of Windows Media Player, iTunes, and RealPlayer. Instead of listing the content and library types on the left, they are listed across the top. You can browse down to individual songs by going from left to right.

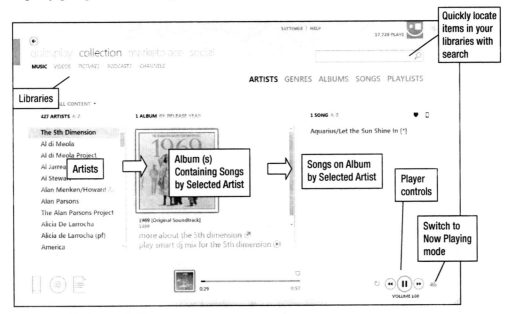

Figure 11–6. *The Zune collection page*

If you want a more interesting view in the Zune window, click the Now Playing button shown in lower right corner of Figure 11–6. In Now Playing you'll see the current album highlighted on a background collage of album covers, as shown in Figure 11–7.

Figure 11–7. *Now Playing view, showing the current album and a collage of album art*

Zune, like iTunes, has a handy feature that can put together playlists and mixes of related songs and make suggestions of other songs to buy that are similar. In Zune these features are called **Smart DJ playlist** and **Mixview**.

Zune's **quickplay** page provides several ways to get to your favorite music, as shown in Figure 11–8. You can pin your favorite artists, create playlists, or go to your most recently played artists or playlists.

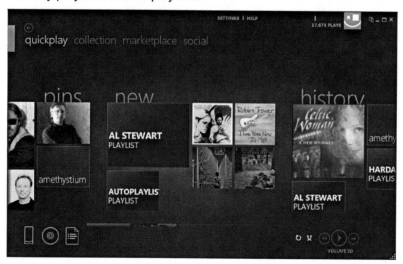

Figure 11–8. *Quickplay makes it easy to get to your favorite songs and playlists*

RealPlayer

RealPlayer is a free media player available from RealNetworks at `www.real.com`. One of RealPlayer's strengths is that it is universal. RealPlayer can play and convert almost any audio or video format. The convertor can also convert content so that it can be used on mobile devices such as Blackberry, iPod, iPad, and iPhone. Even without the convertor, the player is very clean and pleasing to look at, as shown in Figure 11–9.

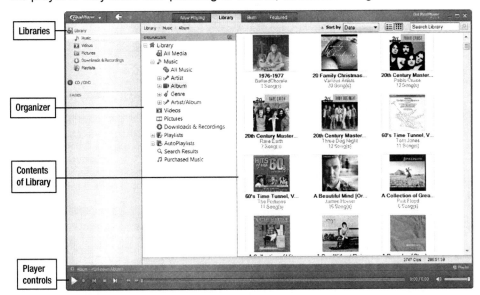

Figure 11–9. *RealPlayer*

You can import music or video you purchased and downloaded from music stores such as Zune, iTunes, and Rhapsody. Though RealPlayer doesn't have its own music store or music subscription plan, it does offer a SuperPass for a monthly fee, which includes $10 (at the time of this writing) per month in music downloads from the Rhapsody mp3 store.

> **NOTE:** RealNetworks owned the music subscription service **Rhapsody** for several years until Rhapsody was spun off as a separate company in 2010.

RealPlayer offers a premium version, RealPlayer Plus, with the following additional features:

- Video transfer to DVDs that you can watch on TV.

- Faster video downloads from video web sites.

- Faster video transfer to smart phones.

- Professional quality music CD production.

Rhapsody

Rhapsody is available at www.rhapsody.com. It is a store and subscription service, but also it provides a free player that you can use to organize and play all of your music, photo, and video content. Like other players, Rhapsody can scan your Music, Photo, and Video folders on your computer for content and add the content to your Rhapsody libraries. You can also import your iTunes library.

The Rhapsody player default view is shown in Figure 11-10.

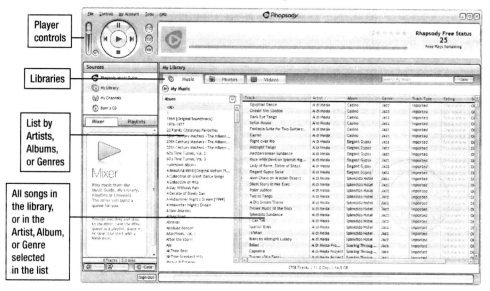

Figure 11-10. *The Rhapsody player is free*

You can compare the Rhapsody store and subscriptions with other stores in the next section, "Music and Video Stores."

Music and Video Stores

One of the reasons why online music and video stores are so popular is that they allow you to get your content in minutes without leaving your computer. You hardly have to move except to fetch your credit card from your wallet or purse. With subscriptions, you can access (borrow) from libraries of music or videos for much less than buying the content outright and owning it. Table 11– describes some of the more popular online music and video stores in the United States. Since copyright laws and licensing are different in each country, some sites are restricted to a specific country, so some of these sites may not be available or may work differently outside of the United States.

Table 11–1. *Comparing Music and Video Stores*

Store	Features and Services
Amazon MP3 Music Store and **Cloud Player**	Available at www.amazon.com
	Amazon offers mp3 downloads for purchase by the song or by album. The store only sells content; it does not offer any kind of subscriptions for unlimited downloads of music. Some songs may only be available as part of an album.
	Amazon recently started a new service, **Amazon Cloud Drive**, that offers 5GB free storage for your audio or video content. This content can be accessed through the Amazon Cloud Player for the Web running in a web browser on any computer and some mobile devices, up to eight different computers or devices combined. There are separate Amazon MP3 Mobile Apps for BlackBerry and Android, and the Amazon MP3 App for Android.
	You can buy a larger storage plan for your Cloud Drive for an annual fee. Any mp3 purchases through Amazon can be stored on Cloud Drive without counting against your 5GB free storage or against any additional storage quota you buy. The Cloud Drive can also be used to store other files such as photos, videos, documents, etc. You can also add music in mp3 or AAC format to your Cloud Drive by uploading it from your computer.
Hulu	Hulu (www.hulu.com) provides free access to many broadcast and cable network shows. It is ad-supported to keep the basic service free so you will see commercials just like on TV. Hulu basic service carries up to five recent episodes of current shows and is only viewable through your PC. Hulu also offers a premium subscription, HuluPlus, to provide access to all current season episodes of many popular shows, HD quality when available, and the ability to watch it on a wide variety of devices such as specially enabled TVs/Blu-ray players, gaming consoles, smartphones, and set-top boxes.

Store	Features and Services
iTunes and **iTunes in the Cloud**	The iTunes store is accessible through the iTunes player. The store only sells content; it doesn't offer any kind of subscriptions for unlimited downloads of music. Soon after Amazon released **Amazon in the Cloud** in 2011, Apple announced a competing product called **iTunes in the Cloud** (www.apple.com/icloud/) coming in Fall 2011. In addition to storing your iTunes purchases, you can store and sync to your apps, books, and documents on all of your computers. Like Amazon, iCloud will be offering 5GB free, but additional storage may cost less than Amazon.
Napster	Napster (www.napster.com) is a legitimate music subscription service owned by BestBuy that provides unlimited streaming of music to your computer or mobile device. You can try Napster on a free 7-day trial. If you decide to buy, their monthly rates are lower than Zune Pass or Rhapsody but don't include a quota of songs you can keep (own) each month like Zune Pass. You do have the option of buying songs that you like and want to keep.
NetFlix	NetFlix (www.netflix.com) is a subscription service that offers unlimited TV episodes and movie streaming to your computer or to a TV through a gaming console or other devices that stream from Netflix. There are no commercials. You can also access your NetFlix subscription through Windows Media Center.
Rhapsody	Rhapsody (www.rhapsody.com) offers a store to purchase mp3s plus subscription plans for unlimited listening to music. You can access your subscription from your computer as well as most mobile devices. You can try the subscription on a free 14-day trial.
YouTube	Though not a store, YouTube is a source for video content. You can use RealPlayer along with the Download This Video plug-in for your browser to save and view the content on your computer; check the RealPlayer help for more information about this feature and the supported web browsers.
Zune Marketplace and **Zune Pass**	Zune (www.zune.net) offers two products. **Zune Marketplace** is where you can buy and download music and videos. **Zune Pass** is a subscription that allow unlimited downloads to your computer, and you can keep (own) 10 songs each month. You can try Zune Pass on a free 14-day trial.

eBooks

Some of you are reading this book as an eBook. Generally, people view eBooks on a dedicated eBook Reader, a device like a Kindle, Nook, Sony Reader, or Kobo, or a reading app on a tablet like an iPad or Android tablet. The format and technology for each is different, so you can't read an eBook created for the Amazon Kindle on a Barnes and Noble Nook. But many of these types of accounts (Barnes and Noble, Amazon, etc.) do allow you to view a copy of your eBook purchase on a PC application. And while most of the eBook devices and tablets can download books directly through Wi-Fi or 3G cellular networks, some have syncing, downloading, or updating operations that you can perform by connecting with a PC. There are no eReader applications provided by Windows 7, but some computer manufacturers may provide software and links for one or more eReader stores.

eBook Formats

Though Kindle, Nook, iBooks and other eBook readers have their own exclusive eBook file format, there are several eBook formats that can be read on almost all or most eBook readers.

Almost all major eBook readers support the PDF format, which can be read on any PC with Adobe Reader and other free PDF reading software. PDF is a universal format that can be read on almost any computer, eBook Reader, smartphone, or mobile device. Most, but not all, eBook readers also support MOBI or EPUB formats, or both. There are software programs available to read MOBI or EPUB formats on your PC.

If you primarily use a specific eBook reader device, you will probably have the best reading experience getting the eBook format made for your device. But if you are feeling left out because you do not have an eBook Reader, want to read eBooks on your PC, or want to view eBooks from sources other than what your eBook Reader can store, PDF eBooks are an option. Also, you can convert your own documents to PDF so that you can read them on your eBook reader device.

> **NOTE:** Most eBooks have some kind of Digital Rights Management (DRM) controls that may restrict how many times or the types of devices you are allowed to use the eBook title on. Some eBook purchases may allow you to view the title on your eBook reader and then view it on your PC or mobile device. Some may only be available on your eReader. Sometimes the reason a title can only be viewed on your eBook reader and not on your PC or mobile device is simply technical, not a DRM limitation: that particular title may not have been converted to a format that could be read on your PC.

eBook Readers and Stores

Table 11–2 compares the major eBook readers and stores and how they work with a PC, if they do at all.

> **NOTE:** You don't need a dedicated eBook reader device or have an account with an eReader store to get eBooks. Most publishers offer their titles in eBook formats that can be viewed on any eReader and on your computer

Table 11–2. *Comparing eBook Readers and Stores*

Store	Features and Services
Amazon Kindle	Kindle devices, books, and reader applications are available www.amazon.com. Kindle devices are available at many electronics retailers.
	Amazon provides free apps so that you can read your content on other devices besides your Kindle. **Kindle for PC** allows you to read your Kindle books on your PC.
	> **NOTE:** Some books and magazines are only available for the Kindle device and thus aren't available for viewing in Kindle for PC.
	You can also connect your Kindle directly to your PC via USB cable to upload some types of documents like PDF files from your PC to your Kindle.
Barnes & Noble Nook	Nook devices, books, and reader applications are available at www.barnesandnoble.com. Nook devices are also available at many electronics retailers.
	Nook provides free apps so that you can read your content on other devices besides your Nook. Nook for PC allows you to read your Nook books on your PC.
iBooks by Apple	iBooks are purchased through the iTunes store. At this time, you can only view iBooks on iPad and iPhone or iPod touch with iOS 4 or later. There are no iBooks applications for the PC or Mac.
Kobo Reader	The Kobo devices, books, and reader applications are available at www.kobobooks.com.
	Kobo provides free apps so that you can read your content on other devices besides your Kobo Ereader. The **Kobo Desktop Application** allows you to read your Kobo books on your PC.

Store	Features and Services
Sony Reader	You can download the **Reader Library Software for PC** from `http://ebookstore.sony.com/download/`. Some models of Sony Reader don't have wireless capability; books must be downloaded from the web to a PC, and then transferred from the PC to the Sony Reader by USB.
	The Sony Reader Library software can also be used to access Google books, which contains over a million public domain books.

eBooks Directly from Publishers

The idea of offering books in digital form was around long before the Kindle, Nook, and other dedicated eReader devices. Most book publishers offer their eBooks in all three formats: PDF, MOBI, and EPUB. For example, Apress, the publisher of this book, offers eBook versions of their books in PDF, MOBI, and EPUB format through their online store at `www.apress.com`.

Online eBook Repositories and Subscriptions

There are also several online eBook repositories that offer access to thousands of books in eBook formats. Two of the largest are Safari Books online at `www.safaribooksonline.com`, and Books24x7 at `www.books24x7.com`. Paid subscriptions provide access to thousands of technical and business book titles online. They offer a range of plans, like unlimited access to their entire library, limited access to a set number or titles per month, and access to specific categories. These plans are available to individuals, small groups or businesses, educational institutions and libraries, and large corporations.

Other services, such as SpringerLink at `www.springerlink.com`, offer access to thousands of technical, academic, and scientific books, journals, and articles.

eBook Magazine and Newspaper Subscription

Many national and international magazines and newspapers are available for eBook readers by subscription. Many publishers choose not to convert their content in eBook formats for viewing on the PC or other non-reader devices, probably because of production costs and availability of much of that content as web pages on their web site.

eBook Checkout from Public Libraries

The content you read and use doesn't all have to come from the device maker's eBook store. If you explore a little bit, you may find that your local library system offers eBook titles for checkout, just like hardcopy books.

Public Domain eBooks Available through Google Books

You can access public domain eBooks through http://books.google.com, and they can be read on your web browser, Android, Kindle, iPhone, iPad, Sony, Nook, and so on. Finding public domain books on the Google Books web site is not obvious, but once you know where to look, it's easy.

To access public domain books on Google Books

1. In your web browser, go to http://books.google.com.

2. On the Google Books page, click the button **Go to the Google eBookstore**.

   It's a bit confusing to look for free books in an eBookstore. Stores sell things, they don't give things away.

3. Scroll down to almost the bottom of the page, until you see the section **Best of the free.**

4. Many of these books are classics, like the works of Mark Twain, Jane Austen, Sir Arthur Conan Doyle, Jules Verne, etc.

5. Scroll through the books. When you find one you like, click it. The description of the book will tell you which eBook formats are available and will provide links to view or download it.

You can also just do a search of all Google books for a particular subject. On the **Search Results** page, you can narrow down your search criteria to **Price: Free only**.

Free eBooks by Project Gutenberg

Another good source for free eBooks is Project Gutenberg at www.gutenberg.org. They offer titles in a variety of eBook formats, from EPUB to Kindle. This site also links to many other resources for free eBooks.

Managing Your eBook Library

If you accumulate a lot of eBooks, especially from outside of your device's own store, you may need help managing and converting the titles. One program you may find useful is **caliber**, a free open-source program available from http://calibre-ebook.com/about. This program features tools for managing your library; converting eBooks; syncing to eBook readers; and viewing eBook content from most of the major eBook formats.

Summary

In this chapter you have learned about

- Media players like Windows Media Center, Windows Media Player, iTunes, Zune, RealPlayer, and Rhapsody.

- Online music and video stores.

- eBooks—the major formats and devices, how they interact with your computer, and where to buy or download free eBooks.

Next Steps

You may find these related chapters useful:

- Chapter 2 explains more about the Music, Video, and Picture libraries. Most of the media players look in those locations first when importing into the player. Knowing how the Windows 7 libraries are organized and where they are located will help you point your media file imports in the right direction.

- Chapter 4 will help you with selecting the default programs for your music, video, and photo files. Often when you install a new media player, it tries to make itself the default program for the media files. If a newly installed program takes over and you want to return to your previous defaults, you can do that through Programs and Features.

- Chapter 5 has many useful tips and recommended practices that are applicable to installing media players.

- Chapter 16 explains how to back up your computer and your document libraries. If you have a large music, video, or picture collection, you'll want to make sure that you back those up regularly, and back them up before you do any media file conversions or imports into another media player.

Chapter 12

Setting Up and Transferring User Accounts

The first time you started Windows 7, you created your first *user account.* Hopefully, you also created a password (and, more importantly, memorized it). Every person who will be regularly using your computer should be assigned their own account. User accounts serve several purposes.

- Personalization: Everybody can set their own desktop colors, background pictures, taskbar arrangement, and music, picture, and video collections.

- Privacy: Everybody can keep e-mail and social network accounts; web favorites; and work, personal, and school documents separate. Privacy doesn't mean that somebody has something to hide; on a very practical level, it allows each user to organize their documents and files and to protect them from accidental deletion or changes.

- Parental Control: User accounts allow you to monitor and control computer usage. You can control the time of day and length of time that they can use the computer. You can also control game and web access.

- User Access Control: You can control what each user can change on the computer, such as whether they can install programs or make significant changes to Windows settings, or just provide simpler web access. You can choose from Administrator, Standard User, or Guest.

If you already have user accounts set up on other computers in your household, you can transfer user settings and documents from an older Windows XP or Windows Vista computer, or even another Windows 7 computer. Fortunately, Windows has a program for that: Windows Easy Transfer.

In this chapter, we'll go over:

Setting up a user account

- Assigning an appropriate user level.
- Creating a strong password.
- Adding a user account.
- Changing and resetting passwords.

Transferring user accounts and settings to another computer

- Using Windows Easy Transfer.
- Third-party programs for transferring your programs without reinstalling.

Setting Up a User Account

Every person using your computer should have a user account, and every user account should have a password. When you start your computer, even if you are the only person who uses the computer, you need to set up Windows to require that you log on with a name and password. If more than one person uses the computer, each person must have a username and password. A user account ensures that each person authorized to use your computer has their own settings, libraries, and preferences. In addition, requiring a user account and password restricts who has access to any information on your computer. Before you add a user account, you should do the following:

- Determine the user account level the user needs.
- Understand the importance of a strong password and how to create one.
- Check to see if user accounts are already set up for the user on another computer in your household.

Determining the Appropriate User Account Level

User accounts also provide a way of specifying what level of changes the user can make to the computer. The highest level of permissions is **Administrator**. An administrator has complete access to everything on the computer, can change system settings that affect all users, and can set the permission levels of users. Most users should be assigned to a **Standard** user account, which allows them to install programs and change system settings that don't affect other users on the computer. If you have occasional visitors who just need temporary access, you can also turn on and off a very limited **Guest** account.

Understanding Passwords and Why They are Important

From the moment you turn on your computer, you are bombarded with little boxes that ask who you are and what's your magic password. You need a password to log on to your computer, to view your e-mail, to use instant messaging, to view web sites, and to get access to other accounts and information. It's easy to get overwhelmed with all of the user names and passwords you'll have to remember. Fortunately, there are programs and strategies you can use to help you manage your passwords.

The User Name/Password Model

In the standard user name/password model, you must provide a user name and a password. Usually the user name is clearly visible, and you may have several choices, like the Windows 7 login user tiles. But when you type your password, it usually appears as little dots or asterisks, as shown in Figures 12–1 and 12–2.

Figure 12–1. *Your password is usually hidden as you type so that somebody can't look over your shoulder and see it.*

Figure 12–2. *An e-mail login*

AutoComplete, AutoFill, and Password Managers

There are several ways to reduce how often you need to enter passwords using Windows 7 features or third-party programs.

AutoComplete

This Windows feature is available through Internet Options in Control Panel. It allows Windows to store user names and passwords for web sites, forms, and account logins.

To access AutoComplete settings:

1. Click the **Start** button, and in the Start menu's search box, type **Internet Options**.

2. In the list that appears, click **Internet Options**.

3. In the Internet Options dialog box, click the **Content** tab. In the AutoComplete box, click **Settings**.

4. Select or clear User names and passwords on forms, as shown in Figure 12–3.

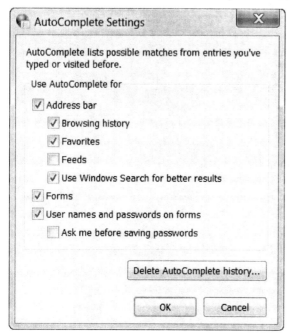

Figure 12–3. *AutoComplete Settings in Internet Options*

Google offers an AutoFill feature in its browser toolbar, similar to the Internet Options AutoComplete.

To use Google AutoFill:

1. Install the Google Toolbar from www.Google.com/Toolbar.

2. In your browser, click the **AutoFill** button on the Google toolbar.

3. Select or clear settings, as shown in Figure 12–4.

Figure 12–4. *Google Toolbar AutoFill settings*

Third-party Password Managers in Security Suites (Not Included with Windows)

Many security suites include a password manager that can store and automatically fill web site username and password fields. If the password manager doesn't have a username and password stored for a site, it can prompt you to save them or automatically save them. Each security suite program is different; these examples show some typical features.

Log into the password manager once, after you login to your Windows user account, as shown in Figure 12–5. The password manager then autofills usernames and passwords for web sites as you visit them.

The password manager may list the accounts and web sites it has stored information for, and allow you to view or change the passwords, as shown in Figure 12–6.

Figure 12–5. *Identity Safe is Norton's password manager. One login allows Identity Safe to store and autofill usernames and passwords*

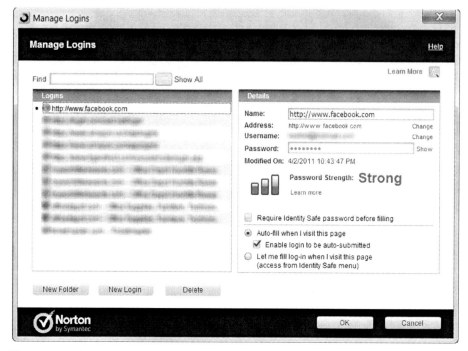

Figure 12–6. *View and manage the stored logins*

Managing Multiple User Accounts on Multiple Computers and a Network

In many households with multiple computers, there may be several users sharing several computers. This could be because they don't all have the same features, programs, or devices attached to them, or one computer is better for some tasks but not as good for other tasks. Though in most cases it is not required, it is a good idea to use the exact same user names and associated password on each computer. If you are sharing files, devices, or storage between several computers on your home network, sometimes you are required to enter a name and password for an account on the other computer. If you always use the same Windows login user name and password on all computers, then you should have no problem knowing which one to enter. Each user should still use their own user name and password on each computer, but be consistent between computers.

Table 12–1 provides an example of the right way and wrong way to create user accounts and passwords that match across multiple computers.

Table 12-1. *Passwords Across Multiple Computers*

	PC1	PC2	PC3
Kevin	User name: **Kevin**	User name: **Kevin**	User name: **Kevin**
	Password: **P@$$w0rd_1**	Password: **P@$$w0rd_1**	Password: **P@$$w0rd_1**
Jason	User name: **Jason**	User name: **Jason**	User name: **Jason**
	Password: **I<3Pizz@**	Password: **sK8bo@rdr**	Password: **n0t_B0urne**
Marie	User name: **Marie**	User name: **Marie**	User name: **Marie**
	Password: **all_G8r**	Password: **all_G8r**	Password: **all_G8r**

Kevin, Jason, and Marie at different times use the computers PC1, PC2, and PC3. Kevin and Marie do not use the same passwords as each other, but use the same user name and password combination on all computers. Jason likes to be original so he created a different password on each computer. Kevin and Marie can log in to any of the home computers and access all of their non-public libraries from any computer with the same name and password. Meanwhile, Jason keeps forgetting which password he used on which computer. Eventually he gets the right password. But when he tries to access his Music library on PC2 from PC1, he runs into the same problem—he has to enter a different password.

If you use the same password for all computers and devices on your network, then you won't get confused. If you have a network attached storage (NAS) device, create user names and passwords for the NAS device that match those you use for your PCs.

Password Security Tips

The following tips can help you choose and manage your passwords carefully.

- Don't use "password" or "123" or anything similar for your password. Those are the first passwords a hacker uses when he tries to break into an account.

- Create *strong* passwords—a combination of upper and lower case, numbers, and symbols. For example, "Mi$t@ke3" contains all four types. The longer your password, the better. Most sites and programs require 8-14 characters.

- Practice typing a potential password several times in Notepad before actually assigning it to a login. That way you can tell if it will be easy to remember and retype. Sometimes a password that looks like it will be a good strong password is actually easy to mistype.

- Don't use words or names in your password that could be found in a dictionary. Sophisticated hackers have large databases of words from the dictionary that they run through to try as passwords.

- Don't use the same password for all of your accounts outside of your home network user accounts. Otherwise, all you have to do is use that password someplace like a friend's computer or a public computer, where it isn't secure, and somebody can get hold of it and try it on other accounts. Yes, it sometimes seems like there are a million password accounts to keep track of. If you want to use the same password over and over again, maybe use one password for one type of account like banks and other very important accounts and another password for less important accounts such as a purely informational site that has no financial data tied to it.

- Rotate your passwords—most companies require that their employees change their network password every 6-12 weeks. That's a good idea for your own personal passwords, too. It also keeps you in practice of remembering your password.

- Be careful about selecting check boxes that say "Remember my password," even if it's your own personal computer at home where you think it is perfectly safe and secure. If your computer were to get stolen, somebody could click their way into your private information without ever having to know your passwords. Allowing Windows to remember your passwords is only as safe as your user account login. If you are using somebody else's computer, you never know what information is being recorded or logged. If the password system itself is not very secure, somebody could hack the computer and find your username and password and use them to enter a secure Web site.

- Don't write down your user name and password—somebody could find that sticky note under your keyboard or in your lost/stolen wallet/purse.

- Is it hard for you to remember your passwords? Create and memorize three easy-to-remember passwords. You can use mnemonic devices like substituting numbers to represent letters. Think of automobile vanity license plates that use numbers to represent letters, drop vowels, or use letters to represent words. For example, 8 could be ate or hate; 4 could be for; 2 could be to or too. You might remember "To be or not to be" as 2Bernt2b .

- Don't give out your user name or password to anybody. Not even to a friend to log in to your account. If you want to give access to your computer or Internet access, create a Guest user account, which will provide built-in limited access.

- If you receive a phone call requesting your user name or password, don't reveal that information! Likewise, if you receive an e-mail message requesting that you click a link to log in to your account because there's been some kind of security breach, don't do it! This is called *phishing*—they take you to a Web site that looks exactly like your bank's online banking site. You log in with your real user name and password for that bank, and then they record that information so that they can log in to the real bank web site and transfer your money out of your account.

- Make sure the Caps Lock key is off on your keyboard.

- Use the password lock hotkeys to lock up your computer—press and hold the Windows key, and then press L. That way, when you know you are going to be away from your computer, you can lock it up without shutting down by pressing the Windows+L keys. If you get called away from your computer longer than you expected and didn't lock the computer when you left, when the screensaver kicks in, it can automatically lock your computer for you.

PASSWORD POLICIES AND FILE ENCRYPTION IN THE WORKPLACE

Microsoft Windows 7 is available in several business editions (Professional, Ultimate, and Enterprise) that offer network and encryption features not available in Windows 7 Basic or Home Premium editions. See Chapter 18 to learn more about:

- Logging onto Windows domains.

- Mandatory password expiration and reset.

- Encrypting files or folders with Encrypting File System (EFS).

- Encrypting entire drives with BitLocker Drive Encryption (Windows 7 Ultimate and Enterprise editions only).

Adding a Password to Your Own Account

You can follow these steps if you didn't create a password during installation or first time setup of Windows 7 on your computer or if someone already created an account for you but didn't create a password for you.

To add a password to your own account:

1. Click the **Start** button, and in the search box type **password**. In the list that appears, click **Change your Windows password**.

   The User Accounts window appears, as shown in Figure 12–7.

2. Click **Create a password for your account**.

   The Create Your Password page appears, as shown in Figure 12–8.

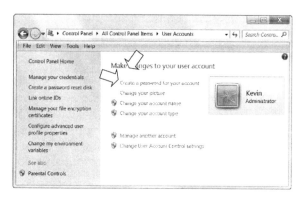

Figure 12–7. *User Accounts Window, Make changes to your user account*

3. Type the new password in both boxes, and optionally type a password hint that will help you remember but not be obvious for others to guess.

4. Click **Create password**.

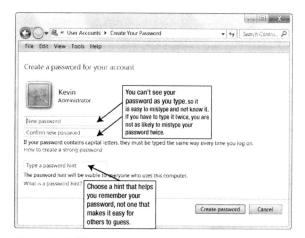

Figure 12–8 *When you create a password, you must type it twice.*

5. When you're done, the user account will now display "Password Protected" under the name, as shown in Figure 12–9.

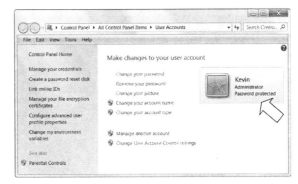

Figure 12–9. *The Administrator account is now password protected.*

Adding a New User

Chapter 1 shows you how to make your computer look unique and individual plus how to set personal preferences to make it easier to use. Imagine you have your Windows desktop background, colors, and taskbar set up just right. The next day when you log on, everything is different! You can't find the files you have been working on, and your computer makes annoying sounds every time you do something with the mouse. And your seven-year-old just looks at you with the sweetest smile.

My personal experience with friends and family over the years is that from the terrible twos to the terrible teens, kids are quite capable of finding new and unique ways to make your computer difficult to use or completely unusable. If every member of the family needs access to a computer and mysterious problems pop up after somebody else has used the computer, one solution is to get each family member their own computer—or at least a separate one for the kids. But many of us can't afford to buy many computers, so the more practical solution is to set up separate user accounts and privileges for each person who uses the computer.

> **TIP:** Are your family computers plagued by the mysterious user **I Don't Know Who Did It?** You should get to know your pals and life savers **Mister Backup** and **Miss System Restore**. They are *time travelers* who can take you back to a time when your computer was working correctly or help you find those files that disappeared sometime in the last couple of days. You can meet Mister Backup and Miss System Restore in Chapter 16.

To add a user:

1. Click the **Start** button, and in the search box type **User Account**. In the list that appears, click **User Accounts**.

   The User Accounts window appears, as shown in Figure 12–10.

2. Click **Manage another account**.

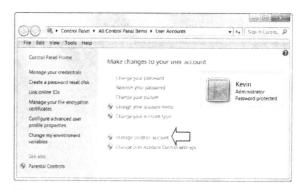

Figure 12–10. *User Accounts Window*

The Manage Accounts window appears, as shown in Figure 12–11.

> **TIP:** If all you want is a temporary account for a visitor, click `Guest`, and you're done.

3. Click **Create a new account**.

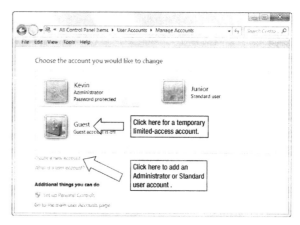

Figure 12–11. *Manage Accounts window*

The Create New Account window appears, as shown in Figure 12–12.

4. Type the new account name, and select **Standard user** or **Administrator**, and then click **Create Account**.

   The new account is displayed, as shown in Figure 12–13.

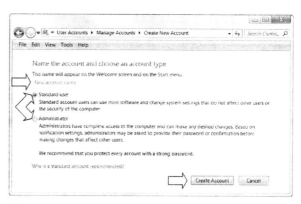

Figure 12–12. *Create New Account window*

CAUTION: Neither of the Standard user accounts in this example are password protected, but they should be.

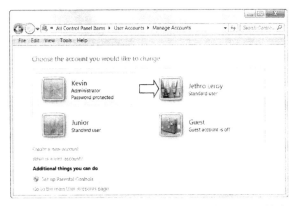

Figure 12–13. *A new Standard user account has been added.*

Setting Password Protection for Each Account

There are several reasons why every account on your computer (except the Guest account) should have a password.

- To protect your computer from other people who have physical access to it.
- To provide each user a sense of privacy for their accounts.
- To provide some protection of the data on your computer in case your computer is lost or stolen.

The password not only protects you against people logging into your account, it also allows you to temporarily "lock" your computer when you are going to be away. You can set your screensaver to automatically lock the computer when you are inactive, or you can manually lock it with a few keystrokes. That way you don't have to shut down your computer to secure it when you need to walk away from your desk for fifteen minutes or a few hours.

After you have created a new account for another user, you or the new user should log in with the new account and add a password. The new user can do this by following the steps shown previously in the "Adding a Password to Your Own Account" section.

Password Lockouts

Many password login systems will only allow you to enter the wrong name and password three times, and then your login session or your account may be locked. This is to prevent hackers or automated programs from trying to guess your password or user name. Usually this lockout is for your current session at the computer. If after three times you still can't get logged in, try cancelling your login attempt completely. If you were trying to log into a network or your computer, try again later. If you are trying to log in to a personal or web e-mail account, try logging in from another computer—this will usually give you three more chances. If you are logging into some other kind of account on a web site, they usually offer a link to a web page where you can reset your password by either answering a secret question you created in the past or by sending reset instructions to the e-mail account you have associated with that web site account.

Creating a Password Reset Disk

As long as people have been logging into computers, they have also been forgetting those passwords. Fortunately, Windows has a nifty little wizard that creates a Password Reset Disk. With the Password Reset Disk, if you forget your user account password or somebody changed it without your permission, you can reset the password.

> **NOTE:** Oops! Somebody at Microsoft forgot to come up with a new name for this. In previous versions of Windows, you needed a *floppy disk* that you could remove from the computer and store someplace safe; now you can use almost any kind of USB flash drive, external USB storage device, or memory card.

Table 12–2 lists the floppy disk alternatives.

Table 12–2. *Password Reset Disk Alternatives*

Storage method	Description
USB flash drive	Recommended. Every Windows computer should have at least one USB slot. These are durable, inexpensive, and easy to safely and securely store so that nobody else can get to it.
Any flash card you can insert in a multi-card reader, such as the memory cards used in digital cameras	Will work, but it would be easy to forget that it has the reset disk and you might accidently erase it by inserting it into your camera.
An external hard drive	Will work, but if several members of the family use this external hard drive, somebody else could accidently delete the password reset disk, or they could also use it to reset the password without your permission.
An ancient floppy disk	Not recommended. Either the disk, the disk drive, or both might be so old that next time you use it, it might not work.

TIP: Even if you don't use a password for your account, if other people have access to this computer, they could create a password for your account. You should still create a Password Reset Disk before somebody else can lock you out of your account.

To create a password reset disk:

5. Click the **Start** button, and in the search box type **password reset**. In the list that appears, click **Create a password reset disk**.

   The Forgotten Password Wizard page appears, as shown in Figure 12–14.

6. Click **Next**.

   The Create a Password Reset Disk page appears, as shown in Figure 12–15.

Figure 12–14. *The Forgotten Password Wizard*

7. Select which drive to store the password reset disk on, and then click **Next**.

   TIP: If you can't tell what each drive letter is, open **Computer** in another window to find descriptions of each drive.

Figure 12–15. *Create a Password Reset Disk page*

   The Current User Account Password page appears, as shown in Figure 12–16.

8. Type your current user account password for this account, and then click **Next**.

   A Progress page will appear.

Figure 12–16. *Current User Account Password*

9. When the Progress page reaches 100%, as shown in Figure 12–17, click Next.

10. When the wizard completes creating the Password Reset Disk, as shown in Figure 12–18, click **Finish**.

Figure 12–17. *It doesn't take long for the Progress page to reach 100%.*

> **NOTE:** Each user must create their own Password Reset Disk for their account.

11. Be sure to mark or label the disk so that you know that it contains the Password Reset information, and also which computer and which user this reset key is for.

Figure 12–18. *This password reset disk is only for this user account.*

Protecting More than One User Account Password

The Password Reset Disk is stored as the file userkey.psw. So if you have several computer users in the household with separate user accounts, and you want to create Password Reset Disks for each of them, you must store them on separate disks. Otherwise, you get a warning message similar to the one shown in Figure 12–19.

Figure 12–19. *You can only store password reset information for one account on a disk.*

If you get this message, click **No,** and then click **Back** so that you can select or insert a different disk. Be sure to label each Password Reset disk, including the computer and user account to which it applies.

Resetting the Password with the Reset Disk

If you forget your password, or somebody else has reset it and you are locked out of your account, you can easily reset it with the Password Reset Disk you previously created. Before you begin, locate the flash drive or memory stick where you stored the Password Reset Disk.

To reset the password with the password reset disk:

1. Attach or insert the drive or disk that contains the password reset disk.

2. At the login screen, select your user tile, leave the password empty, and then click the **Enter** button, as shown in Figure 12–20.

    An error message is displayed with a red and white X: "The user name or password is incorrect" as shown in Figure

Figure 12–20. *Until you enter an incorrect password, there is no way to tell Windows to use the Password Reset Disk.*

Figure 12–21.*Click OK.*

12–21.

3. Click **OK**.

   This time, a new link is added below the password box, "Reset password," as shown in Figure 12–22.

4. Click **Reset password**.

   The Password Reset Wizard is displayed, as shown in Figure 12–23.

5. Click **Next**.

   The Insert the Password Reset Disk page is displayed, as shown in Figure 12–24.

6. Select the drive that contains your password key disk, and then click **Next**.

Figure 12–22. *The Reset password link appears. Click the link to start the Password Reset Wizard.*

Figure 12–23. *The Password Reset Wizard.*

Figure 12–24. *Insert or attach the drive or card that contains the Password Reset disk, and then select the drive.*

The Reset the User Account Password dialog box is displayed, as shown in Figure 12–25.

7. Create your new password and a password hint, and then click **Next**.

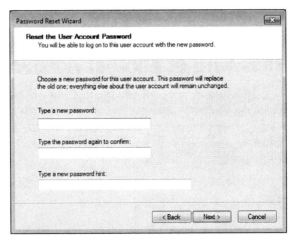

Figure 12–25. *Type the new password twice; the password hint is optional.*

The final page appears, as shown in Figure 12–26.

8. Review the last page of the wizard, and then click **Finish**.

Figure 12–26. *Review the last page of the wizard and then click Finish.*

Using an Administrator Account to Change the Password of Another Account

An Administrator account can change the password of any other user on the computer, including another Administrator. If you attempt to do this through User Accounts, a warning message will be displayed, similar to Figure12–27.

Figure 12–27. *Administrators can change the password of any other user, including another administrator account.*

Windows Basic, Windows Home Basic, and Windows Home Premium do not support creating EFS (Encrypting File System)-encrypted files.

> **NOTE:** Chapter 18 provides more information about using the EFS feature in Windows 7 Professional, Ultimate, and Enterprise editions.

Personal certificates are usually associated with encrypted e-mail and are used mostly in corporate and business environments. Home users are not likely to have either of these, but if they do, they will lose them if you reset their password. They may also lose any stored passwords for web sites or networks. Users can change their own passwords any time without losing any of their encryption certificates or stored passwords.

If you are the administrator for one or more computers in your household, and you are concerned that one or more users may be prone to forget their password, you may want to have each user log into their own account to create a password reset disk, which *you* store safely in case *they* forget their password.

Adjusting User Account Control to an Appropriate Level

User Account Control (UAC) notifies you when you or the programs you are using try to make changes to your computer that might put your computer at risk. It's one of the ways that Windows defends you against viruses and other malware that try to make changes to your computer. When Windows detects a request to make changes to your computer that could be dangerous, UAC alerts you and requires that an administrator approve those changes. If you are not an administrator or if you are logged on as a Standard user, you will be prompted to provide an Administrator username and password. The default setting for User Account Control is suitable for most people, and you should not need to change it.

Some people find these notifications annoying or disruptive and change the UAC settings so that they receive fewer notifications and interruptions. Another reason to change the settings is if you are using programs you know are safe, but UAC does not recommend them as safe.

In the User Account Control Settings dialog box, you can view the different levels of notification available and the consequences of each level.

To change or view your User Account Control settings:

1. Click the **Start** button, and in the search box type **UAC**.

2. In the list that appears, click **Change User Account Control settings**.

3. The **User Account Control Settings** dialog box appears, as shown in Figure 12–28.

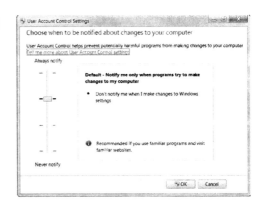

Figure 12–28. *For most users, the default setting provides strong protection without being disruptive.*

4. Move the slider up or down to view a description of each setting. If you want to learn more about UAC, click the **Tell me more about User Account Control** settings link. This opens a separate help window but doesn't close the User Account Control Settings dialog box.

5. Click **OK** if you have selected a different level. Otherwise, if you don't want to make any changes, click **Cancel**.

Applying Parental Controls

Assigning your kids to Standard user accounts is just part of the solution to control access to the computer. Standard user accounts control what programs can be installed and can help prevent or minimize attacks by malicious downloads, programs, or web sites. Parental Controls can be applied to games, the amount of time the computer can be used, and what programs can be used. Most games carry ratings to help you determine if the content is acceptable and age-appropriate. Parental Control settings that can be applied to games include:

- **Time limits**: Set what hours of the day and the week when your child can use the computer.

- **Games**: You can specify whether your child can play games, block or allow games by rating and content types, and block or allow specific games.

- **Allow and block specific programs**: You can apply these settings to your web browser, e-mail programs, instant messaging, or any other program on your computer.

To set up Parental Controls:

1. Log in to Windows with a Computer administrator account.

2. Click **Start**, and in the Search programs and folders box, type **Parental Controls**.

3. In the list that appears, select **Parental Controls**.

    The Parental Controls window lists the user accounts on this computer, as shown in Figure 12–29.

4. In the Parental Controls window, click the user you want to apply the settings to.

Figure 12–29. An Administrator can apply parental controls to a Standard user account. You cannot apply parental controls to an Administrator account.

The User Controls window displays the current settings and allows you to change the settings, as shown in Figure 12–30.

5. Click **On, enforce current settings**.

   The links under **Windows Settings** are now available, and you can adjust as needed.

Figure 12–30. *The User Controls window lists the current settings for this user and provides links to change the settings.*

6. Click **Time Limits**.

7. In the **Time Restrictions** window, select the hours each day that you want to block use of the computer, as shown in Figure 12–31.

   In this example, Jethro Leroy is blocked from using the computer from 9 PM to 6 AM Sunday night through Thursday night, because he has school the next day. On Friday and Saturday nights, he is allowed to use the computer until midnight.

8. Click **OK** when you are done with the Time Restrictions.

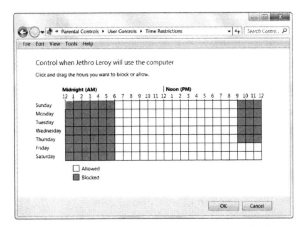

Figure 12–31. *You can block or allow computer use by the hour for each day of the week.*

9. In the **User Controls** window, click **Games**.

   In the Games window you can set restrictions by game rating, content type, or specific games, as shown in Figure 12–32.

10. Click **Set game ratings**.

    The Game Restrictions window appears, as shown in Figure 12–33.

Figure 12–32. *You can restrict game access by rating, content, or game name.*

11. There are three groups of settings for blocking games by rating and content:

    ▪ Allow or block games with no rating. Choose one or the other.

    ▪ Which ratings are ok for user to play. Choose one level. Your selection includes all of the levels above it.

    ▪ Block these types of content. Select none, one, many, or all. By default, none are selected (nothing is blocked). There are about 76 separate checkboxes. Content types are listed alphabetically, not by maturity level.

12. Click **OK**.

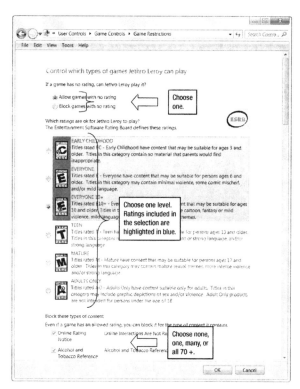

Figure 12–33. *There are three groups of settings for blocking games by rating and content.*

The Game Controls window, shown in Figure 12–34, displays the maximum allowed rating and all of the types of gamed content blocked.

13. Click **Block or Allow** specific games.

Figure 12–34. *The maximum game rating allowed and game content blocked are now displayed.*

The Game Overrides window, shown in Figure 12–35, displays what games currently installed on this computer can be played according to the ratings and content descriptions you selected in the Games Control window.

If you have several ages of users, such as adults, teens, and younger, you may have games that are not suitable for younger users. You can ensure that those games are blocked if they are not already blocked by the rating level or content blocking.

14. When you are done viewing or making changes, click **OK** twice to exit Game overrides and Games Controls.

Figure 12–35. *You can allow or block specific games.*

The User Controls window, shown in Figure 12–36, now lists settings for time limits and game ratings, but no program limits.

15. If you want to block your child from using specific programs, click **Allow and block specific programs**.

The Applications Restrictions window is displayed, as shown in Figure 12–37.

16. Click *User* **can only use the programs I allow**.

It may take a few minutes for Windows to gather a complete list of most of the registered programs on your computer. A list of all programs is displayed, similar to Figure 12–38.

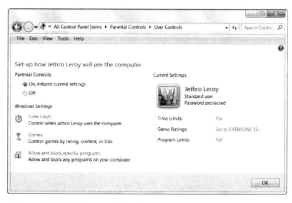

Figure 12–36. *Accessories folder on the Start menu*

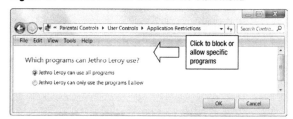

Figure 12–37. *You can control which programs your child can use.*

CAUTION: This list will appear with no programs selected. If you close this window without selecting programs, when this user logs in, many background programs will not run. Instead, your child will see twenty or thirty message boxes from Windows Parental Controls, that Parental Controls has blocked specific programs.

17. A good way to use this list is to click **Check All**, and then clear the check boxes for the specific programs you want to block.

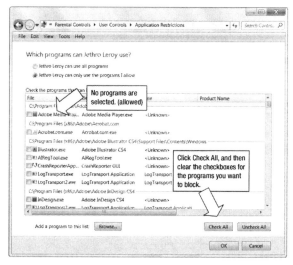

Figure 12–38. *Most programs installed on your computer are listed, but none are selected when the list first appears*

18. Click **OK** when you're done selecting which programs are allowed, and then click **OK** again to close the Parental Controls for this account. Repeat this procedure for each user account you want to set Parental Controls for.

The Parental Controls window is displayed, as shown in Figure 12–39.

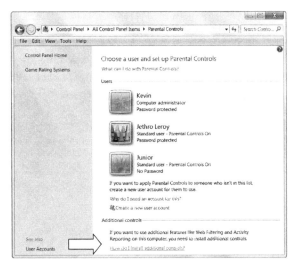

Figure 12–39. *If you want to control access to web sites and web content, you will need to install third-party controls not included with Windows.*

CAUTION: Parental Controls do not include any kind of web or e-mail filtering. Through Parental Controls, you can block specific e-mail programs from running, but you can't block Internet Explorer. You can, however, control access to the web with Windows Live Family Safety, In **Parental Controls**, click **How do I install additional controls**, as shown in Figure 12–39, to learn about installing other third-party controls.

Windows Live Family Safety

Microsoft offers more parental control features through Windows Live Family Safety, which is part of Windows Live Essentials. Many computers come with Windows Live Essentials already installed, but if you don't have it you can download it for free from Microsoft. Chapter 7 tells how to download and install it.

Windows Live Family Safety includes time limits, game restrictions, and program restrictions like Parental Controls, but in addition provides the following features:

- Web filtering
- Web filtering lists
- Activity reporting
- Contact management
- Requests

You can include multiple computers and user accounts, so that you can keep track of all computers in your household. Windows Live Family Safety (Figure 12–40) shows the main web page for monitoring activities. After you have set up Windows Live Family Safety, you can view this web page any time by logging on with the Windows Live ID associated with this account at http://familysafety.live.com.

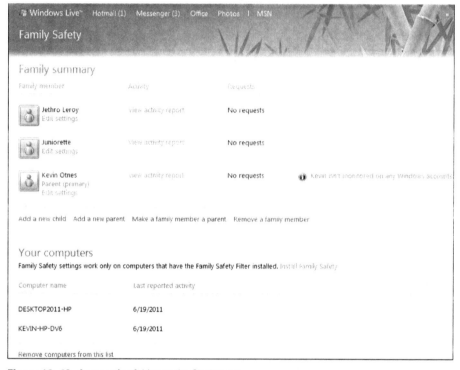

Figure 12–40. *Accessories folder on the Start menu*

You can view and manage individual family member settings from the Windows Live Family Safety web site, as shown in Figure 12–41.

Figure 12–41. *Individual user account settings*

> **NOTE:** In order to monitor all home computers you must set up Windows Live Family Safety on each computer and associate it with the same Windows Live ID account.

To start Windows Live Family Safety for the first time on your computer:

1. Log in to Windows with an Administrator account.

2. Click the **Start** button, click **All Programs**, click **Window Live**, and then click **Windows Live Family Safety**.

   The Windows Live Family Safety sign in page is displayed, as shown in Figure 12–42.

3. Log in with your Windows Live, Hotmail, or MSN ID.

   This account is where monitoring messages and reports will be sent, so make sure this is an account that you have access to but your kids do not.

Figure 12–42. *Windows Live Family Safety sign in*

After you sign in, the Windows Live Family Safety page lists the user accounts on this computer, as shown in Figure 12–43. Any accounts that already have parental controls set up are automatically selected for monitoring.

4. Click **Next**.

Figure 12–43. *User Accounts on this computer that can be monitored*

If you have already set up Windows Live Family Safety on another computer, using the Windows Live ID you just signed in with, you can match up users on this computer with users on the other computer if they are the same people with different account names, as shown in Figure 12–44.

5. Match the Windows accounts on this computer with the Family Safety members as needed.

6. Click **Save** when you are done matching members.

Figure 12–44. *Matching Windows accounts on this computer with Family Safety members*

The monitored accounts and settings are listed, as shown in Figure 12–45.

You can view this window any time by opening Windows Live Family Safety from the Windows Start menu.

7. Click http://familysafety.live.com to view and adjust settings for each member.

Figure 12–45. *Summary of Family Safety settings for monitored Windows accounts*

Since Family Safety monitoring and account information is stored on the web, you can check on all accounts on your computers where you have installed Family Safety and associated it with the same Windows Live ID account, as shown in Figure 12–46.

In order for Family Safety to monitor all computers in your home or home network, you must install and configure Windows Live Family Safety on each computer.

Figure 12–46. *View family activities and settings anytime with your Windows Live ID at* `http://familysafety.live.com`.

Balance Parental Controls and Windows Live Family Settings

It's normal to have to make adjustments to the settings now and then. If the settings are too restrictive, you will constantly be asked to override settings on a case-by-case basis with your administrative account and password. If you relax the settings too much, then you may be defeating the purpose of setting parental controls in the first place.

Using Windows Easy Transfer

Most of us don't like moving. You have to pack things carefully and hope they get to the right place without getting lost or damaged. You may decide to throw some things out before you move because you no longer need them. While things are being moved, you can't use them. When your belongings arrive at the new place, you have to unpack them and sort them out to the rightful owners. Sometimes you hire professional movers to do the moving, which can take some of the load off of you—for a price. That's sort of how it can be with moving to a new computer. Most of us don't want to do it if we don't have to, and it would be nice if somebody else could do it for us.

Fortunately, Windows 7 provides some professional help to make your move to a new computer less stressful: Windows Easy Transfer. With Windows Easy Transfer, you can copy files and settings from your old computer, even another computer running Windows 7, to your new computer running Windows 7.

In this chapter, you'll go through the common tasks associated with getting a new computer, such as moving files and settings with Windows Easy Transfer or alternate methods, installing programs on your new computer, upgrading a computer to Windows 7 from a previous version of Windows, and using or disposing of your old computer.

Moving to a New Computer: The Big Picture

Whether you are upgrading an existing computer from Windows XP or Windows Vista to Windows 7 or moving to a new computer with Windows 7, you probably had your old computer set up just right. You don't need to start all over from scratch to set up your computer the way you want it.

The process for moving from your old computer to a new Windows 7 computer falls into the following tasks:

1. Running Windows Easy Transfer.

2. Installing programs.

3. Connecting printers and other devices.

4. Cleaning up the old computer—reusing, erasing, or recycling.

> **NOTE:** Not sure if your existing computer running Windows XP or Windows Vista can be upgraded to Windows 7? Microsoft provides a free tool you can download to your computer to check whether your system is ready to run Windows 7. Web addresses change frequently, so to find this tool, go to the Microsoft web site at www.microsoft.com and search for **Windows 7 Upgrade Advisor**.

Alternatives to Windows Easy Transfer

Some people don't want or need all of their settings and files migrated to their new computer. But they do want to save things such as pictures, movies, and music. There are many tools and programs that you can use to transfer files between computers that don't require Windows Easy Transfer, such as The Tornado file transfer tool or **Laplink**. You can also use some of the same connection types used for Windows Easy Transfer.

Another alternative is **Laplink PCMover Professional** (www.laplink.com), which can transfer your applications as well as your files, settings, and user accounts. This product sounds promising. I have not used it, so I can't vouch for how well it works. There are several independent articles and reviews on the Web. Some potential problems noted in these articles:

- If you are transferring from a Windows XP computer, some programs might not work on Windows 7.

- If you are transferring from a 32-bit Windows computer to a 64-bit Windows 7 computer, the 32-bit version may not work.

- Some software may need to be reactivated, like Microsoft Office, because the software detects that it is new hardware.

- Other licensing issues. Technically most software is licensed for one computer, so if you transfer your applications to a new computer, you should remove it from the old computer afterwards, or buy another license for the new computer.

- Firewalls and antivirus software may not work well after the transfer.

You may be able to detect some compatibility issues by running the Windows 7 Upgrade Advisor on your old computer. Though this program is meant to check your existing computer to see if it can be upgraded to Windows 7, it may also detect programs currently installed that will not work on Windows 7. It will not help with 32-bit/64-bit issues. You can download the Windows 7 Upgrade Advisor from `http://windows.microsoft.com/upgradeadvisor`.

Reinstall Programs or Transfer Files First?

Which do you do first: reinstall programs or transfer files and settings?

The Windows 7 Windows Help and Support suggests that you install your programs on your new computer and then transfer the files and settings. In several tests of the Windows Easy Transfer, this author found no problems performing the Windows Easy Transfer first, and then installing the programs on the new computer. One advantage of doing it in this order is that after the files and settings transfer, Windows Easy Transfer provides a report of programs that should be installed based on what it detected on your old computer and the documents and settings it transferred over. This takes some of the guesswork out of trying to figure out what you need to install on the new computer by giving you a detailed checklist.

For example, if you had Microsoft Office installed on your old computer but haven't installed it on your new computer, Windows Easy Transfer will still move your Office settings (default file locations, preferences, author information, and so forth) and Office documents (Word documents, Excel spreadsheets, PowerPoint presentations, templates, macros, and so forth) to the new computer. At the end of the transfer, the Windows Easy Transfer report lists the programs you should install based on the settings and documents it transferred and that list would contain Microsoft Office.

Understanding Windows Easy Transfer

Windows Easy Transfer first appeared in Windows Vista, and prior to Vista was preceded by the File and Settings Transfer Wizard. The purpose of these programs is to make it easier to move from an older version of Windows to another computer running the new version without losing your settings, preferences, or files.

The way Windows Easy Transfer works is like this:

1. Run Windows Easy Transfer on your old and new computer. (You may have to download and install Windows Easy Transfer on your old computer if it is running Windows XP. Windows Vista already has Windows Easy Transfer.)

2. Choose a method of transfer—through a network connection, an Easy Transfer cable, or by copying to storage media such as a USB flash drive, external hard drive, or removable discs such as CDs or DVDs.

3. Windows Easy Transfer scans your old computer to determine what can be transferred and the size of the transfer.

4. Choose what to transfer. Windows Easy Transfer suggests what to transfer, but you can customize the list to include or exclude specific files or folders.

5. Transfer the files and settings directly to your new computer (via Easy Transfer cable, or in real time through a network connection) or to a storage location (network share, external hard drive, USB flash drive, or CD/DVD discs) for transfer later to the new computer.

> **NOTE:** Windows Easy Transfer copies only the files and settings from your old computer. If you want to delete the files from your old computer, you must do that yourself. Or you can perform a clean installation of Windows 7, which will delete everything—the Windows operating system, and all documents, pictures, music, data—before installing the new version of Windows.

Using Windows Easy Transfer for a Windows Upgrade Installation on the Same Computer

There are three typical ways to install Windows 7 on a computer:

- Buy a new computer with Windows 7 already installed by the computer manufacturer.

- Upgrade the operating system on your existing computer from Windows XP or Windows Vista to Windows 7. Keep your existing files, settings, and programs on the computer without reinstalling them.

- Install Windows 7 on your existing computer, completely erasing everything on your computer in the process. This is often called a *clean install*.

Windows Easy Transfer can be used for any of these. Throughout the instructions for Windows Easy Transfer in this chapter, the information you see onscreen, and the online help in Windows Help and Support, you will see references to the *old* computer and the *new* computer. It's easy to assume that this means the old computer and new computer are two different machines, such as when you buy a new computer with Windows 7 already installed and you are moving from an older machine with Windows XP or Windows Vista. But Windows Easy Transfer can also be useful when you are upgrading an existing computer to Windows 7.

If you are upgrading an existing computer to Windows 7, in most cases you can do that without losing any of your files or settings, and you won't need to reinstall very many, if any, programs. But in some cases, you may want to do what is called a clean install. In a clean install, Windows erases everything on the computer (cleans) before installing Windows 7; the entire operating system and all of your files, settings, and programs are removed. Some of the common reasons for performing a clean install are as follows:

- Your computer is running poorly under the old version of Windows, and some of the causes may still be there after the upgrade of Windows.

- You have a lot of junk on your computer—files and programs you no longer need or use.

- You don't have much room on your old/new computer's hard drive. A clean install means you won't have any of the old Windows files on your computer.

- You are replacing the hard drive before you upgrade to Windows 7.

If you perform a clean install, Windows Easy Transfer allows you to copy your files and settings to another location that won't be affected by the clean install, such as an external hard drive, a network share, a USB drive, or DVD/CD discs. After performing the clean install, you can then run Windows Easy Transfer on the new computer and transfer the files and settings from wherever you stored them.

Preparing to Move to the New Computer

When you move your files and settings to a new computer, you can and should take some steps to ensure that your move goes smoothly and that everything arrives clean and intact.

One of the nice things about moving to a new computer with a new version of Windows is that you have an opportunity to start clean and fresh. You don't have to move *everything* from your old computer. Over time, a computer accumulates a lot of extra files, clutter, and obsolete files. Maybe you have two years of homework files from each of your kids. Your Programs menu or desktop lists many more program icons than you regularly use. Your Printers folder lists several printers that you no longer own. Some of these don't take up very much physical disk space, but they clutter things up and can slow down your computer. If you have 50 program items on your Start menu Programs list, it will take longer for the Programs menu to appear, and therefore it will take longer for you to find anything.

Preparing the Data on Your Old Computer for Transfer

The following tasks are not required but are highly recommended. Performing these steps is sort of like having a garage sale before you move. Not all tasks are applicable to all versions of Windows, and the ones you do choose to complete don't need to be performed in any particular order:

- In Windows XP, right-click an empty area on your desktop, click **Arrange Icons By**, and then click **Run Desktop Cleanup Wizard**. Many of the icons on the desktop are shortcuts, but some could be actual files and folders.

- In any version of Windows, click the **Start** button and click through the submenus: **All Programs ➤ Accessories ➤ System Tools ➤ Disk Cleanup**.

- Have each user on the old computer go through their My Documents folder and delete documents and files they no longer need or save them to USB flash drives, DVDs, or a hard drive for storage.

- If you have backup software on your old computer, perform a full backup as well as a backup of your documents. Be sure that you have a copy of the backup software on another computer, and test the recovery, in case you need to recover files from the backup.

- If you don't have a backup program on your old computer, copy the contents of your C:\Documents and Settings folder and documents from the Desktop folder to another location outside of your old/original computer. This is not as thorough as running a true backup program, but it will provide something to fall back on if something goes awry in your move to the new computer.

Run Backup Before Using Windows Easy Transfer

Windows Easy Transfer doesn't alter or delete files from your old computer. Backing up your files is just a good precaution in preparation for large file and folder moves. These recommendations are not a substitute for running a real backup program but give you an idea of where to find most document files. Some programs store their data files and documents in separate folders outside My Documents folders. Windows Easy Transfer should detect and transfer program data files and settings even if they are not in the My Documents folders. See Chapter 16 to learn how to back up your entire computer as well as individual files.

Preparing and Verifying a Transfer Method

When you actually run Windows Easy Transfer, you will be prompted to choose how you will transfer the files and settings. You may already have the hardware or connections for the transfer or you may need to purchase items such as a transfer cable, USB flash drive, external hard drive, or blank DVDs.

You may not have a choice of which method you can use because some methods may not be available to you or practical for your particular situation. The following subsections describe each type of transfer method, advantages, requirements, and limitations.

Easy Transfer Cable

Using an **Easy Transfer cable** is the fastest method for Windows Easy Transfer when connected to USB 2.0 ports on both ends. Microsoft worked with several computer cable manufacturers to develop a USB-based cable to connect two computers directly and use the Windows Easy Transfer in Windows Vista. The Easy Transfer cables sold for Vista will work for Windows 7, so don't worry if you can't find an Easy Transfer cable labeled for Windows 7.

The Easy Transfer cable looks like a USB cable with two identical USB-A ends that fit in each computer's regular USB ports. However, this cable is more than a USB cable with two identical ends—the middle of the cable has a small chip that enables the two computers to communicate with each other. A plain USB cable with just the USB-A plug on each end will not work.

The Easy Transfer cable package may include an installation disc with a copy of the Window Easy Transfer program for installation on a Windows XP computer. Windows 7 and Windows Vista come with the Windows Easy Transfer program installed. If you have the Easy Transfer cable but don't have a disc with the Windows Easy Transfer program to install on Windows XP, you can download it for free from Microsoft.

The cable may vary in length, but expect it to be about 8 feet. If you need a longer length, you can use a standard USB extension cable. USB speed and data flow decrease with distance, and you need to be able to interact with Windows Easy Transfer on both computers at the same time, so there are practical limits to how many extensions you can string together. The cost of an Easy Transfer cable is more than a regular USB cable of the same length, but not prohibitive.

Network

There are several ways you can use a **network** for Windows Easy Transfer:

Method	Advantages and Disadvantages
Create an Easy Transfer file and copy it to a shared network location.	The old computer and new computer aren't necessarily connected directly to each other; they just need a connection to the same network location. The transfer is in two steps: The old computer creates the Easy Transfer file on the shared computer. Anytime after the file transfer is complete, you can go to the new computer and transfer the file from the network storage location. Neither the old or new computer will be waiting for or communicating directly with each other. Before you create the Easy Transfer file, compare the estimated size given by Windows Easy Transfer, and make sure enough space is available on the network location.
Use a network connection to perform the transfer in real time directly from the old computer to the new computer.	This method is similar to the Easy Transfer cable method, but not as fast. If the network connection is wireless, it could be much slower, especially if the signal strength is weak or the network speed is slow. This method will not work at all if the old computer and new computer can't find each other on the network, which is not uncommon when you have just started integrating your Windows 7 computer with other non-Windows 7 computers on a home network.
Use a crossover Cat5e cable.	This is a variation of the network connection in real time, and very similar to using the Easy Transfer cable. Both computers must have a regular Ethernet (network adapter) jack. You can directly network the old and new computers by using a crossover Cat5e cable. A crossover cable looks like a regular Ethernet cable, except the wire set order on one end is reversed from the wire set order on the other end. Normally, you connect two computers to each other through a router or network switch box. The crossover cable enables two computers to connect directly to each other without the box in between. Essentially, you are creating a small private network.

Method	Advantages and Disadvantages

NOTE: If one or both of your computers has a Gigabit card, you don't need a crossover cable. You can use a standard Cat5e cable.

In informal testing, using a crossover cable appeared to be comparable in speed to using the Easy Transfer cable. It's not difficult to use, and the crossover Cat5e cable may be available for less than an Easy Transfer cable. The crossover cable works with Windows Easy Transfer but can also be used to perform a file transfer between computers. Because most network cards can work at either 10 or 100Mbps, you can potentially transfer at 100Mbps.

NOTE: If you are using Gigabit cards, your transfer rate will be much quicker than using the USB-based Easy Transfer cable.

The only difficulty in using this method is that you must disconnect both the old and new computer from any other network connections and then reconnect them to their regular network connections when you are finished. Each time you want to change these network connections, you may need to restart the computers in order for them to correctly detect the current network connections.

NOTE: Chapter 15 describes how you can network computers running different versions of Windows (Windows XP, Windows Vista, and Windows 7) by using Ethernet and wireless connections.

External hard disk or USB flash drive

Using an **external disk or flash drive** is similar to using a network location to store a Windows Easy Transfer file. The external hard disk or USB drive is connected to the old computer to receive and store the Windows Easy Transfer file. When the transfer from the old computer is complete, you detach the external device from the old computer and attach it to the new computer. When you run Windows Easy Transfer on the new computer, you specify the external hard disk or USB flash drive as the location of the Easy Transfer file.

If the size of the Easy Transfer file is small enough, it may fit on a large-capacity USB flash drive, or may be broken up to fit several flash drives If the transfer is larger than the USB flash drive capacity, you can fill the drive, copy it to the new computer, go back to the old computer, get the next set of files, and repeat until you have moved all files from the old computer to the new computer. This may be feasible if you already have one or more flash drives available, but it may be not be practical if you have a large transfer that is many times the size of the flash drive capacity. It may be a better buy and more practical to get an external hard drive if the estimated file size is more than 8GB. The price of a 16GB flash drive is fairly close to the price of a 250GB external hard drive. Not only will a 250GB external hard drive make the process less tedious but you can use the drive later for backup of your documents or important files from several computers, or as a place to store lots of files if you have large music, picture, or video collections.

Ensuring that Your Computers Are Not Interrupted During Transfer

Running Windows Easy Transfer may take several hours. During that time, your old and new computers will need all the attention from the computer's resources—memory, hard drive use, and so forth. Also, Windows Easy Transfer needs to run without interruption. After Windows Easy Transfer starts, both computers will display a message warning not to use the computer during the transfer. Even if you don't intentionally use your computer during that time, routine and automatic computer operations may disrupt the transfer process. To ensure that your computer doesn't shut down or get interrupted during the transfer, adjust the following settings before you start the transfer. Otherwise, you may come back to your computers only to find that the transfer did not complete, and you will have to start all over again.

Before you run Windows Easy Transfer, perform or check the following:

- Run your computer on AC power, not your batteries.
- Turn off all sleep, hibernation, standby, and power conservation modes.
- Turn off your screen saver.
- Turn off scheduled virus scans, spyware scans, and backups.
- Close down all other programs.
- Locate installation discs for the programs and devices installed on your old computer.

Run Your Computer on AC Power, Not Your Batteries

If either of the computers is a laptop, make sure they are all running on AC power from your wall outlet. One to two hours is the most many computers will run on just batteries, and you don't want one of your computers to shut down in the middle of the transfer.

Turn Off All Sleep, Hibernation, Standby, and Power Conservation Modes

In Windows XP **Control Panel**, open **Power Options**. On the **Power Schemes** tab, make sure the settings are set to **Never** for **Turn off monitor**, **Turn off hard disk**, and **System Standby** for both **Plugged in** and **Running on batteries**. On the **Hibernate** tab, clear the **Enable hibernation** check box.

In Windows Vista or Windows 7, go to **Control Panel**, open **Power Options**, and then edit or create a power plan that has all settings for **Turn off the display** and **Put the computer to sleep** set to **Never**.

Some computer manufacturers provide their own separate utility in Control Panel for managing power options. In those cases, you'll need to use their utility instead.

Turn off your screen saver

In Windows XP, in Control Panel, open Display. On the Screen Saver tab, in the Screen saver box, select None.

In Windows Vista in Control Panel, open Personalization. In the Screen saver box, select None.

In Windows 7, in Control Panel, open Personalization. Click Screen Saver, and in the Screen saver box, select None.

Turn Off Scheduled Virus Scans, Spyware Scans, and Backups

Any kind of antivirus or backup scans will be competing with Windows Easy Transfer for use of the hard drive, memory, and processor resources. Turn off the automatic scans for these programs or reschedule them to run at a much later time, hours after you expect Windows Easy Transfer to finish.

Close Down All Other Programs

Close down all the programs displayed as open in your taskbar. Also, close programs that might be running in the background, such as instant messaging or mail programs. Check the notification area of the taskbar and right-click icons to see whether they have a **Close** or **Exit** command on the submenu.

Locate Installation Discs for the Programs and Devices Installed on Your Old Computer

You don't need installation discs before or during Windows Easy Transfer. But the Windows Easy Transfer process will take several hours, which might be a good time to start rounding up installation discs. When the transfer is complete, the transfer report will give you a good idea of what programs you'll need to install on your new computer that were on your old computer.

Transferring Files with an Easy Transfer Cable

Transferring files between two computers is a lengthy process—both in time and the steps to complete. You will be going back and forth between two computers because you are running programs on each computer. You can't run this entire process from one computer at one end of the transfer. The transfer itself can take a long time.

To transfer files with an Easy Transfer cable, follow these steps:

1. If your old computer is running Windows Vista or Windows 7, go to step 3.

2. If your old computer is running Windows XP, install the software that came with your Easy Transfer cable. This ensures that your computer has the right hardware drivers installed for the cable. If you are using an Easy Transfer cable for Vista, the installation disc will install the older Vista version of the Windows Easy Transfer software. You will need to update to the Windows 7 version a few steps later in this procedure, but you should still run the cable's installation disc so the drivers are installed.

3. Connect the Easy Transfer cable to the new computer. Windows 7 detects the cable and displays the Windows Easy Transfer screen shown in Figure 12–47.

Figure 12–47. *When the Easy Transfer cable is connected to a Windows 7 or Windows Vista computer, it triggers the Windows Easy Transfer program. This figure is from Windows 7. The screen in Windows Vista is different.*

4. Click **This is my new computer**.

   You are prompted to install Windows Easy Transfer on the old computer, as shown in Figure 12–48.

5. Click **I need to install it now**. Because the old computer doesn't have the software installed that will allow it to communicate with the new computer through the Easy Transfer cable, you can't use the Easy Transfer cable to install Windows Easy Transfer on the other computer. Figure 12–48 displays the choices for installing the Windows Easy Transfer software on the other computer.

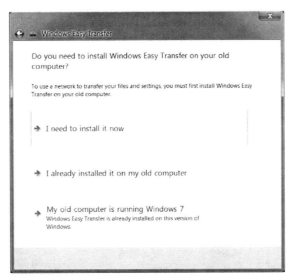

Figure 12–48. *If your old computer is Windows Vista or Windows XP, you will need to install the Windows 7 version of Windows Easy Transfer. Though Windows Vista comes with Windows Easy Transfer, you will need to upgrade to the Windows 7 version on the Windows Vista computer.*

6. If you have a USB flash drive, that's the quickest and easiest choice. Attach a USB flash drive to the new computer and then click USB flash drive.

   —or—

   Attach an external hard drive and then click External hard disk or shared network folder, as shown in Figure 12–49.

7. Click **I need to install it now**. Windows Easy Transfer prompts you to confirm where you want to copy the Windows Easy Transfer software to.

Figure 12–49. *Windows Easy Transfer software is very small. If you have a USB flash drive, that's the quickest and easiest choice.*

After Windows Easy Transfer is copied to the USB flash drive (or external drive), Windows Easy Transfer prompts you to move the USB to the old computer and install it there, as shown in Figure 12–50.

8. Click **Next**. Insert the USB drive in your old computer. Your old computer should autoplay the Windows Easy Transfer installation software. If the installation program doesn't start, follow the instructions shown in Figure 12–50.

Figure 12–50. *Windows Easy Transfer describes how to install the program on your old computer.*

NOTE: In case you need to rerun Windows Easy Transfer on your old computer, copy the Windows Easy Transfer files to a local folder on your old computer. When you run Windows Easy Transfer on your old computer, it's not an installed program, so it doesn't appear on your Programs menu, the desktop, or anyplace else. If you need to run it again, you will need to locate it in your local folder and run it from there.

You will be going back and forth between both computers to follow the prompts. The screen shown in Figure 12–51 is displayed on your new computer.

Figure 12–51. *Windows Easy Transfer on your new computer prompts you to perform steps on your old computer.*

After you install Windows Easy Transfer on your old computer, a Welcome screen lists the types of files and settings that are transferred from the old computer running Windows XP, as shown in see Figure 12–52.

Figure 12–52. *When this Welcome screen appears on your old computer, attach the Easy Transfer cable to the old computer.*

9. Attach the Easy Transfer cable to the old computer. The cable should now be attached to both computers.

10. Click **Next** on the Welcome screen on your old computer. Windows Easy Transfer asks you which computer you are using, as shown in Figure 12–53.

11. Select **This is my old computer** on the old computer. Both computers will try to connect to each other.

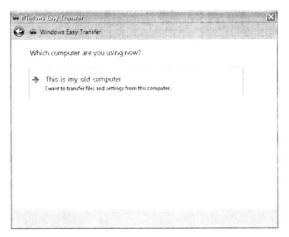

Figure 12–53. *Windows Easy Transfer needs confirmation that this is the computer you want to transfer files from.*

When they are connected, Windows Easy Transfer will check for compatibility between the two computers and then check what can be transferred, as shown in Figure 12–54.

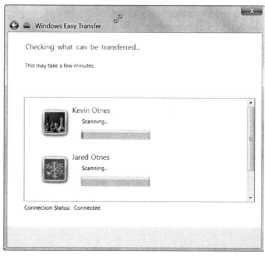

Figure 12–54. *Windows Easy Transfer checks the size of the documents and settings files for each user account on your old computer.*

After Windows Easy Transfer has reviewed what will be transferred, it displays an estimate of how large the transfer will be for each account, as shown in Figure 12–55.

12. Review the settings on this screen. You can change these settings if needed.

- Remove individual users from the transfer by clearing the check box next to a user's name.

- Customize what files are transferred by clicking the Customize link.

- Specify the username to use for each transferred account on the new computer by clicking the **Advanced Options** link.

Figure 12–55. *Windows Easy Transfer selects the accounts and the default files and settings for each account.*

For most people, the default settings don't need adjustment. Some reasons for changing the defaults are to exclude items from the transfer (for example, one of the document-type folders) or to add a folder of content that is not in one of the default user "My..." folders. Clicking Customize under the user's name displays the default folders and settings that have been selected for transfer, as shown in Figure 12–56.

Figure 12–56. *By default, Windows Easy Transfer Windows Easy Transfer selects the default storage folders, desktop, favorites, and other settings.*

13. Review the items that have been selected for transfer. To remove an item from the transfer, clear the check box next to it. For example, the large My Music folder may be a duplicate of the user's entire music collection that is already on another computer. The My Music folder will have a significant impact on how long the transfer takes.

14. If you want to select or remove individual folders on the user's customization list, click the Advanced link for an even greater level of detail, as shown in Figure 12–57.

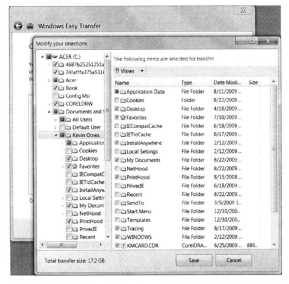

Figure 12–57. *The window for selecting folders for transfer is similar to what you might see in a backup program's window.*

15. When you are finished viewing or changing settings on this screen, click **Save** or **Cancel**, and then click the **Close** button at the top of the user's customization list that was shown in Figure 12–57.

16. In the Choose what to transfer window, click **Advanced Options** at the bottom right of the window. This enables you to select or change the username that will appear for each transferred account on the new computer, as shown in Figure 12–58.

Figure 12–58. *Windows Easy Transfer will try to match up the names on the old computer with account names for the new computer.*

17. If there is no name specified for an account on the new computer, you can create a new name. When you create a new user, you have the option of creating a password, as shown in Figure 12–59.

You can also add new users and set passwords anytime with user accounts, as described earlier in this chapter.

Figure 12–59. *The Create New User dialog box prompts you to create a password for this account. You can leave it blank if you want, and let the user create a password after opening the user account on the new computer.*

Most people typically have only one drive, C:. Windows Easy Transfer automatically transfers files to the same drive letter on the new computer as the one used on your old computer. The Map drives page shown in Figure 12–60 may be useful for advanced users who have multiple drives on their computer; most people won't need to do anything on this page.

Figure 12–60. *The Map drives page specifies which drive letter to use for each drive that is transferred.*

18. When you are ready to perform the transfer, on the What to transfer page, click **Transfer**. The transfer can take several hours to complete. During that time, you can't use the old or new computer, nor can you turn them off, as shown in Figure 12–61.

Figure 12–61. *When the transfer starts, the new computer displays the size of the transfer, but no indication of how long it may take.*

19. When Windows Easy Transfer starts the transfer, it can't calculate how long it will take until it has run a few minutes. In this example, it took approximately 10 minutes before Windows Easy Transfer could make an estimate, as shown in Figure 12–62. The estimates are fairly accurate, although when you are watching the progress, it feels like it takes longer. The size of the transfer, the speed of the connection, and the speed of the hard drives on both computers will affect how long it takes. Using either computer during the transfer will slow down the transfer, or even worse, interrupt and stop the transfer.

Figure 12–62. *It may take 10 minutes or more for Windows Easy Transfer to make an accurate time estimate based on the transfer so far.*

After the transfer begins, you need to leave both computers alone until the transfer is complete. Your screen savers, hibernation, virus scans, backup programs—and anything else that can interrupt the transfer—should all be off. Now is a good time to start rounding up installation discs and product keys for the programs you used on your old computer that you want to install on the new computer. If you will be connecting a printer or other hardware devices to your new computer, locate the installation or driver discs for those, too.

If you installed a program on your computer from an Internet download, you may still have the download or setup program on your computer. You will be able to do a more thorough check of what you need when the transfer is complete and you can view the transfer report.

After the transfer is complete, Windows Easy Transfer displays a screen on which you can choose to view a report indicating what was transferred and what programs you should install, as shown in Figure 12–63..

Figure 12–63. *Use the transfer reports to determine what programs you may need to install on your new computer.*

20. Click **See what was transferred** to make sure there were no problems or errors, and that the things you wanted were transferred, as shown in Figure 12–64.

Figure 12–64. *The transfer report summarizes what was transferred. You can click the Details links for filename-level detail of what was transferred.*

21. Click the **Program report** tab. This is the same information that is displayed when you click the other link shown in Figure 10-65 See a list of programs you might want to install on your new computer. Figure 12–65 shows a summary of the categories.

Figure 12–65. *The program report provides a listing of programs that were installed on your old computer.*

22. Click the down arrow on the left side of the category name to expand it and view the actual lists. Figure 12–66 provides an example of what type of information is displayed. If a program that was on your old computer is already installed on your new computer, a green check mark appears next to the program in the list.

Figure 12–66. *Some of the programs installed on your old computer may already be installed on your new computer. In that case, a green check mark with Already will appear next to the item.*

Transferring Files and Settings via a Network in Real Time

There are two ways you can use a network for Windows Easy Transfer:

- As a real-time direct-connection transfer between the old computer and the new, similar to using the Easy Transfer cable.

- As a storage location between your old and new computer, similar to using an external hard drive or USB flash drive. Transfer the files from the old computer to a network location, external hard drive, or USB flash drive, and then transfer the files from one of these storage locations to your new computer. This takes longer but enables you to break up the transfer process into two stages that can be completed at separate times and locations.

Using a Cable Between the Old and New Computers

We typically think of a network as two or more computers connected to each other through a router or network switch. A network can also be two computers connected to each other directly through a special type of network cable, a **crossover cable**

> **NOTE:** If one or both computers have a Gigabit card, you can use a regular Cat5e (Ethernet) cable; you don't need a crossover cable.

Whichever of these network connections you use, you won't need to install hardware drivers as you do with an Easy Transfer cable. The transfer speed varies depending on your network and connection type. In practice, the fastest connections for Windows Easy Transfer are the Easy Transfer cable or a Cat5e crossover network cable. In actual testing for this chapter, they appeared to be about the same, though technically one is supposed to be faster than the other. A regular network connection appears to be a little slower than the Easy Transfer cable or crossover cable.

Setting Up the Network Connection Between the Old and New Computers

Both computers need to be able to talk to each other through the network connection. Otherwise, the information can't be transferred between them.

To connect the old and new computers through a home network:

1. Connect each computer to the same workgroup, and router or network switch. A wired connection (Ethernet) is much more reliable in speed and quality. Avoid using a wireless connection for your transfer—the connection speeds are usually much slower than an Ethernet connection and more prone to interruptions.

2. Make sure each computer has **network sharing** turned **on**. In Windows XP, you can configure this through File and Printer Sharing. In Windows Vista and Windows 7, use the Network and Sharing Center.

3. Start Windows Easy Transfer on the new computer. If you don't have Windows Easy Transfer installed on your old computer, follow the instructions on your new computer screen to install it.

4. Start Windows Easy Transfer on the old computer.

To connect two computers through a crossover cable:

1. Turn off both computers. Make sure they are close enough to each other that the cable can reach both of them.

2. Connect the crossover cable to the Ethernet jack on each computer.

3. Start both computers.

4. Start Windows Easy Transfer on the new computer. If you don't have Windows Easy Transfer installed on your old computer, follow the instructions on your new computer screen to install it.

5. Start Windows Easy Transfer on the old computer.

Specifying to Use a Network Connection for the Transfer

Although you know what method you want to use, the Windows Easy Transfer wizard doesn't. Now it's time to specify the connection method you just set up.

1. After you have the **Welcome to Windows Easy Transfer** screen on both computers, click **Next**.

    Windows Easy Transfer lists the methods available to transfer files and settings to your new computer, as shown in Figure 12–67. Some options transfer the files and settings in real time directly from the old computer to the new computer. Other options transfer the files and settings to storage on a network share or external device, and then allow transfer to the new computer in a separate operation.

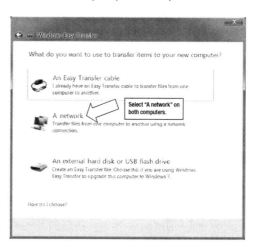

Figure 12–67. *Windows Easy Transfer provides several options for transferring items to your new computer.*

2. Click **A network** on both computers.

3. On both computers, Windows Easy Transfer asks which computer you are using now. Select **This is my new computer** or **This is my old computer** on the appropriate computer.

4. On the new computer, it will ask whether you need to install Windows Easy Transfer on your old computer. Click **I already installed it on my old computer**.

5. Both computers will display messages about getting or entering a Windows Easy Transfer key. Follow the instructions on both screens, as shown in Figures 12–68 and 12–69.

6. On the old computer, write down the key and then click **Next**.

Figure 12–68. *On your old computer, Windows Easy Transfer provides the Windows Easy Transfer key.*

7. On the new computer, click **Next** and then enter the key.

Figure 12–69. *On the new computer, Windows Easy Transfer asks for the key from the old computer.*

8. After you have entered the Windows Easy Transfer key, Windows Easy Transfer will go through a series of screens in the following order to prepare for an actual transfer.

   ▨ Connection established

   ▨ Checking for compatibility

   ▨ Checking what can be transferred (new computer)

   ▨ Transferring files and settings (old computer)

   ▨ Choose what to transfer (new computer)

   The rest of the transfer process via the network is identical to that for transferring via the Easy Transfer cable. To follow through the rest of these steps in detail, start in the previous procedure, "Transferring Files with an Easy Transfer Cable."

Transferring Files and Settings Using a USB Flash Drive, External Hard Disk, or Network Location

This method takes the longest of all but is well-suited for doing a clean install of Windows 7 on an existing computer. Or you can use this process when the old computer and new computer are in different locations that can't be connected directly to each other with a cable or real-time connection.

This is a two stage process.

1. Create a transfer file that contains your files and settings, and store the transfer file on a USB flash drive, external hard disk, or network location.

2. Transfer the Windows Easy Transfer file from the storage location to the new computer.

Creating the Transfer File from Your Old Computer

To create the transfer file from your old computer:

1. Install Windows Easy Transfer on your old computer. You may have to run Windows Easy Transfer on the new computer to obtain the Windows Easy Transfer installation files, and then copy them to a USB flash drive or an external hard drive.

2. Run Windows Easy Transfer on your old computer.

3. After the Welcome screen, when it asks, **How do you want to transfer?**, choose **USB flash drive or external hard drive**. Windows Easy Transfer scans the computer to determine transfer size and accounts.

4. Choose what to transfer from this computer or accept the defaults, and then click **Next**.

    Because this transfer isn't going directly from the old computer to the new computer, it's not as secure. Windows Easy Transfer offers the option to password-protect the transfer file, as shown in Figure 12–70.

5. Specify a password or leave it blank.

6. Click **Save**.

Figure 12–70. *Password protection of the transfer file is optional. You can leave this blank if you want.*

A dialog box is displayed so you can navigate to and select where you want the transfer files to go, as shown in Figure 12–71.

7. Specify the external hard drive, USB flash drive, or network location where you want to save the file. Windows Easy Transfer suggests a filename with the `.mig` extension, **Windows Easy Transfer – Items from old computer <old computer name>.mig**. Click **Save**.

Figure 12–71. *You can specify a USB flash drive, external hard drive, or any network shared folder.*

The **Saving files and settings** screen appears. After a few minutes, the transfer time estimate appears, as shown in Figure 12–72.

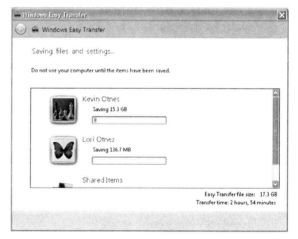

Figure 12–72. *The transfer time estimate does not appear right away, and may change a few times in the first ten minutes after it appears.*

When the transfer is complete, Windows Easy Transfer notifies you and provides instructions for the next steps, as shown in Figure 12–73.

8. Write down the name of the transfer file or files and where to find them.

9. Click **Next** and then click **Close**.

Figure 12–73. *In this example, Brownie is the name of the old computer.*

If you are doing a clean install of Windows 7 on your old computer, making it your new computer, perform the clean install now, before you transfer your files and settings. Note that after you do a clean install, everything that was on the hard disk will be gone permanently, except for what you previously backed up and what you included in the Windows Easy Transfer file.

Transferring the Windows Easy Transfer File from the Storage Location to the New Computer

To finish the transfer, move the Windows Easy Transfer file from the storage location to the new computer:

1. On the new computer, attach the USB flash drive or external drive, or map to the network share where you stored the transfer file.

2. Open Windows Easy Transfer on your new computer.

3. When prompted **What do you want to use to transfer items to your new computer?** select **An external hard disk or USB flash drive**.

4. When prompted, specify that this is the new computer.

5. When prompted **Has Windows Easy Transfer already saved your files from your old computer to an external hard disk or USB flash drive?,** click **Yes**.

6. Browse to the location where Windows Easy Transfer saved your files. By default, it opens to Computer. Besides browsing to devices attached to your computer, you can also browse to other network locations.

7. Look for a folder or icon named **Windows Easy Transfer—Items from old computer <old computer name>.mig**. When you open the file, Windows Easy Transfer checks for compatibility and what can be transferred.

8. Choose what to transfer to this computer. When the transfer is complete, Windows Easy Transfer displays the links to view the reports, as shown in Figure 12–74.

Figure 12–74. *Use the Windows Easy Transfer reports as a guide to what programs you should install on your computer.*

Windows Easy Transfer does not transfer programs, only settings and files. If you've had your old computer a long time, your Programs list on your Start menu may have gotten quite large. The option **See a list of programs you might want to install on your new computer** can save you a lot of time trying to remember or write down all of the programs on your old computer. The report may also be useful in helping you figure out what programs you really need, based on the types of files you transferred.

Carrying Out Post-Migration Tasks

Windows Easy Transfer saves you a lot of work moving your information from your old computer to your new computer, but there are still a few tasks to be done. Unfortunately, Windows Easy Transfer cannot transfer your *programs*, so you will need to reinstall them on your new computer. And you need to make sure you got everything you needed or wanted moved over to the new computer.

> **TIP:** A third-party product that you can purchase, Laplink PCMover Professional, can perform the tasks of Windows Easy Transfer, and transfer your programs to you new computer. See the "Alternatives to Windows Easy Transfer" section earlier in this chapter.

After the transfer is finished, complete the following tasks:

- Start your new computer, and check that everything is there.

- Have each migrated user check his or her login. Each may have to create a new password.

- Reinstall your programs, using the transfer report as a guide.

- Reconnect printers and other devices, and make sure that they work. If not, you may need to reinstall the drivers. Check the device manufacturer's support web site for updated drivers for Windows 7.

- Perform a full backup of your Windows 7 computer, and manually create a System Restore point.

- Check your mail and browser programs. Windows Easy Transfer should catch most of your preferences in the transfer. But sometimes the settings never find a home on your new computer because the old program is no longer used or supported on the new version of Windows. For example, Microsoft Outlook Express was a free mail browser program provided in Windows up through Windows XP. It's no longer supported in Windows, so you would need to find another program. Most mail and browser programs have their own import and export features so you don't lose your address book or bookmarks.

REMINDER: RESTART WHEN PROMPTED BY INSTALLATION

When you are in a hurry to get all your programs reinstalled, it's easy to ignore those messages that say `You must restart your computer....` Don't ignore them. When you get a restart message, do that before you install any more programs. Most of the programs you reinstall should work fine in Windows 7 if they worked in Windows Vista. But occasionally some don't. If you install a bunch of programs at once, and have a problem the next time you start your computer, it may be hard to pinpoint which program is the culprit. Even if the installation program doesn't require a restart, it's still a good idea to do so.

What to Do with Your Old PC

The Web, magazines, and newspapers have lots of articles on what you can do with your old PC, as well as what not to do. Here are just a few ideas:

▪ Use the computer as a print and file server for your home network. Hook up your printers to the PC, and then hook up the PC to your network. Then any PC on your network can print directly to the printers anytime. See Chapter 15 to learn how to share files and printers on a network.

NOTE: While using the old PC as a print and file server allows you to reuse it instead of throwing it away, older PCs may use a lot of power and give off a lot of heat. This will become quite noticeable if you leave it running 24 hours a day. Heat is one of the leading causes of computer hardware failure. Laptops are more prone to heat problems than desktop PCs. Wherever you place the PC, make sure it has good air circulation and fairly stable room temperature.

▪ Don't dump your PC or monitor in the garbage or the dump. Computers contain lots of toxic chemicals that are hazardous to the environment, people, and animals. There are many low-cost or free PC recycling services provided by the government and private industry.

▪ Be careful about passing down to another member of the family a PC that's just a little old and slow. If you are getting rid of your computer because it is slow or has other problems, it's not going to be any better for the person you give it to. And because it used to be your computer, that person may expect that you will know how to repair anything that goes wrong with it.

▪ If you are giving away or disposing of your PC, make sure the data on the hard drive is thoroughly erased. You can buy really strong software to erase your hard drive or take it in to a shop that offers those services.

▪ If you are daring, techie, and curious, and want to venture beyond Windows, you can install Linux on your old PC. Linux is free and can run just fine on older hardware that can't handle Windows 7 or Windows Vista. If you do try this out, it's still a good idea to erase the hard drive on the old PC.

Summary

In this chapter, you learned how to:

- Set up user accounts on a new Windows 7 computer, by creating new accounts or transferring them from your old computer through Windows Easy Transfer.

- Set appropriate level for each user so that they have enough privileges to do what they need on the computer.

- Assign and create strong passwords.

- Retrieve or reset a lost password .

- Apply parental controls and Windows Live Home Safety features to protect and monitor your children's computer usage .

- Move files and settings from your old computer to your new computer with Windows Easy Transfer.

- Choose a connection transfer method: Easy Transfer cable, Ethernet crossover cable, network connection, external hard drive, or discs to transfer the files and settings.

- Prepare your old and new computers for the transfer.

- Finish your migration to your new computer by installing needed programs.

- Move things from your old computer to your new computer with alternatives to Windows Easy Transfer.

- Reuse, recycle, or dispose of your old computer.

Next Steps

After you have everybody set up with their own user accounts on their computers, explore the following chapters for more information about personalization, networks, sharing, and storing your personal documents:

- Chapter 1 explains how to take advantage of the new themes, colors, and personalization provided in Windows 7.

- Chapter 2 shows how you can organize and access your personal files and folders within your user account, such as documents, music, video, and photos.

- Chapter 7 describes how to get Windows Live Home Safety and install it.

- Chapter 16 includes information about personalizing your security settings, passwords, and identity information, as well as how to back up your files and settings.

Chapter 13

Printing, Faxing, and Scanning

It's pretty hard to get by today without at least a printer, but most people also need scanning and faxing capabilities. Happily there are all-in-one printers that print, copy, scan, and fax. And connection options are quite flexible: you can have a printer connected directly to your computer or a wireless printer that can be accessed by any computer in your house.

This chapter will show you how to get the most of these devices. You will look at:

- Choosing printers
- Installing printers on your local computer
- Installing and sharing network printers
- Faxing and scanning with Windows Fax and Scan
- Faxing with other programs
- Scanning with other programs
- Using Optical Character Recognition programs
- Going paperless
- Fun and useful things to do with your scanner

Windows 7 Printer, Fax, and Scanner Features

Windows 7 and the installation programs provided by the hardware manufacturers make connecting and using your hardware fairly easy. Some of the key features that make this happen are discussed in Table 13–1.

Table 13–1. *Connection Options*

Feature	What It Does
Plug and play	When you attach a new piece of hardware to your computer, Windows detects the type, brand, and model of the device and installs the appropriate driver.
Add Printer wizard and Add New Hardware wizard	Most printers and hardware are plug and play: when you attach a new device, Windows detects the device and installs the appropriate driver. If Windows can't find an appropriate driver, or you want to install a printer or device on a network, you can use the wizards to look for updated drivers on Windows Update. You can also use the manufacturer's installation disk.
Windows hardware compatibility	Microsoft maintains a Windows Compatibility site for hardware and software. This site allows you to look up hardware by name, version, or model to determine if it's supported in Windows 7 and how to obtain updated drivers.
Troubleshooters	Windows provides several troubleshooters that can help get your printer or device up and running properly, such as the Printer troubleshooter or the Hardware and Devices troubleshooter.
Windows Fax and Scan	This free program provided by Windows helps you create, save, and share faxes and scanned documents. This program looks a lot like a mail program so many parts are very intuitive.
Other faxing and scanning programs	Most fax and scanner devices include their own software, and many offer additional features not available in Windows Fax and Scan.
Optical Character Recognition (OCR)	Optical character recognition programs convert scanned images into editable pages of text. These programs are not provided by Windows 7 but sometimes are bundled with the scanning software provided by your scanner or all-in-one device manufacturer. OCR programs can be really handy when you only have a paper copy of pages or documents and don't want to have to retype each page. Just scan the page, run the OCR program on the scanned image, and you will have text you can edit in your favorite word processing program. If you are going to do a lot of these conversions, it is worthwhile to upgrade or purchase a good OCR program.

Feature	What It Does
PDF creation or conversion programs	Portable Document Format (PDF) is a file format and open standard created by Adobe Systems. Adobe Reader is a free program that allows you to read, but not create or edit, PDF files. Some scanning or OCR programs offer the capability to save to or print to a PDF file. PDF convertors are also handy if you just want to save content such as a web page or article to a file instead of printing a paper copy.

Printers

Printers are inexpensive. Sometimes when you buy a computer they throw a printer in for free. But printer ink can be expensive, especially color. So having the right printer can save you money, especially if you usually only need black-and-white printing. Table 13–2 describes the most common types of printers available for home use.

Table 13–2. *Printer Types*

Printer type	Purpose
Color and photo printers  **Figure 13–1.** *HP Deskjet Photo Printer*	Color printers usually have individual cartridges for the three primary colors and a separate cartridge for black ink. Most of these printers today use *inkjet* technology, but some now use laser cartridges, which previously were available for only black-and-white printing. Usually you replace the color cartridges as a set and the black cartridge separately. Color printers are versatile because they can print in color or black and white, so they can be used for everything from a plain document to a high-quality glossy photo (comparable to what you would get if you took your photos into the drug store for printing). Photo printers (see Figure 13–1) are like regular color printers except that they are designed to print a little finer detail and often have optional printer cartridges designed especially for photos.

They also usually include camera card slots so that you can plug your camera's memory card directly into the printer and select which photos to print without ever connecting to a computer. Some offer a small screen to help you locate, crop, and edit the photos before printing. Many regular color printers now offer memory card slots. The paper input tray can accommodate paper from standard size 8 1/2×11 inches down to 4×6-inch photographs.

Printer type	Purpose

All-in-one printers

Figure 13–2. *Brother Multi-Function Printer: Print, Scan, and Fax*

All-in-one (or multi-function) printers (see Figure 13–2) are usually color printers with a scanner and fax built in. They are also available as monochromatic (black and white) laser printers. These are handy because most allow you to use them as a straight copier, the scanner allows you to digitize photos or documents from a hard copy, and you can use the scanner to send or receive a page as a fax. The picture quality for color all-in-one printers can be just as good as photo printers.

Though you can share an all-in-one printer on your home network, some models don't let you share the scanner or fax features. To use those features, you must use them from the computer that is attached to the all-in-one.

Personal photo printers

Figure 13–3. *Epson PictureMate Personal Photo Lab*

These printers are much smaller, sometimes about 2/3 the size of a shoe box or tissue box (see Figure 13–3). Their main purpose is to print photos from digital cameras, and they are usually limited to printing 4×6-inch photographs. Because these printers are so small, they are very portable. Some offer rechargeable battery options. With this portability and the capability to download and print directly from the camera or memory card, you can use these much like people used Polaroid cameras to print out pictures on the spur of the moment at parties and get-togethers.

Black-and-white (monochrome) laser printers

Figure 13–4. *Brother monochrome laser printer*

These printers use a single black-ink cartridge, and the technology is similar to that used in copying machines. Monochrome laser printers (see Figure 13–4) will save you huge amounts in printing costs. They print faster than the inkjet color printers, and the ink does not smear on the paper as it does for the first few minutes after inkjet printing. A single cartridge for a laser printer costs more than color printer cartridges, but it lasts many times longer.

Printer type	Purpose
Color laser printers	Like color inkjet printers, color laser printers use a separate cartridge for black, cyan, magenta, and yellow. They are best suited for business color projects like charts and graphs, printing in high volumes and high speed. They are not as suitable for photos because they are not designed to create photo-quality prints or use photo paper. Though laser toner cartridges yield many more copies, the upfront costs of the printer itself and of the cartridges do not make this an economical alternative for the home user.

Printer Use and Purchasing Recommendations

The number of printers you need depends on how much you print and what you print. There may or may not be one perfect printer solution for you or your home network, but the following tips, along with the preceding descriptions of the printer types, should help you choose. Don't rush right out and buy a printer or printers based on these recommendations, but consider these the next time you need to buy expensive ink refills.

- Use a black-and-white (monochrome) laser printer whenever possible. On every computer, make this is your default printer. Otherwise, when people print something, they may not take the extra step to select the black-and-white printer if a color printer is your default printer. A black-and-white laser printer may cost a little more up front, but if you do much printing, it will pay for itself in time.

- Use your local drug store or camera store for printing large quantities of photos, if not all your photos. Studies have shown that printing photos from your home computer costs about the same or more than the regular price of ordering prints from your local drug store or camera store.

- If you must have a color printer, or only one printer, most all-in-one printers offer nearly all the features and quality of a color photo printer.

- If you receive a "free" printer when you buy your computer, and you already have printers you use and like better, consider using the free printer only until the ink needs replacing. Then compare the ink replacement costs of your old and new printers and decide which one makes more sense to keep.

- If you do decide to buy a new printer, get one that offers wired/wireless network connections. Even the least expensive printers often are network ready—you will never again be dependent on a particular computer to access its locally attached printer. And you have more options for where you place your printer—it no longer has to be next to a computer.

Installing a Printer

Most new printers are plug-and-play, which means when you connect the USB cable between the printer and your computer Windows should automatically detect the printer model and install the correct printer drivers. It may be tempting to just hook up the printer and hope that is all you will need to do.

Almost all new printers come with a handy quick start fold-out diagram explaining how to hook up your new printer, and many also include an installation disk. The installation disk usually contains updated printer drivers, and the manufacturer's own printing tools and utilities. While your printer may work without installing anything from the installation disk, you may miss out on getting the use of all features and options of that printer.

You have many options for installing and sharing your printers on a home network. Since USB is the standard for connecting printers, you can connect multiple printers to one computer, or connect printers to several different types of network devices and configurations. Many printers now offer direct connection to your home network through Ethernet or wireless connections.

Figures 13–5 to 13–10 show a variety of ways you can hook up your printer. Reviewing these pictures will help you visualize how you might want to connect printers to your home systems and network. These diagrams describe:

- Connecting a printer locally to your computer.
- Connecting a printer locally to your computer, and then sharing it with other computers in your homegroup.
- Connecting a network ready printer to your network.
- Connecting a printer to your home server.
- Connecting a printer to network attached storage (NAS).
- Connecting a printer directly to a router that has USB ports.

> **NOTE:** Another connection technology option is Bluetooth. Though this wireless technology has been around quite some time, it never caught on for home computing use and is more generally associated with mobile devices. There are very few Bluetooth printers available, and they are primarily aimed at providing printing directly from smartphones and other mobile devices that may not have USB ports or support.

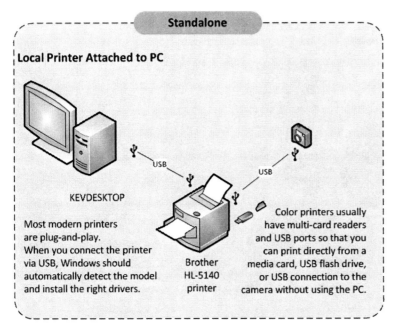

Figure 13–5. *The simplest setup, connecting a printer locally to one computer*

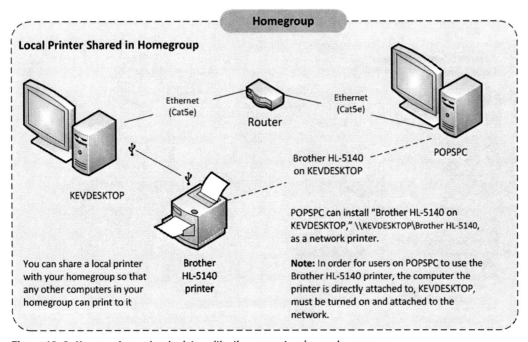

Figure 13–6. *You can share a local printer with other computers in your homegroup.*

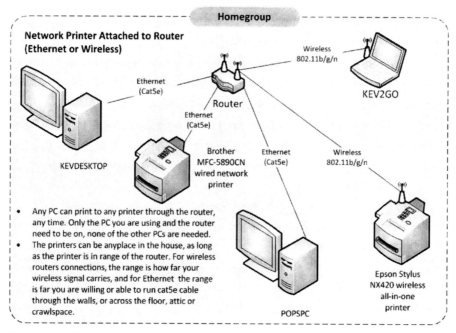

Figure 13–7. *Many new printers are network ready; connect them directly to your network via Ethernet or wireless connection.*

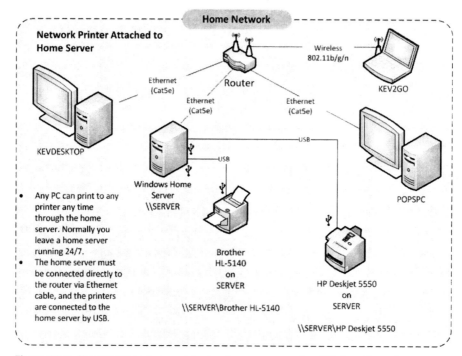

Figure 13–8. *You can connect your printer to a home server such as Windows Home Server.*

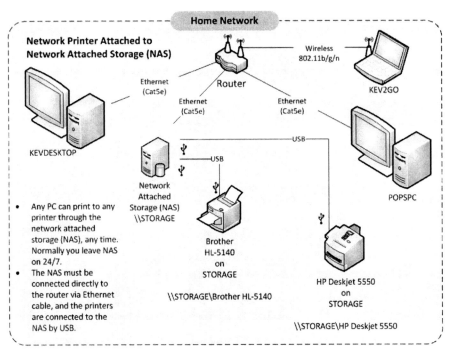

Figure 13–9. *You can connect your printer to a network attached storage device, similar to a home server.*

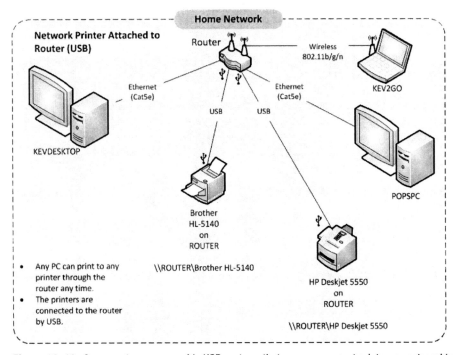

Figure 13–10. *Some routers now provide USB ports so that you can connect printers or external hard drives to your network directly through the router.*

INSTALLING A NEW PRINTER

To install a new printer out of the box:

1. Unpack the printer.

   The box usually contains a power cord, installation instructions, warranty information, and an installation disk. The printer should also include a starter ink cartridge set. The ink cartridges may already be inside the printer.

   > **NOTE:** Most printers don't come with the USB cord to hook up the printer to your computer. There are several types of USB cables, and if you are not sure which to get, see "USB Cable Types" in the Hardware section later in this chapter.

2. Remove all of the wrapping. Some parts may be taped to keep parts from opening or coming apart during shipping.

3. Follow the installation instructions provided by the manufacturer!

   > **NOTE:** There may be several steps to unpacking and installing the printer cartridges before turning on the printer and connecting it to the computer. In some cases, the printer model is so new that there were no drivers for it when Windows was installed. In this case, you will need to use the installation disk or at least have it handy when you first start the printer.

INSTALLING AN OLD PRINTER

Windows 7 includes updated printer drivers for many older printers that were manufactured for Windows Vista or Windows XP. Windows 7 may need updated drivers, but it is the manufacturer's responsibility to create those drivers, not Microsoft. Sometimes Windows 7 has the updated drivers but the original printer tools from the manufacturer don't work in Windows 7.

To install an older printer on a Windows 7 computer:

1. Make sure your computer is connected to the Internet.

2. Try installing from the printer's original installation disk, if available. This step is more for installing the manufacturer's printing tools and utilities. You may get an error message that the tools or drivers will not work in Windows 7.

3. Connect the printer to the computer and turn on the printer.

   If Windows 7 has the drivers, it will automatically install the printer and you will find it in the **Devices and Printers folder**, as shown in Figure 13–11.

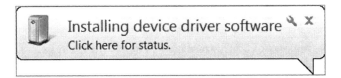

Installing device driver software
Click here for status.

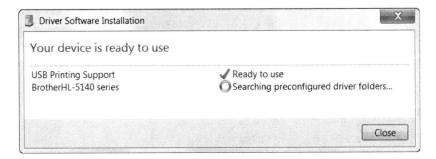

Driver Software Installation

Your device is ready to use

USB Printing Support   ✓ Ready to use
BrotherHL-5140 series   ◯ Searching preconfigured driver folders...

Close

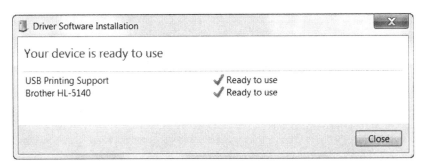

Driver Software Installation

Your device is ready to use

USB Printing Support   ✓ Ready to use
Brother HL-5140   ✓ Ready to use

Close

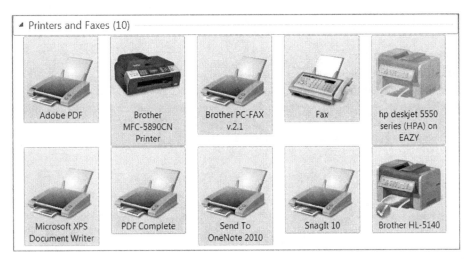

◢ Printers and Faxes (10)

| Adobe PDF | Brother MFC-5890CN Printer | Brother PC-FAX v.2.1 | Fax | hp deskjet 5550 series (HPA) on EAZY |
| Microsoft XPS Document Writer | PDF Complete | Send To OneNote 2010 | SnagIt 10 | Brother HL-5140 |

Figure 13–11. *When a new printer or device is connected to your computer, Windows locates the driver and installs it.*

If Windows 7 can't find the driver, it will attempt to locate a driver from Windows Update. If Windows still can't update a driver, or it's an older printer that connects using the serial or parallel port instead of USB, you can try installing the driver manually.

To manually install a printer driver:

1. Click the **Start** menu. In Search programs and files, type **Add a printer**.

2. In the list that appears, click **Add a Printer**.

    The Add Printer wizard appears, as shown in Figure 13–12.

3. Click **Add a local printer**.

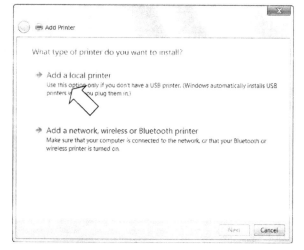

Figure 13–12. *Add Printer wizard*

The **Choose a printer port page** appears, as shown in Figure 13–13.

4. Make sure **Use an existing port** is selected, and then click **Next.**

Figure 13–13. *Select the Use an existing port option*

5. On the **Install the printer driver** page, click **Windows Update**, as shown in Figure 13–14.

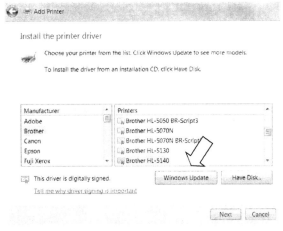

Figure 13–14. *Click Windows Update to get more drivers.*

Windows will check for additional drivers, as shown in Figure 13–15.

Figure 13–15. *Windows locates and downloads new drivers.*

6. Select the printer manufacturer and printer model, and then click **Next**, as shown in Figure 13–16.

7. Complete the wizard, and then click **Finish**.

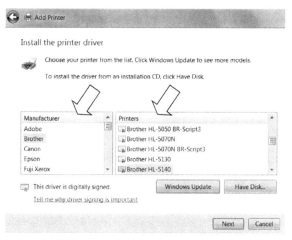

Figure 13–16. *Select the printer from the updated list.*

If you still can't find your printer manufacturer and model in the wizard, search the printer manufacturer's web site and check their Support or Downloads pages for Windows 7 drivers for your model.

Sharing Printers on a Home Network

Have you ever wanted to print a photo, only to realize that the photo printer is attached to another computer, not the one you are using? Do you usually only need plain black-and-white printing, but the (more costly) color printer is more convenient because it's attached to the main family computer everybody uses? If you want to use the right printer for the job, either you have to copy the files to the computer that has the printer you want and print from there, or you have to physically move the printer from the other computer to the computer you are now using.

When you connect and share printers on a home network, you can:

- Print to a network printer from any computer on the network.

- Place your printer anywhere you have wired or wireless access in your house.

- Reduce printer ink and paper costs by using fewer printers.

Table 13–3 describes the most common ways of connecting a printer to a network.

Table 13–3. *Connection Options*

Connection type	Description
Connection to a network computer	Attach a printer to a computer on the network, install the printer on that computer, and then share the printer through your homegroup settings. You can do this with any printer that attaches to your computer with a cable.
Connection directly to your router	If you have a printer that is wired-network ready, you can connect an Ethernet cable from the router to the printer. The only limit on the placement of the printer is how long you want to run the cable from the router to the printer. If you don't have a network-ready printer, some routers also provide USB ports so that you can connect a regular USB printer directly to the router.
Wireless connection to your network	If you have a printer that is wireless-network ready, you can place the printer anywhere within range of your wireless network.
Home server or network-attached storage (NAS) device	The most commonly used home server is Windows Home Server. A NAS device is an external hard drive that attaches directly to your network, usually via an Ethernet cable. Some NAS devices have one or more USB ports, which you can plug your printer into directly.

Installing a Shared Printer

The simplest way to share a printer on a network is to share a printer already attached to one of the computers on the network. Even if you are starting from scratch (meaning you have a printer but have not installed it on any computer), the process to install it and share it on a network is pretty straightforward. You may have already completed some of these steps.

These steps are divided into two sections: attaching the printer to a computer in your homegroup, and then installing the printer on other homegroup computers.

Attaching a Printer to a Computer in Your Homegroup

To attach, install, and share a printer on a homegroup computer, follow these steps:

1. Connect the printer to your computer with a USB cable and then turn on the printer.

   Windows should automatically install the printer on your computer the first time you connect it to your computer with a USB cable. For more detailed printer installation instructions, see "Installing a Printer" earlier in this chapter.

2. After the printer is installed, click the **Start** button, and in the **Start** menu's search box, type **share printers**.

3. In the list that appears, click **Share Printers**. The **Change homegroup settings** window appears, as shown in Figure 13–17.

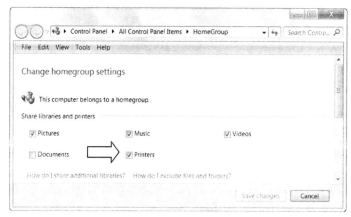

Figure 13–17. *In Change homegroup settings, you can share your computer's local printers with your homegroup.*

4. Make sure the **Printers** checkbox is selected. If it's already selected, you don't need to do anything more in this window, so click **Cancel**. If it's not selected, select it and then click **Save Changes**.

Installing the Printer on Other Homegroup Computers

To install a shared printer on another homegroup computer, follow these steps:

1. On the homegroup computer, click the **Start** button, and in the **Start** menu's search box, type **share printers**.

2. In the list that appears, click **Share Printers**. The **Change homegroup settings** window appears.

   Windows detects that there is a shared printer available in the homegroup, as shown in Figure 13–18.

Figure 13–18. *Windows will detect when a shared printer has been added to the home network and will offer to install it.*

3. Click **Install Printer**. Windows searches for drivers on this homegroup computer or on the computer that the printer is attached to, and installs the printer.

The **Change homegroup settings** window then refreshes, and the Install printer message disappears, as shown in Figure 13–19.

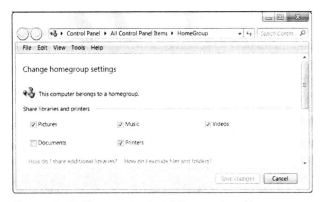

Figure 13–19. *The prompt to install the new shared homegroup printer goes away after the printer is installed.*

4. (Optional) Check to see whether the printer is now available for this computer. Click the **Start** button and then click **Devices and Printers**.

The **Devices and Printers** window shows that the new printer HP Photosmart C4400 attached to the homegroup computer KEVINWIN7 is available, as shown in Figure 13–20. The green check mark means it is the default printer.

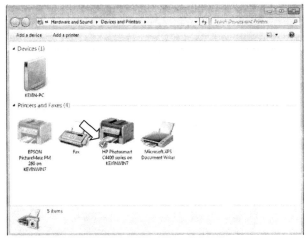

Figure 13–20. *HP Photosmart C4400, shared by another homegroup computer KEVINWIN7, is the default printer on this computer.*

Keeping Shared Printers Available All the Time

Whether you are using homegroup in Windows 7 or File and Printer Sharing in Windows XP or Windows Vista, the computer that the printer is physically attached to must be online and accessible via your network. So how do you make printers and files available to all home network computers all the time? There are several solutions, which may require additional computer devices or using more energy (electricity).

- **Keep one network computer on all the time, and attach all shared printers and store all shared files on this computer.** This is the simplest solution, which requires no new equipment but does require a computer to be on all the time. Not only does this drive up your electrical bill, but it also gives off heat and may warm up your room more than you normally want. Ideally, you could use an older desktop PC that would otherwise be surplus or obsolete, running Windows XP. You could also use a laptop, but they are not as good a choice because laptops are more susceptible to overheating than desktop PCs and tend to have much smaller hard drives for storage. You won't be able to use the homegroup feature with this computer if it's running Windows XP or Windows Vista, but it's not that difficult to set up sharing between Windows 7 computers and Windows XP or Windows Vista. You can minimize the power usage by turning off the monitor when you are not actually sitting at the computer using it.

- **Buy a wireless or wired network printer**. These can be attached directly to your home network router. They are only a little more expensive than printers that offer USB-only connections.

- **Buy a network-attached storage device (NAS).** It can provide access to shared files and printers. These are fairly new to home computer users but have long been in use in corporate networks. For home users, a NAS device is a special type of external hard drive that attaches directly to your network. Many of the examples in this chapter show a device listed as //Storage. That is a NAS device, which happens to also have three printers attached directly to it. The NAS device can be useful if you want to stream music or videos to other devices on your home network, such as a media player to display videos on a TV or certain types of stereo receivers, so that you can share music throughout your house. NAS devices are more expensive than external hard drives but may well be worth it because they provide around-the-clock access to files and printers plus their large capacity provides plenty of space to regularly back up the files on all of your computers.

- **Buy a home server.** Don't be scared by the idea of setting up a server. It's not much more complicated to set up than setting up a regular computer. A home server works similarly to the first alternative of having one computer on all the time. A home server runs on a special version of Windows, Windows Home Server, or another operating system designed to run as a home server. You can't use a home server as a desktop PC to run programs or surf the Web, but it also means that once the server is set up, you can run and administer it from another computer on the network, and you won't need a monitor, mouse, or keyboard attached to the server. A home server offers all the features of a NAS device plus more flexibility to add extra storage as needed.

Installing a Printer That Is Not Attached to a Homegroup Computer

There are several common scenarios where you may want to share printers on your home network but can't do it through the homegroup. Fortunately, Windows 7 provides other ways to install shared printers on your network. The process is similar to the one previously described for homegroup printers: install the printer, share it, and then install it on the individual computers in the home network. You can use this process to share printers that are attached to the home network but not through homegroup computers, such as:

- Wired or wireless printers attached directly to the home network through a router.

- Printers attached to a NAS that is attached to the home network through a router.

- Printers attached to non-Windows 7 computers on the home network running Windows XP or Windows Vista.

The steps in this process are provided in two parts. In the first part, you install the printer so it's available to computers on the home network. In the second part, you install the printer on the other computers in your home network.

Installing and Sharing a Wired or Wireless Printer

For your initial setup, you will need an Ethernet cable, even if you plan to use the printer wirelessly. If you will be using this printer wirelessly, and your network is configured for wireless authentication and encryption, you will also need the wireless encryption key or password. The manufacturer's instructions may vary, but generally follow these steps:

1. Insert the printer's installation disc into a computer on your network.

2. Turn on your printer.

3. Follow the onscreen instructions from the printer manufacturer's installation disc.

4. Attach the printer to the router directly with an Ethernet cable when prompted by the installation program. If you are installing the printer as a wireless device, the installation program will tell you when you can remove the Ethernet cable and use the printer wirelessly.

Checking Signal Strength and Speed with Wireless Printers

Network printers pass a large amount of data between the computer, router, and the printer. Wireless printers are just as susceptible as wireless routers and computers to interference and blockage by walls and devices. After you've completed a wireless setup, print a test page to make sure that your printer location has a strong signal. If you don't have strong signal between your router and printer, printing may take a long time or won't work at all. Move either the printer or the router and try printing the same test page again to see if it works better. If you try multiple locations and still have difficulty, you will need to locate the printer within reach of your Ethernet cable.

Installing and Sharing a Printer Attached to a NAS Device

Check the documentation for your NAS (storage device) to verify that the device supports attaching printers and has a USB port for connecting printers. The exact steps for adding a printer to a storage device vary, but generally follow this process:

1. Attach the printer directly to the storage device via a USB cable.

2. Turn on the printer.

3. Open the configuration program for the storage device. You will need to log in as an administrator on the storage device. Each NAS manufacturer uses their own program for managing their device. Figure 13–21 displays the program used to manage the NAS device on my home network, an Iomega StorCenter ix2.

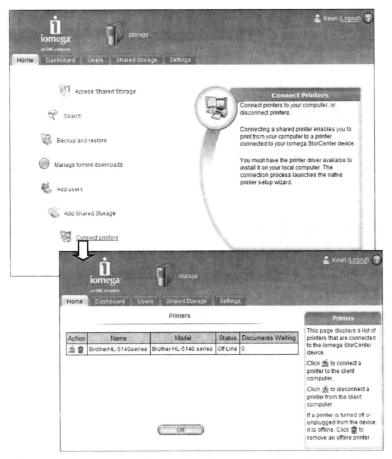

Figure 13–21. *An example of software used to manage a NAS device. Your device's program may be different.*

4. Click the command for managing printers. Check your storage device documentation for the exact command to do this.

5. The printer may be displayed in a list of printers attached to the storage device. Select the printer and select the command to attach the printer. The storage device will not have the printer drivers even if the printer was previously used and installed on the computer from which you are running the storage configuration program.

6. When prompted, insert the printer installation disc. The storage device's configuration program should find the needed drivers on the disc. If you have problems installing a printer on your storage device, consult the storage device documentation.

7. After the printer has been installed on the NAS device, run the Add Printer wizard on your computer, choosing the Network option, as described in the "Adding a Shared Printer to a Windows 7 Computer from a Non-Windows 7 Computer or Device" section.

Installing and Sharing a Printer Attached to a Computer Running Windows Vista or XP

You may need administrator-level privileges to install and share a printer on a Windows Vista or XP computer. Follow these steps:

1. Turn on the computer.

2. Attach the printer directly to the computer via a USB cable.

3. Turn on the printer.

4. Windows may automatically install the printer on your computer the first time you connect it to your computer with a USB cable. Windows comes with printer drivers for most brands of printers, but sometimes it can't find a printer driver that matches your model because the printer is old or very new.

5. If Windows can't find a printer driver, it will offer to search for drivers on another location such as the Web or another folder on your computer. Insert the printer installation disc that came with your printer, and run the printer installation program (the installation screen usually pops up after you insert the disc), or click the **Browse** button in the **Add printer** wizard and navigate to the CD or DVD drive that contains your printer installation disc.

6. If installation is required, complete the **Add printer** wizard or the printer manufacturer's installation program.

7. In **Control Panel**, open **Printers**.

8. Right-click the printer you just installed, and click **Sharing**. The **Printer properties** window is displayed.

9. On the **Sharing** tab, follow the instructions to enable sharing for this printer.

Adding a Shared Printer to a Windows 7 Computer from a Non-Windows 7 Computer or Device

After you've installed the printer on your router (wired, wireless, or direct USB), NAS, Windows Home Server, Windows XP, or Windows Vista computer, and configured it for network sharing, you can add the printer to your Windows 7 computers on your home network. If you want to install and share another printer, you must repeat the preceding procedures for each printer. After a printer is installed and shared on the home network, you can add it to other computers on the network.

To add a shared printer from a non-Windows 7 computer or device to a Windows 7 computer, follow these steps:

1. Click the **Start** button, and in the **Start** menu's search box, type **Printers**.

2. In the list that appears, click **Add Printer**. The **Add Printer** wizard is displayed, as shown in Figure 13–22.

3. Click **Add a network, wireless or Bluetooth printer.**

Figure 13–22. *To a printer that is shared on your network, click Add a network, wireless or Bluetooth printer.*

Windows quickly finds any printers attached to your homegroup. Eventually, it should list all printers on your home network, including those that are attached to non-homegroup computers or devices, as shown in Figure 13–23. In this example, the last printer on the list was attached to a Windows Vista computer named Kevin-PC64HP.

4. Click the printer you want to add and then click **Next**.

—or—

If you don't see the printer you want, click **The printer that I want isn't listed**. Then choose one of the options for locating the printer via

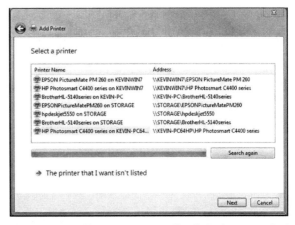

Figure 13–23. *Windows may not at first find printers attached to non-Windows 7 computers or devices. Eventually, Windows should find all printers on the home network.*

browsing, typing the computer name, or typing the IP address. If you still can't find the printer you want, the computer that the printer is attached to might be off, or the printer might not be enabled for printer sharing.

5. After you select or locate the printer, Windows will attempt to connect with it, as shown in Figure 13–24.

Figure 13–24. *Windows attempts to connect to the printer you selected.*

When Windows finds and installs the printer, it will confirm that the installation was successful, as shown in Figure 13–25.

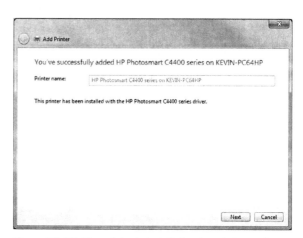

Figure 13–25. *The printer is installed and ready to use from the local computer.*

Repeat the steps in this section for each computer you want connected to the shared printer.

Installing a Printer Attached to a Router via USB

Some home routers now provide one or two USB ports so that you can attach a printer or external USB driver and make it available to all computers on the network. The steps to do this may vary between manufacturers, so they should provide full instructions on how to do it with their products. The installation process may include:

- Using the router's configuration and management utilities to allow computers access to the shared printer or hard drive.

- Installing printer drivers through the router software.

- Running the Add Printer wizard within each computer and choosing the Network option, as described in the "Adding a Shared Printer to a Windows 7 Computer from a Non-Windows 7 Computer or Device" section.

Installing a Printer Attached to a Home Server

Windows Home Server and other home server devices provide documentation on how to attach a printer to the server so that it can be used by any computer on the home network. The installation process may include:

- Running software on each computer to connect the computer to the home server, similar to the process previously described in the "Installing and Sharing a Printer Attached to a NAS Device" section.

- Installing printer drivers on the server itself.

- Running the Add Printer wizard within each computer and choosing the Network option, as described in the "Adding a Shared Printer to a Windows 7 Computer from a Non-Windows 7 Computer or Device" section.

Faxing and Scanning

Windows 7 includes a built-in program for faxing and scanning, **Windows Fax and Scan.** In Figure 13–26, you can see a family resemblance between the Windows Fax and Scan window and Microsoft mail programs such as Outlook and Windows Live Mail.

To access Windows Fax and Scan:

1. Click the **Start** button, and in the **Start** menu's search box, type **Fax**.

2. In the list that appears, click **Windows Fax and Scan**. The **Windows Fax and Scan window** is displayed in the Fax view, as shown in Figure 13–26.

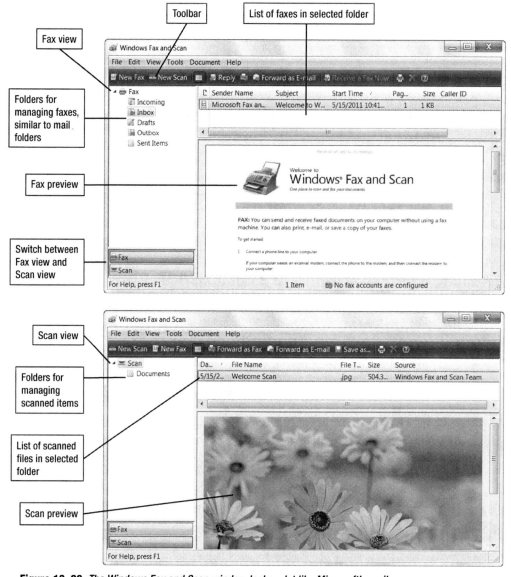

Figure 13–26. *The Windows Fax and Scan window looks a lot like Microsoft's mail programs.*

Sending or Receiving a Fax with Windows Fax and Scan

It might be a little confusing when you look at the image of a fax machine in the Welcome to Windows Fax and Scan message shown in Figure 13–26. Windows Fax and Scan is designed to work with internal or external fax modems and fax servers to allow you to fax directly from programs—not stand-alone fax machines or all-in-one printer-fax-scanners. According to Windows Help and Support, it is possible that the printer manufacturer may have created drivers so that your printer can work like a fax modem with Windows Fax and Scan. Check the printer's documentation or go to the printer manufacturer's support or downloads web site to see if there are drivers you can download.

> **TIP:** Don't feel cheated that you can't use Windows Fax and Scan to fax from your fax machine or all-in-one printer. The manufacturers of those devices usually provide their own fax programs and software that offer more features and capabilities than Windows Fax and Scan. Those features are covered later in this section.

If you want to use your PC or laptop with Windows Fax and Scan to send and receive faxes without a fax machine or all-in-one with fax, you have several choices.

- Use an existing internal fax modem in your computer.

- Install an internal fax modem card in your desktop PC.

- Attach a USB fax modem to your PC or laptop.

- Connect to a fax server set up on your corporate network.

To set up a fax modem or server:

1. Open **Windows Fax and Scan**, and click the **New Fax** button. If you don't have a fax device set up yet, you will be prompted to select one, as shown in Figure 13–27.

   > **NOTE:** If you want to connect to a fax server on your company network, check with your IT department or network administrator for the fax server and name.

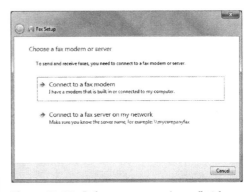

Figure 13–27. *Before you can send your first fax, you must set up a fax device to use with Windows Fax and Scan.*

2. Click **Connect to a fax modem**.

   If the wizard detects a modem, it will prompt you to name the modem, as shown in Figure 13–28. Enter a name for this fax modem, and then click Next. The next screen asks you choose how you want to handle incoming faxes, as shown in Figure 13–30.

Figure 13–28. *Specify a name for this modem, or accept the default*

   If no fax modem is detected, a message like that in Figure 13–29 is displayed. If you think this message is in error, go to the next section, "Troubleshooting an Undetected Modem."

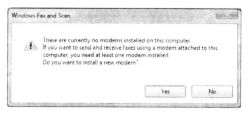

Figure 13–29. *If you think there should be a modem detected, check Device manager*

3. Choose how you want to handle incoming faxes, or click **I'll choose later; I want to create a fax now**, as shown in Figure 13–30.

   The Fax and Scan window appears, as shown in previously in Figure 13–26.

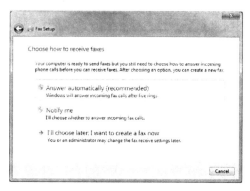

Figure 13–30. *Select how you want to receive faxes*

Troubleshooting an Undetected Modem

If the Fax Setup wizard displays a message that no modems are installed, it might simply mean… you don't have a modem installed! Some new computers don't have a built-in fax card or modem. They are still common for business desktop PCs and business laptops, but many lower price computers for home use skip it to keep costs down. A "budget" computer I purchased two years ago included a fax modem, but I recently purchased a newer model of that line computer from the same manufacturer and it doesn't have a fax modem.

Sometimes your computer has a fax modem but the drivers or software were never configured after you bought the computer, or you upgraded the computer from Windows Vista and new drivers for Windows 7 were never installed or registered.

There are several things to check to verify whether you have a fax modem:

- Check the back of the desktop PC or side of the laptop for a phone jack. The phone jack is slightly smaller than the network (Ethernet) jack. If your computer has a phone jack, it usually has the hardware needed for a fax modem, and you may just need to install the drivers.

- Check Device Manager to see if there is listing for a modem, as shown in Figure 13–31. The easiest way to get to Device Manager is to click the **Start** button, type **Device Manager**, and in the list that appears, click **Device Manager**. If a modem is listed but it has a big yellow? icon next to it, then you need to get updated drivers. For example, if I needed drivers for the modem shown in Figure 13–31, I would search the web for "**LSI PCI-SV92EX Soft Modem drivers**."

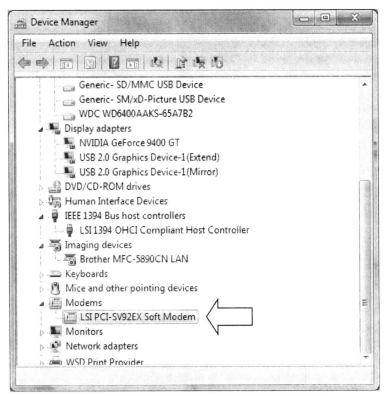

Figure 13–31. *If your computer has a modem, it should show up in Device Manager.*

■ If you didn't find a phone jack or a listing for Modems in Device Manager, than you probably don't have an internal modem. If you really want or need to be able to fax directly from your computer, you can either install an internal fax modem (desktop PC), get an external USB fax modem dongle (desktop PC or laptop), or get an all-in-one printer that includes fax.

When you have a fax modem attached to or installed on your computer or can connect to a fax server, you can use Windows Fax and Scan to create a new fax, similar to creating a new e-mail message. Before you send a new fax, there are several features you may want to set up ahead of time.

■ **Enter Sender Information that can be displayed on the cover page**: On the **Tools** menu, click **Sender Information.**

■ **Create your own cover page**: On the **Tools** menu, click **Cover Pages**.

■ **Create or locate contact information**: On the **Tools** menu, click **Contacts**. You can store frequently used contacts in an address book.

To create a new fax:

1. In Windows Fax and Scan, click **New Scan** in the toolbar. The New Fax window appears, as shown in Figure 13–32.

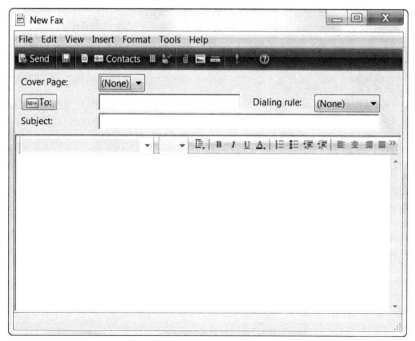

Figure 13–32. *New Fax window*

2. Create your fax message. Select who to send it to, set up a dialing rule if needed, and compose the message itself. Windows Fax and Scan, like most fax software, includes an address book where you can store frequently used fax numbers. You can access your address book from within the New Fax message by clicking the **To** button.

3. To send a document or image, attach it as a file (similar to the BillGates.jpg shown in the **Attach** box in Figure 13–33) or insert the content into the body of the message itself.

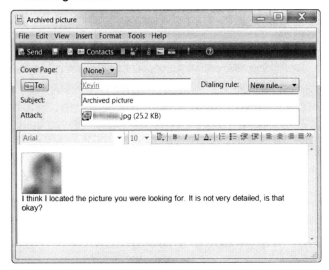

Figure 13–33. *Composing a fax*

4. When you're done, click **Send**.

Using Other Fax Hardware and Software

All-in-one (multi-function) printers usually include both faxing and scanning hardware. All-in-ones are becoming the standard printer for home users and computers, and many small offices because, well, they are multi-function. One device takes the place of several separate devices: a printer, copier, scanner, and fax machine. All-in-one printers usually include their own faxing and scanning software features.

With most all-in-ones, you can use the fax feature without your computer by using controls on the device itself; you can also use those controls and the scanning features to make photocopies of documents or pictures. Faxing technology doesn't depend on a PC or software. You can send and receive faxes with a fax machine attached to your phone line or you can use the software and hardware attached to your computer. Table 13–4 summarizes fax technology and capabilities.

Table 13–4. *Fax Features*

Fax features	Description
Fax modem or device	There are several types of hardware that can send and receive faxes: ▪ Fax machine or all-in-one printer ▪ Fax modem built in to computer ▪ Fax server on a corporate network **TIP:** You can also subscribe to an Internet fax service, which sends and receives faxes over the Internet instead of a phone line. There are a wide variety of services and prices available. To learn more and find service providers, do a web search for "Internet fax."
Software and controls	There are several ways to send and receive faxes: ▪ Physical controls on the fax machine or all-in-one printer, without any PC or software. ▪ Fax programs installed on the PC, such as Windows Fax and Scan, software provide by the fax device manufacturer, or an Internet fax service. ▪ Fax as a printing option (also called Print to Fax). Your fax device is treated as a printer and can be selected when you choose the Print command in a program. Sometimes this command opens up a fax program, or it may just use the settings you already configured in your fax program and just query you for the fax recipient's number and fax cover sheet information.
Managing and storing faxes and settings	For some people and businesses, faxing is just as commonplace for communicating and sharing documents as e-mail. And it's an extension of the telephone. Fax software incorporates features from both e-mail programs and telephone technology to make sending and receiving faxes more automated and convenient. These features are available in **Windows Fax and Scan**. Most fax programs provided by device manufacturers include similar features. ▪ Storage of header and cover sheet information. ▪ An address book or phone number list for frequently used destinations (most fax machines and all-in-ones usually provide phone number storage on the device itself in addition to the software on the PC). ▪ Folders for storing sent and received faxes, similar to e-mail Inbox and Sent folders. ▪ Message preview.

Figures 13–34 through 13–36 are examples of software provided by a printer manufacturer, Brother, for a printer manufactured a couple years ago. Your software will probably look different, even if you have the same brand as this example. But it gives you an idea of what types of features to expect, such as programs to help you send and receive a fax, and an address book so that you can store frequently used fax numbers and contacts.

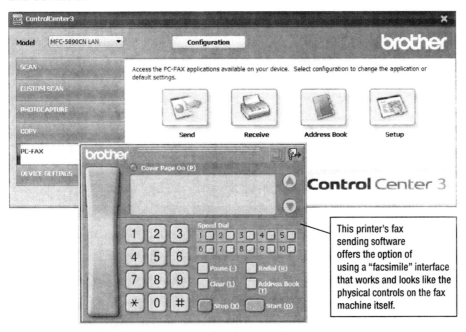

This printer's fax sending software offers the option of using a "facsimile" interface that works and looks like the physical controls on the fax machine itself.

Figure 13–34. *Fax sending software using a "facsimile" style interface for a Brother all-in-one printer (MFC-5890C)*

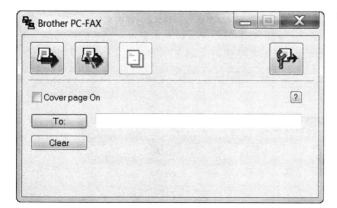

Figure 13–35. *Fax sending software using "simple" style interface*

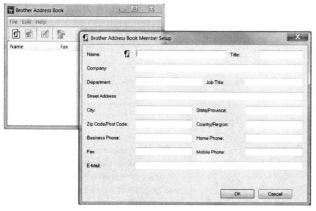

Figure 13–36. *A fax address book and contact entry page.*

Scanning with Windows Fax and Scan or Other Software

Windows Fax and Scan should be able to use any scanning device attached to your computer that is supported by Windows 7. For example, I have an all-in-one printer, but I can't use Windows Fax and Scan for faxes. But Windows Fax and Scan does work with and recognize the scanner in my all-in-one printer.

Scanners are much more dependent on software on your computer. The only scanning feature that does not require any interaction with a PC is when you use the scanner and printing on an all-in-one together as a photocopier.

> **TIP:** While this chapter covers the basics of using a scanner for photos and documents, see Chapter 10: "Organizing and Sharing Pictures and Videos" for more information.

Table 13–5 describes scanning technology, software, and features.

Table 13–5. *Scanning Features*

Scanning Features	Description
Scan to file and type with Windows Fax and Scan	When you scan a document or photo, you may have several choices for saving the scan to a file format and content type. With Windows Fax and Scan, you can scan with different profiles,
	▪ The Photo profile is the default scanning profile and the default file format for photos is .JPG.
	▪ The Document profile default is the .TIF file format, which is better suited for converting to text with an optical character recognition (OCR) program.
	Windows Fax and Scan only offers four file types regardless of whether you choose the Photo or Document profile: .BMP, .JPG, .PNG, or .TIF. Windows 7 does not include any OCR software. With OCR software you have more options for the output file.
Color, resolution, and scan area selection	Whether you are using Windows Fax and Scan or the program provided with your scanner, there are several settings you can adjust when you scan. All of these can affect image quality and file size
	Color vs. black-and-white: Color files are larger than black-and-white. If you are scanning a document, use grayscale or black and white for smaller files.
	Resolution: The higher the resolution, the larger the file. Start with the default settings. For documents, the original may only be 300 DPI, so using the default scan resolution of 200 DPI or bumping up to 300 DPI should give you a comparable quality image. For photos, the higher the quality of the original, the higher the resolution you will need for the scan. Increasing the resolution increases the file size tremendously. Compare the file sizes for a color scan at these different resolutions:
	200 x 200 DPI = 10 MB
	300 x 300 = 23 MB
	600 x 600 = 92 MB
	1200 x 1200 = 367 MB
	Scan area: Most scanning programs allow you to perform a preview scan so that you can select an area for the final scan. This allows you to leave out areas you don't need and reduce the overall file size, as shown in Figure 13–37 and 13–38.

Scanning Features	Description

A preview scan allows you to see what the scan will look like. This allows you to make adjustments such as repositioning the original on the scanner, picking a different resolution, or selecting an area to scan.

The scan area has been cropped by dragging the corners of the dotted line. When you click Scan, only the cropped area will be scanned.

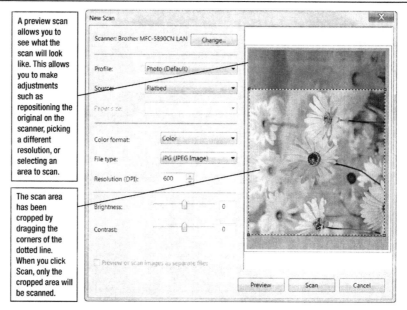

Figure 13–37. *Scan window from Windows Fax and Scan*

Some programs may call the preview by another name, such as PreScan.

In this scanner program, you also get an estimate of the file size for this resolution.

Results from preview scan

The actual area that will be scanned has been cropped and is shown by the dotted lines.

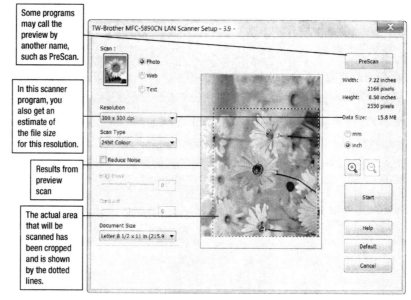

Figure 13–38. *Scan window from the scanning program provided by the scanning device manufacturer*

Scanning Features	Description
Optical character recognition software	Optical character recognition (OCR) software takes a scanned image and converts the bitmap image into text that can be edited. OCR software is handy because it can often convert paper documents to editable document files quicker than retyping or recreating it with a word processing or editing program.
	Even though Windows Fax and Scan does not include OCR software, you can run OCR software after you have scanned to file. Some OCR programs include their own scanner interface so you don't need to use Windows Fax and Scan. Most scanner devices and all-in-one printers provide some OCR software and capabilities with their scanning program. Often the OCR software included is a minimal stripped down version that can be upgraded (at a price) to a full version with more capabilities.
	OCR software may offer the following capabilities and features:
	<ul><li>Scan to Word, Excel, or PDF file formats.</li><li>Recreate page layouts, format, and graphics in-line.</li><li>Specialties like scanning and organizing business cards, receipts, and other types of documents.</li></ul>
	There are many web sites and articles available for comparing the most popular OCR software programs. Some OCR programs offer limited use and timed free trial downloads. Search the web for "OCR software." Some of the more popular choices for OCR software include:
	<ul><li>ABBYY FineReader 9</li><li>FineReader</li><li>OmniPage</li><li>PaperPort</li><li>ReadIRIS</li><li>SimpleOCR</li><li>TextBridge</li></ul>

Compare the results from the OCR software bundled for free with a scanner (at the top of Figure 13–39) to a full-featured OCR program (at the bottom of Figure 13–39). The top example shows several errors in detecting the correct letters and words and doesn't repeat the page layout or formatting of the original. In the bottom example, the conversion looks much like the original, and possible errors are highlighted.

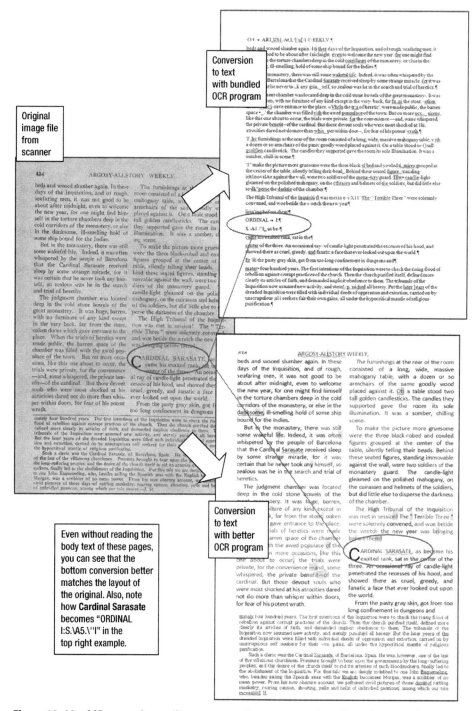

Figure 13-39. *OCR conversion quality can vary, and a poor conversion will require a lot of manual corrections and formatting. The better OCR programs are easy to use, highly accurate, and convert to well-formatted document types.*

Go Paperless: Print and Scan to PDF

The Portable Document Format (PDF) file format and open standard created by Adobe Systems is a great way to save and view documents. It's universal for saving, viewing, and distributing documents, and almost everybody has Adobe Reader (free) on their computer. There are many advantages to using PDFs as an alternate to printing or sending actual document or spreadsheet files in e-mail.

- **PDFs are universal**: Anybody can download a PDF viewer for free and it's available for almost any major operating system including Windows, Mac, and Linux, and in almost any language.

- **Saving web pages**: Printing from any browser often leads to many half empty pages, and trying to save a web page as a file often doesn't work very well either. In your browser, instead of using Save As or printing to an actual printer, print to PDF.

- **Archiving your e-mail**: You can save any e-mail message to PDF by selecting your PDF program in the Print dialog box instead of a physical printer. In some mail programs, like Outlook, you can select multiple messages to print all at once into a single PDF file. It's much easier to work with PDFs than trying to archive or forward e-mail messages if you switch to another e-mail account.

- **Selectable text**: When you scan or print to PDF as selectable text (not an image file), you can use the built-in search feature in Adobe Reader to quickly find text in a PDF.

- **Tax time**: You can scan receipts, bills, statements, and other records to keep better track of them, thereby replacing your tired old shoebox bulging with odd assortments of paper.

> **CAUTION:** Always check with the appropriate professionals, such as accountants, attorneys, bankers, and medical professionals, about what kinds of paper documents you need to retain before destroying a paper copy of a document. Even if you need to retain a paper copies, you may be able to scan and save documents for quick access and put the paper copies in safe storage.

Table 13–6 shows the various ways to create PDFs.

Table 13–6. *How to Create PDFs*

PDF Creation Options	What It Does
Export to PDF	This is similar to Print to PDF. OpenOfficeOrg offers this option. It is similar to Save As in that you're not converting and changing the original document into a PDF; you're creating a copy in the PDF format.
Print to PDF	If you have Adobe Acrobat installed, Adobe PDF will be listed in Devices and Printers. Similarly, when you install other PDF creation programs they may also be listed in Devices and Printers. When you buy a new computer, it may come bundled with a PDF editor. For example, one of my computers came with a free version of a PDF creation program called PDF Complete, and I installed Adobe Acrobat. Both are listed in Devices and Printers, as shown in Figure 13–40.

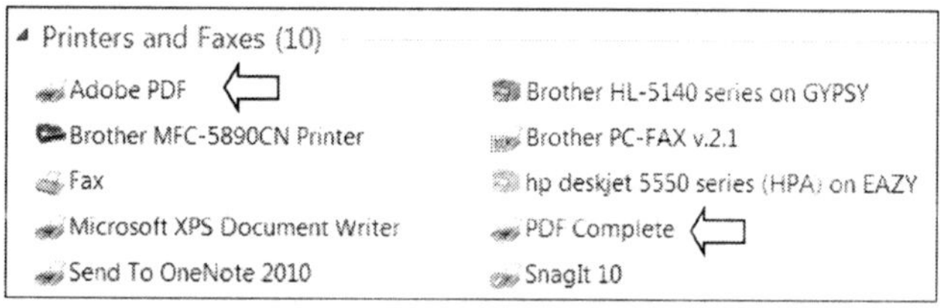

Figure 13–40 *PDF creation/editing programs may be displayed as printers in Device and Printers ➤ Printers and Faxes*

Scan to PDF	The software provided by your scanner manufacturer may include an option to scan to PDF.

> **NOTE** Unless used in conjunction with an OCR program, scanning to PDF may only produce an image that is viewable in a PDF viewer such as Adobe Reader but not actual text that can be selected or copied.

PDF creators or editors	PDF creators range from free programs, such as Primo PDF, to professional PDF editing programs that can cost several hundred dollars, such as Adobe Acrobat. There are many choices in between; programs such as Nitro PDF rival Adobe Acrobat for much less money. Almost all PDF creators that do cost money offer free trial versions or money back guarantees.

CAUTION: As with anything that is offered for free on the web, be careful when downloading free PDF editing programs. Don't just download the first free program you find; research the companies and the programs. There are many reviews of free and paid versions of PDF editing programs.

Keeping It Simple with Faxing and Scanning

If you have a choice of using Windows Fax and Scan (the program provided by your all-in-one device) or purchasing scanning/OCR software, which should you use? Which is best? Windows Fax and Scan seems best suited for business use, with its mail-like interface for storing faxes and scanned images in folders and its support for fax servers. Fax modems are not very common in new computers; most folks at home use an all-in-one printer. The all-in-one printer should come with its own fax program plus buttons and controls on the device itself so that you can fax without using your computer.

The following are recommendations for the home user:

- **For a fax and scanning device**: If you occasionally need to send or receive a fax and scan in photos or documents, the all-in-one printer is a good choice. It takes the place of three different machines: a printer, a fax machine, and a scanner. Most also can be used as a straight copier.

- **For fax programs**: Use the fax software that comes with the device. It was made specifically for your device and it's explained quite well in the manual that comes with the device.

- **For scanning**: Use the software that comes with your all-in-one. The software provided by the manufacturer is just as easy to use as the scanning part of Windows Fax and Scanning—and probably has more features.

I've just touched the surface of what a scanner can do. Here are a number of fun projects and uses for the whole family:

- Convert old photos from photo albums and shoe boxes to digital files so that you can share them with more friends and relatives. Then tag the photos in Windows Live Photo Gallery with the notes and descriptions that was written on the back of the photo.

- Scan the pictures in from your calendars and use them as desktop backgrounds on your computer.

- Scan old documents like your grandparent's wedding license, birth certificates, and diplomas, etc.

- Scan receipts, bills, and records to store and organize them digitally.

■ Even though you can't use OCR to convert old hand written letters, notes and diaries, you can still scan each page in as an image file.

■ Create digital scrapbooks with the family pictures and documents you have scanned.

Summary

In this chapter you have learned how to set up printers, scanners, and fax devices, and how to use them. Your new skills include the following:

■ Adding printers to Windows

■ Connecting and sharing printers locally or through a home network

■ Using Windows Fax and Scan

■ Using other fax and scanner hardware and software

■ Choosing and using Optical Character Recognition (OCR) software

■ Using PDF editors to save documents instead of printing them

Next Steps

You may find the following related chapters useful:

■ Chapter 14: "Connecting Monitors, and Hardware"

■ Chapter 16: "Connecting to the Internet and Home Networks"

■ Chapter 18: "Using Windows 7 at Work and on the Road"

Connecting Monitors and Hardware

Considering how many different companies manufacture monitors, mice, keyboards, web cams, external hard drives and other hardware devices for PCs, Microsoft does a good job at making them all work with Windows 7. With plug and play, all you have to do is connect the device to your computer with a USB or monitor cable, and Windows automatically installs it. Occasionally you may need to help it along with some additional steps or customization.

Although Windows has supported the capability to use multiple monitors for several versions now; many people don't take advantage of the features and benefits available. There are so many ways to physically connect additional monitors; and with LCD and LED monitors so light and affordable, there is no excuse not to use multiple monitors.

In this chapter we'll look at

- Connecting and adjusting your monitor.
- Using multiple monitors.
- Setting up multiple monitors ergonomically.
- Connecting and using hardware and peripherals.
- Managing USB cables and connections.

Windows 7 Features that Help You Connect Devices

It doesn't take long for your computer to find itself attached to a whole bunch of things with cables and funny looking plugs. Even with wireless networks, mice, keyboards, and printers, peripherals and hardware need to be recognized and connected your computer. Fortunately, Windows 7 and the installation programs provided by the hardware manufacturers can make connecting and using your hardware fairly easy. Table 14–1 shows some of the features that make this happen.

Table 14–1. *Hardware Features*

Feature	What It Does
Plug and play	When you attach a new piece of hardware to your computer, Windows detects the type, brand, and model of the device and installs the appropriate driver.
Add New Hardware wizard	Most printers and hardware are plug and play: when you attach a new device, Windows detects the device and installs the appropriate driver. If Windows can't find an appropriate driver, or if you want to install a printer or device on a network, you can use the wizards to look for updated drivers on **Windows Update**, or you can use the manufacturer's installation disk.
Screen Resolution settings	When you connect a new monitor, Windows automatically detects it and sets it to the manufacturer's recommended resolution. You can adjust the resolution, orientation, or multiple monitor positions, through **Screen Resolution**.
Windows Hardware compatibility	Microsoft maintains a Windows Compatibility site for hardware and software. This site allows you to look up hardware by name, version, or model to determine if it is supported in Windows 7 and how to obtain updated drivers.
Troubleshooters	Windows provides several troubleshooters that can help get your printer or device up and running properly, such as **Display Quality** or **Hardware and Devices**.
Device Manager	This Control Panel item lists all of the hardware attached to and recognized by your computer. At a glance, you can quickly identify hardware that is not recognized by Windows, is disabled, or is missing drivers.

For additional help with devices and installation, see "Updating device drivers" in Chapter 17.

Monitors and Displays

Typically when you buy a new desktop PC, laptop, netbook, or tablet, you start with a single display. On a desktop PC, a separate external monitor is attached by a VGA or DVI cable; with a laptop, netbook, or tablet, your display is built in to the computer. The display area can vary from 7" diagonal on a small tablet to 25" for a large external monitor, as shown in Figure 14–1. The sizes shown are the most common ranges by device type. There are high end laptops with 19" screens; and tablets, laptops, netbooks, and convertibles overlap in sizes and capabilities. Many PCs and laptops are sold as media center PCs with high-definition jacks and media-friendly software such as Windows Media Center. There are 27- 32" TVs sold as combination HDTVs/computer monitors. Most large (42-50") HDTVs provide a VGA port plus multiple HDMI ports so you can connect your computer with a VGA or HDMI to VGA cable.

Typical Display Sizes

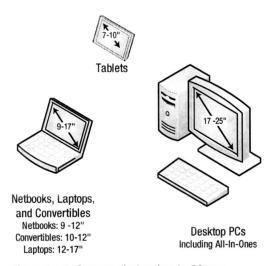

Figure 14–1. *Common display sizes by PC type*

Whether you have one display or multiple monitors, it helps to understand how to adjust your displays. Table 14–2 describes some of the Windows 7 features and related third-party features that help you manage and customize your displays and what you see.

Table 14–2. *Display Features*

Feature	Purpose
Display in Control Panel	**Display** in **Control Panel** provides several different features that adjust how colors and text appear on screen, as well as the resolution and orientation of each monitor attached to your system. In Display, you can access the following features:

- **Adjust resolution/Change display settings** allows you to change the resolution and orientation (portrait or landscape), and for multiple displays, the position of the monitors. You can also access these settings directly from your desktop, by right-clicking the desktop and clicking **Screen resolution**.

- **Make it easier to read what's on your screen** changes the size of text to **Smaller** (100%), **Medium** (125%), or **Larger** (150%).The default size, and sizes available, depends on the size of your display. For more sizes, **Set Custom text size (DPI)** may allow additional settings up to 500%.

- **Adjust ClearType text** works like a wizard. It displays a series of screens where you can compare sets of two to six text samples at the same time and select the sample that looks best to you each time. After three or four screens, you are finished and the text should be optimized according to what looks best to you.

- **Calibrate color** works like a wizard. It displays a series of pages that you use in conjunction with your monitor's on-screen display menu to adjust the brightness, contrast, and color of your monitor. Although many monitors have an auto-adjust feature, using **Calibrate color** may provide even better results.

Later in this chapter you will learn tips and tricks for managing multiple monitors with Screen resolution. See Chapter 1 for the basics of how to adjust the resolution of your display and adjust the size of text on screen.

Feature	Purpose
Personalize	When you use multiple monitors, use portrait mode, or a mix of portrait mode and landscape mode, sometimes the desktop background needs some tinkering. Later in this chapter, you will learn how to use personalization settings to do some cool things like displaying extra-large desktop pictures spanning multiple monitors. See Chapter 1 for the basics of how to use the Personalization settings to change your desktop background.
Third-Party Graphics Card Tools	**Display** in **Control Panel** includes most of the settings you will ever need for adjusting the monitor resolution and orientation. Whether the graphics card is built in to the motherboard, is a separate video card, or is an external video adapter like a USB to VGA adapter, the manufacturer may add their own settings and features. The manufacturer may provide access to these additional features through any of the following: 　▧　Advanced settings in Display ➤ Screen Resolution. 　▧　Adding a menu command when you right-click the desktop, so in addition to Screen Resolution, you may see commands for something like Graphics or Graphics Options. 　▧　Adding an icon to the notifications area on the taskbar. The extra settings provided by the graphics card manufacturer may include additional resolution settings and multiple monitor options not available in the standard Control Panel Display settings. To understand and get the most use of these features, check the online help or documentation provided by the PC or graphics card manufacturer

Multiple Monitors

Multiple monitors allow you to spread your programs and desktop across more than more than one monitor. Numerous studies have shown that computer users increase their productivity when they use multiple monitors. If you use a computer a lot at work or home, it is well worth it to add a second or third monitor. Figures 14–2 through 14–5 show some examples of how multiple monitors can make work or play on the computer more enjoyable.

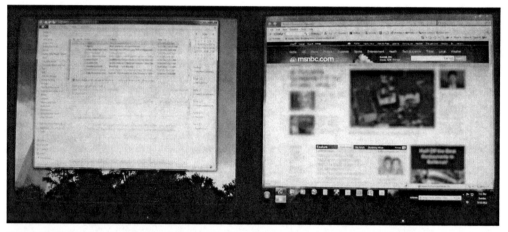

Figure 14–2. *Two identical monitors side by side. Browse e-mail on one monitor and surf the web on the other.*

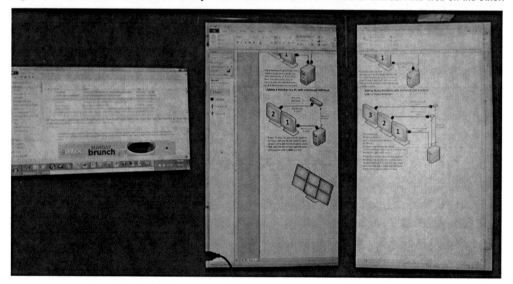

Figure 14–3. *Three monitors: laptop screen on the left and two 20-inch monitors in portrait mode in middle and right. You can spread a program window across two monitors to give a much larger work space, like the drawing program spread across the middle and right monitors. The laptop is on a stand to center the screen to about the same level as the center of the other screens.*

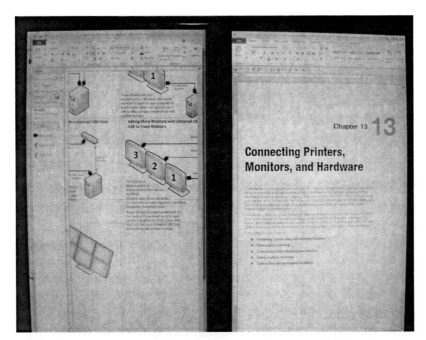

Figure 14–4. *Two 20-inch monitors in portrait mode, displaying the Visio drawing program on the left and Microsoft Word in a full page view on right.*

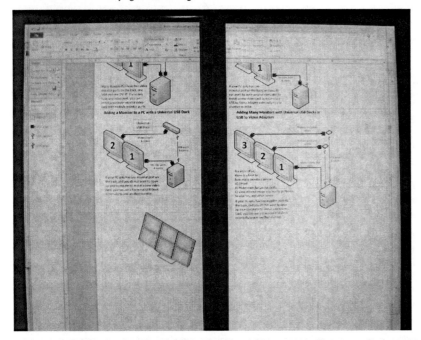

Figure 14–5. *Close-up showing the Visio window spread across both screens. Both are 20-inch monitors, which means they are each approximately 18 inches wide and 10 inches high in regular landscape mode. In portrait mode, the combined work area is 20 inches wide by 18 inches high.*

These figures displayed monitors in *extended desktop* mode, which means Windows treats each screen as separate desktop area. One monitor is your primary monitor and this is the main monitor where your Windows task bar and Start button are visible. Each additional monitor extends your desktop so that you can move or open programs on a separate screen.

You can also use multiple monitors in a *desktop duplicate* mode (sometimes called *mirrored* or *cloned*). In this mode, you see the same Windows desktop and program windows on each screen. Figure 14–6 is an example of the desktop mirrored on two different monitors.

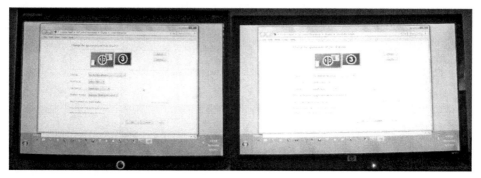

Figure 14–6. *Multiple monitors in mirror mode*

This can be useful if you want to show what is on the screen to more people than can comfortably view one monitor or if you want to control the screen from your monitor or laptop display while others watch it on another monitor.

GETTING THE BEST OF BOTH WORLDS WITH A LAPTOP AND AN EXTERNAL MONITOR

More and more, people are buying laptops as "desktop replacements." And, many companies are equipping their employees with laptops, so that they can take their work with them, on the road, or to meetings, and at the office use a docking station with an external monitor, keyboard, and mouse, so they can do more intensive work at their desks.

It used to be that laptops were more expensive and less powerful than the "tower" design desktop PCs. Today, the price difference is much less, and both home users and business users find that they have all the performance then need with a laptop.

Even without a docking station, you can still take advantage of the laptop's versatility. Add an external monitor, keyboard, and mouse for at home, and it's just like using a desktop PC. Except with the laptop, you also have the mobility to take your computer with you, and just use the laptop's screen, keyboard, and touch pad. Some people (like me) prefer using a mouse, and there are so many choices today for compact wireless mice that it really adds a lot of convenience. If you don't mind the extra weight, you can get laptops with large 17" screens – almost as large as an external monitor. In a few pages, "Adding More Video Ports to Your Computer" will show you several ways you can add multiple monitors to any computer.

Multi-Monitor Hardware

There are many ways to connect multiple monitors to your PC. Before you go out and buy a monitor, check to see what kind of video ports you already have on your computer. You may already have enough ports for multiple monitors and then all you have to do is hook up monitor with the video cable that was supplied with your monitor. If you are not sure if you have the right hardware, Table 14–3 describes what you may need to add multiple monitors. Following these hardware descriptions, you will find a comprehensive illustrated guide showing almost every combination of multiple monitors you might use with laptops, tablets, and desktop PCs.

Table 14–3. *Hardware Necessary to Add Multiple Monitors*

Hardware	Description
Monitors 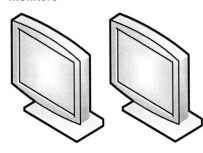 **Figure 14–7** *For best results, when setting up multiple monitors try to use identical size and models.*	If you don't already have your monitor, try to get a monitor that offers both **VGA** (blue) and **DVI-D** (white) input jacks. Most monitors offer both, but some manufacturers only provide a VGA jack on their lowest price models. If you are on a budget, those lowest price models without DVI-D jacks may provide just as good a quality, so don't feel you have to spend extra money to get the DVI-D jack. The size and resolution is up to you. Try to view the monitor in person in a store to compare the picture quality with other monitors on display. If you can, buy your monitors at the same time, getting the same brand and size. Monitors vary in color, saturation, and brightness from brand to brand. Getting the same model should ensure fairly close colors on both. Getting the same size ensures that program windows don't change size as you move them between the monitors (see Figure 14–7).
Video Cables 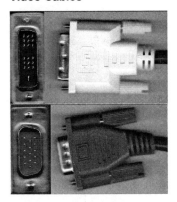 **Figure 14–8.** *The VGA plug is dark blue. DVI-D connects to same color ports on computer*	The most common video cable for computers is VGA, and the second most common is DVI-D. The ends of the video cables have male plugs (small pins) at both ends. The monitor and your computer have female ports (holes); see Figure 14–8. Sometimes the only jack provided on your monitor is VGA and the only port available on your computer is DVI-D because you have already connected the VGA port on your computer to another monitor. In that case, you will need a VGA-to-DVI-D adapter. Most monitors already come with at least a VGA cable and sometimes a DVI-D cable, too. If there is a DVI-D cable, it may also include a VGA-to-DVI-D adapter. If you are hooking up your computer to a large screen HDTV (32" - 50" or larger) typically these may have one or more HDMI jacks, and sometimes a VGA jack, but the TV almost never includes the actual cables.

Hardware	Description
 **Figure 14–9.** *DVI-D to VGA adapter*  **Figure 14–10.** *DVI-D to HDMI adapter* 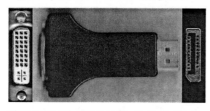 **Figure 14–11.** *DVI-D to DisplayPort adapter*	Most of the time all you need for multiple monitors are VGA and DVI-D cables. But occasionally, the second video port is neither VGA nor DVI-D, but instead **HDMI** or **DisplayPort**. **HDMI** ports are often available on laptops and desktop PCs so that they can be hooked up to High Definition TVs. DisplayPort is not very common now but may be used more in the future. Fortunately, no matter what kind of ports you have on your monitors and computers, there are adapters to convert one type of plug to another. Figures 14–9 to 14–11 show three commonly available adapter plugs: DVI-D to VGA DVI-D to HDMI DVI-D to DisplayPort If you can't find the exact combination you need, you can even combine two adapter plugs as long as the male/female ends match up. For example, you have a laptop with a DisplayPort video port and you want to hook it up to your HDTV. You could combine two plugs: DVI-D to DisplayPort adapter + DVI-D to HDMI adapter. So the connection would be like this: Laptop DisplayPort ➤ DisplayPort to DVI-D adapter ➤ DVI-D to HDMI adapter ➤ HDMI cable ➤ HDMI port on HDTV.
Video Ports 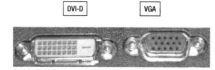 **Figure 14–12.** *DVI-D (left) and VGA (right) monitor ports found on the PC and the monitor.*	Your monitor may have one to three video ports. If there is only one, it's usually VGA (blue). If there is more than one, the second is usually DVI-D (white); see Figure 14–12. Most new desktop PCs have both a VGA and DVI-D port, but if there is only one it usually is VGA also. Laptops, especially those designed to be thin and lightweight, almost always only have one video port. Some, if designed for multimedia entertainment, may have an HDMI port, too. Some Windows 7 tablets don't have a video port or might only provide one on a separate tablet dock.

Hardware	Description

Video Memory

On most computers, the video graphics card is built into the computer's motherboard. Computers built to run Windows Vista or Windows 7 should have sufficient memory to run multiple monitors. If, after hooking up an extra monitor, it appears your screen is slower, it may be that you don't have a lot of video memory. If you have a laptop, there's not much you can do to add video memory, but you may be able to make some improvements through Windows itself. Check the **Windows Help and Support** system for information about improving your computer's performance. If you have a desktop PC, unless it is a mini-desktop PC, you can add a new video card with much higher video memory and multiple ports for hooking up more than one monitor.

> **CAUTION:** Unless you are very careful, skilled, and comfortable with working with the inside of a computer, have your video card installed professionally by a qualified technician; see Figures 14–13 and 14–14.

Figure 14–13. *External video ports for video card inside desktop PC (above)*

Figure 14–14. *Video card inside desktop PC (right)*

Hardware	Description
Pivoting Monitor Stands  **Figure 14–15.** *Nearly identical pivoting monitor stands from 3M and Ergotron*	You are only getting half of the potential of multiple monitors if you don't use a pivoting height-adjustable monitor stand. With multiple monitors, pivoting to landscape or portrait allows you to use the orientation that works best for your programs. E-mail, browsing the web, and spreadsheets often work best in the traditional landscape view. But for reading or writing documents, portrait view may work better. Height adjustment is very important not only for aligning the monitors with each other, but also for setting the right ergonomic position. Figure 14–15 shows two inexpensive but very effective monitor stands from 3M (left) and Ergotron (right). These manufacturers and others provide many other types of stands, such as: ▦ All-in-one stands that hold your desktop PC at the back with the monitor mount on the front. ▦ Articulated arm stands that sit on or clamp to your desktop. ▦ Multiple monitor stands that hold two or more monitors side by side or stacked one on top of the other.

Adding More Video Ports to Your Computer

Sometimes your computer can't support as many multiple monitors as you'd like, either because of the graphics card's limitations or because you just don't have enough ports. There are several options for adding video ports to your computer:

- **Docking station (brand-specific)**
- **Universal docking station**
- **USB2 to VGA, DVI-D, HDMI**
- **Video card upgrade**

VIDEO ADAPTERS ARE INTEGRATED INTO SCREEN RESOLUTION SETTINGS

In Windows 7, most external adapters and docking stations are fully integrated into the Control Panel Display Screen Resolution window. In previous versions of Windows, if you added a monitor through a universal docking station or USB2 to video adapter, you had to use a separate utility provided by the adapter manufacturer. The improvements in Windows 7 for multiple monitors allow adapter manufacturers to integrate their monitor settings into the Screen Resolution so that you can rotate, rearrange, or change the resolution of all monitors at once in one window.

Docking Station (Brand-Specific)

Most laptops designed for business use have optional docking stations that provide both a VGA and a DVI-D port. Dell, HP, and Toshiba are just a few that offer docking stations for their own models. Figure 14–16 shows a Dell docking station that allows you to click your laptop in place and then use external monitors attached to the back.

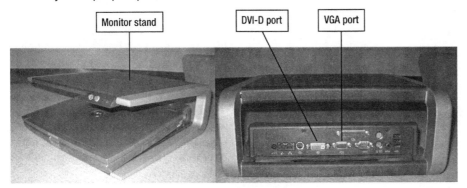

Figure 14–16. *Older model Dell docking station with monitor stand*

Unfortunately, these docking stations may cost another $150 to $200, and are priced more for business use than home users. Also, the video card in most laptops only supports two monitors total, so if you want more you will need to buy a universal docking station or a USB-to-Video adapter.

Universal Docking Stations

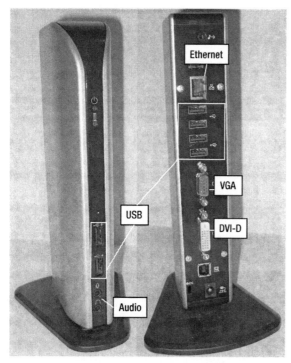

Universal docking stations are similar to the brand-specific docking stations previously described except they are less expensive, and you don't have to buy the same brand as your computer. A universal docking station hooks up to your computer via a USB 2 port and includes jacks for either a VGA or DVI-D monitor. The Toshiba Dynadock in Figure 14–17 is one of many universal docking stations available from a variety of manufacturers. The universal docking station doesn't go through the video card, which allows you to get around the limitation of two monitors that some laptops have. Some universal docking stations themselves have a limitation of only allowing one of their video ports to be used at one time; you can't run separate monitors through the VGA and DVI-D port at the same time even if the universal docking station provides both.

Figure 14–17. *Toshiba Dynadock universal USB docking station*

NOTE: Not all universal docking stations include video/VGA ports; some just provide USB and Ethernet jacks. Also, universal docking stations don't power or recharge laptops. Check product descriptions carefully before purchasing.

There are many other brands of docking station with VGA, DVI-D, or even HDMI ports. Here are just a few of many available online and from computer retail stores:

- **Kensington Universal Notebook Docking Station**

- **HP QuickDock 2.0 Docking Station (KN744AA)**

- **Plugable USB 2.0 Universal Docking Station by Plugable Technologies**

- **Targus ACP50US Universal Notebook Docking Station**

▨ Many more models are listed at www.displaylink.com. DisplayLink provides the USB-to-Video technology used in many of these products.

USB-to-Video Adapters

There are several brands and models of USB-to-Video adapters on the market. While these don't offer the other ports (USB, audio, Ethernet) provided by a universal USB docking station, they are also much less expensive.

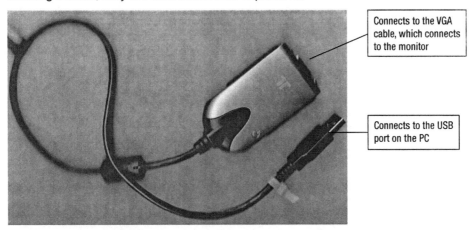

Connects to the VGA cable, which connects to the monitor

Connects to the USB port on the PC

Figure 14–18. *A Tritton SEE2 USB 2.0 to VGA External VGA Video Card*

Figure 14–18 shows a Tritton SEE2 USB 2.0 to VGA External VGA Video Card.

Be sure to follow the manufacturer's instructions for installing the drivers. While Windows 7 may detect and install the right drivers, sometimes there are more current drivers on the manufacturer's support site.

Once the driver is installed, most devices require that you connect your monitor and adapter in this order:

1. Connect the monitor cable to the adapter.

2. Turn on the power for your monitor, if it is not already on.

3. Connect the adapter to a USB port on the PC.

NOTE: If your monitor supports multiple inputs (you can connect more than one video cable, like one VGA and one DVI-D), you may need to push a settings button on the monitor itself to select which video input source to use.

Multiple Monitor Setups

There are many different combinations for connecting multiple monitors to laptops, tablets, and desktop PCs. The following pages diagram some of the most common setups, using internal and external video cards and adapters.

Adding a Monitor to a Laptop with Standard Video Monitor Ports and Cables

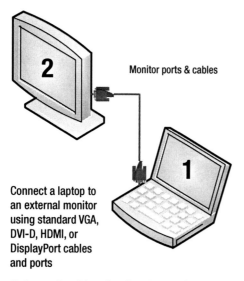

Monitor ports & cables

Connect a laptop to an external monitor using standard VGA, DVI-D, HDMI, or DisplayPort cables and ports

Using a Docking Station Made for Your Specific Model or Brand – Laptop Screen Available

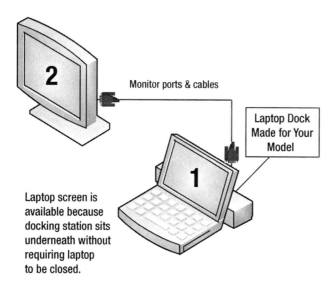

Monitor ports & cables

Laptop Dock Made for Your Model

Laptop screen is available because docking station sits underneath without requiring laptop to be closed.

Adding a Monitor Through a Tablet Docking Station

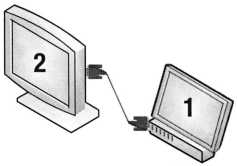

Most Windows 7 Tablets do not usually have video ports, but most include or offer a optional dock. The dock may have a video port, such as HDMI. Or, it may offer additional USB ports and you can use universal USB dock or USB to Video Adapter

Using a Docking Station Made for Your Specific Model or Brand – Laptop Screen Not Available

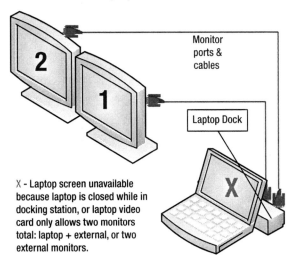

Monitor ports & cables

Laptop Dock

X - Laptop screen unavailable because laptop is closed while in docking station, or laptop video card only allows two monitors total: laptop + external, or two external monitors.

Adding a Monitor to a Laptop or Tablet with no Monitor Ports, with a Universal USB Dock

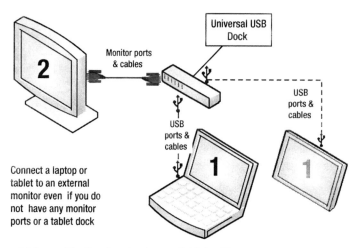

Adding a Monitor to a Laptop or Tablet with no Monitor Ports, with a USB to Video Adapter

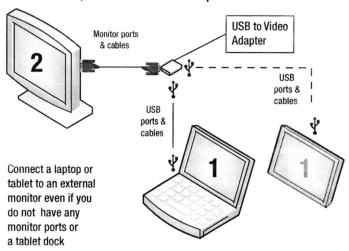

Adding a Monitor to a Laptop with a Monitor Port, with a Universal USB Dock

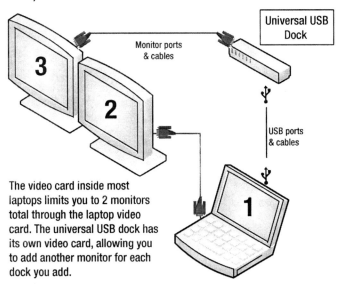

The video card inside most laptops limits you to 2 monitors total through the laptop video card. The universal USB dock has its own video card, allowing you to add another monitor for each dock you add.

Adding a Monitor to a Laptop with a Monitor Port, with a USB to Video Adapter

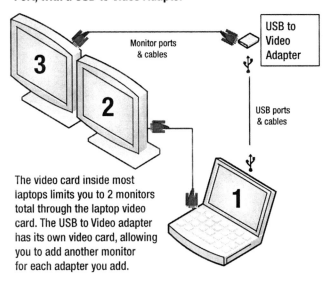

The video card inside most laptops limits you to 2 monitors total through the laptop video card. The USB to Video adapter has its own video card, allowing you to add another monitor for each adapter you add.

Adding a Monitor to a PC with Two Video Ports

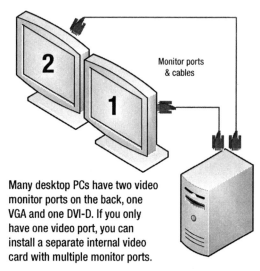

Monitor ports & cables

Many desktop PCs have two video monitor ports on the back, one VGA and one DVI-D. If you only have one video port, you can install a separate internal video card with multiple monitor ports.

Adding a Monitor to a PC with a USB to Video Adapter

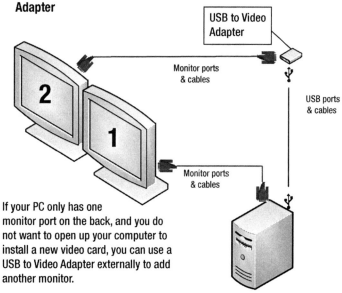

USB to Video Adapter

Monitor ports & cables

USB ports & cables

Monitor ports & cables

If your PC only has one monitor port on the back, and you do not want to open up your computer to install a new video card, you can use a USB to Video Adapter externally to add another monitor.

Adding a Monitor to a PC with a Universal USB Dock

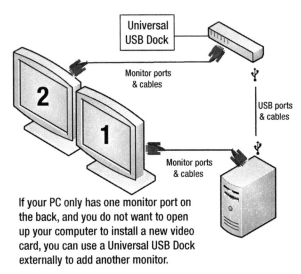

If your PC only has one monitor port on the back, and you do not want to open up your computer to install a new video card, you can use a Universal USB Dock externally to add another monitor.

Adding Many Monitors with Universal USB Docks or USB to Video Adapters

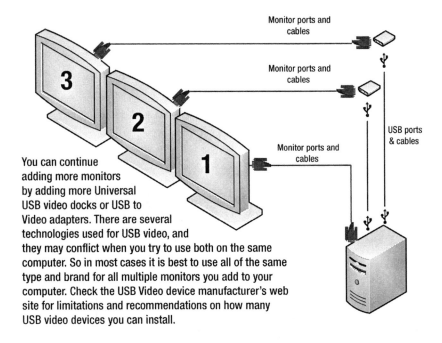

You can continue adding more monitors by adding more Universal USB video docks or USB to Video adapters. There are several technologies used for USB video, and they may conflict when you try to use both on the same computer. So in most cases it is best to use all of the same type and brand for all multiple monitors you add to your computer. Check the USB Video device manufacturer's web site for limitations and recommendations on how many USB video devices you can install.

Adding Really Large Multi-Monitor Arrays

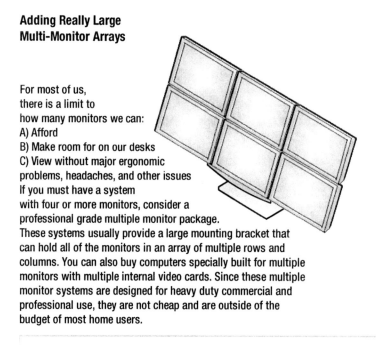

For most of us,
there is a limit to
how many monitors we can:
A) Afford
B) Make room for on our desks
C) View without major ergonomic
problems, headaches, and other issues
If you must have a system
with four or more monitors, consider a
professional grade multiple monitor package.
These systems usually provide a large mounting bracket that
can hold all of the monitors in an array of multiple rows and
columns. You can also buy computers specially built for multiple
monitors with multiple internal video cards. Since these multiple
monitor systems are designed for heavy duty commercial and
professional use, they are not cheap and are outside of the
budget of most home users.

> **NOTE:** There are many practical and common uses for massive multiple monitor arrays. For example, in the financial and trading markets, you may need to check the status of several companies or exchanges at once. Or, you are responsible for monitoring readings on multiple systems or critical equipment. Opening, closing, or moving windows within a monitor screen costs precious time. In any of those cases, the need far outweighs the cost. Not having instant access to all of that information at once could be very costly or dangerous.

Fixing Slowdowns with Multiple Monitors

Adding multiple monitors can slow down your system, depending on how the graphics memory works on your computer. Your computer uses two types of memory:

- System memory (this is the RAM, and usually it is 2, 4, 6, or 8 GB)
- Graphics memory

In most computers, most or all of the graphics memory is "borrowed" from the system memory. This is called *shared system memory*. Since this memory is shared between the system and the graphics, overall performance of your computer may slow down if you are using programs and features that require lots of memory for both of these at the same time. If you have lots of system memory, such as 4GB or more, most of the time there is no problem. But if you have a netbook or tablet with only 1GB or 2GB of RAM to start with, and then the graphics memory borrows some of that, you will experience much slower performance overall. Add another monitor, and your computer must share the graphics memory between each monitor.

Since one of reasons for using multiple monitors is to provide more desktop space to run more programs, when you run more programs, each program eats up some of the system memory.

Monitors attached to external adapters tend to be choppier and slower than the performance on monitors or displays connected directly to the VGA/DVI-D ports on a desktop PC or laptop. The slower performance may be most noticeable when using intensive graphical programs, such as video playback and drawing programs. Or it may take longer to scroll a window or move windows from one display to another.

Don't be discouraged from using or setting up multiple monitors. Table 14–4 details many things you can do improve performance.

Table 14–4. *Performance Fixes*

Task	Action
Adjust for best performance	1. Click the **Start** button, and in the search programs and files box, type **improve performance**.
	2. When the list appears, click Use tools to improve performance..
	3. In **Performance Options**, on the **Visual Effects** tab, click **Adjust for best performance**. This turns off all visual effects including Aero features like transparent glass and Aero Peek.
	4. If you can't live without some of these features, click **Custom** and then select the features you still want and clear all others.
Review Help and Support for tips for improving your computer's performance	1. Click the **Start** button, and then click **Help and Support**.
	2. Search for the topic **Ways to improve your computer's performance**.
Add an internal graphics card (desktop PC only)	See the "Video memory" section earlier in this chapter for information about adding a separate video memory card. These cards come in several different sizes of memory, such as 256MB, 512MB, and 1GB. There is no hard and fast rule on how much memory to add, but I added 1GB video cards to two of my home computers and they work well for running two monitors on each computer. I am not a gamer, but really serious gamers may buy even bigger cards, such as or 4GB, that cost as much as I pay for a moderate computer. Though installing these yourself is not very difficult, any time you open your computer you risk accidental damage to other internal components. If in doubt, have a professional install your card.

Task	Action
Add system memory	If your computer uses shared system memory, adding more RAM can help because it provides more total memory for your system and graphics memory. Adding system memory to a desktop PC is easier than adding an internal graphics card, but make sure your computer can take additional memory or memory upgrades. Some netbooks are not designed for memory upgrades or access by anybody but a qualified technician. Some computers may have all of the memory slots in use already, so an upgrade would require replacing all memory cards with higher memory. For example, a desktop PC might have four slots with 1GB memory in each one, for a total of 4GB system memory. If you want to add more memory, you must replace two of these with 2GB memory for 6GB total system memory, or all four with 2GB memory for 8GB of system memory.
	NOTE: On 32-bit machines Windows 7 only recognizes a total of 3 GB system memory. If you add 4 GB, Windows 7 will only see and use 3 GB. To use 4 GB or more, you need a 64-bit machine. Fortunately most new desktop and laptops (except netbooks) are 64-bit.
	Before purchasing memory, check your computer's documentation or visit a memory manufacturer's web site to see if your computer's memory is upgradeable. Also, check the computer documentation or the manufacturer's site to see if the bios needs to be adjusted so that the graphics card can take advantage of the additional memory. Memory manufacturers often provide tools to determine what memory your model needs. For example, www.kingston.com or www.crucial.com.
Disable your laptop or tablet screen when attached to a larger external monitor	Although this takes away your multiple monitor capability, it may improve your performance and still give you more display area than if you were just using your laptop or tablet screen alone.
Run fewer programs	You can still get the benefits of using multiple monitors even if you are only able to run one or two programs on each monitor.
Make sure your video adapter drivers are up to date	Most video adapter and graphic card manufacturers have upgraded their drivers several times since the release of Windows 7. Check the manufacturer's support site for the latest drivers.
	If you have built-in graphics, check your PC manufacturer's web site for updated drivers.

Task	Action
Try a different external video adapter	There are many different models of USB-to-Video and USB docking stations with video. Some work better than others. If you already have an adapter or are considering buying one, look up the model on an online retailer web site and review customer comments and ratings of the model. Even if you don't want to purchase from Amazon.com, it's a good place to find customer reviews.

> **NOTE:** Some 2D, 3D, game, and graphical programs like Photoshop may experience problems when you use more than one video adapter and may recommend removing additional cards. For example, see this issue and suggestions for Photoshop in the Adobe knowledge base article "GPU, OpenGL support I Photoshop CS4, CS5" at http://kb2.adobe.com/cps/404/kb404898.html.

Enabling and Extending a Monitor

Though your computer may detect the presence of a new monitor, and the size and resolution, it may not automatically enable it. If you just added an external adapter, docking station, or internal card, the product documentation should tell you how to enable and configure your additional monitors. Or, at first you may think something is wrong with your computer or the monitor because you see nothing, you believe you have hooked it up correctly, and the monitor's power light is on. Or, you see the new monitor but it is showing the same desktop and programs as your other monitor. Fortunately, you can usually fix this easily in the Screen Resolution window.

> **TIP:** Most laptops usually provide a *function key* to toggle between single monitor, multiple monitor extended, and multiple monitor mirror modes. There is no universal key that all manufacturers use for this, some use F4, some use F8; some may not provide it at all. Check your laptop's user guide for descriptions of the function keys.

Even if your monitor is enabled, you should fine-tune the alignment of the two display positions next to each other, so that you can move your mouse and windows smoothly from one screen to the other. The following procedure includes steps for aligning the displays with each other.

To enable and extend a monitor:

1. Right-click the desktop, and then click **Screen resolution**.

    The Screen Resolution window appears, as shown in Figure 14–19.

2. Click the new display that is not showing anything on the monitor.

3. In **Multiple displays**, click **Extend desktop to this display**.

4. Click **Apply**.

    After a few moments the new monitor should show the desktop (but not the same programs and windows open as on the first monitor).

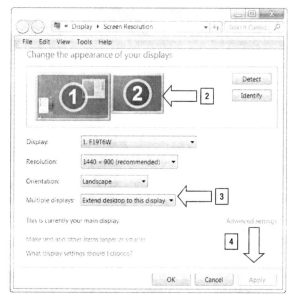

Figure 14–19. *In the Screen Resolution window, you can enable and extend a new monitor.*

5. Click **Identify**.

    The numbers 1 and 2 should appear on your actual monitor screens, similar to Figure 14–20. The order left to right of the physical location of the monitors on your desk should match the Screen Resolution window shown in Figure 14–21.

6. If they don't match, in the Screen Resolution window drag the monitors around until they match the actual arrangement of your monitors, and then click **Apply**. Keep the Screen Resolution window open.

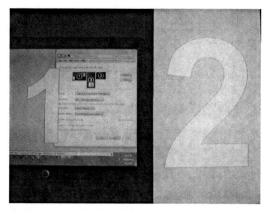

Figure 14–20. *When you click Identify, display numbers appear on each monitor*

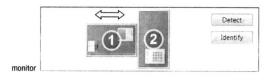

Figure 14–21 *The physical location of the monitors should match the position and location shown in Screen Resolution.*

7. Drag the Screen Resolution window across the displays until it straddles both displays (half of the window on one display and half on the other).

8. If they don't align top to bottom, as shown in Figure 14–22, move the monitors in the Screen Resolution window up and down as needed to match the physical positions of your monitors on your desk, as shown in Figure 14–23.

9. Click **Apply**.

   The Screen Resolution window will jump to one display or the other.

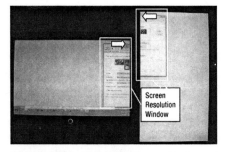

Figure 14–22. *Check the alignment between two screens by dragging the Screen Resolution window so that it stretches over both displays.*

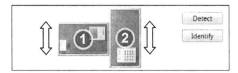

Figure 14–23. *Move the monitor positions up or down in Screen Resolution so that they align, and then click Align. It may take several tries to get it right.*

10. Drag the Screen Resolution window to straddle both displays again.

11. If it is closer but still not exactly even, like Figure 14–24, fine tune the alignment by repeating the rearranging in the Screen Resolution window.

    – or-

    Sometimes you can't get the final alignment correct with just moving the displays around in the Screen Resolution window. Physically adjust the height of the monitors on your desktop, as shown in Figure 14–25, so that the window straddling both displays lines up. If your monitor stands don't have height adjustments, use telephone books, copier paper reams, or something else to fine tune the heights.

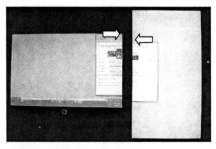

Figure 14–24. *Alignment is better, but to get it more exact you may want to physically raise lower the height of your monitors on your desk.*

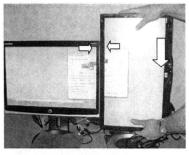

Figure 14–25. *With adjustable height monitor stands you can fine tune the alignment.*

Aligning monitors by the top or the bottom

The previous example showed how to align two monitors that are different orientations. When they are properly aligned, then it is pretty easy to move your mouse pointer or programs from one screen to another. But if you have two monitors in the same orientation, like the two in Figure 14–26, you can align them quite easily in the Screen Resolution window, as shown in Figure 14–27.This is handy when you have programs like spreadsheets, or documents that you want to see multiple pages side by side. Aligning monitors 1 and 2 with different orientations but centered, may require adjusting the physical height of the monitors themselves. Aligning monitors with like orientation and size, like monitors 2 and 3 in portrait mode, can be accomplished by aligning them by top or bottom in the Screen Resolution, while aligning them physically on your desktop. When you align monitors across the top or bottom edges of both monitors, as you move a monitor in Screen Resolution it should "snap" into alignment.

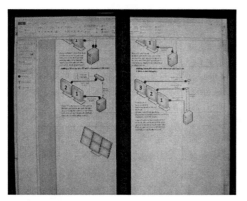

Figure 14–26 *Some programs really work great when you can spread them across multiple monitors, like this example using Visio.*

Figure 14–27 *Aligning monitors along the top or bottom is a snap*

Alignment When Monitors Have Different Resolutions and Sizes

If your monitors don't have the same resolution, even when your monitors are aligned a window might be taller on one display than the other. This often occurs when your monitors are *almost* the same size. In Figure 14–25, one monitor is 19" and 1440 x 600, and the other monitor is 20" and 1600 x 900. Even when the Screen Resolution window is aligned along the top, because of the difference in resolution the window is slightly larger in one display and will not align along the bottom. Most of the time this is not bothersome, but if you want to spread a single program window across both displays, it is more difficult to follow lines of text all the way across the screen.

Cool Desktops for Multiple Monitors: Extra Large Photos and Panoramas

For a really cool desktop background, search the Web for large panorama images that span both monitors. These work best when both monitors are the same size, and in landscape orientation side by side. Search the web for "panoramas for multiple monitors" or "desktop wallpapers for dual monitors." The following example in Figure 14–28 is from the Grand Canyon NPS (National Park Service photostream on Flickr, http://www.flickr.com/photos/grand_canyon_nps/5446235569/sizes/l/in/set-72157626052533148/).

To set your desktop background to a panorama spanning both monitors

One of the keys to making this work right is make sure that the image you select for the background is larger than the combined area of the monitors.

1. Right-click your desktop and then click **Screen Resolution**.

2. If you haven't already, arrange the monitors side by side, as shown in Figure 14–28.

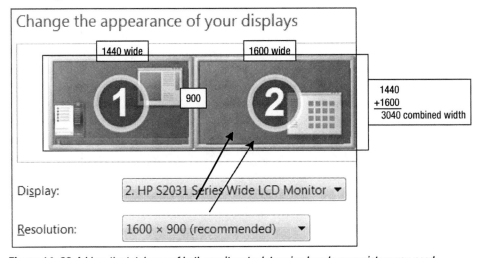

Figure 14–28 *Add up the total area of both monitors to determine how large a picture you need*

3. Click each display to get their resolutions, and then add them up. This will give you the total image area of both screens combined. You will need an image as large as or larger than this image area. In this example, the image area is 3040 wide and 900 tall, or 3040 x 900. So you will need picture that is at least that big.

4. Search the web for a picture that is at least 3040 x 900. How can you tell? If you search for pictures with Google or Bing, it will tell the image size. In this example, I located the image by searching for panoramic pictures, and then looking for the National Park Service site. The Grand Canyon National Park Service photos are available for free through their collection on FlickR.

Figure 14–29 shows an example of what the full picture looks like, and also offers several image sizes. The Original size on the far right is 3940 x 964, which is larger than the area we want to cover across the monitors, 3040 x 900.

Figure 14–29 *Grand Canyon panorama available from Grand Canyon NPS photostream on FlickR*

5. Download the file to your computer, and save it in an easy to find location in your Pictures library. Even though you could right-click the picture and then click Set as background, you will lose this file the next time click Set as background on another picture.

6. Right-click your desktop and click **Personalization**.

7. In the **Personalization** window, click **Desktop background**.

8. Browse to locate the picture.

9. When you have located and selected the picture, in **Picture position**, select **Tile**, as shown in Figure 14–30

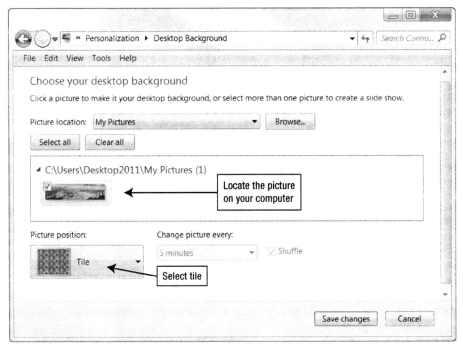

Figure 14–30 *Select tile for picture position. The other choices will just duplicate the picture on each monitor*

10. When you save the changes, your desktop background will show the panoramic picture spanning both monitors, similar to Figure 14–31.

Figure 14–31 *The image spans both monitors. Photo credit for image on monitors, Grand Canyon NPS*

Summary of Multi-Monitor Setup Tips and Tricks

The following tips can help you get the best look and use of your multi-monitor arrangement:

- Make sure that the monitors' physical locations left to right match the order they're shown in Screen Resolution so that when you drag a window off one display it comes out on the display adjacent to it.

- Align the tops or bottoms so that when you drag the window from left to right or right to left, it matches up vertically—the window should move between displays top to top, middle to middle, bottom to bottom.

- Try to match the resolutions of each display pretty closely so that a program window appears to have the same size no matter which display it is on.

- Use the Display ➤ Screen Resolutions window to align monitors with each other, and fine-tune the position of the monitors with an adjustable monitor stand or the good old standbys, telephone books or copier paper reams.

- To get the most out of a multiple monitor setup, buy a replacement monitor stand that allows height adjustment and rotation between horizontal (landscape) and vertical (portrait)

- For desktop computers, if your current computer doesn't have more than one video port (most now include both a VGA and a DVI-D port), your best performance solution is to buy a replacement video card with multiple monitor ports. If you are not experienced with or comfortable with opening up a computer and replacing the graphics card yourself, have a qualified computer technician perform this service.

- If you have a laptop computer or don't want to install a new graphics card in your desktop PC, another alternative is to use a universal docking station that includes video or a USB-to-Video adapter.

- Don't mix different external adapter types. The drivers for universal docking stations may conflict with the drivers for USB-to-Video adapters. If you want to add many multiple monitors, you will usually get the best results if you use the same brand and model for all of them.

- For really large multiple-monitor setups, there are professional-level computer systems that support 4, 8, 16 multiple monitors with multiple video cards and specially designed stands to stack the monitors side by side and top and bottom.

Ergonomics and Multiple Monitors

Whether you use one computer monitor or many, setting up your computer work area to follow good ergonomics is extremely important to your mental and physical health. It is beyond the scope and authority of this book to provide ergonomic guidelines, but fortunately there are many great resources available on the Web to help you. But it is very pertinent to mention a few things to consider about the ergonomic impact of using multiple monitors. Most ergonomic guidelines provide recommendations for making sure that your chair, desk, and computer height are set within a certain range depending on your height and size. With one monitor, it is fairly simple to make sure that it is aligned so that you don't have to tilt your head or swivel your neck over too wide a range.

But with multiple monitors, you have increased your viewing range right to left and top to bottom. You need to move your head much more to view all of your displays. Depending on your total desktop surface available, you may be limited on how much you can arrange the monitors to the optimal height and distance. Ergonomic guidelines usually include recommendations for lighting, placement of monitors in relation to windows and other bright light sources, and avoiding glare. As your display viewing area spreads over a wider area, you are more likely to encounter adverse lighting conditions somewhere in that viewing range. Meanwhile, your keyboard, mouse, and chair probably stay in the same place most of the time.

If your work area is not set up to good ergonomic practices with a single monitor, your health and injury issues will multiply with multiple monitors. I can make some suggestions about how to work with multiple monitor work areas, but ultimately you should educate yourself on sound ergonomic practices and apply them as best you can. Your manager, your company, your family, and your teachers may not be well-versed in ergonomics, so it is up to you to protect yourself.

Though I am by no means an authority on ergonomics, I fully respect and appreciate the need to follow good practices. Writing for a living for over twenty years, I have experienced firsthand what neglecting good ergonomics can do to you. I have worked for many years with multiple monitors—and with multiple computers with multiple monitors—spread over a wide desk area, and have a few recommendations based on my experiences.

- **Locate and use a good ergonomic check list and guidelines**. The United States Department of Labor, Occupational Safe & Health Administration (OSHA), has an excellent ergonomics web site. Visit their Ergonomics web site, "OSHA Ergonomic Solutions: Computer Workstations eTool" currently at `http://www.osha.gov/SLTC/etools/ computerworkstations/index.html`. Web site addresses can change frequently and without notice, so if this web site address changes, try searching the web for OSHA Ergonomic Guidelines or something similar. You may find other similar guidelines from state and local agencies, your employer, or colleges and universities.

▤ **Use adjustable monitor stands on every monitor. Do not think of this as an option, think of it as a requirement.** The 3M and Ergotron monitor stands shown in this chapter are great and cost $50 to $60. Whenever I add a monitor, I consider that as part of the cost of a new monitor. The holes for mounting the brackets are standardized across the monitor industry so you can move them to your new monitors as you replace old monitors. For large sets of multiple monitors, spend a little more on ergonomically designed multiple monitor stands. There are multiple monitor stands for as few as two monitors, and they may be a better choice for you than individual monitor stands.

▤ **Use an adjustable stand for your laptop, and use a separate keyboard.** Personally, I think laptops are an ergonomic nightmare. If you position your laptop so that the keyboard is at the right ergonomic height and distance, your laptop screen will be too close and too low. If you position the laptop screen to the right distance and height, you have to stretch your arms to reach the keyboard. When I take my laptop any place where I expect to spend more than an hour, I bring a separate 88-key keyboard and mouse. At my desk, a laptop stand allows me to raise the screen to a good height and place it alongside my other monitors so that it is not jarring going from your full size monitor to your laptop display and back.

▤ **Use multiple keyboards and mice, or an easily moveable wireless keyboard and mouse.** When I am using several monitors over a wide arc across my desk, I have several keyboards positioned so that I can pivot my entire body to directly face the monitor I am currently working on. If your desk space is small, try a smaller 88-key keyboard, which will allow you to place additional keyboards in a smaller space. The keys and spacing are full sized; you just don't have the numeric keyboard. Omitting the numeric keypad also reduces how far you have to move your hand from the keyboard to your mouse.

▤ **Position your best, largest, or main monitor directly in front of you.** If you have several sizes of monitors, you probably use your largest monitor the most. Place the monitor you use most, running the programs you use most, directly in front of you. Then use the monitors directly on either side of the main monitor for the next most used programs. This puts the least used programs farthest from center, reducing the amount of time you must turn from the center of your vision.

▤ **Do not wait until you have neck, shoulder, arm, or wrist pain to set up your work area ergonomically.** By the time you get to that point of discomfort, you may have already sustained permanent or long term injury that may require physical therapy.

Hardware

Adding hardware can be as simple as connecting a device to your computer with a USB plug, or more complicated like opening up your computer and inserting a new card or component. Some types of hardware are easy to install yourself; other types are best left to professionals unless you are very skilled and experienced working with the insides of a computer or electronics.

> **NOTE:** Prior to installing hardware, perform a full backup of your computer to a drive outside of your local computer, and create system restore points. See Chapter 16 to learn how to perform backups and set system restore points.

Some parts of the installation process are the same whether the hardware is internal or external. But there are some important differences in the complexity and who is qualified to perform the installation.

> **NOTE:** Before adding any hardware, external or internal, make sure that it is compatible with Windows by visiting the Windows Hardware compatibility web site.

Let's take a look at some of the differences, starting with external hardware.

External Hardware	Description
Common Peripherals: ▪ Printers, scanners, and fax ▪ Modems ▪ External hard drives ▪ USB flash drives ▪ Wireless network USB cards ▪ Universal docking stations, USB hubs, and USB-to-Video adapters ▪ Web, digital, and video cameras ▪ Keyboards, mice, and other input devices ▪ USB audio cards ▪ MP3 players, cell phones, PDAs, and eBook readers	External hardware components are more often referred to as computer peripherals, or devices. External hardware installation is mostly about making sure you have the right drivers and good USB connections. Most of these devices are attached to and used by your computer all the time. Some devices, such as USB flash drives, cameras, cell phones, PDAs, and eBook readers, may be attached when you need to download or transfer information between the device and the computer. Figure 14–32 displays a wide variety of devices typically connected to computers via USB. How many can you identify?

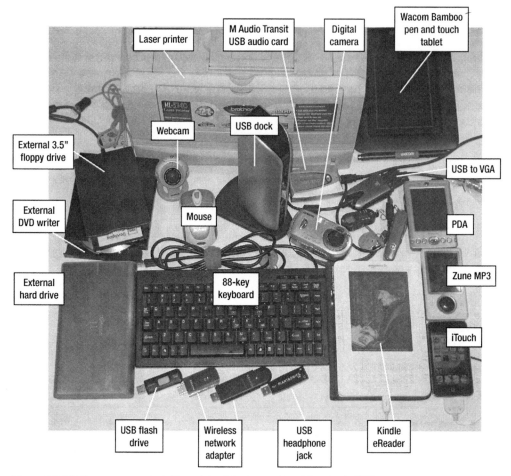

Figure 14–32. *You can connect a wide variety of devices and peripherals via USB.*

TIP: USB cords, connections, and devices can be finicky. Some types of USB devices are very sensitive to the quality and strength of the connection. Don't panic if your computer doesn't see or install your USB device. See "Managing USB Connections and Devices" for tips and recommendations on how to tame your USB devices.

External Peripheral Installation

Almost anything you connect to your computer via a USB connection should not require much installation, if any at all. Windows 7 should automatically detect the make and model of the device and retrieve the necessary drivers from your computer. If Windows can't find the right drivers, it may prompt you to insert an installation disk or it can look for drivers on the Web.

While Windows 7 should smoothly and automatically locate or install the necessary drivers, sometimes you may have to look for the drivers yourself. "Updating Device Drivers" in Chapter 17 provides steps for getting updated drivers.

For most external peripherals, installation:

- Is usually Plug and Play.

- Is usually do-it-yourself; you should not need professional installation.

- May require updated drivers; make sure you have installation disks handy, and access to the Web.

- Doesn't usually require turning off the computer or disconnecting the power; sometimes it may require a restart after installing or updating drivers.

NOTE: Many slim or compact desktop PC cases, and even some full sized cases, may offer little or no room for adding internal cards like video cards or additional internal hard drives. When you are considering a new PC, it's usually cheaper to pay more now for lots of hard drive space than to add or upgrade later.

Internal Hardware Installation

Installing or upgrading internal hardware is more complicated than connecting external USB devices. There are fewer things you can change inside the PC, and the ones you can have much more impact on your computer's performance and capabilities.

Internal Hardware	Description
Common Components: ▦ Memory (Most desktop PCs, some laptops and netbooks) ▦ Graphics card (Desktop PCs only; not upgradeable in laptops or netbooks) ▦ Internal modem (Desktop only) ▦ Ethernet or wireless network card (Desktop PC only) ▦ Internal hard drive (Desktop PCs, some laptops or netbooks) ▦ Extra USB or Firewire ports (Desktop PCs)	Most of these components are user-accessible in a desktop PC, and advanced users may be able to perform the installation. Laptops are not accessible, and some components can't be replaced. Generally, you install these components to upgrade your computer's performance (memory and graphics cards, for example), add capacity or storage (larger or additional internal hard drive), or add capabilities (modem, network cards, USB or Firewire ports). Figures 14–33 and 14–34 show the back and inside of a standard desktop PC case.

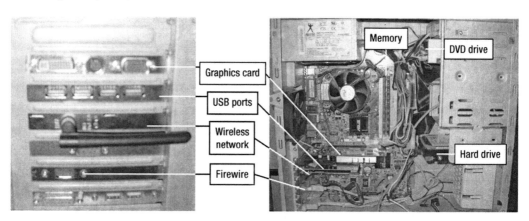

Figure 14–33. *The back of this desktop PC shows some of the components you can install.*

Figure 14–34. *The inside of this desktop PC shows more components that can be installed or upgraded.*

Advantages of Internal Hardware over External Hardware

Not everything can be installed as either external or internal hardware. But for the hardware you can install internally, there are several advantages over their external cousins.

- **Graphics cards**: If you want to add or improve multiple monitor capabilities on your computer, an internal graphics card is usually more stable, more powerful, and less expensive than an external USB-to-Video adapter or USB docking station.

- **Hard drives**: Internal hard drives are cheaper, offer greater capacities, and are faster than external hard drives connected through USB ports.

- **Extra USB ports**: Most computers have three or more USB ports, but sometimes you need more. You can add external USB hubs, but they may not have enough power for hi-speed devices like external hard drives, DVD/CD drives, or scanners. You may be able to add extra USB ports and/or Firewire ports with an internal card. Since the card is connected directly to your computer's motherboard and power supply, it is usually stronger than an external USB hub.

Internal Hardware Installation Recommendations

The following list is not numbered because you should read the entire list before attempting any kind of internal hardware installation.

> **CAUTION:** It is very easy to accidently damage your computer or injure yourself if you are not careful or familiar with safe practices. If in doubt, have a professional perform installations and upgrades.

- Perform a full backup of all disks before installing any hardware. See Chapter 16 to learn how to back up your computer.

- Read the device manufacturer's installation instructions before doing anything with your computer or the device you are installing.

- Check your computer's documentation or online support for special instructions for opening the computer case or installing this type of device.

- Check your computer's documentation for instructions on BIOS setup. Some hardware, such as graphics cards or new hard drives, may require changes in setup prior to booting in Windows.

- Get a wrist grounding strap. This prevents accidental static electricity discharge, which can damage your computer's boards and memory.

- Check your computer's warranty; some warranties are void if you open the computer yourself.

- If required by the manufacturer, install software or drivers; some devices require that you perform the software/driver installation before physically connecting the new hardware.

- If you encounter problems with drivers, the "Updating Device Drivers" section in Chapter 17 provides steps for getting updated drivers.

- Unplug the computer from all power.

- Unplug the power for any peripherals attached to the computer, including printers, monitors, external hard drives, etc.

Getting Help During or After Installation

Whether you are installing internal or external hardware, Windows 7 provides several features to help if you have problems. "Windows 7 Features that Help You Connect Devices," describes these resources. Also, see Chapter 17.

Managing USB Connections and Devices

While USB is great most of the time for connecting all sorts of devices to your computer, sometime it does funny if not annoying things. It is really frustrating to follow all of the instructions for installing or connecting your device, and your computer does not "see" the device. It does not show up in Device Manager, or in Printers and Devices, yet it worked okay a few days ago or on a different computer. You have installed, uninstalled, reinstalled, or updated the drivers; the device power is on; and the USB cable is connected solidly on both ends.

> **NOTE:** The most common version of USB used today is USB 2.0, which transfers data 40 times faster than the previous version, USB 1.1. Older computers may have only USB 1.1, or a mix of USB 1.1 and USB 2.0 ports.

Quite often the problem is your USB connection. If the connection is not strong between your computer and the USB device, Windows may not see it. Yet when you look at the connection, everything looks correct.

Some types of devices, like video adapters, wireless network cards, external hard drives, DVD drives, printers, and scanners, require the maximum speed and strength from your USB connection. They are designed for USB 2.0 connections. All it takes is a weak link between your computer and your device, and it may not work. Here are some common but not always obvious things to check:

- **Did you get a popup notification that the device will run better if it is connected to a USB 2.0 port?**
  If you click that notification, it will take you to Device Manager so that you can see if there are any high-speed USB 2.0 ports on your machine. Unfortunately, Device Manager does not tell you exactly which physical locations on your computer are USB 2.0 hubs. If Device Manager does indicate that high-speed USB ports are available, then you probably are currently connected to a USB 1.1 port or through a USB 1.1 external hub, and you should try connecting your USB cable to a different USB port on your computer until the notification goes away and the device connection works.

- **Is the USB cable going directly from your device to the computer, or is it going through an external USB hub?**
  A USB hub can be too weak if it is a USB 1.1 hub, does not have its own power (running only off the computer's power), or has too many USB devices connected to it. Try connecting the device directly to your computer without going through any hub. If you were using an unpowered hub, try using a powered USB 2.0 hub.

  If you have a direct connection and still nothing happens, try using a different cable. Though you will not find USB cables marked as USB 1.1, some cables apparently were designed for this slower speed, before USB 2.0 came out. Or the cable itself could be defective. If you do find that replacing a cable solves the problem, throw away the defective cable. Otherwise, you will repeat the same problem again in the future.

- **Are you connecting to a netbook or an inexpensive laptop?**
  Sometimes netbooks have underpowered USB ports. Even though the ports are USB 2.0, and powered by the netbook, sometimes too many USB devices can really affect performance. Try reducing the number of USB devices connected to the netbook or try using a powered USB hub.

- **How long is the total USB cable length between the computer and the device?**
  The maximum recommended cable length is 5 meters (16.4 ft.). You may have exceeded that maximum length if you have connected two or more USB extension cords or if you have connected several USB hubs together in a chain.

■ **Are you connected through the same USB port on your computer as you did the last time you used this device on this computer?** Sometimes Windows doesn't recognize a USB device right away if you connect to a port other than the one you used the last time you connected the device to the computer. It may take a few minutes for Windows to relocate the driver, and sometimes you have to manually locate or reinstall the driver.

For best results with USB devices, follow these simple rules:

■ Connect high demand devices like printers, scanners, external hard drives, external DVD drives, wireless network cards, and USB-to-Video adapters directly to USB 2.0 ports on your computer.

■ Try to use unpowered USB external hubs only for lower power devices like keyboards and mice.

■ Use powered external USB hubs if you need more connections than are available through direct ports on the computer, or if you have a netbook or laptop that may be underpowered.

■ Disconnect USB devices that are not in constant use or needed on demand all the time, and only connect them when you need to use them.

■ Avoid extra-long USB cords and runs. For most devices, a 6 to 8 foot cord should be long enough

■ Throw away USB cords that don't work for some devices but work for others

Taming the USB and Computer Cable Jungle

Remember when you were a kid and you had special drawers where you threw all of your important keepsake stuff, and every once in awhile you had to clean it out because you had too much stuff? The same thing can happen with your computer, peripherals, speakers, printers, monitors, and all of the USB, video, power, and network cables connecting them.

Over time, you wind up with a messy tangle of cables across, below, and behind your desk. If you have one computer with many cables, or several computers with many more cables and you often need to move devices between them, it can be a nightmare. Figure 14–35 shows a very mild example of wires crossing each other with no organization or central connection point.

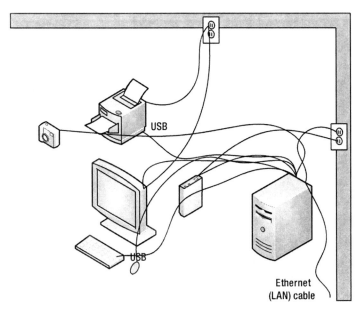

Figure 14–35. *USB, video, and power cables can clutter your desk and workspace.*

I frequently move monitors and devices between several computers, and occasionally add new devices. Every so often, it gets out of hand—much worse than shown in Figure 14–35. After some experimenting and thinking about this, I came up with some strategies that help me clean up my cable messes and make it easier to keep less cluttered. The two guiding principles here are:

- Place your computer, peripherals, and desk accessories where they are most convenient for you.

- Make the cables, hubs, power cords, and power outlets fit where you place things.

To clean up and reorganize a cable mess:

1. **Disconnect all cables and cords from everything.** Make sure any unusual or unique cords or cables are labeled so that you can match them up later.

> **TIP:** Those little power bricks and oversize AC adapter plugs that power a lot of little things often have labels on them that do not match up with the brand or model they are connected to. Before disconnecting these, or whenever you get a new device with one of these oversized plugs, put a label on it or attach a tag with the name of the device it is actually for. So when you find that brick that says Lite On or ACME Electric on it, you can read your label and know it is actually for your printer, scanner, laptop, or stereo speakers.

2. **Count how many USB cables and devices you have.** Compare that to how many USB ports you have on your computer. If you have more USB devices than you have USB ports on your computer, you will need to add more ports through USB hubs.

3. **Count how many power cords you need to plug in for your computer and peripherals.** Don't forget other electrical items around your desk: desk lamps, clocks, paper shredders, telephones, etc., and other electrical devices that may occasionally require a plug, like a vacuum cleaner. Compare that to how many wall outlets are within reach of your computer and components. With typical American electrical code standards, you probably have four, possibly six outlets within reach of your computer. If you have more power cords than outlets, you will need to make up the difference with power strips.

4. **Place your computers, keyboards, mice, speakers, printers, and peripherals *without cords attached*, exactly where you want them.** This is where many of us get into trouble. Instead of placing things where they work best for us, we let the length of our cords, location of the computer, and our wall outlets dictate where we place things.

5. **Measure or eyeball the distances between your computer and your peripherals.**

   You want to be able to bring the USB hubs as close to the peripherals as possible and still be within reach of the computer. If you have lots of peripherals spread across your desk, you may want more than one hub. You will have less cord tangle if you place hubs closer to the peripherals, so that you span most of the distance between the computer, hubs, and peripherals with one long length of cord between the computer and the hub, and multiple short lengths bundled up between the hub and each peripheral.

6. **Measure or eyeball the distances between electrical items and wall outlets.**

   Same principle as with the USB hubs. Bring the power strips as close as possible to the electrical devices with a long power strip cord, and the cords from the devices to the power strip as short as possible.

7. **Make a shopping list for items you will need from your computer/office supply store, and pick up these items as needed:**

   ▨ **Power strips with surge protection**. If you have a lot of oversize adapter plugs add in a few extra outlets for ones that will be covered over by adjoining plugs, or look for specially designed strips that provide extra spacing between plugs. Buy strips with longer cords than you think you will need. Some power strips include USB ports for charging devices without connecting them to your computer while it is on.

- **Powered USB 2.0 hubs**. Be sure to allow a few empty "guest" plug openings for devices like your camera or MP3 player that you occasionally need to connect for downloads but don't leave connected all the time.

- **Hook and loop strips, for bundling together your cords**. Among the chain computer stores, the product I found works best are from Staples: they come in multiple colors, they are reusable, and they are long enough for bundling just about any length of cords.

8. **Plug in the power strips and place the plug-in outlet ends as close to the electrical devices as possible.** When you have the distance set, unplug the power strips from the wall.

9. **Plug in the USB hubs to the computer, and place them as close to the peripherals (not the computer) as possible.**

10. **Working one electrical device at a time, re-attach the power cord to the device, and then plug it into the power strip. Bundle the extra cord length on the power cord with the hook and loop strips, closer to the device than the power strip.**

11. **Connect the USB or monitor cables on each device starting at the device end, and then connect to the computer port or USB hub. Bundle the excess cable length closer to the device than the hub or computer.**

12. **Plug in any other electrical devices such as phones or desk lamps. Bundle the cords closer to device than the wall outlet or power strip, but leave extra slack so that you can move these around easily on your desk.**

Your devices should all be connected to the power strips and USB hubs or ports and the excess cord bundled closer to the device than the power strip or hubs.

13. **Plug in the power strips to the wall.**

14. **Turn on your devices, and make sure they all have power.**

15. **Log on to your computer, and make sure all of the devices and the USB hubs are connected.**

Figure 14–36 is an example of a desktop area cleaned up by relocating some devices to more convenient locations, centralizing the power and USB connections, and bundling excess cables and cords. You can also eliminate cords by using wireless devices and networking.

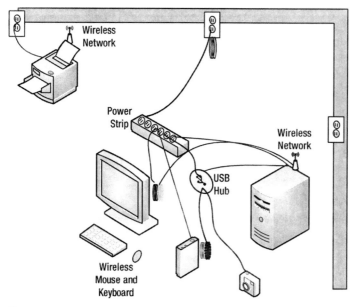

Figure 14–36. *The desktop area is much cleaner because some items have been relocated to more convenient locations, the cords and cables are centralized and bundled, and some devices are now using wireless connections.*

CAUTION: Do not daisy-chain power strips (plug one strip into another). It is a fire hazard, an electrical hazard, and a fire code violation in most locales. Buy strips with as many outlets and as long a cord as possible, so that you can connect fewer strips directly into more wall outlet locations.

Additional cord clutter tips:

- Use wireless keyboards and mice to reduce cords on desktop working area. If you buy a matched keyboard and mouse set, you will also reduce cord clutter because both of these devices will share one transmitter attached to the USB port, instead of two corded connections for a wired mouse and a wired keyboard.

TIP: Don't forget the batteries! Wireless mice and keyboards have batteries that need to be replaced occasionally.

- Use a network printer or wireless printer if you have a home network. This allows you to place your printer in another room instead of the same room as your computers.

- Use a wireless network adapter or card for your computer, instead of a wired Ethernet connection.

NOTE: In some cases, a wireless connection for networking or network printers may be noticeably slower than a wired connection. The newer Wireless N (802.11n) routers and cards can be fairly fast. Sometimes, location can affect performance. So if your wireless networking device is slow, moving the device or your wireless router to a different location may improve performance.

- Move other non-essential electrical devices to another room. You don't have to place your paper shredder in your home office or right next to your desk.

- Combine and reduce devices when possible. With an all-in-one printer, you can reduce four devices (a printer, a fax machine, a scanner, and a copier) down to one device, one USB or network cord, one power cord, and one phone line.

- Reduce your total number of printers. If you only do occasional color photo printing, and your all-in-one printer is satisfactory for regular photos, ditch the separate photo printer and use the drug store or camera shop printing services for large quantities.

Summary

In this chapter you learned the following:

- How to connect monitors and hardware to your computer.

- Windows 7 features that help you connect monitors and hardware.

- Multiple monitor setups.

- How to add more video ports for multiple monitors.

- Aligning monitors so that you can smoothly move from screen to screen.

- Setting up multiple monitors ergonomically.

- Differences between external and internal hardware.

- How to install external peripherals.

- How to install or upgrade internal hardware.

- Managing USB connections and devices.

- Organizing your USB and power cables.

Next Steps

You may find the following related chapters useful:

- Chapter 1: "Customizing And Personalizing Windows"
- Chapter 5: "Installing Programs"
- Chapter 13: "Printing, Faxing, and Scanning"
- Chapter 15:"Connecting to the Internet and Home Networks"
- Chapter 16: "Protecting Your Computer and Data"
- Chapter 17: "Troubleshooting and Maintaining Your Computer"
- Chapter 18: "Using Windows at Work and On the Road"

Connecting to the Internet and Home Networks

It is hard to imagine using a computer without some kind of connection to other computers or the outside world.

An *Internet connection* lets you do all those fun things like surf the Web, e-mail, instant message, and shop online, as well as keep your computer updated with Windows Updates. In this chapter you will learn about connecting to the Internet, including:

- How to connect through wired, wireless, and other connection types.

- How to connect away from home or at work.

A *network* allows you to share your Internet connection with other computers on your network and share files, printers, and storage between the computers. Even if you only have one computer, there are many advantages to creating a small home network. In this chapter, you will learn about the following:

- Creating, changing, or leaving a homegroup.

- Sharing folders and libraries.

- Excluding folders or libraries from homegroup sharing.

- Introduction to sharing printers (See Chapter 13: "Printing, Faxing, and Scanning" to learn all the different ways to set up network printers).

- Viewing, sharing, and storing files and folders with non-Windows 7 computers and devices, such as Windows XP, and Windows Vista, Xbox, Windows Home Server, and Network Attached Storage (NAS).

> **NOTE:** A network is also very important for running and storing backups of all of your computers. See Chapter 16: "Protecting Your Computer and Data" to learn several ways to set up a good backup plan with a home network.

Windows 7 Internet and Network Features

Connecting to the Internet and to a network isn't that complicated. Table 15–1 will help you get familiar with some of the features and hardware you need to set up your Internet and network connections.

Table 15–1. *Necessary Hardware for Connecting to the Internet*

Feature	What It Does
Network and Sharing Center	Displays your current Internet and network connections, connection status, type of connection (wireless or local connection) settings for new network connections, homegroup, adapters, and advanced settings. In Figure 15–1 the Network and Sharing Center shows a good Internet and network connection.

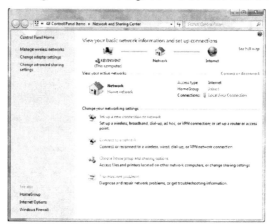

Figure 15–1. *Network and Sharing Center*

Notification Area Icons	Windows 7 Network and Sharing Center provides icons in the notification area, which you can view or click for more information on your connection status, or to open the Network and Sharing Center. There are separate icons for wireless and local (Ethernet, wired) connections. Figure 15–2 shows these icons in their normal state and when they indicate a problem.

 Wireless good, full strength   Wireless trying to connect

 Local connection good   Unidentified network

Figure 15–2. *Icons and their meanings*

Feature	What It Does
Current Connections	When you click a wireless or local connection notification area icon, the corresponding current connections are displayed, depending on the connection type, as shown in Figure 15–3.

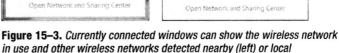

Figure 15–3. *Currently connected windows can show the wireless network in use and other wireless networks detected nearby (left) or local connections (right)*

Device Manager	Sometimes newly added wireless adapters or network cards are not recognized by Windows. Or, a network adapter may have been turned off. You can check the state of all wireless and Ethernet adapters under Network Adapters, as shown in Figure 15–4.

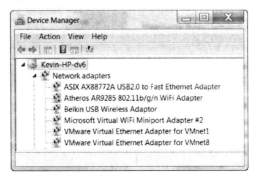

Figure 15–4. *All wireless and Ethernet adapters are listed under Network adapters in Device Manager.*

> **TIP:** To get to Device Manager, click the **Start** button, and in the **Start** menu's search box, type **Device Manager**. In the list that appears, click **Device Manager**.

Feature	What It Does
Troubleshooters	Windows provides several troubleshooters that can help diagnose Internet, network connection, and Homegroup issues: ■ Internet Connections ■ HomeGroup ■ Network Adapter You can access troubleshooters from the **Network and Sharing Center**, or from **Troubleshooting** in **Control Panel**.

Internet and Network Hardware

In addition to the Windows 7 features, there are several key pieces of hardware you need to connect to the Internet and connect your home network. Figure 15–5 shows a simple but typical home network connected to the Internet.

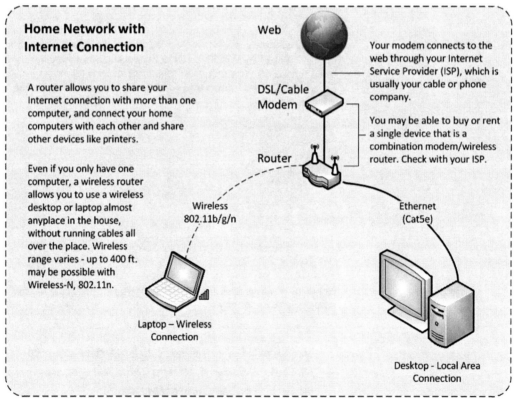

Figure 15–5. *Home network connected to the Internet*

Table 15–2 describes some of the hardware devices and cables used to connect to the Internet and your network.

Table 15–2. *Hardware Devices*

Hardware	What It Does
DSL/Cable modem	A *broadband modem* connects your home network or computer to the Internet. At home, this connection is usually through DSL or cable.
Router	A *router* allows you to share your Internet connection with more than one computer and connect your home computers with each other and share other devices like printers. A router usually has four to six Ethernet jacks, which allows you to connect to devices using Ethernet (Cat5e) cables.
	A *wireless router* allows you to connect computers wirelessly through the router when the computer has a wireless card or adapter. The router may support about six wireless devices and may also provide Ethernet jacks for wired connections. Wireless routers are usually labeled by the wireless standards they support. Most new routers are either wireless G or wireless N. The wireless standard makes a difference because older routers may be much slower than newer ones. Wireless N is the newest and fastest standard. The differences are covered in the "Wireless B/G/N" section.
	Some routers also offer one or two USB jacks so that you can connect an external hard drive or USB printer so that all computers on the network can use them.
Network adapters	Network adapters are the devices on or attached to your computer that provide the network connection to the router. There are two types, wireless and Ethernet.
	Wireless adapters can be internal, built in to the computer, or external (attached via USB or PCMCIA cards). Most wireless adapters are either wireless G or wireless N.
	Wireless networks have grown quite a bit in popularity over the past couple of years, especially with the higher speeds offered by wireless N. Not too long ago, wireless adapters and Ethernet adapters were both standard in laptops, while desktop PCs usually only had Ethernet adapters. If you wanted a wireless adapter on your desktop PC you had to install an internal wireless card, or use a USB wireless adapter. Now it's quite common for desktop PCs to include both Ethernet and wireless adapters.
Wireless B/G/N	There are several different standards for wireless networks. Their long technical names are 802.11b, 802.11g, and 802.11n. Sometimes they are referred to as Wireless B, Wireless G, and Wireless N. There is another standard, 802.11a, but it is rarely used or found in home wireless equipment. Most new computers include support for wireless N, as well as backward compatibility with the older wireless G and wireless B.
	Wireless B is the oldest of the three, and the slowest. Under the best conditions, the network speed is up to 11 megabits per second (Mbps). It has a weaker signal and uses a radio frequency that is prone to interference by cordless phones and microwave ovens. Wireless G is faster, up to 54Mbps,

Hardware	What It Does
	but uses the same radio frequency as wireless B and is still susceptible to interference. Wireless routers and cards that work with wireless G will also work with wireless B, but not the other way around. If you do use a computer with only wireless B on a wireless G network, it will slow down the entire wireless G network to the slower 11Mbps of wireless B.
	Wireless N, or Draft-N, is the latest generation, but it is not a formally approved standard. It promises much faster speeds, greater distance, and less interference. The major wireless manufacturers have different implementations of the wireless N technology, so a wireless N router from one manufacturer may not work as well with a wireless N adapter from another manufacturer. For example, when I use the wireless N adapters built into my newest laptops and desktop computers with a wireless N router by another manufacturer, my network speed is usually 150Mbps. That's much better than my previous 54Mbps wireless G router, but when I use wireless N USB adapters that are the same brand as my wireless N router, my network speed jumps to 300Mbps. So there can be some performance benefit to using the same brand of wireless N adapter as your router.
	Even without matching brands, you should still see much better network speeds with any mix of wireless N adapters and routers over the older wireless G.
Cat5e (Ethernet) cable	The cable used for Ethernet connections is called Cat5e cable. The outside covering of these cables is not color coded, so whether they are gray, blue, or yellow makes no difference. Some manufacturers use different colors to differentiate their cable grades for interior, exterior, straight runs, or for lots of turning inside walls and ceilings.
	You can buy pre-cut Cat5e cable in just about any length, but it can get quite costly if you need many cables or extra-long cables.
	With a little patience and a few tools you can make your own custom length cables for as much as you would pay for a few long precut cables from your local computer store.
	NOTE: Cat5e cable quality can vary. You probably can't always tell good quality from bad by looking, but poorer quality cable may not be able to carry the signals as fast or strong. So your network will seem slow or flaky. One way to test your cable is by switching out a known good cable and a good connection with the suspect cable. If you are buying cable in bulk to make your own, check with your retailer which of their products seem to work best.
	For more information, see "Making Your Own Network Cables" at the end of this chapter.

Hardware	What It Does
Network switch	These little boxes may look a lot like routers because they have a row of Ethernet ports, and more of them. They are different from routers because they are for connecting computers and devices within your network, not used as a gateway to your modem. Figure 15–6 illustrates a home network with a network switch. Most home users will never need more ports than the four to six found on a typical router. But if you have lots of computers and devices and you need or want all of them to have wired connections, a network switch can add much more capacity. Some common sizes for home and hobbyist use are 4, 8, and 16 ports. On a much larger scale, if you use a computer at work, most likely there is a computer room or electrical utility closet with racks of these network switches than can connect hundreds of computers and devices to your network.

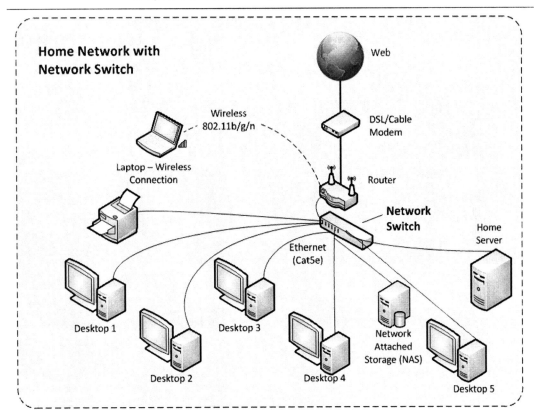

Figure 15–6. *Network switch box connecting multiple PCs, a printer, a server, and a network attached storage device to each other in a network*

Checking Your Current Network Connections

Whether you have one computer or five, one of the first things you'll want to do is connect to the Internet. An Internet connection isn't just for e-mail or surfing the Web. Windows also depends on an Internet connection to activate your copy of Windows—which you may have already done the first time you started Windows 7—and to get the latest Windows updates.

> **TIP:** Chapter 16: "Protecting Your Computer and Data" describes Windows updates and how to apply them to your copy of Windows 7.

Windows 7 provides a handy place to manage your network settings and tasks: the **Network and Sharing Center**. Even if you have not set up a home network, you can get a quick look at what kinds of network connections are already in place. For example, you may have already connected your computer to a digital subscriber line (DSL) or cable modem to connect to the Internet. The first time you start a new computer, it looks for Internet or network connections and attempts to configure them for you. If you don't have a network, the Network and Sharing Center is where you can set it up.

To check your current connections, go to the Network and Sharing Center:

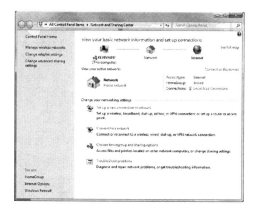

1. Click the Windows **Start** button, and in the **Start** menu's search box, type **Network**.

2. In the results list, under **Control Panel**, click **Network and Sharing Center**. The Network and Sharing Center appears, as shown in Figure 15–7.

Figure 15–7. *The Network and Sharing Center provides a snapshot of your current connections and links for connecting or changing network settings.*

3. In Figure 15–8, the diagram under **View your basic network information and set up connections** shows a computer connected through a network to the Internet. This page doesn't really tell you whether the network uses just a broadband modem or whether there is also a router. Normally, the first time you start your computer, Windows looks for a wired or wireless network connection and prompts you for information to connect to it. However, if you did not set up an Internet connection, your basic connection may be similar to that shown in Figure 15–8.

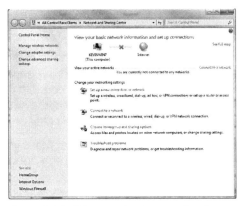

Figure 15–8. *This computer has no network or Internet connection.*

Connecting to the Internet

To connect to the Internet, you need Internet access (usually via DSL or cable) and a broadband modem, or dial-up access through a phone line. If you want to share that Internet access with more than one computer, or you want your computers to share libraries or printers on a network, you will need a router. Technically, you could use a switchbox, but for a few dollars more you can get a wireless router.

> **TIP:** Usually the broadband modem and the router are two separate devices, but some cable or phone companies also offer a combination modem/router or can suggest models you can buy that work with their system.

The router takes the Internet access from your modem and then provides that access to each computer connected to the router. Your computers can connect to the router through a wired connection (also known as an *Ethernet connection*) or a wireless connection (sometimes referred to as *Wi-Fi*).

For wireless connections, you need a wireless router and a wireless card on the computer. Wireless routers also include Ethernet jacks so you can use a wired connection to your computer. The most popular choices for connecting computers in a home network are wired and wireless. In addition, two other wired options use the existing electrical or phone wiring in your house: HomePNA and power line.

Connecting Through a Wireless Network

One of the advantages of a wireless network is that it enables you to use your computer almost any place in the house without having to run long lengths of wires or drill holes through your walls. You can also connect other devices to your wireless network, such as wireless network printers. You can even have your laptop on, move around your house from room to room, and still stay connected.

In many cases, the only extra equipment you need to buy for a wireless network is a wireless router. Almost all new laptop computers have wireless cards built in. You can also use desktop PCs on a wireless network. If your desktop PCs does not have a wireless card built in, you can easily install one or plug in an external Universal Serial Bus (USB) wireless adapter. A USB wireless adapter can be used with laptop computers as well.

> **TIP:** An older computer may already have a wireless card, but it may be wireless G. It will work with newer wireless N routers, but to get the full benefit of the faster wireless N router, upgrade your PCs wireless card or USB adapter to wireless N, too.

If you do need to add a wireless adapter or card, be sure to run the installation program provided by the wireless device manufacturer. If your computer comes with a wireless card already built in, the drivers and software to use it should already be installed.

The **Network and Sharing Center** provides a wizard to walk you through connecting to a wireless network. Before you connect, review the following list to make sure everything else is ready:

- Your wireless router is turned on and is connected to your broadband modem.
- Your computer has a wireless card that is turned on.
- The computer and the wireless router do not have too many walls or too much distance between them.

First Time Wireless Router Setup

If you are setting up the wireless router for the first time, check the documentation provided with the router. For the initial router setup, you may want to connect the router directly to the computer with an Ethernet cable and complete the router setup before attempting to set up a wireless connection.

> **CAUTION:** When setting up a wireless router, always set an encryption password to prevent unwanted guests from tapping into your network, hacking into your computers, or intercepting data wirelessly between your computer and your router or the Internet.

There are several standards for wireless encryption with very similar sounding acronyms: Wired Equivalent Privacy (WEP), Wi-Fi Protected Access (WPA, and WPA2). WEP is the oldest and the least secure and is not recommended. WPA2 is the most secure and highly recommended. Your wireless router manual and online setup will show you how to set the encryption for your model of router.

It is illegal to tap into somebody else's private wireless network without their permission, even if all you want to do is use it for a free Wi-Fi connection.

To connect to your wireless network:

1. Make sure your broadband modem is on.

2. In Windows on your computer, click the **Start** button, and then type **Network** in the **Start** menu's search box.

3. Click **Network and Sharing Center**.

4. Click **Set up a new connection or network,** as shown in Figure 15–9.

Figure 15–9. *Click Set up a new connection or network*

5. Click **Connect to the Internet** and then click **Next,** as shown in Figure 15–10.

Figure 15–10. *Click Connect to the Internet*

6. In the Connect to the Internet window, click **Wireless**, as shown in Figure 15–11.

Figure 15–11. *Click Wireless in the Connect to the Internet Window*

Windows will detect any nearby wireless networks and list them. If you live in a densely populated area, you may see other wireless networks listed besides your own. Figure 15–12 lists two possible wireless networks. The green bars indicate their signal strength. The more green bars, the stronger the signal.

Figure 15–12. *Viewing available networks*

7. Click a wireless network, as shown in Figure 15–12.

The network entry will expand to show a Connect button, as shown in Figure 15–13.

8. Select **Connect automatically** (if this is your own network and you plan to use it all the time when you are at home), and then click **Connect**.

If you set up security protection when you previously installed your wireless router, you will be prompted for a network security key. Type the network security key

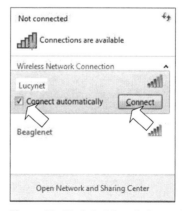

Figure 15–13. *Select the wireless network you want to connect to and then click Connect.*

and then click **OK**. If you don't remember your network security key, check the documentation that came with your wireless router on how to reset the security key.

When your computer is successfully connected to the Internet, your connection will be similar to Figure 15–14.

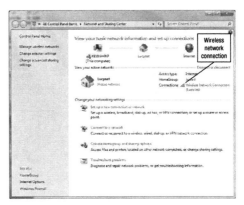

Figure 15–14. *The computer is now connected to the wireless network.*

Extending Your Wireless Network Range with an Access Point

The range of your wireless network (how far from the wireless router your computer can pick up a strong enough signal) depends on the type of wireless technology and the structures in between. Wireless-N has the widest range and is less affected by interference from other electronic devices or physical structures than the older wireless-G or wireless-B.

Sometimes you may not be able to get a good signal for all wireless devices within a large house, in an outlying structure (like a guest house, boat house, workshop), or because you have to place the router at one end of the house where the modem is.

You can extend your range by adding an *access point.* An access point device is either another wireless router that can be configured as an access point or a wireless device designed strictly as an access point. An access point extends the range of your existing wireless network without creating a new wireless network, as shown in Figure 15–15.

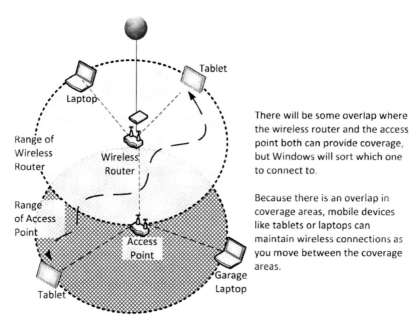

There will be some overlap where the wireless router and the access point both can provide coverage, but Windows will sort which one to connect to.

Because there is an overlap in coverage areas, mobile devices like tablets or laptops can maintain wireless connections as you move between the coverage areas.

Figure 15–15. *Extending wireless range with access points*

Adding an access point is not much more complicated than setting up a router. In theory, most access point models should work with any brand or model of wireless router. However, for best results, use an access point by the same manufacturer as your wireless router. With some routers, you can use the same model for both the router and the access point. For more information about access points, start with the documentation for your router or go to your router manufacturer's web site.

Connecting Through a Wired Network

A wired network requires a separate network cable from your router to each computer. If you are adding a wired network to an existing house, that may mean running a hundred or more feet of network cable, possibly through your attic, through a crawl space, outside your house, or through walls. Sometimes you can make this less noticeable by bringing the cable through the ceiling or floor of a closet and then running it openly on the floor along a wall.

Newer Construction May Already Be Pre-wired for Home Networks

Some new homes and building construction are already pre-wired with cabling for computer networks, just like your electrical lines, telephone lines, and cable TV. The cable used for home networks, Cat5e, can also be used for telephone wiring. However, there is also wire made only for telephones that can't be used for computer networks because it has fewer wires. The Cat5e cable contains eight color-coded wires, and electricians use different combinations of these wires depending on whether they are for your phone or your computer network. If you are fortunate enough to already have this network wiring prewired, hooking up your computer is a snap—connect your router to a central location where all of the room cables come together, and then hook up your computer to a jack in one of the rooms.

Ethernet Jacks

Almost all computers, laptop or desktop, have an Ethernet jack (also known as RJ-45), so you rarely have to add anything to the computer except the cable. The network cable can be quite expensive if you buy premeasured lengths with the jacks on both ends ready to connect. But if you are running long lengths of network cable throughout your house, it will be worth your time to learn how to make your own cables. The Cat5e cable is available in bulk at most home improvement centers in rolls from 50 to 100 feet. To complete the cable, you'll need plastic jacks and a special crimping tool to hold the wires in the jacks. For the price of two precut 25-foot lengths of network cable, you can almost pay for a 500-foot roll, the jacks, and the crimping tool. For more information, see "Making Your Own Network Cables" at the end of this chapter.

For a wired network, you can use either a wired-only router or a wireless router. Wireless routers usually have about four to six jacks for wired connections plus the wireless connections.

Because most houses aren't already wired for computer networks, a wired network may seem like a lot of extra work. However, there are several reasons for using a wired network or connection:

- A wired network is faster than wireless-G or wireless-B networks. Depending on the router and network switch (if used), wired networks can run at 10, 100, or 1000Mbps. The common speed for most wired home networks has been 100Mbps, or almost twice as fast as the 802.11g wireless network's 54Mbps. Wireless-N can potentially run much faster than a 100Mbps wired network—150, 300, or more depending on how the manufacturer designs its implementation of wireless-N.

- Wired networks aren't affected by interference from other devices in the house. If you work from home and connect to your work through a virtual private network (VPN), a wireless network connection may occasionally drop your connections long enough that you have to reconnect to your VPN.

■ Some networked devices, like Network Attached Storage (NAS), networked hard drives, or home servers like Windows Home Server require a wired connection to your router—you can't use a wireless connection for those devices. If you download or upload many files or large files, a wired connection is much more reliable because it has twice the speed of, and almost never drops connections like, a wireless network. And if you play online games with your PC, Xbox, or PlayStation, the speed and reliability of the wired connection may give you a slight competitive advantage.

Gigabit (1000Mbps) Connections

Many newer computers, especially those designed for business use, support 1000Mbps (also called 1-gigabit) network connections, and many wired and wireless routers are available that support this faster speed on the wired connection. When shopping for routers or switches that support 1GB speeds, look for labels or specifications such as 10/100/1000 or Gigabit router or switch. Don't worry about whether computers and networks will work with each other if they have different speeds. The routers and network switches will automatically adjust to each other to use their highest common speed.

Connecting To a Wired Network

After you have all of the network wires and outlets in place in your house, connecting to a wired network is even simpler than connecting to a wireless network. When you connect a network cable to your computer, Windows automatically detects the network and connects to it. You will not be prompted for a network security code because it is assumed that anybody who has physical access to connect your router and a computer with an Ethernet cable must be trustworthy.

To connect to the Internet through a wired connection:

1. Turn on your broadband modem if it is not already on.

   Broadband modems are intended to be on and connected to the Internet all the time. Generally, you do not turn off your modem unless you are having problems and want to reset it by turning the power on and off.

2. Connect your broadband modem to your router, using the Ethernet jacks on the modem and the router. If you have the option of using either an Ethernet connection or a USB cable connection, use the Ethernet connection; it's more reliable.

3. Connect the computer to the router with an Ethernet cable.

4. Click the **Start** button, and then type **Network** in the **Start** menu's search box.

5. Click **Network and Sharing Center**.

If all of the wires are connected correctly between the modem, router, or network switch and the computer, your connection should look similar to Figure 15–16.

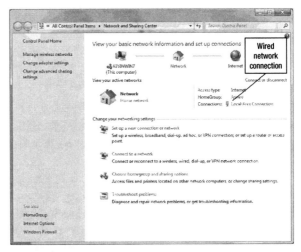

Figure 15–16. *The Network and Sharing Center shows that this computer is connected to the network through a wired Local Area Connection.*

If the connection is not working, your connection may look similar to Figure 15–17 or Figure 15–18.

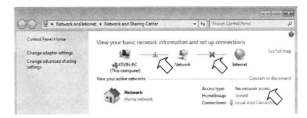

Figure 15–17. *A previous local area connection is broken, and there is no network access.*

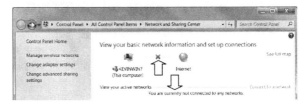

Figure 15–18. *Windows did not detect any current or previous wired or wireless network connections.*

Generally, after you've connected all of the cables from your modem to your router to your computer, that's all you need to do for a wired network connection.

Troubleshooting Home Network Connections

If your network information is similar to one of the examples in Figures 15–17 or 15–18, check the following:

1. In Network and Sharing Center, click Troubleshoot problems, or go to Troubleshooting in Control Panel and try the Internet Connections, HomeGroup, or Network Adapter troubleshooters.

   - Are all of the cables connected—from the cable coming into the house to the modem, from the modem to the router, and from the router to your computer?

   - Is your broadband modem on? Is the router on? On most modems and routers, small, green LED lights indicate that the connections are working. If there are no lights, your modem power may be off. If there are yellow or red lights, there is a problem at the device. If all the lights are green but the connection is still not working, one of your cable connections may be faulty. Try plugging and unplugging each cable or replacing each cable with another cable to see whether you can isolate a defective cable or connection. Sometimes you may need to reset the modem or router by turning it off for a minute or so and then turning it back on. Check the documentation for the modem or router.

   - Contact your cable or DSL provider to make sure their network is working. Occasionally their networks go offline because of problems or for regular maintenance. Usually these providers try to schedule maintenance for the least busy times of the week, such as very late night or early morning.

Connecting Through a PowerLine or HomePNA Network

Though not as common as Ethernet or wireless networks, PowerLine and phone line (HomePNA) networks are alternatives. A PowerLine network uses the electrical wiring in your house to carry network data between computers. A HomePNA network (not to be confused with phone dial-up or DSL) uses the existing phone wiring and jacks to connect your computers. One of the advantages of either of these systems is that they require no new wiring in your house, and the adapters to connect your computers to the network are fairly inexpensive—comparable in cost to the adapters and equipment used for wireless networks. The network speeds vary but are comparable to wired and wireless network speeds.

Some networking equipment manufacturers offer systems that can use a combination of PowerLine or HomePNA networks with wireless networks.

> **NOTE:** PowerLine and HomePNA adoption and equipment availability varies worldwide. Since electrical current standards and voltages vary, not all equipment works in all locales. Check with your local computer retailers for equipment that is compatible with your local power and telephone utilities.

Connecting to a Homegroup

Windows 7 introduces **homegroups** as an easy way to share files and printers with other computers in a home network. The HomeGroup feature is available only on Windows 7 computers and works only with other computers that are running Windows 7. If you have other computers on your home network running Windows Vista or Windows XP, you can still share files and printers by using the File and Printer Sharing features in those systems.

When you first start a computer running Windows 7, it will automatically create a homegroup if it doesn't detect one already in place on your home network. If a homegroup already exists, Windows 7 will prompt you to join that homegroup.

The purpose of joining a homegroup is to share files and printers among Windows 7 computers in a home network.

There are many options for sharing in a homegroup. You can specify whether to join the computer to the homegroup, but users must specify what they want to share from their libraries and printers: pictures, music, videos, documents, and printers.

Creating a Homegroup

A homegroup is created the first time you start the first Windows 7 computer on your home network. After the homegroup is created, when you add other Windows 7 computers to your home network and go to the HomeGroup settings, you will be prompted to join the homegroup created by the first Windows 7 computer.

To create a homegroup for the first Windows 7 computer on your home network:

1. Click the **Start** button, and then type **homegroup** in the **Start** menu's search box.

2. Click **HomeGroup**. Since this is the first Windows 7 computer on your home network, you will be prompted to create a homegroup, as shown in Figure 15–19.

Figure 15–19. *Windows can guide you through setting up a homegroup.*

3. Click **Create a homegroup**. The next screen prompts you to choose what you'd like to share with other computers in your homegroup, as shown in Figure 15–20. Most items are preselected, except for Documents, which tend to be more private or individual. You may want to select Documents if you regularly work on many of your documents from more than one computer in your homegroup.

The settings for what you select to share apply only to the current user. Each user must specify their settings by logging on to the computer under his or her own account.

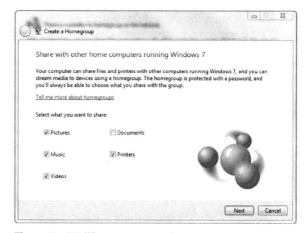

Figure 15–20. *When you create a homegroup, you can specify what you want to share from your computer with other computers in the homegroup.*

4. Select or clear the check boxes to specify what to share and then click **Next**. In the next screen, shown in Figure 15–21, Windows displays the password for your homegroup. You will need to type this password on each computer in your home network to join the homegroup. The password is case sensitive.

5. Follow the instructions on your screen and then click **Finish**.

After you have set up the first computer in a homegroup, when you add other Windows 7 computers to your home network, they will detect the homegroup and offer to join it.

Figure 15–21. *Windows generates a homegroup password that other Windows 7 computers in your home network will need in order to join the homegroup.*

DIFFERENCES BETWEEN HOMEGROUPS AND WORKGROUPS

In previous versions of Windows, membership in a home network was through workgroups. Like homegroups, workgroups provided file and printer sharing, but not as easily or smoothly.

You can have more than one workgroup in a home network, though each computer can belong to only one workgroup at a time. Windows and other programs or devices that access home networks often used the workgroup name Workgroup or MSHOME. You can also create a workgroup with a name of your own choosing. In the past, people had problems sharing files or printers in a home network because the computers were using different workgroup names. If you wanted to share through a workgroup, you had to add all of the computers to the same workgroup. On each computer that you changed the workgroup name, you had to restart the computer so that it could join the new workgroup.

In Windows 7, there is only one homegroup in a home network. You don't have to worry about which name to specify because all the computers in a home network use the same homegroup. To add a computer to a workgroup, you just need to provide the homegroup password created for the first homegroup computer, and then specify what you want to share from each computer.

Joining a Homegroup

To join a Windows 7 computer to the homegroup:

1. Click the **Start** button, and then type **homegroup** in the **Start** menu's search box.

2. Click **HomeGroup**. Windows detects that another computer has already created a homegroup and offers to join the homegroup, as shown in Figure 15–22.

Figure 15–22. *Windows notifies you that another computer has already created a homegroup that you can join.*

3. Click **Join now**. The next screen is similar to the one shown when you create a homegroup. It prompts you to choose what you'd like to share with other computers in your homegroup, as shown in Figure 15–23. Most items are preselected, except for Documents.

4. Select or clear the check boxes to specify what to share and then click **Next**.

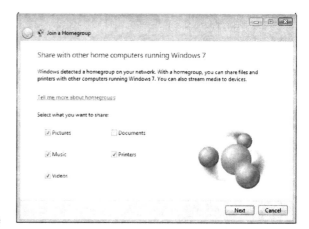

Figure 15–23. *When you join a homegroup, you can select what you want to share with other computers in the homegroup.*

5. In the next screen, shown in Figure 15–24, Windows requests the homegroup password. If you don't know the password, click **Where can I find the homegroup password?** and follow the instructions to locate it.

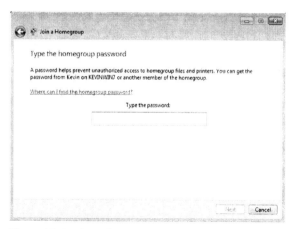

Figure 15–24. *Type the homegroup password, or click the link to find it.*

6. Type the password that was created by the first computer in the homegroup, as shown in Figure 15–25.

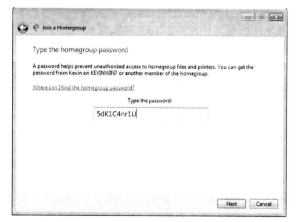

Figure 15–25. *To join the homegroup, enter the homegroup password.*

Windows verifies the password and then confirms that you have joined the homegroup, as shown in Figure 15–26.

7. Click **Finish**.

Figure 15–26. *You have successfully joined the homegroup.*

Changing Homegroup Settings

When you create a homegroup or add a computer to a homegroup, the settings are applied to the current user. If you have several other users on the computer, each will have to specify what to share by logging in to his or her own user account.

You can change the sharing, password, and other advanced settings through the **Change homegroup settings** page.

To change the homegroup settings:

1. Click the **Start** button, and in the **Start** menu's search box, type **homegroup**.

2. In the list that appears, click **Choose homegroup and sharing options**. The **Change homegroup settings** window appears. Yours will be similar to Figure 15–27, but the options and commands listed vary depending on whether any sharing settings were previously specified, or whether this is the first time you have viewed the homegroup settings.

Figure 15–27. *The Change homegroup settings window provides links to change or view the homegroup passwords and sharing selections.*

Leaving the Homegroup

The most common reasons for joining a homegroup are to share files and to share printers. If you have no need to share either, you can leave the homegroup. This does not remove or delete any files; it only removes them from access by the homegroup.

To leave the homegroup, click the **Leave the homegroup** link on the **Change homegroup settings** page.

Excluding Files or Folders from Sharing

Sometimes you may want to exclude specific files or folders from sharing—without blocking an entire library type. For example, you may have a Documents library that you want to share, except for a few confidential or private documents. Even if you select to share your Documents library, you can still exclude files or folders in that library from sharing.

To exclude or limit specific files or folders from sharing:

1. Navigate to the folders or files you want to exclude.

2. Right-click the file or folder, and on the **Share with** menu, click one of the following:

   ▓ **Nobody**: If you don't want to share this file or folder with anybody.

   ▓ **Homegroup (Read):** If you want people to be able to read but not change the file.

   ▓ **Homegroup (Read/Write):** If you want people to be able to read or change the file.

   ▓ **Specific people:** If you want to select specific people with whom to share it.

You can't exclude files or folders within the Public folders, for example `C:\Users\Public`.

Upgrading to Windows 7 to Use Homegroup

The preceding section described how to share files through a homegroup, and the following section describes how to share printers through a homegroup. But what if you have computers in your home network that are not running Windows 7? If computers in your home network are running Windows XP or Windows Vista, you can use their version of file and printer sharing. Or if your other computers are running Windows Vista (and none are running Windows XP), you might also consider upgrading the Windows Vista computers to Windows 7. According to Microsoft, most computers that can run Windows Vista should also be able to run Windows 7 just as well if not better.

For most people, though, upgrading computers to or replacing them with Windows 7 is not necessary. The "Installing a Printer That Is Not Attached to a Homegroup Computer" section in Chapter 13: "Printing, Faxing, and Scanning" and the "Sharing Files with Computers or Devices that Are Not Part of a Homegroup" section in this chapter describe how to do this without upgrading or replacing computers, or buying any extra equipment.

Sharing Printers on a Home Network

There are several reasons to connect and share printers on a home network. You can:

- Print to a network printer from any computer on the network.
- Place your printer anyplace you have wired or wireless access in your house.
- Reduce printer ink and paper costs by using fewer printers.

See Chapter 13: "Printing, Faxing, and Scanning" to learn how to:

- Choose printers.
- Install printers on your local computer.
- Install and share network printers attached to home servers and network attached storage (NAS).
- Use printers with homegroups in Windows 7, and with File and Printer Sharing in Windows XP and Windows Vista.

Sharing Files with Computers or Devices that Are Not Part of a Homegroup

If all of your computers on your home network are running Windows 7, you can manage file sharing with a homegroup. If you have a mixture of Windows 7, Windows Vista, and Windows XP computers on your home network, you can still share files, but the steps are slightly different for each version of Windows.

Because you can't use a homegroup, in order for the computers to recognize and share files with each other, they need to belong to the same workgroup. The default name that Windows assigns to workgroups is MSHOME, so most if not all of your computers may already belong to that workgroup. If some computers belong to different workgroups, you can change the workgroup name on each computer until they all have the same workgroup name.

Viewing and Changing the Workgroup Name on Windows XP

To view and change the workgroup name on a Windows XP computer:

1. On your Windows XP computer, click the **Start** button, right-click **My Computer**, and then click **Properties**. The **System Properties** page is displayed, as shown in Figure 15–28.

Figure 15–28. *The System Properties page in Windows XP*

2. On the **Computer Name Changes** page, type the workgroup name you want to use for all computers on your home network and then click **OK**, as shown in Figure 15–29. Click **OK** again to close the **System Properties** dialog box.

Figure 15–29. *Change the workgroup name to the name you want to use for all computers on your home network.*

Viewing and Changing the Workgroup Name on Windows Vista or Windows 7

To view and change the workgroup name on a Windows Vista or Windows 7 computer:

1. Click the **Start** button, right-click **Computer**, and then click **Properties**. The **System** page is displayed, as shown in Figure 15–30.

2. If the workgroup name is correct, close this window. If it is not correct, under **Computer name, domain, and workgroup settings**, click **Change settings**.

Figure 15–30. *The Windows Vista System page looks identical to the Windows 7 System page.*

3. Click **Continue** if prompted for permission by **User Account Control**. The **System Properties** page **Computer Name** tab is displayed, as shown in Figure 15–31.

4. Click **Change**. The **Computer Name/Domain Changes** window appears, as shown in Figure 15–32.

Figure 15–31. *Windows Vista System Properties Computer Name tab. Windows 7 displays an identical page.*

5. On the **Computer Name/Domain Changes** page, type the workgroup name you want to use for all computers on your home network, and then click **OK** twice.

After you have changed all computers to the same workgroup, and restarted them so that the name takes effect, all computers should be able to detect each other on the network. When all computers on your home network belong to the same workgroup, they can share folders and printers.

Figure 15–32. *The Computer Name/Domain Changes window provides text boxes for renaming the computer or workgroup.*

Viewing and Accessing Shared Folders on Your Network

Each version of Windows has a slightly different way of displaying the shared folders and computers on your home network. You can check to see what's shared, so if there is something that you want to share that's hidden, or something that's shared that you want private, you can go back to the computer that contains the folders and change the sharing settings.

Accessing Shared Folders from Windows XP

To view from a Windows XP computer what computers are available and what they are sharing on your network, follow these steps:

1. Click the **Start** button and then click **My Network Places** to display the folders that are shared and on what computer, similar to Figure 15–33.

2. Perform any of the following tasks to see what is available:

   - Double-click a folder icon to open it and access files in the folders that are shared.

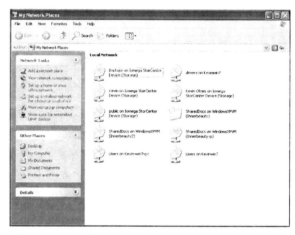

Figure 15–33. *Windows XP lists shared folders on computers and network storage devices on your home network.*

3. View what is in your workgroup, by computer or device. In the **Network Tasks** list in the left column, click `View workgroup computers`. Figure 15–34 displays the computers and storage devices in the MSHOME workgroup. There are fewer icons displayed here than in the previous figure of shared folders, because some computers or storage devices in the previous figure had more than one shared folder.

Figure 15–34. *A list of computers and storage devices in the MSHOME workgroup*

- Open a computer or device in the list and view the shared folders and printers, as shown in Figure 15–35.

Figure 15–35. *The workgroup computer Kevinwin7 contains several folders and printers that are shared.*

Accessing Shared Folders from Windows Vista

To view from a Windows Vista computer what computers are available and what they are sharing on the home network, follow these steps:

1. Click the **Start** button and then click **Network**. The **Network** window displays the computers and devices that are shared on the home network, similar to Figure 15–36. Windows Vista also displays other devices besides computers and storage devices. In this example, the **Network** list includes a wireless router, WGR614V9.

Figure 15–36. *Shared network devices as displayed on a Windows Vista computer*

2. Double-click a computer or device to view what folders and printers are shared. Windows Vista displays the contents, similar to Figure 15–37.

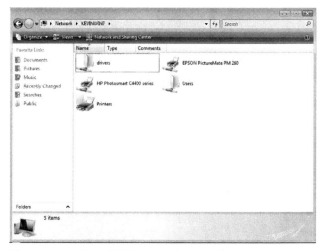

Figure 15–37. *Shared folders and printers available on the computer KEVINWIN7*

Adding the Network Command to the Start Menu for Easy Access

1. You can make it easy to access your network by adding the `Network` command to the **Start** menu:

2. Right-click the **Start** button and then click **Properties**.

3. On the **Start Menu** tab, click the **Customize** button.

4. In the **Customize Start Menu** dialog box, scroll through the list until you find the **Network** check box, and then select it.

Accessing Shared Folders from Windows 7

To view from a Windows 7 computer what computers are available and what they are sharing on the home network, follow these steps:

1. Click the **Start** button, and in the **Start** menu's search box, type **Network**. In the list that appears, click **Network**.

    The Network window displays the computers and devices that are shared on the home network, similar to Figure 15–38. Windows 7 provides grouping and more detail about the devices on the network than Windows Vista.

    Figure 15–38. *Windows 7 groups network devices by type in the Network window.*

2. Double-click a computer to view what is shared. Windows 7 displays the shared contents, similar to Figure 15–39.

    Figure 15–39. *Folders and printers shared on the computer KEVIN-PC64HP, as seen from a Windows 7 computer*

Sharing a Folder If It Does Not Appear Available From Another Computer

After you've added all of your computers to the same workgroup, you may still need to mark folders in order for them to be shared with other computers in the workgroup. There are three ways to share files in Windows 7:

- Create or join a homegroup, as described previously in this chapter. This method is available only for Windows 7 computers.

- Add folders to a public or shared folder. You can do this with Windows XP, Windows Vista, and Windows 7 computers. You can share a folder locally with other users on the same computer, or you can share the folder with other users on this computer and users on the network.

- Specify who can view or change a folder. You can do this with Windows Vista and Windows 7 computers.

The easiest way to broadly share files and folders with other users on your computer or any computer on the home network is to place them in special folders called Shared Documents (Windows XP) or Public Documents (Windows Vista and Windows 7).

> **TIP:** See Chapter 2: "Checking Out Libraries" to learn more about public folders and libraries.

In Windows XP, the shared folder is named Shared Documents in the folder list of **My Computer** and is usually located at `C:\Documents and Settings\All Users\Documents`.

There are more options for sharing than just adding the Shared Documents folder, such as sharing the folder on the network and giving it a share name. The following procedures provide additional sharing options:

- Sharing a Folder on Windows XP

- Sharing a Folder on Windows Vista

- Sharing a Folder on Windows 7

Sharing a Folder on Windows XP

To share a folder on Windows XP, follow these steps:

1. Navigate to the folder in Windows Explorer.

2. Right-click the folder and then click Sharing and Security. The properties for the folder are displayed, similar to Figure 15–40.

If some options are grayed out, that means they are not available. Follow the instructions and links in the dialog box to enable sharing as needed. In this example, the

Curling League folder is automatically made private because it is inside another folder, My Documents, which is private.

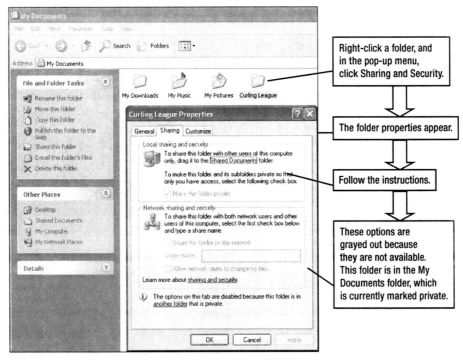

Figure 15–40. *The sharing settings of a folder in My Documents*

TIP: For more information sharing and hiding folders in Windows XP, search the Windows XP help. Click the Start menu, and then click Help.

Sharing a Folder on Windows Vista

To share a folder on Windows Vista, follow these steps:

1. Navigate to the folder in **Windows Explorer**.

2. Right-click the folder and then click **Share**. The **File Sharing** dialog box appears.

3. Click the down arrow to the left of the **Add** button, and then click who you want to give sharing access to. Figure 15–41 shows the list of users who can be given access on this computer. As the user logged in to the computer at this time, you automatically have full access.

Figure 15–41. *You can share a folder with any, all, or no users on this computer.*

4. Click **Add**. When the name appears in the list, you can change the permission level. By default, when you add a user, the permission level is Reader. Continue adding users if needed.

5. After adding your last user, click **Share**.

Sharing a Folder on Windows 7

To share a folder on Windows 7, follow these steps:

1. Navigate to the folder in **Windows Explorer**.

2. Right-click the folder and then click **Share with**. A submenu appears, as shown in Figure 15–42.

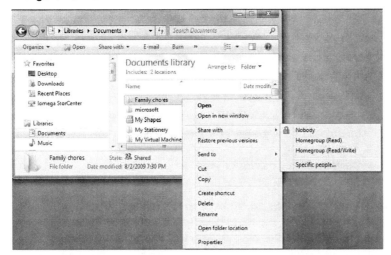

Figure 15–42. *Windows 7 provides several options for sharing a folder.*

3. Click one of the following:

   ▪ **Nobody:** To keep the folder completely private. Only you will be able to access it when you are logged on to this computer. If you select this option, Windows applies it and you are finished.

   ▪ **Homegroup (Read):** To allow any user in the homegroup to read but not add, change, or delete files in the folder. If you select this option, Windows applies it and you are finished.

   ▪ **Homegroup (Read/Write):** To allow any user in the homegroup to read, add, change, or delete files in the folder. If you select this option, Windows applies it and you are finished.

   ▪ **Specific people**: To select users and their permission level from the list of users on this computer. If you select this option, the **File Sharing** dialog box appears, just like the one in Windows Vista. Click the down arrow to the left of the **Add** button, and then click who you want to give sharing access to.

Enhancing Network Security

Networks connect computers to each other and to the outside world (the Internet). This exposes your computer and network to all sorts of threats from outside, and even from other users within the network. This section highlights some security issues and solutions specific to home networks.

> **NOTE:** See Chapter 16: "Protecting Your Computer and Data" to learn how to set up anti-virus and anti-spyware software plus firewalls to protect your computer and your network from attacks and intrusion, as well as how to protect your data from loss and hardware failures with a good backup, recovery, and disaster recovery plan.

A home network is only as safe as its weakest link, whether that link be a particular user or a particular machine. The following list of ten good ways to make your network safer is by no means all that you should do to protect your network, but they are good practices that are worth the time and effort.

- **Use a wireless encryption key for your wireless router.** When you install a wireless router, follow the instructions to create a wireless encryption key. Though there are several types of encryption methods offered with similar-sounding names, avoid using WEP, which is older and not very secure. Use WPA2. If you don't encrypt your wireless router, anybody can tap into your wireless network if they can get within range. Some of the newer wireless routers have a very large range. For example, when I turn on a laptop at home with wireless networking turned on, my computer detects anywhere from one to four other wireless networks from neighboring houses. If I can see their wireless networks, they can see mine. If you live in a higher-density neighborhood, such as apartments or dormitories, you will see many more nearby networks, and more people will detect yours.

- **When using public wireless hotspots, assume the worst and use the highest security settings.** When you first connect to a wireless hotspot, Windows may prompt you to verify whether you feel safe connecting to this new unknown connection. Even if you do trust the Wi-Fi service provider, use the Public profile recommended by Windows. Whether it be a free service at your library or a subscription service at your local coffee shop, assume that somebody could intercept your data as you surf the Internet or use your e-mail. Do not perform any kind of banking, financial, or shopping tasks from a public hotspot.

- **Restrict what types of programs users on your network can download and install.** Free doesn't always mean free. A free screensaver program may have a virus or spyware embedded in it. Popular file-sharing services for swapping videos or music files may require unsafe access through your Windows firewall, and some of these services may violate copyright laws. Downloading many videos may soon take up a lot of your hard disk or storage space.

- **Make sure all computers on the network are up-to-date with the latest Windows updates, antivirus, and antispyware software.** Turn on automatic updating for any of these types of programs. One unprotected computer on your network can easily infect other protected computers on your network because computers within a network trust each other more than they do computers outside the network. For more information, see Chapter 9: "Surfing the Web."

- **Make sure all users have their own accounts, and that all accounts on all computers require a password.** If your laptop or desktop PC gets lost or stolen, it does no good to have passwords for most of the user accounts if one has no password. Hackers could access your password-protected accounts by logging on with the account that has no password. For more information about creating user accounts, see Chapter 2: "Checking Out Libraries," and for keeping your computer safe, see Chapter 9: "Surfing the Web."

- **Make sure you have a password reset disk for every computer on your network.** If everybody or most users have administrator-level permissions on a computer, they may be able to change the passwords of other users on the computer. With a password reset disk, you can recover control over your computer.

- **Do not give anybody any passwords for any account on your computers.** Set up a guest account for limited access to web browsing or e-mail. Typically, when you log in with your user account, you also have other programs that have your personal user accounts such as e-mail, instant messaging, web sites, shopping sites, and so forth. Some of these accounts, or Windows itself, may offer to remember to save your name and password so that you don't have to enter it the next time you visit the site or check the e-mail account. If you give somebody access to your user account, you also give them access to any account with a saved password. If you have a short-term visitor, you can set up a limited guest account. If they are going to be visiting longer term, you can set up a regular user account on the computer, and then remove the account when they leave. For more information, see Chapter 2: "Checking Out Libraries."

- **Back up every computer and storage device with another computer or storage device.** Windows 7 provides backup and recovery software that will help you protect the data on your computer. The Windows operating system and applications can be reinstalled from the original disks. But unless you back up your pictures, files, documents, music, videos, and so forth, you won't have any way to recover them if your computer crashes, is stolen, or is irreparably damaged. Saving all of your important files on an external drive or storage device is not enough. If the only place you store important files for long-term storage and safekeeping is a single storage device, you need to back up that storage device, too. Most backup programs send the backups to a separate location from the original place the data came from. Many external hard drives and storage devices (such as network-attached storage) come with or have built-in backup and recovery programs. Use them. For more information about backup and recovery, see Chapter 6: "Using WordPad, Paint, and Accessories."

- **Do not share everything with every user on the home network.** People accidently delete or move files all the time. One of the reasons for having separate user accounts is so that you can control access to your files. If a member of your family has just about filled up the hard drive with downloaded videos, you don't want them to start deleting your stuff to make room for their downloads. Use Public folders for files that you want to share with other users or be selective (such as sharing your music, pictures, and video folders, but not your other documents).

- **Encourage every user on your home network to use the same user account name and password on every computer they use in the network.** This is partly practicality and partly security. Sometimes when accessing files, printers, or devices on another computer in your network, you may be prompted for an authorized user account and password. If you use the same username John on every computer and the same password with it, you won't have to worry about which password was used with which John account on each computer. For more information, see Chapter 2: "Checking Out Libraries."

Making Your Own Network Cables

There are many names for the network cables used to connect computers and devices to routers, switchboxes, modems, and each other. Ethernet, LAN cables, Cat5e, Cat6, or network patch cables are the most common names. Most home users rarely need more than a few of these, and you can buy them in convenient standard lengths from 7' to 25' with the plugs already on the end. Those are usually more than long enough for connections within a room.

> **NOTE:** Cat6 cable is more expensive and harder to work with than Cat5e cable. For most do-it-yourself home use, Cat5e is just fine. If you are having your house professionally wired, the installer may want to use Cat6 because is rated for higher speed and bandwidth than Cat5e.

There are some situations where you can't use wireless connections and must use a network patch cable. If you need more than a few cables, or longer lengths, it's much cheaper to buy the tools and supplies and make your own cables.

The most common reasons for using and making your own network patch cables are:

Purpose	Explanation
Connect a home server or network attached storage	Most home servers or network attached storage devices require a wired connection to a router or network switch.
Faster connection speeds than wireless connections	Ethernet connections can operate at 10, 100, or 1000Mbps, depending on your network switch, router, and network adapter in your computer. Almost all equipment supports at least 100Mbps, and many also support 1000Mbps (1 Gigabit). Even at 100Mbps, Ethernet is faster than wireless-B (11Mbps) and Wireless-G (54Mbps). Wireless-N is faster than 100Mbps Ethernet, with speeds of up to 150, 300, or 450Mbps. But at its fastest, wireless-N is slower than 1 Gigabit Ethernet.
More stable connections than wireless connections	Even with strong wireless connections using a wireless-N router and adapters, sometimes wireless connections just drop. It could be interference by another electronic device, problems with the wireless card in your computer, or some other phantom problem that pops up from time to time. With a wired network connection, it usually takes less time to get to the Internet after you start up your computer. My experience with wired network connections is that the only time I lose a connection is when I physically disconnect a network cable.

Network Cable Tools and Supplies

Your shopping list is very short and sweet. All of these items are available at most home improvement stores, hardware stores, and computer stores. The items you need are shown in Figure 15–43.

Figure 15–43. *Tools and parts needed for making your own Ethernet cables*

Table 15–3 describes these tools and parts in more detail.

Table 15–3. *Tools and Parts for Creating Your Own Cables*

Item	Description
Cat5e cable	Usually sold in spools. In smaller lengths like 100 feet, it may be rolled up in a package. Inside the cable are eight color-coded wires, twisted together in pairs.
	When you connect the cable to plugs, these wires need to be untwisted and arranged in a specific order in the plug.
	The example shown here was a 250 foot roll; it cost approximately $30 at local home improvement store. Online, the same chain offers a 1,000 foot spool for approximately the same price. Your home improvement may offer other choices, such as:
	▓ **Cable by the foot**. Many home improvement stores sell just about every kind of electrical cable by the foot. It may be cheaper per foot when you buy a large roll of 250-1,000 feet, but if you do not need that much cable, you can still save money by buying just the quantity you do need.
	▓ **"Plenum" or "Riser" Cat5e cable in rolls**. This is for more for wiring an entire house during construction. You can use this for indoors, but it will cost more; for most in-home use, it's not necessary.
	▓ **Cat6 cable**. This is like Cat5e cable but rated for extremely high and intensive network traffic, which you are not likely to encounter in home use. You can use it in place of Cat5e cable, but it is more expensive. Cat6 cable is also trickier to work with and may require a lot more skill splicing wires and connecting plugs.
RJ-45 data plugs	These are the connector plugs where the eight tiny wires from the Cat5e cable go in one end, and the other end has eight contacts (pins) similar to a phone jack (which only has six and is smaller). That end goes into your computer, wall jack, or router. The plugs are usually sold in packs of 25 or 50, and cost about $10-$18. It takes some practice to make your own cables, so it's better to buy more than you think you will need for your current projects.

Item	Description
Modular Data Plug Crimping Tool	Cat5e cable + RJ-45 plugs on each end = Network cable.

Well, almost. You need a special tool to cut the cable wire and crimp the plug after you insert the wire. This tool does four things:

■ Cuts the cable to length from the spool.

■ Strips the outer sheathing without cutting the wires inside.

■ Trims the ends of the individual wires as needed.

■ Crimps the plug after the wires are inserted. This holds the wires in place in the plug and closes the contacts on the wires inside.

The example shown here, the Ideal 33-296 Modular Plug Kit, includes the crimping tool, 10 RJ-45 data plugs, 10 RJ-11 phone plugs, and interchangeable crimping inserts for both types of plugs. This model costs about $25 at the local home improvement store.

There are other brands and models available; make sure that you don't get a television coaxial cable crimping tool, which may look similar and be in the same general area of a store. |
| **(Optional) Plug boots** | These are not necessary but are helpful in keeping your wires from being bent and strained as they come out of the plug. If you do use these, you must place them on the cable before putting the RJ-45 plugs on the end.

Cost: $6 for package of 25. |

The total cost for tools and parts for 250 feet of network cable: a little less than $80. That's the price I would pay for three precut 25' cables or one 100' cable in a package with the plugs on each end. Instead, I can make ten 25' cables or two 100' cables plus one 50' cable.

Color Coding and Order for RJ-45 plugs

The modular RJ-45 plug has eight pins—the metal contacts you see at the end. There is a specific order that the colored wires must go into those pins, so there are two agreed upon wiring schemes, called T568A and T568B (AT&T). You can use either scheme, as long as you use the same scheme on both ends of the network cable. I use T568B, because that is the scheme I found used on my store-bought cables. Table 15–4 illustrates the two wiring schemes, and Figure 15–44 shows an RJ-45 plug using T568B.

Table 15–4. *Wiring Schemes*

Pin	Wire ColorT568A	Wire ColorT568B
1	white/green	white/orange
2	green	orange
3	white/orange	white/green
4	blue	blue
5	white/blue	white/blue
6	orange	green
7	white/brown	white/brown
8	brown	brown

Figure 15–44. *RJ-45 plug using T568B wiring*

To make a network cable:

1. Cut the cable to desired length with the crimping tool, as shown in Figure 15–45.

    Measure twice, cut once. It is better to add extra than to come up short and have to start all over again with another cable.

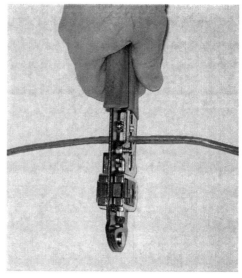

Figure 15–45. *Measure the amount of cable you need, and then cut it.*

2. Strip about 1.5 inches of the outer sheathing off of each end, exposing the eight inner wires as shown in Figure 15–46.

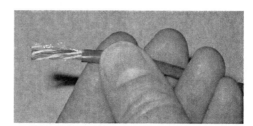

Figure 15–46. *Remove the sheathing without cutting the wires inside.*

3. (Optional) Place plug boot on end of cable before separating the wires, as shown in Figure 15–47. Slide it up the cable, and leave loose for now.

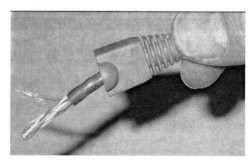

Figure 15–47. *Place boot plug on cable before untwisting the wires.*

4. Untwist each pair, and separate them down to where they come out of the sheathing, as shown in Figure 15–48.

   They will need to be straightened out and arranged in a specific order before they can be inserted into the modular jack.

Figure 15–48. *Untwist and separate the four pairs of wires.*

5. Straighten each wire. The best technique I found is to place the wire between your thumb and a pen (or something skinnier), and gently pull outward. This will leave the wire curved a bit, but it will remove the small kinks.

6. Arrange the wires in order according to the wiring scheme for T568A or T568B, as described in "Color Coding and Order for RJ-45 plugs." In Figure 15–49, T568B is used.

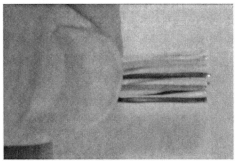

Figure 15–49. *Straightened wires in T568B wiring scheme*

7. Trim back the wires as needed so that only about ½" sticks out of the sheathing. Make sure all wires are the same length. Figure 15–50 illustrates wires that are just a little too long and should be trimmed. The sheathing should come up to just inside the plug. If the wires are not of an even length, then the shorter ones may not get in far enough to make contact.

8. After trimming, check your wires to make sure they are still in order.

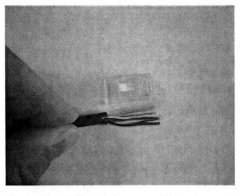

Figure 15–50. *These wires are a little too long and uneven, so they will need to be trimmed.*

9. Insert the wire set into data plug, as shown in Figure 15–51. If they are straight and flat, each wire should slip into their separate pin holes inside. Push the wires as far as they will go.

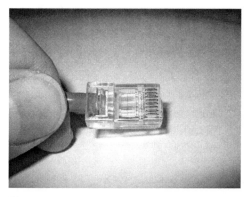

Figure 15–51. *Cat5e wire fully inserted into data plug; note that the sheathing goes partially inside the plug.*

10. Visually inspect the wires through the plug. Even though the wires are small, you should see a pattern of solid-stripe-solid-stripe alternating all the way across. If you see two solids or two stripes together, the wires are out of order. You can still pull the wires out and rearrange them because you have not crimped the plug yet.

11. On the other end of the cable repeat the process of stripping the sheath, separating, and organizing the wires, and inserting them into the plug.

12. Check the wires again, this time comparing both plugs side by side. They should look identical.

13. Figure 15–52 shows two plugs that have different wiring. At least one of these is wrong, and the cable will not work until it is fixed.

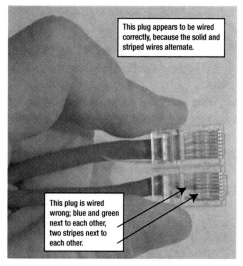

This plug appears to be wired correctly, because the solid and striped wires alternate.

This plug is wired wrong; blue and green next to each other, two stripes next to each other.

Figure 15–52. *You can quickly spot some wiring problems: if plugs look different, or if the colors are not alternating solids and stripes all the way across.*

14. When you are sure that both plugs are correct, crimp each end as shown in Figure 15–53.

15. Test the network cable by connecting a computer to a router with it. Check the network icon in the status bar. If it shows any kind of error, then you will need to redo one or both ends of your cable. Don't be discouraged if your first attempt fails; keep trying and practicing.

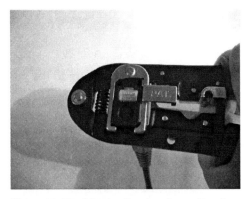

Figure 15–53. *Crimping the plug pierces the wires and puts them in contact with the pins.*

When the cable tests as good, gently disconnect it from the computer and the router or switch, and then slide the protective modular plug boot to the end of the plug. Reconnect the cable if you are going to use it now; otherwise, roll it in wide loops to bundle and store it. Avoid kinking or bending the cable.

Making a Model Cable Connection for Future Projects

You will probably be making more network patch cables in the future for yourself or friends. Before you put the tools and parts back on a shelf and forget about them, there are a couple things you can do to help you the next time you need to make more cables:

- Write down the color code order you used in a way that makes it easy for you to remember. Photocopy the page from this book listing the wire order or write a note out for yourself.

- Make a mockup of the plug connections, similar to Figure 15–54. This makes a quick visual reference not only of the wire order, but also in lining up the wires with the right side of the plug up.

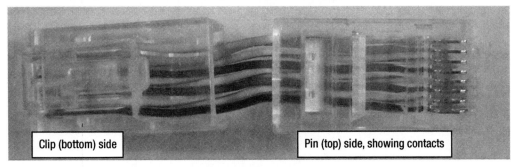

Clip (bottom) side   Pin (top) side, showing contacts

Figure 15–54. *Two plugs connected can help you remember which direction and order the wires go.*

Summary

In this chapter you learned how to:

- Connect your computers to the Internet.

- Connect your computers to a network through wireless and wired connections.

- Extend your wireless network range with access points.

- Create and join a homegroup.

- Share files with Windows 7, Windows XP, and Windows Vista computers all on the same home network.

- Make your own (Ethernet) network patch cables.

- Protect your network from common security problems and issues.

Next Steps

You may find the following related chapters useful:

- See Chapter 13: "Printing, Faxing, and Scanning" to learn how to set up and share printers on a network.

- See Chapter 16: "Protecting Your Computer and Data" to learn how to use your network for backup and recovery of all of your computers.

- See Chapter 17: "Troubleshooting and Maintaining Your Computer" to learn how to fix other problems that affect your network.

- See Chapter 18: "Using Windows at Work and On the Road" to learn how to connect to the Internet on the road, using mobile Wi-Fi, or public hotspots, and how to use corporate networks and Windows network logon.

Chapter 16

Protecting Your Computer and Data

It's easy to take for granted that your computer will always work well, and that everything you store on it will be kept safe for your own use and no others. But you will be in a world of sadness, anger, and frustration if you can no longer access your pictures, music, documents, videos, games, or email messages. There are many things that can happen in a blink of an eye that either take away what you saved on your computer or make your computer entirely unusable:

- Your hard drive crashes. It's not a question of "if," it's a question of when. Eventually, every hard drive fails. We just hope it doesn't happen while we still own that computer.

- It can take less than a minute for hackers or other computers on the Web to attack an unprotected computer connected to the Internet.

- One short electrical surge that barely blinks your lights may be enough to fry your computer's motherboard and circuits.

- You only turn your back for a brief moment at the library or the airport security checkpoint, and your laptop disappears.

- You hear a familiar voice greeting you at the coffee shop, and when you turn to see who it is, you knock over your cup – spilling it all over your laptop keyboard.

- You click a link in an email message from a friend, and all of a sudden weird stuff happens on your computer because you just downloaded a malicious program.

There is no bullet-proof protection that can guarantee no harm will come to your computer or your data. But there's a lot you can do with Windows 7 and with how you use your computer and programs to minimize the risks. This chapter shows you how to back up your computer so that your files are not lost, and how to set up security so that your computer and files resist attacks and security threats.

Your two main lines of defense are:

■ **Backup and Recovery** Set up frequent backups with a reliable backup and recovery program.

■ **A Security Suite** Set up continuous protection for your computer with a good security program and frequent Windows updates.

Backup and Recovery

Sometimes people need a little convincing that backup and recovery is necessary and that it's not difficult.

If you need some persuasion, the following sections cover

■ Backup and Recovery FAQ

■ Excuses for Not Setting Up Backup and Recovery

■ Learning from Personal Experience

If you are already sold on backup and recovery, get down to the nuts and bolts with

■ Windows Backup and Recovery

■ Using Third-Party Backup and Recovery Programs

■ Creating a Disaster Recovery Plan

Backup and Recovery FAQ

It's a crime to be without a good backup and recovery plan in place. Let's investigate and get some answers to basic questions about backup and recovery.

Question	Answer
Who needs to do a backup?	You. Even though your computer came with at least Windows Backup and Recovery, backup doesn't happen by itself. You need to set up the backup and recovery program, decide what you want to protect, and then set up a schedule to run the backups.
What should I back up?	There are several types of backups, for different purposes:
	System image Also known as *disk image, image copy, entire computer, full backup,* or *full system backup*. This backs up your entire computer so that if everything is wiped out, you can restore everything at once. This is most often used for *disaster recovery* when your entire hard disk is corrupted, infected with a virus, crashed, or physically damaged. In most cases, you would replace the hard drive with a new hard drive that's identical or close to the model and size it is replacing, and then restore the computer from your disk image backup.

Question	Answer
	Files and folders You can select individual files, folders, or entire drives to back up. Depending on the backup and recovery program you are using, you may be able to select for backup any of the following:

- An entire drive For example, C:

- **Specific folders or directories** For example, *C:\Users\Kevin\Documents\Writing Projects*

- **My Music, My Pictures, My Documents** Select by library or select one of these named document "containers."

- **File or content type** Specify by file type such as System and Applications, Pictures, Music, Movies, Office documents, etc.

> **NOTE:** The default settings in Windows Backup will back up everything for you: it will create a system image and back up folders and files so that you don't have to sort out what to back up if you want to protect everything

Question	Answer
When should I back up my computer?	Depending on how often you use your computer and what you use it for, you may want to back up everything weekly or monthly, and back up files you use quite frequently daily or weekly. Most backup and recovery programs allow you to perform immediate backups and schedule backups to occur on specific dates and times.
Where do I store these backups?	It depends on how much you need to store and why you are performing a backup.
	If all you want to back up are documents, pictures, music, and other files, you can store these on flash drives or DVDs.
	If you want to back up your entire computer in case something happens to the computer hardware, you will need some kind of storage that holds several times more data than your computer's hard drive. For example: an external desktop or portable hard drive, a network hard drive or network attached storage, or a home server.
	If you want to back up anything because of the physical location of your computer, you may want to place your external hard drive, *network attached storage* (NAS), or home server in a different part of your house than your computer. Or, you may want to use an online, or *cloud*, backup service to safely store data completely outside of your home.

Question	Answer
Why should I back up my computer or files?	Backup is kind of like insurance. You hope you never need to use it to restore or recover files, but you should perform backups before you need them. Here are some of the common reasons for performing backups: ▦ Hard drive crash ▦ Virus or corruption ▦ Theft or damage (fire, water, extreme heat, electrical) to the computer ▦ Accidental deletion ▦ Disaster recovery
How do I perform backups and recoveries?	Use a backup and recovery program such as: ▦ **Windows Backup and Restore**, included with Windows 7. ▦ Backup and recovery programs provided by an external hard drive or network attached storage manufacturer. ▦ Backup and recovery programs provided by a home server, such as **Windows Home Server**. ▦ Online recovery services like **Mozy** or those provided by the computer manufacturer or computer protection suites.

Excuses for Not Using Backup and Restore

Sometimes it takes the loss of irreplaceable memories such as photos, or the frustration of having to recreate your old computer system, before it sinks in how important backup and recovery is for everybody who uses a computer.

Excuse	Solution
I won't know what to back up	Though each backup and recovery program may use different names, windows, and features, they are not too different. Almost all offer a choice of backing up either specific files and folders, or the entire computer. The explanations they provide on their setup pages are usually pretty clear. You should not have any problem selecting what you want to back up.
I tried it once and it took too long.	The first time you run a full backup, no matter what backup program you use, it takes a very long time. That's because it must back up everything. After the first backup, backups are much quicker because you are only backing up what has changed since the last backup. For example, one of my computers took 2.5 hours to complete its first backup. The next 3 backups, 5-7 days apart, each took less than 30 minutes.
When backup is running, I won't be able to do anything else.	When a backup is running it may slow down other programs on your computer, but you do not need to stop working. Since almost all backup and recovery programs allow you to set a schedule, you can specify a time when you are not using the computer. Many programs by default suggest a backup time like midnight, or a range of hours when you are probably not using the computer such as between 2 am and 6 am. You still need to leave the computer on during that scheduled time.

Some backup programs are designed to automatically run in the background when your computer is on but idle. |
| **I don't want to have to leave my computer on all night.** | Many backup programs have an option to automatically shut down the computer when backup is complete. Or, start your home computer before you leave in the morning, and then start a manual backup. |
| **I'm afraid that if I try to do a recovery or restore files, I'll accidentally delete or erase some files that I want.** | You should see plenty of warnings if you click a button or link that might erase a bunch of files. There are a few types of recovery that will erase everything on your hard drive. All of these are for *disaster recovery*, where the contents of your hard drive are corrupted, or destroyed, you can't start your computer or Windows, and you can't access any of the files on your computer:

A disaster recovery disk designed to reset your computer back to the original factory settings You will have to reinstall all programs that you installed after you bought your computer, and then transfer music, photo, video, and document files from previous file backups. |

Excuse	Solution
	A clean install of Windows 7 In a clean install, you reformat your hard drive, reinstall Windows 7, reinstall all of your applications, and then transfer music, photo, video, and document files from previous file backups.
	A disk image recovery This erases your hard drive and copies over the complete image of your computer from a previous full backup.
	A more common daily use of backup and recovery is to recover a few files that were accidently deleted. Locating and selecting the files you want to recover, and where to recover them to, is pretty straightforward.
	Windows Backup and Restore, like most other backup and recovery programs, allows you to specify a different location to restore your files to without overwriting the current files at the original location. This allows you to view the recovered files to make sure they are the ones you want, and compare them to the current files in the original location. Then you can delete the files you do not need, and if you need to keep two different versions of files, you can rename one set.
Storing all of those backups will take up a lot of space – I'll have to buy a separate hard drive.	If it was worth putting on your computer, it's probably worth saving and protecting. The most valuable part of your computer is not the memory, hard drive, motherboard, any of the hardware, or even the software. It is the information you store on your computer: your pictures, your music, your videos, and your documents. Every part of your computer, or the entire computer, can be replaced with something similar or better. Software can be reinstalled. But your personal documents and media can't be purchased. You may be able to fit your entire photo library and documents on a single DVD or USB flash drive. Though your music and video collections could be quite large, there is a practical side to backing up your entire music collection to DVDs or a flash drive, in case you just want to transfer or copy it to another computer. If you can't back up your entire computer, you can still back up the things that are most valuable and not replaceable.

Learning from Personal Experience

You've seen the forensic crime shows on television where the computer expert is able to recover data from a damaged or encrypted hard drive. Sometimes they get frustrated because it takes them several hours. I'm not criticizing these shows, but that is not how it works in the real world. It is an expensive, time-consuming, and often unsuccessful ordeal to try to retrieve data from a damaged hard drive.

A few years ago, I was using an external hard drive to store backup copies of Word docs that I was working on, and to store my photo and music collection. This external hard drive was used both as storage for these collections, and as a backup destination.

Unfortunately, the physical hard drives in an external hard drive are just as likely to crash as the hard drives in your computer. It's easy to forget or not even realize that external hard drives can fail, because they often outlive several computers. But one day, my external hard drive died. Here is where reality separates from the TV crime shows.

- Recovering data from a damaged hard drive is not a do-it-yourself job, even for people with a lot of electronics skills. You need to send the drive to a company that specializes in recovering data from hard disks that have crashed.

- **Recovering data from a hard drive will take some time**. There are only a few companies across the United States, and probably the same internationally, that specialize in this type of recovery so it is not likely one will be in your town or nearby. Expect a couple days to ship it to the recovery company, a couple days for them to work on a diagnosis, days or weeks to do the repair, and then a couple more days to ship a new hard drive that contains the recovered data.

- **Diagnosing the problem is not free**. Besides the shipping costs, expect to pay several hundred dollars for the recovery company to diagnose the problem and propose a solution.

- **Recovery can start at $2000**. The recovery company I sent my hard drive to said they might be able to recover most of the data from the disk, but it would cost almost $2000 dollars if they were successful. If they could not retrieve any data, there would be no charge.

Did I pay for the repair, and was it successful? I did not, so we will never know if they would have been successful.

What about my eight+ years of digital photos, my music collection, and my doc files for several books I was working on? All was not lost. In fact, near as I could tell, I was able to recover everything that had been on the external hard drive from other sources.

- **Photos** I had recently copied my entire photo collection from my external hard drive to my Zune. The only photos I didn't have on my Zune were really recent photos I'd downloaded to several of my personal computers and had not gotten around to moving to the external hard drive. I was able to download all of my pictures from my Zune back to my personal computer.

- **Music** I did not lose my music files. I regularly sync my Zune with my collection on my computers. I'm also really old school: most of my music was ripped from CDs that I owned, so if worst came to worst, I could rip every CD to the hard drive of one of my computers. But the external hard drive was not main storage for my music collection. I had my entire music collection on my Zunes and several computers.

- **Documents** I was working on several writing projects, and every few days I backed up my Documents folder (excluding photos and music) to a USB flash drive, to a folder on another computer, or to DVDs.

This experience reinforces several lessons:

- All hard drives eventually crash.

- If you are backing up your computer files to another device – an external hard drive, NAS, or home server – those devices need to be backed up too. Or, you should have an alternate backup system to another device or to an online storage service (the cloud).

- No single device should be the only location for any files, data, or media that is valuable. If you have some kind of media server for your music and video, you need to back up the content on that server.

- Your iPod, Zune, or personal MP3 player can be a secondary backup for your music, picture, and video files. Or you might consider your portable device to be the main source for these files, and keeping the device synced with your personal computer allows your collection to be backed up on the computer.

Using Windows Backup and Restore

Windows 7 includes **Backup and Restore** for free. It's fairly simple to use and set up. With Backup and Restore, you can

- Create a schedule to automatically perform a backup daily, weekly, or monthly

- Create a system image for recovering your entire computer

- Back up libraries, folders, or selected files

- Send backups to an attached external drive or internal DVD-RW drive (all editions of Windows 7)

- Send backups to a network location (Windows 7 Professional, Ultimate, and Enterprise editions only)

- Recover the entire computer, or restore selected folders or files

- Restore all users' files or just your own

- Restore files to their original location or to a different location

NOTE: Make sure you have enough disk space on the hard drive or network location where you will be storing your backups. For a full computer backup you will need at least as much space as your computer currently uses, plus more space to store multiple backups. There is no hard and fast rule, but I recommend starting with backup storage space equal to twice the space your computer currently uses.

Setting up Backups

With the Windows 7 Home Premium edition, you can back up your computer locally to an attached external drive or internal DVD/CD drive; if you have one of the business editions of Windows such as Professional, Ultimate, or Enterprise, you can back up to network locations as well.

> **TIP:** This is a Microsoft design choice, not a technical limitation. Microsoft chose not to offer a network destination option for the Home Premium edition. Most third-party backup and recovery programs allow you to back up your data and files to network locations in all versions of Windows 7. We'll show you some of those programs later in this chapter, in the section "Using Third-Party Backup and Recovery Programs."

This section covers separate procedures for backing up to both local and network locations.

To back up your computer locally to an attached external drive or internal DVD/CD drive:

1. Click the **Start** button, and in the search box type **Backup and Restore**. In the list that appears, click **Backup and Restore**.

    The **Backup and Restore** window appears as shown in Figure 16–01.

Figure 16–01. *The Backup and Restore window*

2. Click **Set up backup**.

3. The **Set up backup** wizard appears. If you are using Windows 7 Home Premium, it lists local external hard drives, USB flash drives, and internal DVD or CD drives attached to your computer, as shown in Figure 16–02.

4. If you are using Windows 7 Professional, Ultimate, or Enterprise, you will also have a link to select a network location, shown in

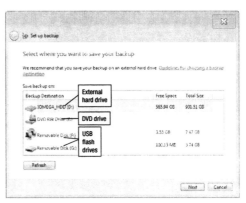

Figure 16–02. *The backup wizard only allows local backup locations in Windows Home Premium edition.*

Figure 16–03. There are a few extra steps to save backups to a network location, so those are explained in the next procedure, "To back up to a network location."

Figure 16–03. *Backup wizard in Windows 7 Professional, Ultimate, and Enterprise editions also allows backups to network locations, in addition to local backup locations.*

5. Select a location from the list of internal or externally attached local drives, and then click **Next**.

    Or, if you don't see your drive here because you forgot to attach it to your computer, attach it now and then click **Refresh**. Select the drive, and then click **Next**.

    The next page of the wizard asks you to select what you want to back up, as shown in Figure 16–04.

6. Accept the default, **Let Windows choose**.

    This will give you a full backup of all of your files, including a system image. When you finish this wizard, and backup starts.

7. Click **Next**.

8. The next page in the wizard, where you schedule your backups, is shown in Figure 16–05.

Figure 16–04. *The default option Let Windows choose is good for your first backup.*

9. Select how often to perform the backup and when. Select a time when you know your computer will be on for several hours. Click **OK** when you are done.

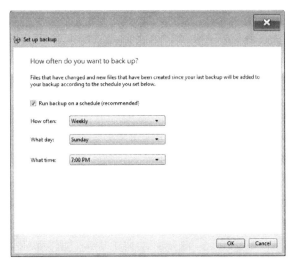

Figure 16–05. *Schedule when and how often to run backup.*

A confirmation page is displayed so that you can review what you have selected to back up and where it the backup will be stored, as shown in Figure 16–06.

10. Click the **Save settings** button.

If the button said **Save settings and exit**, your settings are saved, and the main **Backup and Restore** window is displayed as shown in Figure 16–07. Click **Back up now**. Backup will begin.

If the button said **Save settings and run backup**, then backup will begin immediately.

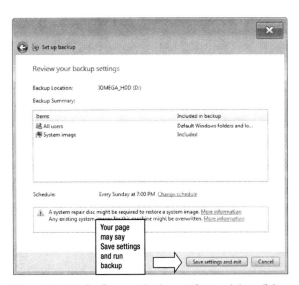

Figure 16–06. *Confirm your backup settings and then click Save settings.*

Note If you selected removable media such as DVDs or a USB flash drive, if that media fills up during backup, you will be prompted to replace it with another blank disk or flash drive.

11. When backup completes, click **Create a system repair disk**.

    You will need a blank CD or DVD for this, as shown in Figure 16–08.

12. Follow the instructions in the wizard and then click **Create disc**.

When you have finished creating the system repair disk, as shown in Figure 16–09, be sure to label it and store it in safe place where you can easily find it if you ever need it.

The system repair disk is a special boot disk that allows you to start your computer without running Windows on your hard drive. This allows you to restore your entire computer from a disk image.

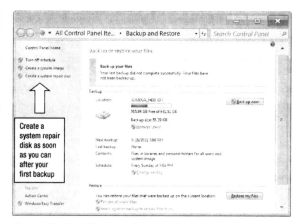

Create a system repair disk as soon as you can after your first backup

Figure 16–07. If backup did not start after you completed your settings, click Back up now.

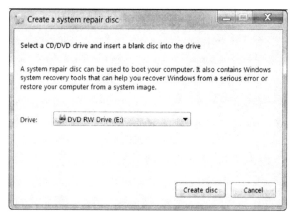

Figure 16–08. Creating a system repair disc is very simple and only takes a few minutes.

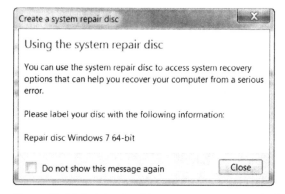

Figure 16–09. Label and safely store your system repair disc.

Windows 7 Professional, Ultimate, and Enterprise are primarily used in the business environment, where large networks are common. In business, you are more likely to back up your computer to a network location than a local drive. You can, of course, purchase an Anytime Upgrade to get the Professional or Ultimate versions for your home computer. One of the features you get with these business editions is the capability to back up your computer to a network location. There are a few extra steps to selecting a network location for your backups. At home, you can use this to connect to a NAS device, networked hard drive, or home server.

To back up your computer to a network location:

1. Click the **Start** button, and in the search box type **Backup and Restore**. In the list that appears, click **Backup and Restore**.

   The **Backup and Restore** window appears as shown in Figure 16–10.

2. Click **Set up backup**.

   The **Set up backup** wizard appears, as shown in Figure 16–11. There are a few extra steps to save backups to a network location.

3. Select a location from the list of network locations, and then click **Next**.

   -or-

   Click **Save on a network**.

   The **Select a network location** dialog box appears as shown in Figure 16–12.

Figure 16–10. *Backup and Restore window*

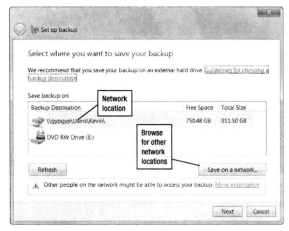

Figure 16–11. *Backup wizard in Windows 7 Professional, Ultimate, and Enterprise editions also allows backups to network locations, in addition to local backup locations.*

Type or browse to a network location.

Your network location does not have to be a server or network attached storage, it can also be one of your other computers on your network if you have enabled network sharing. Figure 16–13 displays a mix of computers, a server, and a NAS device. If you choose another computer on your network, be sure that it is on when your backups are scheduled. Otherwise, you will get an error that backup failed.

4. Type a username and password that has access to this network, and then click **OK**.

Figure 16–12. *When you select a network location, you must also provide a username and password for access to the network .*

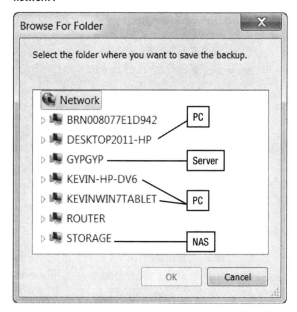

Figure 16–13. *Your network location can include other PCs.*

NOTE: If you set up your home network so that you use the same username and passwords on all computers, home servers, and NAS devices, then entering the Username and Password should not be difficult. However, if you use different names and passwords on different computers or the server in your home network, you may have a few rejected password messages similar to Figure 16–14, until you figure out the right set to use.

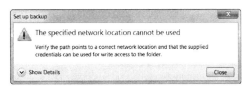

Figure 16–14. *Use the same username and password on all computers and servers in your home network, and you should not see this message unless you just lost your network connection.*

The rest of setting up and running the backup is the same as if you were backing up to a local drive or location.

5. The next page of the wizard asks you to select what you want to back up, as shown in Figure 16–15.

6. Accept the default, **Let Windows choose**.

   This will give you a full backup of all of your files, including a system image. When you finish this wizard, and backup starts.

Figure 16–15. *The default option Let Windows choose is good for your first backup.*

7. Click **Next**.

   The next page in the wizard is where you schedule your backups, as shown in Figure 16–16.

8. Select how often to perform the backup and when. Select a time when you know both your computer and your backup destination will be on for several hours. Click **OK** when you are done.

Figure 16–16. *Schedule when and how often to run backup.*

A confirmation page is displayed so that you can review what you have selected to back up, and where it the backup will be stored, as shown in Figure 16–17.

9. Click the **Save settings** button.

   If the button said **Save settings and exit**, your settings are saved and the main **Backup and Restore** window is displayed as shown in Figure 16–18. Click **Back up now**. Backup will begin.

   If the button said **Save settings and run backup**, then backup will begin immediately.

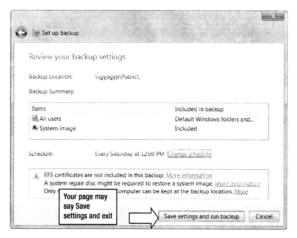

Figure 16–17. *Confirm your backup settings and then click Save settings.*

10. When backup completes, click **Create a system repair disk**.

You will need a blank CD or DVD for this, as shown in Figure 16–19.

Figure 16–18. *If backup did not start after your completed your settings, click Back up now.*

11. Follow the instructions in the wizard and then click **Create disc**.

When you have finished creating the system repair disk, as shown in Figure 16–20, be sure to label it and store it in safe place where you can easily find it if you ever need it.

The system repair disk is a special boot disk that allows you to start your computer without running Windows on your hard drive. This allows you to restore your entire computer from a disk image.

Figure 16–19. *Creating a system repair disc is very simple and only takes a few minutes*

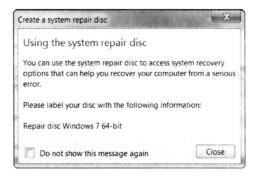

Figure 16–20. *Label and safely store your system repair disc.*

Advanced Backup Tasks

If you have followed the steps in one of the previous procedures for backup, you should be set with a fairly safe backup plan and schedule. Those were the basic "set it and forget it" steps. But you may still want to monitor your backups, adjust settings, or perform other types of backup.

- **Manage space** Windows Backup is set to save as many backups as it can, until it uses thirty percent of the space available on your backup disk. Then it starts deleting the oldest backups as needed to make room for new ones. You can adjust these settings, and delete old backups manually. On the **Backup and Restore** page, click **Manage space** This opens the **Manage Windows Backup disk space** page. If you need additional information, click the **How do my backup settings affect my disk space?** link.

- **Adjust settings** You can change your schedule, what is backed up, and where it is stored at any time. On the **Backup and Restore** window, click **Change settings**.

Check Your Backups

Windows Backup and most other backup programs provide a number of ways to notify you if the backup was not successful, such as the examples shown in Figures 16–21 and 16–22.

Figure 16–21. *Backup was cancelled.*

Figure 16–22. *Backup did not complete successfully.*

You can usually track down what is wrong by clicking **More information** and running the troubleshooting options.

Even if there are no error messages or warnings and your backups appear to be successful, they may not be backing up what you think they are. For example, though mapped drives and libraries make it easy to use folders and files that are actually on other computers as if they were local, folders on other computers, servers, and network attached storage are not included in backups:

- Windows Backup does not back up drives mapped to other folders on other computers. For example, if your computer *ComputerY* has drive V: mapped to a shared folder on another computer on your network, \\Kevin-HP-DV6\Users\Kevin, the backup for *ComputerY* will not include drive V: because those folders are on the computer Kevin-HP-DV6. To back up any folders on Kevin-HP-DV6, you must set up a backup on Kevin-HP-DV6.

- Windows Backup does not back up the folders in libraries on your local computer, even if they appear in your Documents, Music, or Photos libraries. You must back up the computers where those folders really reside.

You can review what is in your backups through Restore, without actually completing the restore. In the next section, you'll see how to perform a basic file restore to help you get comfortable with this process and to understand how to use it *before you actually need it.*

Restore

The default settings for Windows Backup perform a combination of disk image and data file backups. Disk images are not created as often as data file backups, so if you use the default settings, the pattern Windows Backup uses is similar to the following:

- Backup #1:   Disk image backup, including data files
- Backup #2:   Data file backups
- Backup #3   Data file backups
- Backup #4   Data file backups
- Backup #5   Disk image backup, including data files
- Backup #6:   Data file backups
- Backup #7   Data file backups
- Backup #8   Data file backups

Just as you have several choices for what you can back up, you also have several choices for what you can restore.

- With *data file backups*, you can restore individual files, folders, your own user folders, or all user folders if they have previously been backed up. This type of restore will give you the option of restoring files to a different location so that you do not delete or overwrite existing data.

▨ *Disk images* are an exact copy of a drive, which allows you to restore
the entire computer: your system files and settings, all programs
you've installed, and all of your data files. Restoring from a disk image
deletes everything from your computer and replaces it with your disk
image from a previous backup. You can't browse or select individual
items for restore from a disk image; it is all or nothing. In most cases,
this is used for disaster recovery. Since disk images are not created as
frequently as data file backups, after you recover with a disk image
you will want to follow up with restoring from the latest data file
backup. For example, if you recovered your computer with Backup #5,
there were several data file backups after that. You would want to
follow up with a restore of data files from Backup #8.

Restoring Data Files

You can only restore what you previously backed up. That may sound obvious, but it is
a reminder that if you do not follow a regular backup schedule and include all of your
standard data files such as music, pictures, and documents, you will not be able to
restore them later.

Your data file backups are browsable, which means your backups are in a folder
structure you can sift through, and they are searchable, which means you can search by
file or folder names.

To restore data files:

1. Click the **Start** button, and in
    the search box, type **Backup
    and Restore**. In the list that
    appears, click **Backup and
    Restore**.

    The **Backup and Restore**
    window appears, as shown in
    Figure 16–23.

2. Click **Restore my files**.

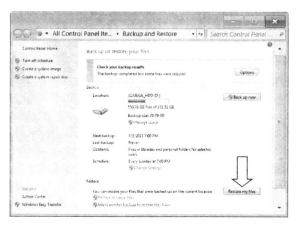

Figure 16–23. *The Backup and Restore window*

The **Restore Files** window appears, as shown in Figure 16–24.

3. Choose how you want to locate and select items to restore:

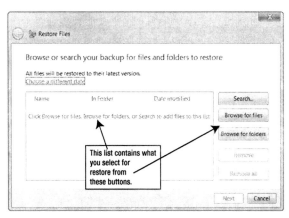

Figure 16–24. *The Restore Files window*

Click **Search**, if you know the name or part of the name of a file or folder you are looking for. The **Search** window is shown in Figure 16–25.

Type what you are looking for, and then click **Search**.

In the list that appears, select the checkbox for each file you want to restore, and then click **OK**.

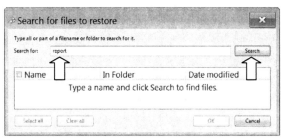

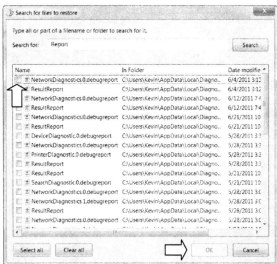

Figure 16–25. *Searching the contents of a backup by filename or folder name*

Click **Browse for files** if you want to select individual files. The **Browse** window is shown in Figure 16–26.

Navigate through the folders to locate the files you want to recover.

Select the files you want, and then click **Add files**.

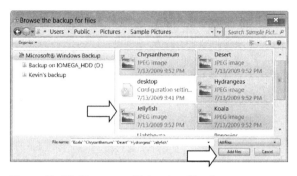

Figure 16–26. *You can multiple select files for recovery.*

Click **Browse for folders** if you want to select entire folders. The **Browse for folders** window is shown in Figure 16–27.

Navigate to the folder you want to add to the restore, and then click **Add Folder**.

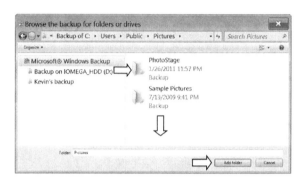

Figure 16–27. *Selecting folders to restore*

You can repeat selecting through the Search or Browse buttons as many times as you want.

4. When you are finished, click **Next**, as shown in Figure 16–28.

The Restore Files page will ask you where you want restore the files to, as shown in Figure 16–29.

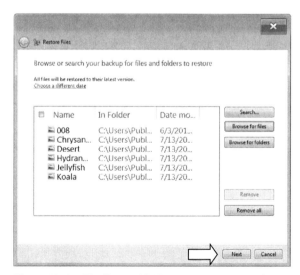

Figure 16–28. *The files and folders you have selected for the restore are listed in the Restore Files window.*

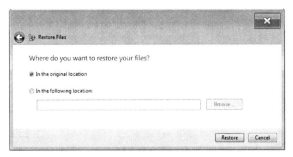

Figure 16–29. You can choose where to restore your files to, if you don't want them to overwrite existing files.

5. Select **In the original location** to overwrite and replace the files currently at that location with the copies you are restoring from backup. If you select this option, during the recovery a message box will pop up to confirm that you want to keep only the old file, keep only the new file, or keep a copy of both, as shown in Figure 16–30.

If you do elect to keep both, the original folder will show both the copy and the original, as shown in Figure 16–31.

Figure 16–30. If you choose the original location, when you start the restore you will still have options that do not overwrite the file currently at that location.

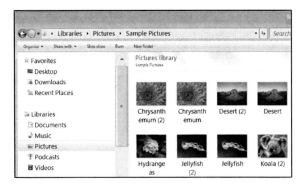

Figure 16–31. If you choose to keep both copies, the copied file is renamed.

–or–

Select **In the following location** and then type or browse to the alternate location. This can be very handy if you are trying to locate multiple versions of the same file and want to check the recovered files before committing them to the original location.

6. Click **Restore**.

When the restore is complete, a confirmation message is displayed, as shown in Figure 16–32.

7. Click **View restored files**.

If you selected to restore to a different location, you will find that the path mimics the path of the original file location. This helps you locate the current copy so that you can compare it to, or replace it with, the recovered copy.

Compare the paths in the original location with the recovered location in the examples in Figures 16–33 and 16–34.

Figure 16–32. *When restoring to a different location is complete, the confirmation message includes a link to the location of your restored files.*

Figure 16–33. *Original file location*

Figure 16–34. *Restored file location*

Recovery

You are probably wondering, aren't *restore* and *recovery* the same thing? Though they seem to be used interchangeably, there really is a difference when it comes to your computer. When you restore files, you are returning them to their original condition. Think of restoring a house or a car. When you recover, you are fixing something that was damaged, injured, in poor health. In this case, you are recovering your computer or system to a healthy state. Some of the feature names in Windows can add to the confusion. In Windows, **System Restore** is a *recovery* method. There are other recovery methods available in Windows.

To review your recovery options:

1. Click the **Start** button, and in the search box type **Recovery**. In the list that appears, under Control Panel, click **Recovery**.

   The **Recovery** window appears, as shown in Figure 16–35.

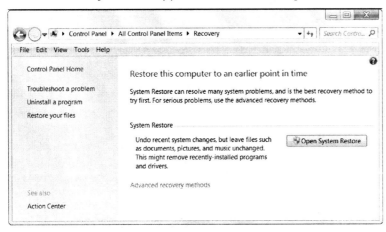

Figure 16–35. *In the Recovery window you can start System Restore, or go to Advanced recovery methods.*

TIP: See Chapter 17: "Troubleshooting and Maintaining Your Computer" to learn how to use System Restore to fix problems.

2. Click **Advanced recovery methods**.

   In the **Advanced Recovery Methods** window, you have two options, shown in Figure 16–36.

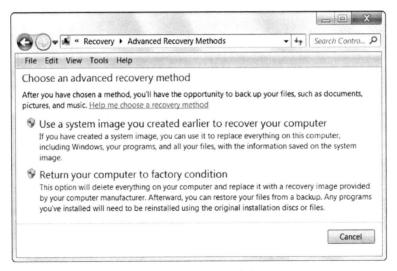

Figure 16–36. *The Advanced Recovery Methods window*

The *system image* method uses a system image backup as described in "To back up your computer locally" and "To back up your computer to a network location" earlier in this chapter. At the end of those procedures, you will also find instructions for creating a system recovery disk.

The *return to factory condition* method usually requires that you create a disaster recovery disk according to the computer manufacturers' instructions. Some manufacturers provide this disk with your computer, but most do not. See Chapter 5: "Installing Programs" for more information about creating your disaster recovery disk.

Using Third-Party Backup and Recovery Programs

Windows Backup and Recovery is not your only option. You may already have other backup and recovery programs installed or available on your computer. You may also find backup programs:

- Built in to your security suite. Many Internet providers (cable, DSL) offer a security suite for free or low cost to their subscribers.

- Bundled with your external hard drive.

- Integrated into your home server or network attached storage device.

- Integrated with online backup services like Mozy, iDrive, and Carbonite, or services offered by your computer manufacturer.

- Available for purchase from a wide variety of software publishers.

There is nothing wrong with Windows Backup and Recovery, and if used correctly it should provide all the protection most people need. But maybe you want more control over the scheduling, like having more than one backup set. Or maybe you want to use the same backup program for all of your computers, and you have a mixture of different versions and editions of Windows. Or, you want a program that makes it easier to select what you want to back up. When considering another backup and recovery product, consider the following:

- Does it offer full backups, including image copy, or just file and folder backup?

- Does it have a "backup now" option?

- Is it easy to use and understand?

- Do you have to buy a copy for each computer, or can you buy one license that covers all of your computers in your home?

NOTE: Backups made by one program can't be restored by another program from another publisher. It is okay to try out several backup programs at a time, but settle on one and use it for all of your computers.

Figures 16–37 to 16–39 are just a few examples of other backup programs.

Windows Home Server provides a console that allows you to set up, monitor, and run backups for all computers on the network, from any computer on the network.

Figure 16–37. *Windows Home Server can manage backups for all of your computers on your home network.*

MozyHome Online Backup Online backup services charge by the month or year, and by how much storage space you want. Many services offer 2-5 GB storage for free.

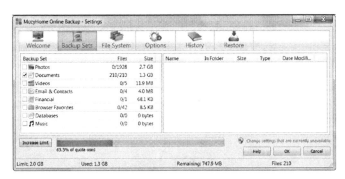

Figure 16–38. *MozyHome Online Backup*

Norton Security Suite makes it easy to see your backup settings at a glance.

Figure 16–39. *Norton backup provided by Norton Security Suite*

Creating and Using a Disaster Recovery Plan

A *disaster recovery plan* just means that you've already taken steps before disaster strikes to protect your data and programs so that you can restore them to your computer after the disaster. Disaster can strike your computer in many ways:

▨ **Your computer is lost or stolen** Your car is broken into, you lose your laptop at the airport, or your home is burglarized.

▨ **Your computer is damaged by electricity, heat, cold, or water** A power surge or spike can damage the chips, board, or hard drive in your computer; your computer is left in a car on a very hot day or on a very cold day; or your house is flooded or a water pipe bursts.

▨ **Your computer's hard drive fails, and you can't access any of the data on it** It's not a question of if, but when, your hard drive will fail.

▨ **Your computer is attacked by a virus, worm, or Trojan horse**: Even with good antivirus protection, some of these still get through to people's computers. Sometimes the only way to fix your computer is wipe everything clean and reinstall Windows and all of your programs.

To prepare for disaster recovery before you need it:

- Create a system repair disc.

- Put your original Windows installation discs (and your product key) in a safe place. If you bought a computer with Windows 7 already installed, your computer may have either a Windows recovery disc or a hidden partition on the hard drive that you can reinstall Windows from. Check the documentation that came with your computer.

- Keep the installation discs for any programs you installed in a safe place.

- Schedule a weekly backup of your entire computer (system image) using Windows Backup. Back up the data to an external hard drive or storage, not the hard drive on your computer.

- If you store most of your information on an external drive already, back up that external drive to another drive or storage.

- Perform daily backups of important files, such as documents you are actively working on. For small backups (not the entire computer), you can use data CDs, DVDs, or USB flash drives (sometimes called **memory sticks**, **USB thumb drives**, **USB fingers**, or **pen drives**). A data CD can hold up to 600MB of data, a standard data DVD can hold 4.7GB (8.4GB dual layer), and USB flash drives are available in a wide range of capacities such as 1GB, 2GB, 4GB, 8GB, 16GB, 32GB, and 64GB.

- Whenever possible, keep your backups in a different physical location than the computer the data came from. Another alternative to backing up your computer or files to a hard drive or disks is to use an online backup service like Carbonite Online Backup (www.carbonite.com), IDrive Online Backup (www.idrive.com), or Mozy Online Backup (www.mozy.com), to name a few.

Security Features that Protect Your Computer

Setting up user accounts and setting up a backup plan are vital to the overall health and security of your computer, but once you are logged onto your computer, you need protection against threats from outside your computer. The Internet hosts all sorts of threats, such as viruses, spyware, hackers, phishing, and spam. Fortunately, Windows and other programs can protect you against all of these.

The following tools and features are the basis for your protection. We'll provide much more information about these features and settings through the rest of the chapter:

- **Action Center** provides the status of your current security settings and notifies you if there is a security issue that needs attention. Third-party Internet security suite programs often provide their own security center page that lists the overall security status of your computer and any issues that need attention.

- **Windows Firewall** blocks unauthorized access to your computer by other computers on the Internet. Windows 7 comes with the Windows Firewall built in and already on the first time you start your computer. You need, and can use, only one firewall on your computer. Many third-party Internet security suites provide their own firewall programs as well.

- **Windows Update** downloads and installs the latest Windows patches and security fixes.

- **Virus protection** scans your computer, downloaded files, and e-mail attachments for viruses and dangerous file types, then blocks or removes them. Microsoft does not provide virus protection software; you must obtain it from a third party. You can use only one virus protection program on your computer. If you want to use a different program, you must uninstall your old one first.

- **Spyware protection** detects and removes programs that may be collecting personal information or hijacking your Internet search and home pages. Windows 7 includes Windows Defender, but Internet security suites often include their own spyware protection. You can install and use more than one spyware protection program on your computer.

- **E-mail filtering of dangerous attachments, junk mail, phishing, and spam** is not a feature of Windows itself but is usually provided by your e-mail program or provider. Some Internet security suites also include filtering or scanning of e-mail messages and attachments when you try to view or open them on your computer.

■ **Browser security settings** in Internet Explorer, Mozilla Firefox, and most other browsers provide their own security features. These features include managing cookies, blocking pop-ups, and blocking dangerous code on web pages.

Security Suites

Windows 7 includes its own firewall, Windows Firewall, and its own spyware protection program, Windows Defender. It does not provide virus protection software, so you must obtain a third-party virus protection software program. Some companies offer a virus protection program by itself or as part of an Internet security suite. Security suites usually include their own firewall that replaces Windows Firewall, spyware protection, and their own security center page that tells you at a glance what the status of your system is. See "Getting virus protection software" later in this chapter for more information, including how to get this software for free or at low cost.

Checking the Security Status of Your Computer

You can check your security status in several ways. You can wait until Windows detects something wrong and displays a notification, or you can check it yourself anytime.

Windows 7 provides several types of security notifications on your desktop.

When you start your computer, you may see a notification pop-up similar to the one displayed in Figure 16–40. The message in Figure 16–40 is a general message that doesn't tell you specifically that there is a security issue.

Or, you might see a more specific message like Figure 16–41 or Figure 16–42.

Whether or not you see one of these notifications, you should check to see what the status is of your security settings.

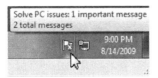

Figure 16–40. *The red and white x on the notification flag tells you there is an important message in the Action Center.*

Figure 16–41. *A notification appears if you do not have an antivirus program installed.*

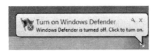

Figure 16–42. *A notification may appear if a security feature is turned off.*

To check your security status:

- Right-click the notification icon in the taskbar, and then click **Open Action Center**.

  – or–

- Click the **Start** button, and in the search box type **Security status**. In the list that appears, click **Check security status**.

The Action Center appears. It may indicate that there are security issues that need addressing, as shown in Figure 16–43.

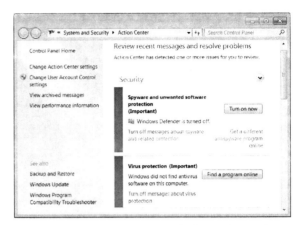

Figure 16–43. *If there are any security issues that need attention, they will be listed in the Action Center.*

If everything is OK, the Action Center may list the current status of your security features, as shown in Figure 16–44. Figure 16–44 also illustrates how Windows will report the status of security features even if they are not provided by Microsoft or Windows.

If you have installed third-party protection software such as an Internet security suite that contains its own spyware protection or firewall, those will be listed. In Figure 16–44, a McAfee security suite has been installed and is providing the virus and spyware protection. McAfee Security is one of many products that you can buy for protection. McAfee Security is not provided by Windows or Microsoft.

Figure 16–44. *All the necessary security features are set to the proper safety levels and settings. Third-party security programs may be included in the security status.*

Fixing Security Issues

The two most likely security issues you may see when you start your new computer are that you need to obtain or turn on virus protection and that you have no spyware protection because Windows Defender is turned off. During setup of your computer, you are asked to turn on Windows Update. If you did not turn it on then, it will also show up as a security issue. Your firewall should always be on. It is really rare for anyone to turn off the firewall, either by accident or on purpose. If you are installing a program that requests that you turn off or open the firewall, Windows may warn you and discourage you from doing it. If the software is from a legitimate company, visit the company website and check its support pages to see if the company provides more information about issues you may encounter with Windows blocking firewall changes. You may also want to check Microsoft's support site to see if it has any information about this issue. Go to www.support.microsoft.com and search for articles about this particular product. If you are not sure that the program or its request to open the firewall is safe, do not do it.

If your security status shows several issues, which do you fix first, and which can you put off until later? The short answer is: fix all of them as soon as you can. Virus protection is the only issue that may require you to purchase additional software that is not already available on your computer.

Adjusting Windows Update

Microsoft is constantly improving Windows to make your computer more secure and to fix bugs. You don't have to wait for a service pack or the next version of Windows to get these improvements. Microsoft makes them available on an ongoing basis through Windows Update. With Windows Update, you can set up your computer to automatically download and install new updates whenever they are available. Or you can choose to download the updates automatically, and Windows will wait for you to install them.

Important and Optional Updates

Windows Update classifies the updates as either *Important* or *Optional*.

Important updates	Important updates usually fix security problems or other issues in Windows that could cause loss of data or prevent programs from working correctly. If an update is classified as important, you should install it. Often, viruses and other harmful programs get on computers because the user did not install an update that would have prevented it.
Optional updates	Examples of optional updates include noncritical updates to Windows or Microsoft programs you use on your computer, updated drivers for devices attached to your computer, and language packs that help Windows display the characters and symbols of a specific language on your computer. If an update is optional, you might skip it if it pertains to a program, feature, or device that you don't really use, and if you don't want to tie your computer up with running the download and installation. For example, you may be notified that 35 new language packs are available for Windows. If you do not browse websites or receive mail or documents in languages other than the one you currently use on your computer, you may not want or need to install other language packs.

Setting Windows Update to Automatically Install Updates

Most of the time, Windows can install the updates in the background and not disrupt you while you are using your computer. But the inconvenience, if any, can't compare to having a computer disabled by a virus or security vulnerability.

> **CAUTION:** Some large updates, with multiple items, may require several restarts. If you are not there, Windows may automatically reboot even though you had some other program running in the background. If you do not want Windows to reboot while you are not there, set Windows Update to **Download updates but let me choose whether to install them** or **Check for updates by let me choose whether to download and install them.** While this means more commitment on your part to keep up with installation, it also means less potential disruption due to unexpected shut downs and reboots.

To set Windows Update to automatically install updates:

1. Click the **Start** button, and in the search box type **Windows Update**. In the list that appears, click **Windows Update**.

2. In the left column of the **Windows Update** window, click **Change settings**.

   The Change settings window appears, as shown in Figure 16–45.

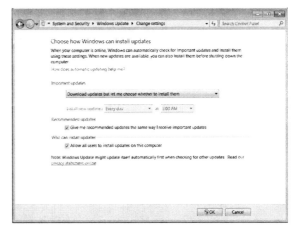

Figure 16–45. *The Change settings window allows you to change how to handle downloading and installing updates.*

3. Click the drop-down list under **Important updates**, and then select **Install updates automatically (recommended)**, as shown in Figure 16–46.

Figure 16–46. *With Install updates automatically, you don't have to remember to check for updates, download them, and install them. Windows can do that for you.*

4. If desired, set how often you want Windows to install updates and at what time, as shown in Figure 16–47.

If your computer is not on at the scheduled time, Windows will install the updates the next time your computer is on.

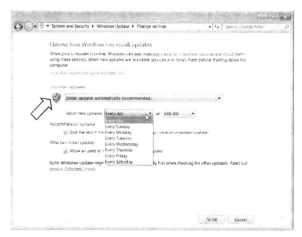

Figure 16–47. *When you choose Install updates automatically (recommended), you can specify how often and at what time to install new updates. Note the green shield with a check mark, indicating that this is an approved safe setting.*

Hackers Exploit Computers that Are Not Up to Date

How often have you read about a virus or Trojan that is expected to hit computers tomorrow? How do they know this, and why didn't they stop it? Often Microsoft or the virus protection software already fixed it, and the fix was included in a Windows update (or the virus protection software company's updates). But the computer attackers know that a percentage of computer users do not install updates. That's what the attackers are counting on.

Checking for New Updates Available for Download or Installation

If you do not have automatic updates turned on, you should check at least once a week to see whether any new updates are available. As a reminder, you can set up a Windows notification to tell you when new updates are available.

To turn on Windows Update notifications in the notification area:

1. Right-click in the notification area at the bottom right of the desktop, and click **Customize notification icons**, as shown in Figure 16–48.

Figure 16–48. *You can customize a notification to let you know when new Windows updates are available.*

2. In the Notification Area Icons window, scroll down to Windows Update, and click the down arrow to view the options available, as shown in Figure 16–49.

Figure 16–49. *You can use a Windows Update notification to let you know when updates are available.*

3. Choose how you want Windows Update notifications displayed.

Figure 16–50. *The Windows Update icon is the icon to the left of the flag icon.*

   If you choose **Only show notifications**, the Windows Update icon will be displayed in the notification area only when there are new updates available. A **New updates are available** notification will pop up when there are updates available, similar to Figure 16–50.

If you select **Show icon and notifications**, the Windows Update icon will always be displayed in the notification area, like the first icon shown to the right of the up arrow in Figure 16–51. When an update is available, a **New updates are available** notification will pop up, as shown in Figure 16–50.

Figure 16–51. *With Show icon and notifications, the Window Update icon is the same as what is shown in Only show notifications, but the icon doesn't go away when the notification is gone.*

4. Click **OK**.

To install updates that have already been downloaded:

1. If you don't know if there are updates available because you have turned off Windows Update notifications, click the **Start** button, and in the search box type **Windows Update**. In the list that appears, click **Windows Update**.

    Alternatively, if you do have notifications on, click the Windows Update icon in the notification area.

    The **Windows Update** window appears, as shown in Figure 16–52.

2. Click **Install Updates**.

    –or–

    Click the **important update** or **optional update** links to view and select the individual items in the update.

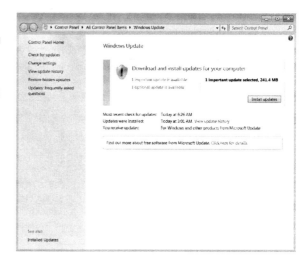

Figure 16–52. *If Windows Update is not set to automatically install updates after downloading, you will need to select and install them yourself.*

Sometimes when you select to install the updates, Windows may need to download additional files for the update. Depending on the type of update, you may be prompted to restart your computer. Or, Windows may need to install the files after you choose to shut down your computer. In that case, after you've logged off, the screen may read "Installing update x of x." Do not turn off your computer yet.

Adjusting Windows Firewall Settings

A *firewall* is a barrier that restricts the flow of information in and out of your computer across the Internet or a network. Think of it as a castle wall, meant to keep the enemy from coming in or taking things out.

You should always have Windows Firewall on, unless you are using another firewall from an Internet security suite.

Windows Firewall works by identifying what types of programs and traffic to allow in and out of your computer. If a program attempts an *unsolicited request*—a request that you didn't make or authorize a program to make—Windows Firewall blocks the connection. It then allows you the opportunity to unblock the program. If you unblock it, Windows Firewall creates an exception and won't ask you the next time that particular program requests information from your computer.

You can change whether Windows Firewall is on or off, change what programs are allowed to communicate through the firewall, and open specific ports in the firewall that are required by a program. If you use several different networks, such as at home and on a public network, you can also customize the firewall settings for each type of connection.

The default settings in Windows Firewall or the firewalls provided by third-party security suites will work quite well without you having to make any adjustments. Even though you can turn the firewall on or off and change other settings to allow programs access to your computer, most of the time you should not need to do anything with the firewall. Do not turn off the firewall or change the settings unless instructed to do so by a person or program you trust.

To check the status of the firewall on your computer:

- Click the **Start** button, and in the search box type **Windows Firewall**. In the list that appears, click **Windows Firewall**.

The Windows Firewall settings are displayed. There are three possible states for the firewall, as shown in Figures 16–53 to 16–55.

In Figure16–53, Windows Firewall is on, and the status of the firewall is good.

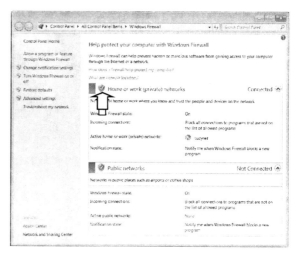

Figure 16–53. *Windows Firewall is on and working normally. The green shields indicate that the status of the firewall is good.*

In Figure 16–54, Windows Firewall is off, but the computer is using another firewall program. This is still OK.

Figure 16–54. *Windows Firewall is off, but your computer is using another firewall. The red shields don't mean there is a problem; in this example, it means Windows detects that a firewall from a third party is in use.*

■ In Figure 16–55, Windows Firewall is off, and there is no third-party firewall on either. This is a security hazard and needs to be fixed right away.

Figure 16–55. Windows Firewall is off, and there is no other firewall on. This is dangerous and should be avoided.

To turn Windows Firewall on or off:

■ In the **Windows Firewall** window, click **Turn Windows Firewall on or off**. The **Customize Settings** window is displayed, as shown in Figure 16–56.

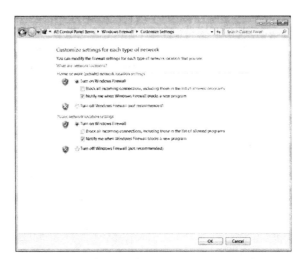

Figure 16–56. Windows Firewall recommended settings are Turn on Windows Firewall.

NOTE: If you are using a third-party firewall program, you will need to go through that program to change firewall settings.

Windows Firewall and Network Connections

By default, Windows Firewall is on for all network connections. If you use more than one network, Windows Firewall provides separate settings for each type of network. For example, if you use your laptop on a work network, your local coffee shop, or your home network, each of these network locations requires different Windows Firewall settings. Depending on what types of networks Windows detects, your Windows Firewall settings may display separate settings for home networks, work networks, public networks, or domain networks. The settings for a domain network are controlled by a domain network administrator and can't be changed by the individual from his or her own machine.

Adding or Removing Programs from the Windows Firewall Allowed Programs and Features List

Windows keeps a list of software programs and Windows features that are allowed through the firewall. There are three common ways programs and features get added to the firewall allowed list:

- **Windows automatically adds it** When you turn on or enable Windows features such as File and Printer Sharing, HomeGroup, and Remote Desktop, Windows adds them to the allowed list. Since these are part of Windows, they are known to be safe and trustworthy.

- **Windows asks whether you want to unblock a program that is currently blocked by Windows Firewall** When you install a program that is not part of the operating system, Windows may display a security message notifying you that Windows Firewall is blocking the program or parts of the program and ask whether you want to unblock the program. Some common programs that require access through the firewall include instant message programs such as Windows Live Messenger, Yahoo Messenger, or AOL Messenger; media players such as Windows Media Player; backup programs; and antivirus programs.

■ **You manually add them to the allowed list** Sometimes Windows automatically blocks a program and does not offer to add it to the allowed list. While programs should register themselves and automatically be added to the allowed list, sometimes the installed program is using outdated credentials or security certificates, or has none at all. If this is a known issue that the program publisher can't fix in their program or installation for some reason, the troubleshooting or issues section on the product's support page may provide instructions to manually add the program to the allowed list. You can also remove programs from this list and select different settings for a program depending on what type of network you are on. You should add programs to this list on an as-needed basis. When you view the list, you will see many programs listed that are not selected as allowed. Every program allowed through the firewall presents a potential risk, so be careful about adding programs to the allowed list.

To add or remove programs from the allowed programs and features list:

1. Click the **Start** button, and in the search box type **Allow a program**. In the list that appears, click **Allow a program through Windows Firewall**.

    The **Allowed Programs** window is displayed, as shown in Figure \=16–57.

    If the list items are grayed and you can't select or clear a checkbox, that may mean you are using a third-party firewall or your settings are controlled by a network administrator.

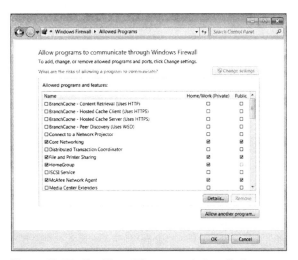

Figure 16–57. *The Allowed Programs window displays programs and features and whether they are allowed through the firewall.*

2. If the **Change settings** button is not grayed, click the button to see whether that gives you access to the list items. If the **Change settings** button is grayed, then you must use the third-party firewall or security suite program to change these settings or contact your network administrator if you are on a company network. See the documentation or online help provided by the third-party software for instructions.

3. Locate the program or feature you want to change.

If the program you want to change is not on the list, click **Allow another program**. In the **Add a Program** dialog box, select the program from the list or locate it with the Browse button, and then click **Add**.

4.   In the **Allowed Programs** window, select the check box next to an item to allow it through the firewall, or clear the check box if you don't want to allow the item.

5.   When you are done with your changes, click **OK**.

Protecting Against Spyware

OK, scary stuff first. In its most malicious form, **spyware** (sometimes called **adware**) can record the websites you visit and your keystrokes—such as what you type in your login name and password boxes—and send that information to thieves or criminals on the Internet. For example, when you log on to your online banking account, spyware can record your username and password and send that information to somebody else on the Internet. A thief can then log on to your banking account and wreak havoc.

> **CAUTION:** There's another tactic for getting your online bank account information via a faked website called **phishing**. You can find out more about phishing and how to avoid it later in this chapter; see "Surfing the Internet and Exchanging E-mail Safely."

In most cases, spyware isn't as dangerous as viruses, but it can be quite annoying. Once on your computer, spyware can do things without your permission:

- Change your home page in your browser
- Add toolbars to your browser
- Change your preferred search service
- Display pop-up advertisement windows
- Slow down your computer

Those are the things you see. In the background, spyware may be gathering personal information by tracking the websites you visit or, worse yet, recording keystrokes.

How Does Spyware Protection Work?

A spyware protection program works similarly to a virus protection program. It offers a multipronged approach to detecting, intercepting, quarantining, and deleting spyware:

- It scans your computer for known spyware programs.
- It detects and notifies you of suspicious activities or downloads that might be spyware actions.

- It quarantines suspicious programs so that you can decide whether to remove them or allow them to perform on your computer

- It automatically updates the antispyware signature files on your computer, which are used to detect and deal with new spyware programs as they appear on the Internet.

Window 7 includes its own antispyware software, Windows Defender. Many antivirus programs and security suites also include antispyware. You can run more than one antispyware program, unlike virus protection or firewalls. You only need one, but if you use more than one, they usually do not interfere with each other.

How Did Spyware Get on My Computer?

Spyware often comes in the front door as part of some other program or service you agreed to download to your computer. A site may offer something free, such as emoticons for e-mail messages, screen savers, program "skins," and so on. During the installation process, you may be asked to allow the service to install other programs as a condition of receiving their services for free. This may be spelled out in a lengthy license agreement, which most people just click through without reading what they are agreeing to. Once you realize something is wrong, it may be impossible to get rid of the spyware by yourself. Even when you go into the Internet Options or search preferences settings, you can't get back your preferred home page or search service.

Fortunately, Windows Defender and other antispyware programs are designed to fix this.

Using Windows Defender for Spyware Protection

Windows 7 includes its own antispyware program. The first time you run Windows Defender, you'll want to do a full scan of your computer. After that, you can set up a schedule to automatically scan your computer daily, weekly, or however often you want.

If you use another antispyware program, the commands, buttons, and menus will be different, but the general process is the same:

1. Turn on the spyware protection program or feature.

2. Set up a schedule for daily or weekly scans, usually a quick scan.

3. Adjust how the program should deal with any issues it finds.

4. Run a full scan the first time, and then let the schedule you set up automatically run scans on a regular basis.

Using Windows Defender for spyware protection is optional but is highly recommended if your antivirus program does not already provide spyware protection.

Turning on Windows Defender

If you already have a third-party security suite installed, that program may have its own antispyware program and will have automatically turned off Windows Defender. Or, somebody in your household turned it off. With antispyware, it is okay to have more than one program in use and installed. Generally, antispyware programs do not interfere with each other.

> **NOTE:** Antivirus software is different. You should only have one antivirus program installed and in use.

To turn on Windows Defender:

1. Click the **Start** button, and in the search box type **Windows Defender**. In the list that appears, click **Windows Defender**.

   If you have not turned on Windows Defender, you will be prompted to turn it on, as shown in Figure 16–58. If you see this message, click the **click here to turn it on** link.

Figure 16–59. *Windows Defender is usually in a turned-off state when Windows 7 is installed.*

   If Windows Defender was already on or you just turned it on, the **Windows Defender** window is displayed, as shown in Figure 16–60.

2. In the toolbar, click **Tools**, and when the **Tools and Settings** window appears, click **Options**.

   The **Options** window appears, as shown in Figure 16–61.

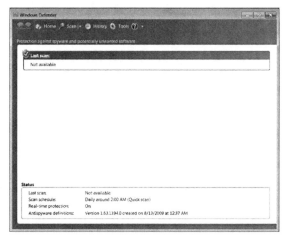

Figure 16–60. *The Windows Defender window provides the current status of your scans, as well as toolbar buttons to run, schedule, view, or configure scans.*

3. Make sure **Automatically scan my computer (recommended)** is selected, and then choose your options to schedule the scan.

4. Click the down arrow for **Frequency**, and then choose **Daily**, or a day of the week if you want to run it weekly. If you connect to the Internet daily, schedule a daily scan for the best protection.

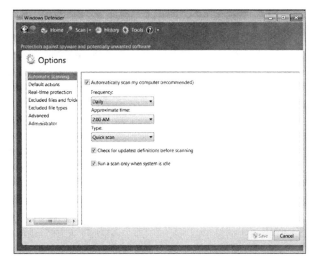

Figure 16–61. *The Options window allows you to set a schedule for automatically scanning your computer.*

5. Click the down arrow for **Approximate time**, and then choose a time when your computer is normally on. The scan can't run when your computer is off.

6. Click the down arrow for **Type**, and then choose **Quick scan** if you will be running the scan frequently, such as daily, or **Full scan** if you will be running the scan less frequently, such as weekly.

7. Select **Check for updated definitions before scanning**. This is how you keep Windows Defender automatically updated. Windows Defender will check the Web for new definitions before running the scan. Microsoft and other antispyware programs are constantly discovering new threats, and these updates allow the program to detect and deal with these new threats.

8. Select **Run a scan only when system is idle**. The scan can slow down your computer, so this setting minimizes the effect on your computer by running it only when the computer is on but you are not actively using it.

9. Click the other options in the left column to see other settings you can configure.

    You may not need to change or set any other options for now; for most people, the default settings are OK. If you want Windows Defender to notify you of issues but not take any actions without your approval, you can change that in **Default actions**.

10. Click **Save** when you are done changing options.

Run a Full Scan as Soon as You Can

The first time you turn on and use Windows Defender, it is a good idea to run a full scan. A full scan takes several hours, so be sure when you start the scan that you can leave your computer on for as long as Windows Defender needs to complete it. That may mean leaving your computer on overnight when nobody is using it. If you leave your computer on but unattended, you can lock the computer by pressing Windows+L. Also, if you're leaving your computer in an idle state while the scan is running, make sure that in the **Control Panel** item **Power Options**, the settings for **Put the computer to sleep** are set to **As long as possible** or **Never**. You can access these settings by typing **change when the computer sleeps** in the **Start** menu's search box.

Scanning your computer for spyware

To scan your computer for spyware:

1. In Windows Defender, click **Home**.

2. Click the arrow next to **Scan**, and select **Full Scan**, as shown in Figure 16–62.

   When the scan is complete, a summary is displayed similar to Figure 16–63.

   When Windows Defender detects spyware, it uses an alert level system to let you know how severe the problem is and what you should do about it. If you get an alert from the scan and are not sure what the levels mean, click the help icon (the round blue and white question mark button) to the right of **Tools** on the toolbar.

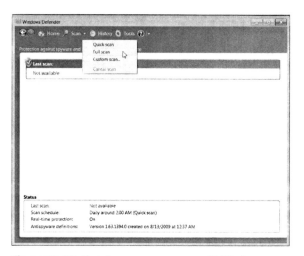

Figure 16–62. *If you've never run a scan with Windows Defender or have not run one for quite a while, run a Full scan.*

If you do not want to see these alerts in the future, you can click the **Tools** button, click **Options**, and then click **Default actions**.

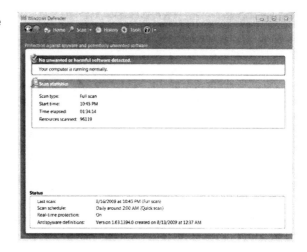

Figure 16–63. *The larger the hard drive, the longer it will take the scan to complete. A full scan takes much longer than a quick scan.*

Choosing an Antivirus Program

The cost of this software is very small compared to the cost of the time you can lose fixing your computer or redoing lost work. If your computer did not come with a virus protection program, you can buy the software either in a retail box with an installation disc or as a software download from a website. Or, you may be able to get it free or at a low cost from your Internet provider.

Once you've installed it, you will receive free updates to the software for a set subscription period, usually a year. This subscription is a very important part of your protection. Just as Microsoft releases patches and updates on a regular basis through Windows Update, your virus protection program checks for regular updates from the virus protection program service. Like Windows Update, most virus protection programs allow you to schedule these updates so that they download and install automatically in the background, without any action required on your part.

Getting Security Software for Free or Cheap

Many companies offer antivirus software separately or in security suites that include a firewall, antivirus software, and antispyware. You can purchase and download this software directly over the web, through Microsoft's referral site, or in a retail box from a store.

However, you may be able to get this software for free or inexpensively. Make no mistake about this—you do need this software, and it is well worth it even if you have to pay for it.

> **NOTE:** Free or cheap still means a legal, licensed copy of the software. Borrowing, copying, or loaning software without a license for each installed copy is illegal.

Tips for Getting Security Software

Here are some tips for obtaining security software:

- **Look for free versions already on your computer**. Check your computer for free or trial versions provided by your computer manufacturer. Check the **Programs** menu, your desktop icons, or any extra program disks that came with your computer for antivirus, virus protection, or security suite programs. You may be eligible for a free 30-day to one-year subscription.

- **Get free software from your Internet service provider**. Check with your Internet service provider or your broadband provider—many offer free security software with their service, which you can install on all your computers in your household.

- **Get free software through your work**. Some companies buy a site license, which allows employees to install a copy of the software on their computer at home. If you use a computer at home for your work, your company may pay for the cost of security software even if they don't have a site license.

- **Purchase a family pack**. Every computer in your home should have security software. Many security software companies offer a discount when you buy several copies at the same time. These "family packs" usually include three to five licenses so that you can install it on all of your computers. Most antivirus programs or security suites are available for multiple versions of Windows so that you can install it on your Windows 7 computer as well as older versions of Windows such as Windows Vista or Windows XP.

- **Don't overbuy**. You only need one firewall and one antivirus program on each computer. If you run more than one of each of these, they will not work together, and you'll have to uninstall or disable one. Microsoft already provides a good firewall, automatic updates, and antispyware program free with Windows. You really only need to purchase and install an antivirus program—if there aren't any free ones available on your computer, from your Internet service provider, or from your employer.

Getting Antivirus Software through Action Center

If you do not have antivirus protection, *Windows Action Center* can help you locate third-party security suites, antivirus, and spyware protection. Action Center provides links to pages where you can purchase, download, and install this software without leaving your desk.

Before you install any virus protection or security suite program, make sure you will be able to leave your computer on for several hours after installation. Typically, these programs prompt you to run a full virus scan when installation is complete. Some programs even run a scan before installation to make sure there aren't viruses already on your computer that could block or interfere with your virus protection software installation. A full virus scan can take several hours, but it is really important that you run this as soon as possible. After the first full virus scan, you usually have an option to schedule quick scans daily or weekly. Even with frequent quick scans, it is a good idea to run a full scan once in awhile. Many people find it convenient to run the full scan overnight while they are asleep.

To get antivirus software through Action Center:

3. Right-click the notification icon in the taskbar, and then click **Open Action Center**.

   If you do not have a virus protection program installed, Action Center provides a link to obtain a program online, as shown in Figure 16–64.

4. Click **Find a program online**.

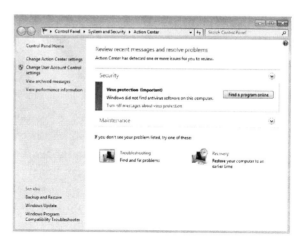

Figure 16–64. *The Virus protection alert and Find a program online button are displayed when there is no antivirus program installed.*

Windows will connect to the Internet and access a Microsoft web page similar to Figure 16–65. The programs listed will be compatible with Windows 7.

Note Web pages change frequently, and the list of companies may change at any time.

5. Click the company logos to go to the websites and view the offerings. Most offer a free 30-day trial so that you can install the program and try it before you buy it.

6. When you find one that you like, follow the instructions on your screen to purchase, download, and install the software.

Figure 16–65. *Security software providers that are compatible with Windows 7. Microsoft may change the list of programs displayed here from time to time.*

During installation, you may need to allow the program to shut down other programs that might interfere with the installation. If you already have another virus protection or security suite installed on your computer, you may be prompted to uninstall it. After you download and install the antivirus or security suite program, you will be prompted to run a full virus scan.

Using the Security Center from a Third-Party Internet Security Suite

You don't have to use Microsoft's Action Center or security programs. Your computer may have come with other security programs or an alternate security center. The important thing is to make sure that you have these basic security features installed and scheduled to run automatically:

- Firewall

- Virus protection

- Spyware protection

- Windows Updates from Microsoft

- Security software updates from the security program or security suite vendor

The Windows Action Center and third-party security centers or overview pages display the security status of all your security features at a glance and the expiration date for your subscription. In general, green is good and means you don't need to do anything. Red is not good; it means something is off, something needs updating, or a scan hasn't been run recently. The example in Figure 16–66 illustrates one of the many different ways these programs may present the status and tools.

Figure 16–66. *The Norton Security Suite summary page*

Running and Maintaining Virus Protection

The previous examples of security centers show that each vendor has its own tools, set of features, and status information. The setup and use of virus protection varies, so it's not possible to use an example of one program to demonstrate how all of them work or should work.

The overall process you should follow is similar for most virus protection programs. Consult the documentation or online help for your program for specific steps:

1. Run a full scan soon after you install the security software. No matter which software vendor you use, the first full scan usually takes several hours.

2. Schedule regular virus scans for at least once a week or several days a week. You can use quick scans most of the time and then once in a while run a full scan.

3. Set up automatic updates of the virus signature or detection files. The default setting (meaning it will do this without you having to specify the setting) for most programs is to automatically check the Internet daily for updates when you turn on your computer.

4. Specify what you want the program to do when it detects a virus or issue. Your options vary depending on the vendor, but usually they include creating a report of problems detected for you to review and then waiting for your approval to fix the problems, automatically fixing all the problems for you, or providing a report afterward of the problems that were detected and fixed.

Surfing the Internet and Exchanging E-mail Safely

Virus protection and spyware protection help protect your computer by detecting bad things on your computer. A firewall is good at preventing outside programs or code from running on your computer or from accessing it. But viruses and spyware don't just magically appear on your computer. They usually get there through e-mail attachments or downloads from web pages. Fortunately, there are many ways that security suites, browsers, e-mail programs, and servers can protect you.

Defending Against E-mail Threats

You first line of defense is your mail service provider. The better services filter out junk mail and mail with dangerous attachments before the messages even reach your mail inbox. Some junk mail may get through and be sent to a junk mail or spam folder in your e-mail account folders. You can usually adjust the sensitivity of how mail is sorted to your junk mail folder if too much junk mail is getting through to your inbox or too many legitimate e-mail messages are going straight into your junk mail folder instead of your inbox. If you still get too much junk mail after adjusting your junk mail settings, you may want to try switching to another e-mail provider. The e-mail program itself may block certain types of mail attachments, for example, blocking any file with the filename extension .exe. But sometimes, the danger is in the links or text of the e-mail message itself.

Many security centers or security suites include e-mail scanning features. That means that when you open an e-mail message you just received, the security software will scan the text and attachments of the message for dangerous links or commands that might not be readily visible to you when you look at the message. Often, pictures in an e-mail message have viruses or dangerous scripts that run when you click or view the picture. So, some e-mail programs automatically hide the pictures in the message but offer you the option to view them.

To Protect Yourself Against E-mail Threats

This is not a complete list of everything you can do, but just following a few guidelines can make your e-mail much safer:

- **Use the junk mail filtering features in your e-mail program** Adjust the settings, and if you are still having problems with junk mail, try another e-mail provider. If the program offers something like a **Mark as junk** command, use it on any junk mail that gets through to your regular inbox. Some e-mail programs "learn" from what you mark as junk mail and use that to improve the filtering.

- **Turn on** e-mail message scanning if it is available in your security software, or consider getting a security suite that includes it.

- **Do not open a mail message even if you do recognize the sender, if the message subject line looks suspicious** Often the subject lines are blank, just say RE:, or FW:, are poorly written, misspelled, typo-filled, or just don't make sense. Drag it or move it to your junk mail folder without opening it, if you can.

- **Add senders you do want to your safe senders list or mail address book** This will reduce the chance of legitimate mail from a new e-mail contact going into your junk mail folder.

- **Beware of suspicious e-mails** Beware of anything that looks like a message from your bank asking you to click a link in the message and log on to your bank account to check or fix something; this is called *phishing*. These e-mails, and the sites they link to, are an attempt to get you to provide your login and password so that somebody can log into your accounts and transfer money out of it. If something looks like it needs immediate attention or you are not sure if the website is legitimate, call your bank on the telephone. Many have 24-hour telephone customer service, including technical support for their website and online bank.

Safe Surfing on the Internet

Windows 7 provides much of its Internet security through the settings in Internet Options in Control Panel. These settings control what kinds of programs and features on web pages can run on your computer, what kinds of information can be stored on your computer (cookies), and how programs are downloaded and run from the Internet. The default security settings should be safe for most people without being too restrictive. Occasionally the browser's security settings block an action it deems unsafe, and you may need to temporarily change some settings to allow a program to work.

Internet security suites from third-party vendors provide additional protection. They are not mandatory like the firewall, virus and spyware protection, and Windows Update. But if your security suite offers additional Internet protection, make use of it. If you find that it is blocking too much, you can usually adjust settings to be less restrictive.

Security Check List

The following checklist summarizes things you can do to help protect your computer and make it safer to use:

- Assign all users on the computer to password-protected user accounts, at the appropriate user level of standard or administrator, as described in Chapter 12: "Setting Up and Transferring User Accounts."

- Set the **User Account Control** to an appropriate level.

- Perform regular backups of your computer, as described at the beginning of this chapter.

- Along with performing your regular backups, be ready for disaster recovery in case your computer is lost, stolen, or irreparably damaged.

- Ensure that Windows Firewall is on in the Windows Action Center, or install and turn on a third-party firewall.

- Use caution when a program requests permission to access your computer through the firewall. Allow only the programs you trust.

- Ensure that Automatic Updates are enabled in the Action Center, and accept the recommended settings to automatically download and install updates daily.

- Turn on virus protection and spyware protection:

  - Scan your computer immediately for viruses and spyware.

  - Set the programs to automatically download the latest virus signatures, spyware definitions, and software updates.

  - Schedule follow-up weekly scans.

  - Accept default settings to enable protection each time you start your computer.

- Use your junk mail features in your e-mail program and service.

- Use e-mail scanning features if they are available in your security suite.

- Avoid opening suspicious e-mail messages.

- Use the default security settings in Internet Options unless specifically told to change them by a person or program you trust.

- Use any additional Internet security settings offered by your security suite.

Summary

In this chapter, you have learned:

- The value and importance of backups

- The two types of backup: data files and disk image

- How to set up Windows Backup and Restore to store backups locally or on a network

- How to check your backups to make sure they are saving the data files you want protected

- How to restore data files

- How to recover your computer with System Restore and advanced recovery techniques

- Third-party alternatives to Windows Backup and Restore

- How to create a disaster plan: locate your original Windows installation disks or media, and your product key; schedule regular backups of your entire computer as well as important document files; regularly store your backups in a location physically separate from your computer, or on an online backup service

- How to check your overall security status with Action Center

- How to view or change your Windows Firewall and Windows Update settings

- How to get virus protection software, which is not included in Windows 7. Microsoft provides a website where you can compare, download, and try or buy virus protection software from third-party vendors. Schedule the virus protection software to regularly scan your computer for viruses, and allow the virus protection software to automatically download and install updates

- How to set up spyware protection by setting up Windows Defender, included with Windows 7, or other antispyware programs. Just like virus protection software, schedule regular scans of your computer and automatic download and installation of updates

- How to explore and set up e-mail filtering of spam and junk mail, detection of phishing sites, and detection of dangerous attachments. The protection features vary with each e-mail program

- How to explore and set up the security settings in your Internet browser programs, such as Microsoft Internet Explorer, Mozilla Firefox, and others.

Next Steps

You may find the following related chapters useful:

- Chapter 5: "Installing Programs" to learn how to create a disaster recovery disk, and tips for organizing, storing, and protecting your program installation disks

- Chapter 12: "Setting Up and Transferring User Accounts" to learn how to protect your computer by controlling access with user accounts and passwords

- Chapter 17: "Troubleshooting and Maintaining Your Computer" about starting in Safe Mode, performing System Restore, and troubleshooting crashed hard drives

- Chapter 18: "Using Windows at Work and On the Road" to learn how to use BitLocker to secure your hard drive, corporate backups and network security.

Troubleshooting and Maintaining Your Computer

An ounce of prevention is worth a pound of cure.

—Benjamin Franklin

The more time you put into protecting and maintaining your computer, the less time you will need to spend fixing things. Unfortunately, a problem that rears its big ugly head often gets your attention better than gentle nudges and reminders about taking care of your computer. Sometimes computers have problems. If you are prepared, you can minimize the damage and disruption caused by your computer not working right.

This chapter will cover

- Using Windows troubleshooters, Safe Mode, System Restore, and Advanced Recovery to diagnose and fix problems

- Fixing problems and mistakes in programs and documents

- Getting help from within Windows and from the Web

- Maintaining your computer and equipment

- Preventing problems before they happen

Fixing Problems from A to Ctrl+Z

Table 17–1 provides a quick reference for common problems and solutions and where to get more help.

Table 17–1. *Common Problems and Solutions*

Problem Areas	Solutions
Documents and files	In this chapter, see Fixing Things at the Document Level.
	Also, see:
	▧ Chapter 12: "Setting Up and Transferring User Accounts"
	▧ Chapter 15: "Protecting Your Computer and Data"
I made a mistake in the current document I am working in.	▧ Try using the **Undo** command (Ctrl+Z).
	▧ Try using the **File ➤ Save As** command to save the current file with a different name and then reopen the original file.
	▧ If you are experimenting or trying something new, work on a copy of the file, not the original file.
My program just crashed while I was working on a file and I think I lost my changes.	▧ Try restarting the program, and opening the file you were working on. Microsoft Office, OpenOffice.org, and many other programs usually have an auto recovery option that saves changes to your file as you are working. This option may not be on by default, so check the program's Save options.
	▧ Open up a backup copy. Some programs provide the option to always create a backup copy whenever you are working on a file.
	▧ If you are experimenting, trying something new, try making lots of changes, and manually save your file frequently.
	▧ If none of the above work, you can use your backup and recovery program to retrieve your last backup of that file. It will not have any changes made since your last backup.

Problem Areas	Solutions
I worked on a file I received in an e-mail and now I cannot find it.	▨ If you opened a file attachment from an e-mail message, it was temporary unless you saved it to a folder on your computer. When you open and work on a file attachment, it is stored in a temporary folder. Even if you saved the file before closing it, it may have only been saved to the temporary files folder. The temporary files folder generally empties when you shut down the computer. The next time you use your computer the file will be gone.
	TIP: When you open a file attachment, immediately save the attachment to a regular folder on your computer. Open the file from the regular folder location before doing any work in the file.
I did not get an e-mail message I was expecting from somebody.	▨ Sometimes mail programs get a little overzealous and send legitimate mail to the Junk or Spam folder. Check your Junk or Spam folders whenever you open your mail program. If you find a message in a junk mail folder that is legitimate, drag or move the message to your Inbox, and add the sender to your mail program's safe sender list.
When I try to use a downloaded installation file it does not work.	▨ You may need administrator-level permissions to run the installation program.
	▨ Your security settings in your Internet Protection or Security Suite may be blocking the file because it is an unsafe file type or a virus has been detected in the file.
	▨ Sometimes installation programs and downloads are buggy.
	▨ When you download a program and select the Run option instead of Save and it doesn't work, try downloading the file to your computer first and run it from your computer location.
	▨ When you download a program and select the Save option instead of Run and it does not work, try downloading the file again and use the Run option instead.

Problem Areas	Solutions
Programs	In this chapter, see Using Programs and Features to Fix Problems Also see: ▪ Chapter 4: "Exploring Programs and Features" ▪ Chapter 5: "Installing Programs" ▪ Chapter 17 "Using Windows 7 at Work and on the Road"
When I try to run a program it crashes a lot. **I cannot get the program to run at all.** **I cannot run a program that worked on previous versions of Windows, such as Windows XP or earlier.**	▪ Try uninstalling and reinstalling the program, or if available, use the Repair option in Programs and Features. ▪ Try running the program in compatibility mode. ▪ Try a troubleshooter: **Control Panel ➤ All Control Panel Items ➤ Troubleshooter ➤ Programs.** ▪ Download and run the Windows 7 Upgrade Advisor from the Windows 7 Compatibility Center at `www.microsoft.com` to make sure that the program is supposed to work in Windows 7. ▪ Check the program publisher's support site to see if there is an update you need to install in order for it to run in Windows 7. ▪ If the program just started "misbehaving" recently, try a System Restore to a restore point before the problems started. ▪ Try installing a virtual machine player, such as Windows Virtual PC (available for Windows 7 Professional and Ultimate [not Home Ultimate]) editions, or VMware Player (free at `www.vmware.com/tryvmware`)
When I try to run the program, I get an error message that I need a 64-bit version of the program.	▪ Unfortunately, many of the programs that trigger this error message are very old and it is not likely that the publisher will ever create an update to work on 64-bit. Your best bet is to try to run the program in a virtual machine such as Windows Virtual PC or VMware Player.

Problem Areas	Solutions
Network problems	In this chapter, see Using Windows Troubleshooters
	Also see Chapter 14: "Connecting to the Internet and Home Networks"
I cannot access printers, files, or other computers on my network.	▓ Check to make sure all computer devices are on, connected to the network, and on the same Homegroup.
	▓ Check the document and printer sharing settings for the computers you want to connect.
	▓ Try a troubleshooter: **Control Panel ➤ All Control Panel Items ➤ Troubleshooter ➤ Network and Internet ➤ Access shared files and folders on other computers**.
My backups keep failing to complete because they cannot connect to the network location I specified for the destination.	▓ Make sure the storage location is online and connected to the network.
	▓ Make sure your computer is connected to the network.
	▓ Check to see if the storage location requires a password to access it. If it does, in your backup program's settings there should be a place where you can specify a log-in name and password that has access to the storage location or server.
	▓ Check to make sure your storage location has enough disk space for your backup. You may need to add another storage device or drive, or delete your oldest backups from your storage device.
I get a message when I start up that Windows cannot reconnect to all network drives.	▓ Click the notification message to see which network location it is referring to.
	▓ Check to make sure your computer and the network drive is online and connected to the network.
	▓ Check to see if you need a user name and password to access the network drive. It may be different than the user account you use to log in to Windows on the computer you are currently using.
I cannot connect to a wireless network.	▓ Check to see if you need an encryption password to connect to the network. If you can see the network listed on your list of wireless networks, and it says it is a secured network, you need to supply an encryption password.

Problem Areas	Solutions
	▦ If you can see the wireless network on your list of networks, but it only has one bar, try moving your computer to a different location that is closer to or on a more direct line of sight to the wireless router.
	▦ Your wireless card or adapter may be disabled. If your wireless card is built in to the computer, the computer manufacturer usually provides their own utility for managing wireless adapter settings.
	▦ If you are using an external wireless adapter, like a USB adapter, you may need to install or update drivers specific for that adapter.
Hardware/device	In this chapter, see Updating Devices and Driver Also see Chapter 13: "Connecting Printers, Monitors, and Devices"
A device does not work properly or does not work at all.	▦ Check **Action Center** in the notification area of the Windows taskbar to see if there are any notifications related to this issue and device.
	▦ Download and run the Windows 7 Upgrade Advisor from the Windows 7 Compatibility Center at www.microsoft.com to make sure that the device is supposed to work in Windows 7.
	▦ Go to the device manufacturer's support web site and make sure you have the latest drivers for Windows 7.
	▦ Update or reinstall the device drivers.
	▦ If it is a USB device, check that the USB cable is securely connected.
	▦ Try connecting the device through a different USB port. If it is connected through a USB hub, try connecting directly to the USB port on the computer.
	▦ Try a troubleshooter: **Control Panel ➤ All Control Panel Items ➤ Troubleshooter ➤ Hardware and Sound.**
The battery on my laptop runs down really quickly.	▦ Check your laptop's current power plan settings in **Control Panel ➤ All Control Panel Items ➤ Power Options.** Switch to the **Power saver** plan. If you are already using that plan, adjust the settings to use even less power.

Problem Areas	Solutions
Display problems	In this chapter, see: ▓ Running Windows 7 in Safe Mode ▓ Using System Restore to Fix Problems ▓ Using Advanced Recovery ▓ Maintaining your computer and equipment ▓ Preventing problems before they happen Also see Chapter 15: "Protecting Your Computer and Data"
I cannot get the cool Aero effects.	▓ Try a troubleshooter: Control Panel ➤ All Control Panel Items ➤ Troubleshooter ➤ Appearance and Personalization ➤ Display Aero desktop effects. ▓ A program or device you are currently using requires a downgraded resolution and so Aero effects are temporarily not available.
When I turn on my laptop, the screen is dead.	▓ Connect your laptop to an external monitor. If it displays Windows, your laptop screen probably needs replacing. Unfortunately a replacement screen may cost nearly as much as a new inexpensive laptop. If you need the functionality of a laptop, copy your files and data from the old computer to a new laptop. If you only use it at your desk, use an external monitor.
I cannot get multiple monitors to work. **I cannot align or arrange my multiple monitors.**	▓ Check display settings in Screen Resolution: Control Panel ➤ All Control Panel Items ➤ Display ➤ Screen Resolution. ▓ See Chapter 13: "Connecting Printers, Monitors, and Devices" for tips and tricks for setting up and using multiple monitors.
I started a program and it appears in the taskbar, but I cannot find it anywhere on the screen.	▓ This sometimes occurs when using multiple monitors. If you move a laptop between two different locations, or connect and disconnect monitors at one location, your computer may be opening the program window on a display that is not in use or is not connected. Check display settings in Screen Resolution: Control Panel ➤ All Control Panel Items ➤ Display ➤ Screen Resolution. Make sure the settings match what you actually have in use.
The title bar or top part of a	▓ Sometimes you can trigger the window to resize

Problem Areas	Solutions
window is off screen and I cannot grab it or move it.	and move the top of the window down by dragging one of the sides of the window.

■ Sometimes you can use the Move command and the arrow keys to move the window back on screen: hover over the program's icon in the taskbar, until the "peek" window appears, right-click the peek window, and then click **Move**. Then you can use the arrow keys on the keyboard to move the window. The program I encounter this problem most often with is Microsoft Word. Figure 17–1 describes how to get to the Move command.

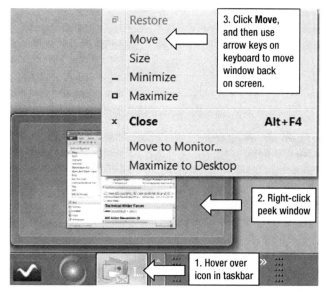

Figure 17–1. *Accessing the Move command for a program window that is partially off screen*

TIP Sometimes you cannot get to the context menu through steps 1. and 2. If that happens, click the window of the program you are trying to move and then press ALT and the SPACEBAR at the same time. The context menu should appear and then you can click the **Move** command or press M.

Problem Areas	Solutions
Windows and PC performance problems	In this chapter, see: ▥ Running Windows 7 in Safe Mode ▥ Using System Restore to Fix Problems ▥ Using Advanced Recovery ▥ Maintaining your computer and equipment ▥ Preventing problems before they happen Also see Chapter 15: "Protecting Your Computer and Data"
My computer recently started acting funny.	▥ Try using System Restore to restore your computer settings to a restore point prior to the date you first noticed problems. ▥ You may have a virus or spyware. Run a scan of your computer with your security or Internet protection program.
My computer seems to be slower.	▥ Try a troubleshooter: **Control Panel ➤ All Control Panel Items ➤ Troubleshooter ➤ System and Security >➤ Check for performance issues**. ▥ Try a PC tune-up program. Many PC manufacturers provide one when installing Windows on your computer; you may also find them in Internet protection or security software suites.

> **TIP:** I have not tested and compared a variety of PC tuneup programs, but I have been very satisfied with **System Mechanic**, available from www.iolo.com. I have used it for over three years on all of my computers, and it is especially helpful in clearing up system clutter and low memory problems.

▥   If you've had your computer for a while, your hard drive may be starting to fill up. The more data you add to your hard drive, the more your hard drive can get cluttered. Run **Disk Cleanup** and **Disk Defragmenter**; both are at **Start ➤ All Programs ➤ Accessories ➤ System Tools**.

Problem Areas	Solutions
After I log in to Windows, it takes a long time before I can do anything with my desktop.	▓ You may have several programs that are set up to run automatically when you start your computer. Check the **Startup** folder in **Start ➤ All Programs ➤ Startup**, and remove any programs that you do not think you need to automatically start. Deleting a program from the Startup folder does not delete the program from your computer.
	▓ If you have programs that use the Internet, like e-mail and instant messaging, they may be trying to connect to the Internet as soon as you start Windows. Sometimes in home networks, it takes a while for your computer to connect to the Internet and in the meantime these programs are waiting in the background. Check the options in your e-mail and instant message programs, to see if there is an option selected to automatically start the program when you start Windows. Clear those options and see if your startups go more quickly.
	▓ Your computer may be running an antivirus scan in the background. Or, it may be running a scheduled backup. You can change the schedule and frequency of these tasks within in your antivirus and backup programs.
My computer will not start Windows.	▓ Try starting your computer in Safe Mode.
	▓ If you can get it to run in Safe Mode, but cannot get it to work in regular mode, perform a System Restore.
	▓ Try Advanced Recovery.
	▓ Try the Disaster Recovery disk provided by your computer manufacturer or that you created yourself.
	▓ Use your Backup and Recovery program to perform a full Disaster Recovery.
My computer will not start at all.	▓ Check the power supply. Make sure the power cable is fully connected from your computer to the power source.
	▓ Sometimes if a laptop battery is dead it will not even start with AC power. Remove the battery and then try to start the computer. If that works, reinsert the battery while the power is on, and leave the laptop on for a while until it gets partially charged. Then shut down the computer and allow the battery to recharge. If your battery cannot get fully

Problem Areas	Solutions
	charged or charged enough to use on battery power alone, you probably need to replace the battery.

> **NOTE:** If your model of laptop requires opening the computer case to access the battery, take the laptop to a qualified repair technician or shop.

Problem Areas	Solutions
My hard drive crashed.	▓ Replace the defective hard drive and reinstall everything—Windows, all programs, and the backups of all of your documents, pictures, videos, music, etc.
	▓ If you have a full image backup you may be able to restore from that using your backup and recovery program.
	▓ As a last resort, send your hard drive to a Data Retrieval Service. Sometimes they can recover the data from the disk inside by repairing the reading heads and other mechanical parts inside. If they are able to retrieve any data, it may cost several thousand dollars.

Using Windows 7 to Fix Problems

Oops! You did something wrong. You lost something. Or so you think. The sooner you discover something is wrong, the easier it is to fix it. There is no panic button that will magically make everything right again. But a few Windows features and good practices will help a lot.

So let's say that one day your computer works fine, but the next day it is slow or some programs do not work right. There are several possible causes:

- ▓ A new program you installed
- ▓ A new device you added
- ▓ Changes or customizations you made through various Windows settings
- ▓ A virus or spyware infection on your computer

Windows 7 provides several features that can help you fix your computer. They can help you at every level—from Windows not starting right, to Windows starting but the computer not running as fast or as smoothly as before. Some of the most useful tools and features for fixing Windows problems are as follows:

- **Windows troubleshooters:** Windows provides troubleshooters to help you fix common problems. You can access these through the Help system, or they may pop up when Windows detects specific problems.

- **Programs and Features:** This Control Panel item enables you to uninstall, change, or repair programs or updates already installed on your computer.

- **Safe Mode:** When you start your computer in Safe Mode, Windows runs with the minimum number of drivers and settings so you can uninstall programs or devices or make other changes

> **NOTE: Drivers** are small files that tell Windows and your device how to work with each other. Almost every device in or attached to your computer has some kind of driver. Some of these may not be necessary when your computer requires only a few basic functions—for example, when your computer is running in Safe Mode. By loading only the basic drivers for devices such as your keyboard, mouse, and video card, Safe Mode enables you to fix problems that are occurring when your computer is operating in a normal state with all of the drivers running.

- **System Restore:** If your computer worked fine a few days ago but started running poorly after installing some programs or devices, you may be able to fix it with System Restore. System Restore enables you to go back in time to a point when your computer was working properly, and restore your computer to the state it was in then. System Restore does not remove or delete document or content files created after the restore point. It is not a file or image backup, like the backup and restore features described in Chapter 6.

- **Backup and Restore:** If you perform regular backups of your system image and your files, you can restore the entire computer or just your files.

> **NOTE:** See Chapter 15: "Protecting Your Computer and Data," to learn how to set up a recurring backup plan so your computer files and computer images are backed up daily, weekly, monthly—whatever you choose. For most people, backing up your computer one or more times a week is safe and sufficient.

- **Recovery disc:** This is provided by the computer manufacturer, not Microsoft or Microsoft Windows. This recovery disc contains the complete Windows installation files, and resets your computer back to the settings and state it was in when it left the factory. This will erase all data on your computer, and you will need to reinstall all programs that you installed after you bought the computer.

NOTE: Some computer manufacturers don't provide a DVD with all of the Windows installation files, and instead create a separate hidden partition on your hard drive and store the files there. To access the recovery disk (partition), you may need to have created a separate boot disc beforehand, or select a special command when you start your computer. If you don't receive a recovery disc with your new computer, contact your computer manufacturer. Upon request, some will send you a recovery disc, even if your computer already has a hidden recovery partition on the hard drive.

Using Windows Troubleshooters

Windows 7 provides **troubleshooters** to solve a wide variety of Windows, software, and hardware problems. When Windows detects a problem with Windows, a program, feature, or device, it will attempt to fix the problem or start a troubleshooter that might fix the problem.

If you have a problem and want to try a troubleshooter, there are several ways you can view a list of troubleshooters and the types of problems they address. Windows often offers several ways to do the same thing, and that is true with accessing troubleshooters:

- **Opening the troubleshooter in Control Panel**: This method enables you to start with broad groupings and then work your way down through more-specific lists to one or more troubleshooters that seem to match your problem.

- **Accessing troubleshooters through Help and Support**: This method is more direct if you know which troubleshooter you are looking for, or you know of a problem and want Help and Support to search for troubleshooters that best match your problem.

Either method is just as good; the choice is a matter of preference. Explore both and use the method that works best for you.

Opening the Troubleshooter in Control Panel

To open the troubleshooter in **Control Panel**, follow these steps:

1. Click the **Start** button, and in the **Start** menu's search box, type **Troubleshooting**. In the list that appears, under **Control Panel** click **Troubleshooting**. The **Control Panel** item **Troubleshooting** is displayed, as shown in Figure 17–2.

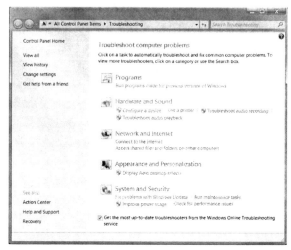

Figure 17–2. The Troubleshooting page in Control Panel groups the troubleshooters into categories such as Programs and Hardware and Sound, and lists the most common problems under each category.

2. Under a category, click a task that matches your problem. If you don't see a task that matches your problem, click a category name to view a larger list of problems in that category. For example, click **Programs**. Windows will check the Internet for new troubleshooters in addition to the ones already installed on your computer, and then display a list of problems in the **Programs** category, as shown in Figure 17–3. If you are not connected to the Internet, Windows 7 will just display the troubleshooters already installed on your computer.

Figure 17–3. Many troubleshooters are available to help with problems with programs.

3. Click a task to view a troubleshooter. If, after viewing the first screen of the troubleshooter, it does not appear to be what you want, you can click **Cancel**.

Accessing Troubleshooters through Help and Support

To access troubleshooters through Help and Support, follow these steps:

1. Click the **Start** button, and then click **Help and Support**. **Windows Help and Support** is displayed, as shown in Figure 17–4.

2. In the **Search Help** box, type **Troubleshooter** and then press the **Enter** key.

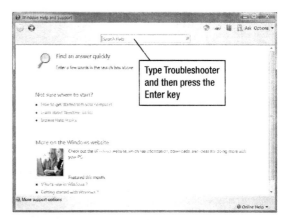

Figure 17–4. *Windows Help and Support includes help with using troubleshooters.*

A list of troubleshooting topics is displayed, as shown in Figure 17–5.

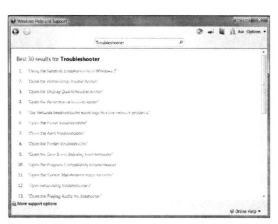

Figure 17–5. *The search results for Troubleshooter in Windows Help and Support provide a longer list of troubleshooters than is displayed in the Troubleshooting page in Control Panel that was shown in Figure 17–2.*

Using a Troubleshooter to Fix Problems with Hardware

A common problem people encounter with a new computer is that hardware or devices that worked with their old computer do not work with the new computer. You can use the Hardware and Devices troubleshooter to guide you through possible solutions.

To use the troubleshooter to identify and fix problems, follow these steps:

1. Scroll down the list of topics as described in the previous section and click **Open the Hardware and Devices troubleshooter**. A Help topic describes the troubleshooter, as shown in Figure 17–6, and provides a link to open the troubleshooter itself.

2. Click the link **Click to open the Hardware and Devices troubleshooter**. When you run this particular troubleshooter, it looks for problems with any hardware or devices on your computer. The troubleshooter will display a series of messages such as the following:

Figure 17–6. *The Help topic describes the problems addressed by the Hardware and Devices troubleshooter, and provides a shortcut link to start the troubleshooter.*

- Detecting problems

- Checking for missing driver

- Resolving problems

- Scanning for hardware change

- Searching for device driver

If the troubleshooter detects that a device is disabled, it will offer to enable it. In the example shown in Figure 17–7, the troubleshooter has detected that a wireless networking card on the computer is not enabled. The person using the computer had turned off wireless networking because the computer was already connected to the home network with a wired (Ethernet) connection.

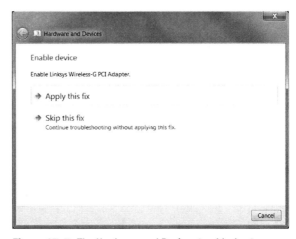

Figure 17–7. *The Hardware and Devices troubleshooter detects a device connected to the computer that was not enabled.*

3. **Apply** or **Skip** the fix as appropriate. The troubleshooter continues detecting problems and displays the next issue. In the example shown in Figure 17–8, the troubleshooter has detected a device that is missing a driver, and offers to install it.

Figure 17–8. *The troubleshooter detects another device that does not have a driver installed.*

4. If the troubleshooter cannot find a driver, a message may be displayed in the notification area. Click the notification link for more details, and a message window is displayed, similar to Figure 17–9.

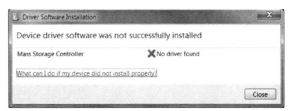

Figure 17–9. *Clicking the notification message that the device did not install correctly displays a message with more details and a link to more help.*

5. Click the link **What can I do if my device did not install properly?**? to open a **Windows Help and Support** page similar to Figure 17–10 that provides more-specific things you can do.

Figure 17–10. *There are several things you can try if Windows cannot find a suitable driver for your device.*

TIP If you did not see any notification message like that shown in Figure 17–9, you can view the help shown in Figure 17–10 by searching **Windows Help and Support** for **What to do when a device isn't installed properly**.

Whether or not you click the notification messages for more information, the troubleshooter continues. When the troubleshooter has completed, it summarizes what was and was not fixed, as shown in Figure 17–11.

Figure 17–11. *When the troubleshooter is done, it displays a report of issues, changes, and fixes.*

The **Explore additional options** link displays a page with other places to look for possible solutions, as shown in Figure 17–12.

Figure 17–12. *You can try these other links for suggestions on how to solve this problem. Windows Communities can be helpful because, if other people have had a similar problem with the same device, they may have found a solution and posted a message to share with others.*

Using Programs and Features to Fix Problems

After you get a new computer or upgrade your existing computer to Windows 7, you may have many programs that you want to install. It is a good idea to install your programs one at a time, restarting your computer between each installation even if the installation program does not require it. If you have a lot of programs to install, spending a little extra time being cautious during installation will save a lot of time and aggravation later. Installing too much, too fast, can give your computer the equivalent of indigestion from eating too much that doesn't agree with it.

Programs and Features in **Control Panel** enables you to uninstall, change, or repair programs or updates already installed on your computer. If after installing a program or programs your computer doesn't work right, you can systematically remove your most recently installed programs until you have figured out which program is causing the problem and can remove or repair it.

> **TIP:** **Programs and Features** isn't just for fixing problems. It's also useful for removing programs you no longer use or for clearing disk space. Chapter 4: "Exploring Programs and Features" provides more information about adding and removing programs on your computer.

If you cannot start your computer, or if it runs very poorly, you may want to start the computer in Safe Mode and then remove the programs while in Safe Mode. If you are not sure which programs are causing problems but have a good idea of when the problems started, you may want to use System Restore instead.

> **TIP:** Later in this chapter, "Running Windows 7 in Safe Mode" describes the trick to getting to Safe Mode when you start up your computer.

To remove a program, follow these steps:

1. Click the **Start** button, and in the **Start** menu's search box, type **remove programs**. In the list that appears, click **Add or remove programs**. The **Programs and Features** window is displayed, as shown in Figure 17–13.

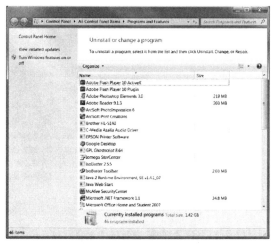

Figure 17–13. *The Programs and Features window displays the programs that are installed on your computer.*

2. Select the program you want to remove, and then click **Uninstall** in the toolbar above the list, as shown in Figure 17–14.

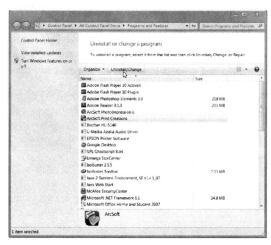

Figure 17–14. *When you select a program in the list, the* **Uninstall** *button appears above the list. Some programs only offer* **Uninstall**, *and some may also offer Change or Repair.*

3. When you click **Uninstall**, the program's *installation* program may start up even though you are *uninstalling*. The installation options for the program displayed in Figure 17–15 include **Modify** and **Repair**, in addition to **Remove** (uninstall). Sometimes you don't need to completely uninstall the program to fix a problem. You may want to try reinstalling the program if that option is available. In this program, you can reinstall with the **Repair** option.

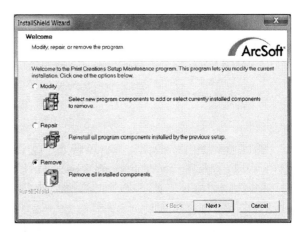

Figure 17–15. *Some programs offer a repair or reinstallation option.*

4. If you are having problems with a program that worked before on another computer, or that you think should run on this computer, try the repair or reinstallation option, if available. Not all programs offer a repair option. Other programs may offer only an **Uninstall** option, as shown in Figure 17–16.

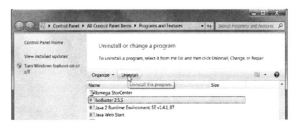

Figure 17–16. *Some programs offer only an **Uninstall** option.*

5. If the program offers only **Uninstall**, click the **Uninstall** button. Windows or the installation program may immediately start uninstalling the program, as shown in Figure 17–17, or may ask you to confirm that you really want to uninstall the program.

Figure 17–17. *The uninstall process may take several minutes, depending on the size and complexity of the program being removed.*

The message and option displayed varies depending on how the software manufacturer designed the program.

When the repair or removal is complete, you may be asked to restart the computer. Even if you aren't asked to, it is a good idea to restart your computer anyway.

> **NOTE:** Many installation programs require that you restart the computer at the end of installation. If you are installing several programs at once, it may be tempting to wait to restart until you have installed several or all programs. Unfortunately, if you install multiple programs and then have problems after restarting your computer, you may not be able to tell which program is causing the problem. Then you'll have to uninstall all of the programs that you just installed.

Running Windows 7 in Safe Mode

Safe Mode starts Windows with a bare minimum of drivers and settings so you can uninstall programs or devices, run System Restore, or make other changes.

> **TIP:** You don't have to be in Safe Mode to use System Restore. "Using System Restore to fix problems" later in this chapter describes how to access System Restore as you would any other program from the **Start** menu.

To get into Safe Mode, you must run it when you first start or restart your computer, before the computer displays the **Starting Windows** screen with the Windows logo on the black background (see Figure 17–18).

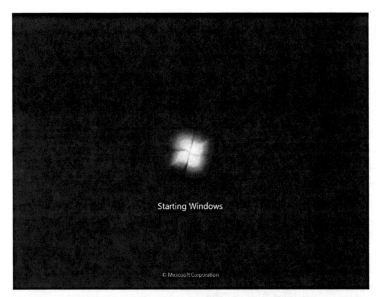

Figure 17–18. *To start in Safe Mode, you must press F8 (usually repeatedly) before this Starting Windows screen is displayed. If this screen appears, you need to restart your computer and try again.*

NOTE: Each computer is different, so some computers get to the **Starting Windows** screen sooner than others. If you miss pressing F8 soon enough and your computer goes to the **Starting Windows** screen shown in Figure 17–18, restart your computer. Wait until the user login screen appears, click the down arrow on the red shut-down key at the bottom right of the screen, and then click **Restart**.

To access Safe Mode, follow these steps:

1. Start or restart your computer.

2. As soon as the screen starts displaying the BIOS information, press the **F8** key repeatedly. If your computer displays a keyboard error message or beeps, or both, ignore it and keep pressing **F8** until the **Advanced Boot Options** screen is displayed, as shown in Figure 17–19.

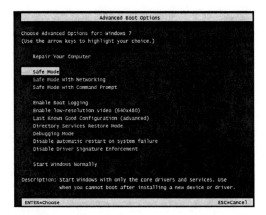

Figure 17–19. *For most purposes, on this screen you'll want to select Safe Mode.*

3. Press the down arrow key on your keyboard to highlight **Safe Mode**, and then press **Enter**. Windows loads the minimum operating system features and drivers needed to run Windows in a very simple mode. As Windows loads drivers and files, the filenames roll down the screen, as shown in Figure 17–20.

Figure 17–20. *It will take a few moments for Windows to load the files it needs to run in Safe Mode.*

When Windows finishes loading the files, it opens in Safe Mode: you see a black screen with the words **Safe Mode** on each corner of the screen. **Windows Help and Support** automatically opens and displays a Help topic on using Safe Mode, as shown in Figure 17–21.

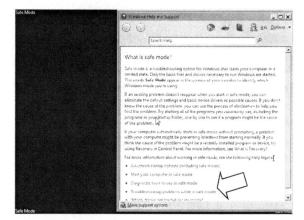

Figure 17–21. *When Windows opens in Safe Mode, the screen isn't pretty but it is functional.*

4. In the Help topic, click **Troubleshooting problems while in safe mode**.

   The troubleshooting page is displayed, as shown in Figure 17–22.

5. If one of the problems listed matches what you are experiencing, click the link for possible solutions. If you are fairly certain that a program you recently installed is causing your problems, you can uninstall the program through **Programs and Features**, using the steps in "Using Programs and Features to fix problems."

Figure 17–22. *You can try several fixes while in Safe Mode.*

SYSTEM RESTORE VS. UNINSTALLING A RECENTLY INSTALLED PROGRAM

The Safe Mode troubleshooter suggests using System Restore if Windows is not working correctly after you installed a program. Another option is to uninstall the program you suspect is causing the problem, instead of using System Restore.

System Restore is safe and reliable, but may take longer than uninstalling a suspect program. The more severe the problems, the better it is to use System Restore instead of uninstall. Sometimes it is easier to identify when your computer last worked okay and the problems started, than to pinpoint what program installation caused the problems. System Restore will usually be a better choice then.

System Restore does not identify what programs or settings are not running correctly, so it restores the settings and programs (good or bad) back to their state at the chosen restore point. You may not know which programs or settings are causing the problems either. After the System Restore is complete, you can carefully add programs back in and restore other settings.

Using System Restore to Fix Problems

If your computer worked fine a few days ago but started running poorly after installing some programs or devices, you may be able to fix it with **System Restore**. System Restore enables you to go back in time to a point when you know your computer was working properly, and restore your computer to the state it was in then.

System Restore automatically creates restore points every week as you use your computer, and whenever you install or remove programs or updates, or make other changes to Windows settings. These checkpoints are called **restore points**. They are a snapshot of the state of your Windows settings and programs at a specific point in time. You can also manually create your own restore points at any time.

> **NOTE:** For most people, the automatic restore points created by Windows are sufficient. However, some programs or setting changes may not automatically generate a restore point, or you may be making changes that you think may be risky. In either case, you may want to manually create a restore point. To create a restore point, click the **Start** button, and in the **Start** menu's search box, type **create a restore point**. In the list that appears, click **Create a restore point**. The **System Properties** dialog box appears. On the **System Protection** tab, click **Create** and follow the instructions on your screen.

To restore your computer to an earlier point in time, follow these steps:

1. Click the **Start** button, and in the **Start menu's search box**, type **recovery**. In the list that appears, click **Restore your computer to an earlier point in time**. The **Recovery** window is displayed, as shown in Figure 17–23.

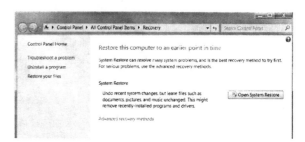

Figure 17–23. The Recovery window describes using System Restore to restore the computer to an earlier point in time when the computer was working normally.

2. Click **Open System Restore**. System Restore appears, as shown in Figure 17–24.

    When you access System Restore from Safe Mode, the page may vary slightly from Figure 17–24, in that it may not include the message that "Recently installed programs and drivers might be uninstalled."

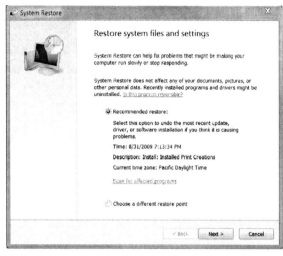

Figure 17–24. *System Restore will recommend a recent restore point on the assumption that you just started experiencing problems. You can select another restore point if you think the problem started before or well after the suggested restore point.*

3. Click **Next** if you want to use the recommended restore point, or select **Choose a different restore point** and then click **Next**. If you select this option, the next page will display a list of recent restore points, as shown in Figure 17–25. Select a restore point and then click **Next**.

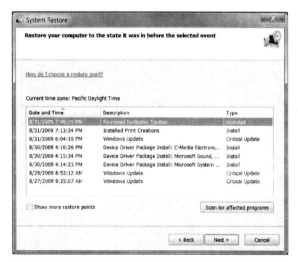

Figure 17–25. *If you want to choose a restore point instead of accepting the recommended restore point, System Restore can display a list of recent restore points and associated events.*

Figure 17–26 is an example of the screen System Restore will display to ask you to confirm your selection and prompt you to close any open programs

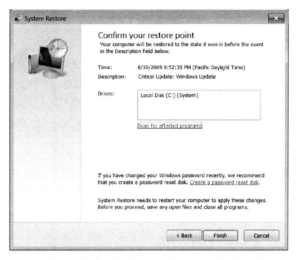

Figure 17–26. *System Restore confirms your choice of restore point before starting the restore.*

4. Click **Finish**. System Restore displays one more screen providing an opportunity to cancel System Restore, as shown in Figure 17–27.

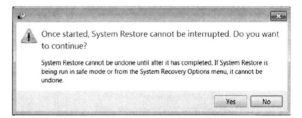

Figure 17–27. *This warning tells you not to interrupt System Restore, and that in some circumstances you cannot undo the restore afterward.*

NOTE: The warning about not being able to undo System Restore is not meant to scare you. If you are running System Restore from Safe Mode or from the System Recovery Options menu, it usually means you were already in an unstable situation. You may not have any better or safer options except running System Restore.

5. Click **Yes**. System Restore starts and displays the screens shown in Figures 17–28 and 17–29.

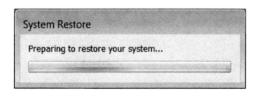

Figure 17–28. *Once System Restore starts, do not try to use your computer, turn it off, or shut it down.*

CAUTION: Once System Restore starts, do not try to use your computer, turn it off, or shut it down.

Figure 17–29. *Windows displays this System Restore screen while performing the restore. System Restore will restart the computer when it has finished.*

After Windows restarts and you log on, System Restore displays a message that it is complete, as shown in Figure 17–30.

6. Check your computer to see whether it is now running correctly and the problems are gone.

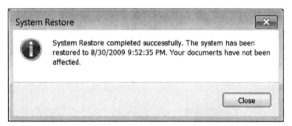

Figure 17–30. *System Restore completed successfully.*

If you are still experiencing the same problems or new ones, run System Restore again and use an earlier restore point. If there are no earlier points available, or you've tried several restore points and none of them have fixed the problem, you may need to try Advanced Recovery. See the "Using Advanced Recovery" section.

NOTE: If you get a message that System Restore was not successful or did not complete, you may need to run System Restore again with a different restore point, or try a more advanced recovery option.

Updating Device Drivers

Device manufacturers usually provide the drivers that enable your computer to work with printers and other devices that you attach to or install inside your computer. Microsoft may provide device drivers if they apply to a wide variety of products in a category.

Sometimes a new version of Windows leaves some older devices behind. If the device is several years old, the manufacturer may not have an updated driver available for Windows 7 right away. When you attach that device to your new Windows 7 machine, it may not work if it needs a new driver for Windows 7. Generally, almost all device drivers that worked in Windows Vista will work in Windows 7.

> **NOTE:** Usually it is the responsibility of the hardware manufacturer, not Microsoft, to provide those updated drivers. Unfortunately, some drivers are never updated because the hardware is several years old and is no longer sold or manufactured.

Examples of Devices That May Need Updated Drivers

This is not an exhaustive list, but it gives you an idea of the wide variety of devices that may need updated drivers:

- Printers
- Scanners
- Web cams
- Wireless network cards and adapters
- Wireless routers
- USB switchers (for connecting a device to more than one computer at a time)
- USB multicard readers
- Digital cameras
- MP3 players
- External hard drives
- DVD drives
- Network-attached storage

> **TIP:** A new computer with Windows 7 installed at the factory should have all the drivers for the devices and hardware that are installed in the computer. You should not have to update drivers on a Windows 7 computer when you take it out of the box. Sometimes the computer manufacturer or the store selling the computer bundles it with other external hardware such as multifunction printers. This added device might need updated drivers to run on Windows 7.

You may discover that you need new drivers in the following ways:

- You use Windows Easy Transfer, and the Transfer Report lists devices that need updated drivers.

- You run the Devices and Printers troubleshooter, and it detects devices that need updated drivers.

- You attach a device to your computer, and the **Add New Hardware** wizard cannot find the right driver.

- A notification appears in the notification area of the taskbar.

- In **Devices and Printers** in **Control Panel**, or in **Device Manager**, one of the devices has a yellow warning icon.

When Windows detects that it needs a driver, it will check the drivers stored on the computer or, if you allow it, will look for drivers on the Internet. Sometimes all that is needed is the device installation disc.

Most devices that work on Windows Vista should work on Windows 7. But if you are moving from Windows XP (or older) to Windows 7, you are more likely to run into a few devices that don't work right away.

Getting the correct drivers to your computer can be the tricky part. After you have the updated drivers, installing the drivers on your computer usually is a cinch.

Locating Updated Drivers

Try any of the following to locate updated drivers:

- Install the device with the device's installation disc.

- Run the Devices and Printers troubleshooter. Sometimes the device just needs to be enabled. The troubleshooter can fix that. If the troubleshooter detects a missing or outdated driver, it can check your computer and the Internet for updated drivers.

- Go to the device manufacturer's web site and check the support area for a downloads or drivers section. Look for updated device installation programs or drivers for Windows 7. If there is no Windows 7 device installation or driver listed, see if there is one for Windows Vista. Download and install the Windows Vista version.

- If the manufacturer doesn't have a Windows 7 driver but is working on one and hopes to release it soon, you could wait for the updated driver.

- Search Internet user forums for drivers or postings from other people with the same problem. For example, there didn't appear to be an updated driver for an older sound card on an older computer that was upgraded from Windows XP to Windows 7. Searching for **Sound Card Name drivers** produced a list of user web sites where this particular sound card was discussed. Sifting through the messages posted on these sites provided several possible solutions:

  - Download the Vista or Windows XP device installation program or drivers and install them using the Program Compatibility troubleshooter.

  - Buy and install a new sound card that is compatible with Windows 7.

  In this example, installing the drivers through the Program Compatibility troubleshooter solved the problem.

Updating the Drivers on Your Computer

To update the drivers on your computer, complete the following steps:

1. Locate and install the device drivers from the device installation disc or a download from the Internet.

2. Click the **Start** button, and in the **Start** menu's search box, type **Device Manager**. In the list that appears, click **Device Manager**.

3. Locate the device with the yellow warning icon, right-click it, and then click **Update Driver**. Figure 17–31 displays a warning on a Mass Storage Controller device.

4. Click **Update Driver Software**.

Figure 17–31. *When you right-click a device, you can update the driver, disable the device, or uninstall the driver.*

Windows asks where to search for the driver software, as shown in Figure 17–32.

5. Click **Browse my computer for driver software**. Figure 17–33 displays your options for finding the driver software.

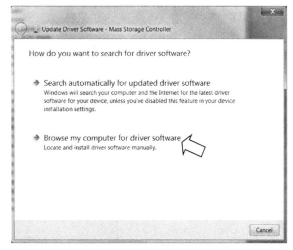

Figure 17–32. *If you've already downloaded the drivers, you still need to direct Windows to the location on your computer.*

6. Click **Let me pick from a list of device drivers on my computer**.

Figure 17–33. *When drivers have been installed on the computer, sometimes all that is needed is to tell Windows where to find the driver for a device.*

A list of device types is displayed, as shown in Figure 17–34.

7. Select the device type and then click **Next.**

A list is displayed of the manufacturers of the type of device you selected, as shown in Figure 17–35.

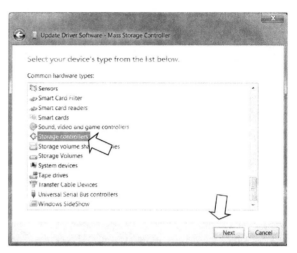

Figure 17–34. *Scroll through a list of device types until you find one that matches your device.*

8. Select the **Manufacturer** and then a **Model** from that manufacturer, or click **Have Disk** if you have the device's installation disc or a driver disc.

9. Click **Next**.

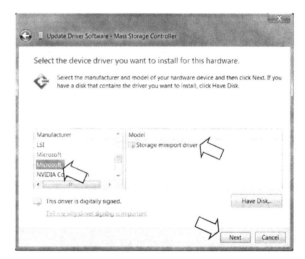

Figure 17–35. *Click a manufacturer and then select a model from that manufacturer.*

10. If you select a driver that Windows does not think is a good match, Windows will display a warning similar to Figure 17–36.

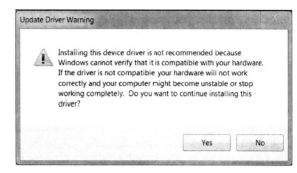

Figure 17–36. *Installing the wrong driver could cause problems with your computer.*

If you proceed anyway, Windows will try to install the driver software. If it is the wrong driver, the device may not even start, as shown in Figure 17–37. In this case, you may need more information to correctly identify the manufacturer and model, so you can download the right drivers.

Figure 17–37. *If the wrong driver is installed, the device may not work.*

If the correct driver is installed, you will get a notification in the taskbar that the installation was successful, as shown in Figure 17–38.

Figure 17–38. *Successful device driver software installation*

Using Advanced Recovery

Sometimes none of the previous methods can solve your problem. You've tried troubleshooters, uninstalling or updating device drivers, uninstalling programs, and System Restore.

There are two basic advanced recovery methods, both of which may cause you to lose data on your computer. Before you use any of these methods, it is very important that you completely back up all important files and documents to a location outside your computer, such as an external hard drive or network storage.

Before you can use one of these methods, you'll need a system image backup from before your problems started, or your Windows installation or recovery disc provided by your computer manufacturer.

Using a System Image to Recover

A **system image** is a backup of your entire hard drive. When you restore your system image, it includes everything that was on the image. You cannot selectively restore parts of your system image. You must have created system image backups before you started experiencing problems. After you have problems, you cannot really make a good system image backup because it will still have the problems on it.

> **TIP:** For information about how to create a system image, see Chapter 16: "Protecting Your Computer and Data."

Using a Recovery Disc

The recovery disc is provided by the computer manufacturer, not Microsoft. This disc resets your computer back to the settings and state it was in when it left the factory. This will erase all of the data on your computer, and you will need to reinstall all programs that you installed after you bought the computer. Check your computer's documentation for information about disaster recovery and recovery discs. Some manufacturers provide a recovery disc that contains all of the Windows installation files, and some just provide a disc you can use to start the computer, and the actual Windows installation files are on a hidden section of your hard drive.

Whichever recovery method you choose, you should plan on it taking several hours. You may not need to attend to the computer directly during the whole time, but you will want to make sure that the computer is not turned off or needed during that time. Also, if you are using a laptop, make sure it is plugged in and not running off battery power. Otherwise, the laptop could run out of power before recovery is complete.

Performing an Advanced Recovery

To start an advanced recovery, follow these steps:

1. Click the **Start** button, and in the **Start** menu's search box, type **Recovery**. In the list that appears, under **Control Panel** click **Recovery**.

2. On the **Recovery** page, click **Advanced recovery methods**. The **Advanced Recovery Methods** page is displayed, as shown in Figure 17–39.

3. Select a recovery method, or click **Help me choose a recovery method**.

4. Carefully read and follow the instructions on your screen.

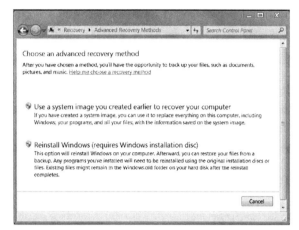

Figure 17–39. Advanced recovery is drastic. Most, if not all, information on your hard drive is erased. No matter which method you use, be sure to back up files such as documents, pictures, music, or any other kind of document file that contains content or information.

> **TIP:** For information about how to back up all files, see Chapter 15: "Protecting Your Computer and Data."

Fixing Things at the Document Level

A few Windows features are almost universal in any type of program and can get you out of a jam really quickly. Mistakes are usually pretty easy to fix, and working carefully can take the fear out of losing information from your documents.

Undoing

The Undo command, Ctrl+Z, is often available even if you don't see it listed on a menu in the program you are using. Typically, you will find it listed on the **Edit** menu. If you accidently cut, delete, or paste something in your program, press Ctrl+Z before you do anything else. Some programs offer multiple undos. For example, in Microsoft Office 2007 programs, you can undo and redo up to 100 actions. Some drawing and graphic programs may also offer multiple undos.

The Undo command can also come in handy when typing in or pasting into text boxes, web addresses in your browser, search boxes, and so forth. Some programs also redo. So if you undo something, and then decide that you didn't want to undo it after all, you can use the Redo command, Ctrl+Y. Not all programs that allow undo also allow redo.

Using Save As

If the Undo command is not available, or you didn't discover something was wrong until much later, another alternative is to immediately save the file you are working on with a new filename via the **File ➤ Save As** command. This saves all the changes you've made since your last save of this file in a new file, while keeping the original file unchanged under the original name.

Some programs offer a similar solution with a Revert command, which reverses all your changes since you opened this file in the current session. But with the Revert command, you will lose all changes made since the last time you saved this file.

Using the Save As command provides an opportunity to open both the new and old versions of the file and selectively add the changes from your new file back into the original.

Using Autosave and Saving Regularly

If your program offers an autosave feature, turn it on (before your computer or program crashes). Occasionally, a program you are using crashes in the middle of working on a document, or the computer is shut down by a person or power outage before you have saved your latest changes. If the program has an autosave feature and you had it turned on before the accident, the next time you open the program or file that crashed, it will offer to open a recovered copy of the file.

Even with autosave or autorecovery, it is a good idea to save your files regularly as you work on them. How often you should save your document depends on how many changes you make as you work. If the power went out, how much of your latest work can you afford to lose? How drastic and risky are the changes you are making as you work on your file? The greater the number or severity of changes, the more frequently you should save your work.

Creating Copies of the Original

If you are going to be making a lot of changes and don't want to lose the original document, start with a copy of the file. As soon as you open the document, use the Save As command to make a copy of the file. Then work on the copy, not the original.

Saving Your Scraps

If possible, open a separate file or document to store information that you've removed from your document. As you delete or remove text or data, paste it into the scrap document. Later, if you decide you didn't want to remove the information after all, you can open your scrap document and retrieve it.

Getting Help from Within Windows

Windows 7 provides a lot of information onscreen as you use programs and features. If you do not understand a screen or window, look for underlined blue links indicating Help topics related to that page or screen.

For example, in the **Advanced Recovery Methods** window, each method is described (as shown previously in Figure 17–39).

If you need further help, you can click the link **Help me choose a recovery method** for a more detailed explanation of the features and options. The contents of these **Windows Help and Support** topics are shown in a separate window, so you don't lose your place in the window or feature you were using, as shown in Figure 17–40.

Figure 17–40. *Windows Help and Support can provide more information if the screen you are viewing is not clear or you just need to know more.*

Accessing Help and Support

Windows Help and Support is not just for providing extra information about a particular window or feature. You can browse or search for information, just as you would on the Web. Much of the Help information is stored on your computer, but Help and Support also links to additional content on the Web.

To access **Windows Help and Support**, click the **Start** button and then click **Help and Support**. **Windows Help and Support** is displayed, as shown in Figure 17–41.

Figure 17–41. *Windows Help and Support home page*

Getting Additional Online Help from Microsoft

Microsoft Support now offers a free new online resource called **Microsoft Fix it**. The online troubleshooters it provides do more than diagnose and suggest solutions, they can also automatically repair problems. So instead of telling you what to do, you can tell Fix it to do it for you. This new service was launched long after the release of Windows 7, and can solve problems with Windows, Internet Explorer, Windows Media Player, Xbox, Office, and other products. You can access the Fix it Center at http://support.microsoft.com/fixit/. Figure 17–42 displays the opening page, where you can find solutions by product type or problem type.

Figure 17–42. *The new Microsoft Fix it Center*

When you find a problem and solution, you can select **Run Now** to automatically diagnose and repair the problem, or **Learn More** to read what this solution fixes before deciding whether to us it. Figure 17–43 shows the type of information you will see if you click **Learn More**.

Figure 17–43. *The Learn More button displays a page describing what this Fix it repairs.*

Once you select to run the solution, you will be prompted to Run or Save the program that will do the actual diagnosis and repair, similar to Figure 17–44.

Figure 17–44. *Fix it downloads or runs a program that diagnoses and repairs the problem.*

When you run Microsoft Fix it, it creates a restore point so that later if you need to you can use System Restore to undo the changes. Depending on the complexity of the problem, it might only take a few minutes for Microsoft Fix it to repair the problem. Some Fix its may require additional input from you as it diagnoses or repairs the problem. Figure 17–45 shows a really simple and quick Fix it repair.

Figure 17–45. *Microsoft Fix it is sometimes as easy as 1-2-3.*

Getting Help from the User Community

Sometimes you have a problem that is not in any book and not in the Help and Support Center in Windows. Chances are, among the millions of Windows users out there, others have run into the same problem and somebody has found a solution. There are lots of user forums on the Web for Windows users. You can make use of user forums in several ways:

- Search for problems and solutions similar to your own.

- Post your problem and see if somebody else can suggest a solution.

- Answer other user postings and share your own solutions.

One user community forum you can start with is **Microsoft Answers** at
http://answers.microsoft.com/en-us (English, United States—this site is also available in other languages), as shown in Figure 17–46.

Search for similar
problem and solutions
from others.

Post a question to
see if somebody
else has an answer.

You can change the
region to many other
languages.

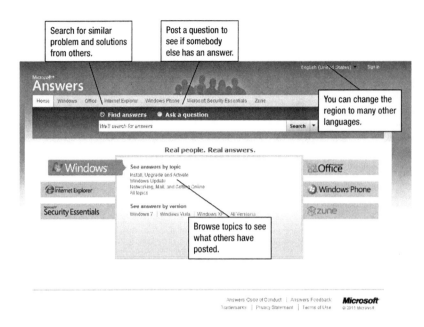

Browse topics to see
what others have
posted.

Figure 17–46. *The Microsoft Answers user forum is free and anybody can join or browse.*

One of the common rules when using forums is to always search existing postings in the forum for a solution before posting your own. Most forums have a FAQs (frequently asked questions) section or a FAQs thread within a feature area. Check those too before posting your question.

There are many other forums for PCs and Windows 7 users. You can search for other Windows forums through your favorite web search program. Figure 17–47 shows the search results for searching with Bing for "windows forums."

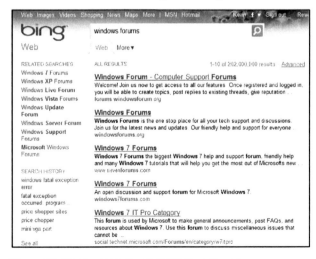

Figure 17–47. *Searching for other Windows forums*

Searching the Web for Error Messages or Notifications

Error messages and notifications are often cryptic or do not provide solutions. If you get an error message you do not understand, copy or write down the text of the message and then search the Web for that text. For example, you get an error message that says "Fatal exception occurred. Program will exit." You have no idea what it means, but those were the last words you saw on your computer before the program crashed. If you search the Web for those words, you will find web sites and forums that discuss and possibly solve the issue, as shown in Figure 17–48.

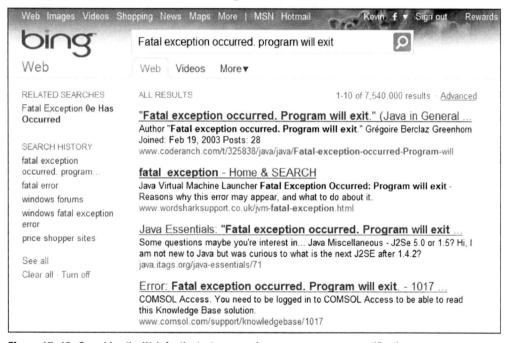

Figure 17–48. *Searching the Web for the text you saw in an error message or notification*

CAUTION Some web sites are set up to appear like they will answer your problem, but they turn out to be advertisements to buy their software to solve your problem. Or, other sites may have links which are actually downloads for viruses or other nasty stuff you do not want on your computer.

You can learn a lot more about using search services like Bing and Google and tips for using the Web safely in Chapter 9: "Surfing the Web."

Maintaining Your Computer and Equipment

Just like your home or your car, your computer needs routine maintenance and proper treatment to keep working for you. Good maintenance improves performance and keeps your computer running well with fewer problems. Table 17–2 lists good practices and recommendations.

Table 17–2. *Recommended Maintenance Tasks*

Task	Purpose
Run Disk Defragmenter and Disk Cleanup regularly, about once a month.	■ Running these programs regularly improves your computer's performance.
	■ The first time you run Disk Defragmenter, it may take hours to complete. But if you run it regularly after that, it will not take nearly as long. Before Disk Defragmenter actually does defragmentation, it checks to see if your disk even needs it.
	■ Disk Cleanup scans your computer for files and folders and suggests files you can delete from your computer to free up disk space.
	■ You can access these settings in Control Panel > Performance and Information.
	NOTE Many security protection suites and computer protection programs automatically schedule these tasks to be performed weekly, monthly, or automatically in the background when your computer is on and idle. Your computer may already have these tasks scheduled. Check **Control Panel** settings to be sure.
Keep Windows and programs current.	■ Make sure you are set up to automatically download and install Windows Updates. Many viruses and computer attacks occur because people do not install updates that could have blocked or prevented it.
	■ Keep other programs current too. Most virus protection programs require regular updates to keep up with the newest viruses.
	■ Program updates can also fix bugs or problems with the software.

Task	Purpose
Keep your computer away from extreme heat, cold, and moisture.	▓ Overheating can permanently damage your computer motherboard. With laptops, use a notebook cooler. With desktop PCs, make sure the vent holes on the outside and the fans on the inside do not get clogged with dust. There are special vacuum cleaner attachments available for cleaning the vents and inside of the computer case. You can also use compressed air cans to blow out dust.
	▓ When not in use, keep the computer away from direct heat. Do not leave your notebook in a hot car on a sunny day.
	▓ Extreme cold can also affect your computer. If you leave your computer in your car when it is freezing cold, when you bring it back inside allow it to get back to room temperature before you start it up.
	▓ Keep drinks and liquids away from your computer. External keyboards are easily replaced. But if you spill soda on your laptop's keyboard, you may need to replace much more than the keyboard.
Protect your data with regular backups.	▓ For most people, once a week should be sufficient. Hard drives do not last forever. No matter how well the hard drive is built or taken care of, eventually every hard drive fails—it's just a matter of when. See Chapter 15: "Protecting Your Computer and Data."
Allow your virus programs to do their job.	▓ Sometimes when your virus protection is scanning your computer, it seems to slow everything else down. You may be tempted to stop the scan. But if a virus gets through, your computer won't just slow down, it may come to a complete stop. See Chapter 15: "Protecting Your Computer and Data."
Shut down your computer properly.	▓ Turning the power off on your computer before Windows has completed its shutdown can lead to file corruption that makes your computer hard to restart.
Protect your computer from dropping.	▓ When you take your laptop with you, make sure you have it in a protected carrying bag or a padded laptop sleeve. Dropping a laptop can damage the screen or the hard drive.

Summary

In this chapter you learned how to fix many common computer problems and how to use many Windows tools for diagnosing and fixing more complex problems, such as

- Windows Troubleshooters
- Safe Mode
- System Restore
- Advanced Recovery
- Uninstall
- Updating device drivers
- Help and Support
- Getting help on the Web from Microsoft, the user community, and error message searches
- Turn Windows features on or off

Next Steps

You may find the following related chapters useful:

- Chapter 5: "Installing Programs"
- Chapter 13: "Connecting Printers, Monitors, and Hardware"
- Chapter 15: "Connecting to the Internet and Home Networks"
- Chapter 18: "Using Windows 7 at Work and on the Road"

Part III

Using Windows at Work and On the Road

Windows 7 is available in several business editions. Windows 7 Professional, Ultimate, and Enterprise provide extra features to meet the stronger network, security, and protection needs in the workplace. Even if you never use your PC outside of the home, some of these extra business features may be useful to you. Whether you are a home user or business user, there are several features available in all editions of Windows 7 that you will find useful when using your computer outside of the office or home. This chapter will look at:

- **Using Windows 7 in Business**
    - Windows 7 business features and what they do
    - Corporate network, security, and computer usage policies
- **Protecting your Computer's Data**
    - Encrypting File System (EFS)
    - BitLocker Drive Encryption
- **Setting up Virtual Machines to Run Legacy Software**
    - Windows XP Mode
    - Windows Virtual PC
    - VMware Player
- **Connecting Outside of the Office or Home**
    - Virtual Private Networks
    - Public Networks and WiFi
- **Physically Protecting your Computer**

Using Windows 7 in Business

Almost all of the features and programs described in this book are available in the home editions:

- Windows Starter
- Windows 7 Basic
- Windows 7 Home Premium

As well as in the business editions:

- Windows 7 Professional
- Windows 7 Ultimate
- Windows 7 Enterprise

In this chapter, you'll learn about the features that are only available in business editions, which include:

- Network domain login
- Backup and recovery to a network
- Encrypting File System (EFS)
- **BitLocker** encryption (Ultimate and Enterprise, not available in Professional)
- **Windows XP Mode** and **Windows Virtual PC***

***Windows Virtual PC** is available for all versions of Windows 7.

There are a few other features that you get with the business editions but that this book doesn't cover. One of these features, which may be of interest to global and international users, is the Multilingual User Interface (MUI) pack, which is available in the Ultimate and Enterprise editions. The MUI pack allows you to easily switch between any of 35 languages.

Windows 7 Ultimate and Windows 7 Enterprise are nearly identical in features. Windows 7 Ultimate is the retail version that anybody can buy. Windows 7 Enterprise is sold through volume key licensing to companies.

Upgrading to a Business Edition with Windows Anytime Upgrade

For home users, there are several features that may make it worthwhile to upgrade from Windows 7 Home Premium to Windows 7 Professional or Ultimate.

- **Backup to network** In Windows Home editions, you can only back up files to a USB flash drive, a USB external hard drive, or to DVD-Rs. If you have a home network, it is a safer practice to back up files to a disk that is away from your computer. If some kind of physical disaster (fire, water, electrical surge, etc.) occurs with your computer, it will probably also strike any drives attached to it. There are other alternatives for backing up a Windows 7 Home Premium computer to a network using third-party products. See Chapter 16: "Protecting Your Computer and Data" to learn more about other ways to back up your files.

- **Encryption** With Windows 7 Professional, Ultimate, and Enterprise editions, you can encrypt files and folders using Encrypting File System (EFS); with Ultimate and Enterprise editions, you can also encrypt entire drives with BitLocker.

Microsoft makes it easy to upgrade from Windows 7 Home Premium to Windows 7 Professional or Windows 7 Ultimate, or from Windows 7 Professional to Windows 7 Ultimate. It is easy, but it is not cheap. What makes it easy is that the version you are upgrading to is already installed on your computer; all you have to do is buy the update product key to unlock it. Once you enter the new product key, it takes about 10 minutes to complete the upgrade. No disks to insert, no programs to reinstall, and none of your data files are affected.

You can purchase and download the update product key online.

To upgrade to another version:

1. Click the **Start** button and in the **Search** box, type **Anytime**.

2. In the list that appears, click **Windows Anytime Upgrade**.

   The Windows Anytime Upgrade page appears. There are several pages to help you decide which version you want. You can compare the features of your current version with the features in the available upgrades, and compare prices.

> **NOTE:** Opening the Windows Anytime Upgrade page does not commit you to purchasing anything. You can just window-shop and close it without buying.

3. If you want to upgrade now, click the **Buy** button. If you want to upgrade later, you can come back to this page or you can buy an upgrade key from an electronics/computer store.

Complying with Corporate Network Security and Policies

When you use a computer on a corporate network, your computer has more protection but you may have less control over some parts of it. Your personal computer at work is not quite as private as your personal computer at home – your employer or organization usually owns the PC, data, programs and even corporate email accounts.

Your employers must protect their legal liability and networks by addressing a number of serious concerns:

- Hacking and intrusion from outside into corporate servers and PCs

- Preventing confidential, proprietary, and trade secret information from getting into the wrong hands

- Accurate financial record keeping, in compliance with the Sarbanes-Oxley Act and other government regulatory requirements

- Preventing use of equipment for illicit or immoral purposes, from pornography to personal or political expressions that do not reflect corporate beliefs

- Prevention of sexual harassment from the display of sexually explicit or offensive content, even if the content is legal

- Abuse of company time and resources; loss of productivity due to excessive use of browsing, email, instant messaging, or social networks for personal use

- Viruses and other damaging software, which can quickly spread throughout the company network to individual PCs and workstations

- Use of unlicensed or illegally obtained software on company computers

- Use of new but untested updates to approved software that may not work with custom internal programs

When you ignore or disobey policies designed to protect you, your equipment, and your company, you put both your company and your employment at risk. Following policies is not just better for you, it also makes it easier for the IT Support and Help Desk technicians to fix your computer problems when they arise.

Differences Between Using Windows in the Workplace and at Home

There are many Windows features that may be different or even unavailable in the workplace:

User login to your computer through a network Instead of logging in with picture tiles for several people on your computer, who may even share the same account, each person using a PC on the network should have their own network user name and password. You cannot just make up your user name; it will be assigned to you by a network administrator.

Stricter password requirements In most companies, you must change your password every 90 days. You cannot reuse passwords previously used on the network, and you must create strong passwords: usually at least one each of lower case letters, upper case letters, symbols, and numbers.

Antivirus and firewall protection Your company will usually provide an antivirus program for all employees to use. Since all of your external connections to the outside world (the Internet) are through company servers, your firewall may appear turned off on your computer because there is a bigger, stronger one on the corporate network.

Port and firewall blocking Open and unprotected ports are one of the ways that hackers gain access to computers. You may find that some types of external file sharing, audio and video chats, instant messaging, and other connections are disabled.

Group policies Windows network administrators can create *Group Policies* that specify what users can and cannot do on their computers. So you may find that some settings for firewall and port blocking are controlled by the network and cannot be changed locally on your computer.

User account privileges You might only have a *standard* user account, not *administrator*, and might not be able to make changes to your computer at the system level. Some companies may also place restrictions on whether you can add or remove programs.

Program installation There are huge fines for companies that are found to have unlicensed software on their computers. Many companies have auditing software that checks individual PCs to make sure that there are licenses on record for any software installed on the computer. If unlicensed software is detected, you may be asked to provide the license number, have your manager purchase a license, or remove the software from your computer.

Software upgrades While you may think that the newest version of Internet Explorer or Firefox is really cool and you use it a lot at home, many programs need to be tested with internal company programs to make sure they still work. If you upgrade to a version that has not been approved by your IT department, they may not be able to help you until you uninstall the new version and reinstall the old approved version. It happens quite frequently that internal company programs like online payroll time cards need to be updated to work with new browser or operating system versions. If you cannot fill out and submit your timecard online, you might have problems getting a paycheck until you fix it.

Windows Update Sometimes Windows Update causes problems with internal company programs. Many companies disable your personal Windows Update settings and replace them with a group policy that allows the IT department to send you the updates once they've been tested and approved. This centralized update control also ensures that users who ignore or turn off Windows Update on their own will still be required to install updates. Many of the worldwide virus and Trojan attacks are successful because users did not install a security update that was released months earlier to prevent it.

Website access External websites have many potential dangers and liabilities to a company network. You should always assume that a company server has a record of your Internet browsing history. It is also likely that servers are used to filter and block inappropriate web sites. They usually have a constantly updated list of websites to block, and when you try to go to one of those sites you will get a warning message on your browser that a website has been blocked by corporate policies. If you see these types of messages frequently, you should review your company's web access policies, and adjust your browsing behavior so that this doesn't happen very much. Or, sometimes you need to talk to get your company to adjust the filters and settings on their servers, because they are blocking legitimate sites you need access to in order to do your job.

Personal email accounts may be blocked Any kind of email coming into a company network has the potential to be dangerous. Company email servers, like Microsoft Exchange, can filter and protect against spam and harmful mail attachments in company email. But just about all email accounts, like Hotmail, Gmail, Windows Live Mail, Yahoo! Mail, etc. are web browser based. Many companies have no choice but to block access to webmail because they cannot filter or detect dangerous messages like they can through an email server. While the potential for wasting company time and resources may play a small part in companies blocking personal mail, most of the need for limiting or blocking email accounts is the danger from unfiltered mail.

If you must keep in contact and check your personal email throughout the day, you may need to set up your own personal smartphone to send and receive email.

Instant messaging Instant messaging requires extra ports to be open on your computer, which means more vulnerability to malicious programs that may try to use those ports too. IM can be a useful communication tool for internal communications. Many companies are employing unified communications servers that control an internal messaging network. Programs like Office Communicator can tie together your email, phone, and IM networks so that you have several options for communicating with your coworkers.

Protection with scheduled backups Most companies use network-based backup and recovery systems to ensure safer and timelier backup of data and files on user's machines. Do not assume that backups are automatically taking place, but when they are you shouldn't need to create and run your own backup system locally on your computer. Check your computer support group or IT department to find out how desktop computers are backed up and to make sure your computer is on their backup schedule.

Personal documents and media files For most employers, there is nothing wrong with putting headphones on and listening to music as you work at your desk. Using Windows Media Player or other music software, it is easy to access and use music stored on your computer. Even though a computer is assigned to you, be careful about putting a lot of personal files on it. It should not be your only or primary location for storing personal pictures, videos, documents, or your music collection. A large music collection can use up a lot of room on a computer with a small hard drive. Also, you never know when your computer might crash, get stolen, or be replaced with little or no warning. Or you may leave your company. In any case, you may suddenly no longer have access to those files. For personal documents and pictures, regularly make backup copies on a DVD or USB drive and save the copies on your home computer. You can also get very large USB flash drives that may be able to hold all of your music. Just plug your USB drive into your PC and listen away. Or, get an iPod, MP3 player, or smartphone and carry your music on that device.

Network group policies that block external USB storage devices Group policies are rules and controls placed on your computer from outside of your computer through network settings. Sometimes, companies implement group policies on all employees to restrict or block access to your computer or network through external USB storage devices. Data coming into your computer or leaving your computer can pose security risks to your computer, network, and corporate data. An external storage device could have Trojans, viruses, or infected files. Since these devices are considered local to your computer, Windows security grants those files more access to your computer than files from the web or even your local network. External storage can also be a liability to a company because they could be bringing in illicit, offensive, or pirated material. External storage could also be used to copy, steal, or leak confidential, proprietary, or private data. Even if you are copying information to work on at home, once the data is on a portable storage device, it is physically outside of the control and protection of your work computer or network. If you believe you have a legitimate business need to store and transport data with a USB device, talk with your manager, IT department, or network administrator about adjusting or overriding the group policies on your computer. Another option that may provide reassurance and protection for external drives is to apply volume (drive)-level encryption with BitLocker or a similar third-party encryption program. The next section provides more information about file-level and volume-level encryption.

Protecting Your Computer Data

Every few months, there seems to be another news story about a stolen or lost laptop that just happened to be holding a large database containing the names, social security numbers, and account information of tens of thousands or even millions of customers. Identity information, personal financial information, proprietary information – they're all easy to steal when you squeeze a lot of data on a single computer.

Windows 7 Professional, Ultimate, and Enterprise versions provide options for protecting your data with encryption. Encryption scrambles your data so that it can only be unscrambled (and readable) with a certificate or key to unlock it. **Encrypting File System (EFS)** encrypts files and folders on your hard drive. **BitLocker** encryption encrypts entire drives.

EFS AND BITLOCKER ARE VERY POWERFUL FEATURES FOR ADVANCED USERS

Though the home power user can use these features, there are many features that are optimized to work within corporate networks. If you are using your computer in a business organization, contact your IT department or network administrator for additional policies that may apply to the use of EFS or BitLocker. Microsoft provides extensive documentation on using EFS and BitLocker in corporate networks on the TechNet web site, `http://technet.microsoft.com`. Microsoft also provides extensive documentation in the Help and Support Center on your computer.

Table 18–1 compares the features, availability, and requirements of each technology.

Table 18–1. *EFS and BitLocker features and requirements*

Feature	Encrypting File System (EFS)	BitLocker
What it protects	Folders and files at user level on local computer.	Entire volumes (drives): ▦ Internal hard drives ▦ External (removable) hard drives and USB flash drives
Requirements	One of the following versions of Windows 7: ▦ Windows 7 Professional ▦ Windows 7 Ultimate ▦ Windows 7 Enterprise	One of the following versions of Windows 7: ▦ Windows 7 Ultimate ▦ Windows 7 Enterprise *Trusted Protection Module* (TPM) enabled, or configuration to work without TPM

Feature	Encrypting File System (EFS)	BitLocker
Sharing	Encrypted files or folders can be shared with other persons by adding their certificates. Can be shared with other computers by exporting EFS certificates from the original computer and importing the EFS certificates into the other computers. These advanced tasks are described thoroughly in Microsoft Help and Support on your computer.	Encrypted removable drives can be unlocked on other Windows 7 computers or computers using a password, smartcard, or recovery key. When using BitLocker To Go, encrypted removable drives can be opened on Windows XP or Windows Vista computers as a read-only listing of the files and folders; files must be copied to a local folder to actually open the content. These advanced tasks are described thoroughly in Microsoft Help and Support on your computer.

CAUTION: Before you encrypt files with EFS or drives with BitLocker, make sure you understand the dangers and loss of data that can occur if you lose your encryption key. Both EFS and BitLocker provide ways to protect your keys with copies, backups, or recovery keys. The methods available for protecting your keys differ for EFS and BitLocker. Search Windows Help and Support for "encrypted file system" or "BitLocker" for extensive documentation on using both of these features.

Practice EFS encryption and BitLocker encryption with test files and USB flash drives!

Encryption provides great protection for your data, but there is one large risk: if you encrypt data and then forget, lose, or damage the password or encryption key, you will never be able to access that data again. Both EFS and BitLocker provide ways to back up the encryption keys. To ensure success with encryption, follow these steps:

1. Read the online help about these features in Windows Help and Support Center.

   a. Click **Start**, and then click **Windows Help and Support**.

   b. In the **Help** search box, type **encrypted file system** or **BitLocker** and read all of the topics you can find about these encryption methods. It is important to understand how to:

   ▧ Encrypt and decrypt with the tool

   ▧ Back up, copy, or create a recovery key or certificate

- Work with encrypted files or drives when they are moved or viewed from another computer.

2. In addition, for BitLocker, review the extensive documentation on **Microsoft TechNet**. Go to http://technet.microsoft.com and search for the topic **BitLocker Drive Encryption in Windows 7: Frequently Asked Questions** or review the **Windows BitLocker Drive Encryption Step-by-Step Guide** (http://go.microsoft.com/fwlink/?LinkId=140225).

3. Check the requirements at the beginning of the sections "Using EFS" or "Using BitLocker," immediately following the section you are now reading, to make sure your version of Windows 7 supports the feature.

4. Create test data to practice with until you understand how to perform encryption and decryption and how to work with the encrypted data.

   - For **EFS**, create a test folder and test files that do not contain valuable data. For example, copy sample pictures from your Pictures library to a new folder, so that you can try the encryption features without risking any real data. Optionally, get a USB flash drive so that you can practice moving encrypted files off your computer and reopening the files on another computer. This will allow you to make sure that you can successfully access and use encrypted files when and where you need them.

   - Similarly, with **BitLocker**, create some sample files and folders and add them to a small capacity (256 MB to 1 GB) USB flash drive. Test encrypting and decrypting the flash drive, and then move it to a Windows XP, Windows Vista, or one of the other editions of Windows 7 that do not support *creating* an encrypted drive. You should still be able to *read* the encrypted USB flash drive on another computer through the **BitLocker To Go Reader**.

Using a small USB flash drive for practicing and testing is useful because:

- The USB flash drive is inexpensive. If you somehow encrypt something and then are unable to read or decrypt it, you haven't spent a lot of money.

- You can test and practice all of the features with a USB flash drive that you can with an external hard drive.

- Encrypting or decrypting a large hard drive with BitLocker can easily take several hours or even much longer; encrypting or decrypting a small USB flash drive can take as little as a few minutes.

- It allows you to explore what happens to encrypted files or drives when the data is moved to another computer.

Using EFS

Encrypting File System (EFS) is available on Windows 7 Professional, Ultimate and Enterprise editions. EFS allows you to encrypt files and folders on your hard drive. This prevents hackers or others from accessing the files from outside of the user account that encrypted them. For example:

1. I log on to my computer with my user account name, "Kevin."

2. In my Documents library I have a folder called Contracts, and I want to protect all of the files in it.

3. I encrypt the folder, and it creates a certificate file on my computer that contains the encryption key for this folder.

   Now that this folder is encrypted, the only way it can be viewed or changed is when I am logged on with my user account Kevin, the account under which I encrypted the folder.

   However, if I want to allow somebody else to access this Contracts folder, I can add their EFS certificate to the files or folder. That way they can access the files when they log onto my computer under their own account, or if it is shared, they can access the files from another Windows computer where they are logged with their own account.

   If another user on my computer uses an administrator account to change my password, all EFS-encrypted files in my account will be lost. However, if you change your own password, as most companies require users to do every 60 to 90 days, you will not lose access to your EFS files.

   If my computer gets lost or stolen, unless somebody has my password, they cannot access or decrypt the files just by getting physical access to my computer. Hackers have ways of accessing the contents of a hard drive. If they change my password so that they can log in to my account, they may access unencrypted files in that account but they will never be able to access the encrypted files.

Encrypting folders or files

The steps for encrypting folders or files are very similar to changing the read and write permissions on folders or files.

> **TIP:** Practice encryption on a test folder or file. Create a new folder, and then add some blank documents to the folder. Then try out encrypting and decrypting the files and folders. That way if you make a mistake, you won't lock yourself out of important files or folders. Also, this is a good way to see what happens when you move or copy files to other encrypted and unencrypted locations.

To encrypt folders or files:

1. In a Windows Explorer or library window, navigate to the files or folders you want to encrypt.

2. Right click the folder or the file, and then click **Properties**, as shown in Figure 18–1.

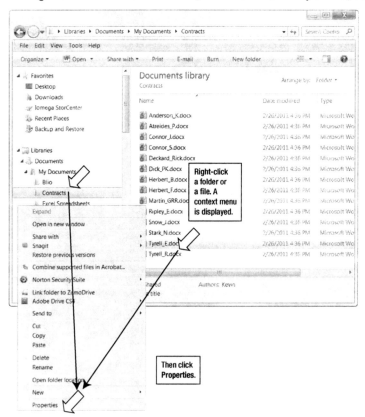

Figure 18–1. *You can encrypt folders or files.*

3. In the **Folder Properties** dialog box, click **Advanced**, as shown in Figure 18–2.

Figure 18–2. *Click the Advanced button to set encryption.*

4. In the **Advanced Attributes** dialog box, check the **Encrypt contents to secure data** checkbox, and then click **OK**, as shown in Figure 18–3.

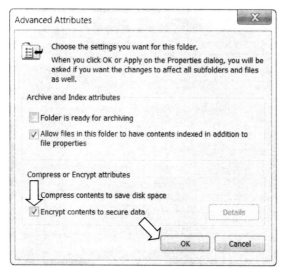

Figure 18–3. *Selecting* **Encrypt contents to secure data**

5. Click **OK** again to close the **Folder Properties** dialog box.

The **Confirm Attribute Changes** dialog box appears, as shown in Figure 18–4. In this example, a folder was selected, so now you have the option of encrypting just the folder or the folder and all contents within it.

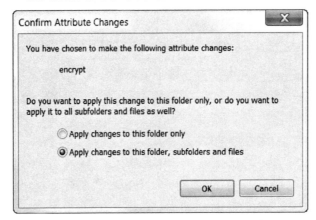

Figure 18–4. *Select how you want to apply the encryption.*

6. Select how you want to apply the encryption:

Apply changes to this folder only means that the encryption key is only needed to open the folder. Think of it as locking the door to a room full of filing cabinets; once you have unlocked the door to the room, you have full access to the filing cabinets and files because they are unlocked. After encryption, the folder name will change colors from black to green, as shown in Figure 18–5, but the unencrypted files within the folder will still be black.

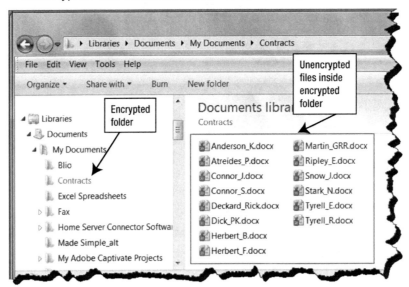

Figure 18–5. *Encrypted folder with unencrypted files*

Apply changes to this folder, subfolders and files means that each item at each level within the folder is encrypted. Think of this as unlocking the door to a room full of filing cabinets, but each filing cabinet is locked too. And all of the files within each filing cabinet are locked. After encryption, the folder name and the file names are both green, as shown in Figure 18–6.

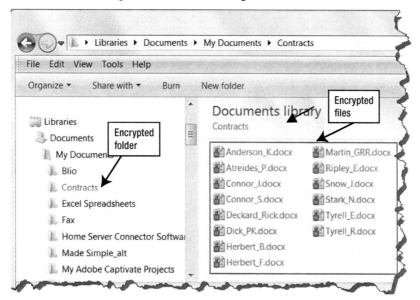

Figure 18–6. *Encrypted folder and files*

Decrypting folders or files

You can decrypt entire decrypted folders and all of the folders and files within them, or you can selectively decrypt individual folders or files. The steps for decrypting are almost identical to encryption, except you clear the option to encrypt.

To decrypt folders or files:

1. In a Windows Explorer or library window, navigate to the files or folders you want to encrypt.

2. Right click the folder or the file, and then click **Properties**.

3. In the **Folder Properties** dialog box, click **Advanced**.

4. In the **Advanced Attributes** dialog box, clear the **Encrypt contents to secure data** checkbox and then click **OK**, as shown in Figure 18–7.

Figure 18–7. *Clearing Encrypt contents to secure data*

5. If you are decrypting a folder and the **Confirm Attribute Changes** dialog box appears, select how you want the decryption applied.

    Click **OK** as needed to exit the **File** or **Folder Properties** dialog box and complete the decryption.

> **TIP:** Even if you didn't practice encrypting and decrypting test files, now would be a good time to try out moving and copying the files and folders in ways that you might typically do with your files. That way, you can ensure that you know how to access to your files when and where you need them. Also, be sure you have set up a recovery method in case your original encryption keys get lost or stolen.

Using BitLocker

BitLocker encrypts entire volumes (drives), such as your hard drive, external hard drives, or USB flash drives. It is only available on Windows 7 Ultimate and Enterprise editions. Unlike EFS, BitLocker is not available on Windows 7 Professional. However, with Windows Vista or Windows XP and the other editions of Windows 7, you can use the **BitLocker To Go Reader** to open and read the content of external hard drives or USB flash drives that have been encrypted with BitLocker in Windows 7 Ultimate or Enterprise.

To use BitLocker, you need the following:

- Windows 7 Ultimate or Windows 7 Enterprise

- A computer with a *Trusted Platform Module* (TPM) that is compatible and turned on in the BIOS

    - or -

    Enable BitLocker to protect drives even when the computer does not have a TPM.

Turning on BitLocker Drive Encryption

BitLocker does not require Trusted Platform Module (TPM) 1.2, but it is recommended for the best protection of the integrity of the early startup components of the operating system. A TPM device, if available, is built into the system hardware inside your computer. Most computers sold for the home or non-business users do not have TPM; it is usually found in computers that are designed primarily for business use.

To turn on BitLocker Drive Encryption:

1. Click **Start**, and in the **Search** box type **BitLocker**.

2. In the search results list that appears, click **BitLocker Drive Encryption**. Do not be alarmed if you see a message that "Compatible TPM cannot be found."

   - If your computer does have a TPM, it may be turned off, and you'll need to turn it on in the BIOS or when you first boot. For detailed instructions on how to turn TPM on in the BIOS, go to Microsoft TechNet (http://technet.microsoft.com), and search the TechNet Library for "To turn on BitLocker Drive Encryption on an operating system drive."

   - If your computer does not have a TPM, Microsoft has documented a workaround so that you can still use BitLocker even if you do not have a TPM device. Go to Microsoft TechNet (http://technet.microsoft.com) and search for "BitLocker Drive Encryption in Windows 7: Frequently Asked Questions." Locate the section "Can I use BitLocker on an operating system drive without a TPM version 1.2?" for instructions on how to change settings so that you can use BitLocker without TPM.

   Once you have turned on TPM or configured your computer to use BitLocker without it, you can access the **BitLocker Drive Encryption** window, similar to Figure 18–8.

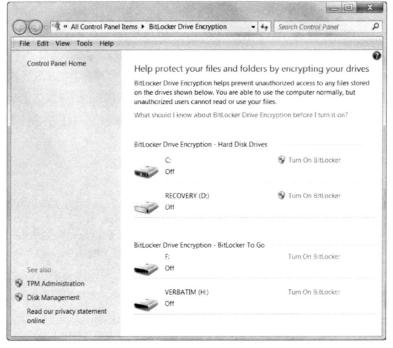

Figure 18–8. *The BitLocker Drive Encryption window lists the hard disk drives, external drives, and USB flash drives available for encryption.*

TIP: If this is the first time you have used the BitLocker feature on any computer, practice encrypting a USB flash drive. It is a little simpler and much quicker than encrypting a large internal or external hard drive.

3. Locate the drive you want to encrypt, and select Turn On BitLocker.

■   If you select an internal hard drive, the BitLocker setup wizard will need to shrink your operating system drive and create a new and separate system partition for system files that are needed for starting and recovering the operating system but cannot be encrypted. When the wizard is done creating the system partition, you will need to restart the computer and start the BitLocker Encryption again. During the restart, BitLocker will check other settings to make sure the computer meets other BitLocker requirements and is ready to begin encryption. Review the Microsoft documentation for additional requirements for minimum partition size for BitLocker and Windows Recovery Environment, in the Microsoft TechNet Library (http://technet.microsoft.com). Search for the topic "Scenario 1: Turning On BitLocker Drive Encryption on an Operating System Drive (Windows 7)."

■ If you have already created the separate partition, or you selected an external hard drive or flash drive, the wizard will prompt you to select a method for unlocking the drive, as shown in Figure 18–9.

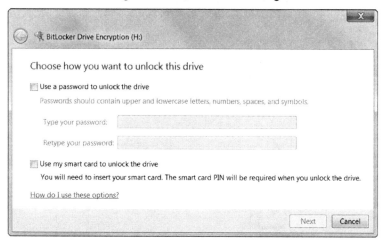

Figure 18–9. *Selecting whether to use a password or a smart card to unlock the drive*

4. Select **Use a password to unlock the drive**, type and retype your password, and then click **Next**.

If you're using a smart card, check with your IT department or the group that administers the card for any additional steps you many need to take besides those in the wizard.

The next page in the wizard allows you to specify how to store your recovery key, as shown in Figure 18–10.

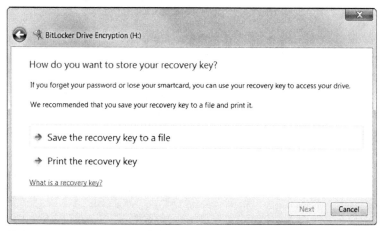

Figure 18–10. *Recovery key options for storing a recovery key file or printing the recovery key*

5. Select a recovery option and then follow the steps in the wizard for specifying the save location or the printer for the recovery key. You can use more than one option. If you select to save it to a file, the file name that BitLocker generates contains a unique identifier number so it will be quite long, as shown in Figure 18–11.

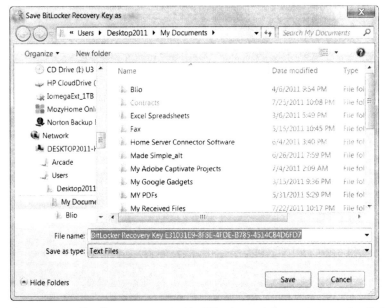

Figure 18–11. *The file name generated by BitLocker contains a unique number that makes it quite long*

After you save or print the recovery key, the BitLocker wizard returns you to the page for selecting a recovery key method. This is the same page shown in Figure 18–10, except now the Next button is clickable.

6. (Optional) Select another method or make another copy to a different location. You can repeat this step as many times you want.

NOTE: Microsoft recommends that you use more than one method, make multiple copies of the recovery key, and store recovery keys apart from the computer. The recovery key is unique to each drive, so you cannot use the recovery key to unlock a different drive than the one it was created for.

7. If you only want to store or print one copy of the recovery key, or you are done making alternate copies, click Next.

The next page, shown in Figure 18–12, is the last step before encryption begins.

Figure 18–12. *This page launches the actual encryption process, which could take several hours for a large hard drive.*

> **CAUTION:** Before you start encryption, make sure you will be able to safely leave your computer on for three hours or more, and that your power controls will not shut down your computer after a period of no activity. Encrypting a large hard drive such as your internal drive or an external hard drive will take hours.

8. Click Start Encrypting.

    A progress message box is displayed, as shown in Figure 18–13. The progress is reported in percentage completed; there is no estimate provided as to how long it will take to complete.

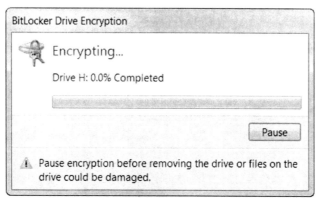

Figure 18–13. *The progress bar shows the percentage of encryption completed, but provides no time estimate.*

A message is displayed when encryption is complete, as shown in Figure 18–14.

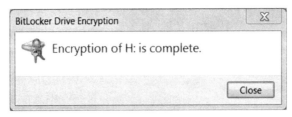

Figure 18–14. *Encryption is complete.*

In the **Control Panel**, the **BitLocker Drive Encryption** page displays the encryption status of all of your drives, as shown in Figure 18–15.

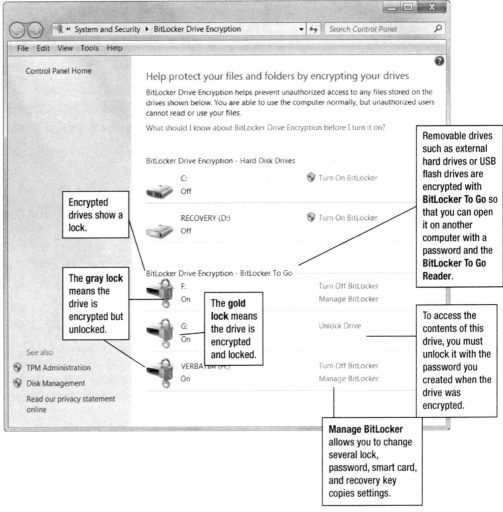

Figure 18–15. *The BitLocker Drive Encryption window shows the encryption status of all attached drives on your computer, and provides links for changing the settings for each drive.*

Viewing BitLocker-encrypted drives from your computer or another Windows 7 computer

To open a BitLocker-encrypted drive:

1. If it is on the same computer you encrypted it from, open the drive through a folder window or Windows Explorer. You will be prompted for the password, as shown in Figure 18–16.

2. If you want to open the drive from a different computer, attach the external hard drive or USB flash drive. Windows 7 automatically detects a BitLocker-encrypted drive when you attach it to the computer, and opens the **BitLocker Drive Encryption** page, which requests a password as shown in Figure 18–16.

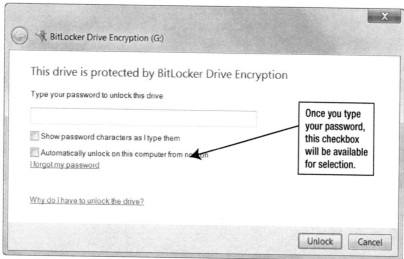

Figure 18–16. *Password request to unlock a drive on a Windows 7 computer*

3. Type your password.

If your home or main location where you use your computer or external drive is secure, you may want to use the **Automatically unlock this drive on this computer from now on** feature. When you take your laptop or external drive outside of the secure environment, the drive will be locked again until you enter the password or recovery key at the new location, unless you previously selected the **Automatically unlock this drive on this computer** feature at the new computer location.

> **NOTE:** When you turn on automatic unlock, anybody who has access to a user account on this computer can access the drive. If you want to control access to specific files or folders, use EFS.

After you enter the password, make your selections, and click **Unlock,** the drive is unlocked and you can access it like any other unencrypted drive or folder on your computer, as shown in Figure 18–17.

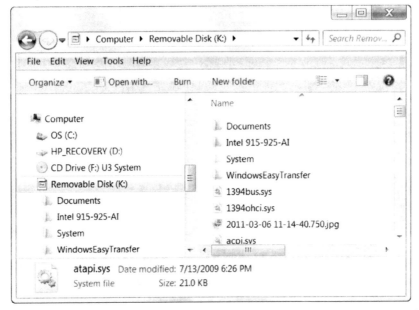

Figure 18–17. *An unlocked BitLocker-encrypted drive on a Windows 7 computer is accessible like any other drive.*

When you remove this drive, it is locked again until you insert it into another computer and enter the correct password or recovery key.

Viewing BitLocker-encrypted drives on a Windows Vista or Windows XP computer

There are several differences between accessing the encrypted drive on another Windows 7 computer and accessing it on a Windows Vista or Windows XP computer:

- **In Windows 7** Once the drive is unlocked, you can add, remove or edit files just as you would any other folders or files on your computer.

- **In Windows Vista and Windows XP** You must use a separate program, BitLockerToGo.exe, to unlock the drive. Once unlocked, you can only copy files from the drive to your computer. You cannot add, edit, or delete files within the drive.

To access BitLocker-encrypted drives on a Windows XP or Vista computer:

1. Attach the external hard drive or USB flash drive.

   Windows XP and Vista require BitLocker To Go. If Windows does not open AutoPlay and offer BitLockerToGo.exe as an option, locate that file on the encrypted drive. Though the contents of the drive are encrypted, BitLockerToGo.exe and related files will be accessible.

2. Open BitLockerToGo.exe.

   The **BitLocker To Go Reader** password dialog box is displayed, as shown in Figure 18–18.

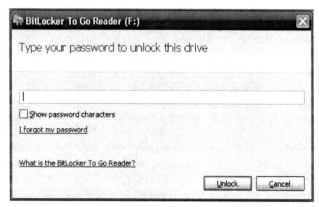

Figure 18–18. *BitLocker To Go Reader password request*

3. If you do not have the password, you can use the recovery key instead by clicking the **I forgot my password** link.

   The **BitLocker To Go Reader Recovery** dialog box is displayed, as shown in Figure 18–19.

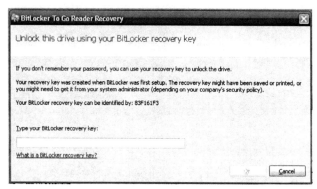

Figure 18–19. *If the password is unavailable, you can use the recovery key instead.*

Once the drive is unlocked the experience is different from Windows 7. A special view-only window is displayed, similar to Figure 18–20. You cannot open any folders or files directly from this window; you must first copy them to a location on your computer.

Figure 18–20. *BitLocker To Go Reader only allows you to see, but not open, folders and files.*

4. Drag and drop the files or folders you want to copy to your desktop or another location on your computer.

The items you copied to your computer will not be protected on your local computer, but all of the items on the encrypted drive will remain unchanged.

Decrypting or turning off encryption

Decrypting, or turning off encryption, completely removes the encryption from the drive. Decrypting is basically one giant undo of encryption. It will take as long to decrypt the drive as it originally took to encrypt it. For a large operating system hard drive, it could take four, six, or eight hours, or more.

Unlocking the drive does not remove the encryption. It unlocks the drive for your current connection to this computer. Access to these settings was described previously in "Viewing BitLocker-encrypted drives from your computer or another Windows 7 computer."

To decrypt a drive:

1. Click the Start menu, click Control Panel, and then click BitLocker Drive Encryption.

2. Locate the drive you want to decrypt, and then click Turn Off BitLocker, if available, as shown in Figure 18–21.

3. f the Turn Off BitLocker link was not displayed, you will need to click Unlock Drive and provide the password or recovery key. Then the Turn Off BitLocker link will be available.

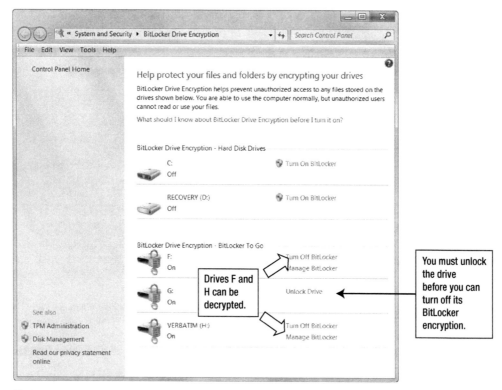

Figure 18–21. *Encryption for drives F and H can be turned off; to turn off encryption for drive G, you must unlock the drive first.*

A dialog box is displayed to confirm that you want to decrypt this drive, and to advise that it may take a long time, as shown in Figure 18–22.

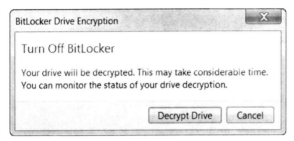

Figure 18–22. *This page launches the decryption process, which could take many hours for a large hard drive.*

4. Click Decrypt Drive.

   A progress message box is displayed, as shown in Figure 18–23. The progress is reported in percentage completed; there is no estimate provided as to how long it will take to complete.

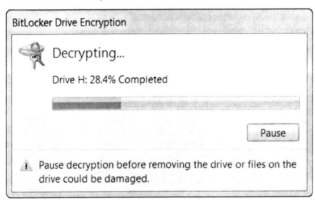

Figure 18–23. *The progress bar shows the percentage of decryption completed, but provides no time estimate.*

A message is displayed when decryption is complete, as shown in Figure 18–24.

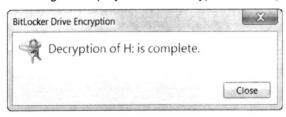

Figure 18–24 *Decryption is complete.*

In the future, if you want to encrypt the drive again, you can go to BitLocker Drive Encryption in Control Panel, or you can right-click the drive in **Computer** and then click **Turn on BitLocker** as shown in Figure 18–25.

Figure 18–25. *When BitLocker is set up on your computer, you can enable it on any drive through the Computer window by right-clicking the drive and then clicking Turn on BitLocker.*

Other Uses for Encryption

EFS and BitLocker are features available in specific versions or Windows 7. There are other companies that provide individual and corporate encrypting technologies and implementations. For example, you can get encryption similar to BitLocker with programs like **TrueCrypt**. If you use a Virtual Private Network (VPN) to connect to your company network from home, your remote network sign in may require a *SmartCard* or an **RSA SecurID key FOB**. There are also *email encryption* products which encrypt email messages and attachments.

Encryption Features Summary

Microsoft Windows 7 provides two encryption features, **Encrypting File System (EFS)** for user file and folder encryption and **BitLocker** for drive-level encryption. If you work for a large company, your organization may have policies and guidelines for the use of encryption. In some industries, encryption may be required to ensure compliance with government regulations for record keeping and archiving, confidentiality of patient records, and protection of personal ID and financial records.

EFS and BitLocker are powerful features that can provide solid protection for the data on your computer. They do pose a risk if not used correctly, because you could lock your data and be unable to unlock it later because of lost passwords, recovery keys, or certificates.

Before attempting any of the encryption procedures in this chapter, be sure to thoroughly read the Windows Help and Support topics for EFS and BitLocker. In addition, read the Microsoft TechNet library articles for BitLocker. Go to Microsoft Technet (http://technet.microsoft.com) and search for "BitLocker Drive Encryption in Windows 7: Frequently Asked Questions" to start.

Setting Up Virtual Machines

Windows XP was the standard operating system for PCs for ten years, and most companies have a wide variety of customized software that is designed for internal use with Windows XP only. Even when Windows Vista came out, many companies did not adopt Vista for employee use, and stayed with Windows XP. For this reason, a lot of programs that worked in XP may not have been updated to work in Windows 7.

At home, you may have some programs or devices that worked with Windows XP but do not work with Windows 7.

Fortunately, there are several solutions available that use *virtual machines*. Virtual machines allow you to run a complete Windows machine within a program window or full screen on your computer. You can easily copy and paste information and files between programs running on Windows 7 and programs running inside of the virtual machine.

In Windows 7, Microsoft offers two virtual machine options, **Windows Virtual PC** and **Windows XP Mode**.

In addition to these options from Microsoft, you can use third-party virtual machine programs like **VMware Virtual Machine Player**. In the section "Installing VMware Player," this chapter also explains virtual machine appliances and using virtual machines to try out other operating systems, like Linux.

Virtual Machine Hardware and Software Requirements

Though a virtual machine is not a physical machine, it does consume physical resources on your host computer. You can run multiple virtual machines at the same time, but each one takes a part of your memory and hard drive space. Before installing virtual machines, check to see if you will have enough of both kinds of resources.

Memory Requirements

You need memory for your host (physical) Windows 7 computer, plus the sum of the memory each virtual machine's operating system requires.

For example, your Windows 7 host (physical machine) needs at least 2 GB of memory. You want to be able to run up to three of your virtual machines at the same time, and depending on the operating system version, you need 1-2 GB for each virtual machine. So to run Windows 7 plus three virtual machines, you would need 5-8 GB of memory installed on the physical machine. If you have several virtual machines open and are already at the limit with the total amount of memory they need, if you try to open another virtual machine you may get a message that there is not enough memory available.

Also, if your video card is built in to the computer motherboard, it uses part of the system memory as video memory. If you are using graphics-intensive programs, you will have even more demands on the total memory installed on your computer.

In actual use, your computer may not need all of the memory required for each virtual machine. For example, while writing parts of this book, sometimes it has been necessary for me to open multiple Windows 7 and Windows XP virtual machines on a Windows 7 laptop with 6 GB of memory. There was no noticeable drop in speed or performance, even though all of the machines (physical and virtual) required the availability of all of the installed memory.

You will likely have performance problems if you start with a computer that has the bare minimum required for the physical machine itself. Windows 7 can run on 2 GB, but even if you have 3 GB that may not be enough to also run a virtual machine.

Hard Drive Requirements

Each virtual machine needs physical disk space. When creating a new virtual machine, the virtual machine program (**Microsoft Virtual PC** or **VMware Player**), will recommend the minimum amount of disk. The size depends on the operating system. You also have the option of allowing the virtual machine to expand its disk space as needed. Most experts I know recommend a set disk size because, in a corporate environment running multiple virtual machines on a server, a few virtual machines could start hogging all of the shared physical drive space. Unless you need to install and run a lot of programs in your virtual machines, generally you can allocate 20-40 GB to each virtual machine. Though your virtual machine may not use up all of that space, the virtual machine file size will carve out the allotted space on your physical hard drive.

Installing Windows Virtual PC and Windows XP Mode

Windows Virtual PC and **Windows XP Mode** are not pre-installed on Windows 7, but you can download them free from Microsoft. You can install both or just **Windows Virtual PC**, depending on your edition of Windows 7:

- If you are using Windows 7 Professional, Enterprise, or Ultimate, you can install both XP Mode and Virtual PC.

- If you are using Windows 7 Starter or Home Premium, you can only download and install **Windows Virtual PC**.

To install **Windows Virtual PC** and **Windows XP Mode**:

1. Go to www.microsoft.com/windows/virtual-pc/download.aspx.

2. To install both **Windows Virtual PC** and **Windows XP Mode**, follow the instructions on the page to select your edition of Windows 7 and language, and then start the download.

3. To install only **Windows Virtual PC**, click the link **Don't need XP Mode and want VPC only? Download Windows Virtual PC without Windows XP Mode**. When the new web page for downloading Windows Virtual PC is displayed, follow the instructions on the page to select your edition of Windows 7 and language, and then start the download.

When installation is complete, you will find Windows Virtual PC on your Start menu, as shown in Figure 18–26.

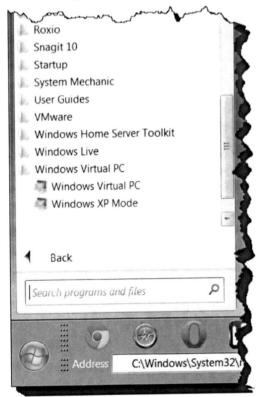

Figure 18–26. *You can access Windows Virtual PC through the Start button.*

Windows Virtual PC

Microsoft officially supports running the following guest operating systems in **Windows Virtual PC**: Windows XP (SP3) Professional, Windows Vista Enterprise and Ultimate, and Windows 7 Enterprise and Ultimate. Figure 18–27 shows an example of a virtual machine window on a Windows 7 desktop.

> **TIP:** You can also run a virtual machine full-screen so that it completely covers the Windows 7 desktop. Using it full-screen on multiple monitors will allow you to view your virtual machine on one monitor and your Windows 7 desktop on the other.

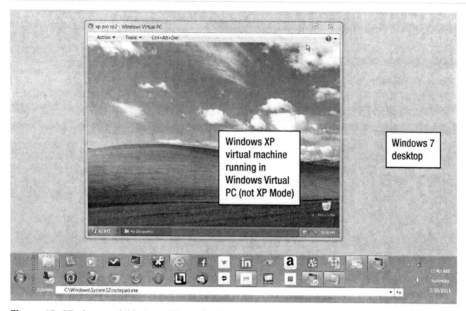

Figure 18–27. *A copy of Windows XP running in a Windows Virtual PC window (not XP Mode)*

> **NOTE:** Each virtual machine is considered a copy of the operating system, so you need a separate operating system license for each virtual machine.

You can also install other non-Windows operating systems like one of the Linux distributions in **Windows Virtual PC,** though this requires advanced skills and knowledge. Search Linux community forums on the web for information from others who have successfully installed Linux in Virtual PC.

Once you have created a virtual machine, you can install applications on the virtual machine using the CD/DVD drive attached to the host (Windows 7) computer, or from an installation file saved to a folder within the virtual machine. After installing a program, you can open it up and run it within the virtual machine. Though you cannot drag a program window out of the virtual machine window onto the Windows 7 desktop, you can copy and paste files, folders, and items between programs in Windows 7 and the virtual machine.

Windows XP Mode

Windows XP Mode is a preconfigured virtual machine with Windows XP all ready to run. It is only available for Windows 7 Ultimate and Enterprise editions. Windows XP Mode does not require a separate license because it is considered part of the Windows 7 license on that machine. Figure 18–28 shows Windows XP Mode on the Windows 7 desktop. Other than the desktop background, the **Windows XP Mode** window doesn't really look much different from the Windows XP installed in **Windows Virtual PC** in Figure 18–27.

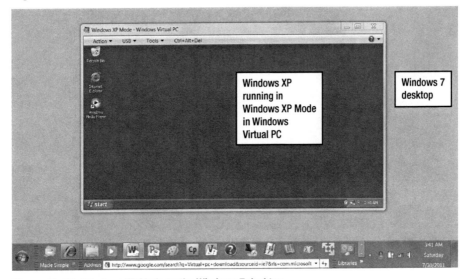

Figure 18–28. *Windows XP Mode on the Windows 7 desktop*

However, what makes **Windows XP Mode** really different is that you can run an application in *Windows XP Application Mode:* instead of appearing as a program window within the virtual machine, all you see is the application window on top of the Windows 7 desktop.

Whenever you install a program within a **Windows XP Mode** virtual machine, it is displayed as a separate program on the **Start** menu, as shown in Figure 18–29.

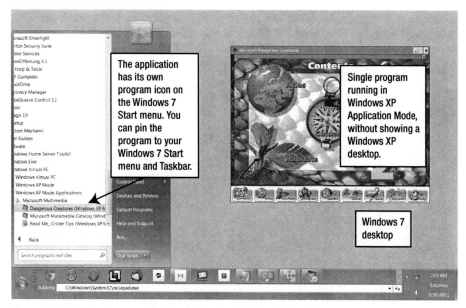

Figure 18–29. *Running an application in Windows XP Application Mode*

In the example in Figure 18–28, **Microsoft Dangerous Creatures**, a multimedia CD-based program created for Windows 95, is running in Windows XP Application Mode. This program can be opened directly from the Windows 7 **Start** menu, without opening a **Windows XP Mode** window.

For further learning about Windows Virtual PC and Windows XP Mode

Microsoft offers some very helpful demonstrations and guides for using Windows Virtual PC. Visit the Windows Virtual PC home page at http://www.microsoft.com/windows/virtual-pc/.

Installing VMware Player

The **VMware Player** is a free virtual machine program available from VMware. It allows you to create virtual machines much like how you create them with **Windows Virtual PC**. **VMware Player** runs on all editions of Windows 7, as well as many other versions of Windows and non-Windows operating systems. **VMware Player** can also import Windows XP Mode, but it is limited to Windows 7 Professional, Ultimate, and Enterprise just like Windows XP Mode in **Windows Virtual PC**. To import Windows XP Mode into **VMware Player**, you must have already downloaded and installed Windows XP Mode from Microsoft.

To install **VMware Player**, go to www.vmware.com/products/player/overview.html and follow the instructions for downloading the **VMware Player**.

Figure 18–30 displays a regular Windows XP virtual machine running in the **VMware Player**. Figure 18–31 displays Windows XP Mode in the **VMware Player**.

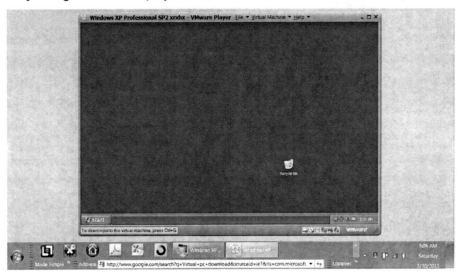

Figure 18–30. *Windows XP virtual machine in VMware Player*

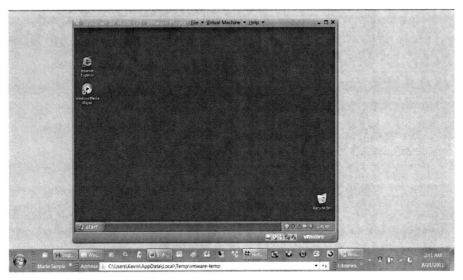

Figure 18–31. *Windows XP Mode in VMware player*

KEY DIFFERENCES BETWEEN WINDOWS XP MODE AND WINDOWS XP IN A VIRTUAL MACHINE

Though for most appearances Windows XP in a virtual machine looks like Windows XP Mode in a virtual machine, a significant difference is in installation and licensing. For the editions of Windows 7 that support Windows XP mode, you do not need to purchase or use a separate license for Windows XP running in Windows XP Mode; it is licensed as a part of your Windows 7 license. But if you install Windows XP in a regular virtual machine, on any edition of Windows 7, you will need a separate license for each Windows XP virtual machine. Also, with Windows XP Mode, you do not need to supply an installation disk, but with Windows XP in a regular virtual machine you will need Windows XP installation disks.

VMware Player has an application-only mode similar to the application mode in **Windows Virtual PC**'s Windows XP Mode. But VMware does not require the imported Windows XP Mode. In VMware this application-only mode is called **Unity**. Figure 18–32 shows an example of an older multimedia program, "Microsoft Complete Gardening," displayed in Unity. The Complete Gardening program is installed on a Windows XP virtual machine in **VMware Player**. Just the application window is displayed, without the virtual machine desktop.

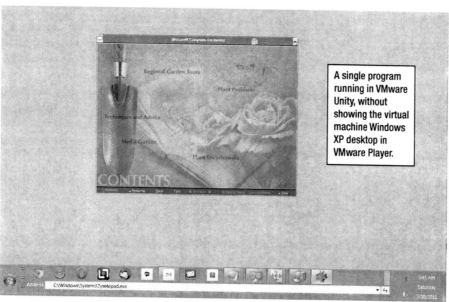

Figure 18–32. *Application-only mode using the VMware Unity feature*

Another neat feature of VMware is the availability of a wide variety of *Virtual Appliances*. These are ready-to-go virtual machines. You don't need to open a new virtual machine and run the operating system installation program. The virtual appliance provides the operating system already in virtual machine form, so all you have to do is download the virtual machine files. You can access the virtual appliances through the VMware Virtual

Appliance Marketplace, shown in Figure 18–33. You can browse the Virtual Appliances store at `www.vmware.com/appliances/`.

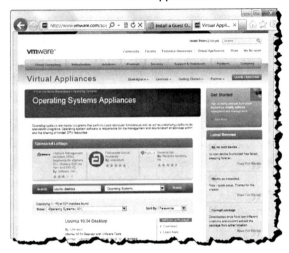

Figure 18–33. *The VMware Virtual Appliances store*

The appliances vary from operating systems to applications, including many free or evaluation virtual machines. For example, Figure 18–34 is a free Ubuntu Linux desktop distribution. Many major Linux desktop operating system distributions are available for free in the Virtual Appliance store.

Figure 18–34. *An Ubuntu desktop operating system virtual machine created from a virtual appliance*

Microsoft offers some virtual appliances in the Microsoft Virtual Hard Disk (VHD) format, but they are mainly used to provide companies with evaluation copies of Windows Server and applications like Exchange Server, or SharePoint, and usually require Hyper-V to host them. The advantage of virtual appliances in evaluations is that you can quickly open and use the evaluation system without extensive installation and configuration.

Summary of Virtual Machine Options and Uses

Virtual Machine players such as **Windows Virtual PC** and **VMware Player** have many practical uses at home and at work. Here are key points to remember about virtual machines:

- Though virtual machines allow you to run instances of Windows (or other operating systems) without a separate physical computer for each instance, you still need to allot memory and dedicate hard drive space for each virtual machine.

- You can use virtual machines to run legacy corporate programs that do not run on Windows 7 but will run on Windows XP inside a virtual machine.

- You can use virtual machines to run older games and programs that worked up through Windows XP, but no longer work in Windows 7.

- You can use virtual machines to experiment with other operating systems like Linux without buying additional hardware or software.

Between **Microsoft Virtual PC** and **VMware Player**, there is at least one virtual machine option for every version of Windows 7.

Network Connections Outside of the Office or Home

When you take your computer outside of your home or workplace, your network speeds, connection strength, and security situation change. Connecting from a public place with WiFi is slower and can be less secure than connecting at home. Connecting to a work network from home can be slower and less secure than a direct connection to a corporate network at your office.

Virtual Private Networks

A *Virtual Private Network* (VPN) is used to provide secure and direct connections across the Internet between a remote location and a company network. VPN is often used to enable workers to "remote in" from home or outside of the office to their company network or their office computer. Creating a VPN is not something you do on your own; these are usually set up by your employer. Part of that setup includes installing a *VPN client* on your computer. The VPN client will contain one or more connection profiles, which provide web address and authentication information to locate and connect to the VPN host (remote server) on your corporate network. Large companies may have multiple hosts that you can connect to, so if you cannot connect through one you can try to connect to another.

Windows 7 fully supports VPN, but sometimes the client you or your company uses may need to be upgraded in order to work with Windows 7. If you upgrade an existing computer to Windows 7, or you get a new Windows 7, the client you used in Windows

XP may not work in Windows 7. You may be able to upgrade the client yourself by going to the VPN client software publisher's web site. If your company's VPN client doesn't support Windows 7 yet, you may be able to download and install another VPN client. You should be able to import your existing connection profiles into the new client.

If you have other problems with VPN and are not able to get help from your company help desk because of your VPN problems, you can do some troubleshooting through **Windows Help and Support**. There may be network settings on your computer that can be adjusted. Click the **Start** button, and then click **Help and Support**. In the **Windows Help and Support** search box, type "VPN problems." In the search results you should see a topic "Why am I having problems with my VPN connection?" Open that topic and try the solutions listed there.

Public Networks and WiFi

Most laptops are WiFi-enabled, so you can easily connect to hotspots in public places and businesses outside of your home or work. Some hotspots are free, and some require that you subscribe to a service. Connecting to a WiFi or wireless hotspot can be as simple as your computer detecting it and offering to connect, or it may require setting up and subscribing to a service. Most WiFi and hotspot locations provide short instructions with the network name (SSID) and any other sign in information that may be needed. You may need to add the network through the **Network and Sharing Center**.

You can quickly check the status of your wireless connection through the wireless network icon in the notification bar. Hover over the icon to see a tooltip listing the current wireless network connections, as shown in Figure 18–35.

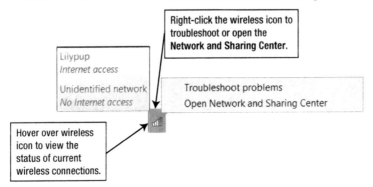

Figure 18–35. *Hover over the wireless icon to view the current wireless connection status; right-click to troubleshoot or open the Network and Sharing Center.*

Right-click the icon, and then click **Network and Sharing Center** for more detailed information or to change settings.

"Chapter 15: Connecting to the Internet and Home Networks" provides detailed steps on accessing the **Network and Sharing Center** in the topic "Checking your current network connections."

CAUTION: Wireless hotspots and WiFi locations are prime hunting grounds for hackers and ID theft. If the wireless signal from the hotspot is strong enough, a hacker could be sitting in a car out in the parking lot, not across the room in the coffee shop. For any connection outside of work or home that is not through VPN, make sure the connection is set as a Public Network in Network and Sharing Center. The Public Network provides the strongest security and reduces your vulnerability.

Table 18–2 describes some of the more common wireless options. Depending on your geographic location, cellular providers, and service provider coverage areas, many but not necessarily all of these connection types might be available.

Table 18–2. *Common wireless connection types*

Connection type or location	Description
Libraries and other public facilities	Usually free. May require that you sign in with a universal name and password (all users use the same sign-in information). If the wireless signal is strong enough, you may be able to access the network after hours outside of the building from the parking lot. Usually supports wireless 802.11b, g, and possibly n, so you can use your built-in or USB wireless adapter for access.
Coffee shops, fast food, restaurants	Some are free, and some may require a subscription to a service like AT&T or Verizon Wireless. Even if you subscribe to a service, you may still need to create a new connection for this location. Usually supports wireless 802.11b, g, and possibly n, so you can use your built-in or USB wireless adapter for access.
Hotels, motels, convention centers	Many lodging and meeting facilities offer complementary wireless Internet access for their guests. Some may also have in-room Ethernet jacks. To cover the entire facility with one wireless network, they may employ several access points, or separate networks for each zone. If you have several to choose from, pick the one that shows the strongest signal (the most bars). Usually supports wireless 802.11b, g, and possibly n, so you can use your built-in or USB wireless adapter for access.
Airports, bus stations, train stations	Most of these facilities offer one or more WiFi/hotspot providers that you can purchase a subscription to or buy a one-time use of hours, or a day. Usually supports wireless 802.11b, g, and possibly n, so you can use your built-in or USB wireless adapter for access.

Connection type or location	Description
Cellular networks	Most cellular networks offer Internet access (data) plans so that you can connect your computer (not just your cellphone) for Internet access. The cost is based on how much data (in gigabytes) you want to download each month. There are three ways to connect your PC to a wireless network:
	Tethering: Your cellphone acts as a modem, and then you connect your PC to the cellphone. Some cellphone providers charge extra for this, even if you have an Internet access data plan for your cell phone.
	External PC card or USB cellular adapter: Looks like a regular wireless b/g/n adapter, except it connects to the cellular network instead.
	Personal hotspot: A small device, about the size of a smartphone, that connects to the cellular network. The device then acts as a wireless router so that you can connect up to five computers.
	Some cellular plans also include WiFi service, so that if you do not have a strong cellular signal or you don't want to use up your data plan allotment, you can use a WiFi connection where available.
Free hotspots web sites	There are many web sites where you can find free hotspots listed or labeled on a map worldwide. For example, `http://free-hotspot.groopli.com`.

Physically Protecting Your Computer

You can protect the data on your computer with a good backup plan, and encryption through EFS and BitLocker. However, even with those in place it can still be quite painful and disruptive if something physical happens to your computer. There are many things you can do to minimize those risks. The following list is not exhaustive, but should help you think about how you can and should protect your computer.

- **Use a computer cable lock** If you are in any public place, like a library, coffee shop, or airport, all it takes is turning your head away for just a moment and somebody can grab your laptop and run off with it. While a determined thief can easily cut through a cable with bolt cutters, if your laptop is locked to a table, you are buying time that a thief may not want to spend. They'll just move on to find an easier opportunity.

- **Protect your laptop when it is in your car** Avoid leaving it in direct sunlight or inside a hot or cold car during temperature extremes.

- **Avoid leaving your laptop in plain view** The time to move your laptop bag from the front seat to your trunk is not when you are getting out of your car in the shopping mall or exercise club parking lot after work. Stow the laptop in your trunk when you first get in the car, before you drive off to your next destination.

- **Use a padded notebook bag, attaché, or computer backpack.** Protect against dropping, other things hitting it, and weather conditions as you carry it between your car and house or work.

- **Protect access even in places you think should be safe** If you need to leave your desk for a minute, and other people in the immediate area have or could get access to your computer, lock Windows so that nobody can view your files, email, or accounts. Press the Windows key + L to lock the computer when you leave your desk or computer for a minute. If you are going to be gone longer, like several hours, save your work and shut down your computer. While you are gone, any number of accidents might occur and you could lose unsaved work or possibly have corrupted files. The power goes out for a moment; somebody spills a beverage on your laptop keyboard or PC; or somebody turns off the power on your PC because they see a blank screen and want to save power.

Summary

In this chapter you looked at several Windows 7 features that are very relevant to business use and when you are away from your desk or home office:

- Windows 7 features designed primarily for business use

- How corporate policies and networks affect Windows features and how you may use your computer

- How to use Encrypting File System (EFS) and BitLocker to protect your computer files, folders or drives with encryption

- How to download and set up virtual machines to run legacy software

- Tips and recommendations for physically protecting your computer

Next Steps

You may find the following related chapters useful:

- "Chapter 4: Exploring Programs and Features" for how to install Windows features that might have been removed because of policies, or install features that may be useful in the business environment

- "Chapter 5: Installing Programs" for help with installing programs from disks or the web, and selecting the default programs to use for specific file types and protocols

- "Chapter 9: Surfing the Web" for how to use and install alternative browsers

- "Chapter 13: Printing, Faxing, and Scanning" for how to connect to network printers and use fax features in Windows

- "Chapter 15: Connecting to the Internet and Home Networks" for how to view and change your Internet connections

- "Chapter 16: Protecting Your Computer and Data" for how to set up backup plans and protect your computer with antivirus and firewall programs

- "Chapter 17: Troubleshooting and Maintaining Your Computer" for how to troubleshoot programs that are not running correctly, including using Program Compatibility to make older programs run in Windows 7.

Index

Y

CPSIA information can be obtained at www.ICGtesting.com
Printed in the USA
LVOW050744290212

270925LV00002B/5/P